6/08

Encyclopedia of Chinese-American Relations

Encyclopedia of Chinese-American Relations

EDITED BY YUWU SONG

McFarland & Company, Inc., Publishers

Jefferson, North Carolina, and London

LIBRARY OF CONGRESS CATALOGUING-IN-PUBLICATION DATA

Song, Yuwu
Encyclopedia of Chinese-American relations / edited by Yuwu Song.
p.   cm.
Includes bibliographical references and index.

ISBN 0-7864-2406-0 (illustrated case binding : 50# alkaline paper)

1. United States—Foreign relations—China—Encyclopedias.
2. China—Foreign relations—United States—Encyclopedias.
I. Song, Yuwu.
E183.8.C5E53   2006   327.7305103—dc22   2006007824

British Library cataloguing data are available

On the cover: Eagle ©2006 Flat Earth; Dragon ©2006 clipart.com

Manufactured in the United States of America

*McFarland & Company, Inc., Publishers
Box 611, Jefferson, North Carolina 28640
www.mcfarlandpub.com*

Contents

I dedicate this book to my parents,
Song Yuexun and Zhao Guolun,
who raised me to be what I am

Preface

American interest in China began in 1784 when the American ship *Empress of China* arrived in the Chinese city of Guangzhou on August 28. From the American missionary quest to transform China in the 18th century to the confrontation over the spy plane incident at the beginning of the 21st century, the development of Chinese-American relations has been full of ups and downs. In spite of all of these trials and tribulations, the two countries' relationship has changed for the better.

In the past century, the United States has established its influence worldwide. At the same time, Chinese influence is spreading around the globe. With a quarter of the world's population and near double-digit economic growth, China is changing rapidly and is becoming a world power. It is obvious that the Chinese-Americans relations may significantly affect world politics in the coming years. Because of substantial mistrust and misunderstanding on both sides nowadays, better understanding of one another is becoming extremely important, and a solid and friendly relationship should be a primary goal for both the Chinese and the Americans. However justified the positions of the two countries may be, dealing with each other will require cool realpolitik and scholarly know-how. It is hoped that this book, as a serious academic reference work, will contribute to better understanding of the relations between the two great nations on earth.

This book offers the user in an easily digestible form a summary of what happened between China and the United States in the past two centuries. The work includes more than 400 descriptive entries of important events, issues, personalities, controversies, treaties, agreements, organizations, and alliances in the history of Chinese-American relations.

The intended readership can be divided into two segments. The first includes students and scholars in history, sociology, political science, ethnic studies, education, Sino-American relations, foreign relations, area studies, and other related subjects. The second segment includes general readers who want information on international relations in general and Sino-American relations in particular.

The encyclopedia was compiled from primary and secondary sources with the aim of providing the clearest possible interpretation. The editor and the contributors examined the people and the events from both Chinese and American perspectives. Two maps of China and Taiwan are provided to enhance understanding of the events and people discussed. There is also a chronology, a list of Chinese ambassadors to the United States since the normalization of relations, a list of American ambassadors to China, a selected bibliography, and an index. The Wide-Giles/Pinyin Conversion Table is provided for identifying names.

This book would not have been possible without the help of many people. I express my heartfelt thanks to all the contributors for their hard work, dedication,

1

and professionalism. The contributors are from 10 countries and regions: the United States, China, Taiwan, Japan, India, Germany, Great Britain, Canada, Egypt, and Portugal. I also want to thank Ms. Noreen Herring who proofread part of the entries. I owe a lot to the University Libraries at Arizona State University, which provided me with research funding for this project. Finally, I would like to acknowledge my debt to the professors who not only taught me history but also steered me toward the right track of historical scholarship. They are:

Dr. Edwin E. Moise (Clemson University)
Dr. Steven Marks (Clemson University)
Dr. Richard L. Saunders Jr. (Clemson University)
Dr. Donald M. McKale (Clemson University)
Dr. Alan Grubb (Clemson University)
Dr. Howard Jones (University of Alabama at Tuscaloosa)
Dr. Ron Robel (University of Alabama at Tuscaloosa)
Dr. Lawrence A. Clayton (University of Alabama at Tuscaloosa)
Dr. David Beito (University of Alabama at Tuscaloosa)
Dr. Maarten Ultee (University of Alabama at Tuscaloosa)
Dr. Paul Gorman (University of Alabama at Tuscaloosa)
Dr. Gary Mills (University of Alabama at Tuscaloosa)
Dr. John Beeler (University of Alabama at Tuscaloosa)
Dr. Lawrence F. Kohl (University of Alabama at Tuscaloosa)
Dr. George W. McClure (University of Alabama at Tuscaloosa)

Chronology

1784	American ship *Empress of China* arrives in the Chinese city of Guangzhou
1800	John Jacob Astor's first fur trading voyage to Guangzhou
1840	First Opium War in China
1842	Treaty of Nanjing U.S. naval squadron arrives at Guangzhou
1844	Treaty of Wangxia signed between the United States and China, giving the United States use of five Chinese ports for commerce and conferring legal rights on Americans living in China
1845	U.S. Commodore James Biddle exchanges ratifications of the Treaty of Wangxia at Guangzhou
1846	Peter Parker becomes the American Commissioner to China
1851	The Syi Huiguan and the Sanyi Huiguan, the first Chinese community associations founded in San Francisco Taiping Rebellion occurs
1853	Chinatown emerges out of Gold Rush
1856	Second Opium War (Arrow War) in China Peter Parker proposes American take-over of Taiwan
1858	Treaty of Tianjin signed between the Western powers and China opening ten new treaty ports in China
1861	China forms Zongli Yamen Anson Burlingame becomes the first American minister to China
1862	Frederick Ward establishes the Ever-victorious Army to fight the Taiping rebels Russell and Company forms the Shanghai Steamship Navigation Company Zongli Yamen sets up Tongwenguan, a foreign language academy
1867	Charles LeGrande launches punitive attack on Taiwan
1868	Burlingame Treaty signed between the United States and China
1869	Frederick Low named the American minister to Beijing
1870	YMCA (Young Men's Christian Association) starts operating in China
1872	First Chinese students arrive in the United States for academic study
1880	Angell Treaty (Chinese Exclusion Treaty) signed between the United States and China restricting the entrance and naturalization of immigrants from China
1881	Zongli Yamen withdraws Chinese Educational Mission from the United States
1882	The Chinese Exclusion Act passed in the U.S. Congress posing restrictions on Chinese immigration to the United States Chinese Consolidated Benevolent Association formed in the United States
1885	Rock Spring Massacre of Chinese workers in Wyoming
1890	YWCA (Young Women's Christian Association) starts operating in China

1894   Sino-Japanese War. China loses control over Korea and Manchuria. The U.S. begins to see China as a new Africa, where foreign powers scramble for territory
        Renewal of Angell Treaty

1895   China loses Taiwan to Japan

1898   The American Asiatic Association formed

1899   Secretary of State John Hay delivers first set of Open Door Notes to the powers with interests in China demanding equal access to China market, "protecting" China from external abuse

1900   Boxer Rebellion begins with Chinese nationalist uprising against foreigners, the representatives of alien powers, and Chinese Christians with the ultimate objective of the expulsion of all foreigners An expedition consisting of British, French, Japanese, Russian, German, Italian, and American troops relieves the besieged quarter and occupies Beijing in August

1901   Secretary of State John Hay delivers second set of Open Door Notes to the powers with interests in China.
        Beijing accepts the Boxer Protocol (large indemnity, commercial concessions, and the right to station foreign troops to guard the legations)

1904   Russo-Japanese War begins

1906   Shanghai Drug Conference convenes

1908   The United States remits Boxer Indemnity to the Chinese government

1909   Knox Neutralization Scheme initiates "Dollar Diplomacy" in China, which encourages U.S. bankers and industrialists to invest in China

1911   Establishment of the Republic of China (ROC) with Dr. Sun Zhongshan elected as the Provisional President

1913   U.S. recognition of the government of the Republic of China
        California passes Land Law discriminating against Asian Americans
        United States withdraws from the Six Power Consortium

1914   World War I starts

1915   Japan forces its Twenty-One Demands on China
        United States announces non-recognition of forcible changes in the status quo in China that affect American interests

1919   May Fourth Movement starts
        Peking Union Medical College opens with funding from Rockefeller Foundation

1921   Washington Naval Conference convenes with talks about a limitation to naval armaments generally and to promote better relations among nations with conflicting interests in the Pacific Ocean and the Far East
        Chinese Communist Party founded

1922   Nine Power Treaty signed affirming the Open Door Policy in China

1924   California passes law prohibiting Asian immigration

1925   Outbreak of May Thirtieth Movement protesting unequal treaties in China
        Journalist Anna Louise Strong arrives in China

1927   U.S. Secretary of State Frank B. Kellogg's statement expresses sympathy with Chinese nationalism and the American policy of non-interference in Chinese internal affairs

1928   United States signs treaty with China restoring tariff autonomy
        Journalist Agnes Smedley makes her first trip to China

1931   Mukden Incident occurs

1932   Puyi installed by the Japanese as the ruler of the puppet state of Manchukuo under the reign
        title Datong
        U.S. Secretary of State Henry Stimson announces U.S. policy of non-recognition of forcible
        changes in the status quo in China
        Lytton Commission from the League of Nations starts to investigate the Manchurian crisis

1936   Silver Agreement signed between the United States and China
        Xian Incident occurs with Jiang Jieshi kidnapped by his generals

1937   Marco Polo Bridge Incident
        Claire Lee Chennault starts working for the Chinese government
        Release of the film *The Good Earth*
        Rape of Nanjing
        USS *Panay* sunk by the Japanese

1938   Edgar Snow's *Red Star Over China* published

1941   U.S. Congress passes Lend Lease Act
        China signs a stabilization Fund Agreement with the U.S.
        U.S. and Britain announces that they would give up all extraterritorial privileges in China
        after the war

1942   General Joseph W. Stilwell named as the Chief of Staff of Chinese Nationalist leader Jiang
        Jieshi's Joint Staff and the U.S. Army Representative in China
        Hump operations begin providing U.S. aid to China through flights from India
        Jimmy Doolittle's air raid on Japan launched
        Lend Lease agreement signed between China and the United States
        China's First Lady Song Meiling travels in the United States publicizing China's war against Japan

1943   U.S. Congress repeals Chinese Exclusion Acts
        Cairo Conference of Franklin D. Roosevelt, Winston Churchill, and Jiang Jieshi convenes on
        joint war plans, post-war conditions such as the restoration of lost Chinese territories, in-
        cluding Taiwan and Penghus
        Sino-American Special Technical Cooperative Organization (SACO) established

1944   Dixie Mission
        General Patrick Hurley appointed as personal representative of President Franklin D. Roosevelt
        to China
        Recall of General Joseph W. Stilwell from China
        General Albert Wedemeyer becomes military advisor to Jiang Jieshi

1945   Yalta Conference convenes
        President Harry S. Truman issues General Order Number 1
        The statement of U.S. policy in China issued by President Harry S. Truman, who expresses his
        desire to see China peacefully unified as a democratic state
        Establishment of Committee for a Democratic Far Eastern Policy
        Civil War in China begins
        Claire Lee Chennault starts Civil Air Transport in China
        U.S. Ambassador Patrick Hurley escorts Mao Zedong to Chongqing for negotiations with
        Jiang Jieshi
        Appointment of General George C. Marshall as President Harry S. Truman's representative to
        China announced
        Resignation of Ambassador Patrick Hurley

1946   George Kennan outlines the containment policy
        President Harry S. Truman reaffirms American belief in a "united and democratic China" and
        the U.S. policy of non-involvement in Chinese civil strife
        Theodore White's *Thunder Out of China* published

1947   Guomindang troops massacre Taiwanese in the February 28 Incident

President Harry S. Truman instructs General Albert Wedemeyer to proceed to China on a fact-finding mission
Truman Doctrine formed

1948   U.S. Congress passes China Aid Bill
First National Assembly under the new Constitution meets in Nanjing with Jiang Jieshi elected by the National Assembly as the President of China
Under China Aid Bill the Chinese government receives $275 million for non-military supplies and $125 million for use at its discretion
Sino-American Agreement for the establishment of Joint Commission on Rural Reconstruction in China signed

1949   President Jiang Jieshi announces his temporary retirement.
Communist forces occupy Nanjing
U.S. State Department releases the China White Paper on U.S. relations with China
The People's Republic of China (PRC) founded in Beijing
Nationalist government moves its seat to Taibei
U.S. diplomat Angus Ward arrested in China

1950   President Harry S. Truman announces the end of American involvement in the civil war in China
President Jiang Jieshi resumes the presidency in Taibei
Russians begin boycott of the United Nations for refusing to let the People's Republic of China replace the Republic of China
Secretary of State Dean Acheson makes National Press Club Speech
Red Scare spreads in America
Sino-Soviet Pact of Friendship and Alliance signed
Tibet made an autonomous region in China
Korean War starts
President Harry S. Truman sends the Seventh Fleet into the Taiwan Strait
Truman imposes ban on trade with China
General Douglas MacArthur appointed commander of the United Nations Command
Chinese troops cross the Yalu River to fight in the Korean War
John Service fired from the State Department as security risk

1951   United Nations condemns China for aggression in Korea
U.S. announces its assignment of the military assistance advisory group (MAAG) to Taiwan
O. Edmund Clubb dismissed from the State Department as security risk
United Nations approves moratorium resolution on discussing Chinese representation for the first time
General Douglas MacArthur recalled
Korean War armistice negotiations resume at Panmunjom
China announces liberation of Tibet

1952   China condemns the United States for germ warfare in Korea
China Committee (CHINCOM) founded to restrict trade with the People's Republic of China
Stalemate of negotiations over POWs in Korea
China expels foreign missionaries
Committee for a Democratic Far Eastern Policy dissolved

1953   President Dwight D. Eisenhower announces the de-neutralization of the Taiwan Strait
China announces Five Principles of Peaceful Coexistence
Korean armistice signed

1954   President Dwight. D. Eisenhower refers domino theory
State Department fires John Paton Davies
Outbreak of the first Taiwan Strait Crisis
U.S.-China Mutual Defense Treaty signed in Washington

1955   Formosa Resolution passed by U.S. Congress
Ambassadorial level meeting starts between China and the United States in Geneva

1956	U.S. Secretary of State John Foster Dulles visits Taibei
1957	Anti-American revolt in Taibei takes place
1958	Second Taiwan Strait Crisis occurs President Jiang Jieshi and U.S. Secretary of State John Foster Dulles issue a joint communique reaffirming solidarity and stating that Jinmen and Mazu islands are closely related to the defense of Taiwan under present conditions Ambassadorial level meeting between China and the United States moves to Warsaw from Geneva
1959	Air America formed from Civil Air Transport Tibetan revolt against Beijing's rule Dalai Lama flees to India
1960	President Dwight D. Eisenhower visits Taibei Soviet technicians withdrawn from China
1961	Congress passes Fulbright-Hayes Act U.S. Vice President Lyndon B. Johnson visits Taibei President John F. Kennedy holds meeting with Chen Cheng, Vice-President of the Republic of China
1964	Beijing conducts first nuclear test
1965	U.S. and the Republic of China conclude in Taibei an accord to establish a Sino-American fund for economic and social development in Taiwan U.S. phases out economic aid to Taiwan
1966	U.S. Vice President Hubert H. Humphrey visits Taibei. Great Proletarian Cultural Revolution starts in China
1967	China conducts first H-bomb test
1969	U.S. Secretary of State William P. Rogers visits Taibei Chinese and Soviet troops clash on Ussuri River in Heilongjiang border
1970	Vice President Spiro T. Agnew visits Taibei
1971	Ping Pong diplomacy begins President Richard Nixon announces end of trade embargo against China President Nixon's Assistant for National Security Affairs Henry Kissinger and Premier Zhou Enlai have talks in Beijing Henry Kissinger visits Beijing to arrange the agenda and itinerary to Nixon's forthcoming trip to Communist China United States advocates UN representation for two Chinas UN votes to admit Communist China, expel Nationalist delegates
1972	President Nixon arrives in mainland China for an eight-day visit A joint communique issued in Shanghai pledges that both parties would work for a normalization of relations
1973	Liaison offices opened in Washington and Beijing
1974	George H. W. Bush becomes the head of Liaison Office in Beijing
1975	Jiang Jieshi dies President Gerald Ford visits China
1976	Mao Zedong dies
1978	Joint communiques issued in Washington and Beijing announce establishment of U.S.-PRC diplomatic relations and termination of U.S.-ROC ties and Mutual Defense Treaty

Senator Barry Goldwater and 14 other legislators file suit in U.S. District Court to prevent termination of ROC Mutual Defense Treaty

U.S. delegation, led by Deputy Secretary of State Warren Christopher, confers in Taibei on future ROC-U.S. relations

China ends all aid to Vietnam

1979   Chinese leader Deng Xiaoping visits the United States

U.S. and PRC mark resumption of diplomatic ties with ceremonies in Washington and Beijing

President Jimmy Carter's December memorandum to U.S. agencies sets terms for continued U.S.-Taiwan relations on "unofficial" basis

President Carter signs Taiwan Relations Act

1980   State Department announces U.S. will sell $280 million in defensive arms to the Republic of China on Taiwan, but no advanced fighter jets for now

Pentagon announces U.S. will sell PRC non-lethal military equipment

U.S.-China Commission on Scientific and Technical Cooperation holds first meeting in Beijing

Chinese officials warn that Ronald Reagan's stand on Taiwan could harm U.S.-PRC relations as well as endanger world peace

1981   PRC–U.S. scheduled air service resumes after 32 years

U.S. Nuclear Regulatory Commission approves export of 3 nuclear reactors to ROC

Secretary of State Alexander M. Haig, Jr. announces U.S. decision in principle to sell arms to PRC

U.S.-PRC cultural exchange pact signed in Beijing

1982   U.S. approves sale of additional F-5E fighter aircraft to ROC, but rules out sale of more sophisticated warplanes

PRC warns Reagan administration that Sino-American relations will suffer "grave consequences" if U.S. insists on making "long-term" arms sales to ROC

U.S. announces sale of $60 million in military spare parts to ROC

Vice President George H. W. Bush visits PRC

U.S. and PRC sign joint communique governing both nations' relations with ROC

Former President Richard M. Nixon visits PRC to commemorate 10th anniversary of Shanghai Communique

1983   China applies to replace Taiwan at Asian Development Bank

China charges U.S. with violating spirit of 1982 U.S.-Chinese agreement on reduction of U.S. arms sales to Taiwan

U.S. grants asylum to Chinese tennis star Hu Na

U.S. announces plans to sell $530 million in new arms to Taiwan

Secretary of Defense Caspar Weinberger visits China, exploring opportunities for increased U.S.-Chinese military cooperation

1984   Premier Zhao Ziyang and President Ronald Reagan sign agreements extending current scientific exchanges and initiating new cooperation in industry and trade

Reagan visits China and meets with Chinese leader Deng Xiaoping

U.S. at end of visit by Chinese Defense Minister Zhang Aiping, announces agreement "in principle" on sale to China of U.S. antiaircraft, antitank weapons

White House warns that U.S.-Chinese nuclear cooperation accord will not be sent to Congress without new guarantees that China will not aid emergence of new nuclear-weapon states

1985   Chinese President Li Xiannian visits Washington announcing signing of pact allowing sale of American nuclear reactors and nonmilitary technology to China

Vice President George H. W. Bush visits China

1986   Reagan administration informs U.S. Congress of intent to sell PRC $550 million in aviation electronics

Three U.S. Navy warships make a port visit at Qingdao, first American military vessels to visit China since 1949

1987   U.S. announces it will not sell certain high-technology products to China in retaliation for China's sale of Silkworm missiles to Iran

1988   Jiang Jingguo, Taiwan's president since 1978, dies

1989   Tiananmen Square Massacre
Chinese political dissident Fang Lizhi takes refuge in American embassy in Beijing
President George H. W. Bush announces sanctions against Chinese government, including suspension of military sales
U.S. mission headed by National Security Adviser Brent Scowcroft and Deputy Secretary of State Lawrence S. Eagleburger arrives in Beijing for meeting with Chinese leadership
Former President Richard Nixon travels to China for private talks with Chinese leaders
President Bush vetoes bill passed by Congress to permit all Chinese citizens in U.S. on student visas to remain until June 1990

1991   U.S. Under-Secretary of State Reginald Bartholomew visits Beijing to seek curb on arms sales to Third World countries, a growing irritant in U.S.-PRC relations
U.S. Secretary of James Baker visits Beijing to discuss issues on trade, human rights, and arms sales in the bilateral relationship
CBS airs documentary of prison labor in China

1992   U.S. extends Most Favored Nation status to China

1993   China conducts an underground nuclear test at the Lop Nur test site in northwest China
President Bill Clinton proposes establishment of a "New Pacific Community"
Galaxy Incident

1994   President Bill Clinton's letter to congressional leaders on rhinoceros and tiger trade by China and Taiwan
Trade sanctions against Taiwan (under the Pelly Amendment)

1995   Chinese dissident Wu Hongda expelled from China
Chinese dissident Wang Dan re-arrested and sentenced to an 11-year term for "plotting to subvert the government"
Li Denghui visits Cornell University

1996   China conducts military exercise in the Taiwan Strait

1997   President Bill Clinton meets Chinese President Jiang Zemin in Washington, D.C. asking for the release of Chinese dissidents Wang Dan and Wei Jingsheng
Release of Chinese dissident Wei Jingsheng from prison

1998   Release of Chinese dissident Wang Dan from prison
U.S.-Taiwan market access agreement signed in Washington, D.C.
President Bill Clinton meets President Jiang Zemin in Beijing to challenge China on human rights issues
President Bill Clinton issues statement on the "Three Noes" in Shanghai

1999   Chinese Premier Zhu Rongji first official visit to the United States
NATO forces bombs the Chinese Embassy in Belgrade
President Bill Clinton cautions Taiwan and China to resolve differences peacefully
U.S. and PRC announce agreement on terms for China's WTO accession
Wen Ho Lee arrested for allegedly passing nuclear information to China

2000   U.S. Trade and Development Agency (TDA) announces reopening of grant assistance program in China suspended since 1989
The full House passes HR 1838, the Taiwan Security Enhancement Act
President Bill Clinton signs the Permanent Normal Trade Relations for China
Chen Shuibian, the pro-independence leader in Taiwan, elected president

2001   A Chinese F8 fighter collides with a U.S. Navy EP-3 reconnaissance plane over the South China Sea
President George W. Bush authorizes the sale of defense articles and services to Taiwan, including Diesel-Powered Submarines, Anti-submarine Air Craft, and Destroyers
Beijing awarded the right to host the 2008 Olympic Games
China formally joins the World Trade Organization (WTO)
U.S. and China commences a counter-terrorism dialogue after September 11
President George W. Bush visits China

2002   China receives Permanent Normal Trade Relations from the United States
U.S. Commerce Secretary congratulates Taiwan on WTO membership
President George W. Bush visits China
President George W. Bush and Chinese President Jiang Zemin discuss Iraq, North Korea at Bush Ranch, Crawford, TX
Chinese leader-to-be Hu Jintao visits the U.S.
North Korean Nuclear Program arouses concerns in China and the United States

2003   President George W. Bush meets with Chinese Premier Wen Jiabao
Secretary of State Colin Powell makes remark that "U.S. relations with China are the best" since President Richard Nixon's ice-breaking visit to Beijing in 1972
Total two-way trade between China and U.S. grows from $33 billion in 1992 to over $180 billion in 2003

2004   Chen Shuibian, the pro-independence leader in Taiwan, reelected president
President Hu Jintao meets with U.S. Vice President Dick Cheney who says that the United States does not support "Taiwan Independence" and is against any unilateral action from each side to change the existing situation across the Taiwan Strait
U.S. Navy stages war exercises off China's waters

2005   North Korea announces it owns nuclear weapons

Abbreviations and Acronyms

AIT	American Institute of Taiwan
APEC	Asia Pacific Economic Cooperation
ASA	Association of Southeast Asia
ASEAN	Association of South East Asian Nations
AVG	American Volunteer Group
CAT	China Air Transport
CBI	China-Burma-India Theater
CCBA	Chinese Consolidated Benevolent Association
CCP	Chinese Communist Party
CDFEP	Committee on a Democratic Far Eastern Policy
CER	Chinese Eastern Railway
CHINCOM	China Committee
CIA	Central Intelligence Agency
CIC	Chinese Industrial Cooperatives
CMB	China Medical Board
CMC	Central Military Commission
COM	The Committee of One Million Against the Admission of Communist China to the United Nations
CPV	Chinese People's Volunteers
DPP	Democratic Progressive Party
DPRK	Democratic People's Republic of Korea
FBI	Federal Bureau of Investigation
FSO	Foreign Service Officer
GDP	Gross Domestic Product
GMD	Guomindang
GNP	Gross National Product
IMF	International Monetary Fund
IPR	Institute of Pacific Relations
ITO	International Trade Organization
JCRR	Joint Commission on Rural Reconstruction
MFN	Most Favored Nation
NATO	North Atlantic Treaty Organization
NPT	(Nuclear) Non-Proliferation Treaty
OSS	Office of Strategic Services
PLA	People's Liberation Army
POW	Prisoners of War
PRC	People's Republic of China
PUMC	Peking Union Medical College
ROC	Republic of China
SEATO	Southeast Asia Treaty Organization
TRA	Taiwan Relations Act
UCR	United China Relief
UK	United Kingdom
UN	United Nations
USC	United Service to China
VOA	Voice of America
WTO	World Trade Organization
YMCA	Young Men's Christian Association
YWCA	Young Women's Christian Association

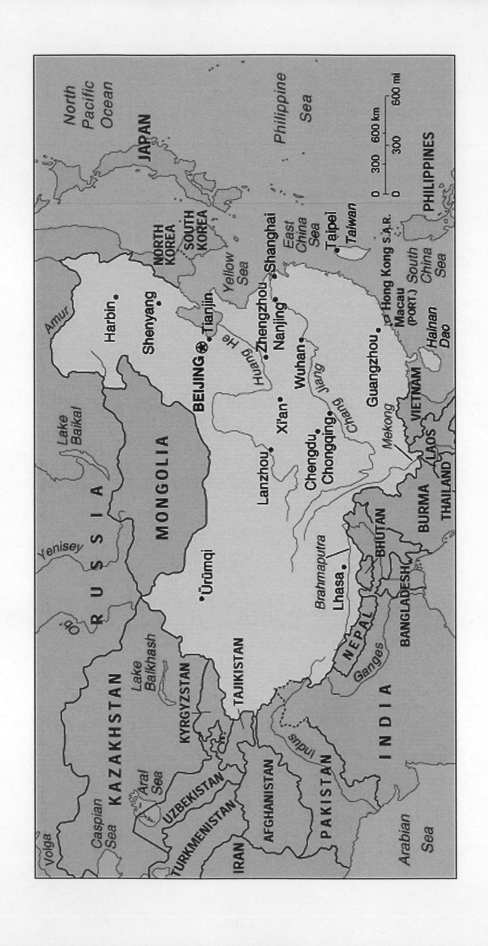

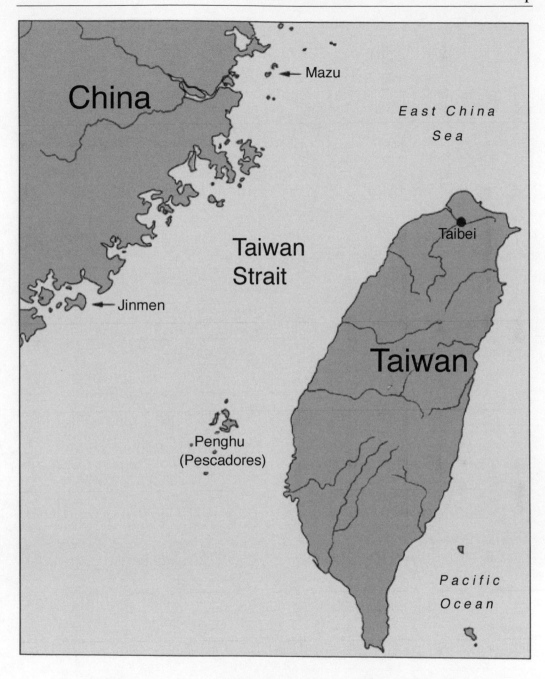

THE ENCYCLOPEDIA

Acheson, Dean (1873–1971)

Dean Acheson served as the Secretary of State for the Truman administration from 1949 to 1952, during the peak of the cold war. Providing counsel to the President on matters of foreign relations, Acheson sought to maintain America's political interests that included considerations of support for its Allies following the end of World War II. During Acheson's tenure he helped implement policies to advance Truman's containment doctrine that reflected the overarching foreign policy of resistance in any advance of Communism through diplomatic and military action. Initially concentrating on the threat of Soviet Communist expansion after the end of World War II, Acheson was soon confronted with the crisis of the looming victory of the Communist army over the Nationalists in China. Even as China's civil war was leaning toward a Communist victory, Acheson was much more concerned with rebuilding Europe as a bulwark against expanding Soviet control of central and eastern European states. Acheson was the American framer and signatory of the North Atlantic Treaty Organization (NATO) on April 4, 1949 creating a coalition of a dozen countries that would collaborate in military defensive action in the event of an armed attack against one or more of them. This served as a much stronger and effective deterrence against the Soviet Union in military actions.

At the same time, Acheson placed the rebuilding of Japan as critical for economic development and trade and as military ally in the Pacific. In fact, Japan's gradual rebuilding during Occupation that was headed by General Douglas McArthur-Supreme Commander Allied Powers would stabilize the region and create a buffer against the Soviet Union. To accomplish this Acheson supported an expansion of Chinese and South Korean trade to rebuild war devastated Japan. Acheson also was concerned by the faltering British economy so by rebuilding Japan, it could resume trade relations beneficial to Britain. This preoccupation of Acheson revealed his priorities; however events would force Acheson to pay more attention to China.

By 1949, however intelligence sources in Asia confirmed that the Communist victory was assured and that Mao Zedong would eventually take power. Acheson understood that Nationalist leader Jiang Jieshi as a corrupt leader who had squandered millions in U.S. military aid. By the spring of 1949, Acheson did not support American intervention to prevent Communist takeover in China. With strained financial resources in the U.S., he concentrated on rebuilding Europe and Japan, and resisted the slings and arrows from the China advocates in Congress and the supporters of Jiang from the private sector lobby. Eventually Jiang escaped to Taiwan following his defeat on mainland China, and soon established the government of the Republic of China (ROC) on Taiwan asserting it was the legitimate Chinese government. Acheson sought to distance American support from Jiang and at the same time maintain democracy in Taiwan. This enabled him to show more neutrality to induce the Chinese to initiate ties with the U.S. Acheson's initial foreign policy toward China was based on the assessment that China being an undeveloped country had little immediate strategic importance or international clout. It was clear that the Chinese would seek economic aid and technical assistance from the Soviets to modernize this poor, densely populated country. Acheson's analysis was that long-term relations between the Soviets and the Chinese would sour and eventually they would develop areas of disagreement. It was this shrift that Acheson sought to exacerbate through his policy of flexibility and accommodation. His aim was to separate these Communist powers from building a stronger and threatening coalition.

Precisely how the Communists would respond to the West was an open question for Truman and Acheson, for initially they both consented that the United States would not attempt to engage in a war against China. The political climates of cold war anxieties eventually lead many to blame Truman for assenting or even deceiving America by the Communist takeover in China and Acheson worked to deflect these attacks. Major policy differences, however, were revealed by the relatively swift recognition of the Communist government by Britain in contrast to an absence of recognition by the United States. Acheson also used the Chinese Communist's abuse and imprisonment of American Consulate officials in 1949 as his rationale to not recognize the Chinese government as official. Rejecting the use of sanction and blockades, Acheson simply issued formal protests accusing the Chinese of illegalities in the treatment of U.S. diplomats. His aim was to convey to the Communists that they should observe their international responsibilities. The Communists showed further dismissal of treaty obligations by retaking American property established by a 1901 protocol. Acheson also managed to retain U.S. neutrality by avoiding actions in the UN that would openly reveal their opposition to recognizing China and intent to steer China to respect the U.S. The outbreak of the Korean War and the movement of American troop across the 38th parallel effectively estranged diplomatic relations between China and the United States. As American troops pushed toward the Yalu River, Mao, with the consent of Stalin, directed nearly three quarters of a million Communist troops to reinforce the North Koreans.

Acheson's foreign policy with China has been scrutinized by numerous scholars that range in assessment that his China policy was extraordinarily successful to those who indicate he didn't achieve his aims. Ultimately the Truman administration's foreign policy and covert Central Intelligence Agency's activities in Korea could not prevent the events leading China to assist Communist North Korea during the Korean War.

See also Cold War; Korean War; Acheson's National Press Club Speech.

REFERENCES: James Chace, *Acheson: The Secretary of State Who Created the American World* (New York, 1998); Nancy Bernkopf Tucker, *Patterns in the Dust: Chinese-American Relations and the Recognition Controversy 1949–1950* (New York, 1983); Ronald L. McGlothlen, *Controlling the Waves: Dean Acheson and U.S. Foreign Policy in Asia* (New York, 1993).

James Steinberg

Acheson's National Press Club Speech

On January 12, 1950, Secretary of State Dean G. Acheson sought in this speech to refute Republican charges that the Truman administration had not done enough to prevent Communist control over China. By late 1949, President Harry S. Truman had concluded that the People's Republic of China (PRC) would conquer Taiwan in the near future and destroy the last remnants of the exiled Guomindang government. On January 5, 1950, he announced that while the United States would continue economic aid to the Nationalists, military aid and advice would cease. Acheson, in his address, denied that the statement constituted any reversal of U.S. policy. The United States, he explained, had recognized Taiwan as Chinese territory in World War II and would not violate past agreements. Far more important, Acheson insisted that military aid would not help Jiang Jieshi's regime because the United States could not give "a will to resist and a purpose for resistance to those who must provide it for themselves." The Truman administration was preparing to establish normal relations with the PRC.

A second objective of Acheson's address was to build support for U.S. policy in the Republic of Korea (ROK). Since the summer of 1949, Congress had been reluctant to authorize a three-year program of economic aid to South Korea. In his speech, Acheson was trying to explain why Korea deserved aid when Jiang did not. The Secretary of State claimed that in Asia, the military threat was not as immediate as the challenge of political "subversion and penetration." Communism exploited conditions of economic dislocation and social upheaval to advance the Soviet strategy for world domination. With American economic aid, technical skill, and administrative advice, however, Asian countries could develop democratic institutions capable of meeting popular needs and desires. But U.S. aid alone was not enough, since Asian leaders themselves had to demonstrate the will to improve conditions. In China, for example, Jiang had not worked to improve political and economic circumstances and the Chinese people had "brushed him aside."

Asians considered national independence and self-government as vital, Acheson continued, in the struggle to overcome economic privation and foreign domination. The United States always had worked for Asian independence, while the Soviet Union sought to rob Asians of control over their own affairs. It was therefore imperative to avoid any actions that obscured Communism as the spearhead of Russian imperialism. For example, with U.S. aid, South Korea had "a very good chance" of resisting Communist expansion. But the United States could not provide a pledge of military protection because the ROK was outside its "defensive perimeter." In the event of open aggression beyond Japan, the Ryukyus, and the Philippines, "the initial reliance must be on the people attacked to resist it and then upon ... the United Nations which so far has not proved a weak reed to lean on by any people who are determined to protect their independence...." Acheson in his speech was describing an intelligent policy of limited containment that the United States followed in Asia before the Korean conflict militarized the Cold War.

Critics later claimed that Acheson's speech gave North Korea a "green light" to invade South Korea because it implied that the United States would not defend the ROK. To date, released Soviet documents record just one discussion among Communist leaders about the address. On January 17, 1950, Soviet Foreign Minister Vyacheslav M. Molotov told Mao Zedong at a meeting in Moscow that Acheson's remarks on "China, USSR and their mutual relations are a clear slander against the Soviet Union and were designed to deceive directly public opinion." He then quoted from a translation of the speech, with emphasis on Acheson's claims that the Soviet Union had incorporated Outer Mongolia and had begun to partition Manchuria. Mao replied that "until now, as is known, these fabrications were the job of all kinds of scoundrels, represented by American journalists and correspondents." That the U.S. Secretary of State was now doing "the dirty work" showed how "the Americans are making progress!" As for the North Koreans, they at first thought Acheson had placed South Korea *inside* the U.S. defensive perimeter.

See also **Acheson, Dean (1873–1971); Civil War (1945–1949); Cold War; Korean War.**

REFERENCES: Dean G. Acheson, *Present at the Creation: My Years in the State Department* (New York, 1969); Bruce Cumings, *The Origins of the Korean War*, Vol. II: *The Roaring of the Cataract, 1947–1950* (Princeton, NJ, 1990); James I. Matray, "Dean Acheson's Press Club Speech Reexamined," *Journal of Conflict Studies* (Spring 2002); David Rees, *Korea: The Limited War* (New York, 1964); William Stueck, *The Korean War: An International History* (Princeton, NJ, 1995).

James I. Matray

Air America

Air America was the airline company owned and used by Central Intelligence Agency (CIA) for covert logistical, intelligence gathering, even military operations in Asia during the 1950s and 1960s. Air America's predecessor was Civil Air Transport (CAT), a Chinese airline established after World War II. General Claire L. Chennault, the hero of the Flying Tigers, played an important role in starting and organizing CAT. In 1950, CIA bought CAT. For the U.S. government, the legitimate company could help American clandestine operations for the support of anti-Communist forces in Asia such as Chinese Nationalist troops in Burma, the South Korean government, and the French troops in Vietnam. In 1959 Tibetans began to revolt against the Chinese Communist rule. Air America secretly provided logistical support for the Tibetan resistance movement. Air America was also heavily involved in the Vietnam War. One of its most critical missions was in the spring of 1975 when its helicopters were used to evacuate Americans and South Vietnamese from Saigon as the Vietnamese Com-

munist troops began to launch their final assaults to capture the capital. By 1976, with the ease of Cold War tensions, the situation in Asia had changed drastically. Since there was little value of a secret air transport capability, CIA then sold Air America to private companies.

See also **Civil Air Transport (CAT).**

REFERENCES: C. Robbins, *Air America* (New York, 1979); W. M. Leary, *Perilous Missions: Civil Air Transport and CIA Covert Operations in Asia* (Tuscaloosa, AL, 1984).

Yuwu Song

Alsop, Joseph (1910–1989)

Joseph Alsop worked as a newspaper columnist at a time when print journalists commanded respect and wielded immense influence in American politics. A graduate of Harvard University, he began his newspaper career in 1935 and wrote with a forceful eloquence and acerbic wit that gained him many readers. As a member of a socially prominent family, Alsop prowled the corridors of power with a confident ease few of his journalistic peers could match. He was equally effective on world-spanning tours that took him to palaces and outposts in Africa, Europe, and Asia.

As the Cold War unfolded after 1945, Alsop established himself as a proponent of deploying unrelenting military power to defeat world Communism. Alsop urged unconditional support of the Nationalist regime in China and blasted officials who doubted the viability of the Guomindang (GMD) regime. Alsop threw his pro-Nationalist campaign into high gear after the Truman administration published its China White Paper. Alsop was able to utilize classified documents he received from General Albert Wedemeyer to assert that Chinese Communism was underestimated by American officials and that the Nationalists represented the only hope for halting the spread of Communism in Asia. Alsop also edited dispatches drafted by his brother Stewart Alsop during a spring 1949 tour of China to highlight the danger of Chinese Communism and blast the complacency of American expatriates in China. Alsop continued to criticize the Truman administration until President Harry S. Truman decided to defend South Korea in June 1950. Although Alsop lauded Truman's decisive move, he also mentioned that the North Korean invasion was a direct result of the failure to take a stand against Communism in China. Alsop went to Korea to report on the war and believed the U.S. had an opportunity to inflict a crippling defeat on Communist China. Alsop was bitter when the Eisenhower administration negotiated a truce with China instead. He charged that the truce emboldened the Chinese Communists to launch an all-out assault that led to the Geneva Conference of 1954, an event that Alsop characterized as a "Far Eastern Munich."

Alsop continued his relentless criticism of President Dwight D. Eisenhower's policies in Asia throughout the 1950s, saying that the U.S. proclaimed support for Nationalist Taiwan but pulled back when Communist China acted aggressively.

With the election of John F. Kennedy, Alsop believed America finally would take a firm stand against Communism. Alsop was a fervent supporter of the Vietnam War, a disaster that sapped the willingness of the American public to support military action to combat Communist subversion. The American public turned to television for its information, and Alsop became a reminder of a bygone era when an elite group of print journalists wielded immense clout. At one point, Alsop's commentary ran in 200 newspapers with a circulation of 25 million. By the time of his death in 1989, he was a symbol of the "Eastern Establishment" that had overextended American power in Asia, a pundit whose biting wit exceeded his political wisdom.

See also Civil War (1945–1949); China White Paper; Korean War; Cold War.

REFERENCES: Joseph and Stewart Alsop, *The Reporter's Trade* (New York, 1958); Robert Merry, *Taking on the World* (New York, 1996).

Michael J. Polley

Ambassador Duke [fictional]

Ambassador Duke was a literary character, who familiarized many Americans with China at the end of Mao Zedong's life and during the normalization of Sino-U.S. relations. Duke, a character in the popular American daily comic strip *Doonesbury*, by Gary Trudeau, was loosely based on the so-called "gonzo" journalist Dr. Hunter S. Thompson. The character Duke represented the libertarian impulses that had also been part of the counter-culture of the United States in the 1960s and early 1970s.

The character Duke was first introduced in July 1974 as a writer for *Rolling Stone* magazine, latter serving as the appointed governor of the U.S. territory of American Samoa. Following President Gerald R. Ford's trip to the People's Republic of China (PRC) and the normalization of diplomatic relations, Trudeau had the character reassigned as the U.S.'s first ambassador to China. Duke believed that his assignment came to send a message to the Chinese that Detente was a two-way street. Duke was openly suspicious of the Chinese, referring to them as "an especially tricky people." He assumed that he had been chosen for the post in part because his experience in American Samoa had shown his ability to work with "minorities." Trudeau himself traveled to China in December 1975 as part of the press corps during President Ford's official visit. In the strip, the character Duke arrived in China in January 1976. Through the daily comic strip many Americans became aware of the new political reality between the U.S. and the PRC. Duke informed the U.S. State Department of rising tension on the Sino-Soviet border. His pained boredom with Chinese revolutionary operas explained well the difficulty Chinese culture had in reconciling traditional arts within a socialist framework. Duke sought to understand the workings of the Chinese government, learning of the rise and fall of Chinese leaders, by interpreting posters in Shanghai. He was aided by his translator who had been furnished by the Chinese government, a Chinese woman he called "Honey." Honey Huan was very loosely based on Tang Wensheng, who had served as translator for President Richard Nixon during his first trip to China in 1972. In June 1977 Ambassador Duke left China to be replaced by the very real Leonard Woodcock and move onto new and increasingly seedy adventures in other parts of the world. When informed by Honey that Leonard Woodcock had shown great sensitivity to the working class, Duke replied, "all labor leaders are sensitive to the working class, that's how they avoid being part of it."

Although a fictional character in a daily comic strip, Duke provided Americans with a view into the workings of the Chinese government near the end of Mao's life. Duke's adventures in the PRC presented to Americans a China that, although different and perplexing, was far less threatening than earlier images. In recognition of the popularity of the character and the impact of the strip on Americans' perception of normalization of relations, the U.S. embassy in Beijing commissioned Trudeau to paint an official portrait of Duke in 1977 for the embassy gallery of former ambassadors.

Honey remained linked with Duke during the following decades. She defected from China and reunited with Duke, with whom she had fallen in unrequited love. She returned to Beijing to attend her college reunion when the Tiananmen Square massacre occurred. She escaped by hiding in the U.S. embassy. Duke returned to China in 1990 to marry her to get her out of the country. In later years Duke and Honey continued to have adventures, from drug running, to operating a for-profit orphanage, to operating a bar in Kuwait during the 1991 Persian Gulf War.

REFERENCES: Gary B. Trudeau, *The Bundled*

Doonesbury: A Pre-Millennial Anthology (Kansas City, KS, 1998); Gary B. Trudeau, *Action Figure!* (Kansas City, KS, 1992); Gary B. Trudeau, *An Especially Tricky People* (New York, 1977).

Barry Stentiford

Amerasia (Magazine)

A magazine founded by Philip J. Jaffe, a businessman, in the late 1930s in an effort to publish information on China's struggle against Japan. As its chief editor, Jaffe exhibited sympathies with the Chinese Communists when analyzing the nature of the second united front between Jiang Jieshi's Nationalist government and Mao Zedong's Communist forces. The editorial staff and contributing writers of this narrowly-circulated magazine included several specialists on East Asian affairs and the so-called China Hands who covered wartime China expansively. Most notable among them was John Stewart Service, a young career diplomat who observed and analyzed the China situation during World War II for the State Department, and who made policy recommendations that were deemed as sympathetic to the Chinese Communists. *Amerasia* published many intelligence reports and diplomatic dispatches on China and other parts of Asia, and was regularly read by the State Department and the Office of Strategic Services (OSS) officials. On March 11, 1945, the office of *Amerasia* in New York City was raided by OSS agents on suspicion that it had published classified government documents. Over 1,700 documents were seized, many of which concerned U.S. policy toward China, including correspondence between President Franklin D. Roosevelt and Chinese leader Jiang Jieshi, and reports on the weakness of Jiang's government and the strength of Mao's movement. Three months later, six people associated with *Amerasia* were arrested on charges of espionage for the Chinese Communists, including Jaffe and Service. Jeffe and his assistant were found guilty of illegal possession of government documents, while Service and others were cleared.

The *Amerasia* case was revived by Senator Joseph McCarthy in 1950 and cited as an example of the alleged infiltration of the State Department by Communists. As a result, despite being cleared again by a congressional investigation, Service was nonetheless fired by the State Department in 1951. He did not resume his diplomatic post until 1957 upon winning the court case. In 1970, Anthony Kubek, a China scholar and professor of history at the University of Dallas, prepared a two-volume book entitled *Amerasia Papers: A Clue to the Catastrophe of China*, for the Senate Judiciary Committee and Senate Subcommittee on Internal Security. He wrote a 113-page introduction for the book in an attempt to interpret the more than 300 selected documents, one third of which were either written by John Service or came from his personal collections. Service was singled out primarily because of his sharp criticism of General Patrick J. Hurley's failed attempt at mediating between the Chinese Nationalists and Communists and his view that it was inadvisable for Washington to render unconditional support to Jiang Jieshi's government.

The renewed attack on Service prompted him to respond in 1971 with his own book entitled *The Amerasia Papers: Some Problems in the History of U.S.-China Relations*, in which he refuted Kubek's assertions and allegations regarding the sources, intentions and impact of the so-called "*Amerasia* Papers" and accused Kubek of deliberate deception in the selection of the *Amerasia* documents as well as his erroneous interpretation of Sino-American relations during World War II and Chinese Civil War of 1945–1949. In addition, Service reiterated his analysis, made in most of his earlier diplomatic dispatches, that the wide spread corruption and factionalism within Jiang Jieshi's government and, above all, Jiang's reluctance to employ all his forces against Japan made him an ineffective ally. Service was highly critical of Hurley's role in the failure of U.S. policy in China due to the latter's ignorance of China's domestic politics, his misrepresentation of Washington's official position, as well as his personal ineptitude and diplomatic blunder, which compounded the existing problems facing American policy makers. Service concluded that an independent and flexible China policy, unburdened by an unwise commitment to the Nationalist government, and a realistic assessment of the nature and strength of the Chinese Communist movement would have altered the course of post-World War II American relations with China. The *Amerasia* case has remained a subject of historical inquiry since its first appearance over fifty years ago, as scholars continue to analyze and debate the merit and legacy of the case in their effort to dissect its impact on American domestic politics and foreign relations.

See also China Hands; Service, John Stewart (1909–1999); Jaffe, Philip Jacob (1895–1980); McCarthyism; Civil War (1945–1949).

REFERENCES: *The Amerasia Papers: A Clue to the Catastrophe of China* (Washington, D.C., 1970); Harvey Klehr and Ronald Radosh, *The Amerasia Spy Case: Prelude to McCarthyism* (Chapel Hill, NC, 1996); John S. Service, *The Amerasia Papers: Some Problems in the History of U.S.-China Relations* (Berkeley, CA, 1971).

Yi Sun

America-China Society

The America-China Society is a unique network of influential individuals whose goals include the promotion of friendly relations between the United States and the People's Republic of China. The Society is unique in that its members are distinguished citizens from the U.S. who have all played key roles in the development of Sino-American relations.

Included in the group's ranks are former U.S. President Richard M. Nixon, Secretary of State Henry Kissinger, former President Jimmy Carter and Jimmy Carter's Secretary of State, Cyrus Vance, who is the co-chair of the organization. Also in association with the group are former ambassadors, former Secretaries of State and State Department officials. Each member has contributed, and continues to contribute, resources to the development of further Sino-American relations. Richard Nixon's activity with China is well known from his visit to China in 1972. During the visit, Nixon succeeded in negotiating the lowering of economic, social and cultural barriers. In the midst of the Cold War, Nixon and Kissinger began devising a negotiation strategy with China as early as 1970. Finally in July of 1971, Kissinger's secret trip to China helped bridge the then widening gap between the two states. President Jimmy Carter helped to open diplomatic relations and settle on terms for the exchange of ambassadors. While Vance did play a more minor role in the establishment of Sino-American relations under Carter, he played a more active role as the co-chairman of the America-China Society until his death in 2002. Kissinger remains the chairman of the Society. Vance said about the America-China Society that, "the role of the organization is political, social and trade development overall, not work for individual firms." It was important for Vance to state the intentions of the group, because some of its corporate members such as Coca-Cola, Chase Manhattan Bank and American Express could lead some skeptics to believe that the America-China Society is oriented purely for market oriented agendas. The work of the America-China Society is indeed multifaceted and is characterized by its dedication towards building new bridges and maintaining already established connections and networks.

REFERENCES: Lori Wallach, and Patrick Woodall, and Ralph Nadar, *Whose Trade Organization? A Comprehensive Guide to the World Trade Organization, Second Edition* (New York, 2004); Society for Historians of America, *Perspectives in American Diplomacy: Essays on Europe, Latin America, China, and the Cold War* (Washington, D.C., 1975).

Arthur Holst

American Asiatic Association

The American Asiatic Association was an organization of American business interests created to lobby the U.S. State Department on East Asian policy issues as well as shape public opinion in support of a forward policy in the Pacific and China. Formed in June 1898 in the midst of both the Scramble for Concessions and the Spanish-American War, it was the leading advocate of an open door policy in China. Despite the initial reluctance of the McKinley administration, the Association pressured relentlessly for the annexation of Hawaii and the Philippines as stepping-stones to the China market.

Through the energetic leadership of John Foord, the fortnightly articles of the *Journal of the American Asiatic Association* and the insider connections of members Willard Straight, W. W. Rockhill and Charles Denby, the organization played a major role in shaping U.S. China policy in 1899 and 1900. The business community acclaimed the critical role of the Association in urging Secretary of State John Hay to issue the first Open Door notes in September 1899. By March 1900, however, John Foord was again warning President William McKinley of the dire threat to the open door posed by both Boxer disturbances and Russian machinations in Manchuria. Again Washington reacted by dispatching 5,000 troops to join the international expedition in suppressing the Boxer Rebellion in July. In addition, a second circular note to the powers insisted on preserving "the territorial and administrative integrity" of China, thus completing the structure of the Open Door Policy. Aware that the China market was linked to American treatment of Chinese immigrants at home, the American Asiatic Association played a prominent, but eventually futile, role in opposing the worst excesses of the Chinese exclusion movement. The result was the 1905 anti-American boycott, which is regarded as one of the first major manifestations of early Chinese nationalism. The Association's influence on policy waned during President Theodor Roosevelt's Administration as Washington sought to protect the open door through balance of power diplomacy with Britain and Japan.

REFERENCES: J. Lorence, *Organized Business and the Myth of the China Market: The American Asiatic Association, 1898–1937* (Philadelphia, PA, 1981); Charles S. Campbell, Jr., *Special Business Interests and the Open Door Policy* (New Haven, CT, 1951); Michael H. Hunt, *The Making of a Special Relationship: The United States and China to 1914* (New York, 1983).

Errol Clauss

American China Policy Association

With the start of Sino-Japanese War in China from the mid-1930s onward there were a variety of contending voices of support and opposition to the Nationalist Chinese government. During World War II the supporters and opponents of the Chinese Nationalist government continued their war of words to win influence for their position. In the war against fascism uncritical support was given to the Soviet Union and to the Chinese Communists. In the politics of the time the show case scenes allowed to reporters or others by the Communists made them appear far more desirable as the future rulers. In contrast there were frequent accusations made against the Nationalists including corrupt practices such as nepotism, bribery, and wasted American aid, and more. The facts behind these charges were often unavailable, but accusations were accepted as facts in some quarters, but not by William Kohlberg. He was an import-export merchant who traveled to China to investigate the reports. His report that the accusations were not true was not accepted by some in the State Department.

In 1946 the American China Policy Association (ACPA) was founded by J. B. Powell who had been a correspondent in China and Helen Loomis, who had been a missionary and teacher. The mission of the organization was to further American interests. Consequently only Americans could belong or participate in meetings where policy discussions were held. In 1946 Kohlberg joined the American China Policy Association (ACPA) to promote aid for the Nationalist Chinese. It began its criticism of the American policy of neutrality in the Chinese Civil War between the Communists and the Nationalists. It eventually became the organization that led the charge in both volume and directness of its attacks on American China policy. In 1947 Powell, President of ACPA died. Clare Booth Luce, wife of the owner and publisher of *Time*, *Life*, and *Fortune* magazines served for the next year as President of ACPA. She was followed by William Loeb, owner and publisher of *Union Leader* of Manchester in New Hampshire.

In 1949 the Chinese Communist Party took control of mainland China. With Soviet expansion in Eastern Europe and with the Cold War now underway the American China Policy Association and other supporters accused the State Department of "losing China." Between 1946 and 1953 The ACPA issued a huge body of literature. Letters, pamphlets, brochures, press releases, and book reviews were addressed to the public at large and opinion leaders in particular. The ACPA even issued as facsimile reprints Chinese Communist party materials that would reveal their policies and how these were at odds with American interests. The work of the ACPA was managed by Alfred Kohlberg, an active member of the China Lobby, at No. 1 West 37th Street in New York City. Publications also carried that address. Most of the literature issued by the ACPA was signed by Kohlberg, although some was signed by Helen Loomis, William Loeb, and several others. Some of the very active members of the ACPC were Freda Utley, Irene Kuhn, Max Eastman, Representative Walter H. Judd, Geraldine Fitch, the Reverend William R. Johnson, Isaac Don Levine, and Margaret Proctor Smith. Others who were less active supporters included Dr. Maurice William (ACPS vice-president), Major General David P. Barrows, William Henry Chamberlin, George Creel, and Roscoe Pound. All of these individuals were members of the APCA's Board of Directors. Creel was famous for his government information management during World War I. And Pound was one of America's most prominent jurists.

Eventually American foreign policy changed to APCA's view that more support should be given to the Nationalist Chinese in their battle with the Communist Chinese. In 1945 there was no criticism of American policy towards China and an absence of support for increasing aid to the Nationalists. By 1953 support and aid for them became an entrenched part of America's China policy. The policy advocacy of the APCA and the battle with the Chinese Communists during the Korean War effectively changed the policy orientation.

See also Civil War (1945–1949); Kohlberg, Alfred (1887–1960); China Lobby.

REFERENCES: Ross Y. Koen, *The China Lobby in American Politics* (New York, 1960); Freda Utley, *The China Story* (Chicago, IL, 1951).

Jack Waskey

American Committee for Non-Participation in Japanese Aggression

In May 1938, two missionary educators and brothers, Harry and Frank Price, met with a group of predominantly American businessmen, educators, journalists and missionaries and formed the American Committee for Non-Participation in Japanese Aggression. The group later chose Roger Greene, a former U.S. diplomat with numerous political connections in Washington, to be chairman. Henry Stimson, the former Secretary of State under the Hoover administration, served as the committee's honorary president.

The Committee was appalled by the Sino-Japanese War especially the atrocities committed by the Japanese military in Nanjing from December 1937 onward. More importantly, the Committee believed that the United States was complicit in Japan's aggression in China because American merchants sold the raw materials to Japan that aided its war effort in China. The Committee sent representatives around the United States on speaking tours, and produced booklets including "America's Share in Japan's War Guilt," and "Shall America Stop Arming Japan?" The thrust of the Committee's message was that the United States should place an embargo on the export of war materials, particularly scrap iron and oil, to Japan. By denying the Japanese war machine of its lifeblood, Japan's advance into China and elsewhere without endangering U.S. security by cutting off trade with Asia. Moreover, the U.S. could retain such raw materials to prepare for its own defense. The Committee also argued that maintenance a strong and independent China was critical to U.S. national security. It did not condemn, but rather condoned, the providing of aid to Nationalist China by the United States even though such an act was hardly neutral.

In February 1941, the Committee ceased to function. Just a few months before, the U.S. Congress passed the National Defense Act of 1940 which gave the President authority to embargo any materials deemed necessary to the national defense. American public opinion almost unanimously supported an embargo on war materials, but the extent to which the Committee can be credited for changing American attitudes is unclear. The extent of the Committee's impact on government policy is likewise unclear. Although the Committee played a role in convincing Washington, for example, to embargo aviation fuel and parts, the Roosevelt administration consistently rejected placing an embargo on oil exports to Japan. Not until July 1941, after the Committee dissolved and Japanese forces moved into southern Vietnam, did the administration take that fateful step.

See also Price, Harry (1905–2002); Price, Frank (1895–1974).

REFERENCES: Donald Friedman, *Road to Isolation: The American Committee for Non-Participation In Japanese Aggression* (Cambridge, MA, 1968).

Stephen Craft

American Emergency Committee for Tibetan Refugees (AECTR)

American Emergency Committee for Tibetan Refugees (AECTR) was founded in 1959 to provide aid and political support for Tibet's religious leader, the fourteenth Dalai Lama and Tibetan refugees who had fled to India in 1959 to escape Chinese Communist aggression in Tibet. Seeking to oppose Chinese Communist expansion, AECTR engaged in public relations campaigns in support of the Tibetans. Prior to the establishment of AECTR were many pro-Chinese Nationalist organizations referred to as the China Lobby. During the early 1950's they were extremely active in their encouragement of the United States government to engage in assistance and in some cases military action against Chinese Communism. A plethora of private organizations mushroomed in reaction to the emergence of the Cold War and resulting uncertainties. There were many agendas of these organizations, however, resistance to recognizing Communist China in the United Nations, continuing support of defeated Nationalist leader Jiang Jieshi, and military support for South Korea in response to Communist support of North Korea's initiation of the Korean War were common themes.

The Chinese military incursions into Tibet began earlier in October 1950, a year after Mao Zedong declared the founding of the People's Republic of China. Initially attacking the town of Chamdo, the larger Chinese forces overwhelmed Tibetan military defenses and by 1951 Chinese troops had reached the Tibetan capital city of Lhasa, which contained the theocratic center — the Potola Monastery Palace — the symbol of Tibetan Buddhism. The Chinese troops stationed garrisons in major cities, while the Dalai Lama sent a delegation to Beijing to negotiate an end to Chinese military invasions and to discuss a resolution of the conflict. The Dalai Lama, however, was to learn that his delegation had been allegedly pressured by the Chinese to sign the seventeen points of agreement that according to the Chinese ended Tibetan political independence. The agreements involved the gradual incorporation of Chinese political changes and reorganization of the military and brought a new Chinese presence to Tibet. In reaction to this change of events the U.S. discussed the situation with the Dalai Lama and supported his rejection of the agreement and recommended that he go into exile. This would generate Asian Buddhist's rejection of Chinese Communist expansion consistent with American containment policy. The Dalai Lama was determined to make the best of the situation and returned to Lhasa from Yatung where he had hidden due to the threats on his life. From 1952 to 1959 the Chinese gradually started making radical reforms, which included aggressive prosecution of Tibetan officials that dissented with Chinese occupation commanders. It was the Dalai Lama's brother, Guyalo Thondrup who recognized that the Chinese were entrenched in Tibet. He trekked to the Indian border and set up an opposition organization in Calcutta, and sought support for resistance of the Chinese in Tibet from the American government and Jiang Jieshi, the President of the Republic of China on Taiwan. Chinese occupation continued to tighten its grip on Tibet by increased taxation, weapons confiscation, removal of private property and harassment of monks. The mayhem proved deadly as struggle sessions and executions were reported. The transition to socialism had begun to be tested by the fiercely independent Tibetan Golok and Khampa clans. Their resistance led to Chinese military reprisals in the bombing of villages, executions and the destruction of sacred monasteries. At the same time, on July 27, 1953 the American military concluded an armistice agreement over the Korean War and by 1956 the Central Intelligence Agency initiated covert operations to train and later equip Tibetans in their resistance against the Chinese forces.

The antagonisms were pre-empted by the escape of the Dalai Lama to India on March 17, 1959, who was granted political asylum in that country and eventually created his government in exile in Dhramsala, India. Many American non-governmental organizations (NGO) sympathized with the Tibetans and their persecution at the hand of the Communists. Echoing the sentiments of the 1947 Truman Doctrine, which expressed that the United States will resist Communist expansion world-wide, these organizations raised funds to assist the plight of the Tibetan refugees that were escaping into India. AECTR was known as an influential organization composed of well-known Americans such as Senator William Knowland, Henry Luce (founder of Time-Life Publishing), and author Lowell Thomas. The organization sought donations for their cause until 1970, primarily funding medical and educational aid and major public relations efforts to free Tibet from Chinese Communists. Initially the organization's goal was to encourage dissent in mainland China to usher the return of Jiang Jieshi and the return of a democratic China. The organization coordinated with Catholic Relief Services and the Central Relief Committee for Tibetans. AECTR also collaborated with the Dooley Foundation, a non-governmental organization in providing aid to the Tibetan refugees in India.

See also Tibet; Dalai Lama.

REFERENCES: Nancy Bernkopf Tucker, *Patterns in the Dust: Chinese-American Relations and the Recogni-* *tion Controversy* (New York, 1983), John Kenneth Knaus, *Orphans of the Cold War: America and the Tibetan Struggle for Survival* (New York, 1999), Kenneth Conboy and James Morrison, *The CIA's Secret War in Tibet* (Lawrence, KS 2002).

James W. Steinberg

American Institute in Taiwan (AIT)

The American Institute in Taiwan (AIT) was established after the passing of the Taiwan Relations Act on April 10, 1979. The AIT serves as a de facto embassy for the United States in Taiwan. After President Jimmy Carter broke formal diplomatic relations with Taiwan, the United States saw it necessary to still maintain an embassy-like presence there.

The AIT is a non-profit, private corporation. The AIT's purpose is the "continuation of commercial, cultural and other relations between the people of the United States and the people on Taiwan." In addition, AIT provides, "any programs, transactions, or other relations conducted or carried out by the President or any Agency of the United States Government with respect to Taiwan shall, in the manner and to the extent directed by the President, be conducted and carried out by or through the American Institute in Taiwan." The American Institute in Taiwan is funded primarily by the U.S. Department of State. AIT also operates under U.S. Congressional jurisdiction, as mandated by the Taiwan Relations Act. AIT has three offices, one in the United States, one in Taibei and one in Gaoxiong. The U.S. office is relatively small and is located in Arlington, Virginia. The Taibei office is significantly bigger and is the hub of activity. The Taibei office employs over 300 people and participates in various duties including trade and consular services, agricultural sales and inter-cultural exchanges. The Gaoxiong office provides many of the same services as the Taibei location, except on a more local scale. The United States' "One China Policy" restricts it from having an embassy in Taiwan. Since Jimmy Carter's administration, the United States does not recognize Taiwan as an official state. Recognition would grant Taiwan the ability to house a formal U.S. diplomatic program. However, China sees the movement of Taiwan towards democracy as a separatist movement.

The U.S. since Jimmy Carter has walked a fine diplomatic line between the ever-tense relations between China and Taiwan. Washington adopted the "One China Policy," while maintaining ideological support for Taiwan. The American Institute in Taiwan is a brick on the path of that line, and is categorical of the United States' position of what has been called, "strategic ambiguity." Militarily, the situation flared in 1996 when China fired missiles into the sea surrounding Taiwan, in order to influence a presidential election. The U.S. responded by sending warships into the region. The AIT's objectives are to maintain stable relations between Taiwan and the U.S. and strive for peace in the region.

See also Taiwan Relations Act (1979); One China Policy.

REFERENCES: I. M. Destler, *The New Politics of American Trade: Trade Labor and the Environment* (Washington, D.C., 1999); James R. Lilley, and Chuck Downs, *Crisis in Taiwan Strait* (Washington, D.C., 1997); Suisheng Zhao, *Across the Taiwan Strait: Mainland China, Taiwan, and the 1995–1996 Crisis* (New York, 1999).

Arthur Holst

American Military Mission to China (AMMISCA) *see* Magruder Mission

American Military Observer Group (Yanan)

In 1943, American officials had very real concerns about the Nationalist Chinese regime headquartered in Chongqing. In addition to evident corruption and inefficiency, Nationalist leader Jiang Jieshi had assigned some 500,000 of his best troops to maintain a blockade of Communist forces at the Yanan base camp. In this environment, some American military and diplomatic officers felt a need to establish contact with the Chinese Communists at Yanan. The only previous official U.S. contact was in 1938, and, given existing plans to invade the Chinese coast to prepare for the invasion of Japan, it made sense to have a working relationship with this strong and effective anti-Japanese resistance group.

In 1944, the U.S. government authorized the Dixie Mission, a group of mid-and lower-level military officers, OSS agents, and diplomatic officials, to travel to the Communist base area at Yanan. There was a primary purpose, to gain Communist assistance for the rescue of downed American flyers, primarily B-29 crews from Claire Chennault's air forces in China. There were a series of secondary purposes, including gaining intelligence about the Japanese and the Chinese Communists. The first men arrived in July 1944 in a landing that destroyed their plane, and the last men left in March 1947 as Nationalist forces were about to seize Yanan while Lin Biao and the Communists were winning in Manchuria. From 1944 to 1946, the team was called the Yanan Observers Group; from 1946 to 1947 it was the Yanan Liai-

son Group. From the outset, the Dixie Mission was different from the larger American mission with the Nationalist army. Unlike advisors assigned to Nationalist units, Dixie Mission experts did not provide training. When they accompanied Communist guerrillas into action, they did so only to observe. Few Japanese troops ever surrendered to Americans in the Pacific war; but hundreds and hundreds of Japanese troops—and a rich mine of intelligence information—came over because of more effective Communist propaganda. Dixie Mission members were interested in Communist techniques. Mao Zedong supported the Dixie Mission, at least initially, in hope it would lead to greater U.S. recognition, and perhaps U.S. support for a Communist presence at a postwar discussion about the future of China. Even when the Communists realized that these younger and more junior officers, agents, and officials could not exert much influence on overall U.S. policy, they continued to treat the Americans well until the mission ended as the Civil War began anew after Japan's surrender.

In later years, critics claimed the Dixie Mission members were duped. Certainly, many members recognized that Mao and his colleagues worked very hard and lived austerely without the gross corruption and inefficiency that characterized Jiang's Nationalist regime. They also appreciated the ability of Communist cadres to organize peasants into effective fighters and convince enemy soldiers to desert. They likely did not anticipate, for few in that period could anticipate, the horrors that Mao's regime would visit on the Chinese people in the 1950s and 1960s in various failed social and economic efforts that caused millions and millions to die. And there were strongly anti-Communist mission members who decried any effort that benefited the Communists. But the majority of members felt the United States would have been well served to send a senior officer to visit Yanan and meet with Mao Zedong and other Communist leaders.

The Dixie Mission members would be the last American government officials to spend extensive time with Chinese Communist leaders until Richard Nixon's historic trip to China in February 1972. Many of them would pay a heavy career price, including fewer opportunities for promotion and being caught up in the Red Scare that accompanied the McCarthyism frenzy. Sadly, the ensuing confrontation and lack of contact may have led to external intervention — American and Chinese — in the Korean and Vietnam conflicts, and thus highlight one price to pay for the failure to build upon the work of the Dixie Mission.

REFERENCES: David M. Barrett, *Dixie Mission: The*

United States Army Observer Group in Yanan (Berkeley, CA, 1970); Carolle J. Carter, *Mission to Yanan: American Liaison with the Chinese Communists, 1944–1947* (Lexington, KY, 1997); Margaret S. Denning, *The Sino-American Alliance in World War II. European University Studies, Series III* (New York, 1986); William P. Head, *Yanan! Colonel Wilbur Peterkin and the American Military Mission to the Chinese Communists, 1944–1945* (Chapel Hill, NC, 1987).

Charles M. Dobbs

American Red Cross (ARC)

In 1881, well-known nurse Clara Barton founded the American Red Cross as a national branch of the international relief organization headquartered in Geneva, Switzerland. The ARC had a hybrid identity as a private association that was chartered, but not funded, by the American government.

In 1905, leadership of the association passed to a group of Progressives led by Mabel Boardman. Many of the new leaders had a personal interest in China, as well as a commitment to socially progressive philanthropy. Over the next two decades, until a new leadership retrenched from global activities, this dual interest nurtured a series of charitable and reform activities within China. The ARC's programs differed in an important respect from most early 20th century American philanthropic initiatives (such as those of the YMCA) in China: they had no formal ties to any religious missionary movement. At the height of collaboration between the government and the ARC, Presidents William H. Taft and Woodrow Wilson served simultaneously as President of the American Red Cross. The two institutions had a symbiotic relationship, whereby the ARC was able to seek government endorsement of various projects while the government felt its image among the Chinese people benefited from those projects. In 1906–1907, the American Red Cross undertook its first major project in China, relief from a famine that resulted from flooding in the eastern part of the country. Its next major project was the provision of relief from the 1910 plague in Manchuria. In 1911, the ARC became more ambitious, seeking to contribute not just to alleviation of China's successive natural disasters, but to social reforms that might prevent future disasters, as well as mold Chinese society in an American Progressive image. In its most ambitious China initiative, the ARC sought from 1911–1916 to design, fund, and implement a Huai River Conservancy Project that would improve China's physical infrastructure, stabilize its social structure, and inculcate American ideals of efficient organization and honest administration. Because of inability to secure American financing, political chaos in the wake of China's 1911 Republican Revolution, and the advent of World War I, the project never came to fruition. A more modest "work relief" response to the 1912 famine in Manchuria also was stymied by local and international factors. In the 1920s, Americans (both the public and its government) retreated from international concerns, while China was in the grip of ongoing civil war and the rise of anti-foreigner nationalism. New leaders in the United States steadily withdrew the ARC from activities in China, ultimately closing their operations in that country in 1929.

Despite failure to achieve its most ambitious goals, the American Red Cross left a considerable legacy in China. Between 1905 and 1929 it spent $2,500,000 on 23 relief projects. During this period, China accounted for 26 of the ARC's 80 foreign relief projects. Further, the ARC helped nurture the Chinese Red Cross and other relief organizations and attracted the activism of an energetic core of Americans resident in China. These progressive activists became more committed to relief and reform in China, even as ARC headquarters in New York was retrenching. In the 1930s, they found other institutional channels for their reform impulses.

REFERENCES: Karen Lynn Brewer, *From Philanthropy to Reform: The American Red Cross in China, 1906–1930* (Ph.D. Dissertation, Case Western Reserve University, 1985); Foster Rhea Dulles, *The American Red Cross: A History* (New York, 1950); Noel Pugach, *Paulg S. Reinsch: Open Door Diplomat in Action* (Millwood, NY, 1979).

Norty Wheeler

American Volunteer Group (AVG)

Also known as the "Flying Tigers," the American Volunteer Group consisted of a small number of American pilots who volunteered to fight against the Japanese for China in the Sino-Japanese War (1937–1945). The AVG existed for less than a year and always operated at a distinct numerical disadvantage.

Initially formed at the request of Nationalist leader Generalissimo Jiang Jieshi and his wife Madame Jiang, head of the country's air force, the AVG was conceived as a response to the unchallenged Japanese bombing raids on southwest China in 1939. Retired American Colonel Claire Lee Chennault, who had been serving as a consultant to China's air force when the Sino-Japanese conflict broke out in 1937, organized the group's enlistment in the U.S. and its operation in China. The AVG operated through a series of clandestine mechanisms that allowed the United States to retain its official neutrality towards Japan in the months before Pearl Harbor. U.S. President Franklin D. Roosevelt issued an executive order allowing pilots and mechanics to resign their positions in the U.S. military and join the AVG with the understanding that they would be reinstated at comparable or higher rank and compensated for time served upon their return from China. In addition, AVG personnel were hired in China by the Central Aircraft Manufacturing Company (CAMCO), a front intended to prevent U.S. personnel from being employed directly by the Chinese government. Pay for AVG personnel ranged from $600 to $750 a month, in addition to an unofficial $500 per plane bounty on Japanese aircraft destroyed. Aircraft were purchased stateside through a similar corporation under Chinese Defense Supplies, run by Chinese envoy Song Ziwen. Procuring aircraft proved extremely difficult for the Chinese since American industry was supplying aircraft to the war in Europe at the time. Eventually, however, the British government was convinced to give up their claim on 100 Curtiss Hawk P-40C aircraft, a model deemed too slow to face German planes over Europe. The United States' Lend-Lease program developed soon after this initial transfer in order to facilitate future exchanges of this nature.

Although the Japanese aerial assault on China began in January of 1939, Chennault and the first wave of American pilots did not arrive in China until the latter months of 1941. Eventually based in Kunming, China, the AVG initially leased the Kyedaw airfield in Burma from the English colonial government for the purpose of ground training and flight instruction. Pilots were trained in the P-40 aircraft and taught Chennault's unique method of aerial warfare, a method that eschewed the concept of single plane-to-plane combat in favor of an approach utilizing teams of two aircraft. AVG pilots also studied Japanese tactics and maneuvers extensively due to the fact that Chennault did not agree with the common conception of the Japanese as inferior and mechanical pilots.

Following their attack on Pearl Harbor on December 7, 1941, the Japanese quickly moved to attack Burma, and the AVG first engaged Japanese fighter planes over Rangoon in December of 1941. Estimates of Japanese losses against the AVG have varied over the last fifty years, with high estimates at around 300 planes (confirmed) and more recent estimates coming in at around 115. In his autobiography, Chennault claimed that only 12 P-40's were lost in combat. In the end, however, the AVG was unsuccessful in its attempt to stop the Japanese invasion of Burma, and its overall statistical importance in the Sino-Japanese war

has been questioned. Whatever their statistical accomplishments, the AVG provided a beacon of success against overwhelming odds at a time when Japan seemed invincible. In July of 1942, with the permission of Generalissimo Jiang, the AVG and Chennault were incorporated into the U.S. 14th Air Force in the China-Burma-India theatre under the command of U.S. General Joseph W. Stillwell.

See also Chennault, Claire L. (1890–1958).

REFERENCES: Charles Bond, Jr. and Terry Anderson, *A Flying Tiger's Diary* (College Station, TX, 1984); Claire Lee Chennault, *Way of a Fighter* (New York, 1949); Daniel Ford, *Flying Tigers: Claire Chennault and the American Volunteer* Group (Washington, D.C., 1991); Barbara W. Tuchman, *Stillwell and the American Experience in China, 1911–1945* (New York, 1970).

Robert Elder

Angell, James Burrill (1829–1916)

James Burrill Angell was born in Scituate, Rhode Island, in 1829. As a young man he gravitated toward academic study, attending Brown University and specializing in the fields of natural science, philosophy, and international politics. He married Sarah Caswell, daughter of an influential faculty member at Brown, Alexis Caswell, who later served as the President of Brown University (1868–1872). Angell himself extended his studies into the field of denominational religion, and was ordained as a Congregationalist minister.

During the American Civil War, Angell was an ardent advocate for President Abraham Lincoln's policies, expressing his Federalist opinions as the editor of the *Providence* (Rhode Island) *Journal,* the state's most influential newspaper. His academic accomplishments and political connections soon won him the presidency of the University of Vermont, a position he held from 1866 until 1871, when he moved to Ann Arbor, Michigan, to become President of the University of Michigan. In part through the efforts of a former U.S. envoy to Beijing, Anson Burlingame, who had briefly attended one of the University of Michigan's regional "branch" schools, Angell was appointed as the U.S. Minister to China in 1880. President Rutherford B. Hayes, under pressure from California's congressional delegation to reduce the influx of Chinese laborers in the Far West, instructed Angell to conclude a new agreement with China's imperial government cutting off legal immigration to the United States from China.

After arriving in China with his wife in mid-1880, Angell found that his mission was unexpectedly assisted by the presence in north China of a woman medical missionary, Dr. Leonora Howard King, who had trained at the University of Michigan. Under Angell's leadership, the University had begun admitting women as students in 1870, and many like King had qualified as physicians and taken up missionary work. In China, King had opened a hospital for women and children, and was the personal physician to the wife of Li Hongzhang, the most important adviser to the imperial court. With King's endorsement in hand, Li gave Angell a favorable hearing. Because of multiple foreign and military policy problems at that time, Li was under extreme pressure to acquiesce to the demands presented by Angell, and he eventually helped secure imperial approval for a new treaty with the United States. The 1880 treaty agreement, often referred to as the "Chinese Exclusion" or "Angell" Treaty, marked a turning point in Sino-American relations. It ended free Chinese immigration to the United States and opened the way for a new type of domestic American legislation. The 1882 Chinese Exclusion Act became the first of a series of restrictive anti-immigration laws that virtually suspended Chinese immigration, permitted monitoring of ethnic Chinese in the United States, and outlawed the naturalization of foreign-born Chinese as U.S. citizens. The 1882 Act established a pattern of immigration restriction that persisted until the 1940s. Angell returned to Ann Arbor in 1881, but throughout his career he maintained an active interest in Chinese affairs. He encouraged large numbers of Chinese students to enroll at the University of Michigan, including the first two Chinese women to study at an American university, Mary Stone (Shi Meiyi) and Ida Kahn. Both became physicians and returned to China to practice medicine.

Angell's longstanding interest in China and the widely publicized accomplishments of Stone and Kahn in China led a wealthy Regent of the University, Levi Barbour, to create a scholarship program at the University of Michigan to fund the education of Asian, including Chinese, women at the University. The Barbour Scholars Program, founded in 1917, continues to attract Asian women to study at the University of Michigan, with the understanding that they return to their home countries to apply their knowledge. Angell also served as the U.S. Minister to Turkey in 1897–1898. James Angell retired as the President of the University in 1909, and died in Ann Arbor in 1916.

See also Angell Treaty; Chinese Exclusion Act of 1882.

REFERENCES: James B. Angell, *The Reminiscences of James Burrilll Angell* (New York, 1912); Margaret Negodaeff-Tomsik, *Honour Due: The Story of Leonora Horward King* (Toronto, 1999).

Laura Calkins

Angell Treaty

Signed on 17 November 1880, the Angell Treaty made it possible for Congress to end the free immigration of Chinese to the United States. Discovery of gold in California in 1849 had created an enormous demand for unskilled and cheap labor, resulting in the so-called coolie trade that brought thousands of Chinese to the West Coast. In July 1868, Anson Burlingame, an American acting as Imperial China's envoy, and U.S. Secretary of State William H. Seward, negotiated a treaty that granted reciprocal rights of immigration and residence for citizens of both countries. Thousands of Chinese laborers came to the United States to help build the transcontinental railroad. Completion of the railroad and the decline of gold mining, however, contributed to a large surplus of labor. American labor leaders began to complain that Chinese immigrants worked for low wages and stole jobs, causing a decline in living standards. Moreover, they made the racist claim that the Chinese were incapable of assimilation. Anti-Chinese hostility and violence had existed since the 1850s, but now moved toward a crescendo. California became the center of a movement to prohibit Chinese immigration.

During the 1876 presidential election, the California Committee of the Republican Party passed a resolution proposing revision of the Burlingame-Seward Treaty. Congress responded to such pressure with bills to exclude the Chinese, but President Rutherford B. Hayes vetoed each one as a violation of the 1868 accord. In 1880, Hayes decided to seek renegotiation of immigration rights with China, fearing that the next President might bow to public demands and sign an exclusion act. To conduct the negotiations, he appointed as U.S. commissioner James B. Angell, who was President of the University of Michigan. He also named John F. Swift of California and William H. Trescott of South Carolina as co-commissioners, each politician representing a state that had strong interest in limiting Asian immigration. Reflecting California's greater militancy on the issue, Swift wanted total exclusion. Trescott, however, joined Angell in deciding to pursue only revision of the terms of the Burlingame-Seward Treaty.

Angell and his associates arrived at Beijing in early August 1880. The Chinese government appointed Baoyun and Li Hongzhang as representatives to negotiate with the U.S. mission. On October 13, during the opening session, Angell stated that more than 100,000 Chinese laborers were residing at American ports and this threatened the security of the United States. He recommended that China restrict immigration of certain classes of undesirables that did not include laborers. He then threatened that Washington would exclude Chinese laborers unilaterally if China did not cooperate then in modifying the Burlingame-Seward Treaty. The Chinese diplomats responded that if the United States could impose restrictions on Chinese in spite of treaty commitments, then China could do the same to Americans. At last, the Chinese relented, agreeing that the U.S. government might "regulate, limit or suspend," but not "absolutely prohibit," the entry and residence of Chinese laborers into the United States. Only those Chinese intent on "trade, travel, study or curiosity" would have the permanent right to enter the United States.

On May 5, 1881, the U.S. Senate ratified the Angell Treaty, which had four parts. Regarding restrictions on labor immigration, the English version provided that the United States had the right to "regulate, limit, or suspend such coming or residence," but that "limitation or suspension shall be reasonable and shall apply only to Chinese who may go to the United States as laborers, other classes not being included in the limitation." This provision was the most important in the treaty because it resulted in Congress passing the Chinese Exclusion Bill in 1882. Beijing reacted with surprise and anger to the legislation because between the two translations of English and Chinese the word "suspend" did not appear in the Chinese version of the treaty. Despite Chinese protests, the U.S. Bureau of Immigration thereafter would reject even Chinese of the expert class by making a laborer of anyone who it could establish as having performed literally any kind of manual work. The Angell Treaty was a watershed in the history of Sino-American relations not least because it exposed the insincerity of U.S. claims to be the benevolent patron of China.

See also Angell, James Burrill (1829–1916); Coolie Trade; Chinese Exclusion Act of 1882.

REFERENCES: David L. Anderson, *Imperialism and Idealism: American Diplomats in China, 1861–1898* (Bloomington, IN, 1985); James B. Angell, *The Reminiscences of James Burrill Angell* (New York, 1912); Mary Roberts Coolidge, *Chinese Immigration* (New York, 1909); Michael H. Hunt, *The Making of a Special Relationship: The United States and China to 1914* (New York, 1983); Tyler Dennett, *Americans in Eastern Asia: A Critical Study of the Policy of the United States with Reference to China, Japan and Korea in the 19th Century* (New York, 1922).

James I. Matray

Anglo-American Medical Mission to China (1943)

Before World War II the exchange of medical information between medical scientists and physicians was a common occurrence. Medical publication circulated freely. However, the war had interrupted this flow of information. In 1943 the Soviet Union requested an exchange of medical information in order to deal with the wartime injuries.

In July of 1943 a group of Canadian, American and British medical personnel visited the Soviet Union and China in order to exchange information on battlefield treatments for burns, trauma wounds, frostbite and other common injuries. In addition they sought information on how the Soviets and Chinese were managing the prevention and treatment of illnesses as a cause of military causalities. The Anglo-American Medical Mission was led by Wilder Graves Penfield (1891–1976), who was an internationally known brain surgeon. Penfield as the time was the director of the Neurological Institute at McGill University in Montreal. Other members of the Mission were also well-known surgeons and physicians or medical administrators. In July of 1943 the Mission spent three weeks in the Soviet Union visiting hospitals, field medical units, and medical institutes. The exchanges were eventually rated as good although the Soviets were less than fully forthcoming. Later in 1943 Penfield was able to make a very fast paced tour of Free China as the guest of Generalissimo Jiang Jieshi's government. He counted his meeting with Jiang and Madame Jiang Jieshi as the high point of his tour. He was impressed enough by them to believe that they were a bulwark against Japanese aggression. He later said that Jiang Jieshi was the George Washington of his country, holding it together during the long dark years of war. With the military conditions unstable Penfield and the others spent most of their time in Chongqing. While there he met with General Victor Wentworth Odlum (1880–1997), who was the acting Canadian ambassador (1942–1946). He also met Dr. Robert McClure who was a famous medical missionary to China and India serving with the United Church of Canada. With Dr. McClure's assistance Penfield was able to tour a number of Chinese hospitals. His medical assessment of the Chinese medical situation was very exacting. He described the supply of medical personnel, facilities and supplies as woefully inadequate to treat the great numbers of battlefield causalities. Even more serious in Penfield's estimation was the loss of Chinese solders to malnutrition and consequent infectious diseases, especially malaria. It was his judgment that more deaths occurred from malnutrition and disease than from battle wounds. He was also made aware that neither the Chinese hospitals nor the Western medical mission hospitals could cope with this problem. Penfield also decided that the Chinese Army Medical Service would operate in its own independent manner no matter what science or information was provided. There would consequently be little that could be done to effect change. Penfield's report was received by the Canadian, American, and British governments. Very little was done in response beyond continuing the shipment of medical supplies to China.

REFERENCES: Donald Avery, "Wartime Medical Cooperation Across the Pacific: Wilder Penfield and the Anglo-American Medical Missions to the Soviet Union and China, 1943–1944," *Pacific Science* (July 2000).

Jack Waskey

Anti-American Boycott of 1905

The anti-American boycott of 1905 was a direct outgrowth of friction over U.S. immigration policies. In the late 19th century, the U.S. Congress enacted increasingly restrictive immigration measures against the Chinese, culminating in 1904 with a measure that excluded Chinese workers for ten years. Although the treaties recognized the difference between workers and Chinese elites, both groups were often treated poorly. Outraged Chinese of all classes, particularly in south China, immediately protested prompting negotiations between the Chinese government and Washington. To express their outrage and help pressure the United States, Chinese merchants in cities throughout China began to boycott American products in the summer of 1905. Although U.S. pressure on the Qing government led to an imperial decree at the end of August that largely quelled the boycott in cities outside the south, boycotts continued into 1906.

This boycott was critical to the development of anti-imperialism and nationalism in China for four reasons. First, it inspired a long series of anti-imperialist boycotts. Second, it was the first boycott of national scope, demonstrating the possibility for national cooperation and coordination. Earlier boycotts against foreigners had been considerably more circumscribed. But in 1905, at least ten provinces and many major cities throughout China (and within Chinese communities abroad such as San Francisco) participated. Third, the boycott cut across class lines. Because U.S. immigration officials had mistreated all Chinese—from manual laborers to aristocrats—all social classes supported the boycott, and the

United States became a common enemy for more than just a single native-place association or a single industry. Fourth, as with the other Chinese social movements in this decade, the boycott fostered popular participation in anti-imperialist and nationalist activities. Protestors used different media to reach as many people as possible. Newspapers targeted the cultural elite; songs, lectures, slogans, drama performances, and cartoons of mistreated Chinese reached a wider audience; and handbills, leaflets, and placards written in the colloquial language informed intermediate groups.

The economic impact of the events of 1905–1906 is debatable. Sino-American trade actually peaked. Although monthly statistics do not exist for the period 1904–1905, imports from America grew during 1905 by over 250 percent. This suggests the boycott was a tremendous failure. Yet, three items imported into regions largely unaffected by the boycott—copper, plain gray cotton sheeting, and cotton drills—accounted for much of the increase. In contrast, U.S. export statistics show a reduction of over 50 percent between April and October. Again, this was probably a result of more than simply the boycott. In other places, particularly Guangzhou and Shanghai, the boycott was very effective, and it did achieve part of its goal. Although the United States continued to exclude Chinese laborers, it started to treat non-working class Chinese visitors with more respect.

REFERENCES: Karl Gerth, *China Made: Consumer Culture and the Creation of the Nation* (Cambridge, MA, 2003); Kikuchi Takaharu, *Chu¯goku minzoku undo¯ no kihon ko¯zo¯: Taigai boikotto no kenkyu¯ [The Historical Background of the Chinese National Movement: a Study of Anti-foreign Boycotts]* (Tokyo, 1974); Wang Guanhua, *In Search of Justice: The 1905–1906 Chinese Anti-American Boycott* (Cambridge, MA, 2001); Sin Kiong Wong, *China's Anti-American Boycott Movement in 1905: A Study in Urban Protest* (New York, 2002).

Karl Gerth

Arms Sales to Taiwan

Taiwan was a Japanese colony from 1895 to 1945. After the defeat of Guomindang (GMT) at the hands of the Chinese Communist Party (CCP) in the Chinese Civil War (1945–1949) on the mainland of China, the American embassy shifted to Taibei in 1949 when Jiang Jieshi's Nationalist government fled to Taiwan. Initially, America had adopted a neutral stance towards Taiwan, which in American perception had "no special military significance."

But the geopolitical environment changed with the outbreak of the Korean War on June 25, 1950. The Beijing leadership decided in October

1950 to cross the Yalu River and enter the Korean War. This prompted the U.S. President Harry S. Truman to order the Seventh Fleet into the Taiwan Strait to guarantee the security of Taiwan. From then onwards, America looked upon Taiwan as an "important shield" against the Communist advance to the western Pacific. With the establishment of the U.S. Military Assistance Advisory Group in Taiwan in May 1951, Taiwan received military and technological assistance worth $4.2 billion from America. In 1954, U.S.-China Mutual Defense Treaty was signed between the United States and Taiwan, which acted as deterrence against a full-fledged war between China and Taiwan over Dachen and Jinmen islands in mid-October 1954. The U.S. Congress passed Joint House Resolution 159 in January 1955, authorizing President Dwight D. Eisenhower to deploy American forces to protect Taiwan. However, following the establishment of diplomatic ties with the People's Republic of China (PRC) in 1979, United States abrogated the Mutual Defense Treaty with Taiwan.

On the other hand, American Congress passed the Taiwan Relations Act on April 10, 1979, obliging the United States to ensure Taiwan's security against Chinese threat by providing it with arms of a "defensive character." In December 1979, America sold 500 Maverick missiles worth U.S. $25 million to Taiwan followed by sale of various types of missiles, including Hawk and Sea Chaparral missiles, worth a total U.S. $280 million and 14 M110A howitzers worth U.S. $3.7 million in 1980. Although under the August 1982 Joint Communique signed between China and the United States, the Reagan administration agreed to reduce the quantity of military weapons to Taiwan, it continued with the policy of arms transfer to Taibei not only for meeting any potential threat from China but also to defend its own economic and security interests in the region. In continuation of this policy, the military sales continued, which included radar equipment for F-5, F-104 and C-130H transport aircraft, F-16 combat aircraft, the Black Hawk S-70 helicopter, M60A3 tanks. Thus military sales worth $628 million in 1983 touched the figure of $6 billion in 1993. This apart, the Pentagon in January 1993 confirmed the sale of 200 Patriot surface-to-air missiles and related equipment worth U.S. $10 billion followed by the sale of four E-2 early warning aircraft worth U.S. $900 million in March 1993. In October 1994, President Bill Clinton signed legislation authorizing the lease of two New Port-class tank-landing ships to Taiwan. Further, in 1996, the Pentagon confirmed the sale of 1,299 Stinger missiles and related equipment

worth U.S. $420 million and of 110 torpedoes worth U.S. $66 million to Taiwan. In 1997 the U.S. supplied 700 DMS anti-missile air defense missiles to Taiwan. In the fiscal year of 1998 the U.S. supplied to Taiwan U.S. $1.5 billion worth of arms, mainly F-16 fighters. In April 2000, the Clinton administration approved the sale of Maverick air-to-ground missiles, advanced medium-range air-to-air missiles (AMRAAM) and Pave Paws radar. In September 2000 the Pentagon approved the plan to sell Taiwan arms worth $1.3 billion, which included 200 AIM-120C (AMRAAM), 146 155mm howitzers, 71 Harpoon anti-ship missiles. In a marked contrast to the preceding administrations, President George W. Bush emphatically declared that America would do "whatever it takes" to help defend Taiwan itself. In April 2001, America announced the sale of sophisticated weapons to Taiwan, which included 4 Kidd-class destroyers; 12 P-3C Orion aircraft, 8 diesel submarines, AA V7A1 Amphibious Assault Vehicles; Mk 48 torpedoes without advanced capabilities.

China, while registering its protest over the U.S. arms sales to Taiwan, maintains that it is a clear-cut violation of 1982 Communique on arms sales. Moreover, China fears that enhancement of Taiwan's military capability would make its task of national reunification further complicated. Whereas, America defends its arms sales to Taiwan for the latter's security under the Taiwan Relations Act of 1979.

See also Taiwan; Taiwan Strait; Taiwan Relations Act (1979); Taiwan Security Enhancement Act (1999).

REFERENCES: Shirley Kan, "Taiwan: Major U.S. Arms Sales Since 1990," *Congressional Research Service Report* (Washington, D.C., April 2003); Michael Tsai and Martin Edmonds (eds.), *Defending Taiwan* (London, 2003); Zhou Bian, "The Issue of U.S. Arms Sales to Taiwan: A Hot Potato," *Beijing Review* (March 29, 2001); Winberg Chai, "The Taiwan Factor in U.S.-China Relations: An Interpretation," *Asian Affairs: An American Review* (Fall 2002).

Romi Jain

Arrow War (1856–1860) *see* Second Opium War (1856–1860)

Asia Pacific Economic Cooperation (APEC)

Asia Pacific Economic Cooperation (APEC) was established in 1989 with an objective of creating an Asia Pacific community in order to promote prosperity in the region by establishing a free trade regime through liberalization of economy, trade and investment. It is a group of 21 members comprising Australia, Brunei, Canada,

Chile, China, Hong Kong, Indonesia, Japan, the Republic of Korea, Malaysia, Mexico, New Zealand, Papua New Guinea, Peru, the Philippines, the Russian Federation, Singapore, Taiwan, Thailand, the United States and Vietnam. Its headquarter is in Singapore. All decisions in the APEC are taken unanimously. It accounts for more than a third of the world's population, 60 percent of the world's GDP, and nearly 47 percent of world trade. It is also the most economically dynamic region in the world generating nearly 70 percent of global economic growth. China and the United States, as the two major economic powers in the world, have a bigger role in promoting free trade and investment among APEC member nations. Since its membership to APEC in 1991, China has been playing an important role in shaping the trade and investment climate as well as in forging partnership among its member nations. America also perceives China's cooperation essential for translating APEC's objectives into reality on account of consistently maintaining highest economic growth rate as well as burgeoning foreign exchange reserves and foreign direct investment.

At the Shanghai Summit (2001), American President George W. Bush and his Chinese counterpart Jiang Zemin expressed their common commitment to promoting open markets, structural reforms and increasing trade capacity building within Asia — Pacific region. APEC leaders endorsed the U.S.-proposed "Shanghai Accord" under which they committed themselves to develop and implement the APEC transparency standards, reduce trade transaction costs in the Asia-Pacific region by 5 percent over 5 years, and pursue trade liberalization policies relating to information technology goods and services. Since the 9/11 terrorist attacks, war on terrorism has occupied a priority in APEC's agenda. APEC leaders at the Shanghai summit pledged counter-terrorism cooperation, designed to protect key Pacific Rim infrastructure — trade, finance and information systems—from terrorist exploitation and attacks. Also, at APEC's Santiago summit in 2004, Chinese President Hu Jintao pledged to fully support the APEC's determination to strengthen "counter-terrorism cooperation" in the interest of regional peace, prosperity and stability.

Energy is another area of cooperation between the United States and China in APEC since both countries are heavily dependent on oil from external sources. It may be noted that China has fast emerged as the second largest consumer of energy after the United States. While dwelling on future challenges before APEC, China called upon its member nations not only to improve energy efficiency, but also to ensure accessibility of the poor to energy products at "affordable price." Besides, China favors international economy and trade in the interest of poor developing nations. Whereas, America has been accusing China for its failure to honor WTO obligations by ending protectionism as well as liberalizing its exchange value regime. As regards security issues in APEC, China and the U.S. have divergent perspectives and contrary approaches. For example, both countries have diametrically opposed views on the question of sovereignty to the South China Sea's Spratly and Paracel Islands, as well as APEC's action plan for controlling shoulder-fired anti-aircraft missiles. At the APEC's meeting in Santiago in 2004, Chinese President Hu Jintao reiterated that smooth functioning of APEC required a strict adherence by each member, while hinting at America, to the principles of "respect for differences," "equality," "mutual benefit," and voluntary participation and "consensus." Being economic heavyweights in the APEC, both China and the United States would naturally determine the future course of APEC.

REFERENCES: Laurence J. Brahm (ed.), *China's Century: The Awakening of the Next Economic Powerhouse* (Singapore, 2001); Donald C. Hellman and Kenneth B. Pyle (eds.), *From APEC to Xanandu* (Armonk, NY, 1997); Nicolas R. Lardy, *Integrating China into the Global Economy* (Washington, D.C., 2002).

B. M. Jain

Asiatic Fleet

Beginning in the early 19th century the U.S. Navy started patrolling the western Pacific and China coast. The Navy established a permanent East Asian patrol in 1835 to protect American commercial interests in the region. To sailors the duty became known as the Asiatic Station and the ships, which comprised the patrol, became the Asiatic Squadron. During the Spanish-American War of 1898 the squadron, under Commodore George Dewey, defeated the Spanish fleet off Manila Bay and established American control over the Philippine archipelago. Two years later the ships and sailors of the Asiatic Squadron took part in the China Relief Expedition. In 1902 the Navy renamed the squadron the Asiatic Fleet and charged it with protecting all U.S. interests in the western Pacific.

The Asiatic Fleet encompassed not only ocean going warships but also river bound gunboats and the fleet oversaw U.S. operations on the Yangzi River. These gunboats were built in Chinese shipyards for the U.S. Navy's Yangzi River patrol. To the gunboats fell the task of protecting American interests in China and safeguarding the nation's Open Door Policy. U.S.-Japanese tensions prompted the withdrawal of all battleships from the fleet in 1904, which left it a composite of cruisers, destroyers, and gunboats. Three years later, as relations between Tokyo and Washington reached a crisis point, the elements of the Asiatic Fleet were incorporated into the U.S. Pacific Fleet, as its First Squadron. This arrangement did not last long and in 1910 the First Squadron once again became the Asiatic Fleet charged with protecting American interests from the Philippines to China.

Following the Washington Naval Conference of 1921–1922, the Navy reorganized, as a result of the reductions in naval armaments the treaty required. With the greatly reduced Atlantic and Pacific Fleets combined into the U.S. Fleet, the Asiatic Fleet became the sole American naval presence from Guam to China and to it fell the protection of the Philippines. As a consequence, U.S. naval forces were concentrated in the archipelago and the gunboats assumed the role of safeguarding American interests in China, a duty the Navy termed the China Station.

The gunboats of the Asiatic Fleet, therefore, became the American presence in much of China. For the boats and their crews this meant a mission wrought with danger because it was common for both sides in the Chinese civil wars in the 1920s and 1930s to fire upon them. With the onset of the Sino-Japanese War in 1931 the position of the gunboats became more precarious, as the United States maintained its official neutrality but supported the Guomindang, nonetheless. After the Japanese attacked Nanjing, the gunboats were used to evacuate Americans from the city. To avert a Japanese air attack the commander of the USS *Panay* had two large American flags laid out on the vessel's upper deck. Yet the ship came under Japanese attack and was sunk on December 12, 1937. Subsequent Japanese claims that the pilots were unable to identify the vessel's markings because of their altitude were exposed as false when newsreel footage showed that the planes attacked at low-level and then strafed survivors in the water. Shortly thereafter Tokyo apologized to Washington and paid a $2 million indemnity.

As U.S.-Japanese tensions increased and the two nations moved towards war, the Asiatic Fleet, woefully ill-equipped for the task at hand, failed to receive reinforcements. After the Japanese attacks of December 8, 1941 the fleet's ships became involved in the defense of the Philippines. During the Battle of the Java Sea in early 1942 the cruiser USS *Houston* sunk with its guns still firing, as units of the Imperial Japanese Navy sank most of the remaining ships of the Asiatic Fleet.

REFERENCES: George W. Baer, *One Hundred Years of Sea Power: The U.S. Navy, 1890–1990* (Stanford, CA, 1994); Thomas H. Buckley, *The United States Navy and the Washington Naval Conference, 1921–1922* (Knoxville, TN, 1970); William R. Braisted, *The United States Navy in the Pacific, 1897–1909* (Austin, TX, 1958) and *The United States Navy in the Pacific, 1909–1922* (Austin, TX, 1971); Kenneth J. Hagan (ed.), *In Peace and War: Interpretations of American Naval History, 1775–1984* (Westport, CT, 1984); David M. Kennedy, *Freedom from Fear: The American People in Depression and War, 1929–1945* (New York, 1999); Allan R. Millett and Peter Maslowski, *For the Common Defense: A Military History of the United States of America* (New York, 1994); Gerald E. Wheeler, *Prelude to Pearl Harbor: The United States Navy and the Far East, 1921–1931* (Columbia, MO, 1963).
Paul D. Gelpi, Jr.

Association of South-East Asia (ASA)

Foreign Ministers of Malaya, the Philippines and Thailand issued a joint "Bangkok Declaration" establishing the Association of South-East Asia (ASA) on July 31, 1961. Mirroring that acronym, *asa* (or *qasa*), means "hope" in Bahasa, Tagalog and Thai. Desiring regime stability, foreign ministers of an Islamic parliamentary federation, a mostly Christian republic and a Buddhist constitutional monarchy found common cause in "regional cooperation." Non-Asian states did not belong to ASA. Thus, the Association was the first of its kind in post-World War II Asia. Shared anti-Communism and fear of agrarian revolution united officials of the three nation states with different ethnic, cultural and historical circumstances.

Mutual cooperation in ASA on specific projects was usually bilateral. Economic and cultural collaboration in ASA also had a geopolitical context. On the one hand, increasingly bitter Sino-Soviet antagonism was underestimated. On the other hand, China's relatively cautious military-security foreign policy was not appreciated. Meanwhile, overlapping alliances in the South-East Asia Treaty Organization (SEATO) and bilateral treaties with the U.S. and UK fell short of fully addressing the desires of the ruling parties in the three ASA states to undercut revolutionary nationalist movements at home. ASA foreign ministers claimed not to be aligned with the West. However, overt and covert U.S. support for ASA and Southeast Asian "regionalism" weakened their claim. In the U.S. Congress, China Lobbyists like Walter Judd endorsed columnist Edgar Ansel Mowrer's praise for ASA as a link in a chain of geopolitical alliances containing the spread of Communism from China. During the 1960s, *The New York Times* and the U.S. Department of State periodically expressed their support for ASA. China's foreign-language communications media occasionally characterized ASA's claims of neutrality as deceitful. Evidently, however, ASA did not appear unduly threatening. Internal strife nearly tore ASA apart. In 1962, President of the Philippines Diosdado Macapagal (1961–1965) resurrected a longstanding claim to Sabah (North Borneo). The claim was at odds with a plan by the UK and Malaya to include North Borneo in an expanded collection of British colonies and former colonies to be called Malaysia. Despite U.S. President John F. Kennedy's endorsement of the expansion, in 1963 Macapagal refused to extend diplomatic recognition to the new Malaysia. Macapagal's rebuff slowed ASA's activities to a standstill. ASA teetered on the edge of self-destruction. Following the expulsion of majority-Chinese Singapore from Malaysia on August 8, 1965, Singapore chose not to exercise its option of participating in ASA. Quiet, persistent bilateral engagements with Malaysia and the Philippines by Thailand's Foreign Minister Thanat Khoman are credited with resuscitating ASA. The 1966 meeting of the ASA Standing Committee in Bangkok formalized ASA's revival. Subsequently, President of the Philippines Ferdinand E. Marcos (1965–1986) normalized relations with Malaysia.

Originally planned for mid-August 1967, an ASA ministerial conference was postponed to schedule for a meeting of the South East Asian Association for Regional Co-operation (SEAARC) earlier that month. SEAARC renamed itself the Association of South East Asian Nations (ASEAN). On August 29, 1967, the ASA Foreign Ministers decided to transfer ASA technical and cultural cooperation programs to ASEAN. The Association of South-East Asia's existence as a distinct organization ended a few months later. Overall, ASA reinforced mutual understanding and support among anti-Communist government officials from Malaya/Malaysia, the Philippines, and Thailand.

See also Association of South East Asian Nations (ASEAN).

REFERENCES: Association of South-East Asia, "Bangkok Declaration Establishing ASA," *Bangkok Post* (August 1, 1961); Edgar Ansel Mowrer, "New Asian Agreement Will Help Stop Reds," in "Extension of Remarks by Hon. Walter H. Judd," U.S., 87th Cong., 1st Sess., *Congressional Record, Vol. 107, No. 28.* (August 22, 1961); "'Neutral' Malaya," *Peking Review* (March 1961); ASA National Secretariat of the Ministry of Foreign Affairs of Thailand, *Fifth Year of ASA-1966* (Bangkok, 1965); Vincent K. Pollard, "Two Stages in American Promotion of Asian Regionalism: United States-Southeast Asia-Japan Relations, 1945–1970," Association of Asian Studies, Japan, *Ajiagaku-ronsô [Bulletin of Asian Studies], Vol. 5* (1995).

Vincent Kelly Pollard

Association of South East Asian Nations (ASEAN)

The Association of South East Asian Nations (ASEAN) was initiated by the foreign ministers of Indonesia, Malaysia, the Philippines, Singapore and Thailand on August 8, 1967. Like its predecessor the earlier ASA, the media presented ASEAN to elite and middle class readers of English-language Southeast Asian newspapers as a hope for economic cooperation but also to reinforce domestic counterinsurgency. At the time, ASEAN was envisioned by some Americans as complementing U.S. strategy in "containing" China. But conservative anti-Communist governments in South East Asia were capable of pursuing their own agendas. Thus, there was an overlap of interests. Although ASEAN claimed that foreign military bases would not be permanent, it placed no obstacles to continued U.S. presence in the Philippines. And American bases remained there until 1992.

In August 1967, China's Ministry of Foreign Affairs fell under control of the Cultural Revolution Group. Early that month, Xinhua (New China News Agency) condemned ASEAN. In a turnaround, initiatives taken by U.S. President Richard M. Nixon to play the "China card" against the Soviet Union (or "Soviet social imperialism" as *People's Daily* called it) began altering the balance of forces in Asia. One by one, ASEAN members extended diplomatic relations to China. Although China preferred bilateral relations, it warmed up to ASEAN after the Socialist Republic of Vietnam's invasion of Democratic Kampuchea (Cambodia) in late 1978. Vietnam was viewed as an agent of the Soviet Union. China invaded Vietnam in 1979 but was repulsed in six weeks. To bring greater pressure on Vietnam, China embraced an informal diplomatic and military alliance with ASEAN, the U.S. and the Coalition Government of Democratic Kampuchea — a three-party united front brokered by ASEAN and dominated by Pol Pot's Khmer Rouge. In 1988, Vietnam agreed to withdraw its troops from Cambodia and did so over a period of several years. Since the 1980s, China has actively asserted its jurisdiction over South China Sea islands, reefs and ocean resources overlappingly claimed by Vietnam, other governments in Southeast Asia and Taiwan. Shifting the balance in 1995, Vietnam broadcast its desire to join ASEAN. By 1999, ten countries of Southeast Asia had joined. By mid-2004, only Timor Leste was not a member.

With a population more than double that of ASEAN, China's willing cooperation testifies to ASEAN's prestige and to China's opportunity to offset U.S. influence. In July 1996, China became a full dialogue partner at the twenty-ninth ASEAN Ministerial Meeting. In 2003, China's accession to ASEAN's Treaty of Amity and Cooperation was approved. Despite earlier militarized confrontations with Vietnam in the South China Sea, China renounced the use of force in the region in favor of negotiation and consultation. ASEAN's dialogue with China extended to the ASEAN Regional Forum and Joint Cooperation Committee. Import-export trade and foreign direct investment (FDI) in both directions has increased in the 1990s, although FDI flowed more heavily into the People's Republic of China. In 2001, China's trade with the ASEAN countries (5.9%) was worth less than one fourth its trade with the U.S. (24.8%). Nonetheless, trade, communications and development projects taking advantage of Chinese expertise were underway by 2004.

See also Association of South-East Asia (ASA)

REFERENCES: Bernard K. Gordon, "East Asian Regionalism and United States Security," *Paper (RAC-P-45)* (McLean, Strategic Studies Department, Virginia: Research Analysis Corporation, October 1968); Vincent K. Pollard, "South East Asian Regionalism: Containment, Counterinsurgency, and the Nixon Doctrine," *Journal of Contemporary Asia, Vol. 1, No. 4.* (1971); Vincent K. Pollard, "Spreading the Risks: Co-marketing ASEAN in a Contested Election," in *Globalization, Democratization and Asian Leadership: Power Sharing, Foreign Policy and Society in the Philippines, and Japan* (Aldershot, UK, 2004); Yoichiro Sato, "Mixed Feelings: East Asia's Debate about China's Economic Growth and Regional Integration," in Satu Limaye (ed.), *Asia's China Debate* (Honolulu, HW, 2003); Susumu Yamakage, "ASEAN no kessi to chiiki kyoryoku," ["The Formation of ASEAN National Incentives to Regional Cooperation,"] *Tonan Ajia Kenkyu, Vol. 19.* (1981).

Vincent Kelly Pollard

Astor, John Jacob (1763–1848)

John Jacob Astor was a critical actor in U.S.-China trade from 1800 to 1817. It was his China trade that got him on the road to become America's first multimillionaire. When he died in 1848, Astor was the wealthiest person in the United States. Indeed, his personal fortune constituted almost one percent of the total wealth of the nation. (As a point of comparison, Bill Gates has had a long run as the wealthiest individual in the world, but his personal fortune constitutes about

six-tenths of one percent of the nation's total wealth.) A German immigrant, Astor made a fortune in the fur trade, became involved in the China trade, established himself as a prominent banker, and acquired extensive real estate holdings, in particular in Manhattan, that he developed to great profit.

Born on a farm outside Waldorf, a town near Heidelberg, Germany, Astor first emigrated to Great Britain when he was in his mid-teens. His brother had started a business there, manufacturing musical instruments, and when Astor was twenty years old, he then emigrated to the United States, generating his initial investment capital from a consignment of those instruments. Over the next two decades, Astor, with an equal mixture of imagination and relentlessness, established the American Fur Company as the major competitor on the continent to the British Hudson's Bay Company. The company's business agents and trappers were largely responsible for asserting the American presence along what is now the border with Canada, from the upper Great Lakes region to what is now the American Northwest. Ultimately, through the American Fur Company and several subsidiary companies, Astor would control the fur trade from the Mississippi to the Pacific and from the Canadian border to the Mexican. When styles changed and the fur trade began to become less profitable, Astor used Astoria, the trading station near the mouth of the Columbia River that he had established to dominate the fur trade in the region, as a base for entering into the increasingly profitable clipper-ship trade with China. Starting with a fleet of twelve ships, Astor immediately became a major player in the trade. Indeed, in trading furs and other products of the American interior (eventually including cattle hides from California ranches) for Chinese silks, porcelain, spices, and tea, Astor did much to promote the mid-19th century American fascination with all things "Oriental." Astor's involvement in the China trade was not, however, without controversy, for it included some participation in opium trading.

When the trade with China became less profitable, Astor shifted focus again, buying up much of Manhattan, developing the properties commercially and residentially and then selling long-term leases that would provide an ever-increasing income to his heirs as the city grew exponentially in the second-half of the 19th century. In the last years of that century, a half-century after Astor's death, his descendants were earning almost $10 million annually from just the long-term leases on the Manhattan properties that he had developed. Many of the family's properties have become landmarks in the city. The Astor Library, funded by a $400,000 bequest in John Jacob Astor's will, eventually became the New York Public Library, and the Waldorf-Astoria became the most prestigious of the family's sizable holdings in the hotel industry.

REFERENCES: John D. Haeger, *John Jacob Astor: Business and Finance in the Early Republic* (Detroit, MI, 1991); Axel Madsen, *America's First Multimillionaire* (New York, 2001); Kenneth W. Porter, *John Jacob Astor, Businessman* (Cambridge, MA, 1931); Arthur D. Howden Smith, *John Jacob Astor, Landlord of New York* (Philadelphia, PE, 1929); John Upton Terrell, *Furs by Astor* (New York, 1963).

Martin Kich

Baker, James Addison, III (1930–)

James Addison Baker, III was born in Houston, Texas on April 28, 1930. Serving as White House Chief of Staff from 1981 to 1985, Baker was also a member of Reagan's National Security Council, a senior foreign policy adviser, and he served as Treasury Secretary through 1988. Baker was appointed as U.S. Secretary of State under the Presidency of George H.W. Bush. Baker showed great tenacity and diplomatic skills as he handled the issues regarding Tiananmen Square protests of 1989 in China.

Following the Chinese authorities' suppression of demonstrators in June 1989, the State Department, on Baker's direction, issued a travel advisory for China. Meanwhile he helped to enact measures to express the American condemnation of China's violation of human rights. The U.S. suspended a large number of governmental exchanges with China and weapons exports from the U.S. to China. Baker pushed the U.S. to impose a number of economic sanctions. New trade activities in China were suspended from June 1989 until January 2001, when President Bill Clinton lifted the suspension. Baker also pressured the International Monetary Fund not to support credits to China except for projects that address basic human needs. The Overseas Private Insurance Corporation suspended any new activities beginning in June 1989 as a result of Baker's request. Shortly afterwards, Baker issued a statement to Congress and the American public, indicating that his policy recommendations were working since the Chinese lifted martial law, permitted international travelers to return, and released more than five hundred political prisoners.

In the summer of 1990, Baker led what came to be known as the G-7-Houston Summit. At the Houston Summit, Baker called for renewed political and economic reforms in China. As a result of this Summit and further talks, Baker was able to get China's support of the first Gulf War. In September 1991, Baker traveled to China in an effort to improve human rights in China and prohibit further proliferation of nuclear weapons. However, this trip proved unproductive as China rebuked Baker's criticism of China's treatment of human rights.

REFERENCES: Robert L. Suettinger, *Beyond Tiananmen: The Politics of U.S.-China Relations, 1989–2000* (Washington, D.C., 2003); James A. Baker, *The Politics of Diplomacy: Revolution, War, And Peace, 1989–1992* (New York, 1995); Jason Ritchie, *Secretaries of State: Making Foreign Policy* (Minneapolis, MN, 2002); Jean Edward Smith and Herbert M. Levine, *The Conduct of American Foreign Policy Debated* (New York, 1990); Jean Edward Smith, *George Bush's War* (New York, 1992).

Steven Napier

Bamboo Curtain

The phrase "bamboo curtain" refers to the political and ideological barrier separating the West and the People's Republic of China (PRC) and its allies in North Korea and North Vietnam much as the Iron Curtain referred to a similar barrier separating the former Soviet Union and its European satellites from the nations of Western Europe, the United States, and Canada.

In the months immediately following Mao Zedong's pronouncement of the People's Republic of China on October 1, 1949, Great Britain and Canada had recognized the PRC as the government of the Chinese people. It appears that in the winter and spring of 1950, the United States was considering recognizing the PRC and thus withdrawing recognition from Jiang Jieshi's Nationalist government in exile on Taiwan, if only to give Mao and his supporters an alternative to relying solely on the Soviet Union. The North Korean invasion of the Republic of Korea (ROK) and, more importantly, the Communist Chinese intervention in late November 1950 as U.S. and ROK units neared the Yalu River separating North Korea and China's Manchurian region, changed American opinion from a grudging respect for the accomplishments of Mao's Communist followers and a willingness to recognize that they, as a practical matter, controlled China, to a harsh view that condemned virtually anyone who proposed dialogue with Chinese Communist leaders. Thus, Under-Secretary of State at that time (and later Secretary of State), Dean Rusk, commented that "the leaders of the PRC fail the test because they are not Chinese, they are Communists." And Secretary of State John Foster Dulles refused to shake hands with PRC Premier and Foreign Minister Zhou Enlai during the Geneva negotiations in 1954 to end the French-Viet Minh conflict. During the McCarthy Era in America, U.S. diplomats who recognized the likelihood of a Communist victory when the Chinese Civil War resumed in earnest after Japan surrendered, found themselves hounded from office in the acrimonious and largely pointless debate in America over "who lost China?"

One sign of the power of the image of a Bamboo Curtain was the use of the term "Red China," where few in American politics referred to the USSR as "Red Russia." Another sign was the U.S. failure to interact with China as America began its long and costly involvement in Vietnam. That is, the U.S. government never tested its assumptions, which involved the government in Beijing, because it had no easy way to conduct diplomacy with that Chinese government and there would be a great political cost to pay at home. Interestingly, while American and some other Western leaders had great fears about China's intentions along its long borders, Chinese leaders held fears about the USSR and its intentions along its long borders in Asia. To improve their government's bargaining condition, Chinese leaders built a vast underground city in Beijing, largely unknown to most Chinese and to virtually all foreigners, to help some 300,000 Chinese leaders and key individuals survive a nuclear attack they feared Russia might be planning.

When President Richard Nixon traveled to the PRC in February 1972, the phrase, Bamboo Curtain, lost its power. During the height of the Cold War in Asia, many Western observers, perhaps reflecting at least a degree of anti-Asian prejudice, saw the Chinese as inscrutable, willing to accept massive loss of life, and completely antithetical to the West. But, in the aftermath of the ping-pong diplomacy that preceded Nixon's historic trip and Nixon's trip itself, Americans rediscovered their fascination with the Middle Kingdom. Thereafter, a steadily increasing number of American tourists traveled to China; Chinese students and scholars came to American universities and vice versa; and Sino-American trade increased amidst prospects of even greater trade. The Bamboo Curtain thus had fallen, and a new U.S.-China-Soviet Union strategic triangle would arise, with all the possibilities and tensions that triangles can have. Of course, that the old fears in the West had eased did not mean that relations with China were positive. There was the status of the island of Taiwan and its government, increasingly seeking to proclaim its independence from the mainland; there were issues of trade policy and currency valuation; and there would be from time to time provocations that threatened to re-institute the old harsh and cold relations. But China was as handy a counterweight to Russia for the United States as America was a counterweight for China.

See also Cold War, Korean War; Civil War (1945–1949); Nixon's Visit to China; Strategic Triangle of U.S.-Soviet-China Relations.

REFERENCES: Alexander Bevin, *The Strange Connection: U.S. Intervention in China, 1944–1972* (New York, 1992); Gordon H. Chang, *Friends and Enemies: The United States, China, and the Soviet Union, 1948–1972* (Stanford, CA, 1990); Robert A. Garson, *The United States and China Since 1949, A Troubled Affair* (London, 1994); Jan Hallenberg, *Foreign Policy Change: United States Foreign Policy Toward the Soviet Union and the People's Republic of China, 1961–1980* (Stockholm, 1984); Chen Jian, et. al., *The Cold War in Asia* (Washington, D.C., 1996).

Charles M. Dobbs

Beijing Spring

Beijing Spring is the name given to a burst of intellectual freedom and political liberalization in the People's Republic of China. There have been several periods in recent history that have been labeled as Beijing Spring, perhaps derived from the infamous Prague Spring in 1968. An earlier period known as Beijing Spring was during 1977 and 1978, immediately after the Mao era, when intellectual freedom meant the ability to criticize the Chinese government. Most of the criticism concerned the events of the Chinese Great Proletarian Cultural Revolution of 1966–1976 and the actions of the Gang of Four, the radical leaders in the Chinese Communist Party (CCP). The criticism was largely publicized through the use of the Democracy Wall and big-character posters. The government ended the movement when the criticism was extended from past government mistakes to current government policies. In 1998, some Chinese intellectuals called the more relaxed political atmosphere in China a new Beijing Spring. However, this period of political liberalization also ended, this time with trials of some political dissidents.

The most notorious recent period to be named Beijing Spring refers to the events that developed during the spring of 1989 in and around Beijing's Tiananmen Square. Beijing Spring is better known in the United States as the Tiananmen Square Incident or Massacre. While Hu Yaobang, the General Secretary of the Chinese Communist Party, had earlier supported political liberalization simultaneous with economic liberalization, his political downfall and death on April 15, 1989 dimmed the hopes of those who supported political liberalization. Hu Yaobang's funeral sparked student demonstrations that ultimately focused on the great changes that occurred in China as a result of economic reforms, specifically the emerging social problems of inflation, internal migration to cities, and official corruption. Students and intellectuals began to demand greater political reforms to meet the challenges of the emerging social issues. They gathered in Tiananmen Square, the time-honored place to protest against the government. After the students had occupied Tiananmen Square for about a month, the Chinese government declared martial law on May 20, 1989. The students still refused to leave the Square even after meeting with the soon to be deposed Zhao Ziyang, Party General Secretary, who had replaced Hu. The result was a confrontation that resonates as one of the most notorious standoffs of the 20th century. In the early hours of June 4, 1989, Chinese soldiers entered the square and opened fire.

Americans became acquainted with Beijing Spring, or the Tiananmen Square Incident, through repeated images on CNN and Western newspaper coverage. The media coverage focused mainly on the later days of the student demonstrations and featured images like the *Goddess of Democracy* and the lone man standing before a tank. Many Americans interpreted the demonstrations as an attempt to set up an American-style form of government. As footage of the military firing on the demonstrators circulated throughout the global press, governments responded with strict trade sanctions on China. While the Japanese government, for instance, lifted sanction after three months, the U.S. still continues some of the sanctions imposed at that time including those on military hardware and dual-use technology. For many in the U.S. government, this event continues to influence their perception of China as a harsh dictatorial regime. **See also Tiananmen Square Massacre.**

REFERENCES: Michel Oksenberg, Lawrence R. Sullivan, and Marc Lambert, *Beijing Spring, 1989: Confrontation and Conflict: The Basic Documents* (New York, 1990); Gail Copeland, *Spring Winds of Beijing* (Lakewood, CO, 1992).

Elizabeth Van Wie Davis

Belgrade, Bombing of the Chinese Embassy (1999)

On May 8, 1999 NATO forces mistakenly destroyed the Chinese Embassy in Belgrade, Yugoslavia with airborne bombs. The bombing killed three and injured twenty-seven people. NATO military spokesperson Major General Walter Jertz said that the forces had misidentified the embassy as a "legitimate military target." Chinese UN ambassador Qin Huasun immediately acted and declared that the attack was a "crime of war."

Anti-American sentiments rose to a fevered pitch in Beijing, where protesters gathered en masse around the U.S. Embassy and proceeded to pelt it with rocks and debris. Attempts were made by the protesters to set fire to U.S. vehicles. Students made up the majority of protestors. Busses from nearby universities were loaded with students, who traveled to the U.S. Embassy and other U.S. associated firms to protest. Americans in China during the period were told to remain home, and not to venture out too often, due to the newly heightened security risks posed to them by the angry groups of protestors. NATO instigated military action in Yugoslavia and was bombing Belgrade in particular to force the government to sign an agreement to allow peacekeeping troops to enter Kosovo. The ethnic Albanians were a minority, and were being systematically destroyed by Slobodan Milosevic and the Serbian military. The bombing in Belgrade was largely successful, in that it brought the Yugoslav military to its knees. However, the Chinese Embassy bombing and a similar mistake involving the death of several civilians marred the entire campaign.

Despite the immediate anti-American response after the bombing, relations were normalized formally when Secretary of State Madeleine Albright visited President Jiang Zemin, Premier Zhu Rongji, and Foreign Minister Tang Jiaxuan in Beijing on June 22, 2000. Taiwan was the focus of the talks, but the Chinese Embassy bombing was still an important topic among many. The Chinese government's role in the sentiment of the Chinese people over the accidental bombing of the Chinese Embassy in Belgrade should not be underestimated. On the day of the event, Communist party officials organized the students in busses to protest. In Chengdu, rioters destroyed the home of the U.S. Consul General with a firebomb. On the anniversary of the event, however, the Communist Party held no such protests and coordinated no such actions. The anniversary of the bombing came at the same time that the U.S. Congress was to vote on opening more trade with China. *The People's Daily*, a Communist Party publication, encouraged people in China not to protest, but to instead go to work.

REFERENCES: Garreth Byrne, "China: Campus Reactions to the NATO Bombing in 1999," *Contemporary Review* (February 2003); "Profile: Madeleine Albright's Meeting with Chinese Leaders," *All Things Considered* (June 22, 2000); Matt Forney, "China Plays Down Bombing Amid Trade Debate," *Wall Street Journal* (May 9, 2000); Mark Leong, Yang Lian, and Peter Hessler, *China Obscura* (San Francisco, CA, 2004); Peter H Gries, *China's New Nationalism: Pride, Politics, and Diplomacy* (Berkeley, CA, 2004); Andrew J. Nathan and Bruce Gilley, *China's New Rulers: The Secret Files* (New York, 2003).

Arthur Holst

Beveridge, Albert Jeremiah (1862–1927)

Albert Jeremiah Beveridge was a U.S. Senator, lawyer, and historian, and a dedicated member of the Progressive movement. Beveridge was born in Ohio on October 6, 1862. He made his reputation as a GOP campaign speaker, and in 1899 Beveridge became a U.S. Republican Senator for two consecutive terms. Beveridge became a supporter of U.S. expansionism and wanted a large U.S. Navy to protect America's interests in China. During the administration of President William McKinley, Beveridge supported an imperialistic doctrine abroad, especially in its application toward China, because Beveridge felt that China was almost an unlimited market for U.S. products. He believed that finding additional markets for U.S. products was essential to get the American economy going again. Beveridge is on record in the U.S. Senate of recommending friendly relations and free trade with China even if the U.S. had to act unilaterally setting example for other nations. In 1901, Beveridge conducted a tour of China for the U.S. Senate. He was appalled by the lack of fresh food and quality products. Beveridge's visit to China only strengthened his desire to open their markets for U.S. goods and help to improve Chinese living conditions. Under President Theodore Roosevelt, Beveridge was continually at odds with Roosevelt over trading issues relative to child labor. Beveridge wanted free trade but only if the Chinese would guarantee that the products produced were without the use of child labor. He supported a tariff agency to monitor the flow of products from China into and out of the U.S. Beveridge was an advocate of free trade. He repeatedly sought to reduce tariffs instituted by prior administrations on goods produced in China. In 1910, he lost the election for what would have been his third term in the Senate largely because his free trade philosophy toward China was out of touch with the American public. The dominate view of the American citizenry at the time believed that free trade would hurt manufacturing and ultimately cause a loss of jobs at home.

Beveridge's ideas on foreign policy align with the philosophy of Leo Straus, because he thought that the U.S. should liberate the people of the Orient. By taking his stand on such policies he was able to move many conservatives in the Republican Party toward pushing for human rights and better conditions throughout East Asia. In 1912, when Theodore Roosevel left the Republicans and ran for president on the Progressive Party ticket, Beveridge joined Roosevelt and was the keynote speaker at the GOP national convention of which U.S.-China policy was one of its central themes.

During the Presidency of William Howard Taft, Beveridge was constantly at odds with the administration's foreign policy toward China. Beveridge fought hard against some Chinese products that the Taft administration tried to monitor with strict protective tariffs. In 1914 Beveridge made an unsuccessful run for the United States Senate as a Progressive candidate on an imperialist platform. He pushed for the U.S. to continue to be more involved with China in both its domestic and international objectives. Not necessarily for what was in the interest of the United States at the time but also what would be of best interest for the Chinese people. In his final campaign in 1922, Beveridge won the GOP Senate primaries, but lost in the general election. Beveridge continued to take a firm stand against totalitarian oppressive regimes that had been in control of the Orient for thousands of years. In addition to politics, Beveridge was a scholar of Oriental history. The American Historical Association has subsequently named an award in his name that examines the best work produced on East Asia.

REFERENCES: Albert J. Beveridge, *The State of the Nation* (Indianapolis, IN, 1924); John Braeman, *Albert J. Beveridge: American Nationalist* (Chicago, IL, 1971); Arthur T. Vanderbilt, ed., *Studying Law: Selections from the Writings of Albert J. Beveridge (And Others)* (New York, 1945); Jean Edward Smith and Herbert M. Levine, *The Conduct of American Foreign Policy Debated* (New York, 1990); John A. Coffin, *Senatorial Career of Albert J. Beveridge* (Indianapolis, IN, 1928).

Steven Napier

Biddle, James (1783–1848)

United States naval officer James Biddle was born in Philadelphia and educated at the University of Pennsylvania. He enlisted as a midshipman in 1800. He obtained a leave of absence in 1807 in order to sail to China as first officer of a merchant ship. He reenlisted and ultimately reached the rank of Commodore in Atlantic, Mediterranean, and Pacific commands.

In 1845 the United States Senate ratified the first Sino-American treaty, "Treaty of Wangxia," which had been negotiated by Caleb Cushing in the previous year. President James K. Polk appointed Alexander Everett to succeed Cushing as American commissioner to China and to exchange treaty ratifications. Polk placed the ship-of-the-line *"Columbus"* and sloop-of-war *"Vincennes,"* both under the command of Biddle, at Everett's disposal. They embarked from New York in June 1845. Everett became ill, abandoned his assignment at Rio de Janiero, returned to the United States, and entrusted his mission to Biddle, who reached Macao just before the expiration of the period fixed for the exchange of the ratified treaties. On December 31, an American delegation assembled at Guangzhou consisting of Biddle, the principal officers of the *"Columbus,"* and United States Consul Paul S. Forbes. Dr. Peter Parker served as interpreter. The Imperial Chinese delegation included Jiying (Kiying), the three high officials who assisted him in negotiating the treaty, and the prefect of Guangzhou. The commissioners exchanged ratified copies of the treaty and signed and sealed certificates of exchange, which had previously been prepared in both Chinese and English.

Under the terms of this and other Sino-Western treaties, Guangzhou was designated as the venue for diplomatic contact between China and all other Occidental countries except Russia. The Emperor sent a high commissioner to reside in Guangzhou. Biddle established the American legation in the foreign settlement outside the city walls. He presided there until April 15, 1846, when he transferred his powers as commissioner to Parker. Biddle also visited Xiamen, Chusan, Ningpo, and Shanghai, where he reported that American trade was "considerable." On July 7 he sailed for Japan in an unsuccessful attempt to open that isolated nation to American trade. His ships returned home in time to participate in the Mexican War.

See also Treaty of Wangxia (1844).

REFERENCES: Curtis Henson, *Commissioners and Commodores* (Tuscaloosa, AL, 1982); Charles O. Paullin, *Diplomatic Negotiations of American Naval Officers* (Baltimore, MD, 1912).

Jonathan Goldstein

Bombing of the Chinese Embassy *see* Belgrade, Bombing of the Chinese Embassy (1999)

Boxer Protocol

The Boxer Protocol was signed on September 7, 1901 by the Qing government with foreign powers after the end of the Boxer Uprising. The terms of the Protocol were mainly punitive. Those pro-Boxer officials were severely punished. The foreign powers demanded the death of eleven senior Chinese officials, and in the end settled for the execution of Yuxian, the Governor of Shandong province and the deaths of Prince Zhuang and four other senior officials by suicide. There were as many as a hundred Chinese officials punished for their anti-foreign and anti-missionary actions. The civil service examinations were suspended in the Boxer areas.

Under the Protocol, some twenty-five forts had to be demolished by the Qing government, including the Dagu forts stationed outside Beijing. Foreign troops were allowed to station at important lines of communication and at major strategic areas, including a large area of the Inner City of Beijing, known as the Legation Quarter. For two years, China was not permitted to import any arms. Taking advantage of China's weakness, Russia seized the whole of Manchuria, which sowed the seeds of the Russo-Japanese War in 1904–1905. The most devastating impact of the Protocol was huge indemnities. The 450,000,000 tael indemnity, equivalent to $333 million, which was more than four times the annual revenue of the Qing government and about one tael for each Chinese subject, had to be paid to foreign powers over a period of thirty-nine years at an annual interest rate of four percent. The annual payments made up one-fifth of China's national budget. Some foreign governments, notably Britain and the United States, used some of the indemnity to sponsor the education of Chinese students abroad, who were called Boxer Indemnity Scholars. The financial burden, the humiliation associated with infringements on sovereignty and intervention into China's internal affairs in the provisions of the Boxer Protocol completely undermined the credibility of the Qing government, and gave rise to a series of anti-Manchu revolutionary movements in China.

See also Boxer Rebellion (1900).

REFERENCES: Paul A. Cohen, *History in Three Keys: The Boxers as Event, Experience, and Myth* (New York, 1997); Joseph W. Esherick, *The Origins of the Boxer Uprising* (Berkeley, CA, 1987).

Joseph Tse-Hei Lee

Boxer Rebellion (1900)

The Boxer Rebellion broke out in northwestern Shandong province on the flood plain of the Yellow River, a densely populated area notorious for its long history of banditry, village feuds and sectarian movement as well as for its lack of government control. Throughout the 1890s, German Catholic priests of the Society of the Divine Word (Societas Verbi Divini or SVD) were aggressively recruiting converts and building Catholic villages in North China. On November 1, 1897, two German SVD missionaries were murdered in southern Shandong, and the incident provided the pretext for Germany to seize by force the Jiaozhou leased territory on the Shandong promontory. This in turn escalated the "scramble for concessions" by foreign powers in China, a crisis that provoked strong Chinese resistance against Western imperialism.

Faced with the problem of imperialism, some rural communities in Shandong defended their interests through secret societies and sectarian groups. In 1898, a Yellow River flood followed by disastrous drought led to famine in North China. Many rural communities blamed Western missionaries and Chinese Christians for their suffering. But the outbreak of anti-foreign and anti-missionary violence led foreign powers to put pressure on the Qing government to protect Christian interests in lawsuits and disputes. It is against this background of external and internal crises that the Boxer Rebellion began to take shape in Shandong. Joseph W. Esherick's seminal study published in 1987 traces the Boxer origins to two peasant traditions in northwestern Shandong, which were the technique of the martial arts or "boxing" and the practice of spiritual possession. The Spirit Boxers, later known as *Yihetuan* (Boxers United in Righteousness), successfully combined these two traditions. By observing appropriate rituals, Boxers believed to be invulnerable to swords or bullets, and therefore, were ready for combat. Anyone could be possessed by the spirit and so become a Boxer leader for the moment. No hierarchical organization was needed for the Boxers. The Boxers' agenda was simple and direct: "Support the Qing, destroy the foreigners." The Boxer Rebellion spread from northwestern Shandong across the North China Plain. Rather than suppressing it, the Qing government, and especially the Empress Dowager Cixi, decided to exploit the Boxer Rebellion against Western imperialism.

In the spring of 1900, some Legation guards went out attacking the Boxers in order to intimidate them, but the attack provoked much anger among the Boxers. Large numbers of the Boxers entered Beijing and Tianjin on June 13–14, destroying Christian churches, attacking Western missionaries and Chinese Christians, and looting. On June 10, over 2,000 foreign troops marched from Tianjin to defend the legations in Beijing but they stopped halfway. On June 17, a foreign fleet attacked the forts outside Tianjin. On June 21, the Chinese imperial court declared war on all foreign powers. The Boxers' siege of Beijing in the summer of 1900 was well known because many foreign diplomats, missionaries and journalists were besieged for eight weeks, from June 29 to August 14, in the Beijing Legation Quarter. The Eight-Power Allied Forces, comprised of troops sent by Britain, the United States, France, Germany, Japan, Italy, Russia, and Austria, were sent to suppress the Boxers. Faced with the foreign attack, the Empress Dowager, with the Emperor, left for Xian by cart. The Allied Forces looted Beijing and terrorized the surrounding towns, where the Boxers killed many thousands of Chinese Christians and 250 foreigners, mainly missionaries.

Throughout the Boxer Rebellion, the Chinese provincial governor-generals, such as Li Hongzhang at Guangzhou, Zhang Zhidong at Wuhan, and the others decided in June to ignore Beijing's declaration of war on foreign powers. By condemning the whole event as a "Boxer Rebellion," they compromised with the Allied Forces, secured peace, and kept foreign troops out of Central and South China. The War of 1900, the largest that the Qing government fought with foreign powers in the late 19th century, was largely confined to North China. The fighting ended with the signing of the Boxer Protocol on September 7, 1901.

See also Boxer Protocol.

REFERENCES: Paul A. Cohen, *History in Three Keys: The Boxers as Event, Experience and Myth* (New York, 1997); Joseph W. Esherick, *The Origins of the Boxer Uprising* (Berkeley, CA, 1987); R. G. Tiedemann, "Christian Civilization or Cultural Expansion? The German Missionary Enterprise in China, 1882–1919," in Ricardo K. S. Mak and Danny S. L. Paau (eds.), *Sino-German Relations Since 1800: Multidisciplinary Explorations* (Frankfurt, Germany, 2000).

Joseph Tse-Hei Lee

Brussels Conference (1937)

After outbreak of the Sino-Japanese War in July 1937, the League of Nations took up the question of whether an act of aggression had occurred and what, if anything, the League members should do in response. Japan withdrew from the League in 1933 in reaction to the League's adoption of the findings and suggestions of the Lytton Report. Around the time of Japanese withdrawal, the League Assembly created and charged the Advisory Committee, composed of the Committee of Nineteen and two non-league members, with the task of settling the dispute between Japan and China. Four years later, China, which was a member of League, called for economic sanctions. On October 1, the League Advisory Committee refused to support sanctions, but instead suggested that a meeting of the Nine Power Treaty states would be more effective in dealing with the Sino-Japanese dispute.

The Nine Power Treaty was a product of the 1921–1922 Washington Naval Disarmament Conference. Belgium, the British Empire, China, France, Italy, Japan, the Netherlands, Portugal, and United States agreed, among other things, to respect China's territorial and administrative integrity and to maintain the Open Door or the "principle of equal opportunity for the commerce and industry of all nations throughout the territory of China." Going into the conference, the

Chinese were hopeful that the United States would take a leadership role in rallying the powers against Japan. In October, President Franklin D. Roosevelt gave the "Quarantine Speech" in Chicago in which he asserted that "The epidemic of world lawlessness" had to be quarantined. Initially, Roosevelt considered taking measures to deal with Japan should mediation fail, but the isolationist backlash to Roosevelt's speech cooled any notions of taking serious measures. The U.S. delegation was warned ahead of time that public opinion would not support sanctions against Japan.

On November 3, eight of the nine powers gathered in Brussels. Although not a signatory, the Soviet Union participated as well. An invitation was extended to Japan to accept the powers' mediation of the Sino-Japanese conflict only to be rejected. Chinese representatives for the Nationalist government argued that Japan had committed aggression against China and had to be punished. France opposed imposing sanctions against Japan, but instead tried to use the conference to secure an American commitment to defend Europe now faced with the threat of Nazi Germany. Britain refused to act in Asia without U.S. assistance and feared sanctions would only drive the U.S. deeper into isolation. And true to their instructions from Roosevelt, the U.S. delegation rejected taking the lead or supporting sanctions because of public opinion and because U.S. interests in China were not viewed as vital. Only Nationalist China and the Soviet Union called for collective security in Asia. On November 24, the conference came to a close. The Brussels Conference's last resolution stated that its sessions had been temporarily suspended and would meet again when it could be "advantageously resumed," but the conference never resumed again.

See also Open Door Policy; Quarantine Speech (1937).

REFERENCES: Dorothy Borg, *The United States and the Far Eastern Crisis of 1933–1938: From the Manchurian Incident through the Initial Stage of the Undeclared Sino-Japanese War* (Cambridge, MA, 1964); Robert Dallek, *Franklin D. Roosevelt and American Foreign Policy, 1932–1945* (New York, 1979).

Stephen Craft

Bryan, William Jennings (1860–1925)

William Jennings Bryan, the "Boy Orator of the Platte," represented the Populist sentiment of American politics in the late 19th and early 20th centuries. Bryan came from Nebraska, and his rural, Protestant Mid-Western origins shaped his world-view. To his end, he believed that American democracy sprang from the innate character of small town and rural Protestant America. As a result, he maintained a firm record of opposition to anything that he believed threatened small town America, including big business, foreigners, imperialism, militarism, Marxism, and agnosticism.

Bryan rode to national prominence with his backing of the demands of Midwestern farmers that the government base currency on silver as well as gold. Bryan's Cross of Gold speech at the 1890 Democratic National Convention is a classic of American political rhetoric. In the speech he likened the oppression of workers by big business to the suffering of Jesus on the cross. He later admitted that he understood little of the economics involved in the issue; the farmers back home were for silver and thus he was for silver. The Democratic Party nominated him as their candidate for the Presidency in the 1896, 1900, and 1908 elections, all of which he lost. After the 1896 election, Bryan moved from strictly rural Populism to embrace the more general reform movement known as Progressivism. Unlike the Populists, the Progressives embraced the city and championed urban reform. Bryan bridged these two disparate movements. He backed a platform of reform that, although today seems mild compared to Franklin D. Roosevelt's New Deal a generation later, represented a major shift from traditional free market capitalism. Bryan supported reforms such as federal ownership of the railroads and a graduated income tax. He backed federal guarantees for savings in banks. He also sought such fundamental changes to the Constitution as single term presidency, women's suffrage, and voter initiates. Despite his championing of these reforms, he never lost his faith in small-scale capitalism. Bryan sought to reign in the large capitalists, especially the railroads, which had a stranglehold on small farmers. Although Bryan opposed war in general, he took a commission as a colonel of Nebraska Volunteers once the U.S. declared war on Spain in 1898. His regiment never left the U.S., and Bryan resigned from the military soon after the signing of the peace treaty with Spain. Bryan then became the leader of the anti-imperialist movement in the U.S. He became incensed by the annexation of the Philippine Islands. He believed that the Philippines would never be populated by American farmers and thus would become a colony in the sense that the European imperialist nations held colonies. This he believed would lead to militarism and end the moral authority of the U.S. Instead he urged the United States to maintain only a small coaling station and harbor in the Philippines to facilitate trade with the islands and with China. Two years later he decried as imperialistic President William McKinley's decision to send American soldiers to China to join the Europeans and Japanese in suppressing the Boxer Rebellion.

His appointment as President Woodrow Wilson's Secretary of State presents the spectacle of one of the most xenophobic American political leaders in charge of the department charged with maintaining relations with other nations. With Wilson he saw the hope for the world in making other peoples become more like Americans. His scruples led him to oppose the Preparedness movement, which sought to make the American military stronger either to avoid entering the Great War, or failing that, being ready to win it. He resigned from the administration from what he saw as Wilson's overly militaristic leanings. After he left the administration he would increasingly be relegated to the political wilderness, battling anything he saw as threatening to Fundamentalist Christianity. He championed the spread of the English language in China, which he believed would bring with it Protestant Christianity, but he believed this could best be done through trade, missionary work, and by example, rather than colonialism.

Although today it is common to ridicule Bryan for his part in the prosecution of the schoolteacher John Scopes for teaching evolution in Dayton, Tennessee's, infamous Monkey Trial near the end of his life in 1925, his service to American political development is far more profound. His opposition to both Communism, and the big business capitalism that he believed was making America fertile ground for Communism, showed a middle way between Communist revolution and exploitative market capitalism.

REFERENCES: Louis W. Koenig, *Bryan: A Political Biography of William Jennings Bryan* New York, 1971); Paul W. Glad, *The Trumpet Soundeth: William Jennings Bryan and His Democracy 1896–1912* (Lincoln, NE, 1966); William Jennings Bryan, *The Memoirs of William Jennings Bryan* (Port Washington, NY, 1925).

Barry Stentiford

Brzezinski, Zbigniew (1928-)

Zbigniew Brzezinski was born on March 28, 1928 in Warsaw, Poland. He is one of the most prominent American political scientists and public officials during the Cold War era. The son of a diplomat, he was raised in Canada. After earning his BA and MA degrees from McGill University in Montreal, he came to the United States in 1953. He was awarded the Ph.D. at Harvard in 1958. From 1960 to 1977 he taught international relations at Harvard and Columbia University. He became an influential voice on political affairs in the Com-

munist world. During Carter's administration, he served as national security adviser (1977–1981). In 1981, he resumed his teaching career. Later he was associated with the Center for Strategic and International Studies in Washington D.C. He wrote numerous books on U.S. strategic relations and eventually on the collapse of Communism. Through his prolific writings he expounded his philosophies as well as his political beliefs and ideals.

Of the accomplishments of the Carter administration, Brzezinski was proudest of its success in the normalization of relations with the People's Republic of China (PRC). In contrast with the other diplomatic initiatives of the Carter administration, Brzezinski almost single-handedly engineered the U.S. diplomatic recognition of the PRC on January 1, 1979. To some extent, Brzezinski finished the progress in Sino-American relations, started by Henry Kissinger, President Richard Nixon's National Security Advisor, in his successful trip to Beijing in July 1971. In his memoirs, Brzezinski drew the parallels between his trip to Beijing in May 1978 and Kissinger's: "I could not help but think of the strange coincidence that the Sino-American relationship was being forged in the course of a single decade by two U.S. officials who were of immigrant birth with larger strategic concerns in mind. I was determined to succeed in transforming that still-tenuous relationship into something more enduring and much more extensive." These "larger strategic concerns" caused frictions between Brzezinski and Cyrus Vance, the Secretaries of State. They both believed that it was necessary to develop full diplomatic relations with China, however, they had different views on the rationale. Vance wished to establish relations for their own sake, Brzezinski, on the other hand, shared the opinions with Nixon and Kissinger. He intended to play the "China card" as a counterweight against the Soviets whose relations with the Chinese had deteriorated in the 1960s. Vance was concerned that a sudden move to American recognition of Red China would anger the Russians, Brzezinski, however, believed that playing on the fears of the Soviets was beneficial to the United States. He told Chinese leader Deng Xiaoping, "my inclination to be fearful of offending the Soviet Union is rather limited. I would be willing to make a little bet with you as to who is less popular in the Soviet Union-you or me." Brzezinski even went as far as wishing to provide China with technologies with dual civilian and military uses, and proposing that the United States remain silent if Europeans were going to sell weapons to the mainland.

With this mind-set, Brzezinski sought the invitation to Beijing, believing that the Secretary of State's 1977 trip to China was a failure. Although Carter initially leaned toward Vance's strategy, by the end of 1978, Brzezinski appeared to have prevailed. He persuaded the President into setting a deadline for establishing full diplomatic relations with Beijing. After tough negotiations about American relations with Taiwan, the Carter administration reached its goal before the deadline of New Year's Day of 1979. The United States and China finally agreed that the U.S. break off relations with Taiwan in exchange for having the right to sell weapons to Taiwan and a vague promise from China not to use force to invade the island. The making of the decision to normalize relations with Beijing marked the ascendancy of Brzezinski and the increasing alienation of Vance from the policies of the administration. In his book, *The Grand Failure* published in 1989, Brzezinski suggests that Communism's failure in the world was caused by the political, social, and economic failure of the Leninist prototype, the model, which most Communist countries had adopted. Reforms proposed by Soviet leader Mikhail Gorbachev in the Soviet Union, he believed, would be unsuccessful. On the other hand, Brzezinski felt that China is liable to achieve success with its reforms because the Chinese leaders are more pragmatic and willing to abandon Marxist and Leninist ideologies and experiment with capitalist economics.

See also China Card.

REFERENCES: Gaddis Smith, *Morality, Reason, and Power: American Diplomacy in the Carter Years* (New York, 1986); Zbigniew Brzezinski, *The Grand Failure: The Birth and Death of Communism in the Twentieth Century* (New York, 1989); Zbigniew Brzezinski, *Power and Principle: Memoirs of the National Security Adviser, 1977–1981* (New York, 1983); Zbigniew Brzezinski, *The Grand Chessboard: American Primacy and Its Geo-Strategic Imperative* (New York, 1998).

Yuwu Song

Buck, Pearl S. (1892–1973)

Pearl C. Sydenstricker was born on June 26, 1892 in Hillsboro, West Virginia, while her Presbyterian missionary parents temporarily returned from China. Three months later they moved to Zhenjiang, a port city on the Yangzi River. There, as Buck later claimed she became fluent in Chinese before English. During the Boxer Rebellion, the family fled to Shanghai and returned to their home in Zhenjiang in 1902. From 1907 to 1909, Buck attended a Western boarding school in Shanghai. During her early years in China, she often contributed articles to the children's edition of the *Shanghai Mercury*.

In 1909 Buck left China and visited Europe and Great Britain before enrolling in Randolph-Macon College in Lynchburg, Virginia in 1910, graduating in 1914. She remained at the college to teach, but returned to China to care for her ailing mother in November 1914, where Buck taught school and trained Chinese women teachers. She married John L. Buck in 1917, who worked for the Presbyterian Church in China teaching modern agricultural methods, and moved with him to a small town in northern China. Her next several years here served as an inspiration for her novel, *The Good Earth*. In 1921 the couple moved to Nanjing where he accepted a position at the University of Nanjing. She also taught English literature as well at the university and at several other colleges over the next few years. The Bucks returned to the United States in 1925 to seek medical treatment for their retarded daughter, and enrolled at Cornell University. She worked on her MA in English winning a prize for her history essay "China and the West." The family returned to China in 1926, and barely escaped with their lives during the 1927 Nanjing Incident during the Northern Expedition's attempt to reunify China. The Bucks moved to Japan for a year until matters settled down in China. In 1929 she returned to America and published her first successful novel, *East Wind: West Wind*, short stories about Chinese life. She traveled back to Nanjing where she began work on *The Good Earth*, which, she claimed, she completed in three months, and published in 1931. It became an instant success, and won her a Pulitzer Prize. It would be expanded into a trilogy with *Sons* (1932) and *A House Divided* (1935). She also translated the classic Chinese novel, *Shui Hu Zhuan* as *All Men Are Brothers* (1933), and wrote another novel about the life of a Chinese peasant woman, *The Mother* (1934). She returned permanently to the United States in 1934, and divorced her husband but retained his last name after marrying Richard J. Walsh, President of the John Day Company that published many of her books. In 1936 Buck published biographies of her parents: *The Exile* and *The Fighting Angel*. For her body of work, she received the Nobel Prize in Literature in 1938, making her an "expert" on China. From 1941 to 1946, she and her husband published *Asia*, a general magazine about life in that continent. During the Second World War, Buck worked for the Office of War Information and the United China Relief, while continuing to write *Dragon Seed* (1942) and *Promise* (1943), novels about the Chinese effort against the Japanese. She also organized the East and West Foundation to sponsor exchanges and dialogs for mutual understanding especially between the United States and Asia. In

1949 she founded Welcome Home, an adoption agency for American children of mixed Asian descent. In 1964 she established the Pearl S. Buck Foundation for Ameri-Asian children abroad. Shortly before her death, she gave up the rights to most of her written works so that the proceeds would benefit the Buck Foundation. She died on March 6, 1973 in Danby, Vermont.

Buck was a prolific writer producing about 100 books and countless articles. Besides her famous novels, she also wrote children's books and novels about American life under the pseudonym John Sedges. She is one of the most widely translated American authors.

See also *The Good Earth*.

REFERENCES: Nora B. Stirling, *Perl S. Buck: A Woman in Conflict* (Piscataway, NJ, 1983); Theodore F. Harris, *Pearl S. Buck: A Biography in Consultation with Pearl S. Buck* (New York, 1969–1971); Paul A. Doyle, *Pearl S. Buck* (New York, 1965).

Greg Ference

Burlingame, Anson (1820–1870)

Lawyer, congressman, U.S. minister to China, and Chinese envoy, Anson Burlingame was born in New Berlin, New York. He received a bachelor's degree from the University of Michigan (1841), and a law degree from Harvard University (1846). Shortly after being admitted to the bar and practicing law in Boston, Burlingame entered politics, serving in the Massachusetts Senate (1852–1854) and as a delegate at the state constitutional convention (1853). He then won three consecutive elections to the U.S. House of Representatives, first as a Free Soiler (in a fusion ticket with the American party) and later as a Republican congressman (1855–1861).

During his tenure in Congress, Burlingame emerged as a vocal opponent of slavery. He became a northern hero by denouncing Preston Brooks' caning of Charles Sumner and accepting a challenge to a duel from Brooks (Brooks later rescinded the challenge). In 1856, Burlingame, one of the organizers of the Republican Party in Massachusetts, supported John C. Fremont for president. In 1860, he strongly supported Abraham Lincoln's candidacy for the President to the neglect of his own reelection bid, causing his defeat to William Appleton. Lincoln rewarded Burlingame by appointing him U.S. minister to Austria, but the Austrian government declared him *persona non grata* because of Burlingame's earlier support for both the Hungarian revolutionary Louis Kossuth and Sardinian independence. Secretary of State William H. Seward then appointed Burlingame as U.S. minister to China (1861–1867).

Arriving in Beijing in mid-1862, Burlingame became the first American diplomatic minister to reside in China's capital. His respect for Chinese culture and civilization influenced his efforts to address the "unequal treaty system" which gave foreigners economic and legal privileges (control of China's tariffs and extraterritoriality) that violated Chinese sovereignty. Seward, concerned about British and French support for the Confederacy in the American Civil War, instructed Burlingame to cooperate with both powers in China so that the United States could continue to benefit economically from its most-favored-nation status secured in the Treaty of Wangxia (1844). Influenced by his opposition to slavery, Burlingame decided to change Western policy toward China by favoring restraint over force. He did not eliminate the unequal treaties, but Burlingame gained an agreement with the British, French, and Russian ministers to pursue a "cooperative policy," namely, that the government in Beijing be treated as a sovereign power. This policy won Burlingame the gratitude of the Chinese government, which relied on the American minister to solve such difficulties as the Lay-Osbourne flotilla debacle, the appointment of Robert Hart as Foreign Inspector of Maritime Customs, and the suppression of the Taiping Rebellion.

After resigning as U.S. minister to China in November 1867, Burlingame accepted a commission as China's first official envoy to the Western powers (1867–1870) to convince them to drop their demands to revise the Treaties of Tianjin (1858). He led a Chinese delegation to the United States, Britain, France, Germany, and Russia seeking agreements to ensure the continuation of the "cooperative policy." His lone success occurred in the United States where he and Seward concluded the Burlingame Treaty (July 28, 1868) in which the U.S. government agreed to recognize China as a sovereign nation. Britain and Germany offered only modest pledges to continue the "cooperative policy" toward China. France refused to issue any such pledge. After reaching St. Petersburg, Burlingame developed pneumonia and died.

Burlingame relied on personal diplomacy to promote a common policy to solve Western problems in China. He sought recognition of China's independence in order to make it more receptive to Western civilization, especially trade. The shortcoming of Burlingame's diplomacy is evident in the demise of the "cooperative policy" following his death. Yet, his effort may have prevented the partition of China in the late 19th century amongst the Western powers and Japan.

See also Treaty of Wangxia (1844); Extrater-

ritoriality; Treaty of Tianjin (1858); Treaty Tariff.

REFERENCES: David A. Anderson, *Imperialism and Idealism: American Diplomats in China, 1861–1898* (Bloomington, IN, 1985); Tyler Dennet, *Americans in East Asia: A Critical Study of the Policy of the United States with Reference to China, Japan, and Korea in the 19th Century* (New York, 1922); S.S. Kim, "Burlingame and the Inauguration of the Co-operative Policy," *Modern Asian Studies Vol. 5:4* (1971); Martin Robert Ring, *Anson Burlingame, S. Wells Williams, and China, 1861–1870: A Great Era in Chinese-American Relations* (Ph.D. Dissertation, Tulane University, 1972).

Dean Fafoutis

Burlingame-Seward Treaty (1868)

The signing of the Burlingame-Seward Treaty for Peace, Amity, and Commerce between the United States and China in 1868 provided a clear expression of the importance of Chinese labors to the prosperity and development of the Frontier West. Article V of the treaty affirmed for each country, "the mutual advantage of the free migration and emigration of their citizens and subjects respectively from one country to the other...." In Article VI, the treaty continued with the provision that "Chinese subjects visiting or residing in the United States, shall enjoy the same privileges, immunities, and exemptions in respect to travel or residence as may there be enjoyed by the citizens or subjects of the most favored nation." The treaty further pledged in Article VIII that the United States would not intervene in the domestic or economic affairs of China without China's consent. The treaty reflected the views of Secretary of State William Seward, who wished to treat China as an equal among world powers. He opposed the nativism and discrimination that overlooked the benefits which Chinese immigrant laborers provided to the developing economy of the U.S. West Coast. Anson Burlingame had served as Seward's envoy in China since the early 1860s, and the treaty was concluded when Burlingame returned to the United States with Chinese government officials.

At first, little organizational opposition existed to the treaty. However, the open immigration provisions of the treaty would increasingly become a source of contention in the subsequent years as economic conditions soured. White laborers worried that the Chinese would take the available jobs because of the perceived willingness of the Chinese to work for lower wages. Politicians and labor leaders began to exploit these feelings. Since the Chinese could not vote in California, their concerns did not effect the decisions of politicians. The state passed laws depriving the Chinese of the ability to become naturalized citizens, to testify in courts against whites, to attend white public schools, and to actually block the immigration of the Chinese into the state. However, discriminatory laws were found to be in violation of either the Burlingame-Seward Treaty, the existing Civil Rights legislation, or the equal protection clause of the Fourteenth Amendment.

Because California politicians found little success through local action, they began to appeal to the United States Congress to repeal the Burlingame-Seward Treaty and to enact restrictive immigration laws. California politicians viewed this as a necessary course of action to resolve economic problems, threats of violence, and the threat of losing the support of voters. In 1876, both California political parties cooperated in the state Senate to create an appeal to Congress calling for a national exclusion policy. The U.S. Congress responded with the creation of a special joint committee in 1876, which traveled to California in order to study Chinese immigration. The committee concluded that the President should modify the Burlingame-Seward Treaty to apply only for commercial purposes, and that Congress should then limit Chinese immigration.

The U.S. Congress successfully enacted Chinese exclusion legislation for the first time in 1879. It was the Fifteen Passengers Bill. The bill prohibited any ship from bringing more than fifteen Chinese passengers to the United States in any one voyage. President Rutherford B. Hayes vetoed the bill, arguing that it violated the open immigration policies of the Burlingame-Seward Treaty. Hayes believed that Congress could not unilaterally abrogate treaties. He also viewed this bill as a threat to America's trade relations with China, which he saw as an essential component of continued economic prosperity. He did not see the situation on the West Coast as volatile enough to warrant the abrogation of the treaty. Nonetheless, enough opposition existed so that the treaty was modified in 1880 to allow for limits on immigration, paving the way for subsequent exclusionary policies.

See also Burlingame, Anson (1820–1870).

REFERENCES: Warren I. Cohen, *America's Response to China: A History of Sino-American Relations* (New York, 2000); Mary R. Coolidge, *Chinese Immigration* (New York, 1909); Shirley Hune, *The Issue of Chinese Immigration in the Federal Government, 1875–1882* (Washington, DC, 1979); Elmer C. Sandmeyer, *The Anti-Chinese Movement in California* (Urbana, IL, 1939).

Wade D. Pfau

Burma *see* Guomindang Intervention in Burma

Burma Road

The name Burma Road refers to the overland connection between Kunming in southwest China and Lashio, Burma built to supply China during World War II. The name is often extended, generically, to include the Ledo or Stilwell Road from Assam, India to Bhamo, Burma built to bypass Japanese-held territory and connect with the original Burma Road.

In 1937 the Chinese Nationalist leader Jiang Jieshi realized that the loss of eastern ports to the Japanese would cut China off from all outside supply, apart from the trickle through Hanoi into Yunnan and via truck from Soviet central Asia. His choice was to connect Kunming with British Burma at Lashio by motor road. Lashio was connected by rail and waterway to the port of Rangoon. The 600-mile truck road followed some ancient trail networks and local roadways, but about half was entirely new. Zigzagging over 8,000 foot mountain ridges of solid rock down through thick jungle valleys, it crossed the Mekong and Salween Rivers and innumerable waterways. 4,500 bamboo culverts and 500 bridges were built, many single-span suspension bridges. Financed by the U.S. and Britain despite Japanese objections, it was built principally with Chinese labor using hand methods reminiscent of the American transcontinental railroad of 1862–1869. It was a huge logistics endeavor to support up to 20,000 men at any one time 200 miles from supply depots. An astounding 36 million cubic yards of earth were moved, 4 million yards of rock cut and 600 miles of roadway surfaced with one-inch rock, all done by hand. Even the huge limestone rollers were pulled by hand. There were many casualties before completion in December 1938.

Much of the roadway was one lane and conditions permitted a top speed of only twelve miles per hour, taking up to six days each way. Three round trips wore out a truck. Monsoon rains necessitated continual maintenance and cut traffic as much as 85% seasonally. In 1941, with more new trucks from the U.S. and Britain, tonnage reached 10–15,000 tons per month. Going in was military equipment, ammunition, cement, steel, motors, copper wire, machine tools and petroleum. Going out to balance China's trade balance was tungsten, antimony, wolfram, tung oil, and silk. Russia, after the Ribbentrop Pact, cut its Asia supply route (1940) and Japan pressured Vichy France to close the supply line through Indochina (1940). In the summer of 1940 the Japanese succeeded in pressuring Britain to limit port access to China. The road was also under attack by Japanese-backed Burmese guerrillas. It was U.S. pressure that got the British to reopen the road in early 1941 as part of an evolving Roosevelt policy of sustaining the anti-Axis forces that later became Lend Lease. China and its Burma Road link were integral to that strategy. The initial deployment of the American Volunteer Group (Flying Tigers) in 1941 was to Burma to protect Rangoon and the Road. When Japan invaded Burma, Chinese forces were sent under the command of General Joseph W. Stilwell to supplement British defenses. As the Japanese surged northward, the Chinese troops were pushed out, part into China and part into India. Lashio fell on April 1942, and the road link was cut. The danger to China's war effort was taken seriously, so Stilwell, backed by General George C. Marshall, advocated a reconquest of Burma. This strategy, based on the two Chinese forces, an increasing American presence and somewhat reluctant British efforts, became the Burma Campaign, one of the most difficult of the war.

As part of the Burma campaign and to provide an alternative link to reopen the Burma Road, a route was conceived from Ledo in India's Assam province to Bhamo, Burma. Called the Ledo Road, it would have to be pushed in the face of stubborn Japanese resistance. Begun in 1942 as a planned 478 miles of all-weather gravel, it was one of America's engineering triumphs of the war. Called "Pick's Pike" after its engineering officer, General Lewis Pick, it was said to have cost "a man a mile." The linkup with the old road was made in January 1945, with only seven months until the war's end.

See also Stilwell, Joseph W. (1883–1946); China-Burma-India (CBI) Theater; Stilwell Road.

REFERENCES: Donovan Webster, *The Burma Road* (New York, 2003); Leslie Anders, *The Ledo Road* (Norman, OK, 1965); Ray McKelvie, *The War in Burma* (London, 1948); Nathan Prefer, *Vinegar Joe's War: Stilwell's Campaigns for Burma* (Novato, CA, 2000); S. Woodburn Kirby, *The War Against Japan Vol. IV, The Reconquest of Burma* (London, 1965).

Dave Egler

Bush, George H. W. (1924-)

President from 1989 until 1993, George H. W. Bush presided over the interruption of Sino-American relations following Tiananmen Square Massacre and their subsequent slow resumption, the last becoming a principal goal of his administration. The son of Connecticut Senator Prescott Bush and, in common with most China Hands of his generation, a Yale graduate, Bush made international affairs the focus of his public career from his election to the House of Representatives in 1966 from the 7th congressional district of

Texas onwards. He entered the Nixon administration as ambassador to the United Nations from 1971 to 1972, stepping down to serve as chair of the Republican National Committee from 1972 to 1973, and first encountered China serving there from October 1974 as first chief of the United States Liaison Office. Bush continued in this post until January 1976, when he returned to Washington to become Director of Central Intelligence Agency until the close of the Ford administration. While in Beijing he developed great affection for the nation; he cycled to work on a bicycle Chinese associates dubbed the Flying Pigeon, and his daughter Dorothy was christened in Chongwenmen Christian Church.

Upon assuming the presidency, Bush lost no time in returning to China, first doing so in the context of a trip to Asia for Emperor Hirohito's funeral in February 1989. While there, he reiterated his commitments to the three communiques of 1972, 1979, and 1982 and proposed a bilateral relationship premised on facilitation of increased trade through intellectual property protection, legal protection for investors, and greater market access on both sides; cooperation on regional security, narco-trafficking, and counter-proliferation; and expanded cultural and educational exchanges and military cooperation. This blueprint for a close bilateral relationship was quickly disrupted with the suppression by Deng Xiaoping's government on June 3 and 4, 1989 of student protests in Tiananmen Square, which commemorated the reformist legacy of deceased former Communist Party General Secretary Hu Yaobang. For President Bush, who prided himself on special familiarity with the country's leaders and his personal role in the Sino-American rapprochement of 1972–1979, the preferable American response would have imposed limited sanctions to protect the bilateral relationship from more drastic measures by China critics in Congress, then returned the relationship as soon as practicable to one of close bilateral ties managed personally at a high level by leaders of the two nations. This policy met with substantial congressional opposition, spurred by Senate Majority Leader George Mitchell and in the House by Representative Nancy Pelosi in her first full term. Bush faced a substantial defeat in Congress over the symbolic issue of immigration, with Congress passing without a dissenting vote the Emergency Chinese Immigration Relief Act of 1989, Pelosi's legislation permitting Chinese students to remain in the country after the expiration of their visas. Bush was only able to sustain his veto after granting the same legal protection to the students by executive order, and even so, secured a margin of only four votes in the Senate, with even this requiring considerable pork to sway marginal votes.

Bush nonetheless secured his goal of shepherding the relationship back to a state of normalcy, with a secret mission by National Security Advisor Brent Scowcroft in June 1989 laying the groundwork for restored relations, although doing so required expenditure of tremendous political capital. Chinese cooperation was marked in the lead-up to the Persian Gulf War, with Beijing supporting UN Security Council Resolutions 660 (condemning the invasion of Kuwait) and 661 (imposing sanctions), and agreeing not to veto Resolution 678, which authorized military force. Bush's internationalism became a political vulnerability when high unemployment and low GDP growth caught public attention, and Bush's public approval falling to 29 percent during the summer preceding his election. He was defeated by Governor William J. Clinton in November by 370 electoral votes to Clinton's 168, and left office in January 1993.

See also Tiananmen Square Massacre; Scowcroft-Eagleburger Mission (1989).

REFERENCES: George H. W. Bush and Brent Scowcroft, *A World Transformed* (New York, 1998); Patrick Belton, *Congressmen as Diplomats: Congress and the Politics of China and Russia Policy* (Ph. D. Dissertation, Oxford University); David M. Lampton, *Same Bed, Different Dreams: Managing U.S.-China Relations, 1989–2000* (Berkeley, CA, 2002); Robert L. Suettinger, *Beyond Tiananmen: The Politics of U.S.-China Relations* (Washington, DC, 2003).

Patrick Belton

Bush, George W. (1946-)

Serving as U.S. President from January 2001 and reelected to a second term in November 2004, George W. Bush's China policy underwent several pronounced shifts during his presidency. From entering office, viewing China as a "strategic competitor," after the terrorist attacks of September 11, 2001, his administration recast China as an ally in global counter-terror efforts. For its part, the Chinese government hoped within a stable relationship grounded upon counterterrorism it could secure gains on such issues as American arms sales to Taiwan.

As candidate, Governor Bush sought to distance himself from the Clinton administration's Sino-American engagement, pledging to reduce the importance of China in American foreign policy in favor of greater attention to Taiwan, Japan, and South Korea. In the campaign, his foreign policy advisor Condoleezza Rice noted Chinese cooperation with Iran and Pakistan in proliferation of ballistic-missile technology and termed China a "potential threat to stability in the Asia-Pacific region" and "a great power with unresolved interests," making military deterrence of Chinese attempts at forcible reunification with Taiwan a principal national goal. In the closer relationship that followed September 11, President Bush met more frequently with his Chinese counterparts during his first two years as President than any of his predecessors did in their entire administrations. American engagements in Afghanistan and Iraq required Chinese acquiescence in the Security Council. An early irritant, when a U.S. Navy reconnaissance plane collided with a Chinese naval aviation over the South China Sea on April 1, 2001, was accordingly forgotten. For its part, Beijing found in American attentiveness to counterterrorism an opportunity for suppressing dissent in Muslim communities within its Xinjiang-Uighur Autonomous Region and influencing Bush to further dissuade Taiwanese President Chen Shuibian from making moves toward Taiwanese independence. Accordingly, in December 2003 following a meeting with visiting Chinese Premier Wen Jiabao, Bush criticized Chen in language which went beyond historical precedents, saying "the comments and actions made by the leader of Taiwan indicate he may be willing to make decisions unilaterally that change the status quo, which we oppose." Conversely, Bush encountered some success in bringing pressure to bear upon China over several key imprisoned political dissidents, leading to their early release from prison. These include Xu Wenli and Wang Youcai (co-founders of the short-lived China Democracy Party), Tibetan nun Phuntsog Nyidron, Tibetan scholar Ngawang Choephel, and Uighur businesswoman Rebiya Kadeer.

Though conflicted, in 2004 the Chinese government quietly supported Bush's reelection to a second term. His controversial administration created a diplomatic vacuum which permitted Beijing to build up influence in a historically pro-Washington Asian region. Furthermore, his willingness to rein in pro-independence tendencies in Taiwan contrasted with Beijing's fears that Democratic presidential candidate John F. Kerry could have been more vulnerable to calls from congressional Republicans for symbolic concessions to Taiwan, as well as to pressure from organized labor to oppose Chinese trade practices.

REFERENCES: Kerry Dumbaugh, "China-U.S. Relations," *CRS Report for Congress* (May 20, 2004); Wily Lam, "The End of the Sino-American Honeymoon?" *China Brief 4* (June 24, 2004); James Mann, *Rise of the Vulcans: The History of Bush's War Cabinet* (New York, 2004); Condoleezza Rice, "Promoting the National In-

terest," *Foreign Affairs* (January/February 2000); Patrick Belton, "How World Leaders See Bush and Kerry," *The Hill* (November 2, 2004).

Patrick Belton

Cairo Conference

Cairo Conference, code-named Sextant, was held from November 23 to 26, and December 3 to 7, 1943. The conferees included British Prime Minister Winston Churchill, U.S. President Franklin D. Roosevelt, and Chinese Generalissimo Jiang Jieshi. It was the high point of collaboration among the three leaders. The major discussions at the conference focused on Southeast Asia and Jiang Jieshi's wish to have the Western Allies launch amphibious attacks in the Bay of Bengal to coincide with a Chinese intervention in Burma. Churchill was uninterested in these discussions. Despite Britain's cold attitudes, Roosevelt promised Jiang that the Allies soon would take amphibious actions against the Japanese. In the middle of the Cairo Conference, Roosevelt and Churchill met with Soviet leader Joseph Stalin at Teheran from November 27 to December 2. Stalin did not come to Cairo, because he hesitated to meet with heads of states at war with Japan when the Soviet Union was not. The outcome of discussions at Teheran forced Roosevelt to retract his promise to Jiang.

The main results of the Cairo Conference included an agreement on military operations in China against the Japanese, a promise of postwar return of Manchuria, Taiwan, and the Penghuss to China, and a pledge of freedom and independence "in due course" for Korea. The Cairo Declaration of December 1, 1943 did not mention the future status of the Ryukyus, indicating that the Chinese view that the islands should revert to China was not shared by the Americans and the British. American officials in Washington who had studied the territorial question had concluded that the islands, if thoroughly demilitarized, could be retained by Japan. Nevertheless, the Chinese felt euphoric that at last China was accepted as a world power and assured an important role in the postwar international partnership. They also were gratified that Jiang was viewed as a major leader in the world. But the retraction of the Allied promise for amphibious warfare operations made the Chinese feel betrayed and belittled.

See also Jiang Jieshi (1887–1975); Roosevelt, Franklin D. (1882–1945); World War II.

REFERENCES: Barbara W. Tuchman, *Stilwell and the American Experience in China: 1911–1945* (New York, 1971); John King Fairbank, *The United States and China* (Cambridge, MA, 1948); Tang Tsou, *America's Failure in China, 1941–1945* (Chicago, IL, 1963).

Yuwu Song

Cambodia

From the late 19th century up to World War II, Cambodia was joined with Vietnam and Laos in French Indochina. The first Indochina War, which began in 1945 and 1946, and ended in 1954, was primarily a struggle of the French against the Viet Minh, a Vietnamese nationalist movement under Communist leadership. The war extended into Cambodia to some extent, but this was mainly a matter of Viet Minh forces operating in Cambodia. The Cambodian Communist movement, later to become famous as the Khmer Rouge, was too small to play a major role. The United States backed the French, and the People's Republic of China (PRC) backed the Viet Minh, but neither had a direct role in Cambodia in this period.

When the French chose Norodom Sihanouk as King of Cambodia in 1941, they intended him to be a French puppet, but in 1953 he managed to win genuine independence. The Geneva Conference of 1954 affirmed his government's control of Cambodia, and Viet Minh forces withdrew. King Sihanouk became Prince Sihanouk in 1955. After 1954, Cambodia was officially neutral in the Cold War. Sihanouk sent mixed signals to both sides. In 1955, he signed an agreement with the United States for military aid, but did not accept the U.S. advisers who would normally have accompanied such aid. In 1956, he made a state visit to the PRC, and signed an agreement for Chinese economic aid, but he did not grant diplomatic recognition to the PRC until 1958. But Sihanouk was on very bad terms with America's allies in Thailand and South Vietnam. Gradually, he leaned to the Communist side in the Cold War. He terminated the U.S. military aid program in 1963, and broke off diplomatic relations with the United States in 1965. Communist-led guerrilla struggles against the governments of Laos and South Vietnam began in 1959 and 1960. These gradually grew to become the Second Indochina War. Cambodia at first avoided direct involvement. But in 1964 or 1965, Chinese ships began to deliver weapons and munitions to Sihanoukville, on Cambodia's south coast; these were then hauled across Cambodia by truck and delivered to Vietnamese Communist forces. Sihanouk permitted the Vietnamese Communists to use base areas in Cambodia. In return, the Vietnamese Communists were to avoid intervention in Cambodian politics. Sihanouk eventually became nervous about PRC influence in the ethnic Chinese community in Cambodia, about the growing size of the Vietnamese Communist forces in Cambodia, and about the danger that they might support a small rebellion against him by the Khmer Rouge, which

began in 1967 and 1968. When President Richard Nixon began a very secret program of U.S. bombing of the Vietnamese Communist base areas in Cambodia in 1969, Sihanouk did not protest. Instead he restored diplomatic relations with the United States. In 1970, Sihanouk was overthrown in a coup led by General Lon Nol and Prince Sisowath Sirik Matak, who allied Cambodia with the United States and attempted to expel Vietnamese Communist forces from the country. Sihanouk met in China with representatives of the Khmer Rouge and the Vietnamese Communists, and allied himself with them. A devastating war spread across Cambodia, in which Lon Nol's forces, with U.S. and South Vietnamese aid, fought Communist forces that were mostly Vietnamese from 1970 to 1972, mostly Khmer Rouge thereafter, with Chinese aid. U.S. air support for Lon Nol's forces was terminated by an act of Congress in 1973. The Khmer Rouge won the war in April 1975. Khmer Rouge rule, from 1975 to 1978, was an unspeakable horror. More than a tenth of the Cambodian population died. China was the only significant foreign supporter of the Khmer Rouge. At the end of 1978, Vietnamese forces invaded and overthrew the Khmer Rouge, ending the slaughter. The Khmer Rouge maintained a guerrilla resistance against the Vietnamese forces, based partly in the jungles of Cambodia and partly in Thailand.

The United States and China, both enemies of the Soviet Union (with which Vietnam was allied), united in expressing outrage against the Vietnamese invasion of Cambodia. China briefly invaded northern Vietnam in 1979, in an unsuccessful effort to draw off Vietnamese troops from Cambodia. It was primarily U.S. diplomatic support that allowed the Khmer Rouge leaders to continue representing Cambodia in the United Nations for several years after they had ceased to rule that country. Following withdrawal of Vietnamese forces from Cambodia in 1989, an agreement brokered by the United Nations finally restored something approaching peace, if not prosperity, to Cambodia.

See also Second Indochina War.

REFERENCES: David P. Chandler, *The Tragedy of Cambodian History: Politics, War, and Revolution Since 1945* (New Haven, CT, 2000); Justin Corfield and Laura Summers, *Historical Dictionary of Cambodia* (Lanham, MD, 2003); Qiang Zhai, *China and the Vietnam Wars, 1950–1975* (Chapel Hill, NC, 2000).

Edwin Moise

Carter, James Earl (1924-)

As President of the United States from 1977 to 1981, Jimmy Carter presided over the normalization of relations with the People's Republic of China; a process which began under his Republican predecessors Richard Nixon and Gerald Ford. Carter's policy of normalization with China was complicated by increased tensions between the United States and Soviet Union as well as Congressional passage of the Taiwan Relations Act of 1979.

Carter was born October 1, 1924 in Plains, Georgia to a family of peanut farmers. He graduated from the Naval Academy in 1946. After completing his Naval obligations, Carter returned to his native Georgia, where he farmed and entered state politics. In 1970, he was elected Governor of Georgia in a campaign noted for its emphasis upon removing racial barriers. Carter narrowly defeated incumbent Republican President Gerald Ford in the 1976 presidential election. Although he had little experience in foreign affairs, Carter inherited the Nixon-Ford initiative of normalizing relations with the People's Republic of China. Initially, Carter had his Secretary of State Cyrus Vance take a hard stance that the United States was unwilling to abandon all governmental relations with Taiwan, and talks were placed on hold. As negotiations between the Untied States and Soviet Union stalled over strategic arms limitations, however, Carter attempted to put pressure on the Soviets by reopening discussions with the Chinese. In June 1978, the American liaison in Beijing, labor leader Leonard Woodcock, approached Chinese leader Deng Xiaoping, who assured the Americans that the People's Republic of China would not use force to liberate Taiwan. On December 15, 1978, President Carter announced that the United States would now recognize the Communist regime in Beijing as the official government of China. While there was some domestic opposition to the "abandonment" of Taiwan, the lure of business investment in China dissuaded most critics. To modify those who still harbored doubts about the Beijing regime, Deng flew to the United States and won the approval of many Americans. The Chinese leader even donned a cowboy hat in Houston, Texas. On March 1, 1999, the United States officially extended diplomatic recognition to the People's Republic of China. Relations, however, were strained when the Chinese troops attacked Vietnam, who had overthrown the Chinese-supported Pol Pot regime in Cambodia. This indecisive military engagement, nevertheless, did not prevent the negotiation of a Sino-American commercial treaty in 1979; a move, which further antagonized the Soviets who were denied most favored-nation status under the Jackson-Vanik Amendment to the Trade Act of 1974. The Soviet invasion of Afghanistan in 1979 increased tension between the United States and Kremlin, but Chinese feelings were not spared by the Taiwan Relations Act of 1979. Carter's relationship with the Congress was troubled throughout his Presidency, and the Georgian was unable to prevent inclusion of measures, which antagonized the Chinese. The Taiwan Relations Act pledged military aid to Taiwan and declared that any aggression by the mainland against Taiwan would be a "matter of grave concern to the United States."

In 1980, Carter's re-election bid was terminated by Ronald Reagan, who was now presided over the strained relations with both the Soviet Union and China. Following his electoral defeat, Carter returned to private life. Building upon the Nobel Peace Prize for his peace-making efforts in the Middle East, Carter has used his status as a former president to work for global human rights.

See also Deng Xiaoping (1904–1997); Taiwan Relations Act of 1979.

REFERENCES: James Mann, *About Face: A History of America's Curious Relationship with China from Nixon to Clinton* (New York, 1999); Alexander Moens, *Foreign Policy under Carter: Testing Multiple Advocacy Decision Making* (Boulder, CO, 1990); Herbert P. Rosenbaum and Alexj Ugrinsky, *Jimmy Carter: Foreign Policy and Post-Presidential Years* (Westport, CT, 1994); Gaddis Smith, *Morality, Reason, and Power: American Diplomacy in the Carter Years* (New York, 1986).

Ron Briley

Center for China-United States Cooperation (CCUSC)

The Center was founded in 1998, with support from an alliance between China scholars and Chinese American business professionals in the Denver area. Its official sponsor is the University of Denver's Graduate School of International Studies. The Executor Director is Sam Suisheng Zhao, founder and editor of the *Journal of Contemporary China*. The Center's goal is to improve mutual understanding between the United States and China on all levels—academic, government, and civil society. While newer and smaller than longer-established bilateral relations associations, it is unique in several respects. First, on the American side it has a regional focus in the Rocky Mountains, whereas most other associations are based on the east coast and a few in California. Second, it is the only significant broad-agenda U.S.-China association based on a university campus. Third, it has established a sustained working relationship with the China Institute of Contemporary International Relations, a Premier think tank with close ties to China's State Council.

Center for China-U.S. Cooperation programs include the following. Joint Research: The Center sponsors cooperative research by American and Chinese scholars, particularly on security issues. Public Forums: Since 2002, CCUSC has hosted a monthly forum in Denver, at which a leading political, business, or academic personality from the United States or China discusses an aspect of bilateral relations. Scholarly Exchange: The Center has established partnerships with eight Chinese universities, as well as two Chinese think tanks, and organizes regular visiting scholar exchanges. Annual Conferences: Since 2000, the Center has held an annual conference with a specific theme of importance to China and US-China relations, such as the WTO, Taiwan, and political reform. Executive Training: Intended to provide professional training in a variety of fields, the program began in 2003 with CCUSC providing financial training in Denver to economists and state-owned enterprise executives. Publications: The Center has assumed sponsorship of the *Journal of Contemporary China*.

REFERENCES: Center for China-U.S. Cooperation, *www.du.edu/gsis/china*.

Norty Wheeler

Central Intelligence Agency (CIA)

Established in 1947, The Central Intelligence Agency (CIA) was created to protect the security of the United States by predicting and preventing external threats and attacks. To accomplish this monumental task requires the agency to coordinate its activities with many other military and private agencies. In June 1942, President Franklin D. Roosevelt initiated the Office of Strategic Services (OSS) that was charged with building a network of spies and informants in Europe as well as in Myanmar (previously known as Burma). With the failure to predict the December 7, 1941 Japanese attack on Pearl Harbor, this illustrated the need for improved intelligence. OSS operations lasted from 1942 to 1947 and were disbanded and then Congress started the formation of the CIA. During both the Roosevelt and Truman administrations, war aims focused primarily on Europe particularly about the expansion of Soviet influence in Europe.

Following World War II the spread of Soviet influence solidified Truman's containment doctrine that emphasized steps to prevent the spread of Communism. Several CIA operations were authorized and developed in Tibet, Korea and Myanmar (Burma) whose aim was in general to contain the expansion of Communism. In Burma the CIA collaborated with Nationalist Chinese intelligence to develop covert operations whose aim was to organize and train a force for an invasion of the new Communist People's Republic of China. With the Nationalists recently defeated, the Communists were considered vulnerable and thousands of Nationalist troops remained in Burma for future operations. The CIA was involved in equipping and training these troops in a plan to insert these troops into China and engage the People's Liberation Army. In 1950 several unsuccessful invasions were launched from Burma. The apparent rationale was to generate a grassroots uprising sufficient to bring back Nationalist leader Jiang Jieshi to organize and defeat the new Communist regime in China. The Burma operation involved thousands of Nationalists troops that were easily repulsed by Chinese troops inflicting many casualties. The retreat back to Burma led the remaining Nationalist troops to settle in Burma and with assistance from the CIA allegedly used opium smuggling to finance further covert operations in China and Indochina. CIA operations in Korea started badly since its poor intelligence operations did not warn the U.S. of the invasion of South Korea and the start of the Korean War in 1950. During the Korean War the CIA had covert operatives in North and South Korea involved in espionage and covert action activities starting in October 1949. By early 1951 the CIA airdropped hundreds of trained North Korean refugees in four regions in North Korea to engage the North Korean troops and disrupt their organization. The Burma operations failed to materialize and Chinese troops poured into North Korea resulting in fierce engagements with American troops. After the armistice July 1953, the CIA conducted sea operations in which sea-based guerilla missions continued. At the same time the CIA also supported Tibetan clansmen in their resistance to the occupation of Tibet by the People's Liberation Army. The CIA was involved in establishing communications, recruiting and training hundreds of Tibetan fighters in Colorado and airdropping guerillas and military equipment into Tibet. Once again the aim was to attempt to chip away at the Communist troops in Tibet via guerilla activity. Support for the CIA activity continued as the Communists threatened the Buddhist god-king the Dalai Lama. Once the Dalai Lama escaped from Tibet to India in 1959, a revolt occurred but the Communists were able to defeat the CIA supported Tibetan resistance.

Covert action in China and North Korea continues and the CIA assesses the military threat and keeps an eye on the development of nuclear weapons and raw materials in their production. With the Cold War essentially ended, the CIA has shifted its attention to the more immanent threat of terrorism in comparison to the previous priority of restraining the spread Communism.

REFERENCES: Joseph J. Trento, *The Secret History of the CIA* (New York, 1990); Rhondri Jeffreys-Jones, *The CIA and American Democracy* (New Haven, CT 1998).

Jim Steinberg

Chaffee, Adna Romanza (1842–1914)

Adna Romanza Chaffee was a general of the United States Army. He was born on April 14, 1842 in Orwell, Ohio, and died on November 1, 1914 in Los Angeles California. On July 22, 1861, Chaffee enlisted in the regular army for service in the Union forces during the Civil War. Fighting with the Sixth Cavalry, Chaffee saw combat in over fifty battles including the Peninsular Campaign, Antietam, Fredericksburg, Gettysburg, and Appomattox. During the war, Chaffee rose to the rank of First Lieutenant and afterwards was posted to frontier service in Texas, Kansas, Arizona, and New Mexico. He was selected to become the Indian Agent of the San Carlos Indian Agency, where he apparently attempted to clear the agency of corruption. He returned to frontier service in campaigns against Native Americans by the Sixth Cavalry and rose to the rank of Major in 1888. Appointed to the post of Inspector General of Arizona and subsequently Colorado and then as an instructor at military school at Fort Leavenworth where he reached the rank of Lieutenant Colonel. With the outbreak of the Spanish-American War in 1898, Chaffee was promoted to Brigadier General and fought in Cuba remaining after the war in the post of Chief of Staff to the Military Governor of Cuba.

In 1900 he was promoted to Major General and selected to command American troops of the China Relief Expedition responding to the anti-foreign Boxer Rebellion in Beijing. An allied expedition of American, English, French, Italian, German and Japanese troops marched on the city. Chaffee led a somewhat presumptuous American assault on the Imperial City, forcing through several gates under heavy fire before ordering a withdrawal, however Chaffee's troops did manage to rescue diplomats. The withdrawal was supported over Chaffee's objection for diplomatic reasons, violation of the sacred Forbidden City being seen as an unwise political maneuver for future relations. Once the immediate danger of the rebellion had been extinguished, Chaffee refused to lend his forces to an allied punitive expedition under the leadership of the Germans because he felt such action was an offensive maneuver that would promote hostilities. In fact, Chaffee hoped to withdraw American troops completely once the military object of securing Beijing was accomplished.

Recalled from China in 1901, Chaffee was appointed the military governor of the Philippines and in 1904 selected as Army Chief of Staff by President Theodore Roosevelt. On February 1, 1906 Chaffee retired to Los Angeles, California, where he became President of the Board of Public Works and oversaw construction of the city's aqueduct system, a project necessary for growth. After his death he was buried at Arlington Cemetery.

See also Boxer Rebellion (1900).

REFERENCES: William Giles Harding Carter, *The Life of Lieutenant General Chaffee* (Chicago, IL, 1917); Peter Fleming, *The Siege at Peking* (Edinburgh, 2001).

Linus Kafka

Chen Guangfu (1881–1976)

Known as K. P. Chen or Kwang Pu Chen in the West, Chen Guangfu was a prominent Chinese banker and financier in 1930s and 1940s. He was significant for Sino-American relations in that he was instrumental in negotiating several important financial agreements with the United States before the U.S. entered World War II. These agreements proved to be beneficial to both sides. Chen was well educated in China and the United States. He earned his Ph. D. degree in finance from the University of Pennsylvania in 1909. After he went back to China, he got involved in international business with a concentration on trade with the United States.

During the Chinese currency reform in 1935, Chen led a team of experts to negotiate a loan from the American government. As a result of his financial expertise and his negotiation skills, the Silver Agreement was signed between China and the United States, which helped set up the new monetary system in China. After the breakout of the Sino-Japanese War on July 7, 1937, Japan's army swept through China. Disturbed by the Japanese aggression, the Roosevelt administration was pondering the possibilities to provide assistance to China against Japan. But the Neutrality Act of the 1930s made it very hard for President Franklin D. Roosevelt to do so. In order to get around the Neutrality Laws, the Roosevelt administration secretly invited Chen to Washington to negotiate a financial deal between the two countries. As the chief representative from China, Chen held talks with Henry Morgenthau, Secretary of Treasury in late 1938. In the next few months, Chen succeeded in obtaining for China the Tung Oil Credit of $25 million and the Tin Credit of $20 million. At a time when China was fighting the Japanese juggernaut alone and was suffering from great financial difficulties, these two loans helped a great deal in stabilizing China's war economy.

On returning to China, Chen busied himself with the task of repaying the credits to the United States in a timely manner. His professionalism and dedication as well as his banking entrepreneurship made him a well-respected Chinese financier in the United States. Chinese Nationalist leader Jiang Jieshi even planned to appoint him as Chinese treasury minister, but Chen declined the appointment.

REFERENCES: M. Schaller, *The U.S. Crusade in China, 1938–1945* (New York, 1979); *Kwang Pu Chen Papers 1936–1958*, Rare Book and Manuscript Library, Columbia University.

Yuwu Song

Chen Shuibian (1951–)

Born in rural southern Taiwan, Chen Shuibian emerged as an active politician in 1979 after the pro-independence riot at Gaoxiong. He served as the lawyer to defend the rights for the rioters. Because of his legal and political acumen, dissidents on the island rallied their support for Chen. Soon, he became the symbol of rising Taiwanese nativism (or nationalism, as it is called by some natives) against the mainlander-controlled Guomindang (GMD) central government in Taiwan, which fled to the island in 1949 and ruled there without strong local support since the islanders considered it to be lacking legitimacy.

The time was ripe for the islanders' nativism/nationalism during the later 1970s and early 1980s. The ruling mainlander regime was aged and loosened its control of the island whereas local Taiwanese grew more confident with their promising financial situation and stronger international support. Chen seized this unusual opportunity to represent the native Taiwanese discontents that the ruling regime only served the agendas of mian land Chinese immigrants to Taiwan. Chen took to the street to demonstrate for popular demands and attacked mainlander elites. In 1981 he gained a seat in the Taibei City Council, and, five years later, became a member of the Legislative Yuan, Taiwan's Congress. When the Democratic Progressive Party (DPP) was founded in 1986, Chen was one of the founders. Like other DDP leaders, Chen embraced Taiwanese independence, believing that Taiwan was not a part of China and therefore, Taiwan should return to its own traditions beginning in the Japanese colonial era. Chen also believed that for a new Taiwan to be born, referendum and plebiscite should be held in order to correct all historical wrongs made by the Guomindang government. This view alarmed the pro-unification group on the island and the Chinese Communist regime on the mainland. Surprisingly, Chen was elected as the mayor of Taibei in 1994 when the ruling party split. But he lost the position four years later. However, his defeat did not end his career. In 2000 he harvested the fruit again when the GMD repeated the blunder of split. Chen became the President of the Republic of China on Taiwan with slightly more than one third of the votes. This surprised all of the nations that watched Taiwan's political situation closely. Beijing became more concerned about the future of Taiwan and publicly announced its determination to reunify the country by force if the independence movement in Taiwan went too far under the new leadership. In response to Beijing's reaction, Washington urged Chen to show restraints. Facing great pressure from within the island and without, Chen tried to calm the situation by claiming, "no war, no independence."

However, Chen tried to test Beijing's tolerance by making public an idea of "one side, one country" in 2002 and by raising the issue of referendum and plebiscite for the future of Taiwan, both of which triggered fierce reaction from the mainland. With a full understanding of the implications of Chen's statements, the United States warned the Taiwanese leader against provoking Beijing. As a result, Chen backed down again.

In 2004, in a very controversial presidential election, Chen barely won by some 30,000 votes. The political developments during Chen's presidency has made the future of Taiwan's political status a more contentious issue in the cross-strait and Sino-American relations.

See also Democratic Progressive Party (DPP).

REFERENCES: Chen Shuibian, *The Son of Taiwan* (Taibei, 1999); Dong Zhixin, *Taibei Jingyan [Taibei Experience]— Chen Shuibian* (Taibei, 1998).

Hsiang-Wang Liu

Chen Xiangmei (1925–)

Chen Xiangmei (Anna Chennault) was born in Beijing, China into a distinguished family. Both her maternal and paternal grandfathers were members of the Chinese urban elites who opposed the decaying Manchu rule in the early 20th century, and who embraced modern Western education. Her parents, Sam Chen and Isabella Liao, were both educated abroad before their return to China in the early 1920s. Chen spent her teenage years in Hong Kong before attending Lingnan University. At the age of 20, she worked as the first female wartime correspondent for the Central News Agency. On her assignment to report on the American "Flying Tigers," she met General Claire Chennault who was assisting the Nationalists' anti-Japanese war effort. Despite their age difference, the two began their legendary romance and, overcoming her family's opposition, they were married in 1947.

After the Chinese Civil War of 1945–1949, the couple went to live in Taiwan before coming to the U.S. where Chen became a naturalized citizen in the 1950s. Following her husband's death in 1958, she endured some financial difficulties, moved from Louisiana to Washington, D.C. with their two daughters, and began her involvement in both politics and business. Using contacts on both sides of the Pacific, she quickly became an influential member within the upper echelon of the political and social circles in Washington. In a time when it was still rare for women and minority to wield significant influence in the political and diplomatic world, Chen was able to fuse her gender and ethnicity into an advantage and succeeded admirably as both an "informal diplomat" and a businesswoman. Appointed by President John F. Kennedy as the chairman of the Chinese Refugees Relief Committee, Chen was the first Chinese-American who became a member of the White House staff. Active in the Republican Party politics, she held positions as co-chair of the Republican National Committees' Finance Committee from 1966 to 1983, and chair of the National Republican Heritage Groups Council. As a "secret ambassador" for several Republic presidents, including Nixon, Ford, and Reagan, Chen helped to facilitate U.S. relations with Asian countries, particularly Vietnam and China. Her "informal diplomacy" was highly effective in representing U.S. interest in Asia and in smoothening out some trouble spots in the complex relations among Washington, Taibei and Beijing. She was also instrumental in working out an agreement between Beijing and Taibei that allowed soldiers who left for Taiwan at the end of the Chinese Civil War to return to the mainland to visit their relatives. In addition to her political roles, Chen has also had a successful career in business, particularly in the aviation industry. Since the early 1980s, when mainland China embarked on its road of economic modernization, Chen has become actively involved in promoting the cause of education with her annual Chen Xiangmei Award for Teaching Excellence and generous funding for schools, especially in economically deprived areas in China.

A prolific writer, Chen has written extensively on her life, politics and international events. Aside from *A Thousand Springs*, a highly ac-

claimed autobiographical account of her life with Claire Chennault and her experiences in the U.S., she has recently published in China a nine-volume collection of her writings during the last five decades, including articles on political events, novels, poems, and translated works.

See also Chennault, Claire L. (1893–1958).

REFERENCES: Anna Chennault, *A Thousand Springs: The Biography of a Marriage* (New York, 1962); Catherine Forslund, *Anna Chennault: Informal Diplomacy and Asian Relations* (Wilmington, DE, 2002); Yao Moyu (ed.), *Chen Xiangmei Yanjiu [A Study on Chen Xiangmei]* (Hangzhou, China, 2000).

Yi Sun

Chennault, Anna (1925-) *see* Chen Xiangmei (1925-)

Chennault, Claire L. (1893–1958)

Claire L. Chennault was born on September 6, 1893, in Commerce, Texas, to a cotton farmer. He grew up in northeastern Louisiana and attended Louisiana State University briefly in 1909. He left to attend a teacher's training program at a normal school. In 1910 he became a teacher and married a fellow teacher a year later; the couple had eight children. Unable to support his family on a teacher's salary, he took various jobs before joining the army in April 1917, shortly after the United States entered the First World War. He received a commission and worked with the army air service before earning his flying wings in 1919. Although discharged in 1920, he returned to the army later that year serving in various assignments. He wrote *The Role of Defensive Pursuit* (1935), that argued unsuccessfully particularly for fighter support of bombers; it would later become the basis for his tactics against the Japanese. The army retired him due to health problems in 1937. Shortly after his retirement, the Chinese Nationalist government offered him a two-year contract to develop a modern air force. Arriving in China, he became a personal advisor to Generalissimo Jiang Jieshi, the Nationalist leader. When war broke out between China and Japan that summer, Chennault opened a training school in Kunming, and built the air force by getting American aircraft and recruiting Americans for the American Volunteer Group (AVG), later known as the Flying Tigers.

The AVG had an impressive record against the Japanese making Chennault an American, as well as Chinese hero. After the United States entered the war, in April 1942, the AVG was merged into the U.S. Army Air Corps. It became part of the new Fourteenth Air Force commanded by Chennault as a major general in March 1943.

Having a rash personality, Chennault often clashed with his superiors, but won the loyalty of his men who performed quite well. His differences with General Joseph Stilwell, Jiang Jieshi's chief of staff, and problems with General George C. Marshall, among others, kept him from being promoted to lieutenant general, but they could do nothing else to him since Chennault enjoyed the favor of President Franklin D. Roosevelt. When Roosevelt died in 1945, Chennault's superiors curtailed his power causing him to retire in July, and return to America before the end of the war. Upon his retirement, Generalissimo Jiang Jieshi awarded him China's highest medal for his service. In January 1946, Chennault returned to China establishing the Chinese Nationalist Relief and Rehabilitation Agency, a civilian commercial airline that supported and supplied the Nationalist regime and troops in its civil war with the Communists. Later that year, he divorced his wife, and married Chen Xiangmei, a Chinese reporter with the China News Agency who had covered the Fourteenth Army Air Corps. Two years later he reorganized his air company as the Civil Air Transport that continued to help the Nationalists in their struggle against the Communists. It and Chennault moved to Taiwan when the Communists seized the mainland of China.

A staunch anti-Communist, Chennault allowed the Central Intelligence Agency to secretly buy the airline. The company under Chennault's tutelage dropped spies and supplies to anti-Communists throughout China, supported anti-Communists in Burma and Korea, and flew supplies to the French at Dien Bien Phu before their defeat in 1954. In 1955, the CIA took tighter control relegating Chennault to become a figurehead chairman. After this, Chennault spent his time at his homes in Taibei and Monroe, Louisiana. Two day before he died in New Orleans on July 27, 1958, he received an honorary promotion to lieutenant general.

See also American Volunteer Group (AVG); Civil Air Transport.

REFERENCES: Earle Rice, Jr., *Claire Chennault: Flying Tiger* (Philadelphia, PA, 2003); Joe Archibald, *Commander of the Flying Tigers: Claire Lee Chennault* (New York, 1966); Robert L. Scott, *Flying Tiger: Chennault of China* (Garden City, NY, 1959); Robert Hotz (ed.), *Way of a Fighter: The Memoirs of Claire Lee Chennault* (New York, 1949).

Greg Ference

Chiang Ching-kuo (1910–1988) *see* Jiang Jingguo (1910–1988)

Chiang Kai-shek (1887–1975) *see* Jiang Jieshi (1887–1975)

China Aid Act (1948)

The China Aid Act of 1948 refers to the U.S. legislative bill in which the American government offered aid to the Chinese Nationalist government, which was engaged in a civil war with the Chinese Communists. On February 18, 1948, President Harry S. Truman proposed before Congress an economic aid program for China. The sum of $510 million was for essential civilian needs, such as food, and $60 million was for industrial and transportation purposes. On April 2, 1948, the U.S. Congress passed the aid bill, with adjustments. The sum of $338 million was for economic aid, and $125 million was for the Chinese Nationalist government to use if it was necessary for military purposes. On April 3, 1948, President Truman signed the bill, which became known as the China Aid Act of 1948. It offered aid to be made available for one year from the date of enactment. However, the act was not implemented until after the aid agreement signed between China and the United States on July 3, 1948. Even if the American government granted both aids, the sum would not be big enough to save the Chinese Nationalist government from losing to the Chinese Communists. The Chinese Nationalist government at last lost to the Chinese Communists and retreated to Taiwan. Mao Zedong, on October 1, 1949, proclaimed the establishment of People's Republic of China.

See also Civil War (1945–1949).

REFERENCES: Bevin Alexander, *The Strange Connection: U.S. Intervention in China* (New York, 1992); DuPre Jones (ed.), *China: U.S. Policy Since 1945* (Washington, DC, 1980); Immanuel C.Y. Hsu, *The Rise of Modern China* (Cambridge, UK, 2000); Ernest R. May, *The Truman administration and China, 1945–1949* (Philadelphia, PA, 1975).

Edy Parsons

China-Burma-India (CBI) Theater

As part of its larger offensive in 1942, Japan attacked throughout Southeast Asia, seeking both raw materials and a defensive perimeter behind which to exploit those resources. And, within the several months, Japanese troops had landed on the Kra Peninsula, moved down Malaysia, and forced a British surrender at Singapore; other Japanese army divisions had moved into Burma, and pushed defending Anglo-Indian divisions across the Irrawaddy back to India. Meanwhile, in China, the Japanese took Hong Kong and launched an offensive to seize the north-south corridor from Beijing to Guangdong.

In response, the Allies organized the China-Burma-India Theater. It would always be a place at the end of the long supply chain from America's factories and far from the forefront of Allied planning to defeat the Axis powers. Since China occupied the majority of the Japanese army, there was always a sense in various Allied headquarters that, if only China would attack, Japan would find itself too thinly spread to hold its ill-gotten gains in Asia and the Pacific, especially after the Battle of Midway in June 1942 so greatly weakened the Japanese navy. The British tried to contest Japanese control of Burma, but it was a long and frustrating effort. In October 1942, General Sir Archibald Wavell tried to regain the port of Akyab, but his combined assault failed. Wavell also created a long-range penetration brigade, the Chindits, which received favorable publicity, but accomplished little and suffered high casualties simply moving through the jungles of Burma. U.S. General Joseph W. Stilwell, who served as Jiang Jieshi's chief of staff among other command obligations, wanted to train and equip three Chinese divisions in India and additional, larger Chinese forces in Yunnan province to pincer off the Japanese in northern Burma and reopen the Burma Road to China, but he would have a long and frustrating experience dealing with Jiang. And, probably most importantly, there were real challenges in getting supplies from America (and Britain) to India and in China given the higher priorities for Great Britain, the Soviet Union, and the Pacific Theater. In November 1943, the Allies planned on taking the offensive into 1944. Given the topography of Southeast Asia, the British and the Americans wanted a three-pronged attack. Anglo-Indian forces would attack across the Chindwin toward Indaw; Chinese troops trained by Stilwell, would moved from Ledo towards Myitkyina; finally, Chinese armies in Yunnan province would strike down across the Salween River all designed to reopen the Burma Road, secure ground communications with Nationalist China, and begin the long task of pushing the Japanese back. The attack did not go as planned, for Jiang would not commit quality troops to attack the Japanese. He was largely content to wait out the war and prepare for the resumption of the interrupted civil war with Mao Zedong's Communist movement. However, Stilwell's Chinese divisions operating out of India continued fighting into April 1944, and positioned Stilwell to seek his most significant objective, the center of gravity of the Japanese position in northern Burma at Myitkyina. Stilwell did not pause for the onset of the monsoon season, and he attacked despite the rain, the mud, and the disease all of which made it difficult for his men. In what really was a siege, Chinese troops attacked Japanese positions from May until August 1944, when they drove off the few remaining Japanese troops and seized this key position. Stilwell wanted to continue to attack in the north, but his combative relationship with Jiang and with U.S. General Claire Chennault who commanded the U.S. Army Air Forces in China led to his recall from the CBI. As Stilwell was preparing to attack Japanese rail communications in northern Burma, Japan launched the Ichigo offensive in China, and Jiang and Chennault complained to Washington that Stilwell diverted Chinese troops from the defense of China. Thereafter, the campaign in Burma would be more exclusively an Anglo-Indian effort against Japan and General Sir William Slim pushed forward. The attack still took place, and ran into a strong Japanese offensive thrust. The Japanese decided to move first in the Arakan area. However, this time the Anglo-Indian forces held, and threw the Japanese back, and again, in the Japanese advance on Imphal, the defenders held their ground. By the end of spring of 1945, the Japanese had retreated, and the overland route to China was reopened.

The final stage of conflict in the CBI favored the Allies. U.S. landings in the Philippines cut off Burma and nearby areas from Japan, and local Japanese army units had to survive on what they had and could find locally. Meanwhile, as the need for supplies to Europe lessened and as America's production miracle continued, more and more supplies arrived in the theater. The tempo of Allied attack increased, and the Japanese continued to retreat. However, before the British and Americans could organize an offensive to liberate Malaysia, the atomic bombings had brought about the Japanese surrender.

See also Stilwell, Joseph W. (1883–1946); Burma Road; World War II.

REFERENCES: Raymond Callahan, *Burma, 1942–1945* (London, 1978); Geoffrey Frank Matthews, *The Re-conquest of Burma, 1943–1945* (Aldershot, UK, 1966); Nathan N. Prefer, *Vinegar Joe's War: Stilwell's Campaigns for Burma* (Novato, CA, 2000); E.D. Smith, *Battle of Burma* (New York, 1979); Donovan.Webster, *The Burma Road: The Epic Story of the China-Burma-India Theater in World War II* (New York, 2003).

Charles M. Dobbs

China Can Say No

Published in 1996 and instantly became a Chinese bestseller, *China Can Say No: Political and Emotional Choices in the Post-Cold War Era* was collectively written by a group of mainland Chinese intellectuals who called for their government to stand up against the United States in a new era of global competition. In addition to bashing the U.S., the book also bashes Japan for its "defection" from Asia as well as its pro-American stance. The commercial success of this book represents the growing popularity of anti-American and anti-Japanese sentiments among the Chinese public. Especially, it reflects the growing disillusionment with the U.S. among many young and educated Chinese as China is increasingly integrated into the global economic and political systems.

The authors accuse the U.S. of being nostalgic about the Cold War and pursing conspiratorial foreign policies to suppress the rise of China in global rivalry. Specifically, they cite the frequent invocation of contentious issues such as human rights, nuclear proliferation, intellectual property, environmental protection, and Taiwan by the U.S. as examples of the American efforts to hinder China's progress. Aside from criticizing American foreign policies, the authors also question the American self-proclaimed moral leadership in international affairs by devoting a great deal of the book to pointing out the domestic social and political problems of the U.S. The authors further warn that if the United States continues to pursue its confrontational and condescending foreign policies, China will not be afraid to stand up against American imperialism, including, for example, the use of force to "defend" Taiwan. Ironically, despite its anti-Japanese sentiment, the book was at least partially inspired by the controversial *The Japan That Can Say No* (1991) written by Shintaro Ishihara, a leading Japanese nationalist, who stirred up a storm in U.S.-Japan relationship in the early 1990s by arguing that Japan should acquire greater autonomy by standing up against the U.S.

The Chinese government initially endorsed the general tone of *China Can Say No*, calling it a representation of Chinese public opinion. However, after igniting criticisms in Asia and the U.S., the government quickly condemned the book as irresponsible and causing confusion, temporarily banning it from circulation out of practical political and economic concerns. The same group of authors later published a sequel called *China Can Still Say No* to rebut their critics. Although publications like these do not necessarily reflect the full spectrum of Chinese opinion about the U.S., they often shape the public discourse of Sino-American relationship by reducing it to a narrowly defined "China versus the U.S." dichotomy. For instance, immediately after *China Can Say No* was published, even in overseas Chinese communities where reactions were less sympathetic to the book's simplistic analysis, discus-

sions were often dominated by questions like "Can China say no?" "Why does China want to say no?" and "How does China Say No?"

In addition to its commercial success in China, the book equally created a sensation in the U.S., triggering widespread concerns for China's rising economic and political status, as well as its implications for the U.S. Particularly, for political conservatives and rightwing ideologues, rhetoric like that of *China Can Say No* seems to confirm their suspicion of China's intention to replace the U.S. as the global hegemonic power, prompting them to further argue for the necessity of containing and suppressing China. As such, by emphasizing the differences between China and the U.S. and even their potential collision course, sensational and jingoistic policy discourses from both sides of the Pacific do not just distort, but also shape the reality of Sino-American relationship even though the two countries are indeed closer than ever in an increasingly globalized world.

REFERENCES: Song Qiang, Zhang Zangzang, Qiao Bian (eds.), *Zhongguo ke yi shuo bu: leng zhan hou shi dai di zheng zhi yu qing gan jue ze [China Can Say No: Political and Emotional Choices in the Post-Cold War Era]* (Beijing, 1996).

Tong Lam

China Card

The term "China card" refers to the idea of the United States siding with the People's Republic of China (PRC) against the Soviet Union in the Cold War. It is alleged that Henry Kissinger, President Nixon's National Security Advisor, developed this "China card" concept. In his memoirs, Kissinger categorically denies this allegation, claiming that he was seeking to improve relations with both China and the Soviet Union and was careful to avoid "tilting" toward either Communist giant.

The "China card" idea actually was the brainchild of Michael Pillsbury, a China analyst at Rand Corporation. In early 1970s, Pillsbury had developed a friendship with a Chinese general in the United Nations. During their gatherings, they discussed on issues such as the modernization of the Chinese army and the defense of China against the Soviet Union in a local war. These talks made Pillsbury rethink about the Sino-American relationship. In the fall of 1973, Pillsbury wrote a memo suggesting that the United States might establish a military relationship with Beijing. In his memo, he pointed out that such a relationship would give the United States a new advantage over the Soviet Union because it might help China to become a stronger military power and tie down the Russian troops in Asia, which might be deployed in Europe. He argued that it would also strengthen the Chinese leaders who favored a better relationship with Washington, thus prevent accommodation between Beijing and Moscow. Pillsbury's report began to attract America's national security apparatus. Although some people in the military feared that China might one day reach rapprochement with the Russians and become the enemy of the United States as it had been before, James R. Schlesinger, the Secretary of Defense was intrigued by this novel approach. He ordered a government study of a U.S. defense relationship with Beijing. This was the original concept of "China card." At this time the idea did not produce any quick results in shaping the U.S. foreign policies towards China. But the prospect of playing the "China card" was being explored and was beginning to appeal to a wider audience beyond the circle of the researchers and the national security apparatus. Gradually, top policy makers realized the feasibility of this policy approach.

In 1975 and 1976, the United States took steps down a new path when Henry Kissinger visited Beijing. He focused on the fields of military, technology, and intelligence cooperation with China. Washington now tilted toward Beijing as a means of combating the Russians. By then, the "China card" idea was becoming an important component in mainstream American policy towards the PRC.

See also Brzezinski, Zbigniew (1928-); Kissinger, Henry (1923-).

REFERENCES: REFERENCES: Henry Kissinger, *White House Years* (Boston, MA, 1979); James Mann, *About Face: A History of America's Curious Relationship with China, from Nixon to Clinton* (New York, 1999).

Yuwu Song

China Committee (CHINCOM)

CHINCOM refers to the China Committee, a U.S.-sponsored working group that supervised embargo with Communist countries in Asia within the Coordinating Committee (COCOM) of the Consultative Group (CG) in Paris. The major task of the CHINCOM was to coordinate the multilateral export control against the People's Republic of China (PRC) and other Communist countries in Asia and enforce stricter embargo lists against them than the COCOM list against the European Soviet bloc. This enlarged embargo list was called the "China differential." The CHINCOM was officially established in September 1952 with the United States, Great Britain, France, Canada, and Japan as the founding members.

The United States had hoped to set up a sep-

arate Far Eastern Group including Japan to deal with the Asian trade and export control. But major COCOM members, particularly Britain, France, and Canada, worried that the United States might gain greater control over Asian trade through this new organization independent of the COCOM. They insisted that the new committee be established within the framework of the COCOM. The United States finally yielded on the allies' proposal but successfully persuaded them to accept higher trade and export controls against the Asian Communist states than the Soviet bloc in East Europe. At the same time, in a bilateral agreement with the United States on export control to China signed on September 5, 1952, Japan was required to maintain the embargo of items on three COCOM International Lists and the U.S. Battle Act Lists, which were stricter than the CHINCOM list.

After the end of the Korean War, frictions on the China differential between the United States and other CHINCOM members increased. Although agreeing to relax the COCOM export control on the Soviet Union and its European allies in 1954, Washington insisted on the maintenance of the existing stifling CHINCOM controls. However, other CHINCOM members were dissatisfied because the truce in Korea made continued strict embargo ungrounded. Moreover, their economic recovery from a dragging recession made increase in exports an urgent need. Further, relaxation of the COCOM control virtually made the China differential ineffective because the PRC successfully acquired the embargoed goods of Western origins through its trade with East Europe and the Soviet Union. Thus, major CHINCOM members, particularly Britain, Japan, and Canada, called for relaxation on trade control against the PRC. Unable to persuade the allies to hold the stricter trade control on China, the United States step by step made compromise. In 1954, the Eisenhower administration released Japan gradually from the 1952 bilateral agreement. On May 27, 1957, Britain decided to unilaterally eliminate the China differential. Following Britain, Japan on July 16 also announced that its export controls against the PRC would go down to the COCOM level. The United States began to negotiate with Britain and other allies about revision of the China embargo list. As a result, in June 1958, the CG formally removed the China differential by merging the COCOM and CHINCOM lists into one, which marked the end of U.S. multilateral higher trade controls against China.

See also Trade Embargo.

REFERENCES: Frank Cain, "The U.S.-led Trade Embargo on China: The Origins of CHINCOM, 1947–52,"

The Journal of Strategic Studies, Vol. 18, No. 4. (1995); Simei Qin, "The Eisenhower administration and Changes in Western Embargo Policy against China, 1954–1958," in Warren Cohen and Akira Iriye (eds.), *The Great Powers in East Asia, 1953–1960* (New York, 1990); Sayuri Shimizu, *Creating People of Plenty: United States and Japan's Economic Alternatives, 1950–1960* (Kent, OH, 2001); Shu Guang Zhang, *Economic Cold War: America's Embargo Against China and the Sino-Soviet Alliance, 1949–1963* (Stanford, CA, 2001).

Tao Peng

China Hands

The China Hands were career diplomats such as John S. Service, John P. Davies, George Atcheson, Raymond Ludden and others from the State Department who were stationed in China during World War II. These diplomats had extensive experience and knowledge regarding China. Some of them were raised in American missionary families there. They were fluent in the Chinese language and familiar with Chinese history and culture. After World War II and the establishment of the People's Republic of China, the China Hands were accused of disloyalty, of being sympathetic with Communists, and of contributing to the "loss of China." Although they were exonerated later, they suffered terribly from political persecution.

In World War II, the United States emerged as a major actor in Chinese affairs. As an ally, it embarked in late 1941 on a program of massive military and financial aid to the hard-pressed Guomindang (Nationalist) government. The wartime policy of the United States was initially to help China become a strong ally and a stabilizing force in postwar East Asia. As the conflict between the Nationalists and the Chinese Communist Party intensified, however, the United States sought unsuccessfully to reconcile the rival forces for a more effective anti-Japanese war effort. During the war, the China Hands became disillusioned with the Nationalist government, which they believed to be corrupt, inefficient, and undemocratic. Their observations about Jiang Jieshi and his government led them to argue for a more realistic appraisal of China and a practical policy based on that assessment. Many of the reports sent by the China Hands provided descriptions of life in the Communist controlled area that contrasted sharply with reports of life at Chongqing under Guomindang.

The China Hands were convinced that in the power struggle the Communists would win the final victory. Fearing that a Communist takeover would help the Soviet Union expand its influence in China, they urged the U.S. government to extend its aid to the Chinese Communists. They believed that to provide military aid to the Communists would shorten the war, because U.S. assistance would enable the Communist army to fight more effectively against the Japanese. They also reasoned that the strengthening of Mao Zedong and his government would force Jiang to be more conciliatory regarding a coalition government in China. On February 28, 1945, the counselor of the American Embassy at Chongqing sent to the State Department a cable signed by all the embassy political officers, who recommended that "the President inform the Generalissimo in definite terns that military necessity requires that we supply and cooperate with Communists ... through such policy ... we could expect to hold the Communists to our side rather than throw them into the arms of Russia." U.S. Ambassador to China, Patrick J. Hurley, stubbornly opposed this view. Supported by Presidents Franklin D. Roosevelt and later Harry S. Truman, Hurley's position prevailed. The China Hands in the embassy were eventually dismissed from their China assignments. Hurley's criticism and removal of the embassy staff helped trigger the purge of the China Hands that peaked in the witch-hunt started by Joseph R. MacCarthy in the early 1950s.

See also McCarthy, Joseph R. (1908–1957); Davies, John P. (1908–1999); Service, John Stewart (1909–1999); Hurley, Patrick J. (1883–1963); Clubb, O. Edmund (1901–1989).

REFERENCES: Barbara W. Tuchman, *Stilwell and the American Experience in China: 1911–1945* (New York, 1971); Joseph Esherick, *Lost Chance in China: The World War II Dispatches of John S. Service* (New York, 1974); E. J. Kahn, *The China Hands: America's Foreign Service Officers and What Befell Them* (New York, 1975).

Yuwu Song

China Incident (1937) *see* Marco Polo Bridge Incident (1937)

China Lobby

The China Lobby began in 1940 with the efforts of a wide spectrum of individuals, who united to assist the Chinese Nationalist government in its war against both Japan and the Chinese Communists. Some of the Lobby's more prominent representatives were men like Henry Luce, of the *Time* and *Life* magazines publishing empire, his wife Claire Boothe Luce, and journalists like Roy Howard and Joseph Alsop. These individuals portrayed Americans as having a "special friendship" with the Chinese and fostered an idealized image of Chinese leader Jiang Jieshi and Madame Jiang Jieshi.

The China Lobby can be understood in the context of those holding opposing positions on the Nationalist conflict with the Chinese Communists. Foreign Service Officer John Service argued that the Nationalists should not obtain U.S. support unless they reformed their party's rampant corruption. Service recommended that the U.S. support both Jiang and the morally superior and popular Communists under Mao Zedong. He hoped that the result would be a centrist liberal Democratic Coalition government. Service's views were supported by every political officer in the American embassy, as well as journalists Edgar Snow and Agnes Smedley, diplomatic representative John Davies and General Joseph W. Stilwell. These individuals believed that since the Communists would likely win, the United States should not alienate them and drive them into an alliance with the USSR. General Stilwell was an ardent foe of the China Lobby, as he faced off against both Jiang and "Flying Tiger" commander and Jiang supporter Claire Chennault, as Commander of the Allied Forces in China, Burma, and India during World War II. Stilwell was frustrated with Jiang's repeated requests for more monies and lack of willingness to direct the war against the Japanese, whom Jiang referred to as a "disease of the skin," rather than the Communists, a "disease of the heart." Stilwell grew frustrated by his inability to train Jiang's ground forces, and believing Jiang's fighting tactics reflected insubordination, penned numerous complaints to President Franklin D. Roosevelt. Rather than comply with Stilwell's requests, Roosevelt heeded the advice of the China Lobby, reflected in Chennault's demands for increased reliance on airpower. Hence, many perceive the China Lobby as responsible for the U.S. government's failure to insist upon reform of Jiang's ground forces in return for U.S. support.

Some China Lobbyists saw U.S. security as tied to the Chinese Nationalists' victory. Roosevelt and his cabinet officials and advisors like Henry Morgenthau and Harry Hopkins believed that American national security was hinged upon a China that was independent of the Communist USSR. This view did not acknowledge the possibility of an independent Communist China and prevented the Roosevelt administration from seeing the value of using American aid to force the Nationalists to enter into an equal partnership with the Chinese Communists. The Chinese Communist response to the U.S. refusal to pressure Jiang Jieshi to cooperate led to anti-American propaganda. In response to this propaganda and the belief that American security was tied to what happened in China, the United States would give Jiang unwavering support as he retreated to Taiwan in 1949. This support was coupled with a feeling of betrayal as the China Lobby convinced Americans that there were traitors in various government positions who were responsible for the "loss" of China. These charges fueled members of the China Lobby who would use this "loss" to further their political careers, thus ushering in an era of "red baiting" and what is often referred to as the second "Red Scare" in the United States.

To insure the recognition of Jiang's new regime of 15 million in the island of Taiwan as the legitimate China and the punishment of the Communist Chinese, the China Lobby organized the Committee of One Million. Funded by wealthy importer Alfred C. Kohlberg, who owed his profits to Nationalist China, chaired by ex-missionary Republican Walter Judd of Minnesota, and led by General Claire Chennault and publisher Henry Luce, the Committee succeeded in denying Communist China U.S. recognition and United Nations membership until the Nixon administration reversed this policy with the Shanghai Communique in 1972.

See also Luce, Henry (1898–1967); Judd, Walter H. (1898–1994); Kohlberg, Alfred (1887–1960); Committee of One Million; China Hands.

REFERENCES: Ross Y. Koen, *The China Lobby in American Politics* (New York, 1973); John S. Service, *Lost Chance in China: The World War II Dispatches of John S. Service* (New York, 1974).

Cristina Zaccarini

China Relief Expedition

The China Relief Expedition was authorized by President William McKinley to protect Americans in China from the anti-Western, anti-Christian violence of the Boxer Rebellion. Most of the violence was confined to North China, where 250 foreigners had been killed, much property destroyed, and many Chinese employees and converts killed. McKinley selected General Adna R. Chaffee to command the American contingent of the eight-nation force sent to relieve the siege of the Legation Quarter in Beijing in 1900.

By the time the siege began on June 20, the capital elements of the Imperial Chinese Forces had joined the Boxer military forces on the order of Cixi, the Dowager Empress. The Chinese were protesting the provisions of the treaties, which gave foreigners special rights of habitation and propagation of their faiths in China. Other provisions interfered with Chinese sovereignty. Cixi was not well informed on the military capabilities of the foreigners, nor were the conservative officials who supported her. U.S. Navy ships joined those of other nations off Tianjin to prevent reinforcement by sea of the capital area by the Chinese. Many of the governors of the central and southern Chinese provinces refused to support the Boxers; thus the foreign military contingents could concentrate on the area around Tianjin and Beijing. A small mixed relief force under the British Admiral Sir Edward Seymour, attempted to reach Beijing early in June of 1900. The Boxers had destroyed or damaged the railroad in several places, and attacked the train when it halted. Seymour was forced to retreat to Tianjin with heavy casualties. The Boxers brought forces into Tianjin, where a series of battles with Western troops ensued. By July 13, the city was under Western control, and additional foreign forces had arrived. The eight-nation force began the march from Tianjin to Beijing on August 4. The China Relief Expedition consisted of 8,000 Japanese, 4,800 Russians, 3,000 British, 2,100 Americans, 800 French, 58 Austrians, and 53 Italians. The Germans arrived too late to join in the march. However they were very active in the secondary suppression and punitive expeditions against the Boxers. In the Legation Quarter were 450 guards, 475 civilians, including 12 ministers, 50 Chinese servants, and 2,300 Chinese Christians. The Boxers, in the face of Western forces and many deaths, began to discard their distinctive dress and melt into the population. Additional operations against remnants of the movement were concluded by 1901. The eight-nation expedition occupied Beijing and the surrounding area until the Chinese government agreed to the Boxer Protocols. General Chaffee's orders had been to uphold American prestige, relieve the siege, and retain the goodwill of the Chinese people. After the relief of the Legation, Chaffee enlisted the help of prominent Chinese to restore order, distribute food and establish public health programs prior to the return of the Qing Dynasty officials. Then the American forces began to withdraw, the last of the expeditionary forces had left by May 1901. Much of the world opinion dismissed the uprising as actions of ignorant peasants; the resentment of the Chinese to the extensive foreign presence was ignored.

See also **Chaffee, Adna Romanza (1842–1914); Boxer Rebellion (1900); Boxer Protocol; Cixi (1835–1908).**

REFERENCES: Joseph W. Esherick, *The Origins of the Boxer Uprising* (Berkeley, CA, 1987); Paul A. Cohen, *History In Three Keys-the Boxers as Event, Experience, and Myth* (New York, 1997).

Katherine Reist

China Tariff Autonomy

China's struggle to recover tariff autonomy was one of the most contentious aspects of Sino-foreign relations in the late 19th and early 20th century. China ceded control over tariff rates in the Treaty of Nanjing (1842) and in subsequent "unequal treaties." For nearly one hundred years, China's tariff rate remained at 5.0–7.5 percent of the estimated value of goods. Despite inflation the assessment of the value of imports used price tables that were decades old, resulting in even lower actual tariff rates. Furthermore, once the tariff had been paid, imports were exempted from all further levies, including internal transit tolls (or *lijin*), a privilege that gave imports a distinct advantage over their domestic competitors.

In the initial years following the Treaty of Nanjing, tariff control did not seem to be an important issue. Nor was it clear that the Chinese had ceded such control. However, by the end of the 19th century, as nation-states came to see tariff control as a key to asserting sovereignty and promoting economic growth, recovering tariff autonomy became a rallying point for Chinese reformers and nationalists, especially as China's trade deficit ballooned. China's trade deficit became a symbol of the country's weakness, and trade statistics within elite political and intellectual circles became a primary means of comprehending China's lack of sovereignty. Recovering tariff autonomy so that China could reverse its trade deficit became a widely shared goal, especially after the defeat by Japan in 1895. Likewise, recovery was a key objective of anti-imperialist protests and nationalistic activities within the National Products Movement.

Successive Chinese governments and popular pressure repeatedly brought foreign governments to the bargaining table to discuss tariff autonomy. However, until 1925 the treaty powers refused to negotiate the restoration of tariff autonomy. In 1928, the newly established Nationalist government made achieving economic sovereignty and recovering tariff autonomy a top priority. The Chinese foreign minister, Wang Zhengting, ultimately forced the issue by announcing the new government's intention to terminate all treaties unilaterally in 1928. In response, the U.S. Minister John V. A. MacMurray, acting on instructions from Secretary of State Frank B. Kellogg, negotiated a new treaty, signed on July 25 and effective at the start of 1929. Shortly thereafter, nearly all the other treaty powers followed suit. The new treaty promised to end the era of unequal treaties on tariff matters. But a deal could not be concluded. Because the United States stipulated that the "most-favored-nation" clause remained in effect, the new treaty could not take effect until China renegotiated tariff autonomy with Japan. The Japanese, however, had much more vested in lower rates. Although, as promised, the Chinese government promulgated new rates on February 1, 1929, it could not fully implement them until the Japanese consented in May 1930.

See also Treaty of Nanjing (1842).

REFERENCES: Karl Gerth, *China Made: Consumer Culture and the Creation of the Nation* (Cambridge, MA, 2003); Stanley F. Wright, *China's Struggle for Tariff Autonomy, 1843–1938* (Shanghai, 1938); Hsiao Lianglin, *China's Foreign Trade Statistics, 1864–1949* (Cambridge, MA, 1974).

Karl Gerth

China White Paper

The China White Paper was published by the U.S. Department of State in August 1949 to assure the American public that the collapse of the Nationalist government in the Chinese Civil War (1945–1949) was caused by its own shortcomings rather than a lack of sufficient U.S. aid. Secretary of State Dean Acheson insisted that, "the unfortunate but inescapable fact is that the ominous result of the civil war in China was beyond the control of the government of the United States. Nothing that this country did or could have done within the reasonable limits of its capabilities could have changed that result; nothing that was left undone by this country has contributed to it." The White Paper was published in the midst of bitter partisan controversy over America's China policy, the effort to create an anti-Communist consensus in support of the Truman Doctrine of containment in Europe and the growing Red Scare in American society and culture.

The idea of an explanatory White Paper first appeared in State Department circles in the fall of 1948, the crisis period of the Chinese civil war. Secretary of State George C. Marshall and President Harry S. Truman initially rejected the proposal as detrimental to the Nationalist cause. By the spring of 1949, however, the new Secretary of State, Dean Acheson, convinced Truman that such an initiative was necessary to counter Republican criticism of the administration. President Truman sought two goals with the publication of the White Paper: objectivity and justification. His critics accepted neither and, indeed, Acheson's Letter of Transmittal became the most controversial document in the volume. Both the *New York Times* and *Time* denounced the effort as self-serving. Only Walter Lippman recognized that the United States had had very limited influence over the course of events in China despite the Open Door fantasies of the previous half-century. Surprisingly, the Nationalist government made very little of the White Paper. Gu Weijun, China's ambassador to the U.S., simply acknowledged that China might have been "guilty of acts of commission and omission in the past," while Jiang Jieshi advised against a formal rebuttal. The Chinese Communist Party, however, made the White Paper the center of their first mass anti-American campaign. Mao Zedong himself wrote several articles denouncing the document in an effort to convince urban intellectuals and bourgeoisie of the perfidy of American imperialism in China.

The publication of the White Paper marked the end of an era in American China policy. After Senate hearings in October 1949 involving China specialists, international businessmen, and public figures such as George C. Marshall and George F. Kennan, the Truman administration began a policy of disengagement from China. Washington withheld recognition from the new Beijing government, distanced itself from the Nationalists, yet warned that Communist military activity beyond the borders of China would be considered a threat to peace. The new direction in U.S. policy met with immediate criticism and derision from Republican critics, now heightened by the rhetoric and accusations by Senator Joseph R. McCarthy (R-Wisconsin) of Communist influence in the State Department. The result was the destruction of the careers of a large number of leading China specialists in the U.S. Foreign Service. American Asian policy was in a state of uncertainty when the Korean War began in June 1950.

See also Civil War (1945–1949); Truman, Harry S. (1884–1972); Acheson, Dean (1873–1971).

REFERENCES: The United States Department of State, *The China White Paper* (Stanford, CA, 1967); Tang Tsou, *America's Failure in China, 1941–1950* (Chicago, IL, 1963); Dean Acheson, *Present at the Creation: My Years in the State Department* (New York, 1969); J. Chace, *Acheson: The Secretary of State Who Created the American World* (New York, 1998); R. McGlothlen, *Controlling the Waves: Dean Acheson and U.S. Foreign Policy in Asia* (New York, 1993); W. Stueck, Jr., *The Road to Confrontation: American Policy Toward China and Korea, 1947–1950* (Chapel Hill, NC, 1981).

Errol Clauss

Chinagate

Chinagate refers to the allegations that President Bill Clinton was involved in a fund-raising scandal in which the Chinese government was secretly funneling cash to Clinton's 1996 campaign for re-election in order to buy influence. The major allegations and other related accusations include:

During Clinton's Presidency, the White House has taken a very soft line toward China, despite its violations of human rights and its bad trade records.

Clinton has relaxed trade restrictions on exports of high technology to China. In 1994, Clinton ended the Coordinating Committee on Multinational Export Control, the joint agreement among American allies that they would not sell certain high technology items to countries like China. As a result, proliferation had become a more serious problem than it had been since 1994.

Clinton gave permissions allowing U.S. firms to transfer advanced missile and satellite technologies to China during the launching of American satellites with Chinese rockets.

Clinton granted waivers allowing his top campaign fundraiser's aerospace company to transfer U.S. missile guidance technology to the Chinese.

Clinton ignored or downplayed numerous Chinese arms control violations.

Clinton hosted over 100 Beijing-linked campaign fundraisers in the White House.

Clinton used people with strong Chinese connections such as John Huang, Charlie Trie, Johnny Chung, and James Riady to raise money for the presidential campaign. There were huge campaign gifts supposedly donated by people of very modest means.

Clinton tried to cover up the stealing of America's sophisticated nuclear weapons technology by China.

Because of the allegations, Louis Freeh, director of Federal Bureau of Investigation, assigned Charles LaBella, who became head of the Justice Department's China Task Force, to look into this matter. LaBella and his team spent months investigating the connections, attempting to link the dots with campaign contributions, foreign influences, and White House actions. What LaBella found was put down in a 100-page memo for Attorney General Janet Reno. The memo recommended for the appointment of an independent counsel to carry on the investigation. But Reno rejected the recommendation. It seems that there is not enough criminal evidence to justify such an appointment. So far nothing concrete has been found that would incriminate President Clinton or demonstrate that he and his aides were aware of the Chinese penetration and actively refused to head it off.

REFERENCES: James M. Inhofe, "*End Chinagate Cover-up,*" *Human Events* (July 16, 1999); David Tell, "The Asian Money Scandal: A Primer," *The Weekly Standard* (December 30, 1997).

Yuwu Song

Chinaman

Chinaman is an ethnic slur, taboo in American English; the accepted term, noun (singular and plural) or adjective, is *Chinese.* An echo of the taboo word is in the idiom (now much suppressed as well) *a Chinaman's chance,* which means "no chance at all." The term was used originally in the 1860s to describe the Chinese workers who were building the Transcontinental Railroad in the United States. The Chinese men were treated like slaves and forced to do the most dangerous jobs while getting very little pay.

Racial slurs such as "Chinaman" and "chink" serve to demean an entire race and class of people. For years Chinese-Americans have been working hard to bring education, awareness and sensitivity to the issues of culture, race and stereotyping. However, intentionally or unintentionally, some people in the United States still use the word. The most publicized cases in recent years include the reference to Yao Ming, the Chinese player of NBA, as a "Chinaman" on a TNT telecast and similar remarks made by NBA player Shaquille O'Neal about Yao. Under the public pressure, people involved apologized for the impropriety of using derogatory terms in describing minorities.

REFERENCES: Chinese American Citizens Alliance, *www.cacanational.org.*

Yuwu Song

Chinatowns

Chinatowns have emerged in major cities all over the world, wherever there is a Chinese population. In many cases they emerged as a survival strategy — a center of support and assistance for the unwelcome immigrant facing language barriers, limited employment opportunities, and a hostile local population.

In the United States, the largest of the Chinatowns — those in San Francisco, New York, Los Angeles, and Honolulu — emerged concurrently with Chinese exclusion policies. Chinatowns were the place of residence, the place of work, and the primary place of refuge for a large part of the Chinese community in the United States. Early Chinese immigrants were spread thin across the American West, in small mining communities and railroad towns, moving in pursuit of employment opportunities. As these opportunities began to disappear and anti-Chinese sentiment, founded on American labor concerns about unfair competition, rose in the 1870s and early 1880s, wide-scale urbanization of the Chinese community occurred, and more and more workers gathered in the cities for their mutual aid and protection. As fewer and fewer jobs were available to the Chinese population (itself starting to stagnate in numbers due to harsh immigration restrictions), a Chinatown-centered ethnic economy emerged. An assessment of local needs and opportunities pushed the Chinese into the most traditional Chinatown businesses: markets, restaurants, and laundries. Such businesses could be sustained within the Chinese community if necessary, and they required little capital to establish. With the implementation of the Chinese Exclusion Act in 1882, Chinatowns also became the center of mutual aid societies and the representative voice of the Chinese in America. Native place and surname organizations and the Chinese Consolidated Benevolent Association (CCBA) branches all kept their headquarters in Chinatowns. In New York and San Francisco, the President of the local CCBA was often referred to as the unofficial "mayor" of Chinatown, and spoke for the entire community, representing its interests to the local and federal American governments. For many Americans in the late 19th century, Chinatown represented a taste of the exotic Orient in the heart of an American city. Long infamous for opium and gambling dens, Chinese prostitutes, and the so-called "Tong Wars"—wars among Chinese secret societies—Chinatowns early gained an unsavory reputation as dens of iniquity. In the early 20th century, CCBA and other Chinatown leaders led an effort to "clean up" Chinatowns, presenting them as a tourist attraction and erecting colorful temples, gates, and pagodas for the sake of drawing in the average American. As important as Chinatowns were in the Exclusion era, by the time of repeal in 1943 many had disappeared from small towns and the larger Chinatowns were already experiencing a level of population flight as a result of a combination of urban development plans which often eliminated or cut into Chinatown "slums," and natural acculturation by second and third generation Chinese Americans. In 1947, the Supreme Court ruled that property deeds could not be restricted on account of race, which also led to greater suburbanization. New immigration laws facilitating family reunification and chain migration changed the nature of the Chinese population, so that whole families, many with American-born children, took over from the aging male, foreign-born traditional population.

Today, only a few of the largest American Chinatowns still exist, and many of these are best known as a local tourist attraction. Still, it is important to note that the New York and San Francisco Chinatowns remain major reception centers for new, low-income and illegal immigrants, and the CCBA and other Chinese American or-ganizations continue to maintain headquarters in Chinatowns. Although strong anti-Chinese sentiment no longer makes their presence absolutely necessary, Chinatowns remain an important economic and cultural link to the home country for the Chinese in the United States.

See also Chinese Americans; Chinese Consolidated Benevolent Association; Chinese Exclusion Act of 1882.

REFERENCES: Benson Tong, *Chinese Americans* (Boulder, CO, 2003); Peter Kwong, *The New Chinatown.* (New York, 1987); L. Eve Armentrout Ma, *Revolutionaries, Monarchists and Chinatowns: Chinese Politics in the Americas and the 1911 Revolution* (Honolulu, HW, 1990).

Meredith Oyen

Chinese Americans

The identity of the Chinese American community was first forged in the era of Exclusion; as the only ethnic group ever to be explicitly barred from immigration into the United States, early Chinese migrants faced particular challenges. Although Chinese were at first welcome as a low-cost and industrious labor, anti-Chinese sentiments led by white workers concerned about wages and job availability quickly became the norm. By 1870, Chinese were barred from naturalization, and by 1882 Chinese laborers were excluded from entry to the United States. Because only merchants and diplomats were given the right to bring their wives and families to American shores, the early Chinese community was composed almost exclusively of single, foreign-born men.

In spite of being barred from free entry and naturalized citizenship, Chinese in America quickly demonstrated signs of acculturation, most notably through the use of the American justice system to challenge the laws that controlled their movements and prevented them from forming families in the U.S. Organizations like the Chinese Consolidated Benevolent Association (CCBA) sent test cases through the federal courts and put pressure on the weak Qing government to renegotiate with U.S. authorities treaty restrictions on immigration. In 1895, the first organization composed entirely of American citizens of Chinese descent appeared in the form of the United Parlor of the Native Sons of the Golden State, later renamed the Chinese American Citizens Alliance (CACA). World War II was a turning point for Chinese Americans. From the start of the Sino-Japanese conflict, Chinese and Americans worked together to provide necessary resources to China. After the U.S. entry into World War II, 22% of the adult Chinese men in the

United States enlisted in the U.S. Army. The Chinese Exclusion Acts were repealed in 1943 as a wartime measure, though the Chinese quota was only 105 each year. In the years immediately after the war, a series of new immigration acts gave Chinese unprecedented access to American shores. Most importantly, the 1946 Fiancees Act and 1947 amendment to the War Brides Act ensured that Chinese-American servicemen could bring their brides to the U.S. outside of the oversubscribed Chinese quota. Special quota numbers for Chinese refugees and non-quota preferences in the 1952 Immigration and Nationality Act would also transform the composition of the Chinese Community into full family units. The 1965 amendments to the Immigration and Nationality Act would be the final watershed, eliminating discriminatory racial quotas and providing family reunification preferences that would mean the start of a great chain migration across the Pacific. These improvements in the status of Chinese Americans were to a significant extent linked to American diplomatic goals in the Pacific and the need for a strong partnership with the Free Chinese government in the face of Cold War difficulties. Still, these years were not without challenges for Chinese Americans. Faced with a newly Communist homeland, some Chinese Americans were placed under intense scrutiny and sometimes subjected to persecution and deportation. The sensational reporting of the Chinese illegal immigration racket capable of smuggling Communist spies into the U.S. brought the FBI and INS into American Chinatowns to trace illegal entries. The Guomindang worked through the CCBA and other local organizations to promote its own political agenda, taking advantage of 1950s-era red-baiting of the era to keep Chinese American sentiment strongly its favor.

In the 1960s and 1970s, the anti-war movement, the rising generation of native-born Chinese American youth, and UN recognition of the People's Republic of China combined to diversify Chinese American communities. The concept of "Chinese American" expanded from its roots in Guangdong Province to include people with origins across all of China and Taiwan; this geographic, linguistic, and political expansion ensures that the Chinese American community of the present rarely speaks with a single voice on any issue, including Sino-American relations. Still, many Chinese Americans are politically active on such issues as U.S.-Chinese trade, Chinese human rights, and Cross-Strait relations.

See also **Chinese Consolidated Benevolent Association (CCBA); Chinatowns; Chinese Exclusion Act of 1882.**

REFERENCES: Him Mark Lai, "China and the Chinese American Community: The Political Dimension," *Chinese America, History and Perspectives Vol. 13.* (1999); Peter H. Koehn (ed.), *The Expanding Roles of Chinese Americans in U.S.-Chinese Relations* (New York, 2002).
Meredith Oyen

Chinese Communist Party (CCP)

Advancing policy and constitutional decisions in China, the Communist Party is the dominant political party in China. It represents the ruling party and organization that has selective admission and by 2002 increased its membership to 63 million. The party represents the intellectual and ideological traditions of Marx, Lenin and Mao Zedong, which espouse the advantages of Communism in which the state maintains control and ownership of industry and the economy. This command economy is in contrast to capitalist countries that are based on market economies. Since the end of the Cultural Revolution and the death of Mao in 1976, more moderate leaders launched the Four Modernizations 1976–1986 to accelerate economic development and improve the standard of living.

The Chinese Communist Party started in China in 1921 and has waxed and waned with the currents of regional and world events. The rise of the Nationalist Party in 1924 originally formed a coalition with the CCP and later by 1927 its leader Jiang Jieshi sought to annihilate the CCP in pogroms such as the White Terror. However, CCP members retreated in the legendary Long March and rebuilt its base in the midst of the continuing civil war against the Nationalists in the mid 1930s. The two parties formed a united front during the Sino-Japanese War. Gaining much military experience during the Sino-Japanese War, the Communist Red Army used superior tactics to defeat the Nationalists in 1949. Mao had declared the founding of the Peoples Republic of China on October 1, 1949. With Mao as Chairman, the CCP embarked on a dramatic program to reorganize China's production systems in agriculture and industry. While the First Five Year Plan realized productivity gains, The Great Leap Forward resulted in widespread food shortages and famine. The Great Proletarian Cultural Revolution created near chaos in China as Red Guards attempted to infuse Communist fervor to jump-start the economy. The CCP party organization was ruined, and after a power struggle one CCP leader Deng Xiaoping emerged to embark on a politically stabilizing course of economic and social reform. The party has had to defend its legacy of the abuses generated by Red Guards and the government during the Cultural Revolution and new abuse allegations based on corruption and human rights infringements after the Tiananmen Square massacre. The party has dramatically altered the command economy since 1978 leading to nearly half of state owned industries to privatize or consolidate to assure profits. Additionally it has expanded special economic zones to attract foreign investors. Both developments have created new problems for workers as managers have gained power, new systems of accountability have had to be developed to avoid abuses on workers. Although entrepreneurial activity has mushroomed, the workers from defunct state industries, farmers and migrant workers each face special challenges, experience different privations, and pressure the party for long-term solutions. The Chinese government has three parts: the Party, the State (government) and the Army. Since there are party members in all parts, the Party is pervasive and characterized as an oligarchy. The party's largest body is the National People's Congress (NPC), meeting every five years. One main function of the body is the election of the Central Committee. This committee then elects the key decision-makers of the party: The Politburo (22 members), The Politburo Standing Committee, Secretariat, Central Military Commission and the Discipline Inspection Commission. There are numerous additional departments that carry out specialized functions. The state exercises the power to implement and change policy and consists of the National People's Congress, the President and the State Council (main Party officials: Premier, Vice Premiers, state councilors and ministers and head of state). The majority of the leaders in the state offices also are CCP members who show a centralization of power. Guided by the Constitution, the NPC examines and forwards policy, law, and budget recommendations, however, the Central Committee initiates many policy directives and with its greater authority, may resist changes. The President as of 2005 currently is Hu Jintao, the Vice President is Zeng Qinghong and the Premier of the State Council is Wen Jiabao. Hu Jintao also is the General Secretary of the Politburo Standing Committee.

In the aftermath of the Democracy Movement in 1989, the Party remains vigilant and suppresses negative information and criticism of government policy and actions. Being a one-party authoritarian structure, the party has shown some responsiveness to citizens' grievances however many underground activist groups continue to echo human rights violations, exploitation, and party corruption on a local level. The Party now has a professionally developed website on the World Wide Web in an attempt to disseminate information and maintain legitimacy. The Party will continue to combat party-hostile and human rights websites and literature as it also works to gradually adapt its economy to a coordinated partial-market system. This is evidenced by the imprisonment of leaders of the grassroots movement to found the China Democratic Party in 1998, although some scholars indicate that the political situation has become more tolerant.

See also Mao Zedong (1893–1976); People's Republic of China.

REFERENCES: Wang Gunguwu and Zheng Yongnian, *Damage Control: The Chinese Communist Party in the Jiang Zemin Era* (Singapore, 2003); John King Fairbank and Merle Goldman, *China: a New History* (Cambridge, MA, 1998); Lu Xiaobo, *Cadres and Corruption: the Organizational Involution of the Chinese Communist Party* (Stanford, CA, 2000).

Jim Steinberg

Chinese Consolidated Benevolent Association (CCBA)

The Chinese Consolidated Benevolent Association, or CCBA, is the largest and longest-running Chinese mutual-aid society in the Americas. The CCBA forms a network connecting Chinese Americans to each other and to issues of concern to China.

In the 1800s, the Chinese in the Americas created a variety of organizations to fight the rampant anti-Chinese agitation that ultimately led to harsh and restrictive immigration policies. Locked out of many economic opportunities, prevented from acquiring American citizenship, and discriminated against in ways that often led to violence, the Chinese created their own support networks based on mutual ties in China. *Huiguan*, or native place associations, were among the earliest formal organizations among the Chinese in the Americas. Membership in one's *huiguan* in the United States was not voluntary — upon arrival, one was registered and forced to pay annual membership dues and other fees to the organization, often headed by the wealthier or more established merchant class. In return, the *huiguan* provided a hostel for travelers, maintained funerary facilities, mediated disputes, and controlled exit permits for return to China, which ensured that no return migrant would flee to China leaving debts behind him. In 1882 (the same year as the first Chinese Exclusion Act), in response to both increasing anti-Chinese agitation and urging from the Qing consul in the United States, the *huiguan* of San Francisco created an alliance to address issues of concern to all Chinese in the Americas. At this time there were six predominant *huiguan*, so the resulting alliance was often referred to as the "Chinese Six Companies," and later renamed the Chinese Consolidated Benevolent Association of San Francisco (*Jinshan Zhonghua Huiguan*). The CCBA founded branches in cities across the United States in the years that followed, including in New York in 1883 (called the *Zhonghua Gongsuo*). In this era, when the number of new immigrants was severely restricted and the Chinese government was weakened by a series of internal conflicts, the CCBA became the primary link between the Chinese in the United States and mainstream America. For example, the San Francisco branch became quickly involved in a wide variety of projects, from creatiing Chinese hospitals and schools to providing legal support to a series of cases designed to test the constitutionality of the various Exclusion-related acts. As the Qing Dynasty ended in China and the political situation there became more and more unstable, the CCBA also became increasingly enmeshed in Chinese politics. In the 1920s and 1930s, Nationalist Party (GMD) leaders in the United States recruited party members among CCBA directors in an effort to control the political capital of the Chinese in America. After 1949 and the Communist takeover of the mainland, the CCBA remained steadfastly pro-GMD, forming anti-Communist leagues and organizing propaganda to encourage support of the Jiang Jieshi regime on Taiwan. In 1957, CCBA leaders organized a National Conference of representatives from American CCBAs to discuss immigration issues, including the situation of Chinese refugees in Hong Kong and how to promote continued support for the Taiwan regime.

In the 1960s and 1970s, a series of events—including the liberalization of American immigration laws, the recognition of the mainland regime, and the growth of the native born American population—weakened the role of the CCBA in America. The Chinese in America were no longer concentrated in a relatively few urban Chinatowns and no longer dependent on CCBA leadership to defend against the racisms of white America. Still, the basic concept of a Chinese mutual aid society has been retained, and today's CCBA continues to provide social services and English classes to new migrants, Chinese classes for American-born youth, and leadership on issues related to Chinese politics.

See also Chinese Exclusion Act of 1882; Chinatowns; Chinese Americans.

REFERENCES: Him Mark Lai, "The Historical Development of the Chinese Consolidated Benevolent Association/*Huiguan* System," *Chinese America, History and Perspectives Vol. 1.* (1987); Peter Kwong, *The New Chinatown* (New York, 1996).

Meredith Oyen

Chinese Eastern Railway (CER)

As part of the diplomacy to end the Sino-Japanese War of 1894–1895 and of the subsequent Triple Intervention, China agreed to let Russia construct a railway, the Chinese Eastern Railway, across Manchuria. This railway cut 800 miles off the Trans-Siberian Railway from Moscow to Vladivostok, and the Russian government hoped it would lead to a peaceful, economic penetration and takeover of Manchuria, China's resource rich northeastern-most lands.

While the President of this new company was Chinese, the general manager would be Russian, and Russia would operate and control all aspects of the railroad's operation. The Chinese government could not interfere with Russian troops or military supplies moving on the railroad and company agents (who were Russian) had all rights to protect the railway line and its rolling stock. Thereafter, Russia set about securing more and more control over Manchuria. In the wake of railroad construction, the Russians opened post offices and took over ports and other facilities. As they finished work on the main line across Manchuria from west to east, the Russians moved to develop a line running south from Harbin to the ports of Lushun (Port Arthur) and Dalian (Dairen). There were challenges, especially during the anti-foreign Boxer Rebellion (the so-called Righteous and Harmonious Fists), where Chinese nationalists badly damaged the developing railway. As Russia developed the CER, Japan watched nervously. The Japanese government had an interest in Korea, and considered growing influence in Manchuria as a logical extension of Japan's area of activity. Finally, by 1904, Japan deemed Russia a threat to its imperial aspirations in northeast Asia, and attacked setting off the Russo-Japanese War of 1904–1905. As part of the peace settlement that U.S. President Theodore Roosevelt brokered, Russia let Japan take over and complete development of the spur from Harbin to Lushun. When the United States sought to neutralize railroads in Manchuria to give its own merchants an opportunity for trade, that is extending the so-called Open Door to Manchuria, both Russia and Japan demurred. As Japan descended into militarism, the new Soviet government decided to turn over the CER to its Japanese neighbor. In September 1931, the Japanese Kwantung Army in Manchuria claimed that Chinese "bandits" had damaged the main track of the South Manchurian Railway and, over the course of the next year, from October

1931 to October 1932 the Japanese military used this "Mukden (Shenyang) Incident" to chase Chinese "bandits" and thereby to take control of the entire province. In 1935, Moscow decided to sell its rights to the CER to Japan.

As part of its demands at the Yalta Conference in 1945 and later repeated at the postwar Potsdam Conference, the Soviet Union wanted a restoration of its rights to the Chinese Eastern Railway Company in return for entering the conflict against Japan. At the Yalta Conference, Stalin sought a restoration of Russia's former position in Eastern Asia before 1904 and the loss to Japan. This demand included all of Sakhalin Island, the Kurile Islands north of the main Japanese islands, significant interests in Lushun and Dalian in Chinese Manchuria, giving the Soviet Navy all-year, warm water ports in Northeast Asia, and Russia's former railway holdings, the Chinese Eastern Railway. That is, the price for Soviet intervention would be at least tacit support for Soviet expansionism in East Asia. The United States and Great Britain accepted these demands since, in these months before the successful testing of atomic weapons, the Allies assumed they would have to invade Japan, that Japan still had strong defenses, and that the Allies would suffer at least two million casualties—so any help at virtually any price seemed a good deal.

Finally, on February 14, 1950, as part of a Sino-Soviet friendship treaty, the Soviet Union turned over the Chinese Eastern Railway and all of the Soviet Union's rights to the People's Republic of China. The railroad was renamed and the CER passed into history.

See also Manchuria, Open Door Policy; Mukden Incident; South Manchurian Railway.

REFERENCES: Harry L. Kingman, *Effects of Chinese Nationalism upon Manchuria Railway Developments, 1925–1931* (Berkeley, CA, 1932); George Alexander Lensen, *The Damned Inheritance: The Soviet Union and the Manchurian Crises, 1924–1935* (Tallahassee, FL, 1974); Yoshihisa Tak Mazusaka, *The Making of Japanese Manchuria, 1904–1932* (Cambridge, MA, 2001); R.K.I. Quested, *"Matey" Imperialists? The Tsarist Russians in Manchuria, 1895–1917* (Hong Kong, 1982).

Charles M. Dobbs

Chinese Exclusion Act of 1882

Previous to the discovery of gold in California in late 1840s, there was minimal Chinese immigration into the United States. But over the next two decades, the states along the Pacific coast would attract approximately 60,000 Chinese immigrants. Some were undoubtedly attracted by the gold itself, but others prospered by establishing businesses, such as the proverbial restaurants and laundries, that served the needs of miners.

The largest number, however, came to the United States as a somewhat less direct consequence of the gold rush. The exponential increase in the wealth and population of California made the construction of a transcontinental railroad seemed all the more urgent. During the Civil War, there was a desire to link the Pacific states with the other states in the Union. After the war, the east-west unification of the country by rail seemed a symbolic complement to the political reunification of the North and South. The Union Pacific Railroad was charged with laying the track through the Sierra Nevada range, the great Basin, and the western Rockies, and the Central Pacific Railroad with laying the tracks westward across the central plains and into the eastern Rockies. The Central Pacific could not draw its laborers from a large influx of Irish and other European immigrants into the cities of the Northeast and Midwest. But any Irish who made it to California went to the gold fields. So the Union Pacific resorted to recruiting Chinese laborers. Because the Taiping Rebellion in China in 1850s was then wreaking havoc on large swathes of Chinese society, huge numbers of Chinese were willing to emigrate to the United States, even if doing so meant doing hard and dangerous labor in very difficult terrain and often extreme weather conditions.

The completion of the transcontinental railroad then expedited the movement of Chinese immigrants into other sections of the country. The majority of Chinese immigrants did continue to settle in the Pacific states, where they were typically treated as second-class citizens and regarded as a threat to Anglo-European culture and economic opportunities. Ironically, however, it was the movement of relatively small groups of Chinese into communities in the Midwest and Northeast that made Chinese immigration into a volatile, national political issue. For in these industrial communities, the Chinese were competing with European immigrants for unskilled and low-skilled employment in manufacturing, and in the midst of the growing nativist abhorrence of all immigrants, Asian immigrants seemed especially "alien" to WASP sensibilities. Thus, in their antipathy toward the Chinese, immigrant labor and affluent WASPs found a rare common cause.

In 1882, the United States Congress responded to public pressure by passing the Chinese Exclusion Act, which essentially halted Chinese immigration into the United States. The act followed revisions made in 1880 to the Burlingame Treaty of 1868. The revisions to the treaty allowed the U.S. to suspend immigration. The act excluded all Chinese laborers to the United States for 10 years. In 1884, amendments was made, which tightened the provisions that allowed previous immigrants to leave and return, and clarified that the law applied to ethnic Chinese no matter which they came from. In 1892, the act was renewed for another 10 years, and in 1902 it was renewed again with no terminal date.

The Exclusion Act would remain in force until it was repealed in 1943 by the 1943 Magnuson Act, allowing a national quota of 105 Chinese immigrants per year. But, until its repeal, it created awkward complications in the military alliance between the United States and China. For representatives of the United States could hardly be very outspoken in their condemnation of the Japanese oppression of the Chinese when the Chinese were not even permitted to enter to the United States except for limited visits. The wartime trips of Madame Jiang Jieshi to the United States became, in effect, public-relations tours that aimed at rehabilitating the image of the Chinese in the United States and at defusing, if not entirely reversing, the latent nativist antipathy toward the Chinese. Large scale Chinese immigration did not occur until the passage of the Immigration Act of 1965.

See also Chinese Americans; Chinese Consolidated Benevolent Association; Chinatowns; Transcontinental Railroad.

REFERENCES: Andrew Gyory, *Race, Politics, and the Chinese Exclusion Act* (Chapel Hill, NC, 1998); Xiaohua Ma, "The Sino-American Alliance during World War II and the Lifting of the Chinese Exclusion Acts," *American Studies International* (June 2000); Edward J. M. Rhoads, "'White Labor' vs. 'Coolie Labor': The 'Chinese Question' in Pennsylvania in the 1870s," *Journal of American Ethnic History* (Winter 2002); Elmer C. Sandmeyer, *The Anti-Chinese Movement in California* (Champaign, IL, 1973); Alexander Saxton, *The Indispensable Enemy: Labor and the Anti-Chinese Movement in California* (Berkeley, CA, 1971); Richard J. Walsh, "Our Great Wall Against the Chinese," *New Republic* (November 1942).

Martin Kich

Chinese People's Volunteers Forces (CPVF) *see* Korean War.

Chinese Revolution (1911)

The Chinese Revolution took place on October 10, 1911 in Wuchang, the seat of the Huguang Governor-General and the center of a planned nationwide railway network on the middle reaches of the Yangzi River. The success of the Revolution had more to do with political and social unrest caused by the Qing government's railway nationalization policy in provinces along the Yangzi River, especially in Sichuan province where the Railway Protection Movement led to

large-scale riots, and part of the garrison in Wuchang were sent to suppress the rebels. The uprising broke out after an accidental bomb explosion in the Russian Concession of Hankou. Official investigations and arrests forced the revolutionaries to advance their plans. Because of the absence of the garrison, the revolutionaries quickly seized control of Wuchang on October 10, 1911.

The anti-Manchu sentiments underlying the Railway Protection Movement enabled Chinese local elites in provinces and cities to identify with the republican cause. In November 1911, representatives from seventeen provinces met together and set up the Provisional Republic Government in Nanjing under the command of Sun Zhongshan (1866–1925), founder of the Revolutionary Alliance (Tongmenghui), and Li Yuanhong (1864–1928), a local military commander in Wuchang. Though controlled by the Tongmenghui, the Provisional Government represented only a fraction of different revolutionary groups and political interests, and did not have much control over the country. The Qing government called upon Yuan Shikai (1859–1916), the chief military and diplomatic official in North China, to suppress the revolutionaries. It was clear to the revolutionaries that the success of the Revolution depended on the attitude of Yuan, who was the last hope for the Qing government but also a potential ally of the revolutionaries. In mid-November, Huang Xing, one of Sun Zhongshan's proteges, urged Yuan to join forces with the revolutionaries, and Yuan established contact with the revolutionary forces. From late November to early December, Yuan engaged in secret negotiations with the Provisional Government for the abdication of the Qing emperor. In the end, Yuan came to support the Provisional Government because of the revolutionaries' promise of the presidency. In late December 1911, Sun Zhongshan returned to China after seventeen years of revolutionary exile. On January 1, 1912, Sun became provisional President of the new Chinese Republic. By then, the agreement had been made to turn over the presidency to Yuan in exchange for his arrangement of the Manchu abdication. As a result, Sun resigned in favor of Yuan as the First President of the Republic of China.

Under Yuan and the warlords succeeding him, China remained a republic on paper only. Nonetheless, the Chinese Revolution on October 10, 1911, later known as "Double Tenth," symbolizes the success of nationalistic struggles and marks the end of the imperial dynastic system of government in China.

See also Sun Zhongshan (1866–1925); Yuan Shikai (1859–1916).

REFERENCES: Marie-Claire Bergere, *Sun Yat-sen* (Stanford, CA, 1998); Mary Clabaugh Wright (ed.), *China in Revolution: The First Phrase, 1900–1913* (New Haven, CT, 1968).

Joseph Tse-Hei Lee

Christopher, Warren (1925–)

Warren Minor Christopher was born October 27, 1925, in Scranton, North Dakota. He served as Deputy Secretary of State under President Jimmy Carter and the 63rd Secretary of State during Bill Clinton's first term as President. One of his accomplishments was helping to establish relations with the People's Republic of China. He also chaired the first interdepartmental group on the rights of citizens that dealt with China. After being on shaky grounds for the last several years, relations between China and the U.S. began to improve in 1978. The State Department announced in a December press release that diplomatic relations would be normalized as of January 1, 1979 in which Christopher was very instrumental in accomplishing. Taiwan became the most crucial problem between the United States and China, and remained so throughout Carter's and Christopher's time in office. In establishing relations, Christopher was an essential element in the Carter administration's reaffirmation that the People's Republic was the only recognized government of China and that Taiwan was inseparable to the Chinese government. Spearheading the normalization of U.S. relations with China helped to motivate President Jimmy Carter to award Christopher the Medal of Freedom, the nation's highest civilian honor, on January 16, 1981.

Christopher carried with him a good reputation in dealing in his relationships with the Chinese from the Carter administration, when he was appointed as Secretary of State under President Clinton. At Christopher's confirmation hearings for Secretary of State, he stressed the need for the U.S. to reexamine its policy. At the time of Christopher's tenure Li Denghui, President of the Republic of China on Taiwan, was seen as moving Taiwan foreign policy away from the One-China Policy. Almost as an avoidance issue Christopher tried to take a hands-off approach in Sino-American relations by refusing to refer to them specifically in any of his public statements. China was granted Most Favored Nation (MFN) trading status that was supported and encouraged by Christopher. Christopher visited China a total of twelve times while serving as Secretary of State during Clinton's first term as President. He visited China the first time on March 12–14, 1994, making progress in the implementation of better human rights conditions. Christopher's talks with

the Chinese leadership helped to have prisoners released, release more detailed information on detainees, and China agreed to talk to the American Red Cross about prison conditions. In all negotiations Christopher tried to take a non-direct approach with full knowledge that the Chinese were resistant to pressure. Still Christopher had and still has a strong record on human rights and was able to seemingly improve conditions without offending the Chinese.

In 1994, when Taiwan President Li Denghui's plane had stopped in Honolulu to refuel after a trip to South Africa, the U.S. government had refused Li's request for a visa. Li had been confined to the military airfield where he landed, forcing him to spend a night on his plane. The U.S. State Department called the situation embarrassing and Li complained that Taiwan was being treated as a second-class country. After Li had decided to visit Cornell University in 1995, Christopher assured Chinese Foreign Minister Qian Qichen that a visa for Li would be inconsistent with America's unofficial relationship with Taiwan. However, the humiliation from Li's last visit caught the attention of many pro-Taiwan figures in the U.S. and this time, the United States Congress acted on Li's behalf. In May 1995, resolutions asking Christopher to allow Li to visit the U.S. passed the House 396 to 0 and the Senate 91 to 1. The positions taken by Christopher did much to ensure his confidence and relationship with the Chinese government but the prevailing situations didn't do much for China's relationship with the U.S. as a country. Because of congressional action the State Department was forced to grant Li a visa on May 22, 1995. The Chinese government was furious over the US's policy reversal and resorted to military intimidation. The Chinese announced and followed through with the conduction of several military exercises. On March 8, 1996 the State Department announced that it was sending U.S. naval forces into neutral territory near Taiwan. Tensions erupted further on March 15 when China announced a simulated amphibious assault planned for March 18–25. China's attempts at intimidation were counterproductive. The military tests and exercises also strengthened Christopher's argument for further U.S. arms sales to Taiwan and led to the strengthening of military ties between the U.S. and Japan. Christopher also pushed to increase the role Japan would play in defending Taiwan. Subsequently, tensions in the Taiwan Strait diminished, and relations between the U.S. and China had improved, with increased high-level exchanges and progress on numerous bilateral issues, including human rights, nonproliferation, and trade. As a result, as Christopher was preparing to leave office U.S.-Sino relations had improved somewhat. Largely because of the policies sought by the Clinton administration and Christopher's policies as Secretary of State, Chinese President Jiang Zemin made the first state visit by a Chinese president in 1997 that was followed by a visit by Clinton to China in 1998, which was the first visit by a U.S. president Since Tiananmen Square Massacre.

REFERENCES: John Hamilton, *The Secretary Of State Through Warren Christopher* (Edina, MN, 1993); Warren Christopher, *Fighting Terror, Waging Peace: Twin Challenges For Democracies And Peacemakers* (Washington, DC, 1996); Warren Christopher, *Chances Of A Lifetime* (New York, 2001); Warren Christopher, *In The Stream Of History: Shaping Foreign Policy For A New Era* (Stanford, CA, 1998); Jean Edward Smith and Herbert M. Levine, *The Conduct Of American Foreign Policy Debated* (New York, 1990).

Steven Napier

Civil Air Transport (CAT)

Civil Air Transport (CAT) was formed by General Claire Chennault and Whiting Willauer to provide air transport service in China after World War II. Chennault spent the war in China where he created the American Volunteer Group (AVG) to help fend off Japanese air attacks. The group was known and popularized as the Flying Tigers. He used his connections in China, specifically with Generalissimo Jiang Jieshi, to gain support for the formation of CAT. It started by initially distributing food and supplies coming into the country from the United Nations Relief and Rehabilitation Administration (UNRRA). Approval to start the airline required allowing Chinese businessmen who had existing interests in similar transport companies, to own a large minority share in the company. Once funding and political issues were settled by late 1946, the partners began planning operations. Relief supplies were funneled through the associated Chinese organization, CNRRA. CNRRA Air Transport was shortened to CAT, which later became Civil Air Transport after the liquidation of the UNRRA.

Between its first flight in early 1947 and the culmination of the Chinese Civil War in 1949, CAT provided air support and transport for Jiang's Nationalist (GMD) armies in addition to its role as a private air cargo company. They flew medication, food, seeds, ammunition, and more into the Chinese interior, sometimes providing the only support for cities besieged by Chinese Communist Party (CCP) forces. Return flights moved raw materials for processing and crop surpluses for sale, in addition to serving as an evacuation service for cities and villages in the path of CCP armies. In spite of being an unarmed transport service, the flights often came under fire. Willauer acted as general manager of the business, overseeing operations, management of airstrips, and the financial and legal details. Chennault, meanwhile, managed the more immediate operations, while also ensuring pilots understood the specifics associated with the unique conditions under which they operated. Due to the continued success of the CCP in the civil war, CAT had less and less area in which to operate, which led to serious financial shortfalls. By early 1949, CAT was no longer being paid by the GMD government. General Chennault traveled to the United States to lobby for monetary support and found only one option. Chennault came to a financial and ownership agreement with the recently created Central Intelligence Agency (CIA), which allowed CAT to continue flying as a private airline, while in addition, secretly providing transport services for intelligence collection in all of non-Communist Asia.

CAT continued to play an important role for the GMD right up to the government's departure to Taiwan in 1949, helping to evacuate thousands of Chinese from the mainland. Under CIA operation, CAT continued flying regular passenger flights based out of Taiwan after the CCP victory in the civil war, while simultaneously using other aircraft to fly covert missions. During the Korean War, CAT played a role in transporting war materials for United States and United Nations military operations. In 1959, CAT's name was changed to Air America, and missions included airlifting food, evacuating civilians, and rescuing downed U.S. aircrews in Southeast Asia, particularly Laos and Vietnam. One of the company's most memorable missions was in 1975 when its helicopters were used to evacuate Americans and South Vietnamese from Saigon as the armies of the North finally gained control of the whole country. In 1976, Air America ceased operations.

See also American Volunteer Group (AVG); Air America.

REFERENCES: William M. Leary, Jr., *Perilous Missions: Civil Air Transport and CIA Covert Operations in Asia* (Tuscaloosa, AL, 1984); Martha Byrd, *Chennault: Giving Wings to the Tiger* (Tuscaloosa, AL, 1987); Air America, *www.air-america.org*; William M. Leary, Jr. and William Stueck, "The Chennault Plan to Save China: U.S. Containment in Asia and the Origins of the CIA's Aerial Empire, 1949–1950," *Diplomatic History* (Fall, 1984).

Catherine Forslund

Civil War (1945–1949)

The Japanese surrender on September 2, 1945 signaled a near certain resumption of the Chinese Civil War. When the Second World War ended,

Jiang Jieshi's Guomindang (GMD) armies were located mostly in south and southwest China; Japanese troops still occupied much of east and northeast China; Soviet Red Army troops had sliced through the remnants of the Japanese Kwantung Army in Manchuria on their way to Korea; and Chinese Communist guerrilla formations held much of northwest China near Japanese positions.

There was a momentary pause while U.S. General George C. Marshall attempted to create a coalition government. Marshall's famous mission began in January 1946 and within months he was completely frustrated with the unwillingness of either side to trust the other, and he returned to the United States and the fighting resumed. During Marshall's time in China, Jiang ignored his American advisors and acted contrary to good military strategy. Instead of securing the richer, southern half of the country and then moving gradually against the Communists in the poorer, less populated northern half of China while securing popular support for his government, Jiang had U.S. Marines take the Japanese surrender in North China while he had the U.S. Army Air Corps and the U.S. Navy transport his best, American-trained and-equipped troops to Manchuria. At first, GMD forces were successful, as in the battle at Siping, 70 miles north of Shenyang, where Nationalist armies drove Communist forces back. But, Jiang would throw away his advantages in manpower and equipment, in part, because his opposition had superior leadership, security, and surprise. Jiang concentrated on taking major cities, and thus violated the principles of mass and economy of force. As his troops seized major cities in Manchuria and, thereafter, in North China, including, for a brief time in March 1947, the Communist "capital" of Yanan, Mao Zedong's guerrilla forces retreated into the countryside, content to attack smaller Nationalist units when the Communists outnumbered them and to avoid battle when the Nationalist formations were too strong. It appeared in 1947 that, perhaps, the military issue was in question. Communist armies under Lin Biao concentrated on cutting off Nationalist forces in Manchurian cities, which became dependent on airdropped supplies. At the Songhua River, the Communist People's Liberation Army (PLA) launched four attacks beginning in January. In May they crossed and by late June they had moved 150 miles south, seizing the initiative in Manchuria. Meanwhile, the corruption and inefficiency that had marked the Nationalist regime continued, and a devastating monetary inflation destroyed the economy and turned many undecided Chinese into supporters of Mao's agrarian reform movement. And Communist armies always paused to indoctrinate poor farmers as they passed through areas. In 1948, one after another, the Nationalists lost key Manchurian cities and their forces garrisoned in those cities. In March, Communist armies took Siping; in October, they seized Jinzhou; and, having begun a buildup against Shenyang in December 1947, the Communists tightened the noose in September and remaining Nationalist troops surrendered on November 1, 1948, and, several days later Mao's forces won all of Manchuria, destroyed Jiang's best forces, and gained a great deal of valuable U.S. military equipment that Jiang's men abandoned. At the same time, other Communist armies regained territory lost in North China, including Yanan and Kaifeng, further isolating Nationalist armies in Manchurian cities. In November 1948, Jiang's armies moved to battle in the Huai Hai region north of the Yangzi River, where several months later they suffered a critical defeat. Peasants dug miles of anti-tank traps and thus negated the Nationalist armored divisions that Jiang had long held in reserve. In the end, Jiang lost 66 divisions, including more than half that the Communists claimed surrendered with all their equipment. The Communists soon seized Beijing in January 1949, and the rest of the great North China plain. The Communist tide flooded southern China in 1949. In April, Communist armies crossed the Yangzi River, and they gained Shanghai the next month. As their armies pursued the remnants of Nationalist armies across southern China, Mao Zedong on October 1, 1949, stood atop Tiananmen Gate and proclaimed the People's Republic of China.

On December 10, 1949, Jiang fled to Taiwan, and it appeared the final chapter in the long civil war reaching back to 1927 would take place there. As Communist forces massed in Fujian and Zhejiang provinces opposite Taiwan and prepared for a difficult amphibious invasion across the 100-mile wide Taiwan Strait, the Korean War began. President Harry S. Truman committed the U.S. Seventh Fleet to the Taiwan Strait, and the long awaited last battle was postponed for at least the next five-plus decades.

See also Truman, Harry S. (1884–1972); China White Paper; Marshall, George C. (1880–1959); Marshall Mission; Jiang Jieshi (1887–1975); Mao Zedong (1893–1976).

REFERENCES: Lionel Max Chassin, *The Communist Conquest of China* (Cambridge, MA, 1965); Trevor N. Dupuy, *The Military History of the Chinese Civil War* (New York, 1969); Suzanne Pepper, *Civil War in China.*

The Political Struggle, 1945–1949 (New York, 1999); Odd Arne Westad, *Decisive Encounters: The Chinese Civil War, 1946–1950* (Stanford, CA, 2003).

Charles M. Dobbs

Cixi (1835–1908)

The daughter of a minor Manchu official, Yehonala was born in Beijing on November 29, 1835, and became a concubine to Emperor Xianfeng in 1851. She quickly became his favorite and her influence grew after bearing him his only surviving son in 1856. In 1861, upon the death of the emperor, she along with the late emperor's first wife, Empress Cian, formed a regency for her son Emperor Tongzhi, whereupon her brother-in-law Prince Gong gave her the title of Dowager Empress Cixi, the first two Chinese characters of her long title. Cixi soon became more powerful than her co-regent and worked with Prince Gong to gain control of the imperial government. By the 1870s, the two disagreed on the future of China with Prince Gong leading the Self-Strengthening Movement advocating industrialization and modernization, which Cixi opposed. Although her son became of age in 1872, she remained the power behind the throne, and when he died in 1875, she broke the dynastic succession law by naming her four year old nephew as Emperor Guangxu to retain power, claiming she was his adoptive mother. In 1884, she dismissed Prince Gong taking complete control of the government officially refusing to end her regency until the emperor married in 1889. Despite his marriage, she continued to exercise control over the throne.

The Empress Dowager became more anti-foreign due to encroachments by the Russians in Central Asia, the British and French in South and Southeast Asia, and the Japanese in Korea; the disastrous Sino-Japanese War 1894–1895; and the forced leasing of Chinese territory to France, Germany, Great Britain, and Russia in 1898. As a consequence of these events, the young emperor came under the influence of a group of progressive Confucian scholars who launched the 100 Days Reform in June 1898 trying to modernize China. Although the United States and Great Britain had tried to support the dynasty in recent years out of fear of growing Russian influence, constant interference by American and British missionaries, businessmen, and other citizens in support of reform as well as advocating a constitutional monarchy caused conservatives to view the reform movement as an American, British, and Japanese plot and to rally around the conservative Empress Dowager. In September, after being informed of a plot to arrest her, she seized control of the government, cancelled the reforms, and resumed her regency running the country until her death in 1908.

In December 1898, to try to win foreign support after her actions, Cixi broke tradition by inviting the wives of the diplomatic corps, including Sarah Conger, wife of the American ambassador Edwin Conger, to tea at the Winter Palace against the advice of her advisors. Yet she remained anti-foreign. During this time, she pursued a policy of "divide and rule" between the great powers, as well as her officials. Although the Boxer Rebellion was initially anti-foreign and anti-Manchu, the Empress Dowager manipulated it to become chiefly anti-foreign, and supported the Boxers including a declaration of war against the great powers who defeated the Boxers and occupied Beijing and large sections of northern China. Cixi and the emperor fled to Xian returning to the capital in January 1902. Upon their return, Cixi again broke tradition by allowing the ambassadors from the six chief nations, including Edwin Conger, to present their credentials in an audience within the Forbidden City. In an attempt to save the dynasty in the aftermath of the Boxer calamity, the Empress Dowager allowed a series of reforms including many from 1898, but by this time, many Chinese had turned against it. On November 15, 1908, the day after the emperor died, Cixi died but not before choosing her three-year-old grand nephew Puyi to succeed him, thereby, hoping to continue her hold on the throne.

See also Boxer Rebellion (1900); Boxer Protocol; China Relief Expedition; Chinese Revolution (1911).

REFERENCES: Sterling Seagrave, *Dragon Lady: The Life and Legend of the Last Empress of China* (New York, 1992); Marina Warner, *The Dragon Empress: The Life and Times of Tz'u-Hsi Empress Dowager of China 1835–1908* (New York, 1972); Arthur W. Hummel, *Eminent Chinese of the Qing Period* (Washington, DC, 1943).

Greg Ference

Clark, Mark W. (1896–1984)

General Mark W. Clark was the Commander in Chief of all United Nations forces during the Korean War from May 12, 1952 to July 27, 1953, when the armistice agreement was signed, ending the war. During World War II, Clark had risen to prominence commanding Allied forces during the Italian campaign. Following the end of the war, Clark commanded the U.S. occupation forces in Austria and established an anti-Communist reputation in his dealings with Soviet forces stationed there.

In June of 1950, Clark was named head of the U.S. Army Field Forces at Fort Monroe, Virginia and was primarily responsible for the training of combat troops. When the Korean War began in July of 1950, Clark expressed the belief that the Communists were a ruthless enemy and as a result, instituted a rigorous training program for American soldiers. In Clark's mind, the entry of the Chinese Communists into the war raised the image of a monolithic enemy bent on world domination. Clark advocated the bombing of military targets in mainland China in retaliation and that the United States should take an aggressive stance to stop the spread of Communism in Korea and elsewhere. President Harry S. Truman appointed Clark as the Commander in Chief of U.S. forces in the Far East and of the United Nations Command in May of 1952. Large-scale fighting had ended in stalemate a year earlier and armistice talks between the U.S., North Korea, and China had faltered on the question of repatriating prisoners of war. Although armistice negotiators would continue to meet frequently, no progress was made toward a truce and negotiations were suspended by Clark in October of 1952. Following the suspension of negotiations, Clark strengthened United Nations military positions and intensified the training of South Korean forces. Clark hoped that the election of Dwight D. Eisenhower to the presidency in 1952 would allow the United States to pursue a victorious end to the war by military means. In December of 1952, Clark met with the president-elect in Korea and attempted to persuade him to pursue military victory. Eisenhower, however, would not be persuaded and was resolved that an armistice was the best means for ending the war, although he did allow Clark to bomb some targets previously forbidden, including the North Korean capital Pyongyang. Shortly after the meeting with Eisenhower, Red Cross organizations meeting in Geneva proposed that the warring nations in Korea exchange prisoners of war and sick and wounded. Clark took the opportunity to open up peace negotiations again by discussing the Red Cross proposal with North Korean and Chinese military leaders. The Red Cross proposal, the death of Soviet leader Josef Stalin in March of 1953, and the increased bombing on the part of U.S. forces seemed to compel the Communists to resume peace negotiations in the spring of 1953. On June 8, Communist and United Nations representatives signed a preliminary peace agreement called the Terms of Reference. South Korean President, Syngman Rhee refused to accept the agreement and on June 18, released all Korean prisoners of war who refused repatriation to North Korea. The Communists broke off peace negotiations and Clark attempted to convince Rhee to

accept the peace agreement over the course of the next several weeks. After finally convincing Rhee that there was no other choice for him but to accept the terms of the agreement, Clark and his representatives signed the armistice on July 27, 1953.

During his retirement, Clark expressed the belief that it was his duty to sign the armistice, but that military victory in the Korean War had been possible if the civilian leadership in Washington had been willing to take a more aggressive stance. Clark believed that the U.S. reluctance to increase the number of resources committed and to use atomic weapons doomed the war effort and led to a divided Korea.

See also Korean War.

REFERENCES: Martin Blumenson, *Mark Clark* (New York, 1984); Mark W. Clark, *From the Danube to the Yalu* (New York, 1954); John Toland, *In Mortal Combat: Korea, 1950–1953* (New York, 1991).

Mark Love

Clinton, William J. (1946-)

President from January 1993 until January 2001, William J. Clinton's stance toward China evolved from one of "conditionality" in his first year in office to one of "comprehensive engagement" thereafter. As a candidate, Governor Clinton had adopted a China policy close to, and largely adopted from, the congressional Democratic leadership, strongly criticizing the Bush administration's prioritization of trade over the promotion of human rights. In office, the domestic policy orientation of his early presidency led him to construct his China policy largely in terms of its acceptability to Congress, to preserve political capital for more his health care and budget struggles. On May 28, 1993, Clinton enacted by executive order the proposal of Republican Stephen Solarz for a one-year renewal of trade relations with China, with a series of human rights conditions outlined for China to meet to secure further renewals. The congressional leadership withdrew legislation, which would have enacted that conditionality into law. Clinton's executive order 12850 extended most favored nation status to China until July 3, 1994, and made further renewal conditional on Chinese progress on seven human rights areas. (These corresponded to free emigration, no exportation of goods manufactured with prison labor, the release of peaceful protesters from Chinese prisons, treatment of remaining prisoners in accord with international human rights standards, recognition of the distinctive regional culture of Tibet, permitting international television and radio broadcasts, and observation of human rights specified in UN instruments to which China was a party).

China, however, refused to make any movement toward satisfying the American human rights conditions, and in summer 1994, Clinton admitted defeat and called for a renewal nonetheless of normal trade relations under a revised policy of "comprehensive engagement." Under this retreat from his earlier policy, trade relations were to be "delinked" from China's human rights practices: "I believe the question, therefore, is not whether we continue to support human rights in China, but how we can best support human rights in China and advance our other very significant issues and interests," he said. Facing, however, a resurgent Congress under Republican control from January 1995 onward, Clinton quickly succumbed to congressional pressure over Taiwan. Senators Murkowski and Helms and Representatives Gillman, Lantos, and Gingrich led a cross-bench legislative insurgency which first pushed Taiwanese arms sales and high-level visits on to the political agenda, then forced the administration to conduct a review of its Taiwan policy to appease its calls for an upgraded American relationship, and finally overcame the objections of the State Department to force Clinton to invite Taiwanese President Li Denghui to visit the United States from June 7 to 11, 1995, extending a level of officiality to the U.S.-Taiwan relationship it had not enjoyed since the normalization of ties between the U.S. and mainland China in 1979. The visit dramatically altered the character of the American relationship with mainland China and Taiwan for the remainder of the decade; Beijing "indefinitely" recalled its ambassador on June 16, then suspended missile control talks with the United States and cross-strait discussions with Taiwan. Bilateral relations declined to their nadir during the Taiwan Strait Crisis of March 1996, when to intimidate the populace of Taiwan during their presidential elections, China launched ballistic missiles against points close to the Taiwanese ports of Gaoxiong and Jilong. Clinton ordered the carriers *Nimitz* and *Independence* and their associated battle groups to stand off the Straits. Tensions eased markedly after the end of elections, with both Li Denghui of Taiwan and Jiang Zemin, the Communist leader, calling over the summer for resumption of cross-strait negotiations. Improving thereafter, relations had improved sufficiently by June 1998 to permit a summit visit to China. In Shanghai, President Clinton made a public statement known subsequently as the "Three Noes": "I had a chance to reiterate our Taiwan policy, which is that we don't support independence for Taiwan, or two Chinas, or one

Taiwan-one China. And we don't believe that Taiwan should be a member in any organization for which statehood is a requirement. So I think we have a consistent policy." Though not new (a State Department spokesman had presented a similar catalogue following a 1997 visit by Jiang to Washington), members of Congress perceived the statement as making concessions toward Beijing on the subject of Taiwan. In fact, the President was indeed making more sweeping assurances to President Jiang, though privately: as later emerged, in August 1995 President Clinton had quietly sent President Jiang a letter which indicated the United States would "oppose," rather than merely "not support," Taiwanese independence. Clinton successfully defended his Taiwan policy in February 2000 against congressional challenge in the Taiwan Security Enhancement Act, which Congress withdrew when Taiwan requested it do so, fearing the measure would provoke Beijing.

By the end of his tenure a much stronger president, Clinton in the same month submitted to Congress a Permanent Normal Trade Relations legislation which proposed an end to annual congressional renewal of China's trade relations, and making normal trade relations permanent with Chinese eventual accession to the World Trade Organization. President Clinton marshaled the remaining political resources of his presidency with great focus, treating the vote as the last major contest of his administration, and ordinary lines of political contestation blurred, with daily consultations on legislative strategy between the White House and House Republican Whip Tom DeLay. Appearing evenly matched with the opposition in votes from February to May 2000, Clinton turned with the support of the Republican leadership to House Ways and Means Committee member Sander Levin to craft compromise legislation which would court wavering Democrats without losing Republican votes. The resulting Levin-Bereuter compromise proposed creation of a high-level commission drawn from Congress and the higher levels of the executive branch officials to monitor conditions in China and report to the President and Congress, and swayed ten to fifteen House votes, influencing perhaps a further twenty. In May, the House approved Permanent Normal Trade Relations, including the Levin-Bereuter compromise, by a vote of 237–197. In the Senate, the measure carried in September by a vote of 83–15. President Clinton left office in January 2001.

See also Permanent Normal Trade Relations; Taiwan.

REFERENCES: Philip Auerswald, Christian Dutweiler, and John Garofan, *Clinton's Foreign Policy: A*

Documentary Record (New York, 2003); Patrick Belton, *Congressmen as Diplomats: Congress and the Politics of U.S. China and Russia Policy* (Ph. D. Dissertation, Oxford University); David M. Lampton, *Same Bed, Different Dreams: Managing U.S. China Relations, 1989–2000* (Berkeley, CA, 2002); James Mann, *About Face: A History of America's Curious Relationship with China, from Nixon to Clinton* (New York, 2000); Robert L. Suettinger, *Beyond Tiananmen: The Politics of U.S.-China Relations* (Washington, DC, 2003).

Patrick Belton

Clubb, O. Edmund (1901–1989)

Oliver Edmund Clubb was born on February 16, 1901, in South Park, Minnesota, the son of a cattle rancher. He joined the United States Army during the First World War, after which he attended the University of Washington and the University of Minnesota where he took several classes on China and received a degree in international law. After he passed the foreign service examination in 1928, he was sent to Beijing to study the Chinese language for two years. He served as vice consul in Hankou, Beijing, and Shanghai from 1931 t01940. In 1939, and, again, in 1941, he briefly took charge of the American embassy in Nanjing. In December 1941, he was assigned to the American consulate in Hanoi, in Japanese occupied French Indochina. Shortly after his arrival the Japanese attacked Pearl Harbor and interned him for eight months before he was exchanged for Japanese officials held by the Allies. Clubb then served several months in the consulate in Lanzhou and the embassy in the national wartime capital of Chongqing. He subsequently traveled to Urumchi in Xinjiang to open a consulate and remained until December 1943 when he was recalled to the Department of State in Washington, DC. Due to his knowledge of the Chinese and Russian languages, he was sent to Vladivostok as consul general in 1944. In 1946 Clubb served as consul general in Shenyang, in Changchun 1946–1947, and Beijing in 1947–1950 overseeing the consulate's closing by the Chinese Communists in April 1950. He returned to the United States and in July 1950 became director of the Office of Chinese Affairs at the State Department.

As one of the China Hands, a career diplomat who had extensive knowledge and experience in China, he came under criticism by Senator Joseph McCarthy and his search to uncover alleged Communists and their sympathizers in the American government. Like other China Hands, Clubb warned the American government of the poorly received view of the growing popularity of the Chinese Communists and the corruption of the Nationalist regime. To make matters worse, Clubb, while in Beijing before the closing of the consulate, had met with Communist officials and urged diplomatic recognition of the People's Republic. After returning to the United States, he predicted that the Chinese would enter the Korean War if United Nations forces, including American, invaded North Korea by crossing the 38th parallel. Furthermore, back in 1932 he had visited the offices of a Communist journal in New York City with a letter of introduction from a leftist journalist. Instead of meeting with the editor, he met with Whittaker Chambers. Chambers, a reformed Communist by the early 1950s, identified Clubb as a Communist sympathizer to McCarthy who, in turn, blamed him, among others in the State Department, for the "loss of China." Clubb testified before several government committees, and was seen as a security risk losing his director's position. Although cleared in early 1952, he received a new job in the State Department's historical section. Viewing it as a demotion and a dead-end position, Clubb resigned.

Clubb began to lecture at Columbia University, New York University, Brooklyn College, and the New School. He also wrote several books: *Twentieth Century China* (1964), *Communism in China: As Reported from Hankow in 1932* (1968), *China and Russia: The "Great Game"* (1971), and *The Witness and I* (1974) about his career with the foreign services. In the 1960s, he became an early opponent of the Vietnam War. Clubb died in New York City on May 9, 1989.

See also China Hands; McCarthyism.

REFERENCES: E. J. Kahn, *China Hands: America's Foreign Service Officers and What Befell Them* (New York, 1975); "Oral Interview with O. Edmund Clubb," Truman Presidential Museum and Library, *www.trumanlibrary.org/oralhist/clubb*.

Greg Ference

Cold War

Although most often considered in U.S.-Soviet terms, a concurrent but independent Sino-American Cold War began in October 1949 with the establishment of the People's Republic of China (PRC). Nor was the Cold War in Asia solely a conflict between the United States and the PRC. Beijing and Moscow competed for influence in Hanoi and Pyongyang, as well as in Mongolia, and border clashes marked periods of heightened tensions. Unlike the U.S.-Soviet Cold War, the Sino-American conflict continued despite the collapse of the Soviet Union in 1991. Tensions between Beijing and Washington remained elevated into the 21st century with the fate of Taiwan a frequent cause of conflict.

A hallmark of the U.S.-Soviet Cold War was a destabilizing arms race. In a fashion similar to

Moscow's arms exportation strategy from the 1950s to the 1980s, Beijing supplied nations hostile to the United States with weapons with guided missiles, the most serious threat to U.S. national security. Likewise the United States provided military technology, weaponry, and economic aid, to counterbalance Beijing's power and regional influence, especially Taiwan, as well as Asian nations combating Communist insurgencies.

Several crises defined the Sino-American Cold War. From October 1949 to the June 1950 the United States maintained a cautious ambiguity towards the People's Republic of China. When the North Korean People's Army invaded the Republic of Korea in June 1950, the Truman administration interpreted Pyongyang's actions as directed from Moscow not Beijing. Although Beijing had little say in Pyongyang's decision to go to war the rapid collapse of Communist forces in Korea and their withdrawal towards the Chinese border in the late fall of 1950 prompted Mao Zedong's government to intervene in the Korean War. In October Beijing warned that a continued United Nations' military effort on the Korean peninsula would result in Chinese involvement. Yet, the Truman administration, along with the U.S. military, ignored the warning and were surprised by the Chinese Communist army's offensive the next month. After the entry of the PRC into the war the United States sought to contain Communism within the "bamboo curtain" without widening the conflict in Korea. Although the United Nations' command entered into armistice negotiations with representatives from the Democratic People's Republic of Korea and People's Republic of China in 1951 little progress was made for two years because of Beijing's support for Pyongyang's continuation of the war. The armistice negotiations typified the duplicity and skepticism of Sino-American relations. Only when President Dwight D. Eisenhower implicitly threatened to widen the war and directly attack Communist China, which would entail the use of nuclear weapons and the military backing of Taiwan, did the war draw to a close.

Yet, conflict between Beijing and Washington continued. In 1954 the Chinese People's Liberation Army began an artillery bombardment of the Taiwan-controlled offshore islands of Jinmen and Mazu, along with the Dachens. Eisenhower dispatched units of the U.S. Navy to the Taiwan Strait in support of Jiang Jieshi's Nationalist government on Taiwan. Jiang agreed to cede control of the Dachens to Beijing but refused to do so with Jinmen and Mazu, which were considered central to Taiwan's defense. As 1955 began the U.S. Congress approved the "Formosa Resolu-

tion," which authorized the use of U.S. military force to defend Taiwan. Implicit in the resolution and explicit in Eisenhower's remarks was the threat of a nuclear strike against the People's Republic of China. In April Beijing stopped the bombardment of the offshore islands but refused to recognize the legitimacy of the Taibei government. To contain Chinese influence and surround the PRC with its own non-Communist allies, the United States engineered the creation of the South East Asia Treaty Organization later in 1954. The following spring, Beijing sponsored the Bandung Conference, in Indonesia, of the unaligned nations in Africa and Asia, to curb American influence and extend its own.

Over the next three years American ties to Taiwan were strengthened through dual auspices of the U.S.-China Mutual Defense Treaty of 1954 and the Formosa Resolution, as the United States sought to contain Communist influence in Asia. Beijing's acquiescence, in addition, weakened its influence in the region as it strengthened that of the United States. As Mao instituted his domestic agenda, the Great Leap Forward, he sought a means to unify the nation and distract the populace from the hardships his program caused. The offshore islands offered a means through which to do so, as well as to reclaim the regional influence Beijing had lost. In October 1958 the People's Liberation Army renewed its shelling of the now heavily-fortified Jinmen. Eisenhower refused to appease Communist aggression and ordered U.S. Air Force, as well as Navy, units to the region. Although the U.S. forces did not engage in combat with the Chinese Communists, they did supply Taiwan with much-needed munitions and supplies, including advanced air-to-air missiles. Simultaneously, the U.S. Secretary of State, John Foster Dulles, proposed a draw down of nationalist forces on Jinmen if Beijing ceased hostilities. Both initiatives proved decisive in halting the Communist campaign and eased PRC-American tensions.

Throughout the 1960s the conflict in Vietnam kept tensions between Beijing and Washington escalated. The Nixon administration, however, reevaluated its China strategy and recognized that Moscow and Beijing were more adversaries than allies with military clashes along the Sino-Soviet border and their competition for influence in Hanoi. In the establishment of relations with Beijing, the administration saw a means to curb Soviet influence in Asia, obtain a satisfactory outcome in Southeast Asia, and secure a Chinese counterbalance to the growing power of Hanoi. As the 1970s dawned, the United States, thus, began covert negotiations to establish diplomatic relations with the People's Republic of China and replace the policy of containment with one of detente. An era of detente began with President Nixon's August 1972 trip to China.

See also Korean War; Taiwan Strait; Detente; Nixon's Visit to China.

REFERENCES: Stephen E. Ambrose, *Eisenhower, Volume II: The President* (New York, 1983); Warren I. Cohen, *America's Response to China: A History of Sino-American Relations* (New York, 2000); Rosemary Foot, *The Practice of Power: U.S. Relations with China Since 1949* (Oxford, 1995); John Lewis Gaddis, *Strategies of Containment: A Critical Appraisal of Postwar American National Security Policy* (Oxford, 1982); June M. Grasso, *Truman's Two-China Policy* (Armonk, NY 1987); George C. Herring, Jr., *America's Longest War: The United States and Vietnam, 1950–1975* (Columbus, OH, 2001); Akira Iriye, *The Cold War in Asia: A Historical Introduction* (Englewood Cliffs, NJ, 1974); Shu Guang Zhang, *Deterrence and Strategic Culture: Chinese American Confrontations, 1949–1958* (Ithaca, NY, 1992).

Paul D. Gelpi, Jr.

Committee for a Democratic Far Eastern Policy (CDFEP)

Established in August 1945, the Committee for a Democratic Far Eastern Policy (CDFEP) was a leftist liberal and progressive organization, which objected to American intervention in China, in particular the Truman administration's support for the Guomindang (GMD) government headed by Jiang Jieshi. From 1946 to 1952, the committee members frequently wrote and delivered speeches on current affairs related to China. They published a newsletter *Far East Spotlight* expressing their political views.

During the early 1950s, the CDFEP's support for diplomatic recognition of the People's Republic of China and its opposition to U.S. policy in the Korean War brought its members under close surveillance by the House Un-American Activities Committee and the Attorney General's Subversive Activities Control Board. Membership and contributions decreased rapidly. As a result, the CDFEP was forced to dissolve in August 1952. Undaunted, some activists were determined to continue to write and speak on China, believing that the American people deserved to hear a different voice from the uniform mainstream media coverage of what was going on. With the help of her former CDFEP colleagues and friends, former CDFEP director Maud M. Russell started to publish a newsletter, *Far East Reporter*, a successor to the CDFEP's *Far East Spotlight*. The materials for this publication were from a wide variety of newspapers and magazines ranging from *New York Times, Far East Economic Review, China Reconstructs* to books, photos, slides, and films

sent by friends and supporters of CDFEP in America and China. With the thawing of the icy Sino-American relationship in the early 1970s, the former members of CDFEP found themselves become popular speakers on issues related to China. They drew a big audience in the United States. In early 1970s, some CDFEP activists such as Maud Russell became the first members of the United States-China People's Friendship Association (USCPFA).

REFERENCES: Karen Garner, *Precious Fire: Maud Russell and the Chinese Revolution* (Amherst, MA, 2003); K. S. Chern, *Dilemma in China: America's Policy Debate, 1945* (Hamden, CT, 1980).

Yuwu Song

Committee of 100 (C-100)

A group of socio-economically elite Chinese Americans founded C-100 in 1990, in part in response to the deterioration in official U.S.-China relations that followed the violence at Tiananmen Square in June 1989. According to its website, members are "American citizens of Chinese descent" who have "achieved positions of leadership in the United States in a broad range of professions." Membership is by invitation only. Governors include musician Yo-Yo Ma and architect I.M. Pei, while Chen Xiangmei (Anna Chennault, informal diplomat and widow of Claire Chennault, of World War II Flying Tiger fame) complements a list of business and professional people with prestigious affiliations. In broad terms, C-100 has a two-fold mission. In addition to the transnational aim of working as "cultural ambassadors" outside official state channels to improve bilateral relations, it has the domestic goal of combating all forms of discrimination against Chinese and other Asian Americans. This two-part agenda is complementary, insofar as C-100 argues that the United States has weakened its ability to understand and communicate with China by putting a glass ceiling above Chinese Americans who are well qualified for diplomatic positions.

C-100 uses publicity and quite diplomacy to work toward its goals. In 1998, for example, members briefed National Security Advisor Sandy Berger prior to President Bill Clinton's visit to China. In 1994, they previewed United States government officials on the results of the Wirthlin Report it had commissioned. The Report showed that Hong Kong residents were relatively unworried about the 1997 transfer of sovereignty from the UK to China, even though the majority of Americans assumed that they were very worried. In 1997, C-100 hosted a "fireside chat" in Washington, DC, for visiting Chinese President Jiang

Zemin, so as to help Jiang better understand American policy concerns. One of C-100's recent projects has been the dissemination of journalistic news and analysis on the question of "Outsourcing and Globalization of Trade." While members "share with our fellow Americans concern about the U.S. unemployment rate and the lack of job growth in the current economic recovery," they worry that a misguided over-emphasis on the role of Chinese manufactured products in causing employment stagnation will undermine U.S.-China relations and stir up racist scapegoating attitudes toward Asian Americans.

REFERENCES: Xiao-huang Yin, "The Growing Influence of Chinese Americans on U.S.-China Relations," in Peter H. Koehn and Joseph Y.S. Cheng (eds.), *The Outlook for U.S.-China Relations Following the 1997–1998 Summits: Chinese and American Perspectives on Security, Trade, and Cultural Exchange* (Hong Kong, 1999); Norton Wheeler, "Improving Mainland Society and U.S.-China Relations: A Case Study of Four Chinese American-led Transnational Associations," in Peter H. Koehn and Xiao-huang Yin (eds), *The Expanding Roles of Chinese Americans in U.S.-China Relations: Transnational Networks and Trans-Pacific Interactions* (Armonk, NY, 2002); Committee of 100 Web site, *www.committee100.0rg.*

Norty Wheeler

Committee of One Million (COM)

The Committee of One Million Against the Admission of Communist China to the United Nations (COM) was the public relations arm of the influential Congressional "China Lobby." The Committee dedicated itself to two related efforts which, its sponsors hoped, would hasten the demise of the Chinese Communist regime — to block the People's Republic of China (PRC) membership in the United Nations (this represented the primary element of a larger attempt to completely quarantine Communist China from the international community), as well as garner support in the United States for the continued recognition of Jiang Jieshi's Nationalist regime on Taiwan.

The group began in 1953 as the Committee for One Million in the days following the Korean War armistice. Its name referred to the signature campaign launched to gather names for a petition outlining the group's goals, which had been signed by COM's Congressional members and presented to President Dwight D. Eisenhower. The COM reached the height of its activity in the years immediately following the armistice. It was during the 1954 Geneva Conference on Indochina and Korea that COM member Senator William Knowland (R-California, previously dubbed the "Senator from Formosa") cabled Secretary of State John Foster Dulles that over eight hundred

thousand Americans had formally endorsed the COM's petition. By the following year, both the group's name and mission had expanded. Now the far more cumbersome Committee of One Million Against the Admission of Communist China to the United Nations included opposition to American trade with "Red China" to its platform. Despite the ultimate success of the petition drive to collect a million signatures, the group's active financial supporters never numbered more than forty thousand. In the 1950s, the COM fought for a cause that was generally popular, a fact, which is amply demonstrated by the fact that opinion polls throughout the decade showed that the vast majority of the public, even those who favored a more moderate China policy, opposed PRC membership in the UN. Both leading party platforms endorsed a policy of continued exclusion, and resolutions opposing the seating of the PRC in the UN passed unanimously in both houses of Congress. COM's campaign did keep the issue in the public eye, and this provided the Eisenhower administration with an effective response to criticism from allies increasingly at odds with American policy, namely that granting the PRC UN membership could provoke a domestic backlash that might well result in American withdrawal from the UN.

The driving forces behind the COM were its Executive Secretary, ex-Young Communist League member *cum* successful New York public relations agent Marvin Liebman, and the former China missionary, Congressional Representative Walter Judd (R-Minnesota). Other influential China Lobbyists from both sides of the aisle counted themselves COM members in the 1950s, including Representatives Thomas Dodd (D-Connecticut), Robert Byrd (D-West Virginia), Kenneth Keating (R-New York) and Senators Paul Douglas (D-Illinois), Barry Goldwater (R-Arizona), Jacob Javits (R-New York), William Knowland (R-California), and Mike Mansfield (D-Montana). The fortunes of the COM seemed to follow the general contours of Sino-American foreign relations during the Cold War, in that the organization's influence waned as momentum for a more moderate stance on the PRC (including its participation in the UN) grew in the 1960s. The death or removal from office of key China Lobbyists was also a factor. After a period of dormancy, the COM in October 1970 announced "a nation-wide information program and petition drive," prompted partly by disclosure that "powerful, well-financed groups" were pressing for recognition of the Beijing regime and its admission to the UN. The committee frequently distributed Nationalist China materials to members of Congress, some of which was read on the floor of the House.

In the era following the inclusion of the PRC to the UN in 1971, all pro-Nationalist groups were defunct except the COM, which — now reconstituted as the Committee for a Free China —continued to encourage grass-roots support for Taiwan after normalization of U.S. relations with the PRC until its own demise a few years later.

See also Cold War; Knowland, William Fife (1908–1974); China Lobby; United Nations.

REFERENCES: Stanley Bachrack, *The Committee of One Million: China Lobby Politics, 1953–1971* (New York, 1976); Lee Edwards, *Missionary for Freedom: The Life and Times of Walter Judd* (New York, 1990); Marvin Liebman, *Coming Out Conservative: An Autobiography* (San Francisco, CA, 1992); Ross Koen, *The China Lobby in American Politics* (New York, 1974).

Matthew Young

Committee on Scholarly Communication with the People's Republic of China *see* Committee on Scholarly Communication with China

Committee on Scholarly Communication with China

Founded in 1966 as the Committee on Scholarly Communication with Mainland China, CSCC soon changed its name to the Committee on Scholarly Communication with the People's Republic of China, taking on its current name in 1996. It was established by U.S.-based China scholars, with sponsorship by the National Academy of Sciences, the American Council on Learned Societies, and the Social Research Council. CSCC's initial charter was to open scientific and cultural contacts between the two estranged countries. The Cultural Revolution (1966–1976) postponed significant progress toward this goal until 1971. For the next two decades, the Committee on Scholarly Communication played a prominent and indispensable role in organizing scholarly exchange delegations and programs. Scientists from both countries formed the initial core constituency, starting with reciprocal medical delegations in 1973. Over time, scientists found separate sponsorship and funding, and social science and humanities exchanges became more prominent, with CSCC organizing several early, high profile delegations to China. While it was never the dominant facilitator of U.S.-bound Chinese delegations and students, its role was essential there, too, throughout the 1970s and 1980s.

When China first cautiously opened its doors in the 1970s, it maintained control by approving gatekeeper organizations on each side. By the late 1980s and the 1990s (the Tiananmen Square events of June 1989 notwithstanding), the control over exchanges became increasingly decentralized, with dozens of new facilitators on both sides, including individual academic and research organizations. In this changed climate, CSCC's role became less central to non-state relations between the United States and China. In 1996 it ceased publication of its quarterly magazine *China Exchange News*, and by the end of the decade it scaled back its programming and transferred its headquarters from the National Academy of Sciences to a more modest office at the American Council for Learned Societies, which also provides a Web page. Currently, CSCC sponsors two grant programs for American scholars, a "teacher exchange program" that sends about a dozen American teachers to China each year, and a Program on Social Development in China. The latter sends U.S.-based scholars to China each summer to provide four weeks of intensive training to Chinese sociologists. The seminars are conducted in Chinese, and the program provides a useful alternative for Chinese scholars who cannot study in the United States, whether for financial, linguistic, or other reasons.

REFERENCES: Joyce K. Kallgren, "Public Interest and Private Interest in Sino-American Exchanges: DeTocqueville's 'Associations' in Action," in *Educational Exchanges: Essays on the Sino-American Experience* (Berkeley, CA, 1987); Norton Wheeler, *Bridging the Pacific: The 1990 Institute and Transnationalism in Late-20th Century U.S.-China Relations* (Masters Thesis, University of Kansas, 2002); CSCC Website: *www.acls.org/pro-cscc.htm*.

Norty Wheeler

Communist International (Comintern)

Communist International, known popularly as Comintern, emerged out of the Soviet Union as the Third International. International is the common name for a multitude of socialist organizations. The International is characterized by a supra-national initiative to unite the proletariat across international borders. The First International was founded in 1864 when English and French workers in London formed the International Workingmen's Association in London. Marx, living in London at the time, was accepted with open arms into the association and was elected as the International's provisional general council. An early and important schism occurred early on in the International movement when Mikhail Bakunin, a follower of anarchist Pierre Joseph Proudhon, had to confront Marx's authoritarian plans for the revolution of the proletariat. In 1872 during the Hague Congress, Marx ultimately won out and Bakunin was routed out of the International. The Second International emerged out of the French Revolution in 1889. One of the socialist congresses that met in Paris was Marxist inspired and was known then as the Second International. Once again, the anarchists were expelled, leaving mostly German Marxists in control of the International. Nationalist tendencies during WWI led to the Second International's demise. Members forgave their supra-national allegiances in order to protect their individual nation's military integrity. The Third International, Comintern, lasted from March of 1919 until May 1943. After the Russian Revolution, Lenin organized a new supra-national socialist movement. The first President of the socialist congress was Grigory Zinovyev. After Lenin's death in 1924, Stalin used Comintern as a personal power grab. Less interested in a supra-national worker's movement, Stalin used Comintern as an ideological weapon. Stalin, upon prompting by U.S. and British allies in World War II , dissolved the organization in May 1943.

Comintern representatives Grigori Voitinsky and Yang Mingzhai, visited Li Dazhao and Chen Duxiou in China and set up the first Communist local group in Shanghai in 1920. The Chinese movement was organized primarily around the education of youth into the Communist ideologies. A group of thirty to sixty students traveled to Moscow for education in August 1921. Comintern representatives offered Chen an invitation to the Sixth World Congress of the International in 1929, however Chen declined, because the Communist Party of China did not agree with Stalin's egotistical agenda regarding Comintern. The Communist perspective on the dissolution of Comintern is that Comintern was no longer necessary due to the establishment of Communist parties throughout the world.

REFERENCES: Tim Rees, *International Communism and the Communist International 1919–1943* (Manchester, UK, 1999); C. L. R. James, *World Revolution, 1917–1936: The Rise and Fall of the Communist International* (Norman, OK, 2003); Laszlo Ladany, *The Communist Party of China and Marxism 1921–1985: A Self Portrait* (Stanford, CA, 1992).

Arthur Holst

Comprehensive Engagement *see* Engagement

Conger, Edwin Hurd (1843–1907)

Edwin H. Conger, the U.S. Minister to China who, with other Western diplomats and missionaries, survived the 1900 siege of foreign legations in Beijing during the Boxer Rebellion, began his career as a country lawyer in the American Midwest. Conger was born on March 7, 1843 in Knox County, Illinois, and graduated from the local college, Lombard University, in 1862. Conger enlisted as a private, serving in the 102nd Regiment of the Illinois Volunteer Infantry from 1862 until the end of the American Civil War, ending his military service as a Brevet Major. He then embarked upon legal studies, and ran a small law practice in Galesburg, Illinois, before moving to Dallas County, Iowa, in 1868.

A successful businessman in Iowa, Conger decided to enter politics as a Republican. He was elected twice as Iowa's State Treasurer, in 1880 and 1882, before running for the U.S. Congress. Conger served three terms in the U.S. House of Representatives, resigning on October 3, 1890 to accept the position as U.S. Minister to Brazil. He held this assignment for three years, 1890–1893, and briefly again in 1897–1898, before his selection in January 1898 as U.S. Minister to China. Conger arrived in China at a time of extreme stress for the imperial government of the Qing Dynasty, whose capital was in Beijing. For over fifty years the Chinese government had confronted technologically superior Western countries with expansionist aims in East Asia. As recently as 1895–1896 China's military, which had belatedly begun a modernization campaign, had been humiliated in a clash with Japan. Stunned by this defeat, senior Chinese officials sought to introduce broad social as well as technological reforms, but resistance from both local officials and from the anti-foreign Dowager Empress, Cixi impeded their efforts. Conger arrived in China just as the most vigorous reform attempts of 1898 were introduced. Their failure and Cixi's patronage fostered the growth of a peasant-based millenarian and anti-Western movement known to Westerners as the "Boxers." The Boxers opposed Christian missionaries, Western businessmen, and the local Chinese who cooperated with them. They organized as a militia, violently attacking symbols of Western encroachment on traditional Chinese life. Many accounts attribute to Cixi the Boxers' decision to enter Beijing and attack Western business offices and legations in early 1900. Minister Conger, as head of the American mission, learned in December 1899 that Boxer forces were moving toward the capital city, although he initially discounted missionaries' reports of Boxer violence. Once the Boxers arrived in Beijing civil unrest grew, and despite Cixi's eventual efforts to reign them in, it became clear that Qing officials could not control the Boxers. Small groups of American, Russian, British, French, German and Japanese servicemen fought street battles against

Boxer forces to gather other Westerners and Christian Chinese in the "Legation Quarter," a small area that housed most Western embassies. By June 1900 Conger was telegraphing Washington, D.C. requesting the dispatch of American troops to protect American citizens. Ministers of other countries made similar appeals. In July an allied force of 19,000 troops, including American Marines redeployed from the Philippines, landed and began to march toward Beijing. Boxers had destroyed many telegraph lines, and Conger was unable to contact Washington for several weeks, while the Legation Quarter was besieged by Boxer forces. Just before the allied column captured Beijing in mid-August, Conger was finally able to cable Washington, The Secretary of State, John Hay, suspected the message was a fake, and asked Conger to prove his identity by wiring back his sister's name. Conger replied that his sister was named "Alta." After American newspapers carried the story, along with news of the liberation of the besieged Americans, "Alta" became a popular and patriotic name for newborn American girls.

Conger remained in Beijing, where he and his wife Sarah were frequent visitors at Cixi's court, until their departure from China in 1905. Conger briefly served as U.S. Minister to Mexico in 1905, and died on May 18, 1907.

See also Boxer Rebellion (1900).

REFERENCES: Diana Preston, *The Boxer Rebellion: The Dramatic Story of China's War on Foreigners That Shook the World in the Summer of 1900* (New York, 2000), Sarah Pike Conger, *Letters From China: With Particular Reference to the Empress Dowager and the Women of China* (Chicago, IL, 1909).

Laura M. Calkins

Constructive Engagement *see* Engagement

Containment

Although U.S. statesmen and military strategists had begun articulating a policy of "containment" with regards to the Communist threat in the immediate aftermath of World War II, they focused their efforts on the Soviet Union. As a consequence, a Chinese Communist threat was overlooked until the entry of the People's Republic of China into the Korean War. Indeed, the Truman administration was ambivalent, initially, towards the new government of Mao Zedong. The People's Liberation Army offensive against the United Nations' forces in November 1950, however, surprised both the UN command and the Truman administration. The shock with which Washington greeted the Chinese offensive belied the United States' inability to understand China's role in global Communism, a failing that would characterize Sino-American relations until the early 1970s.

The escalation of U.S.-Soviet tensions from 1946 to 1949 resulted in the American presumption of Russian leadership in the Communist world. Their attention focused on Moscow, the Truman administration, as well as the American people, saw the hidden-hand of Soviet leader Joseph Stalin controlling events in all Communist nations. While this presumption held true for much of Eastern Europe it obscured the very nature of the relationship between Stalin and the Communist world's other leaders, Marshal Tito, of Yugoslavia, and Mao. Neither Tito nor Mao looked to Stalin for approval and both articulated a Communist view of their nations independent of Soviet control. Early on Truman realized that Tito acted independent of Stalin and U.S. policy became one of exacerbating Yugoslav-Soviet tensions whenever possible to minimize Soviet influence in the Balkans. A similar conclusion was not reached with regards to Mao and the United States' failure to recognize the Sino-Soviet rift had dire consequences for American foreign policy not only in Asia but also throughout the world.

Stalin's continued support for the Guomindang should have alerted U.S. analysts to Sino-Soviet divisions but American, as well as European, political leaders were blinkered to a monolithic view of Communism. Truman's ambiguous "two-China" policy presumed Moscow's control of Beijing. To prevent the escalation of the conflict in Korea to a global war, therefore, Truman minimized American support for the Republic of China (ROC) on Taiwan. Upon becoming president, Dwight D. Eisenhower, reversed his predecessor's policy with regards to Taiwan and intimated to the Chinese Communist leadership that the U.S. would countenance Taiwanese entry into the Korean War via an attack on the People's Republic of China. The cessation of hostilities in Korea shortly thereafter suggested the benefit of an aggressive policy of containment towards Beijing. Under Eisenhower, the United States adopted such a policy and sought diplomilitary measures to isolate the People's Republic of China (PRC).

As a result, U.S. analysts understood the conflicts in British Malaysia, Dutch Indonesia, and French Indochina as Beijing-led rather than independent, indigenous Communist movements. In doing so, however, the United States increased Beijing's influence and strengthened ties between the PRC and Asian Communist movements. The 1954 PRC-ROC clash over the islands of Jinmen and Mazu in the Taiwan Strait reaffirmed the correctness of containment for U.S. leaders. To contain Chinese influence and surround the PRC with its own non-Communist allies, the United States engineered the creation of the South East Asia Treaty Organization later in 1954. The following spring, Beijing sponsored the Bandung Conference, in Indonesia, of the unaligned nations in Africa and Asia. Rather than accept the conference for what it was, an attempt by Mao to increase Chinese influence and decrease that of the United States, as well as the Soviet Union, the Eisenhower administration viewed the conference as an attempt by Moscow to gain influence via a Chinese proxy.

Eisenhower, along with his next two successors, would continue to adhere to a policy of diplo-military containment with regards to China. The failure to understand the role of China in Asian affairs, especially in Vietnam, meant lost opportunities for the United States to avert costly wars. President Richard M. Nixon's national security advisor, Henry A. Kissinger, however, recognized the folly of containment. As the 1970s dawned, the United States, thus, began covert negotiations to establish diplomatic relations with the People's Republic of China and replace the policy of containment with one of detente. Kissinger's October 1971 trip to China marked the last days of containment, which ended with Nixon's China trip in February 1972.

See also Cold War; Detente; Nixon's Visit to China.

REFERENCES: Stephen E. Ambrose, *Eisenhower, Volume II: The President* (New York, 1983); Rosemary Foot, *The Practice of Power: U.S. Relations with China Since 1949* (Oxford, 1995); John Lewis Gaddis, *Strategies of Containment: A Critical Appraisal of Postwar American National Security Policy* (Oxford, 1982); June M. Grasso, *Truman's Two-China Policy* (Armonk, NY 1987); George C. Herring, Jr., *America's Longest War: The United States and Vietnam, 1950–1975* (Columbus, OH, 2001); Akira Iriye, *The Cold War in Asia: A Historical Introduction* (Englewood Cliffs, NJ, 1974); Shu Guang Zhang, *Deterrence and Strategic Culture: Chinese American Confrontations, 1949–1958* (Ithaca, NY, 1992).

Paul D. Gelpi, Jr.

Coolie Trade

The term "coolie trade" refers to the importation of Chinese laborers under the conditions of indenture. In exchange for passage from China, wages, and room and board, Chinese laborers in the 1840s and latter half of the 19th century agreed to work for five to eight years, usually for Caribbean and Latin American employers. Although this arrangement was ostensibly a contractual one in which both parties participated freely, many employers used fraudulent and coercive tactics to force the laborers to accept their terms. Some hired "brokers" or "recruiters" whose ruthless tactics included kidnapping Chinese workers to obtain rewards paid per capita.

This practice became common in the1840s and 1850s as the international slave trade dwindled, creating a demand for cheap labor in sugar and tobacco plantations, guano pits, and hotels. Conditions suffered by the Chinese workers were similar in many respects to those of African slaves — shipped aboard vessels with often deadly overcrowding, they arrived in the Caribbean and Latin America to find that the terms of their contracts were not upheld, and they were sold at auction or sent to perform grueling labor. Some scholars estimate that over half of the workers died before obtaining their freedom, from suffocation in the holds of ships, from overwork, and from suicide on learning that they would be virtually enslaved. The laws of the U.S. prohibited the importation of coolies inside its own borders, but many of the ships used in the trade between China and other nations were owned by American companies. Peter Parker, an American physician, Christian medical missionary, and diplomat, lobbied against the inhumanity of the coolie trade in opposition to the companies who profited by participating in it. Parker brought the attention of the United States government to the atrocities that were facilitated by American ships under American trade laws. American participation in the coolie trade ended in 1862 when Congress passed the Prohibition of Coolie Trade Act. In 1868, the Burlingame Treaty (the Supplementary Articles to the Treaty of Tianjin) formalized a relationship between the United States and China in which immigration would be permitted freely, importation by employers would be prohibited, and immigrants would be protected from exploitative practices.

The term "coolie" has also been applied to Indian workers imported along with Chinese laborers during the same period, as well as to Chinese immigrants in America. This latter use of the term is misleading: though some of these immigrants owed large debts for the price of their passage, they came voluntarily and worked freely.

See also Burlingame-Seward Treaty (1868).

REFERENCES: Robert J. Plowman, "The Voyage of the 'Coolie' Ship *Kate Hooper* October 3, 1857-March 26, 1858," *Prologue* (Summer 2001); Shih-Shan Henry Tsai, *The Chinese Experience in America* (Bloomington, IN, 1986).

Tara Robbins

Cox Report

In early 1998, reports began to surface that two U.S. aerospace companies, Hughes and Loral

Space and Communications, provided China with sensitive technical information after the failure of two Chinese Long March rockets carrying US-built satellites. The Loral and Hughes affairs gradually came to light arousing suspicion that U.S. national security interests were damaged. Following the exposure of the affairs, Congress set up the Cox Committee chaired by Congressman Christopher Cox to do investigation on U.S.-Chinese security interaction and make recommendations for official legislative and executive orders in areas such as exerting control over the export of sensitive technology, access to American national laboratories, and the handling of sensitive intelligence information. On December 31, 1998 the *New York Times* and the *Washington Post* carried news about the Cox Report on U.S. National Security and Military Commercial Concerns with the People's Republic of China. It was said that the 700-page report was unanimously approved by the committee. The report discussed how China had replaced the former Soviet Union as America's major military rival — and obtained the means to target missiles on U.S. cities, and how Beijing had pursued a systematic strategy of trade, influence-buying, and espionage to achieve their goal of nuclear leverage over the United States. The Cox Report also accused China of preparing for a war against the United States. The report concluded that since China established diplomatic relations with America in 1979, it had been involved in a serious and sustained effort to steal the most sensitive American military technology, including nuclear weapons designs and high-performance computers.

The Cox Report triggered a new "Red Scare" and witch-hunt at the U.S. National Weapons Laboratory and around the world. As a result FBI and CIA spent thousands of man-hours looking for Chinese spies. The Taiwan-born American scientist Wen-Ho Lee became a suspect during the witch-hunt and was arrested. Since no hard evidence was found against him, Wen was released with an apology from the judge overseeing the case.

See also Wen Ho Lee "Spy" Case.

REFERENCES: United States Congress, House Select Committee on U.S. National Security and Military/Commercial Concerns with the People's Republic of China, U.S. *National Security and Military/Commercial Concerns with the People's Republic of China* (Washington, DC, 1999).

Yuwu Song

Cultural Revolution (1966–1976)

Chinese Great Proletarian Cultural Revolution (1966–1976) was inaugurated by Chairman Mao Zedong of Chinese Communist Party (CCP) in order to purge "capitalist roaders" within the party, who, in Mao's perception, were heading towards capitalist path and thereby, hindering consolidation of socialist system as well as building up the national military and economic power.

The revolution was aimed at preventing the emergence of elitist and "bureaucratized Soviet style Communism." This was given effect by dislodging capitalist roaders from all positions of power in the government and party, persecuting a large number of officials in the CCP and the government, and transforming education, art, and literature on the pattern of socialist ideology. The first three years of the revolution were dominated by the Red Guards who unleashed bloody persecution of Chinese teachers and intellectuals in order to enforce Mao's "cult of personality." However, due to growing anarchy stemming from Red Guard factionalism, Mao ordered the People's Liberation Army (PLA) to suppress Red Guards, facilitating military's upper hand, though temporarily. Its influence faded away by early 1972 following the death of Lin Biao, Mao's successor and a PLA leader who turned Mao's would-be-assassin in 1971, paving the way for power struggle between radical forces and the moderates in the party. The situation took a drastic turn with the arrest of the radical "Gang of Four" in October 1976 by the moderate-led coalition, a month after Mao's death. This finally brought an end to the Cultural Revolution. If seen in hindsight, Mao's decision to launch the Cultural Revolution veered round attacking revisionist policies and rectifying the Soviet style of Communism. This eventually resulted in a severe deterioration in Sino-Soviet relations reinforced by Red Guard's besieging of the Soviet embassy and maltreating its diplomats. Though it might sound paradoxical, the fact remained that Cultural Revolution proved as a boon in improving the long tethered ties between China and the United States. The Johnson administration expressed its desire for improvement in Sino-U.S. relations. If seen in realistic perspective, it was during the consolidation period of the Cultural Revolution that China and America had begun normalizing their relations. This manifested from the U.S. recognition of "One China Policy" in 1972 and as a gesture of goodwill and friendship, China extended diplomatic support to the United States on certain issues in the United Nations. For instance, Mao's spokesman took an identical stance with that of its U.S. counterpart by legitimizing Pakistani military ruler Yahya Khan's iron handed approach to crush the liberation movement of Bangladeshi people during the internal turmoil ensuing during 1970–1971. On another crucial UN Security Council resolution demanding the Israeli withdrawal from Arab lands, the Mao's government, instead of supporting the just cause of Palestinians, toed the U.S.-pro Israel policy. These evidences suggest that in the realm of foreign policy, it was Mao's strategy to seek rapprochement with the U.S. as an anti-Soviet plank. While, the United States used the "China card" to cultivate the Soviet Union through its detente policy, resulting in the conclusion of the historic Strategic Arms Limitation Treaty (SALT I) with the Soviet Union in 1972.

While evaluating the Cultural Revolution in today's context, it is termed as the period of darkness and the "decade of chaos" that not only led to massacre of a large number of officials and intellectuals, but had also proved disastrous for China's economic development and its cultural life.

See also Mao Zedong (1893–1976); Chinese Communist Party (CCP).

REFERENCES: Wang Ming, *Mao's Betrayal* (Moscow, 1975); Jean Daubier, *A History of the Chinese Cultural Revolution* (New York, 1974); Hong Yong Lee, *The Politics of the Chinese Cultural Revolution* (Berkeley, CA, 1978).

Romi Jain

Cushing, Caleb (1800–1879)

Caleb Cushing was an American statesman and diplomat who signed the first American treaty with China in 1844. Caleb Cushing was born in Salisbury, Massachusetts on January 17, 1800. His father, John Newmarch Cushing, was a well-to-do merchant and ship owner who was engaged in the lucrative China trade. His mother, Lydia Dow, died when Caleb was ten years old. In 1802 his family moved to nearby Newburyport, a prosperous shipping town. After graduating from Harvard in 1817, Caleb taught mathematics and natural sciences for two years at his alma mater. Later he studied law and was admitted to the state bar in 1821. Three years later he was elected to the lower house of the Massachusetts legislature, and in 1826 became a state senator. In 1834 he was elected to the U.S. Congress, where he served for four consecutive terms until 1843. Later under President John Tyler he was nominated for Secretary of the Treasury, but the Senate refused to confirm him.

Following China's defeat in the First Opium War (1839–1842) and the signing of the Treaty of Nanjing (1842), the United States began making plans to send a diplomatic representative to negotiate a commercial treaty with China. On May 8, 1843, President Tyler appointed Cushing the first American commissioner to China. Leaving America in July, his small fleet reached Macao in late February 1844. Although the Chinese had already informally granted Americans and other foreigners most-favored-nation privileges, Cushing had been instructed to negotiate a new, separate American treaty. For their part the Chinese authorities in Guangdong stalled talks with the American commissioner for several months, and in retaliation Cushing threatened to sail to Beijing and deal directly with the Chinese emperor. Anxious to avoid further trouble, Qiying, the Chinese imperial commissioner, arrived in Macao and soon afterwards in the nearby village of Wangxia both men signed the Cushing or Wangxia Treaty on July 3, 1844. With the Senate's approval the treaty was formally proclaimed on April 18, 1846. The Cushing Treaty was basically a summary, with some important refinements, of the treaty that China had signed with Britain two years earlier. Cushing's treaty opened up five Chinese ports to American merchants, settled many disputed points regarding tariff and trade regulations, and established the important principle of extraterritoriality, specifying that American citizens living in China should be subject to the exclusive jurisdiction of U.S. laws and courts. By giving explicit definition to extraterritoriality the Cushing Treaty proved to be of great value to all foreigners, because by the most-favored-nations clause the privileges granted to the U.S. were automatically bestowed on other treaty powers. Extraterritoriality, perhaps the most important provision in the treaty, not only provided legal protection to American citizens in China, but also served as an important vehicle for the expansion of Western trade and influence in that country as well.

Cushing left China on August 27, 1844, and after touring America for a few years was once again elected to the Massachusetts legislature in 1847. An avid expansionist, he raised and financed with his own money a regiment, which he led personally during the Mexican War (1847). Between 1850 and 1868, Cushing held a number of public offices both in his home state and in Washington. During the last years of his public career he served as special envoy to Colombia in 1868, and minister to Spain from 1874 to 1877. He died at his home on High Street in Newburyport on January 2, 1879.

See also Treaty of Wangxia (1844); Extraterritoriality.

REFERENCES: Claude Moore Fuess, *The Life of Caleb Cushing* (New York, 1923); P. C. Kuo, "Caleb Cushing and the Treaty of Wangxia," *Journal of Modern History* Vol. 5 (1933); Michael Hunt, *The Making of a Special Relationship* (New York, 1983).

Robert J. Antony

Cushing's Treaty *see* Treaty of
Wangxia (1844).

Dalai Lama (1935-)

The Dalai Lama is the traditional spiritual and political leader of Tibet, as well as the head of the *dge lugs pa* order of Tibetan Buddhists. *Dalai Lama* is often translated as meaning "Ocean of Wisdom." *Dalai* is from Mongolian and means "Ocean" and *Lama* is a traditional Tibetan title for religious teachers. Altan Khan, a Mongolian leader, was the first to use the title referring to his teacher, Sonam Gyatso, who is considered to be the third Dalai Lama. The title was then posthumously applied to his two predecessors. Tibetan Buddhists believe that the Dalai Lamas are the reincarnated physical manifestations of the compassionate bodhisattva Avalokitesvara. After the death of a Dalai Lama, his monks begin searching for his reincarnation, guided through the use of dreams and oracles. When a child is found that appears to be a candidate, the monks test to see if the child can differentiate between the belongings of the previous Dalai Lama and other objects. Once a child is recognized as the incarnation of the Dalai Lama, he is taken to a monastery to be trained as a Buddhist monk. To date, there have been fourteen Dalai Lamas: Gendun Drup (1391–1474), Gendun Gyatso (1476–1542), Sonam Gyatso (1543–1588), Yonten Gyatso (1589–1616), Lozang Gyatso (1617–1682), Tsangyang Gyatso (1683–1706), Kelsang Gyatso (1708–1757), Jampel Gyatso (1758–1804), Lungtok Gyatso (1805–1815), Tsultrim Gyatso (1816–1837), Khedrub Gyatso (1855–1856), Trinlay Gyatso (1856–1875), Tubten Gyatso (1876–1933), and Tenzin Gyatso (1935–present). Scholars in the People's Republic of China regard the thirteenth Dalai Lama, Tubten Gyatso, as a Chinese patriot. He attempted to enact social reforms and also led the effort to limit the expansion of British influence into Tibet from India. However, globally his successor has become the best-known member of the line of Dalai Lamas.

Tenzin Gyatso was born in 1935 and ascended as the fourteenth Dalai Lama in February of 1940. When the Communist Party gained control of China, Mao Zedong declared that Tibet had always been an integral part of China and, in 1950, sent the People's Liberation Army into the region to assert the claim. At the time, the Dalai Lama had not yet assumed his full religious and political responsibilities. He assumed power in November 1950, at the age of sixteen, in hopes that Tibet could retain its autonomy. The following year, China pressured Tibet to sign the Seventeen Point Agreement that declared that Tibet was a part of China. Following an unsuccessful revolt in 1959, the Dalai Lama fled to Dharamsala, India, where he set up a government-in-exile. He has traveled around the world lecturing on Buddhism and speaking out against Chinese mistreatment of the Tibetan people. The Dalai Lama has encouraged the use of non-violent means to attain a form of self-government for Tibet, and was awarded the Nobel Peace Prize for his efforts in 1989. He has expressed a willingness to accept that Tibet is part of China, in exchange for assurance of some self-government for the province and preservation of Tibetan cultural distinctiveness.

The policy of the United States does not recognize Tibet as an independent state. Therefore, the Dalai Lama is not accorded the status of a head of state in exile. However, this has not kept him from meeting with important officials in the U.S. Government, including the President during his frequent visits to the United States. In his capacity as a Nobel laureate and religious leader, the Dalai Lama has met with a number of U.S. officials to voice his concerns about conditions in Tibet. The U.S. government regularly criticizes China for human rights violations in Tibet, and has continued to press the People's Republic to resolve the outstanding issues on Tibet through a dialog with the Dalai Lama or his representatives.

See also Tibet.

REFERENCES: Ram Rahul, *The Dalai Lama: The Institution* (New Delhi, 1995); Ya Hanzhang, *The Biographies of the Dalai Lamas* (Beijing, 1991); Gareth Sparham, "Dalai Lama," *Encyclopedia of Buddhishm* (New York, 2004); Thubten Samphel, *The Dalai Lamas of Tibet* (New Delhi, 2000); Government of Tibet in Exile Website, *www.tibet.com*.

Anne M. Platoff

Davies, John P. (1908–1999)

Part of the group of American diplomats known as the China Hands during the 1930s and 1940s, John P. Davies was intimately involved with the American diplomatic effort in China for almost twenty years, participating in the "Dixie Mission" and serving under American General Joseph W. Stillwell during the Second World War.

John Paton Davies, Jr. was born in Jiading, Sichuan Province, China, in 1908, to missionary parents. Growing up in China during the 1920s, Davies witnessed the country in conflict and became familiar with Chinese culture, history, and politics. Receiving part of his college education at Yenching University in Beijing, Davies traveled to the United States and received a degree from Columbia University in 1931. He immediately took the Foreign Service examination and entered the

U.S. Foreign Service, returning to Asia to serve in a variety of posts until the Japanese attack on Pearl Harbor in December of 1941. During the Second World War, Davies served as a political aide to U.S. General Joseph Stillwell, who was in command of the China-Burma-India Theater. In October of 1944, Davies took part in the famously unsuccessful "Dixie Mission" in Yanan, led by U.S. Colonel David D. Barrett in an attempt to reconcile the Chinese Communist and Chinese Nationalist governments. Accompanied to Yanan by other American diplomats, as well as American journalist Teddy White, Davies' involvement in the mission would prove fateful. Davies began to form the opinion that Nationalist leader Jiang Jieshi was a marginally useful ally for the United States, and wrote memos recommending that the U.S. should attempt to establish some sort of diplomatic contact with the Chinese Communists. Davies also disregarded the commonly held wisdom that Soviet and Chinese Communism were monolithic in their unity and singular in their purpose. In 1945, Davies became the First Secretary at the U.S. embassy in Moscow. In 1947, he was recalled to the United States to become a member of the Policy Planning Staff in the U.S. State Department, working under George Kennan. Beginning in 1948, however, with the accusation of Patrick Hurley, former U.S. ambassador to China, that Davies and other China Hands had "lost" China to the Chinese Communists, Davies was subjected to repeated investigations and reassigned to Lima, Peru. At the urging of U.S. senator Joseph McCarthy, Davies was investigated a ninth and final time in 1954, and found guilty of "lack of judgment, discretion, and reliability." U.S. Secretary of State John Foster Dulles urged Davies to resign and avoid embarrassment, but fired him when Davies refused. Davies and his family lived in Peru and ran a furniture business until 1964, when they returned to the United States and Davies began actively trying to clear his name.

The State Department reexamined Davies case in 1968 and cleared him of any wrongdoing, fourteen years after his expulsion. John Paton Davies, Jr. died in Ashville, North Carolina in December of 1999.

See also China Hands; Stillwell, Joseph W. (1883–1946).

REFERENCES: John P. Davies, *Dragon by the Tail: American, British, Japanese, and Russian Encounters With China and One Another* (New York, 1972); David Halberstam, *The Best and the Brightest* (New York, 1972); E.J. Kahn, Jr., *The China Hands: America's Foreign Service Men and What Befell Them* (New York, 1975); Barbara J. Tuchman, *Stillwell and the American Experience in China, 1911–1945* (New York, 1971).

Robert Elder

Democracy Wall Movement (1978–1979)

The Democracy Wall Movement developed in Beijing by grassroots groups in late 1978 and coincided with economic reforms—The Four Modernizations—advanced by Chinese leader Deng Xiaoping. The period also marked the end of the Chinese Great Proletarian Cultural Revolution and a period of tolerance developed referred to as the Beijing Spring. The Democracy Wall is a wall located in Xidan District in Beijing and it became symbol of the demonstrations demanding democratic political changes. Encouraged by the April 5, 1976 demonstrations in Tiananmen Square ostensibly to honor Premier Zhou Enlai who died in January 1976, the actual public protest was criticism of the abuses during the Cultural Revolution and the "Gang of Four," the radicals. This event signaled one of the first demonstrations in China where citizens took to the streets to publicly share their political opinions. Initially, criticism was aimed at the party's practice in allowing a monopoly of power enjoyed by an elite leadership that was assured positions for life.

The Democracy Wall Movement was the second political movement that criticized the excesses of the Cultural Revolution's absence of human and democratic rights and that permitted torture and mayhem. At the heart of the criticism was the demand for democratic political reforms to allow Chinese citizens expanded human rights, democratic elections, and social and political freedom. Other criticisms were directed at the condemnation of the "Gang of Four" that sought to continue the destructive Maoist revolutionary policies after his death. The activists defended their protests as an expression of their constitutional rights. The 1978 Constitution of the People's Republic of China guaranteed four key rights, freedom of speech, to discuss views publicly, to conduct discussion/debates and free written expression in wall-posters. In 1980, after the movement was repressed, the National People's Congress approved the party's legal revision to deny the four key rights as well as the right to strike. This shows that the party felt open discussions turned criticism toward the Communist Party and its leadership, weakening its legitimacy to maintain political solidarity. The Xidan Wall became the location where political activists initiated debates, framed political issues and was the source of underground magazines and flyers. Since many of the activists were previous Red Guards along with workers they adopted the same struggle strategies they used against the so-called bourgeoisie-leaning establishment during the Cultural Revolution. Displaying the big-character poster was the initial practice that served as a catalyst to encourage many activists to publicly exchange individual political views.

Based on the contagion around the wall, smaller networks of groups spontaneously developed and coordinated around common issues. These groups engaged in extensive poster writing, distributing pamphlets, and publishing black market magazines and literary works. This spread the democratic ideals of the movement far beyond the small number of activists. By 1979 The Democracy Wall Movement spread to several cities including Shanghai and Guangzhou, echoing activist's complaints of abuses of the Cultural Revolution and concerns with economic and political issues. The Fifth Modernization wall poster authored by Wei Jingsheng gained widespread public notice for emphasizing that individual freedom was much more important than Dengist reforms concentrating on economic growth. The Democracy Wall Movement took a serious turn when Wei Jingsheng, also the editor of an underground magazine *Explorations*, severely criticized Deng Xiaoping and called for the overthrow of the party, and the addition of democracy as the fifth modernization (to add to the Four Modernizations inaugurated by the party). Wei was promptly arrested and following a showcase trial received a fifteen-year prison sentence. The party stepped up crackdowns with arrests and imprisonment of other leader-activists as it shut down the Democracy Wall Movement. Considered as an inspiration to other activists the democracy movement and Wei in particular were issues spawning the Tiananmen Square Protests in 1989. Following a severe crackdown involving military intervention resulting in many activists' deaths, was an intermission in economic reforms. Eventually the democratic movement in China has become splintered if not moribund. While draconian steps ended the movement recent social changes in China may cause the movement to remain weak. Scholars report recent relaxation allowing more political expression during the post-Deng era, while reframing commonly used Western language of the pro-democracy protests as "incidents."

Activists in the movements had some memory of the abuses of the Cultural Revolution unlike the younger generation. They have a greater trust of the government and do not fear the resurgence of the disastrous Maoist programs of the past. The aims of the movement being revolutionary demanded an immediate change toward democracy, which many view as too confrontational. In contrast the Chinese government continues to emphasize economic modernization with much more gradual relaxation on legal human rights restrictions.

See also Wei Jingsheng (1950-); Beijing Spring; Cultural Revolution; Four Modernizations; Tiananmen Square Massacre (1989).

REFERENCES: Immanuel C.Y. Hsu, *China Without Mao: The Search for a New Order* (New York, 1990); Craig J. Calhoun, *Neither Gods Nor Emperors: Students and The Struggle for Democracy in China* (Berkeley, CA, 1994); Andrew J. Lathan and Perry Link, *The Tiananmen Papers: Compiled by Zhang Liang* (New York, 2001).

Jim Steinberg

Democratic People's Republic of Korea (DPRK)

Throughout the Korean War and the Cold War that followed, the Democratic People's Republic of Korea (DPRK) or North Korea has been the focus of attention in Northeast Asia between the United States and the People's Republic of China (PRC) as the competing Cold War interests sought to exert influence on the reclusive regime at the center of Northeast Asia.

The founding of the Democratic People's Republic of Korea and the People's Republic of China is closely intertwined. During the Chinese Civil War of 1945–1949, North Korea provided a secure base and staging ground in crucial battles against the Nationalists while as many as 100,000 Koreans fought in the Chinese Communist People's Liberation Army (PLA). In the aftermath of victory of the People's Liberation Army and the establishment of the People's Republic of China in October 1949, many of the Korean troops returned home in hope of liberating Korea. The confrontation between the United States and China over North Korea began at the onset of the Korean War as the United States sought to contain the Communist threat in Asia. Fearing the establishment of a Soviet satellite in Northeast Asia, the United States intervened militarily in the Korean civil war in support of the right-wing government of President Syngman Rhee. Tension gradually built between the United States and China during the early stages of the Korean War as United Nations troops ignored repeated Chinese warnings to halt their advances past the 38th parallel. The continued advance of United Nations troops towards the Yalu River frontier of China triggered a massive Chinese offensive as a 250,000 Chinese "volunteers" crossed the Yalu River in support of Kim Il Sung's beleaguered Korean People's Army. The ensuing military stalemate eventually led to the cessation of hostilities and the solidified the hitherto disputed borders and the permanent division of the Korean Peninsula at the 38th Parallel. Even as hostilities ensued between the United States and China in the years following the Korean War and ensuing Cold War, North Korea adopted an increasingly isolationist policy known as *Juche* (self-reliance). During China's Cultural Revolution, relations between North Korea and China became strained as North Korea criticized China for its hard-line policies while the Chinese Red Guards denounced Kim Il Sung. As a consequence, Chinese aid to North Korea declined substantially. In the years following the Cultural Revolution relations between the PRC and the DPRK improved as Kim Il Sung and Deng Xiaoping sought to normalize relations.

The end of the Cold War saw a softening in the American position towards China vis-à-vis North Korea as the United States and China shared a common interest — stability on the Korean Peninsula — while preserving nuclear nonproliferation. The North Korean nuclear crisis of 1993–1994 provided an opportunity for the former Cold War adversaries to work together. Viewing China as a key player on the Korean Peninsula, the United States sought China's help in seeking a comprehensive settlement of Korean Peninsula issues. Both the United States and China were involved in Four Party Talks process with North Korea. This has, in effect, led China to be a more active participant in international diplomacy. Yet, the level of influence China exerts on North Korean behavior seems to have limits as characterized by the Yang Bin incident in October 1992. China's engagement in inter-Korean relations and its efforts to influence North Korea reflects both its long-term strategic interest and sense of concern regarding a strong U.S. influence on the Korean Peninsula.

See also Korean War; Republic of Korea (ROK); North Korean Nuclear Controversy.

REFERENCES: Lee Chae-Jin, "The Koreans in China: Identity and Adaptation," *Korea and World Affairs* (Fall, 1989); Han S. Park, *China and North Korea: Politics of Integration and Modernization* (Hong Kong, 1990); Suh Dae-Sook and Edward J. Schultz, *Koreans in China* (Honolulu, HW, 1990).

Keith Leitich

Democratic Progressive Party (DPP)

The Democratic Progressive Party (DPP) was founded in 1986. It was a product of Taiwanese nativism or nationalism as it is called by the native Taiwanese. The islanders believed that it was they who owned the natural rights to rule their homeland, not the groups of non-Taiwanese origin. This sense of nativism originated and grew during the Japanese colonial period from 1895 to 1945. After the Japanese left, the government of the Republic of China (ROC) based on mainland China took over the island. In February 1947, clashes occurred between the native Taiwanese and the Guomindang (GMD) government over the rights of the natives. The GMD central government in Nanjing ordered troops to crush the riots and regained the control of Taiwan.

In 1949, Jiang Jieshi's Nationalist regime retreated to Taiwan after losing the civil war to the Communists who founded the People's Republic of China (PRC) on the mainland. With an army of one million strong, the GMD firmly controlled the island. However, the Taiwanese nativist pro-independence movement never died. In 1965, one spiritual leader of the movement, Peng Min-Ming preached Taiwanese nationalism at National Taiwan University, but shortly afterwards he was forced to flee to the United States. The movement went underground until the mid 1970s. Two years after Jiang Jieshi died in 1975, popular demands for Taiwanese rights culminated in a riot at Chung Li City. More severe clashes occurred at Gaoxiong in December 1979. These events showed that it had become more and more difficult for the GMD to rule the island. The early 1980s witnessed the rise of a new class of Taiwanese elites with elevated political and socioeconomic status. The Nationalist regime tried to absorb the new island elites into the government, but opposition forces would not allow this. They quickly formed the Democratic Progressive Party in 1986 and gained 25% of the vote in Taiwan. Ironically, the Nationalist President Li Denghui, who succeeded President Jiang Jingguo in 1988, cooperated with the DPP. The DPP steadily grew and became the most influential opposition party on the island in the 1990s. The mainlanders and their second generation were systemically purged from important government positions. Taiwan was being "nativized" and moved toward independence.

In the 1970s, the nativist movement in Taiwan presented a dilemma for the United States. On the one hand, in the context of the Cold War, Washington needed the GMD government to side with the United States, on the other hand, Americans found that they should support the natives' demands for democracy and freedom and their challenge to the autocratic GMD regime. After the founding of the DPP, more and more Americans were attracted to the party's ideals of political liberalization. By the 1990s, the DPP, the leading party of the independence movement, had developed a close relationship with many American politicians. They helped establish pro-independence student and immigrant organizations and infiltrated into American politics by forming a powerful lobby.

In 2000, the pro-independence DPP leader Chen Shuibian won the presidential election in Taiwan, and was reelected in 2004. It has become clear that the Democratic Progressive Party has evolved into one of the leading forces to shape Taiwan's future. These developments presented a more difficult problem for the cross-strait and PRC-U.S. relations for years to come.

See also Chen Shuibian (1951-).

REFERENCES: Jason C. Hu (ed.), *Quiet Revolution on Taiwan, Republic of China* (Taibei, 1994); Academia Historica, *Documentary Collection on Democratization Movement of Postwar Taiwan* (Taibei, 2000).

Hsiang-Wang Liu

Denby, Charles (1830–1904)

A prominent American diplomat, Charles Denby was born in Virginia and attended college at Georgetown College in Washington, DC, and the Virginia Military Institute. After several years spent as a teacher, he moved to Evansville, Indiana in 1853 to study law and work as an editor for the Democratic *Daily Enquirer*. He was admitted to the bar in 1855 and then elected to the Indiana legislature in 1856. In 1858 he married Martha Fitch the daughter of Senator Graham Fitch.

With the outbreak of the U.S. Civil War in 1861, Denby volunteered for the Union cause. He rose to the rank of Colonel but was discharged in 1863 after being wounded at the Battle of Perryville in Kentucky. He returned to Evansville and over the next twenty years became a successful railroad lawyer and an influential power broker in the Democratic Party. In 1884 Denby supported fellow Indianan Thomas Hendricks for the Democratic vice-presidential nomination on a ticket headed by Grover Cleveland. Cleveland rewarded Denby by appointing him minister to China on May 29, 1885. Denby retained the post through Cleveland's administration, through the subsequent administration of Benjamin Harrison, through Cleveland's second administration and finally through the first year of William McKinley's administration. He resigned his post in August 1898 after thirteen years, an extended period in diplomatic service. At the time of Denby's appointment Chinese relations were becoming increasingly important to the U.S. There was talk of Chinese plans for a national railroad system and Denby, because of his background, was supported by American railroad interests. He was regarded, at least initially and informally, as a promoter of American economic influence in China and sought to gain railroad contracts for American businesses. Denby saw China not only as a boon to American railroad companies, but saw railroad construction as part of a larger plan to dominate the Chinese market which he believed to be a natural extension of the American commercial sphere and a necessary outlet for American overproduction. Denby could not organize the railroad construction project within the terms placed by the Chinese, much to the disappointment of American interests, but Chinese authorities adopted Denby's plan, forming the China Railway Company under a charter based on the railroad incorporation laws of Indiana. Denby's failure to gain ground in China for American corporations was a challenge to his belief that Western civilization was superior to Eastern civilization. However, despite his embrace of Social Darwinism, Denby condemned tactics that he felt violated the spirit of international law. For instance he opposed the Chinese exclusion acts from both a legal stand and out of a fear that such legislation would hurt trade between the countries.

The Sino-Japanese War of 1894–1895, and Denby's role as a supposedly neutral negotiator, gave him renewed opportunities to push his commercial agenda. China's loss to the Japanese saddled the nation with war indemnities, which Denby knew could most readily be met by licensing franchises to American business interests. Here, too, however Denby's assistance to American economic interests was generally unsuccessful, both because of lack of support from the State Department and antagonism from the Chinese, adding to his fears that more organized powers such as the British and the Russians would divide China between them. Not unrelated to his attention to commercial interests, Denby was also a strong supporter of American missionaries in China. Although, as a public official he did not discuss their religious work, he looked upon missionaries as agents of trade who acted as forerunners of commerce. He also considered their humanitarian work a form of compensation for wrongs committed by foreign nations. Privately, he often did not support specific missionary acts that he thought threatened goodwill between the nations. Publicly, he backed missionary claims to preserve the image of American strength and he advocated gunboat diplomacy to suppress antiforeign riots, such as those that broke out along the Yangzi River in 1891.

Upon his retirement from the diplomatic post, Denby was appointed by President William McKinley to the Philippine commission following the Spanish-American War. He died after giving a lecture in Jamestown, New York on January 13, 1904.

REFERENCES: David L. Anderson, *Imperialism and Idealism: American Diplomats in China, 1861–1898* (Bloomington, IN, 1985); David Healy, *U.S. Expansion-*

ism; the Imperialist Urge in the 1890s (Madison, WI, 1970).

Linus Kafka

De-neutralization of the Taiwan Strait

On February 2, 1952, President Dwight D. Eisenhower announced that he was ordering removal of the U.S. Seventh Fleet from the Taiwan Strait. This action reversed President Harry S. Truman's directive of June 27, 1950 at the start of the Korean War that U.S. naval forces should protect Taiwan from any Communist invasion and also required the fleet to prevent Nationalist attacks from the island against the mainland. Republican partisans and American supporters of Jiang Jieshi, leader of the Guomindang government exiled on Taiwan, criticized "neutralization" with increasing intensity, especially after the People's Republic of China (PRC) intervened in Korea late in 1950. At Senate Hearings regarding his recall in May 1951, General Douglas MacArthur had advocated reversal of the policy. A year later, John Foster Dulles in an article in *Life* magazine had called for "de-neutralization" as part of a global U.S. offensive urging people living in Soviet bloc countries to rebel and overthrow Communist domination.

In the 1952 presidential campaign, Republican candidate Dwight D. Eisenhower threatened to "unleash" Jiang's forces to place pressure on Communist China to accept a settlement in the Korean War. He visited Korea after his election, fulfilling a campaign pledge, where U.S. military leaders told him that de-neutralization might force China to redeploy troops from Korea to the southeast coast. But the State Department warned that risking a wider war would alienate U.S. allies. During the return trip, Dulles, who would become Secretary of State, probably secured Eisenhower's approval for de-neutralization when the two conferred on board the cruiser *Helena*. Two weeks after his inauguration, President Eisenhower in his first State of the Union address declared that he was "issuing instructions that the Seventh Fleet no longer be employed to shield Communist China." He denied that this indicated any aggressive intentions against China.

Republicans applauded Eisenhower's announcement, while Democrats expressed misgivings. Press and radio commentary was overwhelmingly positive. The British were very critical, despite U.S. assurances that it would not condone an attack on the mainland. The Guomindang government issued a brief and restrained official statement that praised de-neutralization as "not only judicious but militarily and morally sound." However, the Nationalist foreign ministry instructed its representatives abroad to avoid any suggestions that an assault on the mainland was imminent. The PRC refused to dismiss Eisenhower's remarks as propaganda and placed its forces on alert. "We desire peace," Mao Zedong stated five days later, "but as long as American imperialism does not discard its barbaric and unreasonable demands and its plots to expand its aggression, the resolution of the Chinese people can only be to continue to fight together with the Korean people to end it." At the truce talks, the Chinese informed the U.S. delegation that the Communist side would wait for acceptance of its terms before agreeing to resume negotiations.

Eisenhower wrote in his memoirs that de-neutralization helped force the PRC to accept an armistice in Korea. No evidence exists to support his claim that Beijing feared it could not count on past U.S. restraint. By contrast, Dulles admitted later that the main motivation was domestic politics. "Unleashing" the Nationalists for an attack against the mainland would demonstrate the administration's commitment to achieving its campaign pledges to follow an assertive Asia policy and act boldly to end the Korean War. In fact, the change in China policy was symbolic rather than real. Both Eisenhower and Dulles saw Europe as the prime battleground of Cold War. Neither had any intention to support a Nationalist attempt to re-conquer the mainland. Charge Karl L. Rankin quickly obtained Jiang's informal promise that he would take no major military actions without consulting the United States, an assurance that became a formal commitment two months later. New instructions for U.S. advisors cautioned against engaging in any "precipitate action" that might expand the war with China. Most important, none of the administration's plans for ending the Korean War provided for use of Nationalists troops, whether on the mainland or in Korea. De-neutralization poisoned American politics and Sino-American relations because it kept alive the dream that the Guomindang would again rule all of China.

See also **Neutralization of Taiwan**.

REFERENCES: Robert D. Accinelli, *Crisis and Commitment: United States Policy toward Taiwan, 1950–1955* (Chapel Hill, NC, 1996); Robert J. Caridi, *The Korean War and American Politics: The Republican Party as a Case Study* (Philadelphia, PE, 1968); Dwight D. Eisenhower, *The White House Years: Mandate for Change, 1953–1956* (Garden City, NY, 1963); Karl L. Rankin, *China Assignment* (Seattle, WA, 1964); Qiang Zhai, *The Dragon, the Lion, and the Eagle: Chinese-British-American Relations, 1949–1958* (Kent, OH, 1994).

James I. Matray

Deng Xiaoping (1904–1997)

As one of the most important Chinese Communist leaders in the 20th century, Deng joined the "Chinese Communist Young League in Europe" in 1923. After his return to China, he organized uprisings in Guangxi in 1929 and became a commander and political commissar in the Red Army from 1930 to 1936 and served as an officer at the headquarters of the Eighth Route Army in 1937–1945 during World War II. He led his troops across the Yellow River in 1947 against Guomindang (GMD) offensive campaigns during the Chinese Civil War. His Second Field Army Group and his "Huaihai Campaign" in 1948–1949 eliminated more than half a million GMD troops and enabled Mao to press on to a national victory.

After the founding of the People's Republic of China (PRC) in 1949, Deng became vice premier in 1954 and General Secretary of the Central Committee of the Chinese Communist Party (CCP) in 1954–1966. He was purged in 1966 along with Liu Shaoqi by Mao as the head of the "Bourgeoisie Headquarters within the party" and ousted from the PRC and CCP hierarchy during the Cultural Revolution. Deng was back in power and resumed his vice premier post in 1973. He became the vice chairman of the Central Military Commission (CMC), chief of general staff of the People's Liberation Army (PLA), vice chairman of the Central Committee, and member of the Politburo Standing Committee in 1975. He was dismissed again in April 1976 from all of his posts and faced an anti-Deng campaign until Mao died and the radical "Gang of Four" was arrested later that year.

Following a third comeback as vice premier with firm control of Beijing in 1977, Deng made a historic speech, "Emancipate the Mind," at the Third Plenary Session of the Eleventh Central Committee in 1978 — a declaration of unprecedented seismic reform and an opening to the outside world to bring the Four Modernizations to China. He announced that China and the U.S. would establish full diplomatic relations on January 1, 1979. To achieve economic growth, he emphasized international peace and cooperation, and developed close relations with the U.S. In 1979 he paid a state visit as the first PRC top leader to America, holding talks with Jimmy Carter and signing protocols. His efforts led to the development of full relations between the two countries, including trade, education, technology, and cultural exchanges. Later, Deng met Ronald Reagan and George Bush in Beijing during their state visits, and became CMC chairman in 1981. Deng began negotiations with the British in 1982 over Hong Kong and with the Portuguese for Macao's return. He developed a theory of "one country, two systems" to apply to these territories and Taiwan for peaceful reunification. Meanwhile, a rapid increase of cross-strait trade, visits, and exchanges occurred, and multi-level official talks began between Beijing and Taibei in 1980s. By joining many world organizations and signing numerous treaties with foreign governments, Deng tried to keep China within the international system so as to seek maximum opportunities. In 1987 he resigned from the Central Committee along with other conservative senior party members to ensure continuity of his reform. Retired from official posts, Deng remained in power when the third generation of Chinese leaders faced many difficulties in the late 1980s. The reform was, in Deng's words, to "cross the river by feeling the stones." Unable to solve the reform problems and unwilling to carry it into political aspect, he and other leaders in the summer of 1989 were challenged by pro-democracy student demonstrations asking for political reforms and protesting against corruption. It was approved by Deng that PLA soldiers were ordered to open fire on the students in Beijing on June 4, 1989.

Deng continued his reform with a new theory of "building socialism with Chinese characteristics" in 1992. His health problem soon reduced his active political role. Parkinson's disease and lung ailments made him nearly blind and deaf by the mid-1990s. He died in Beijing on February 28, 1997.

See also Tiananmen Square Massacre.

REFERENCES: Benjamin Yang, *Deng: A Political Biography* (Armonk, NY, 1998); Merle Goldman, *Sowing the Seeds of Democracy in China: Political Reform in the Deng Xiaoping Era* (Cambridge, MA, 1994); Lucian W. Pye, *The Spirit of Chinese Politics* (Cambridge, MA, 1992).

Li Xiaobing

Detente

From the late 1940s onward, U.S. policy towards the People's Republic of China (PRC) was one of containment. The thaw in the Cold War characterized by the spirit of detente embodied in the relationship between the Nixon administration and the Soviet Union under the leadership of Leonid Brezhnev and Alexei Kosygin during the late 1960s and early 1970s, along with the continued Vietnam War prompted President Richard Nixon's National Security Advisor, Henry A. Kissinger, to reevaluate Sino-American relations. Kissinger recognized that Moscow and Beijing were more adversaries than allies with military clashes along the Sino-Soviet border and their competition for influence in Hanoi. In the establishment of relations with Beijing, Kissinger saw a way to limit Moscow's influence in Asia, obtain a satisfactory outcome in Southeast Asia, and secure a Chinese counterbalance to the growing power of Hanoi. As the 1970s dawned, the United States, thus, began covert negotiations to establish diplomatic relations with the PRC and replace the policy of containment with one of detente. Kissinger's October 1971 trip to China marked the last days of containment, and the era of detente began with Nixon's China trip in February 1972. The emergence of detente in Asia, however, marked the apex of detente with regards to U.S.-Soviet relations.

The withdrawal of the last U.S. troops from Vietnam and the return of a portion of those U.S. servicemen held as prisoners of war by the Hanoi government eased Sino-American tensions further. The continued U.S. support of Pakistan, a Chinese ally, moreover, furthered a rapprochement but Sino-American diplomacy remained characterized by mutual distrust. At issue was the United States' Mutual Defense Treaty with Taiwan. Further complicating Sino-American relations was Beijing's support of the Democratic People's Republic of Korea and the permanent U.S. military presence in the Republic of Korea. Nevertheless, the 1970s marked a new era in Sino-American diplomacy.

With the Chinese chastisement of Vietnam for its invasion of Cambodia detente assumed a new meaning for Beijing and Washington. Whereas U.S. military aid to Taiwan had been marked by an indifference to Beijing's security concerns, increasingly American armaments were withheld from Taibei lest they upset the delicate balance of power in the Taiwan Strait. Chinese exportation of military equipment to nations hostile to the United States threatened to undo detente, however.

The collapse of the Soviet Union and the end of the U.S.-Soviet Cold War, in the early 1990s, demonstrated another shift in Sino-American relations. Although economic exchanges between the two countries increased as the 20th century gave way to the 21st, the bombing of the Chinese Embassy in Belgrade in1999, the discovery of Chinese attempts to secure American nuclear weapons technology, the downing of an American spy plane, and an increasingly belligerent Democratic People's Republic of Korea, all increased tensions. Yet, the spirit of detente continued to characterize the relationship between Beijing and Washington.

See also Cold War; Containment; Nixon's Visit to China; Nixon, Richard (1913–1994); Kissinger, Henry (1923-).

REFERENCES: Warren I. Cohen, *America's Response to China: A History of Sino-American Relations* (New York, 2000); Rosemary Foot, *The Practice of Power: U.S. Relations with China Since 1949* (Oxford, 1995); John Lewis Gaddis, *Strategies of Containment: A Critical Appraisal of Postwar American National Security Policy* (Oxford, 1982); George C. Herring, Jr., *America's Longest War: The United States and Vietnam, 1950–1975* (Columbus, OH, 2001); Akira Iriye, *The Cold War in Asia: A Historical Introduction* (Englewood Cliffs, NJ, 1974).

Paul D. Gelpi, Jr.

Dewey, John (1859–1952)

Prominent educator and "pragmatism" philosopher John Dewey traveled to Japan with his wife in 1919. In response to request from former students at Columbia University, now back in China, he altered his plans and added a several-month stay in China to his itinerary. As it turned out, he arrived in China just after the outbreak of the May Fourth Movement. Dewey was such a popular speaker and was so attracted to Chinese culture, that he ended up spending two years in China and delivering over one hundred lectures throughout the country. Both letters he and his wife wrote from China and his lectures provide documentation of his experience. (As a challenge to literary and historical scholars, the lectures exist only as an English translation of detailed notes by some of Dewey's students. His original notes in English are lost.)

Dewey was sympathetic to the democratic, liberal, tradition-challenging ferment of the May Fourth Movement. He balanced celebration of the movement's universal dimensions with a respect for the need for each society to find a path toward social progress that was rooted in its own history and culture. One scholar has believes his experience in China had a formative influence on Dewey's mature philosophy. Cecile Dockser has argued that the May Fourth Movement radicalized Dewey's ideas about social change and that his favorable impressions of Chinese culture solidified an emerging "cultural relativism" in his philosophy.

The dominant theme in scholarship about Dewey and China, though, has been the influence of his ideas on China's educational system. Barry Keenan writes that "no Western scholar had enjoyed such a large influence [in China]," though he qualifies that conclusion in his narratives of the careers of Dewey's most prominent Chinese students— Hu Shi, Jiang Menglin, Guo Pingwen, and Tao Xingzhi. In various ways, all tried to adapt Dewey's ideas about progressive education to Chinese circumstances during the inter-war decades. Tao, for example, argued that Dewey's "education is life" dictum needed a "half-somersault" to become "life education," which for Tao was embodied in the emerging mass education movement in rural China. In the end, Keenan concludes that Dewey's disciples had limited success, largely because they lacked significant political power. After the Communist victory in the civil war, Dewey's ideas came under harsh attack on the mainland as "bourgeois" and remained in disrepute for several decades. Since the beginning of the current reform period in the late 1970s, however, Chinese scholars and educators have begun reconsidering both the history of Dewey's ideas in China and what elements of them might be of practical use today.

See also May Fourth Movement.

REFERENCES: Robert W. Clopton and Tsuin-chen Ou (eds.), *John Dewey: Lectures in China, 1919–1920* (Honolulu, HW, 1973); John Dewey and Alice Chipman Dewey, *Letters from China and Japan* (New York, 1920); Cecile Bahn Dockser, *John Dewey and the May Fourth Movement in China: Dewey's Social and Political Philosophy in Relation to his Encounter with China* (Ph.D. Dissertation, Harvard University, 1983); Barry Keenan, *The Dewey Experiment in China: Educational Reform and Political Power in the Early Republic* (Cambridge, MA, 1977); Lauren Pfister, "The Rise, Fall, and Re-evaluation of Dewey's Philosophy in China," in Priscilla Roberts (ed.), *Sino-American Relations Since 1900* (Hong Kong, 1991).

Norty Wheeler

Dixie Mission *see* American Military Observer Group (Yanan)

Dollar Diplomacy

After issuing the Open Door Notes of 1898–1899 and Hay Circular of 1900, U.S. policy in the Far East focused on how to ensure equality of opportunity of trade in China without resorting to war with Japan. The Roosevelt administration tried to achieve this goal by: (1) seeking to establish a balance of power in the region between Russia and Japan; (2) concluding arrangements that recognized Japan's special interests in the region in return for security guarantees by Japan for America's Pacific possessions (Taft-Katsura Memorandum and Root-Takahira Agreement); and, (3) combining an acknowledgement of Japanese interests in China with a show of naval force in the Pacific.

During the Taft administration, the U.S. sought to preserve the Open Door Policy in China by pursuing "dollar diplomacy." President William H. Taft and Secretary of State Philander Knox encouraged government-sponsored American investments in China to undercut Japanese influence there. The policy actually began taking shape during the final years of the Roosevelt administration after railroad financier Edward H. Harriman had failed to realize his around-the-world transportation scheme due to Japan's nonparticipation in the project. Willard Straight, the American consul-general at Mukden, distrusted Japan, and believed that Japan's control of southern Manchuria threatened American interests there. He convinced Harriman that American investments would increase American influence in Manchuria but the financial panic of 1907 forced Harriman to back away from the plan. In response to a Russian-Japanese agreement (1907) that divided control over Manchuria between the two countries, Straight, now chief of the Division of Far East Affairs in the State Department, renewed his efforts to encourage American investments in Manchuria, but Roosevelt rejected the policy because it threatened to increase U.S.-Japanese tensions in China.

Taft and Knox agreed with Straight's ideas and began sponsoring American investments in China in order to defend the Open Door. Taft succeeded in securing American participation in the Huguang Railroad Loan, or Four-Power Consortium. But Secretary of State Knox failed to realize his "neutralization scheme," an effort to form an international syndicate in order to purchase all of Manchuria's railroads and thus undercut Japanese and Russian influence in the area. The Taft administration then tried unsuccessfully to increase American influence in China by promoting currency reform. Such efforts, especially the Huguang Railroad Loan, proved unpopular with the Chinese populace and contributed to the collapse of the Manchu Dynasty in 1911. The new Chinese government, however, needed money, paving the way for one last effort at "dollar diplomacy" under Taft, the Six-Power consortium. The project ended in failure due to fears that the international market could not handle the loan and the Chinese objections to specific provisions of the loan that infringed on China's sovereignty.

The Wilson administration, with its attention focused on domestic reform, difficulties with Mexico, and the strains of maintaining American neutrality during World War I, pursued a more reactive, hybrid, and improvised Far East policy. It first repudiated Taft's "dollar diplomacy" policy. In removing the U.S. from the Six-Power consortium, President Woodrow Wilson understood that Russia and Japan, who had each failed to observe the Open Door in Manchuria, controlled the group. He also believed that the U.S. would have a better chance of increasing its influence in China through a go-it-alone policy through small bankers. China's acceptance of

Japan's Twenty-One Demands in 1915 shattered such hopes. The Wilson administration announced it would not recognize any agreement that infringed on the Open Door Policy and took two additional steps to contain Japan in China. First, it adopted one of Roosevelt's policies by concluding the Lansing-Ishii Agreement, an ambiguous document that tried to balance Japan's special interests in China with recognition of the Open Door Policy. It then reversed its previous stance on "dollar diplomacy" by creating a new Four-Power consortium in the hope of checking Japanese economic dominance in China. Neither policy proved successful, thus causing the U.S. government to switch tactics to defend the Open Door Policy in China by adopting the Washington Treaty System (the Five-Power Treaty and Nine-Power Treaty) in 1921–1922.

See also Knox Neutralization Scheme, Open Door Policy.

REFERENCES: Roy Watson Curry, *Woodrow Wilson and Far Eastern Policy, 1913–1921* (New York, 1968); Michael H. Hunt, *The Making of a Special Relationship: The United States and China to 1914* (New York, 1983); Emily S. Rosenberg, *Financial Missionaries of the World: The Politics and Culture of Dollar Diplomacy, 1900–1930* (Cambridge, MA, 1999); Charles Vevier, *The United States and China, 1906–1913: A Study of Finance and Diplomacy* (New York, 1968).

Dean Fafoutis

Domino Theory

The domino theory was a Western explanation of global politics applied to Asia primarily during the Cold War, although its roots were much older. As the strategic atmosphere in Asia changed dramatically when China 'fell' to Communism in 1949 and when Communist North Korea invaded South Korea in June 1950, the Truman administration was convinced that all of Asia was in danger of a Communist take over from the Soviet Bloc. As the Cold War momentum built, the domino theory gained credence in American foreign policy during the 1950s and 1960s.

The domino theory asserted that if one country in Asia became Communist then the rest of Asian countries would "fall" to Communism like a line of dominoes. It manifested in concerns about Communism on the Indochina peninsula and was an ideological basis for the American war in Vietnam. If Communism succeeded in Vietnam, it would only be a matter of time before Laos and Cambodia also became Communist. With the Indochina peninsula in Communist control, the dominoes would fall in two directions: to the south through Southeast and South Asia to Thailand and Burma, then Pakistan and India; and to the west through the Middle East

to Afghanistan and Iran, then North Africa and the Mediterranean region. In Western Europe, the concern focused on the fall of dominoes toward North Africa and the Mediterranean. The commander in chief of French Indochina, General Jean de Lattre de Tassigny, during a September 20, 1951 visit to Washington, DC, described a line of dominoes from the Indochina peninsula to Europe: "Once [Vietnam] is lost, there is no real barrier before Suez...."

The United States was more concerned with a domino cascade in Asia and the island chain of defense that proved so vital to the American effort in the Pacific in World War II. The U.S. was particularly concerned about the relationship between Southeast Asia and Japan. With a Communist government now ruling China, Japan was more dependent on Southeast Asia for resources and trade. If the Japanese economy stagnated, there were real fears of Japanese Communists gaining power. According to a 1952 National Security Council (NSC) memo: "In the long run the loss of Southeast Asia, especially Malaya and Indonesia, could result in such economic and political pressures in Japan as to make it extremely difficult to prevent Japan's eventual accommodation to the Soviet Bloc." U.S. Secretary of State John Foster Dulles said in 1953 that if "Indochina should be lost, there would be a chain reaction throughout the Far East and South Asia," posing a "grave threat to Malaya, Thailand, Indonesia, the Philippines, Australia and New Zealand." The domino theory was espoused by U.S. President Dwight D. Eisenhower at a press conference on April 7, 1954: "[T]he "falling domino" principle ... the loss of Indochina, of Burma, of Thailand, of the Peninsula, and Indonesia ... turns the so-called island defensive chain of Japan, Formosa, of the Philippines and to the southward; it moves in to threaten Australia and New Zealand. It takes away, in its economic aspects, that region that Japan must have as a trading area or Japan, in turn, will have only one place in the world to go—that is, toward the Communist areas in order to live. So, the possible consequences of the loss are just incalculable to the free world."

The domino theory continued to be prevalent in the United States under the Kennedy and Johnson administrations in the conduct of the Vietnam War. During his administration, U.S. President Lyndon B. Johnson asserted, "The battle against Communism must be joined in Southeast Asia ... or the United States, inevitably, must surrender the Pacific and take up our defenses on our own shores." It was not until the shift back to geopolitics in the Nixon administration that the domino theory was relinquished as the dominant political theory in Asia.

See also Cold War; Eisenhower, Dwight D. (1890–1969).

REFERENCES: Frank A. Ninkovich, *Modernity and Power: A History of the Domino Theory in the Twentieth Century* (Chicago, IL, 1994); James S. Olson and Randy Roberts, *Where The Domino Fell* (New York, 1996); Stanley Karnow, *Vietnam: A History* (New York, 1983); David Halberstam, *The Making of A Quagmire* (New York, 1964).

Elizabeth Van Wie Davis

Dong Xianguang (1887–1971)

Dong Xianguang's name is also spelled Hsien Kuang Tung. He was best known in the West by the last version of his name. Dong was born into a Christian (Presbyterian) family in Ningpo, Zhejiang Province, China on November 9, 1887. He was educated as a child in Shanghai. In 1908 Dong traveled to Parkville, Missouri, where he attended Park College. To make his name easier for Westerners to pronounce, he anglicized it to Hollington K. Tong. Park College gave Dong an honorary Ph.D. for his journalistic and diplomatic accomplishments decades later.

In 1909 Dong moved to Columbia to attend the University of Missouri. He graduated in the first class of its new journalism school with a BA degree. In 1912 Dong started graduate studies in New York at the new Pulitzer School of Journalism at Columbia University. He attended classes and worked part-time as a newsman. One undercover assignment turned him into a waiter in a cocaine den. He graduated in 1913 with the first class to receive an advanced degree in journalism. Dong returned to China where he became assistant editor of the *China Republican*. From 1914 until 1916 he served as the chief editor of the *Peking Daily News*. In 1915 Dong played an important role in blocking the Japanese attempt to impose its Twenty-One Demands on China. From 1916 until 1925 Dong was assistant editor and Beijing correspondent for *China Weekly*. In the 1920s Dong also accepted the position of associate editor of *Millard's Review of the Far East*. From 1925 to 1931 Dong published *Yung Pao*, a Chinese language daily in Tianjing, China. He formatted the daily after American newspapers. In 1931 Dong moved to Shanghai to work as managing director of the *China Press*. In 1933 he published a book, *Problems and Personalities in the Far East* (China Press). In addition he also published *Men and Events in the Far East* (1933–1934). In 1935 he took over as managing director of the *China Times*, *Ta Wan Pao* and the Shun Shih News Agency. In 1936 as events moved toward Japan's invasion of China, Nationalist leader Jiang

Jieshi appointed Dong as director of the Shanghai office of the National Military Council. He was later made acting minister of the fifth board of the Council. In 1937 he published *Chaing Kaishek: Soldier and Statesman,* an authorized biography. In 1937 the Guomindang government put Dong in charge of its international propaganda activities. Dong established an office to build world support for China's war effort against Japan. During World War II, Dong contacted Carl W. Ackerman of the Graduate School of Journalism at Columbia University about establishing a wartime journalism school in China. Ackerman, a 1913 classmate of Dong's arranged for the project. In addition he got two anonymous gifts totaling $75,000 to fund the project. Staffed by instructors from Columbia University, Chongqing Graduate School of Journalism was secretly funded by the Office of Strategic Services. It began with 32 cub reporters in October 1943. It operated for three years. Dong was the director and Harold L. Cross of Columbia was the dean. In May of 1947 Dong was named head of the Government of Information Office. His activities brought criticism from foreign journalists for the censorship he enforced over their dispatches. In 1948 he was appointed Minster without Portfolio in the Executive Yuan (Council). Also in 1949 he was appointed a member of the central advisory committee of the Guomindang, general manger of the Broadcasting Corporation of China and chairman of the board of directors of the *Central Daily News*. Dong supervised the development of the Nationalist Chinese radio station, the Voice of Free China, in Taibei. It was soon broadcasting in a dozen Chinese dialects, in Russian, and in Korean to oppose Radio Peking, its Chinese Communist antagonist. Dong was busy in 1950. He was appointed Director of the Information Department in the Guomindang's Office of the President. He directed publication of the *China Handbook, 1950*, and he published *Dateline: China*. From 1949–1952 Dong made numerous trips to the United States and to Europe as an emissary for the Republic of China. From 1952 to 1956 he served as its ambassador to Japan. In 1956 Dong was appointed ambassador to the United States, and served until 1958. During this time he often spoke publicly on the dangers of the Communist regimes.

Dong married Ying Hsiang Chao (Sally Chao). They had three sons and three daughters. Dong died in a nursing home in Monterey, California on January 9, 1971.

REFERENCES: Hsien Kuang Tung, *Dong Xianguang Zhuan [Autobiography of Dong Xianguang]* (Taibei, 1974); Zhu Xinquan and Yan Ruping (eds.), *Zhonghua*

Minguo Renwu Zhuan [Who's Who of the Republic of China] Vol. 4 (Beijing, 1984); Max Perleberg, *Who's Who in Modern China* (Hong Kong, 1954); "Obituary," *New York Times* (January 11, 1971).

Jack Waskey

Doolittle Raid

In a attempt to raise American morale after the devastation of the Pearl Harbor attack, Lieutenant Colonel James H. Doolittle was chosen to lead a top secret air raid on Japan. The flyers and crew were all volunteers for this potentially suicidal mission. The military chose mid-range B-25 Mitchell bombers that could take off from an aircraft carrier. The plan called for 20 bombers to fly from a carrier about 550 miles off the east coast of Japan, bomb several cities under the cover of night, and then fly in the morning to airfields in unoccupied China where the planes would be handed over to the Chinese. Fearful that the Chinese would let the secret out, the Americans undertook careful negotiations with Generalissimo Jiang Jieshi's Nationalist government for airfields in eastern China saying only American bombers were flying in. The Nationalists designated several airfields on April 14, 1942, after the mission was underway.

Over 80 men volunteered for the mission, but only 16 B-25s would fit on the deck of the carrier USS *Hornet* where the pilots and crews learned how to say, "I am an American," in Chinese. The carrier encountered a Japanese vessel about 650 miles from Japan, and fearing possible detection sank it and moved up the timetable of the mission. The first plane took off at 8:20 AM on April 18, 1942, and arriving over Japan four hours later. The B-25s came in at treetop level and then rose to drop the bombs on their targets in Tokyo, Yokohama, Kobe and Nagoya encountering ineffective Japanese defenses. The bombers then headed west for China but had to scatter when they encountered a storm. Due to their premature departure, it remained to be seen whether the B-25s could make it to Chinese airfields before their fuel ran out. Furthermore, the airfield at Lishui could not be prepared in time and this information could not be relayed to the *Hornet* for fear of interception. One bomber flew to the Soviet Union landing about 40 miles from Vladivostok where Soviet authorities interned the crew. The crews of the other fifteen bombers either bailed out or crashed landed. Seventy-one of the men survived. The Japanese captured eight and subsequently tried then for crimes against humanity in Tokyo, executing three. Unfortunately, the Chinese phrase the men learned was in the wrong dialect causing several of them to be robbed by Chinese bandits who, upon learning of their true identity, turned them over to the Nationalist forces. Chinese civilians helped the remaining men caught in occupied China to make their way to the Nationalist wartime capital of Chongqing where they were welcomed as heroes and received medals from Madame Jiang Jieshi. President Franklin D. Roosevelt promoted Doolittle to brigadier general the day after the raid, and when the President was asked whence the planes took off, he joked, "Shangri-La," referring to the mythical Tibetan kingdom in the James Hilton novel *Lost Horizon*. The truth would be released a year later.

The Japanese, fearing other such raids, launched an offensive in China to capture the Chinese airfields in Jiangxi Province causing the deaths of approximately 250,000 Chinese, some in retribution for helping the American flyers escape. Although the raid did very little damage to Japan, it provided a great psychological boost to the American war effort. Hollywood produced a well-received docudrama version of the raid in 1944, *Thirty Seconds Over Tokyo*.

REFERENCES: Robert Jackson, *Bomber: Famous Bomber Missions of World War II* (New York, 1980); Quentin J. Reynolds, *The Amazing Mr. Doolittle: A Biography of Lieutenant General James H. Doolittle* (New York, 1953).

Greg Ference

Duke, Ambassador *see* Ambassador Duke [fictional]

Dulles, John Foster (1888–1959)

As Secretary of State during the Eisenhower administration from 1953 to 1959, Dulles was instrumental in formulating and implementing American foreign policies during the critical years of the Cold War. Born into a prominent Presbyterian family in Watertown, New York, Dulles was exposed to the world of diplomacy and public service in his early years. Aside from the benefit of a privileged education, Dulles's family connections placed him on the Washington political scene at an impressionable age. The influence of his maternal grandfather, John Watson Foster, a distinguished diplomat, contributed to Dulles's decision to embark on a diplomatic career. In 1907, at the age of nineteen, he attended the Second Hague Peace Conference and served as the secretary to the Chinese delegation, which his grandfather represented. In 1911, a law degree from George Washington University got him a position at the reputable New York law firm of Sullivan and Cromwell that specialized in international legal affairs.

The year 1944 marked the beginning of Dulles' official entry into Washington politics, when he acted as the foreign policy advisor for the Republican candidate Thomas Dewey during the latter's unsuccessful bid for the presidency. Dulles was actively involved in the planning for the United Nations and played a major role in negotiating the United States-Japanese Peace Treaty during 1951–1952 and in establishing the Southeast Asia Treaty Organization. Dulles' anti-Communist stand was hardened by the Korean War. He began to attack President Harry S. Truman's and Secretary of State Dean Acheson's "Europe first" policy, and proposed to "end the neglect of the Far East." Meanwhile, he proposed to replace Truman's policy of containment with that of liberation during an Eisenhower administration.

Dulles and the policies that he espoused have been the subject of continuing study and scrutiny. Some see Dulles as an ideologue who initiated reckless policies of "brinkmanship" and "massive retaliation" and are critical of his moralistic approach to foreign policy issues. Others deem him as a sophisticated politician who understood the complexities of the Cold War and who personified the contradictions between idealism and realism in American foreign policy making. The contradiction between his stringent rhetoric and policy practices was especially evident in his dealings with the People's Republic of China during the two Taiwan Strait crises from 1954 to 1958. He pushed for the conclusion of the U.S. security treaty with Taiwan in late1954 as well as the Formosa Resolution in early 1955 authorizing President Dwight D. Eisenhower to use military intervention if the security of Taiwan was threatened. At the same time, Dulles made sure that the language used in the treaty and the resolution be kept deliberately ambiguous in order to avoid automatic American military involvement in future cross-strait conflicts. Dulles' practice of militant diplomacy made him one of the most controversial secretaries of state in U.S. history.

See also Eisenhower, Dwight D. (1890–1969); Cold War; Formosa Resolution; U.S.-China Mutual Defense Treaty.

REFERENCES: Richard H. Immerman (ed.), *John Foster Dulles and the Diplomacy of the Cold War* (Princeton, NJ, 1985); Ronald Pruessen, *John Foster Dulles: The Road to Power* (New York, 1982); Robert S. Ross and Jiang Changbin (eds.), *Re-examining the Cold War: United States-China Diplomacy, 1954–1973* (Cambridge, MA, 2001); Mark Toulouse, *The Transformation of John Foster Dulles: From Prophet of Realism and Priest of Nationalism* (Macon, GA, 1985).

Yi Sun

Eisenhower, Dwight D. (1890–1969)

Born in Denison, Texas, Dwight David Eisenhower grew up in Abilene, Kansas and graduated from the U.S. Military Academy in 1915. Following World War I his career languished in the peacetime military but Eisenhower made his reputation as a staff officer and rose to prominence as the architect of the nation's wartime strategy. During World War II he rose to command all Allied forces in Europe and after the war he served as Army Chief of Staff. He retired from the Army in 1948 to the assume presidency of Columbia University, although his tenure in academia was punctuated by service as a national security advisor to President Truman. By 1952, however, he had grown disenchanted with the Truman administration and its national security policy, especially in its seemingly open-ended war in Korea. Thus, he entered electoral politics at the behest of the Republican Party. Elected the nation's 34th president on a platform that promised a new national security policy and an end to the Korean War, Eisenhower undertook both tasks immediately.

Fulfilling his campaign pledge to "go to Korea" and "end the war," president-elect Eisenhower visited Korea. To bring the long-stalled armistice negotiations to a close, he implicitly threatened to widen the war and attack the People's Republic of China directly, which would entail the use of nuclear weapons and the military backing of Taiwan in a conflict between Beijing and Taibei. His threats had the intended effect and an armistice was concluded in July 1953. Although dissatisfied with Truman's overall national security policy, Eisenhower agreed with his predecessor's hard line stance against Beijing. The perceived capitulation of Beijing and Pyongyang in the armistice negotiations convinced him, furthermore, that an aggressive policy of containment was the wisest course of action in East Asia.

Under the Eisenhower national security policy, the "New Look," American conventional forces were de-emphasized in favor of the nation's nuclear arsenal. With NSC 162 as his guide (National Security Council Paper Number 162, a document calling for the use of an atomic strike force capable of deterring the Communists from action), Eisenhower predicated the "New Look" on the development of regional alliance systems to contain Communist expansionism. U.S. forces would provide the nuclear backbone of the alliances and the nation's allies would provide the conventional forces needed to halt Communist aggression. In Asia this translated into an abandonment of Truman's "two-China" policy and the creation of diplo-military alliance, the South East Asia Treaty Organization.

The continued conflict in French Indochina prompted the administration's first post-Korea crisis in Asia. Although his senior military advisors considered intervention, Eisenhower declined direct American involvement. When the French withdrew from Southeast Asia, Eisenhower increased American aid to, as well as U.S. influence in, the region. With Communist insurgencies ongoing throughout East Asia, the Eisenhower administration ascribed control of the independent, indigenous Communist movements to Beijing.

Mao Zedong challenged the United States' new role in the region in 1954 with the artillery bombardment of the Taiwan-controlled offshore islands of Jinmen and Mazu, along with the Dachens. Eisenhower dispatched units of the U.S. Navy to the Taiwan Straits in support of Jiang Jieshi's nationalist Chinese government on Taiwan. Jiang agreed to cede control of the Dachens to Beijing but refused to do so with Jinmen and Mazu, which were considered central to Taiwan's defense. As

1955 began the U.S. Congress approved the "Formosa Resolution" and authorized the use of military force to defend Taiwan. Implicit in the resolution and explicit in Eisenhower's remarks was the threat of a nuclear strike against the People's Republic of China. In April Beijing stopped the bombardment of the offshore islands, which prompted Eisenhower to conclude, for a second time, that the threat of preventive war had resolved the crisis in the United States' favor.

A tense peace lasted for the next three years in the Taiwan Straits and American ties to Taiwan were strengthened through dual auspices of the Mutual Defense Treaty and the Formosa Resolution.

Beijing's acquiescence, additionally, weakened its influence in the region as it strengthened that of the United States. As Mao instituted his domestic agenda, the Great Leap Forward, he sought a means to unify the nation and distract the populace from the hardships his program caused. The offshore islands offered a means through which to do so, as well as to reclaim the regional influence Beijing had lost. In October

1958 the People's Liberation Army renewed its shelling of the now heavily-fortified Jinmen. Eisenhower refused to appease Communist aggression and ordered U.S. Air Force, as well as Navy, units to the region. Although the U.S. forces did not engage in combat with the Chinese they did supply Taiwan with much-needed munitions and supplies, including advanced air-to-air mis-

siles. Simultaneously, the U.S. Secretary of State, John Foster Dulles, proposed a draw down of nationalist forces on Jinmen if Beijing ceased hostilities. Both initiatives proved decisive in halting the Communist campaign. As a result, Eisenhower's policy towards China resumed the cautious ambiguity that had characterized Truman's "two-China" policy.

See also Truman, Harry S. (1884–1972); Korean War; Two China Policy; One China Policy; Domino Theory; Formosa Resolution (1955); Taiwan Strait; Neutralization of Taiwan; Deneutralization of the Taiwan Strait; U.S.-China Mutual Defense Treaty (1954); Jinmen and Mazu Crisis; Cold War.

REFERENCES: Stephen E. Ambrose, Eisenhower, Volume II: The President (New York, 1983); Rosemary Foot, The Practice of Power: U.S. Relations with China Since 1949 (Oxford, 1995); John Lewis Gaddis, Strategies of Containment: A Critical Appraisal of Postwar American National Security Policy (Oxford, 1982); June M. Grasso, Truman's Two-China Policy (Armonk, NY 1987); George C. Herring, Jr., America's Longest War: The United States and Vietnam, 1950–1975, 4th ed. (Columbus, OH, 2001); Akira Iriye, The Cold War in Asia: A Historical Introduction (Englewood Cliffs, NJ, 1974); Shu Guang Zhang, Deterrence and Strategic Culture: Chinese American Confrontations, 1949–1958 (Ithaca, NY, 1992).

Paul D. Gelpi, Jr.

Embargo *see* **Trade Embargo**

Empress of China

Indirect trade between the British North American colonies and China existed throughout the 18th century. It was mainly conducted via London. In 1784–85 the New York ship *Empress of China* became the first United States-flag vessel to make a round trip to China.

After the American Revolution, Great Britain excluded United States ships from trading in British West Indian colonies. Nearly simultaneously, British Captain James Cook's 1776 Pacific voyage fired the imaginations of early American entrepreneurs. Cook observed that the fur, which abounded on the American northwest coast brought hefty prices in Guangzhou, then the only port in China open to Westerners. John Ledyard, a Yankee who served with Cook, published this information in 1783. Ledyard's book caught the interest of Revolutionary War financier Robert Morris, who determined to send out a China voyage of his own. Morris lost interest in Cook's Pacific fur scheme once he learned that investors from Massachusetts had dispatched a sloop to China in 1783 with a cargo of American-grown ginseng, a root, which the Chinese prized as a medicine and aphrodisiac. The *Harriet* got as far as the Cape of Good Hope, where the cargo was purchased by British speculators who also sensed its value.

In February 1784 Morris teamed with New York West Indian merchant Thomas Randall in investing $120,000 in *The Empress of China* and a cargo consisting mainly of Appalachian ginseng. The ship was commanded by Captain John Green, with ex-Revolutionary War Major Samuel Shaw as chief commercial officer and Randall as assistant. They reached Guangzhou on August 28, exchanged goods, and returned to New York on May 11, 1785. Randall recorded that the ship sold "the largest quantity of ginseng that had ever been brought to the Chinese market, more than all the British and Portuguese ships had brought for the year 1784." The sale of the *Empress'* return cargo in New York netted a 25% profit on the original investment. The voyage directly inspired the China trade of many other American merchants, four of whom would become America's first millionaires (the others were John Jacob Astor, Joseph Peabody, and Elias Hasket Derby). Although Americans continued to trade with China via Europe after the *Empress* voyage, this 1784–85 voyage inaugurated direct Sino-American maritime trade, which has continued unbroken except for the "frozen" period of 1949–72.

REFERENCES: Phillip Smith, *Empress of China* (Philadelphia, PA, 1984); Samuel Shaw, *The Journals of Major Samuel Shaw* (Boston, MA, 1847).

Jonathan Goldstein

Engagement

After the end of the Cold War and the collapse of the Soviet Union, the United States crafted a policy of engagement towards China in the emerging new world order. American policy makers realized that in an altered security and strategic environment, it would be in their long-term national interest to engage China in the Asia-Pacific region where China might pose a potential threat to American interests.

Basically, the engagement policy has been designed to integrate China into the international system and global economic system through open dialogue and frequent consultation with China on the critical international and regional issues. Theoretically speaking, it is a policy of maintaining friendly ties and sustaining a comprehensive dialogue with China. In effect, engagement is an instrument or "tactic" rather than an end in itself to realize American national interests. Some key principles of engagement policy comprise peaceful resolution of territorial disputes, refraining from the unilateral use of military force, and re-

spect for human rights. President George H. W. Bush pursued the policy of constructive engagement with China on a wide range of issues that included gradual democratization of China, safeguarding of human rights in Tibet, and fair trade practices. Carrying forward the legacy of his predecessor's policy, President Bill Clinton enunciated the policy of "comprehensive engagement," rather than containment, towards China, in view of the fact that after the demise of the Soviet Union, China had emerged as a major economic power. The rationale behind pursuing engagement policy is rooted in a host of interconnected factors such as China's emergence as an economic power with its increasingly military, nuclear and missile prowess. Since the adoption of economic reforms and "open door policy" during the Deng Xiaoping period, China's trade with the United States and the latter's foreign investment in China has been phenomenally on increase. This has not only benefited American companies but has also opened up vast employment opportunities for American people. Given this, economic engagement with China is considered essential to maximize its economic, trade and investment interests. This is one of the main reasons that the U.S. government not only simplified control procedures to accommodate China's interests but also facilitated China's entry into the World Trade Organization (WTO) in December 2001. In the era of economic globalization, Sino-U.S. strategic engagement is an imperative for improving "macro economic management systems," and making WTO non-discriminatory and effective to address common problems facing both developing and developed nations for a sound development of the world economy. Apart from trade and economic linkages, U.S. strategic engagement with China involves eliciting China's cooperation in resolution of regional and global problems. In realistic terms, as a major power and permanent member of the UN Security Council, China's cooperation is indispensable, for example, in preventing proliferation of weapons of mass destruction in North Korea, in Iran and Syria in the Middle East, in fighting international terrorism, in maintaining peace and stability in East Asia, and to protect environment and combat international crimes.

However, the U.S. engagement policy remains shrouded in ambiguity. Both countries have sharp differences on security and strategic issues like American power projection in the Gulf War, in Afghanistan, and in Kosovo as well as on the U.S. theater missile defense (TMD) and national missile defense (NMD) systems, which are viewed by China as a well calculated move to mute its strategic deterrence capabilities against

America. More importantly, given the primacy of national interests of both countries, it is not yet precisely clear how the two countries would be able to resolve the most problematic issue of Taiwan. Although America has acknowledged Taiwan as part of China, there is a conspicuous ambiguity about the nature of American response in an eventuality of China deploying military means to reunify Taiwan. Similarly, with respect to human rights and democratization of Chinese society, engagement policy is less likely to fructify. Though America may endeavor to engage China politically and culturally in order to influence its political and cultural behavior, it would be a Herculean task for the American leadership to bring about fundamental change in China's domestic structures and institutions. Be that as it may, the future of engagement policy is likely to depend on convergence of well-defined goals and interests of both countries as well as on American "consistent view" of China.

See also Cold War; Bush, George H. W. (1924-); Clinton, William J. (1946-).

REFERENCES: Samuel S. Kim (ed.), *China in the World: Chinese Foreign Relations in the Post-Cold Era* (Boulder, CO, 1994); Zalmy M. Khalilzad, et al., *The United States and Rising China* (Santa Monica, CA, 1999); James Shinn (ed.), *Weaving the Net: Conditional Engagement with China* (New York, 1996).

B. M. Jain

Extraterritoriality

Extraterritoriality is a concept where citizens of one nation are subject to their own country's justice and exempt from legal jurisdiction of the host country while living and conducting business in that host country. In the case of China, it was an aspect of the so-called unequal treaty system from its onset in the aftermath of China's defeat in the Opium Wars in the early 1840s until the Second World War — one hundred years later — when Western nations gave up their treaty rights to encourage the Republic of China to continue to resist Japanese aggression.

The major seafaring powers, as they extracted concessions from China, also demanded extraterritorial rights for their citizens in the belief that China under the Qing Dynasty was uncivilized, and incapable of providing justice for Westerners. British negotiators gained this right in the Treaty of the Bogue on October 8, 1843, and, initially, it extended extraterritoriality only to criminal cases. Later, the American diplomat, Congressman Caleb Cushing, extended this principle to civil cases in the 1844 Treaty of Wangxia, a right soon extended to all the foreign powers under the so-called most favored nation principle.

At first, Qing leaders and Confucian bureaucrats did not consider extraterritoriality to be a major concession. During the height of the Tang Dynasty, Tang rulers permitted foreign communities in the great capital of Changan to rule themselves, and China had a history of magnanimously granting such rights to free itself of having to bother with foreigners. It reflected China's long-standing preference for the smallest, leanest official government. At the same time, Portuguese authorities that had been in Macao for many years claimed exclusive jurisdiction over their citizens, while the British likewise insisted on their own courts at Guangzhou with criminal and admiralty jurisdiction. However, as merchants and missionaries were above local constraints, Chinese at all levels of societies resented this expanded power over all civil and criminal cases involving most foreigners as an infringement of sovereignty. For example, as imperialist powers helped missionary activities, Chinese criminals who at the moment of arrest claimed they had converted to Christianity found support from missionaries who used extraterritoriality to shield these Chinese nationals from their own justice. There were similar issues in business dealings, and in the administration of contracts. To exercise police powers over their nationals and to protect them from the uncivilized Chinese justice system, Western nations established themselves in cities — "concessions" — and stationed troops in China and navies on major Chinese waterways, and thus used extraterritorial rights to further weaken Chinese sovereignty. Still, it seems only Great Britain truly accepted its extraterritorial obligations as well as rights, and provided funds and a mechanism of justice to house the accused, try them, and deal with them after judgment. Extraterritoriality, combined with foreign concessions, the low 5% ad valorum tariff, and the presence of foreign military units on Chinese soil all combined to create a great deal of foreign control over China. Under Sir Robert Hart, the British operated the Chinese Maritime Customs Authority, a virtual government unto itself; foreign navies patrolled the Yangzi and other major Chinese rivers; the imperial powers had concessions in major coastal cities; and the low tariff kept China open to vast foreign imports, weakening China's developing industrial economy.

The end of extraterritoriality finally came in 1946. At the Paris Peace Conference ending the First World War, Germany gave up its rights as part of its renouncing of imperial aspirations. In 1924, the new Soviet Union returned its rights, as an encouragement to colonial peoples across the Third World to rise up against their capitalist oppressors. During the Second World War, Japan and Italy forfeited their rights as members of the Axis alliance. The United States and Great Britain voluntarily gave up their rights on October 10, 1943 (since October 10 supposedly marks Confucius' birthday) to help keep Nationalist China in the war against Japan. Finally, in 1946, the reconstituted French government gave up its rights, and China regained its full sovereignty about one hundred years after the imperialist powers forced it to recognize extraterritoriality.

See also Treaty of Wangxia (1844).

REFERENCES: Wesley R. Fishel, *The End of Extraterritoriality in China* (New York, 1974); G.W. Keeton, *The Development of Extraterritoriality in China* (New York, 1969); Francis Clifford Jones, *Extraterritoriality in Japan and the Diplomatic Relations Resulting in Its Abolition, 1853–1899* (New York, 1970); Raymond Thomas Rich, *Extraterritoriality and Tariff Autonomy in China* (Shanghai, 1925).

Charles M. Dobbs

Fairbank, John King (1907–1991)

Fairbank was born in Huron, South Dakota, on May 24, 1907, the son of a lawyer. He attended Phillips Exeter Academy in New Hampshire, and after graduating, entered the University of Wisconsin. He transferred to Harvard University where he graduated in 1929. He received a Rhodes Scholarship for further study in England and decided to concentrate on China. In 1932, he went to China to learn the language and to work on his doctoral thesis. While there, he traveled extensively and befriended several Chinese intellectuals and American expatriates including Hu Shi and Edgar and Helen Foster Snow. In 1933 Fairbank lectured at Qinghua University in Beijing and began to publish chapters from his dissertation. In 1936 he received his doctorate, and a revised edition of his dissertation later appeared as *Trade and Diplomacy on the China Coast* (1953). That the same year, he began to teach at Harvard University where he worked along side another historian of China and Japan, Edwin O. Reischauer. After the United States entered the Second World War, Fairbank took a leave of absence from Harvard to work in Washington at the Office of Strategic Services. It sent him to the Chinese wartime capital of Chongqing in 1942 where he served as an assistant to the American ambassador and gathered information. He returned to Washington in late 1943 to begin work at the Office of War Information. After the end of the war in 1945, he again visited the country as the director for China of the United States Information Service. In 1946 he resumed his career at Harvard where he published extensively and promoted Chinese studies in America. His most no-

table publications include *The United States and China* (1948), *East Asia: The Great* Tradition (1960) with Reischauer, and *East Asia: The Modern Transformation* (1963) with Reischauer and Albert M. Craig. All went through numerous editions.

During the McCarthy Era, he was attacked as a Communist, but successfully defended himself before a Senate subcommittee. After this episode, he pursued his research and promotion of Chinese studies. He founded the MA Program in Chinese studies at Harvard. In 1955 he became the director of Harvard's Center for East Asian Studies later renamed the Fairbank Center for East Asian Research in his honor upon his retirement in 1977. In the 1960s he became the co-editor of the multi-volume *Cambridge History of China*. Upon the invitation of Premier Zhou Enlai, Fairbank returned to China shortly after President Richard M. Nixon made his historic visit in 1972. He retired from teaching in 1977, and two years later, as part of an official visit by Vice President Walter P. Mondale, he returned to China. He died two days after submitting the manuscript of his final book *China: A New History* (1992) on September 14, 1991, in Cambridge, Massachusetts.

Fairbank received many awards, fellowships, and honors for his work. He was elected in 1950 as President of the Far Eastern Association, in 1958 of the Association for Asian Studies, and in 1968 of the American Historical Association, which, in the same year, inaugurated the John King Fairbank Prize for an outstanding monograph in East Asian history. Fairbank became the "dean" of Chinese studies in the United States and one of the discipline's most respected scholars publishing over twenty books and countless articles while being a mentor to numerous future scholars of China and East Asia.

REFERENCES: Paul A. Cohen and Merle Goldman, Fairbank Remembered (Cambridge, MA, 1992); Paul M. Evans, John Fairbank and the American Understanding of Modern China (New York, 1988); John King Fairbank, Chinabound: A Fifty-Year Memoir (New York, 1982).

Greg Ference

Falun Gong

In 1992, Li Hongzhi (1952-), the so-called Grand Master from northeast China, founded the sect known as Falun Gong. The name of the sect translates literally as "the power of the law wheel." The members of the sect believe that the "law wheel" is a mystical center continually turning in each individual's lower abdomen. This "law wheel" governs the physical health of the individual, and belief in Falun Gong is said to activate its mystical power. To the tape-recorded instruction of Li Hongzhi, members of the sect practice ritual exercises to enhance the influence of the "law wheel" on their own health. These ritual exercises and the Falun Gong philosophy are described in Li Hongzhi's book, *Rotating the Law Wheel*, which has proven more popular in China than any title since Mao's *Little Red Book*. Falun Gong can be viewed as a contemporary revival of the traditional Chinese belief in *qi gong*, the use of exercise to regulate breathing and thereby positively influence the *qi*, or life force, which circulates continually throughout the body. Under Mao, the Chinese Communists banned the practice of *qi gong*. But the traditional belief gradually resurfaced after Mao's death and has even been implicitly endorsed by the party leadership. Deng Xiaoping's longevity was commonly attributed to the practice of *qi gong*. Indeed, many of Li Hongzhi's followers believe that he is able to effect miraculous cures of terrible diseases and disabilities simply by touching the afflicted. But "cures" of less dire conditions such as near-sightedness and baldness have also been attributed to contact with him.

The Chinese government initially seemed willing to regard the sect as a benign phenomenon, the exponential growth in Falun Gong's membership and its increasing political activism led the government to ban it and then to actively persecute its members. Ironically, this persecution seems both to have deepened the fervor of the sect's adherents and to have broadened its appeal to new members. By 1999, the sect claimed more than 60 million members in China, a larger membership than that of the Communist party. In April 1999, 10,000 members of the sect marched in Beijing to protest government oppression. Although government negotiated with the leaders of the protest to convince them to disband peacefully, the size of the protest convinced the government of the need to intensify its broader efforts against the sect.

The post-Tiananmen scrutiny of political oppression in China and the Chinese government's antipathy toward attempts to organize Christian congregations in China have together created a popular reaction against the persecution of Falun Gong in the West, and especially in the United States. Many of those who are protesting the repression of the sect may only vaguely understand the principles of Falun Gong. Few likely would endorse Li Hongzhi's assertion that aliens visited Earth sometime around 1900 and have been busy creating human clones through which they will wrest control of the planet from humanity. But the Chinese government's persecution of the sect has galvanized political and religious groups that may more typically find themselves opposed on most other issues. Indeed, the international attention to the issue has generated an international growth in the sect's membership, with chapters organizing in at least eight countries and almost two dozen American states. In 1995, Li Hongzhi himself left China for the United States, where he has subsequently lived as a permanent resident. The sect has sought to sue the Chinese government through the U.S. courts, but it has thus far been unsuccessful in these efforts.

REFERENCES: Steven Butler and Thomas Omestad, "Why Beijing's Grumpy Old Men Are So Grumpy," U.S. *News & World Report* (August 9, 1999); Bay Fang, "An Opiate of the Masses?," U.S. *News & World Report* (February 22, 1999); Terry McCarthy and Mia Turner, "Inside the Falun Gong," *Time* (August 9, 1999); Kevin Platt, "China vs. Mass Spiritual Thirst," *Christian Science Monitor* (August 3, 1999); Kevin Platt, "No Tiananmen II: This Mass Protest Was Calm," *Christian Science Monitor* (April 27, 1999); David Van Biema and Jaime A. FlorCruz, "The Man with the Qi," *Time* (May 10, 1999); "Why the Exercisers Exercise China's Party," *The Economist* (July 31, 1999); "Worried in Beijing," *The Economist* (August 7, 1999).

Martin Kich

Fang Lizhi (1936-)

At times referred to as China's "Sakharov," Fang Lizhi is a renowned scholar. The son of a postal worker, Fang was born in Beijing in 1936. He excelled in his studies and attended the prestigious Beijing University (Beida) where he studied physics. While at Beida, Fang was involved with the Communist Youth League, earning a reputation as an outspoken and free thinking individual. After graduating in 1956, Fang worked at the Chinese Academy of Sciences' Institute of Modern Physics Research. His career got off to a rocky start, however, as he was targeted in the 1957 anti-Rightists campaign and expelled from the party because of his outspokenness.

Despite his political troubles, Fang's skills made him a valuable man for his country. In 1963 he became a lecturer in the physics department at the Chinese University of Science and Technology (Keda). However, even his academic reputation was unable to protect him during the Cultural Revolution, which broke out in 1966. Accused of being a "reactionary," Fang spent one year in solitary confinement before being "sent down" to the countryside to learn from the peasants. Following the death of Mao and the end of the Cultural Revolution, Fang was "rehabilitated" and allowed to rejoin the party. During the late 1970s and early 80s, Fang became a well-respected and prolific scholar at Keda. Drawing on his academic success, Fang traveled around the world attending various scholarly conferences. Such travels had a profound affect on not only his scholarly views, but more importantly on his political views. In 1984 Fang became Vice President of Keda. Using his new position, Fang called for greater democracy and free speech. In December 1986, the students responded to his call as thousands of them took to the streets in Shanghai, Hefei, and Beijing. The government, obviously caught off guard by such demonstrations, reacted by punishing the assumed leaders of the movement, including Fang. Beijing authorities quickly expelled Fang from the party and transferred him to a research institute in Beijing, far removed from daily contact with students and large audiences. His reassignment, however, did not silence Fang. In January 1989, he wrote a well-circulated letter to Deng Xiaoping asking him to open the Chinese political process and to release political prisoners such as Wei Jingsheng. The next month Fang accepted an invitation from President George H. W. Bush to a state dinner at the U.S. embassy in Beijing (though at the last minute the police prevented him from attending). In April 1989, pro-democracy students gathered at Tiananmen Square to protest against official corruptions and one party rule. The demonstration gathered momentum, dwarfing the earlier marches of 1986. By May, one million individuals had congregated carrying banners and posters, and erecting the now famous "Goddess of Democracy." On June 3, government troops arrived and forcibly cleared the square, leaving an unknown number of students dead.

Though Fang had never participated in the demonstration, he was apprehensive for his own safety. On June 6, he and his wife entered the U.S. embassy in Beijing and asked for asylum, where they would live for the next year. In 1990, party officials finally allowed them to leave the country. Since that time, Fang has accepted a position as a physics professor at the University of Arizona.

See also Tiananmen Square Massacre.

REFERENCES: Melissa August, et al., "Ten Years After Tiananmen," *Time*, (May 31, 1999); Fang Lizhi, *Bringing Down the Great Wall: Writings on Science, Culture, and Democracy in China* (New York, 1990); Fang Lizhi, *From Assent to Dissent: The Memoirs of Fang Lizhi* (New York, 1991); Fang Lizhi and James H. Williams, *Farewell to an Era* (New York, 1991); Arthur Fisher, "Man Without A Country," *Popular Science*, (August 1996); Ma Shu-Yun, "Clientelism, Foreign Attention, and Chinese Intellectual Autonomy," *Modern China* (October 1998).

David Kenley

February 28 Incident of 1947

February 28 Incident of 1947 is a Taiwanese anti-Nationalist uprising beginning on February 28, 1947. Since the first Sino-Japanese War in 1894–1895, Taiwan had become Japan's colony. Following the Cairo Declaration, Taiwan would be return to China upon Japan's surrender. In October 1945, the Nationalists officially took over Taiwan from the Japanese. Although 50 years of Japanese colonial rule and separation from mainland China made Japanese influence diffusive throughout the island, the Taiwanese regarded the mainland as their homeland. After Japan surrendered, they anticipated not only the end of Japanese colonialism but also a prosperous society and an efficient government which would take care of people's well being.

However, ignorant of the political, economic, social and cultural gap between Taiwan and the mainland created by the Japanese colonial rule, the Nationalist government headed by Governor-General Chen Yi was not ready to meet Taiwanese expectations. Although the Nationalists from the mainland expected to be embraced as liberators, they were unable to establish good communications with the Taiwanese and provide the concrete political and economic benefits, which the Taiwanese had hoped. Relying on the mainlanders and excluding the Taiwanese from the politics, the Nationalist authority in the island proved corrupt and repressive. Its misrules caused a drastic slump in living standard and a rapid deterioration of social order and public services, created increasing tensions between mainlanders and the Taiwanese, and finally fueled the 1947 uprising.

The spark for the uprising came on February 27 when the agents of the Taibei City Monopoly Bureau beat up a forty-year-old widow Lin Chiang-mai whom they saw selling what they thought were smuggled cigarettes. Their brutality immediately triggered outrage of the bystanders and caused clash in which a bystander died. On the morning of February 28, about two thousand demonstrators gathered in the streets of Taibei and attacked a branch office of the Monopoly Bureau. Businessmen closed up their stores and employees started a strike. Chen Yi declared the martial law but failed to stop the riots. Within a few days, uprising quickly spread to other cities. By early March, the rebels had controlled much of the island, except the Penghu (Pescadores). Through their major organ—the Settlement Committee—they called for fundamental political and military reforms in their 32 demands. Chen Yi expressed his willingness to accept some of the demands on hope to restore order. At the same time, he made the reinforcement request to Nanjing. On March 8, over 10,000 Nationalist troops landed on Jilong and Gaoxiong and began to suppress the uprising. The reinforcements continued to arrive until March 17. By March 13, the Nationalist troops had occupied every district on the island. The White Terror began. The Settlement Committee was dismissed and all newspapers critical to the government were shut down. People involved in the Uprising were persecuted. It is estimated that at least over ten thousand native-born Taiwanese were killed during the time of terror in March. Most killings occurred from the areas around Jilong, Taibei, and Gaoxiong.

After the uprising was suppressed, the Nationalist government took a conciliatory policy in the island and tried to improve Taiwanese-Mainlander relations by allowing the Taiwanese to share certain local political power. But the brutal suppression of the 1947 Taiwanese uprising left many Taiwanese a deep-seated hostility to the mainlanders. Such hostility finally evolved into a lasting political movement, which aimed to get rid of the rule of the mainlanders and turn Taiwan into an independent state.

See also Taiwan.

REFERENCES: Mei-ling T. Wang, *The Dust that Never Settles: The Taiwan Independence Campaign and U.S.-China Relations* (Lanham, MD, 1999); Lai Tse-han, Ramon H. Myers, and Wei Wou, *A Tragic Beginning: The Taiwan Uprising of February 28, 1947* (Stanford, CA, 1991).

Tao Peng

Feng Yuxiang (1882–1948)

The so-called "Christian general," because of his alleged baptism of troops with a hose, Feng Yuxiang was a warlord who managed to gain positive recognition among the Chinese. As such, Feng's career demonstrates that he was violent but concerned, treacherous yet moral.

Born into a poor family — both parents were opium addicts — Feng was enrolled into the army at ten, making the army both his school and his home. In 1902 he transferred to one of Yuan Shikai's new battalions, one that ultimately helped form the Beiyang Army. Feng's industriousness insured a steady advance in the ranks, and his avid reading exposed him to ideas both traditional and revolutionary. The Chinese Revolution of 1911 provided Feng with the opportunity to form his own brigade. It was also about then that he became a Christian. In Christianity he found not only a moral code often not too different from Confucian thought, but one that provided practical advantages. Connections with the foreign community were one, but another was finding a new perspective that could be used to inspire troops and civilians. Despite his military station, Feng genuinely wished to reform society. To this end, in 1924 he renamed his army the National People's Army of the Chinese Republic, and besides lecturing them repeatedly about morality, entertained various proposals for social reform. Hence his reputation, for even if he didn't manage to fulfill reforms he seemed more promising than other militarists. Feng's later actions repeat this ideological yet practical predilection. While he proclaimed loudly the virtues of a particular course, he was also practical enough to choose his courses at the last moment when things were secure. He supported Yuan Shikai as long as he thought wise, but switched to the anti-monarchical forces in 1916 after engaging them. He later joined the powerful Zhili Faction, but deserted Wu Peifu in 1924 just as Wu was poised to dominate China south of the Wall. Some suggest that despite Feng's fierce anti-Japanese stance he may have been encouraged — and financed — to abandon Wu by Japanese personnel in China. This makes Feng's later collaboration with Guo Songling in 1925 all the more intriguing, for in encouraging Guo to revolt against Zhang Zuolin, Feng was undermining Japanese authority in Manchuria at a time when he was negotiating for Japanese aid in the development of his base area northwest of Beijing. Although Feng lost his command in early 1926, he returned after touring the Soviet Union to lead his old army to the aid of the Northern Expedition. Feng, however, eventually sided with Jiang Jieshi against the Communists, despite the Soviet Union's long support of the development of Feng's northwest base. Feng's history likely encouraged Nationalist leader Jiang Jieshi to force Feng into retirement in 1930, but interest was rekindled in Feng after 1945 among those searching for an alternative to Jiang. Feng himself promoted this during his tour of the United States in 1946–1948. Ostensibly inspecting irrigation and water management, Feng spent most of his time denouncing Jiang's regime and American support of it. In November 1947, Feng and his allies even founded an "Overseas Chinese Association for Peace and Democracy in China," provoking the Chinese government to demand his immediate return. Although Feng ignored the order, his public criticisms faded anyway as growing Communist strength rendered Feng's activities moot. Feng eventually gave up and decided to return home via the Soviet Union. He never did though, as the Soviet press announced his accidental death aboard ship on September 1, 1948.

Unlike many warlords, Feng has been deemed

respectable enough. A book of his poems was published in 1954, and his ashes lie buried on sacred Mount Tai. His is remembered more for his patriotism than for his appropriation of foreign techniques and ideals.

See also Warlordism.

REFERENCES: Hsi-sheng Chi, Warlord Politics in China, 1916–1928 (Stanford, CA, 1976); James E. Sheridan, Chinese Warlord: The Career of Feng Yu-hsiang (Stanford, CA, 1966); James E. Sheridan, "The Warlord Era: Politics and Militarism Under the Peking Government," in John K. Fairbank (ed.), The Cambridge History of China: Volume 12: Republican China 1912–1949, Part I (New York, 1983); Arthur Waldron, From War to Nationalism: China's Turning Point, 1924–1925 (New York, 1995).

Bill Sewell

First Indochina War

The Japanese occupation of French Indochina (Vietnam, Laos, and Cambodia) during World War II disrupted French control of the area. A Vietnamese nationalist movement under Communist leadership, the Viet Minh, was able to develop substantial strength, and proclaimed the independence of the Democratic Republic of Vietnam (DRV) in September 1945. Sporadic fighting between Viet Minh and French forces began almost immediately, and escalated to full-scale war in December 1946.

The French forces, better trained and better armed, quickly defeated the Viet Minh in the early battles, but these forces were not very large. From 1947 to 1949 the war was stalemated; the French did not have the manpower to occupy all of Vietnam, and the Viet Minh guerrillas did not have the weapons to drive the French from the areas they did occupy. The United States, reluctant to endorse a colonial war, withheld military aid from the French forces in Indochina, though providing it to French forces in Europe.

A regiment of the Chinese People's Liberation Army (PLA), which had retreated into northern Vietnam in 1946 to evade Guomindang forces in southern China, provided a little training for Viet Minh forces. But real Chinese aid for the Viet Minh had to wait until the beginning of 1950, when the PLA forces that had won the Chinese civil war reached the Vietnamese border. China granted diplomatic recognition to the DRV in January 1950 (the Soviet Union immediately did the same), and began arming the Viet Minh. Chinese advisers were sent to Vietnam, and camps were established in southern China, where Viet Minh personnel whose training in Vietnam had been limited to guerrilla warfare could learn to operate in larger and more conventionally organized units. The arrival of Chinese advisers in 1950

began the period of greatest Chinese influence on Vietnamese Communism, which was to last until 1956. The United States had already been drifting toward greater involvement in Indochina. The imperative of opposing Communism was becoming powerful enough to outweigh squeamishness about colonialism. In 1950, the United States began providing military aid to the French forces in Indochina, on a scale that increased steadily thereafter. By 1954, the United States would be paying most of the financial cost of the French war effort — more than three-quarters, by some estimates. Also in 1950, the United States granted diplomatic recognition to the State of Vietnam, previously shunned because it was too obviously a puppet of the French. But the French resisted U.S. pressure to strengthen the State of Vietnam, and give it genuine independence.

Many American officials exaggerated the degree of outside influence over the Viet Minh. The widespread belief that the Viet Minh were proxies in a Chinese and/or Soviet effort to take over all of Asia encouraged belief in the "domino theory," according to which if Vietnam (or just the northern portion of Vietnam, the area around Hanoi) were to fall to Communism, this would quickly cause the fall of most of Southeast Asia. The United States, a much wealthier country than China, gave more military aid to the French forces than the Chinese gave to the Viet Minh. But Chinese aid to the Viet Minh had a much greater impact on the war than did American aid to the French, because the French had already been adequately armed, while the Viet Minh had been very deficient in arms before the Chinese aid began. The war had been essentially stalemated at the beginning of 1950; the Viet Minh began to gain ground significantly late in 1950, when units armed and trained by the Chinese became available for battle. The end of the Korean War in 1953 allowed both the United States and China to put more of their resources into Indochina. The United States provided the French with more military aircraft than they could maintain; U.S. Air Force mechanics had to be sent to Vietnam to keep the planes flying. The Chinese greatly increased the Viet Minh's artillery and antiaircraft capabilities; these were crucial at the climactic battle of Dien Bien Phu in 1954.

The war was finally terminated at the Geneva Conference of 1954. The United States urged the French to fight on, rather than sign a compromise peace with the Communists, but the French had lost hope of winning the war and decided to end it. China pressed the Viet Minh not to demand too much, when the details of the compromise were being worked out.

See also Second Indochina War; Cold War; Geneva Conference (1954).

REFERENCES: Bernard Fall, *Street Without Joy* (Harrisburg, PA, 1961); Qiang Zhai, *China and the Vietnam Wars, 1950–1975* (Chapel Hill, NC, 2000).

Edwin Moise

First Opium War (1839–1842)

Precipitated by China's effort to suppress the illegal opium trade, this was the first Sino-British war. It ended in the defeat of China and was followed by a series of humiliating "unequal treaties" with Britain, France, the United States, and other Western nations.

The First Opium War represented a clash of Chinese and Western cultures and the ways in which China and the West conducted foreign relations. For the British the main issues were free trade and diplomatic equality. Prior to the war, Chinese relations with the West were limited to trade, with little in the way of diplomacy. That trade had been strictly controlled by the so-called Guangzhou System, whereby all Western trade with China was carried out through the port of Guangzhou and Western merchants had to deal only with a small group of Chinese firms called the Cohong. By the early 19th century, the Guangzhou System had become a major source of tension between China and the West. Opium was another major cause of tension. Although opium had been introduced into China by Arab and Turkish traders nearly a millennium earlier, it was not until the late 18th century, after British merchants began importing Indian opium into China, that drug consumption had become a serious problem and the Qing (Manchu) emperors began outlawing it. Britain had originally introduced opium as a corrective to the trade imbalance caused by the lackluster market in China for Western goods. By the mid-1820s, however, the balance of trade was reversed and the previous flow of silver into China now began to flow out of the country in order to pay for the ever-increasing demands for opium. After a long debate among high-ranking officials in China, in late 1838 the Daoguang emperor (1821–1850) ordered a stepped-up suppression of opium trafficking. A vigorous campaign against dealers and addicts began and thousands of Chinese were imprisoned and hundreds executed. This was the situation when the emperor appointed a special commissioner, Lin Zexu, with plenipotentiary powers to handle the opium problem at Guangzhou. After arriving at his new post on March 10, 1839, Lin immediately put into action a three-pronged attack against addicts, Chinese dealers, and Western suppliers. In order to force the foreigners to surrender their opium supplies, on March 24 Lin detained the foreign community of about 350 men in the foreign factories in Guangzhou. By late June over 21,000 chests of opium had been turned over to Lin, who then destroyed the contraband. Later after a band of British sailors killed a Chinese villager and Charles Elliot, the British superintendent of trade in Guangzhou, mishandled the case, Lin ordered the expulsion of all British residents from Macao, where the British had already retreated earlier in the summer. On August 26, all British subjects moved to Hong Kong, a sparsely populated island at the mouth of the Pearl River opposite Macao. Actual hostilities began gradually during the autumn of 1839 in a series of skirmishes. The first major clash occurred on November 3, when a British vessel sank a Chinese war junk in the Pearl River. This was followed on December 6 by Lin banning all British trade in China. Finally, on January 31, 1840, war was officially declared. After a lull in fighting, in June the British expeditionary force assembled off Macao, where it first blockaded Guangzhou before the main body of the fleet moved northward up the Chinese coast. By late August the British had defeated Chinese forces near the mouth of the Yangzi River, seized Zhoushan Island, and were threatening Tianjin and the imperial capital at Beijing.

Although involved in the China trade since gaining independence, the war in China reawakened widespread American interest in China. With Britain preoccupied with the war, American merchants in Guangzhou took the opportunity to increase their own share of the opium and other trade in China. Also during the war an American naval squadron remained in Chinese waters under the command of Lawrence Kearny. At this point the emperor replaced Commissioner Lin with Qishan, who persuaded the British to return to Guangzhou to negotiate. After considerable delays and continued fighting, on January 20, 1841, Qishan and Elliot signed the Chuenpi Convention, which promised to cede Hong Kong, provide diplomatic equality and a $6 million indemnity to Britain, and reopen Guangzhou to trade. However, both governments rejected the agreement and both Qishan and Elliot were dismissed. Hostilities were renewed. In May the British attacked Guangzhou but withdrew after securing a ransom of $6 million.

In August 1841 Henry Pottinger replaced Elliot and once again British forces moved north, easily taking the coastal cities of Xiamen, Ningbo, and Shanghai by early summer. Later British troops advanced up the Yangzi River threatening the city of Nanjing. Thereupon the imperial court accepted the futility of continuing the war and on August 29, 1842, reluctantly signed the Treaty of Nanjing. The main articles of the treaty included (1) an indemnity of $21 million dollars; (2) the opening of the five ports of Guangzhou, Fuzhou, Xiamen, Ningbo, and Shanghai; (3) diplomatic equality between Britain and China as well as the rights of British consuls to reside in the treaty ports; (4) the abolition of the Cohong monopoly; (5) fixed tariffs on imports and exports; and (6) the cession of Hong Kong to Britain in perpetuity. Once the provisions of the Treaty of Nanjing and its supplements were made known to the outside world, the United States, France, and other Western countries sent their own representatives to negotiate their own treaties with China. In 1843 President John Tyler sent Caleb Cushing, who in the following year signed the Treaty of Wangxia.

See also Treaty of Nanjing (1842); Treaty of Wangxia (1844).

REFERENCES: Hsin-pao Chang, *Commissioner Lin and the Opium War* (Cambridge, MA, 1964); Peter Fay, *The Opium War, 1840–1842* (New York, 1976); Frederic Wakeman, Jr., "The Canton Trade and the Opium War," in John Fairbank (ed.), *The Cambridge History of China, Vol. 10* (Cambridge, UK, 1978).

Robert J. Antony

First Taiwan Strait Crisis (1954) *see* Taiwan Strait

Fish, Hamilton (1808–1893)

Hamilton Fish was born on August 3, 1808 in New York City. The son of Nicholas Fish and Elizabeth Stuyvesant Fish, Hamilton was named after the nation's first treasury secretary, Alexander Hamilton, who was a personal friend of his father. Fish attended both the Doctor Bancel's French School and, in 1827, graduated from Columbia University. After graduation from Columbia, Fish turned his attention to the study of law. By 1830, he was licensed to practice law in the state of New York and opened a law office in his native New York City.

Public service, however, would be Fish's principal avocation. Fish served in a number of offices for both city and county. He then moved on to national office. In 1842, he was elected as a Whig representative to the United States House of Representatives. This would be the beginning of a long career of prominent state and national offices. These included Lieutenant Governor of New York (1848), Governor of New York (1849–1851), and United States Senator from New York (1851–1857). In 1868, newly elected president, Ulysses Grant, nominated Fish for Secretary of State. While Fish was not the president's first

choice, many historians agree that Fish proved to be an effective cabinet officer and is generally regarded as one of the nation's most successful Secretaries of State. Despite personal misgiving about the appointment, Fish would serve for the entire presidency of Grant, leaving office in March 1877. After leaving government, Fish returned to the legal profession. He died on September 7, 1893. Among Fish's most prominent successes was his negotiations of the agreement between the United States and Great Britain that solved the Alabama claims as well as a number of smaller issues between the countries. The agreement was formalized in the Treaty of Washington, signed on May 8, 1871. Among Fish's more controversial actions was his support of President Grant's attempt to annex the country of Santa Domingo, which put Fish at odds with Senator Charles Sumner, chair the Senate Committee on Foreign Relations.

Preoccupied with the Alabama claims, Santa Domingo, and affairs in Cuba, Fish did not devote a great deal of time to China. Just prior to his tenure as Secretary of State, the United States had ratified the Burlingame Treaty with China. Named after American minister, Anson Burlingame, the first American minister to China, the Burlingame treaty gave the Chinese unrestricted immigration rights to the United States in exchange for the continuation of most favored nation status. Additionally, the United States denied any intention to intervene in China's domestic affairs. Fish's tenure as Secretary of State was characterized by an attempt to maintain American rights under the Burlingame treaty, thereby creating opportunities for American commerce. At the same time, he worked to discourage and restrain Americans who desired to use American power to intervene in the affairs of the Manchu Dynasty. In some respects, Fish's attitude foreshadowed the "Open Door Notes" of later Secretary of State John Hay.

See also Burlingame-Seward Treaty (1868).

REFERENCES: James B. Chapin, "Hamilton Fish and American Expansionism," in Frank J. Merli and Theodore A. Wilson (eds.), *Makers of American Diplomacy* (New York, 1974); Mark Grossman, "Hamilton Fish," in Mark Grossman (ed.), *Encyclopedia of the United States Cabinet* (Denver, CO, 2000); Allan Nevins, *Hamilton Fish: The Inner Story of the Grant Administration* (New York, 1937); David L. Wilson, "Hamilton Fish," in Bruce W. Jentleson and Thomas G. Paterson (eds.), *Encyclopedia of U.S. Foreign Relations* (New York, 1997).

Bruce Tap

Five Power Treaty (1921)

The Five Power Treaty (1921) was an agreement forged between the United States, Great

Britain, Japan, France, and Italy for the reduction and regulation of naval arms. It was one of nine treaties that emerged from the Washington Naval Conference of 1921–1922. The conference was held at the invitation and suggestion of the United States and credit should be given to U.S. President Warren G. Harding's Secretary of State, Charles Evans Hughes, for his initiative in the creation and direction of the conference. Harding and Hughes satisfied the national trend for disarmament and created a degree of protection from foreign threats. The British and Japanese, the primary threats to the U.S., faced similar domestic situations and therefore also wished to avoid an arms race. Originally, the U.S. only invited Great Britain and Japan, the two nations whose Far East policies and Navies most concerned the U.S. At the suggestion of Great Britain, representatives from France, Italy, Portugal, the Netherlands, China, and Belgium, also participated. The U.S. sought to prevent a naval arms race, reduce the risk of future wars, dismantle the Anglo-Japanese Alliance of 1902, and gain acceptance of its Far East policy. The conference began on November 12, 1921 and a total of nine treaties were signed. Two of the notable ones were the Nine Power Treaty regarding China and the sanctity of the Open Door Policy, and the Four Power Treaty, which replaced the Anglo-Japanese Alliance. The Five Power Treaty (1921), however, was arguably the most important, especially for American foreign policy. The Five Power Treaty (1921) agreed to a ten-year limit in the building of capital ships. The ratio 5:5:3:1.67:1.67, represents the tonnage amounts given to the U.S., Great Britain, Japan, France, and Italy respectively. The U.S. and Great Britain were given the same tonnage, the British because they had a world wide Empire to maintain, and the U.S. because they had to defend and maintain their homeland and possessions in both the Atlantic and Pacific Oceans. The Japanese were given less tonnage as their interests were solely in the Pacific. The French and Italians were given the smaller tonnages. The French protested that they had to defend in the Mediterranean and the Atlantic and should have been given tonnage equal to the Japanese. Small ships, such as submarines, destroyers, and cruisers were not included in the restrictions of the Five Power Treaty (1921). The countries placed a limitation on acquiring new bases and fortifying existing ones that respected each power's sphere of influence.

The Washington Naval Conference and the Five Power Treaty (1921) were huge steps towards multi-lateral security. Future conferences were held between the various powers to discuss the shortcomings of the agreements in Washington. The U.S., however, achieved all of its major goals in the Washington Naval Conference. It was a huge success for Harding's Administration and for the history of American diplomacy.

See also Washington Naval Conference (1921–1922); Four Power Treaty (1921); Open Door Policy.

REFERENCES: Jerald A. Combs, *The History of American Foreign Policy, Vol. II: Since 1900* (New York, 1997); Warren I. Cohen, *Empire Without Tears: America's Foreign Relations, 1921–1933* (New York, 1987).

Antonio Thompson

Flying Tigers *see* **American Volunteer Group (AVG).**

Ford, Gerald R. (1913-)

Gerald R. Ford, the 38th President (1974–1977) of the United States, took the oath of office on August 9, 1974 after the resignation of President Richard Nixon following the Watergate scandal that had left an "indelible scar" on American society. Earlier, he spent over two decades as Congressman from Michigan did and less than a year as 40th Vice President of the United States. Ford was sworn in as Vice President of the United States on December 6, 1973 the first time he filled the office mid-term. His unique managerial ability and skill, as a Congressman, won him many friends and admirers in the Congress and outside. Being a non-elected head of state, Ford, however, tried to retrieve the dignity of the White House and restore the national prestige besmirched due to Nixon's offence.

Ford continued with his predecessor's U.S. policy towards China. He retained Henry Kissinger, a key figure in the Nixon administration responsible for rapprochement with China, as Secretary of State. Ford reaffirmed his commitment to "One China Policy" under the 1972 Joint Shanghai Communique signed during President Nixon's visit to China. As a great admirer of Kissinger, Ford had given him a free hand to shape and articulate broad contours of American policy towards China in order to further improve ties between the two countries. Kissinger, during his visit to China in November 1974, set an agenda of discussion with Chinese leaders prior to Ford's official visit to China in December 1975.

President Ford visited China from December 1–5, 1975, and had held discussions with Chairman Mao Zedong and his Vice Premier Deng Xiaoping on international and regional issues of mutual concern and interest. Ford pledged "continuity in the U.S. commitment" to the principles of the Shanghai Communique, without signing new agreements with China. However, his visit was significant from the standpoint of meeting China's new leaders to better understand their perceptions of and expectations from America. Deng Xiaoping, a veteran Communist leader, told him frankly that improvement in Sino-U.S. relations required Washington to undertake concrete steps such as establishing diplomatic ties with Beijing, severance of diplomatic relations with Taiwan, abrogation of U.S.-China Mutual Defense Treaty of 1954 and withdrawal of U.S. troops from Taiwan. On these counts, President Ford could not complete the process of full normalization with China during his brief tenure as he had lost the 1977 presidential election to Jimmy Carter.

REFERENCES: John J. Casserly, *The Ford White House: Diary of a Speechwriter* (Boulder, CO, 1977); John Robert Greene, *The Limits of Power: The Nixon and Ford administrations* (Bloomington, IN, 1992); John Robert Greene, *The Presidency of Gerald R. Ford* (Lawrence, KS, 1995); Gerald R. Ford, *Time to Heal: The Autobiography of Gerald R. Ford* (New York, 1979).

B.M. Jain

Formosa Resolution (1955)

Ratified by the United States Senate on February 9, 1955, the Formosa Resolution pledged the United States to defend Formosa (Taiwan), authorizing the President of the United States to defend Formosa and the Penghus (Pescadores) Islands against armed attacks, including such other territories as appropriate to defend them. The Formosa Resolution was the beginning of U.S. military protection of Taiwan against the People's Republic of China and would define relations between the United States and China over sovereignty of Taiwan.

The origins of the Formosa Resolution lay in the defeat Nationalist forces in 1949 by the People's Liberation Army (PLA). Jiang Jieshi and his Nationalist forces fled to Taiwan and surrounding islands in the Taiwan Strait from where Jiang hoped to attack mainland China. The Communists tried to dislodge the Nationalist forces from the islands in the Taiwan Strait — Dachen, Penghus (Pescadores) Islands, as well as Jinmen and Mazu — with artillery bombardment throughout early 1950 but the outbreak of the Korean War in June 1950 prevented the outbreak of full-scale war as President Harry S. Truman sent the U.S. Seventh Fleet to the Taiwan Strait to deter cross-strait hostilities. Following President Dwight D. Eisenhower's decision to lift the navy blockade of Taiwan in 1953, Jiang reinforced Nationalist troops on Jinmen and Mazu. In response, Chinese Premier Zhou Enlai declared that Taiwan must be liberated. Tensions mounted rapidly as each side's military buildup precipitated small-scale engagements on Jinmen and Dachen Islands. The escalating tensions worried the United States as policymakers became increasingly concerned at the possibility of China controlling the Taiwan Strait and warned China against actions against Taiwan. Despite repeated calls for nuclear strikes against China, President Eisenhower took a calmer approach to the situation and signed the Mutual Defense Treaty with the Nationalist government in Taiwan on December 2, 1954.

In January 1955, the People's Liberation Army seized Yijiangshan Island while fighting continued on Jinmen, Mazu and along the mainland Chinese coastal port cities. Concerned that the existing Mutual Defense Treaty with Taiwan did not apply to islands along the Chinese mainland, U.S. policymakers quickly proposed the Formosa Resolution.

See also Taiwan; Taiwan Strait; U.S.-China Mutual Defense Treaty (1954); Seventh Fleet.

REFERENCES: Yu His Chen, "Sovereignty Disputes Across the Taiwan Strait," in David C. B. Teather and Herbert S. Yee, (eds.), *China in Transition: Issues and Policies* (New York, 1999); Warren Cohen, *America's Response to China: An Interpretive History of Sino-American Relation* (New York, 1990); Lin-chun Li, "The Mutual Defense Treaty and U.S. Policy on China," *Asian Outlook, Vol. 12* (1977); Simon Long, *Taiwan: China's Last Frontier* (New York, 1991).

Keith Leitich

Four Modernizations

Originating from Premier Zhou Enlai in his report to the Fourth National People's Congress in 1975, The Four Modernizations became a catch-phrase for widespread economic, political and social reforms in China. The areas identified for improvements were in agriculture, industry, defense, and science and technology. These goals were a response by the Chinese Communist Party (CCP) leadership to the economic ruins created by Mao Zedong's Cultural Revolution 1966–1976: widespread malnourishment, a budget deficit, high unemployment, outdated technology, and stagnation in science and military sectors. In the general population, this lead to growing credibility questions of Chinese Communist Party leadership in improving China's standard of living.

Zhou Enlai's report was endorsed by CCP leader Deng Xiaoping in a series of documents written in 1975; however his reports were condemned by "The Gang of Four." Consisting of Jiang Qing, the wife of CCP Chairman Mao's and three other ruling Politburo members (Zhang Chunqiao, Yao Wenyuan and Wang Hongwen) they rejected Deng's support of modernization as materialistic and against Chinese Communist principles. Following the death of Zhou Enlai January 8, 1975, Deng was relieved of all responsibilities and suffered his second purge from the party. Following Chairman Mao's death in September 9, 1976, the Gang of Four was arrested and opened the way for the reinstatement of Deng Xiaoping who would become the chief architect in launching the Four Modernizations. The new Chairman Hua Guofeng initiated a push for economic growth and announced a ten-year modernization program in 1978. Goals were identified in key areas in the four sectors, and included specific and ambitious financial investments with projected growth rates.

The first of the four modernizations was agriculture. Agricultural production had been hampered by the collectivization and commune systems. Even with such an abundance of labor and a preponderance of people working on farms, food production rates barely kept pace with population growth. Zhao Ziyang headed the efforts in the agricultural sector and had a record of success in Sichuan Province where farmers rented land and surplus produce could be sold at village markets. This added greater incentive for farmers to maximize production and increase earnings given their freedom to keep profits from farm and sideline production. The new highly effective system was called the contract responsibility system and replaced the commune system. Production brigades also were seen as having potential for developing new rural industrial development to supply industry and export markets. Since agriculture was the basis of the Chinese economy providing over half of total exports and the consumer market, modernization of agriculture and the addition of rural industry would generate income to support part of the growth in the other three modernizations. The industrial sector sought to invest in improvements in steel, oil, coal, electric power and later in the 1980s added foreign investment in special economic zones and privatized state-run organizations. In the steel industry, German and Japanese firms were contracted to build steel production facilities and to upgrade existing facilities to meet the aim of tripling the tonnage to 60 million by 1985. To increase oil production, exploration and the construction of crude oil and natural gas complexes resulting in a quadrupling in production. Coal is still the dominant source of energy in China, and eight new mines and upgrading old mines lead to anticipated doubling of production. Construction of ten coal-fired generating plants was scheduled to handle the increased coal production to meet increased electrical demands. Augmenting coal is pollution-free hydroelectric power and China pursued an expansion to construct twenty additional power facilities. Military modernization while considered important since equipment and technology was outdated was eventually relegated to a lower priority due the expense of purchasing foreign modern weapons systems. Even with this compromise, planners spent approximately $33 billion in 1978. Areas that were developed included computer systems, communication, transportation, conventional weapons and nuclear weapons (established in 1964). There were expansion and upgrading of in-house manufacturing industries for various military needs as well as development of research and development of new cutting edge technologies such as lasers, communications, optics, guidance systems, aircraft and rocket development. The adoption of new technologies also required the reorganization of the military organization, which also required a gradual transition. Scientific and technological modernization centered on increasing the number of scientists and skilled technical workers and developing centers for scientific research and development. The National Science and Technology Commission were formed to identify goals to expand science and technology education in eighty-eight selected universities. Facing a shortage of skilled technicians, China sent advanced scholars overseas for further study and hired foreign technicians to fill the void.

The Dengist era experienced rapid modernization and signaled the incorporation of market mechanisms (capitalist) in socialist structures. The success of decentralization and market mechanisms would pave the way for further economic stimulus for foreign investors in designated special economic zones and gradually lead the Party to balance its authoritarian political grip with use of capitalist management approaches on maintaining profits. President Richard Nixon visited the Republic of China in February 1972 to initiate Sino-U.S. relations with both sides supporting expansion in science, technology, culture, sports and bilateral trade. Normalization of relations is shown in the establishment of Embassies by March 1, 1979. The United States also reaffirmed the 1972 Shanghai Communique and stressed reducing military conflict and recognizing China's position on Taiwan. Given that this coincided with the start of the Four Modernizations, this encouraged the U.S. to pursue regular ties. By 1980 there were growing exchanges not only by the U.S. government but by many private companies initiating business in China.

REFERENCES: Immanuel C. Y. Hsu, *China Without Mao: The Search for a New Order* (New York, 1990); Immanuel C. Y. Hsu, *The Rise of Modern China* (New York, 2000); Lawrence Reardon, *The Reluctant Dragon: Crisis Cycles in Chinese Foreign Economic Policy* (Seattle, WA 2002).

Jim Steinberg

Four Power Treaty (1921)

In the years preceding the Washington Naval Conference of 1921–1922, relations between Britain, Japan, and the United States were marked with tensions. Japan exploited its alliance with Britain and the vacuum created in Asia by World War I to expand politically, militarily and economically on continental Asia and islands throughout the Pacific. Failed efforts to make China a Japanese colony, Japanese intervention into Siberia after the Bolshevik Revolution of 1917, and Japanese threats to not join the League of Nations unless permitted to retain Chinese territory only added to the tension. After World War I, the United States viewed Japan as a potential threat to its Pacific possessions, but worried that the Anglo-Japanese Alliance, which was already waning in importance, prevented Anglo-American cooperation in maintaining Pacific security should it be threatened by Japan. For their part, Japanese policymakers had long recognized that the United States wanted to eliminate the treaty, and were willing to forgo the treaty in favor of a triple entente with Britain and the United States.

On December 13, 1921, Britain, Japan the United States and subsequently France agreed, pending ratification by their various legislatures, to "respect their rights in relation to their insular possessions and insular dominions in the region of the Pacific Ocean." All four powers also agreed to hold a conference should "a controversy arising out of any Pacific question and involving their said rights which is not satisfactorily settled by diplomacy and is likely to affect the harmonious accord now happily subsisting between them." If any of the powers' rights were "threatened by the aggressive action of any other Power," the powers would determine "the most efficient measures to be taken, jointly or separately, to meet the exigencies of the particular situation." Article 4 of the Four Power clearly stated that upon ratification by all contracting powers, "the agreement between Great Britain and Japan, which was concluded at London on July 13, 1911, shall terminate." The treaty was to remain in effect for ten years "and after the expiration of the said period it shall continue to be in force subject to the right of any of the High Contracting Parties to terminate it upon twelve months' notice." All four powers ratified the Four Power Treaty (1921) in 1923.

In its ten years of existence, its signatories never exercised their right to call a conference. In 1931, the Japanese military expanded into Manchuria, threatening the U.S.'s Open Door principles. The next year, Sino-Japanese conflict in Shanghai threatened to blow up into a war involving all the contracting powers. In 1933, Japan issued the Amau Doctrine, which insisted that foreign powers not aid China, and that a Asian Monroe Doctrine made Japan responsible for peace in Asia. Weakened by the Great Depression to the detriment of their militaries, Britain, France and the United States were unable to defend their Pacific colonies. The latter also reverted to an isolationism that rejected the notion that U.S. rights in China were worth fighting a war to defend.

See also Washington Naval Conference (1921–1922); Five Power Treaty (1921); Open Door Policy.

REFERENCES: J.A.S. Grenville and Bernard Wasserstein, *The Major International Treaties of the Twentieth Century: A History and Guide with Texts* (London, 2000); Ian Nish, *Japanese Foreign Policy in the Interwar Period* (Westport, CT, 2002).

Stephen Craft

Fulbright Act (1946)

Begun in 1946 by Senator J. William Fulbright of Arkansas, the Fulbright Act succeeds in funding international educational and cultural exchanges for students and scholars. The Fulbright Program is funded by the U.S. Department of State and was signed by President Harry S. Truman. The policies and guidelines of the Fulbright Program are administered by a 12 member J. William Fulbright Foreign Scholarship Board, who are appointed by the President of the United States.

After the end of World War II, the United States enjoyed a rich economic surplus. Senator Fulbright wished to use some of these resources to foster mutual knowledge and understanding between countries, something he thought was necessary in order to maintain peaceful relations abroad. All of the major countries in Western Europe had signed on to the Fulbright Program by 1952. Graduate students, teachers, advanced researchers, trainees and observers qualify for exchange trips abroad to try and foster this international knowledge and understanding. Under the umbrella "Fulbright Program," there exist multiple grants and programs including: Fulbright Student Grants, The American Scholar Program, The Visiting Scholar Program, The Fulbright Teacher Exchange Program, and The Hubert Humphrey Fellowship Program.

Even though the Western European countries had all signed on by 1952, China was the first country in the world to sign an official Fulbright agreement with the U.S. The first grantee from the U.S. to travel abroad was Derk Bodde, a Sinologist at the University of Pennsylvania in Philadelphia. Bodde's research was in Chinese philosophy. The Fulbright Accord was signed in China by the Nationalist Chinese Foreign Minister Wang Shijie and American Ambassador John Leighton Stuart on November 10, 1947. In 1949, with the establishment of the People's Republic of China, the Fulbright Program with China was disabled. Not until relations were formalized under President Jimmy Carter in 1979 was the Program reinstated. After the initial normalization, the Chinese government used the Fulbright Program solely for the acquisition of Western industrial technology. New terms were negotiated, and soon after, China began accepting scholars in a wide variety of fields, including the more social sciences such as psychology, sociology, law and international relations.

The program in China is administered by the Protocol Between the Government of the United States of America and the Government of the People's Republic of China for Cooperation on Educational Exchanges. The Chinese Scholarship Council chooses students for foreign exchange and the placement of U.S. scholars in China.

REFERENCES: Randall Woods, *J. William Fulbright, Vietnam, and the Search for a Cold War Foreign Policy* (Cambridge, UK, 1998); Randall Woods, *Fulbright: A Biography* (Cambridge, UK, 1995); Haynes Johnson, *Fulbright; The Dissenter* (Garden City, NY, 1968).

Arthur Holst

Galaxy (*Yin He*) Incident

In the early 1990s, allegations of chemical weapon related sales from Chinese companies to Iran began to appear. The American officials became worried that the Chinese exports could help Iran develop its suspected chemical weapon programs.

In the summer of 1993, American intelligence agencies claimed that chemical precursors (thionyl chloride and thiodiglycol) were loaded aboard the Chinese ship *Galaxy* (*Yin He*) at a port in China before leaving for Iran. The U.S. had the Chinese ship on the high seas followed by its warships and taken aerial photos of by its military aircraft. The U.S. also spread information to countries whose ports *Galaxy* was scheduled to call, and demanded that they refuse to let the ship dock and unload its cargo. Finally, the U.S. forced the ship off the high seas and into a port in Abu Dhabi, United Arab Emirates. The Americans conducted an inspection of the ship only to find that there were no chemical precursors aboard. Feeling insulted, China became highly critical of U.S. actions leading up to the inspection. On September 4, 1993, the Ministry of Foreign Affairs of China made a statement claiming, "The *Yin He* incident is the sole making of the U.S. side as a result of its erroneous act based on its false intelligence." It stated that, "This is a show of hegemonism and power politics pure and simple ... , and the *Yin He* incident is only one example in this regard." The Chinese also argued that as a signatory to the Chemical Weapons Convention, China had committed itself publicly not to producing or possessing chemical weapons, nor did it export chemical products that might be used for the purpose of making chemical weapons. In spite of this statement, reports and allegations about Chinese chemical transfers to Iran and the Middle East continued to emerge. The U.S. concern about Chinese chemical weapon related exports to Iran became so strong that in 1997 the Defense Department reported that, "China is an important supplier of technologies and equipment for Iran's chemical warfare program. Therefore, Chinese supply policies will be key to whether Tehran attains its long-term goal of independent production for these weapons." In 2000, evidence surfaced that China's companies kept selling chemical weapon related production equipment to Iran. In June 2001, the U.S. State Department made an announcement that sanctions had been imposed on a Chinese company, the Jiangsu Yongli Chemicals and Technology Import and Export Corporation for violating the Iran Nonproliferation Act of 2000. These sanctions included a ban on all transactions between the Chinese company and any U.S. government entities, as well as a suspension on all business transactions between the company and any American company. Since the *Galaxy* Incident, the issue of China's chemical weapon related materials exports has remained a sensitive area in Sino-American relations.

REFERENCES: Anthony Cordesman, *Iraq and the War of Sanctions* (Westport, CT, 1999); Department of State, Bureau of Nonproliferation, "Imposition of Nonproliferation Measures Against a Chinese Entity Including Ban on U.S. Government Procurement, Public Notice 3707," *Federal Register* (Washington, DC, June 26, 2001).

Yuwu Song

Gauss, Clarence E. (1887–1960)

Having graduated from college in Washington, DC, Clarence E. Gauss started to work for the State Department in 1906. After working in the nation's capital for about a year, Gauss began his long service in China in 1907. He served as Consul at Shanghai, Tianjin, Xiamen, Beijing, and Jinan for over two decades. In 1940, he was appointed as American Ambassador to Australia. His tenure in Australia did not last long because President Franklin D. Roosevelt sent him back to China as the new American Ambassador in January 1941. Only months after his arrival in China, Japan launched its surprise attack on Pearl Harbor. As the United States entered World War II officially, China became a formal ally and Chongqing, the Chinese wartime capital, rose as one of the most important diplomatic outposts for Washington.

Maintaining effective and close relations between the two allies was not an easy task even for a seasoned and knowledgeable diplomat like Gauss. Right after the Americans enter the war, Jiang Jieshi, the Nationalist leader, began to seek $1 billion dollars of loans from the United States and Great Britain to support Chinese currency and ease economic conditions in China. Based on his knowledge about the conditions in China and the nature of the Nationalist government, Gauss recommended that the total loan amount should not exceed U.S. $500 million and that no huge lump sums should be provided without any conditions since he believed that loose lump sum credit would be poorly used to support the retrogressive, self-seeking, and fickle elements in and closely associated with the Nationalist government. At the end, the United States provided a U.S. $500 million loan for China and most of the money was used later to check the runaway inflation in China and the decline of Chinese currency. The alliance was saved, but the relations between the two allies and between Gauss and the Nationalist leaders were damaged.

Gauss had to face a tougher situation in Chongqing when the United States was unable to provide as much military and economic aid to China as requested by the Chinese. Because of the Europe First Strategy adopted by Washington and transportation difficulties created by the Japanese, only limited American weapons and equipments did reach China during the war years. In order to show American support for China's war effort, the State Department developed the China Cultural Program in 1942. Gauss supported the program after giving it a complete overhaul. Under the new program revised by Gauss, Washington provided generous financial assistance to Chinese students stranded in the United States, sent technical experts to work in China, sponsored the visit of Chinese leading scholars to America, and sent microfilmed science journals and books to Chinese universities in the Southwest. With experience and sensitivity, Gauss turned educational exchange into the most effective and successive dimension in the bilateral relations during the war.

While working hard to support China's war effort, Gauss pressed the Nationalist government for political reforms so as to make China a more effective ally. Under the instruction from President Roosevelt, Gauss urged Jiang to form a working agreement with the Communists so that more Chinese troops could fight the Japanese rather than among themselves. He recommended that a war council be established to give various groups and parties representation as well as responsibility. However, Jiang was unwilling to make any serious political or military reforms as suggested by the United States. Unable to achieve any of his major goals in China, Gauss resigned in November 1944, only days after President Roosevelt recalled General Joseph W. Stilwell under the strongest request from Jiang. After retiring from the State Department in 1945, Gauss served as the President of the United States Import and Export Bank.

See also Jiang Jieshi (1887–1975); Stilwell, Joseph W. (1883–1946).

REFERENCES: Herbert Feis, *The China Tangle, The American Effort in China from Pearl Harbor to the Marshall Mission* (New York, 1965); Theodore White and Annalee Jacoby, *Thunders Out of China* (New York, 1946); Wilma Fairbank, *America's Cultural Experiments in China, 1942–1949* (Washington, DC, 1976).

Hongshan Li

Le Gendre, Charles William (1830–1899)

Charles Le Gendre was born on August 26, 1830, in Ouillins, France and studied at the University of Paris, Sorbonne. He came to the United States in 1854 and settled in New York. At the outbreak of the Civil War he helped to organize the 51st NY Volunteers and was commissioned as a major. He was wounded twice and lost an eye at the Battle of the Wilderness in 1864. In 1866 he was appointed American consul at Xiamen, China, a jurisdiction, which included the island of Formosa (Taiwan). In response to the massacre of the shipwrecked survivors of an American ship, *Rover*, in 1867 Le Gendre led an expedition to Formosa and established relations with the tribal authorities. From this, Le Gendre negotiated a convention, which protected American sailors.

In 1872, Le Gendre resigned from the Foreign Service and moved to Japan. There he became an advisor to the Japanese government and used his knowledge of Chinese affairs to promote Japan's imperial aims in China. He was able to help the Japanese in their diplomatic negotiations in Beijing in 1873. He also provided information to the Japanese to prepare them for an invasion of the island of Formosa in 1874, an expedition, which he accompanied. He received the Order of the Rising Sun in 1875 for his service to the emperor of Japan and remained in Japan until 1890. While there he authored *Progressive Japan: A Study of the Political and Social Needs of the Empire*. In 1890 he moved from Japan to Seoul and became an influential advisor to the king of Korea. Le Gendre died on September 1, 1899 in Seoul, Korea.

REFERENCES: Charles William Le Gendre, *Progressive Japan, a Study of the Political and the Social Needs of the Empire* (New York, 1878); Sandra C. Thompson, "Filibustering to Formosa: General Charles Le Gendre and the Japanese," *Pacific Historical Review* (November 1971); Ernst L. Presseisen, "Roots of Japanese Imperialism: A Memorandum of Gen. Le Gendre," *Journal of Modern History Vol. 29* (1957).

Linus Kafka

General Agreement on Tariffs and Trade (GATT)

The General Agreement on Tariffs and Trade (GATT) is a product of the post–World War II era. It began operation in January 1948, after a founding conference in Geneva in 1947. The objective was to create an organization that could facilitate free trade between nations, and the countries that join GATT are expected to work toward this end. Free trade should be achieved by reducing barriers to trade, such as tariffs, quotas, export subsidies, and other hidden protections. Also, GATT members, called contracting parties in GATT terminology, should treat one another as most-favored nations, meaning that GATT members do not discriminate to provide better trade deals to particular members. Some exceptions to these objectives have developed over the years to meet the particular needs of member countries. For example, agricultural products are not included among the eligible goods, and developing countries can be provided with extended time periods to meet the objectives. China was one of the 23 original GATT members, and it officially became a contracting party in May 1948. However, the Guomindang government withdrew China from GATT two years later in May 1950, after moving to Taiwan. Though the government in Beijing did not recognize this withdrawal, GATT accepted it and a long period of separation began for the People's Republic of China (PRC).

By the 1970s, the PRC began to look outward after a period of isolation, and it sought to join a variety of international organizations. In 1984, the PRC obtained permanent observer status in GATT. Economic reforms steadily progressed, and in 1986, the PRC sought to be re-included as a contracting member in GATT. This began a period of negotiations that would last for over fifteen years. The Working Party on China's status began in 1987 under the leadership of GATT to address issues related to the PRC's accession. Issues needing to be addressed during this time period included building a variety of bilateral deals between the PRC and other member countries regarding how to properly expand trade between the countries to meet the requirements of GATT. There were also many issues to resolve regarding the transparency of the Chinese economy and issues for pricing and tariffs that result from non-market factors determining the price of goods in the PRC. Another point of contention was that the PRC wished to be treated as a developing country, and thus be given more time to implement the variety of reforms needed to improve trade conditions. Meanwhile, American negotiators argued that the Chinese economy did not need such protections. Progress in the GATT negotiations was hampered by economic problems in the late 1980s and early 1990s, and by controversy regarding Tiananmen Square Massacre. Early in the Clinton administration, the President joined with Congress to demand political change and improved human rights conditions from the PRC as a condition for joining. Meanwhile, changes in political leadership in the PRC created new questions for the Chinese about what true benefit they could expect to receive from GATT participation. On January 1, 1995, the World Trade Organization (WTO) became the new name for GATT. China would still not become a member until December 2001.

See also World Trade Organization (WTO).

REFERENCES: Harold K. Jacobson and Michel Oksenberg, *China's Participation in the IMF, the World Bank, and GATT: Toward a Global Economic Order* (Ann Arbor, MI, 1990); David M. Lampton, *Same Bed Different Dreams: Managing U.S.-China Relations 1989–2000* (Berkeley, CA, 2001).

Wade D. Pfau

General Conference of Protestant Missionaries

Protestant missionary work in China did not begin until January 31, 1807, when Robert Morrison arrived in Guangzhou. He had been sent to China by the London Missionary Society (Congregational). Despite the hostility of the East India Company to missionaries, he was able to learn Chinese and eventually enter the Company's employ as a translator. From then on the spread of the

Gospel by Protestants (preceded by Roman Catholic missionaries by several centuries) was rapid in both reaching the Chinese and in the number of Protestant missionary groups. By 1900 the growth of Protestant Christianity had been slow and steady. There were thousands of Protestant missionaries from the United States and Europe serving in China representing dozens of mission boards and denominations of Protestants. They were building schools, clinics and other institutions. To create unity of action for the sake of the ministry mission conferences were organized. The first general mission conference was held in Calcutta in September 1855 (The Bengal Protestant Missionaries). It was followed by others including the Bangalore Conference in 1879. A similar missionary conference was held in Japan in 1872 as the "General Conference of Protestant Missionaries." These conferences prepared the way for similar conferences in China.

The first General Conference of Protestant Missionaries was held in Shanghai in May of 1877. There were 126 missionaries present representing 26 missions. In addition there was one Chinese pastor who attended. He was granted the privilege of speaking, but was not received into membership so that he could vote. The first General Conference of Protestant Missionaries of China issued a statement, which declared its zeal for the salvation of Chinese soul. The work was declared to be a faithful fulfillment of the Great Commission. The second General Conference of Protestant Missionaries convened in Shanghai in 1890. It was much larger than the first conference. Among other work it issued a paper that was delivered at the conference in Shanghai, "The Attitude of Christianity toward Ancestral Worship." A general conference held in 1903 adopted the policy that Chinese converts to Christianity were still considered by them to be Chinese citizens and therefore subject to all Chinese laws. Nor was it the practice or policy of Protestant missionaries to enter into lawsuits on behalf of their communicants. The issue of lawsuit interference was due to the practice of the Roman Catholic priests entering to cases on behalf of their communicants. Involvement in lawsuits had been an issue in the Boxer Rebellion. The "Great Conference" was held in 1907 to mark the centenary of the mission work in China. It was the third General Conference of Protestant Missionaries, and was attended by over one thousand missionaries. They represented 63 mission agencies. Voting rights were limited to 509 of those attending. In addition the nine Chinese attending in an honorary capacity were also not granted the vote.

One of the decisions of the conferences was the establishment of "comity" in mission work. The arrival of Protestant missionaries to the Chinese mission field had been without regard for the work of other missions. To prevent competition that wasted resources, and confusion among the Chinese it was agreed at the Shanghai Conference that rural missions would be non-competitive, but that large cities would be areas where competing missions could be conducted.

See also Missionaries (American) in China.

REFERENCES: F. Hartmann, "Orphanages, Asylums for the Blind, Deaf and Dumb, and Other Charitable Institutions in China," *Records of the General Conference of the Protestant Missionaries of China, Shanghai, May 7–20, 1890* (Shanghai, 1890); W. J. Lewis, W. T. A. Barber, and J. R. Hykes, *Records of the General Conference of the Protestant Missionaries of China, Shanghai, May 7–20, 1890* (Shanghai, 1890); A. E. Moule, "Essay: The Use of Opium and Its Bearing on the Spread of Christianity in China," *Records of the General Conference of the Protestant Missionaries in China Held at Shanghai, May 10–24, 1877* (Shanghai, 1878); Stephen Neill, *A History of Christian Missions* (New York, 1964); M. T. Yates, *Records of the General Conference of the Protestant Missionaries of China, Held at Shanghai, May 10–24, 1877* (Shanghai, 1878).

Jack Waskey

General Order Number 1

Drafted by the U.S. War Department and approved by President Harry S. Truman on August 17, 1945, this unilateral declaration was a sweeping American effort to shape the political landscape of postwar East and Southeast Asia. The Japanese wartime Greater East Asia Co-Prosperity Sphere had shattered the prewar colonial order in Asia. Left-leaning national liberation movements emerged in China, Korea, the Philippines, the Dutch East Indies, and Indochina, threatening Washington's desire for an orderly transformation of the region.

After Tokyo capitulated under the simultaneous shocks of two nuclear attacks and the Soviet declaration of war, large numbers of Japanese troops in the Pacific as well as East and Southeast Asia had no legitimate Allied forces to whom to surrender. Fearful of the emergence of victorious Communist-led guerrilla movements in this political vacuum, Washington laid down precise guidelines for Japanese surrenders, in due course, to "appropriate" authorities rather than local armed resistance forces. The Americans sent General Order Number 1 to both Moscow and London for their information rather than approval. General Douglas MacArthur, as Supreme Commander for the Allied Powers (SCAP) was to direct Emperor Hirohito to issue the order delineating the precise forces to whom the Japanese were to surrender in the various theaters of operations. Most crucial for later developments was the decision that all Japanese forces in China (excluding Manchuria) were to surrender to Jiang Jieshi's Guomindang forces exclusively. This despite the fact that Mao's Chinese Communist Party had created a national resistance movement and could claim control over areas containing some 95.5 million people by 1945. Although reluctant, Stalin allowed the CCP into Manchuria, but urged a continued United Front with the Guomindang.

General Order Number 1 also divided Korea into a Soviet and U.S. zone of surrender at the 38th Parallel while French Indochina was divided between a Nationalist Chinese zone in the north and a British zone in the south. Japan and her mandates were to surrender to U.S. forces.

See also World War II; Korean War; Cold War.

REFERENCES: G. Kolko, *The Politics of War: The World and United States Foreign Policy, 1943–1945* (New York, 1968); H. Feis, *Japan Subdued* (Princeton, NJ, 1961); Odd Arne Westad, *Decisive Encounters: The Chinese Civil War, 1946–1950* (Stanford, CA, 2003).

Errol M. Clauss

Geneva Conference (1954)

The armistice of July 27, 1953, ended combat in Korea, but did not officially end the Korean War. The armistice agreement stated that an international conference should be held to work out a more permanent solution. Few felt real hope that the various parties would actually agree on a political settlement. But representatives from the United States, the Soviet Union, China, North Korea, South Korea, and 14 other governments did attend the conference at Geneva, Switzerland, from April 26 to June 15, 1954. No agreement was reached on any aspect of the Korean problem.

This was the first major international conference at which the People's Republic of China (PRC) had been present. U.S. Secretary of State John Foster Dulles was determined not to do anything that might imply recognition of the PRC. There was no conference table — the delegates had chairs, but not the usual large table in the middle on which to place their papers — because Dulles refused to sit at the same table with PRC Foreign Minister Zhou Enlai. On the day of the first session, when Zhou Enlai walked up to Dulles to shake hands and introduce himself, Dulles looked at Zhou's outstretched hand and turned his back. It was suggested that the presence of the foreign ministers of so many important countries in Geneva could provide the opportunity to hold a second conference, on a problem that might actually be capable of being resolved: the First In-

dochina War. The French, receiving American assistance, had been losing ground since late 1950 in their struggle against the Viet Minh, a Communist-led nationalist movement receiving Chinese and Soviet assistance. The main locus of the war was Vietnam, but it spilled over to some extent into Laos and Cambodia, the other components of French Indochina. The Geneva Conference on Indochina lasted from May 8 to July 21, 1954. The United Kingdom and the Soviet Union were the co-chairs. The other governments involved were France, the United States, the PRC, the Democratic Republic of Vietnam (DRV — the official government of the Viet Minh), the State of Vietnam (a puppet government under French control), and the royal governments of Cambodia and Laos, which were associated with the French but had more actual independence than the State of Vietnam.

The United States consented only very grudgingly to the conference on Indochina. The reason a settlement seemed possible was that the French were losing heart and looking for a way out of the war. Dulles feared the conference would produce an agreement embodying unacceptable concessions to the Communists. The United States and the State of Vietnam proposed that the State of Vietnam be given control of Vietnam. Since the State of Vietnam was a junior partner on what was clearly by this time the losing side in the war, this proposal was ignored by the serious negotiators at the conference. The Geneva Accords — separate signed cease-fire agreements for Vietnam, Laos, and Cambodia, and a Final Declaration of the Geneva Conference that was verbally endorsed by some but not all of the delegations — were completed on July 20 and 21, 1954. China and the Soviet Union had pressed the Viet Minh to be conciliatory, despite the fact that they were winning the war on the ground. Vietnam was split at the 17th parallel. The armed forces of the DRV were to regroup to the north of this line, and those of the French and State of Vietnam to the South. In 1956, an election was to be held under international supervision, to choose a government under which Vietnam would be reunited. It seemed obvious in 1954 that the Viet Minh would win such an election, but there was also an obvious possibility that the election would fail to occur in 1956. When the election indeed did not occur, the Viet Minh were left in North Vietnam with less land and less population than what they had controlled in 1954. Cambodia was placed entirely under the control of the French-allied government of King (later Prince) Norodom Sihanouk. The small Cambodian Communist movement later to become famous as the Khmer

Rouge was given nothing. Laos was placed mostly under the French-allied royal government. The Pathet Lao, a substantial Laotian Communist movement, was given two provinces as a temporary regrouping zone, to be reintegrated with the rest of Laos later.

China was satisfied with the Geneva Accords. The United States and the State of Vietnam were not. There is a widespread belief that the U.S. delegate, at the final session of the conference on July 21, promised that the United States would not obstruct implementation of the accords, but this is incorrect.

See also Geneva Conference (1961–1962); Korean War; Cold War; First Indochina War; Second Indochina War.

REFERENCES: *Foreign Relations of the United States, 1952–1954, Vol. XVI, The Geneva Conference* (Washington, DC, 1981); U. Alexis Johnson, *The Right Hand of Power: The Memoirs of an American Diplomat* (Englewood Cliffs, NJ, 1984); Robert F. Randle, *Geneva 1954: The Settlement of the Indochinese War* (Princeton, NJ, 1969).

Edwin Moise

Geneva Conference (1961–1962)

The Geneva Accords, drawn up at the Geneva Conference of 1954, declared Laos a neutral country. From 1956 to 1958, the neutralist Prince Souvanna Phouma was prime minister of Laos. He seemed for a while to be making neutrality real. In mid 1958, however, a rightist government aligned with the United States and Thailand came to power. Guerrilla resistance against this government by the Pathet Lao, the Communist movement of Laos, began in 1959. A coup in August 1960 brought Souvanna Phouma and his neutralist faction briefly back to power, but in December he was forced out by the rightists once more. This led to a war pitting the rightist government in Vientiane, supported by the United States and Thailand, against an alliance of Pathet Lao and neutralist forces, supported by significant numbers of troops from the Democratic Republic of Vietnam (DRV, North Vietnam), with assistance from China and the Soviet Union.

DRV troops opened in 1961 a network of routes through southeastern Laos, collectively known as the Ho Chi Minh Trail, by which the DRV could send men and supplies from North to South Vietnam, bypassing the Demilitarized Zone (DMZ) separating them. From 1959 to 1961, the Ho Chi Minh Trail had gone directly across the DMZ, rather than detouring through Laos. President John Kennedy increased the number of U.S. advisers in Laos, and seriously considered more direct U.S. participation in the war, but decided instead to try for a negotiated settlement. A sec-

ond Geneva Conference began in May 1961, with delegates from the United States, the Soviet Union, the People's Republic of China, the rightist Royal Laotian Government, the Pathet Lao, Souvanna Phouma's neutralists, the DRV, the Republic of Vietnam (South Vietnam), the United Kingdom, Cambodia, Thailand, France, India, Canada, and Poland. The conference offered the occasion for Secretary of State Dean Rusk to shake the hand of the PRC Foreign Minister, something Secretary of State John Foster Dulles had conspicuously refused to do at the 1954 Geneva Conference. But there was not a great deal of interaction between American and Chinese representatives. The Americans conducted their serious negotiations more with the Soviet representatives, mainly Deputy Foreign Minister Georgi Pushkin, than with those of China or the DRV. There was supposed to be a cease-fire in Laos during the conference, but this broke down repeatedly. A major defeat for rightist forces in May 1962 at Nam Tha, in northern Laos, persuaded the rightists to accept terms they had previously rejected. Negotiations elsewhere among the three Laotian factions were important supplements to the conference in Geneva. The most crucial such meeting, in Laos in June 1962, produced an agreement on a coalition government for Laos, with a cabinet made up of eleven neutralists, four rightists, and four Pathet Lao. Souvanna Phouma became both prime minister and minister of defense. The conference in Switzerland produced on July 23 a Declaration on the Neutrality of Laos, under which all foreign military forces were to be withdrawn. If actually implemented in full, the agreement would have been a major victory for the United States. Withdrawal of all DRV military forces from Laos would have meant closing the Ho Chi Minh Trail. Withdrawing the much smaller number of U.S. personnel from Laos would have been a cheap price to pay. Pushkin promised the United States that the Soviet Union would ensure that the DRV actually pulled its troops out of Laos, and it seems likely that the Soviet Union tried to do so, but if so it failed. The DRV signed the agreement but then flagrantly violated it, keeping troops in Laos and continuing to operate the Ho Chi Minh Trail. China supported the DRV in this. The United States, on the other hand, pulled out its troops. This was a major factor causing Souvanna Phouma, who had been allied with the DRV and the Pathet Lao before the agreement was signed, to shift and ally himself with the United States and the rightists soon after.

Many people believe that the United States, in the years that followed, foolishly allowed itself to be bound by the 1962 Geneva Agreement even though the DRV was violating it. This is not really true. The United States was restrained by a desire not to lose its alliance with Souvanna Phouma, the most respected political figure in Laos. Souvanna eventually allowed the United States to carry out a huge bombing campaign in Laos, completely forbidden by the 1962 agreement. But he did not wish to have significant U.S. ground forces there, and the United States respected his wishes.

See also Geneva Conference (1954); Cold War; First Indochina War; Second Indochina War.

REFERENCES: Martin Stuart-Fox, *A History of Laos* (Cambridge, UK, 1997); Qiang Zhai, *China and the Vietnam Wars, 1950–1975* (Chapel Hill, NC, 2000).
Edwin Moise

Germ Warfare (1951–1952)

Germ warfare, or biological warfare, is the use of living organism, such as diseases, against enemy forces and population, to deliver mass destruction. During the Korean War, the People's Republic of China (PRC), Democratic People's Republic of Korea (DPRK), and Union of Soviet Socialist Republic (USSR) made allegations that the U.S. used bacteriological weapons in North Korea and Northeast China against the Korean People's Army (KPA), the Chinese People's Volunteer Forces (CPVF), and civilian populations.

In 1951–1952, the CPVF headquarters warned the Chinese field commanders that U.S. airplanes had dropped different kinds of infected insects such as fleas, flies, mosquitoes, crickets, spiders, and sand flies over CPVF positions in North Korea. Tests by their medical officers identified more than ten types of insect-borne germs and viruses, which might cause diseases like plague, anthrax, cholera, typhoid, dysentery, meningitis, and encephalitis. The Chinese commanders requested their troops in North Korea to apply "emergency measures" to extinguish the insects immediately, adopt preventive methods, and address morale problems. DPRK Foreign Minister first declared a protest statement that condemned the "criminal conduct of using germ weapons by the American invaders" in May 1951 and again in February 1952 and sent a formal statement to the UN Security Council. On March 8, 1952, Zhou Enlai, PRC Premier and foreign minister, accused American military aircrafts of dropping bacteriological bombs in Fushun, Xinmin, and Dandong in Northeast China, and Qingdao in East China on sixty-eight separate occasions between February 29 and March 5. The Central Committee of the Chinese Communist Party (CCP) founded the China Central Commission of Epidemic Pre-

vention in March, chaired by Zhou and joined by other eighteen national leaders. Within one month the commission organized 129 provincial and local prevention teams with 20,000 members. Meanwhile, 5,800,000 kits of vaccine were shipped from China to Korea to meet front line needs. The Red Cross of China and various groups organized the "American Germ Warfare Crime Investigation Team." The Chinese news agency successively issued public statements made by twenty-five captured American pilots concerning the employment of germ weapons. The Chinese and North Korean governments also invited the "International Association of Democratic Lawyers" in March-April and the "International Scientific Commission" in June-August for investigations. Both organizations supported PRC and DPRK allegations in their reports.

U.S. and UN officials, however, denied in early March 1952 any employment of biological or bacteriological agents as a war method to further the goals of the military operations in Korea and China. Dean Acheson, U.S. Secretary of State, and General Matthew Ridgeway, commander of the UN Forces in Korea, denied the claims of using biological agents against the Chinese and North Korean troops and civilians, though the U.S. did not ratify until 1975 the Geneva Protocol of 1925 which outlawed the first use of biological and chemical weapons in warfare, but nations generally reserve the right to use them in retaliation. The Soviet Union reiterated that the U.S. had never ratified the protocol, and the Soviet delegation repeatedly called on the U.S. to do so throughout the UN germ warfare debate in 1952–1953. The Soviets, like the Chinese and North Koreans, provided neither solid information nor material evidence to support their allegations at the time.

Since the end of the Korean War, no documentary evidence or personal testimony in the West has ever conclusively proved that the U.S./UN forces conducted germ warfare. But recent Russian disclosures suggest an elaborate Russian-North Korean hoax. In 1998 some former Soviet documents from the Russian Presidential Archive became available, which indicate that the charges were "contrived and fraudulent." This is the first evidence from the Communist side to refute the longstanding allegations that U.S./UN forces used biological weapons in the Korean War. Though small in number, they certainly show a new direction for further analysis and research of the event.

See also Korean War.

REFERENCES: Xiaobing Li, Allan R. Millett and Bin Yu (eds.), *Mao's Generals Remember Korea* (Lawrence, KS, 2001); M. Leitenberg, *The Korean War Biological Warfare Allegations Resolved* (Stockholm, 1998);

Stephen Endicott and Edward Hagerman, *The United States and Biological Warfare: Secrets from the Early Cold War and Korea* (Bloomington, IN, 1997).

Li Xiaobing

Girard, Stephen (1750–1831)

Philadelphia mariner and merchant Stephen Girard, one of the first four millionaires in the United States, made the basis of his fortune in the China trade. He was born in France in 1750, became active in French-West Indian trade, and sought refuge in Philadelphia in June 1776 when his ship ran into high winds and seas. Shortly thereafter he became an American citizen and shifted the focus of his business to U.S.-Caribbean trade. After 1783, when the British West Indian islands were closed to American commerce, he began to seek other avenues of trade.

At this time the United States tariff schedule was especially favorable to Asian imports. Girard took note of the voyage of *Empress of China*, which made the first commercially successful US-China roundtrip voyage in 1784–1785. After the almost total collapse of his West Indian trade between 1793–1795, he commissioned the construction of four ships specifically for the China trade. His initial cargo to Guangzhou was ginseng root, as was the principal cargo aboard the *Empress* on its 1784 trip. Girard quickly discovered that there was limited Chinese demand for this expensive medicine/aphrodisiac and the market was frequently glutted. Girard sensed that a better export commodity would be opium, an illegal addictive drug, which was widely consumed by the Chinese. By 1815 the smuggling of Turkish opium into China had become the basis of Girard's China trade. In that year, a shipload of Girard opium reached China at a time of market glut — precisely the problem he hoped to avoid by switching from the ginseng business. Even more seriously, Girard's agents ran into a Chinese governmental crackdown. After several more Chinese crackdowns, and China's shut down of all foreign trade during the "Terranova" incident of 1821, Girard never shipped opium again. Howqua, his Guangzhou agent, also withdrew from the China opium trade. The last China trade voyage Girard sent out was that of *North America* in 1824.

Girard nevertheless made a fortune in the China trade. Thereafter, he invested in banking and Pennsylvania's embryonic railroad industry. He clearly understood the seriousness of the Chinese government in its efforts to suppress the opium trade and wisely pulled out after 1821. Unlike other American merchants, Girard was never concerned by the moral implications of his involvement in the opium trade. In his view, Chinese hostility was but one obstacle, which an American entrepreneur had to confront as he won his fortune.

See also *Empress of China*.

REFERENCES: Jonathan Goldstein, *Philadelphia and the China Trade, 1682–1846: Commercial, Cultural, and Attitudinal Effects* (University Park, PA, 1978); Jacques Downs, *The Golden Ghetto: the American Commercial Community at Guangzhou and the Shaping of American China Policy, 1784–1844* (Bethlehem, PA, 1997).

Jonathan Goldstein

Goddess of Democracy

The *Goddess of Democracy* statue was one of the defining images of the Tiananmen Square demonstrations of 1989. The thirty-seven foot (ten meter) tall statue was constructed in a mere four days by student demonstrators using styrofoam and paper. Rather than working from traditional Chinese artistic motifs, this white figure of a torch-bearing woman with windswept hair draws primarily upon the U.S. Statue of Liberty (proper name *Liberty Enlightens the World*) created by French sculptor Frederic-Auguste Bartholdi. However, while Lady Liberty in New York Harbor stands serene and holds her torch aloft, the *Goddess of Democracy* clutches hers in both hands, at once acknowledging the ideal of American-style democracy and the precarious nature of the Chinese democracy movement.

The *Goddess of Democracy* was erected on May 30, 1989, directly before the portrait of Mao Zedong that dominates Tiananmen Square. During the unveiling ceremony, a student read a brief speech acknowledging that the physical statue was of temporary materials that could not last through the ages, but called upon those present to erect her image within their hearts. The assembled students then made repeated cheers for democracy, followed by the singing of *Internationale*, the Communist anthem. Any such reassurances made little impression upon the Communist authorities, who on June 4 sent tanks to crush the pro-democracy demonstrations permanently. The *Goddess of Democracy* statue was hacked to pieces by the soldiers and crushed under the treads of the tanks that had routed the students. Pictures of the destruction of the statue were seen on American television, where the news was received with grief and anger by many who had hoped real change would follow. Although the original *Goddess of Democracy* statue was destroyed, her image became a symbol of solidarity for Westerners sympathetic to the student protesters. On November 16, 1989 the San Francisco Recreation and Parks Commission approved the erection of a statue modeled upon it in Portsmouth Square. Approval from the San Francisco Arts Commission came the following year on April 2, and on June 4 the statue was erected. When it was covered during a visit by Chinese officials two years later, the action drew a storm of protest on the grounds that it was intended not as a diplomatic courtesy, but as a way of allowing the Chinese government to avoid confronting responsibility for their repressions.

Similar statues have also been erected in Washington, D.C. and Vancouver, British Columbia, while a new award for pro-democracy activity takes the form of a small bronze replica of the *Goddess of Democracy*.

See also Tiananmen Square Massacre.

REFERENCES: George Black, *Black Hands of Beijing: Lives of Defiance in China's Democracy Movement* (New York, 1993); Timothy Brook, *Quelling the People the Military Suppression of the Beijing Democracy Movement* (New York, 1992); Craig J. Calhoun, *Neither Gods Nor Emperors: Students and the Struggle for Democracy in China* (Berkeley, CA, 1995).

Leigh Kimmel

Golden Triangle

The term "golden triangle" was coined by Marshall Green, U.S. Assistant Secretary of State, in a press conference held on July 12, 1971 when he referred to the growing of a large amount of opium in an area including North Thailand, Upper Burma and Upper Laos. The golden triangle comprises the border areas of these three countries, which includes Thailand, Burma, and Laos. The golden triangle became famous because of the opium and heroin trade generated from the growing of poppies in these border areas. The physical barriers, such as rivers, terrain, and monsoon rains lasting for several months every year, made this area highly inaccessible. This made suppressing the illegal opium trade activities very difficult. In addition, these countries did not have good relationships. The Burmese government could not control the border between Burma and Thailand ever since its independence in 1948. Rebel groups from Burma controlled the border and gained the profit from border trade via tax. Problems also came from smugglers, opium warlords, and former Chinese Nationalist soldiers who belonged to the Chinese Nationalist Ninety-third Army and fled into Upper Burma after the conclusion of the Chinese Civil War. The American government supported these Chinese Nationalists in Upper Burma mainly because the United States hoped to assist the Nationalists to fight back into China. In the early 1950s, with the aid from U.S. intelligence agencies, the Chinese Nationalists attempted an invasion of China from Burma three times, but failed on each attempt. The United States, nonetheless, continued to support the Chinese Nationalists, which were well armed. These Chinese Nationalist soldiers also had links with certain people from Yunnan Province, China and thus got involved in the opium trade. In 1961, China and Burma took military actions against these Chinese Nationalists and forced them flee to Thailand. The Nationalist troops regrouped in Thailand and continued to deal in the illegal opium trade. The U.S. aid to the Chinese Nationalists in Burma was maintained even after they fled to Thailand.

In the areas of the golden triangle, there were various tribal groups, such as Karen, Mien, Lahu, Hmong, Lisu, and Akha. These tribal groups were originally from China. When these tribal people moved southward from China, some migrated to Laos, Burma and Thailand. They brought with them the seeds of opium poppies and the knowledge of growing opium. Hmong, Mien, Lahu, and Lisu grew opium because the area of the golden triangle contained prime territory for opium poppies to grow in the areas above 850 meters elevation. In 1875, Yunnan Province of China had one-third of its arable land growing opium poppies. By the end of the 19th century, opium had become one of the major crops in southern China. China declared opium illegal in 1949. Opium growing and use was wiped out in China. This forced the opium trade to move south into the areas of the golden triangle. In 1947, the government of Thailand restricted the growing of opium poppies in Northern Thailand, which was a portion of the golden triangle. In 1959, the government of Thailand passed the Opium Law, which made growing and trading opium illegal.

As early as the 1970s, various development programs were held in the golden triangle in order to make tribal people shift from growing opium to other kind of cash crops, such as coffee, potatoes and vegetables. The United Nations also had programs to teach the tribal groups new agricultural techniques and also offered drug treatment. The improvement of the infrastructure and roads helped the transportation in some areas of the golden triangle.

See also Guomindang Intervention In Burma.

REFERENCES: Edward F. Anderson, *Plants and People of the Golden Triangle: Ethnobotany of the Hill Tribes of Northern Thailand* (Portland, OR, 1993); Paul and Elaine Lewis, *Peoples of the Golden Triangle: Six Tribes in Thailand* (New York, 1984); Ronald D. Renard, *The Burmese Connection: Illegal Drugs & The Making of The Golden Triangle* (Boulder, CO, 1996).

Edy Parsons

The Good Earth

American author Pearl S. Buck published her second novel, *The Good Earth* in March 1931. It became an immediate success winning international acclaim, and was translated into over thirty languages, winning her a Pulitzer Prize in 1932 and the Howells Medal of the American Academy of Arts and Letters in 1935. Buck received the Nobel Prize for Literature in 1938 for her various works including *The Good Earth*.

The novel sympathetically portrays early 20th century northern Chinese existence by following the life cycle of a peasant family. The chief characters are Wang Lung, a farmer; his wife O-Lan, a slave brought by Wang Lung's father, who toils in the fields with her husband while keeping the family together; Lotus Blossom, Wang Lung's concubine who O-Lan refuses to allow in her house; Pear Blossom, Wang Lung's slave; Nung En, Wang Lung's oldest son who is in love with Lotus Blossom, but marries the local grain merchant's daughter; Nung Wen, Wang Lung's second son who is apprenticed to the local grain merchant; and the Fool, Wang Lung's retarded daughter. There are also numerous other characters including Wang Lung's father, his other children, his daughters-in-law, Wang Lung's overseer Ching, Wang Lung's uncle, the uncle's wife and good-for-nothing son.

The "good earth" is the source of Wang Lung's livelihood and, later, his wealth before it will claim him in death. The novel portrays the hard life of Wang Lung and O-Lan before the upheavals of the early 20th century. When starvation, caused by locusts and drought, forces the family to move to the city, revolution causes China to fall into chaos. O-Lan steals jewels from a rich urban man enabling the family to buy more land that in turn permits the family to prosper so much that Wang Lung is able to afford a concubine who is detested by his wife. O-Lan dies of a stomach ailment in middle age, after which Wang Lung purchases a pretty female slave, Pear Blossom. Wang Lung's wealth and property are protected during the uncertain times by his uncle, whom Wang Lung dislikes. The uncle has come with his family to live on Wang Lung's farm and is a member of a group of local bandits. Although wealth has made Wang Lung, it is also destroying his family. By the end of the story, Wang Lung is facing death alone except for his daughter, the Fool. His sons want to sell the farm upon their father's death while Wang Lung tries to figure out some way to provide for his retarded daughter knowing his sons or concubine will not do so. In 1932 Buck published *Sons*, and, in 1935, *A House Divided*, which together with *The Good Earth*

forms a trilogy that was published as *The House of Earth,* also released in 1935. Whether deserved or not, Buck's instant success with *The Good Earth* made her an "expert" on China for many Americans. The book became a standard way Americans perceived China until the 1960s, and is still widely read today. The book was criticized for not being representative of Chinese life.

The Good Earth was the best seller in 1931 and 1932 before being turned into a play. In 1937 Hollywood made the book into a movie of the same name, but did not feature any Asian actors in starring roles. Luise Rainer won an academy award for best actress for her portrayal of O-Lan. The film became one of the most successful movies of the 1930s and has withstood the test of time especially the locust scene.

See also Buck, Pearl (1892–1973).

REFERENCES: Paul A. Doyle, *Pearl S. Buck* (New York, 1965); Pearl S. Buck, *The Good Earth* (New York, 1931); Pearl S. Buck, *The House of Earth: The Good Earth; Sons; A House Divided* (New York, 1935).

Greg Ference

Graves, Frederick Rogers (1858–1940)

The Protestant Episcopal Church in the U.S. was among the first American Protestant missions to China and started its ministry right after the opening of five ports to foreigners. Bishop Frederick Rogers Graves, the fifth Bishop of the Church, served in China for 59 years and filled a unique position in the church history in China. Graves was born in Auburn, NY, and received his college education at Hobart College. After several years of training in theology, he started his mission career in China in 1881. On June 14, 1893, he was consecrated Bishop of Shanghai with jurisdiction over the lower Yangzi Valley.

Throughout his ministry in China, Graves represented the hard line mission strategy that resisted the accommodation of the church to its context. In the high tide of Chinese nationalism in the 1920s, Graves held student nationalism in low opinion. In 1925, during the May 30th Incident, he described contemporary students as possessing "a total lack of discipline" and therefore would not allow Chinese students who attended St. John's University in Shanghai to express their sympathy for the incident. His insistence made many teachers and students leave St. John's and to establish another university in Shanghai. Graves evinced a similar attitude toward the issue of school registration. When the Nationalist government required all foreign schools register with the government and be in conformity with the curriculum standards set by the government, Graves never backed down in his resistance of these requirements. Even other bishops of the American Episcopal Church in China allowed Chinese Christians to join to serve as school administrators and made attendance at religious worship and instruction in school voluntary. Nevertheless Graves still stood firm in making no compromise. Christian Schools under his jurisdiction were seriously influenced by Graves' policies. For example, St. John's University became the only unregistered Christian college in the 1930s and lost its leading role in Christian colleges that it used to enjoy. The issue of the National Christian Council of China further illustrates Graves' position in maintaining a mission field. This Council represented the most ambitious efforts of Christian churches trying to make Christianity indigenous to China. Graves saw the efforts of Chinese Christians in this matter as "radical," and "meddling in church affairs with politics." A public statement with the signatures of Graves and 31 other senior missionaries in 1927 criticizing the Council hurt both the reputation and the influence of the Council. The once-prosperous indigenization movement soon collapsed in China.

Graves resigned the bishopric in 1937 because of his age and illness. He lived at the campus of St. John's University until his death in 1940. **See also Missionaries (American) in China.**

REFERENCES: Frederick R. Graves, *Recollections, 1881–1893* (Shanghai, 1928); Edward Yihua Xu, "Religion & Education: St. John's University as an Evangelizing Agency (Ph.D. Dissertation, Princeton University, 1994); Peter Chen-main Wang, "Bishop F. R. Graves and the Changing Context of China in the 1920s," in Peter Chen-main Wang (ed.), *Contextualization of Christianity in China: An Evaluation in Modern Perspective* (Sankt Augustin: Institut Monumenta Serica, 2005).

Chen-mian Wang

Greater China

In December 2002, the respected journal *Business Week* reported a cover story entitled "Greater China." The glossy image on the front of the magazine included three well-dressed businessmen with their arms around each other looking upward toward a bright, endless sky. On their backs were the unmistakable icons of the Peoples' Republic of China, Hong Kong, and the Republic of China on Taiwan. The message was clear: China, Hong Kong, and Taiwan were chummy and equal participants in an emerging economic juggernaut that could best be defined as "Greater China."

In addition to sharing cultural, linguistic, and historic ties, the three areas are increasingly economically linked. Already China has surpassed the United States as Taiwan's largest export market. Conversely, China has now surpassed Taiwan in its production of many types of computer hardware. Many of the Chinese companies that are producing such hardware are Taiwanese owned and managed. As a result, at least 500,000 Taiwanese now live in Shanghai and other mainland cities and many more travel to China for extended business trips. In addition to China-Taiwan integration, Hong Kong is also playing an important role in Greater China. In 1997 Hong Kong reverted from British to Chinese control, but the city still maintains a high degree of autonomy under Beijing's "one country, two systems" policy. For example, China and Hong Kong still have different currencies and passports. Such differences have not stopped economic integration. As with Taiwan, thousands of Hong Kongers have moved to China seeking economic advantages, and not all of them are wealthy investors. Greater China is much more nebulous than simply the three entities of China, Taiwan, and Hong Kong. The concept can also be applied to other areas with high concentrations of ethnic Chinese, including Singapore, Malaysia, Indonesia, and even Silicon Valley in California. Nor is Greater China merely an economic bloc. The capital flows between these locales also carry ideas, cultural icons, and even people. Therefore, it is impossible to delineate the borders of Greater China and it is equally impossible to quantify the "gross domestic product" of such a body.

Furthermore, discussions of Greater China should not mask the very real differences that divide the Chinese communities of Hong Kong, Taiwan, China, and elsewhere. The Taiwan Strait remain one of the globe's most dangerous "hot spots," and the two sides seem to be drifting politically farther apart even as they draw economically closer together. The same can be said of Hong Kong. Many Hong Kong residents feel that China has reneged on its promise of "one country, two systems" and chafe at Beijing's repeated acts of political suppression. Some China watchers have even predicted the political breakup of China proper, as the coastal regions continue to develop more quickly than the poorer interior and western regions. For these reasons, it seems as if Greater China, at least in the near future, will remain an economic ideal and a political fallacy.

See also People's Republic of China; Hong Kong; Taiwan.

REFERENCES: Larry Jay Diamond and Ramon H. Myers (eds.), *Elections and Democracy in Greater China* (Oxford, 2001); Thomas A. Metzger and Ramon H. Myers (eds.), *Greater China and U.S. Foreign Policy: The Choice Between Confrontation and Mutual Respect* (Stanford, CA, 1996); Dexter Roberts, Mark L. Clifford, Bruce Einhorn, and Pete Engardio, "Greater China

How Leaders From the Mainland, Hong Kong, and Taiwan are Creating an Integrated Powerhouse," *Business Week* (December 9, 2002); Chris Rowley and Mark Lewis, *Greater China* (New York, 1996).

David Kenley

Greater East Asia Co-Prosperity Sphere

During the "Great East Asian War" (1931–1945) Japan struggled to rationalize its imperial conquests in a Wilsonian age through an effort to reconcile Pan-Asianist rhetoric with the idea of national self-determination. By 1938 Tokyo had announced a New Order in East Asia based on economic cooperation and a mutual defense of a new "East Asian" culture by the "independent states" of Japan, Manchukuo and Occupied China. In 1940, however, German military successes in Western Europe caused the Japanese to look southward to the raw material-rich colonies of France, the Netherlands, and Britain, which were now defenseless. Accordingly, in the summer of 1940 Japan announced her new Greater East Asia Co-Prosperity Sphere aimed at linking the peoples of the old Sinitic cultural sphere of northeast Asia and the more complex and diverse societies of Southeast Asia. This project might be dismissed as mere imperialistic opportunism, but the reality is more complex. The idea of a Co-Prosperity Sphere served many functions for Tokyo. It could emphasize Japan's leading role in creating a new order to replace the old order of Anglo-American supremacy in Asia. In addition, it would serve as a justification for abandoning liberal democracy at home in favor of the "New Order Movement" (the Imperial Rule Assistance Association). Finally, it provided a respectable ideological basis for collaboration with indigenous elites under Japanese control. Asian nationalism would be reconciled with Japanese regional hegemony.

In the wake of the Pearl Harbor attack, Japan conquered Southeast Asia in a dazzling series of military campaigns that eventually outran her strategic planning for the area. In November 1942, a Greater East Asia Ministry was established by Imperial Ordinance, undermining the authority of the Foreign Ministry as well as promoting discord among competing interest groups. In the newly occupied "Southern Regions" the Japanese eventually reached out to the nationalist elites with an active propaganda campaign aimed at destroying the old order of colonialism, racism, and materialism. Instead, Western ideas were denigrated and Allied civilians humiliated and interned under harsh conditions, while the Japanese language and worldview were promoted. All

public occasions were begun with a collective bow in the direction of Tokyo and Emperor Hirohito. Japan's military prowess caused many Asian nationalist leaders to make pragmatic accommodations with the occupation forces. More important, the Japanese released prewar political prisoners and welcomed dissidents in exile. Local people filled the administrative and managerial vacuum created by the sudden collapse of the empire. A cultural revolution occurred as the Japanese encouraged and promoted the use of native languages in the media. Youth and women found a voice in Japan's "New Order" and were encouraged to participate in mass organizations, parades, rallies, and paramilitary formations. Student exchange programs were initiated, as well as periodic Greater East Asia cultural exchange associations and literary and scientific conferences. Finally, Christians, Buddhists, and Muslims were all invited to participate in the holy war for the soul of Greater Asia.

The year of 1943 was the turning point of both World War II and the Greater East Asia Co-Prosperity Sphere. The Allies had challenged not only Japan's military and naval supremacy, but also her professed ideals in both the 1941 Atlantic Charter and the 1943 Cairo Declaration. In response, Tokyo announced her decision to grant "independence" to Burma and the Philippines. An Indian National Army had been created from among the POWs captured at Singapore and a Burma Independence Army came into being. In addition, volunteer armies were raised all over Southeast Asia. The climax of Japan's effort to transform the region came with the Greater East Asia Conference held in Tokyo during early November 1943. Fifty leading Asian nationalists/collaborators attended, including Puyi of Manchukuo, Wang Jingwei of the Nanjing regime in China, Ba Maw of Burma, Wan Waithayakon of Thailand, Jose Laurel of the Philippines, and Subhas Chandra Bose of the Free State of India. Premier Tojo Hideki addressed the delegates, celebrating the dawning of a new age of harmony and co-prosperity in an Asia cleansed of Western colonialism.

In 1944 and 1945, however, the fortunes of the Greater East Asian Co-Prosperity Sphere ebbed with Japanese defeats. Nevertheless, Japan inadvertently began the revolutionary transformation of Southeast Asia by 1945. Seeking to enlist the loyalties of local nationalist elites, as well as extract strategic raw materials for the inevitable struggle to come, Japan's economic exploitation and terror drove many into opposition, resulting in the emergence of such anti-Japanese national liberation movements as the Vietminh in French

Indochina, the Hukbalahap in the Philippines, and the Free Thai Movement.

See also World War II.

REFERENCES: P. Duus, et al. (eds.), *The Japanese Wartime Empire, 1931–1945* (Princeton, NJ, 1996); J. C. Lebra-Chapman, *Japanese-Trained Armies in Southeast Asia: Independence and Volunteer Forces in World War II* (New York, 1977); C. Thorne, *The Issue of War: States, Societies, and the Far Eastern Conflict of 1941–1945* (New York, 1985).

Errol M. Clauss

Gu Weijun (1887–1985)

Known as V.K. Wellington Koo in the West, Gu played an important role in the establishment of the League of Nations and the United Nations, as well as serving as ambassador for the Republic of China (ROC) to France, England, and the United States. Born into an affluent family, he studied in St. John's University, a prestigious missionary school in Shanghai, from 1901 to 1904. After graduation, he went to the United States and enrolled in Columbia University, where he actively participated in extracurricular activities. He joined a debating team and became an editor of the *Columbia Daily Spectator* and the school's yearbook, the *Columbian*. He was the President of the Chinese Students' Alliance of the Eastern States and served as editor of the *Chinese Students' Monthly* and the *Chinese Students' Annual*. He won the Columbia Philolescean Literary Prize and the Columbia-Cornell Debating Medal. Gu earned a master of art's degree in political science in 1909 and a doctorate in 1912. Columbia University Press published his dissertation in 1912 under the title of "The Status of Aliens in China."

In April 1912, Gu went back to China and served as secretary in the cabinet and then counselor in the Ministry of Foreign Affairs of the newly established ROC. From 1915 to 1919, Gu was Chinese minister to Mexico, the United States, and Cuba. In 1919, he participated in the negotiations for the Versailles Peace Treaty after World War I as a member of the Chinese delegation and was an instrumental figure in negotiating the Shandong Agreement, dealing with the question of Japanese treaty rights in that province. Gu played an important role in helping China become a nonpermanent member of League Council in the League of Nations in 1920, advancing the theory of geographical representation, eventually accepted by the international community. Appointed ROC foreign minister in August 1922, Gu began to negotiate with the Soviet Union over the establishment of diplomatic relations, the settlement of the Chinese Eastern Railway dispute, and the question of the political status of Outer Mongolia. Before talks produced any results, the cabinet he was serving fell to a military clique, forcing him to resign. During the subsequent changes of cabinets during the Warlord Era, he was recalled and served as foreign minister, acting Premier, and finance minister without much accomplishment.

When the Northern Expedition unified China in 1928, the Guomindang (Nationalist) issued an order for Gu's arrest for his collaboration with the former military regime, forcing him into exile abroad. He returned to Shenyang in 1929, where his friend Zhang Xueliang protected him and eventually persuaded Jiang Jieshi to rescind the order for Gu's arrest in 1930. In 1932, Gu was China's assessor in Lytton Commission investigating the Mukden Incident. In that capacity, he worked on China's behalf and submitted a detailed report on Japan's aggression to the commission. That same year, Gu was appointed minister to France and China's delegate to the League of Nations. During 1933 and 1934, he was China's delegate to the Conference on Reduction and Limitation of Armaments at Geneva, the World Monetary and Economic Conference at London, and the Permanent Court of Arbitration at The Hague. After the Marco Polo Bridge Incident in July 1937, he served again as China's chief representative in the League of Nations, defending China's interests there without much success.

When France fell to Germany in 1940, Gu stayed in Vichy for a short time, then went to Britain as ambassador. His achievements during World War II included arrangements of the Sino-British exchange of parliamentary missions in 1942, British relinquishment of extraterritorial rights in China in 1943, and the Sino-British Lend-Lease Agreement in 1944. In March 1945, Gu became a member of Chinese delegation at the San Francisco Conference to create the United Nations. While serving as chairman of China's UN delegation, he was appointed in May 1946 as ambassador to the United States. After Jiang's government fled to Taiwan following the Chinese Civil War, he exerted great efforts to negotiate and sign the U.S.-China Mutual Defense Treaty of 1954. In 1956 he resigned the ambassadorship. Gu became a judge on the International Court of Justice at The Hague in 1957, serving from 1964 to 1967 as Vice President of the body.

Gu's outstanding performance in diplomacy won him many honorary degrees including degrees from St. John's, Columbia, Aberdeen, Birmingham, and Manchester universities. In October 1963, Gu submitted his collection of speeches, diaries, telegrams, and letters to Columbia University. In the early 1980s, Gu arranged with the China Academy of Social Sciences in Beijing for the publication of his multi-volume memoir, *Gu Weijun Hui Yi Lu (Memoir of Gu Weijun)*. Gu died in 1985 at the age of 97. He is recognized by both the Nationalists and Communists in China as a prominent diplomat and true patriot.

REFERENCES: William Tung, *V. K. Wellington Koo and China's Wartime Diplomacy* (New York, 1977); Howard L. Boorman (ed.), *Biographical Dictionary of Republican China* (New York, 1967–1971).

Yuwu Song

Gunboat Diplomacy

Gunboat diplomacy is the pursuit of foreign policy objectives with the aid of conspicuous displays of military superiority. It involves intimidation by threat or use of military force, and usually comes in the form of political application of naval forces. Gunboat diplomacy had its origins in the First Opium War of 1840, when the Chinese rebelled against the British importation of opium into China, and the British response was to send a gunboat up the Yangzi River to intimidate the Chinese. In 1891 anti-foreign riots broke out along the Yangzi River, American diplomats strongly advocated gunboat diplomacy to suppress the riots. But it was not until 1921 that the United States established a Yangzi River patrol to protect American interests, lives, and property. In 1923 Washington acted with other nations by sending warships to Guangzhou in the name of protecting the foreign administration of Chinese customs. In 1927 the Chinese civil war became more intense, the U.S. government dispatched 35 warships, along with the navies of other powers, to Shanghai to protect foreign economic interests. Gunboat diplomacy was effective to some extent but sometimes it aroused more anger than fear among the natives.

REFERENCES: James Cable, *Gunboat Diplomacy 1919–1991: Political Applications of Limited Naval Force* (New York, 1994).

Yuwu Song

Guomindang (GMD)

The Guomindang, otherwise known as the Nationalist Party of China is a political party. It is active in the Republic of China on the island of Taiwan. The Guomindang has a long and active history in China. Established after the Chinese Revolution of 1911 (Xinhai Revolution), the Guomindang retreated to Taiwan in 1949 after its fight with the Communist Party of China for control over the country.

The Guomindang was founded on August 25, 1912 by Song Jiaoren and Dr. Sun Zhongshan. The Guomindang was a synthesis of several revolutionary parties in China including Tongmenghui.

The Guomindang was suppressed after the assassination of Song in 1913. In 1924, they took on Dr. Sun Zhongshan's political theory called the Three Principles of the People: nationalism, democracy, and the livelihood of the people.

The Guomindang aligned itself with the Soviet Union in 1918 and maintained a political structure similar to the Leninist structure well into the 1990's. In 1923, one of Sun's lieutenants, Jiang Jieshi traveled to Moscow to study the Soviet's military and political practices. Dr. Sun died in 1925 and was succeed by Jiang Jieshi. General Jiang instigated the Northern Expedition, a military action against the government in Beijing shortly after Sun's death. For over 20 years, battles were waged throughout China, until the Guomindang fled to Taiwan in 1949. Political turmoil ensued under Jiang in Taiwan. The Guomindang claimed de facto control over all of the China, to the chagrin of the Communist Party. The sovereignty of China in regards to the United Nations has been in dispute throughout the years. The Guomindang held the United Nations seat for China until 1971, and held the positive opinion of the United States until President Jimmy Carter broke formal diplomatic relations with the Republic of China on Taiwan in 1979.

At the turn of the millennium, the Guomindang was more than a political party. It was an economic powerhouse. Estimated at U.S. $6.5 billion, the party was the richest political party in the world. The fine political balance of the Guomindang rests mainly on the distinction between reunificationists and separatists. In the 2000 Presidential election, Lian Zhan's nomination caused dissent among former Party Secretary General Song Chuyu, who instigated an independent bid for the presidency. After being run out of the party, Song formed the People's First Party. The schism worried Lian, who in turn moved the party's platform towards reunification of China. The pattern of isolating issue based parties continued with the subsequent creation of the Taiwan Solidarity Union. As of the 2004 presidential election, Wang Jinping, the GMD's campaign manager said that the Guomindang is no longer opposed to Taiwan's "eventual independence."

See also Sun Zhongshan (1866–1925); Jiang Jieshi (1887–1975); Jiang Jingguo (1910–1988); Li Denghui (1923-); Taiwan.

REFERENCES: Chung-chi Kuei, *The Kuomintang-Communist Struggle in China, 1922–1949* (The Hague, 1970); Thomas Marks, *Counterrevolution in China: Wang Sheng and the Kuomintang* (London, 1996); Steven Hood, *The Kuomintang and the Democratization of Taiwan* (Westminster, UK, 1997).

Arthur Holst

Guomindang Intervention in Burma

During the final stage of the Chinese Civil War in 1949, the Communist forces swept through all over China, forcing Nationalist leader Jiang Jieshi and most of his Guomindang (GMD) troops to retreat to Taiwan. Some of the remnants of Jiang's defeated army in southwest of China fled to Burma. In the summer of 1949, the GMD troops began to reassemble in the border area of Burma. At the beginning, only a few thousand soldiers arrived. By 1952, there were more than 30,000 in the Nationalist bases in Burma. President Harry S. Truman viewed the GMD troops as a defensive force blocking Chinese Communist penetration into Southeast Asia, while more militant leaders such General Douglas MacArthur and members of the China Lobby saw them as an offensive force to be used to harass and destabilize the newly founded People's Republic of China (PRC). They also believed that the GMD anti-Communist fighters could establish a base for another front in case Jiang would attempt to regain the control of the mainland by launching attacks against the Communists from Taiwan.

During the early 1950s, with the help of the Central Intelligence Agency (CIA) and Jiang who supplied arms and reinforcements, the GMD troops in Burma made several attempts to capture Yunnan Province from their bases. But they were repeatedly defeated by the Communist forces. The Burmese government, upset by the presence of a foreign army in Burma, used both military and diplomatic approaches to remove the GMD bases. The Burmese leaders asked the U.S. government to help them with the removal of the Chinese Nationalist troops only to find out that the Americans were actually supporting the GMD intervention in Burma. The Burmese then began to seek assistance from the United Nations. But the situations changed when Dwight D. Eisenhower was elected president. Eisenhower saw little value in supporting and maintaining the GMD troops in Burma. His rationale was that they did not provide a base of operations for a serious military threat against Red China. Gradually, the new administration began to downplay the U.S. role in providing supplies and assistance to the Nationalists in Burma. With the consolidation of power of the Communists in the border areas in Yunnan and the military pressure from the Burmese government to force them out, the GMD forces were facing more and more difficulties surviving. Eventually, they retreated to Taiwan, ending the episode of the joint U.S.-GMD attempts to destabilize the Communist regime in mainland China.

REFERENCES: Robert H. Taylor, *Foreign and Domestic Consequences of the KMT Intervention in Burma* (Ithaca, NY, 1973).

Yuwu Song

Haig, Alexander Meigs, Jr. (1924-)

Alexander Meigs Haig, Jr. was appointed Secretary of State in 1981 during President Reagan's first term in office, but resigned in 1982 amid disagreements with other administrative officials. Haig already had a cordial relationship that he had developed during the Nixon and Ford administrations with the Chinese. Haig had been very involved with the opening up of China during the 1970s and his appointment helped to give a favorable balance to the skepticism of the incoming Reagan administration. One extraordinary and notable feats of Haig was to bring Harvard educated Ji Chaozhu who was only a mid-ranking Chinese official to spend time with President Ronald Reagan. Haig's motives were to influence Reagan in changing an ideological stereotype of the Chinese that had come about as a result of his little contact with China. Also it was people like Ji Chaozhu who would return to China and influence many to look on the U.S. favorably. Most of the officials during Haig's tenure of office were more willing to offend the Chinese than Alexander Haig. As Secretary of State, Haig made a public statement during a visit to China in June, 1981 that the U.S. would now consider the market of a variety of military equipment to China on an individual basis. Coincidentally, it was revealed in Washington that the U.S. and China had instituted an intelligence information gathering facility, largely on Haig's recommendations and influence, in China for a year. The facility was instituted to replace preexisting U.S. operating systems used for this same purpose.

Alexander Haig's policies as Secretary Of State in retrospect, was a tremendous success in terms of the relationship he built with the Chinese. His philosophy toward China was one that was conducted in the open, upfront, and honest and was viewed favorably by China. While Haig held the office United States-China relations went through several twists and turns. By late 1981 China appeared to pull back somewhat from the U.S. as it asserted its independent foreign policy. One of the main issues of contention was the Taiwan Relations Act, passed by the United States Congress in 1979, which provided for continuing unofficial relations between the U.S. and Taiwan. In late 1981 China began to make serious demands that the United States set a firm timetable for discontinuing American arms sales to Taiwan, even threatening to retaliate. Haig visited China in June 1981 in an effort to resolve Chinese questions about America's unofficial relations with Taiwan. Eight months of negotiations produced the U.S.-China joint communique of August 17, 1982. This was the third of such meetings in which Haig stated its intentions of the U.S. to reduce gradually the level of arms sales to the Republic of China on Taiwan, and the Chinese described as a fundamental policy their effort to strive for a peaceful resolution to the Taiwan question. Although the communique forestalled further deterioration in relations, China and the United States differed in their interpretations of it. The Taiwan issue continued to be a dark cloud affecting United States-China relations to varying degrees as it was with previous Secretaries and Haig's entire tenure. In addition to the question of Taiwan, other aspects of United States-China relations created controversy at times during the 1980s, Sino-American trade relations, the limits of American technology transfer to China, the nature and extent of United States-China security relations, and occasional friction caused by defections or lawsuits. Difficulties over trade relations during 1981–1982 included Chinese displeasure with United States efforts to limit imports such as textiles and a degree of disappointment and frustration within the American business community over the difficulties of doing business in China. Haig pushed the administration and was somewhat successful in trying to relieve trade restrictions. The issue of technology transfer came to the fore several times during Haig's term, most often with Chinese complaints about the level of technology allowed or the slow rate of transfer. Nevertheless, scholars generally view Haig's tenure as a tremendous success in Sino-American relations and his leaving office did more to hurt the relationship of the Reagan administration with China than any other single event of Reagan's presidency.

REFERENCES: Alexander Haig, *Inner Circles: How America Changed The World, A Memoir* (New York, 1992); Alexander Haig and Clare Boothe Luce, *Caveat: Realism, Reagan, And Foreign Policy* (New York, 1984); Alexander Haig, *The American Role In Deterring Soviet Aggression: An Address* (Washington, DC, 1981); Jean Edward Smith and Herbert M. Levine, *The Conduct Of American Foreign Policy Debated* (New York, 1990); Nancy Bernkopf Tucker, *China Confidential: American Diplomats And Sino-American Relations, 1945–1996* (New York, 2001).

Steven Napier

Harriman Affair

The "Harriman Affair" refers to the events surrounding the American railroad magnate Edward Henry Harriman (1848–1909) as he attempted to establish a commercial presence in Manchuria, part of his dream of creating an around-the-world transportation line. Although he initially gained tentative Japanese acceptance, he was later rebuffed, an experience that left lingering suspicions among some Japanese and Americans regarding the others' goals in China. The affair also reflects some of the difficulties involved in establishing viable concerns in China.

As the Russo-Japanese War (1904–1905) drew to a close, the Japanese government realized it was going to gain title to the southern section of the China Eastern Railway, which was to become the South Manchurian Railway. Arriving in Japan on August 31, 1905, Harriman began negotiating with the Japanese government to secure partial control of this railway so as to link it with his Pacific Mail Steamship Company and American railroad interests. He envisioned buying later the China Eastern Railway and gaining some kind of concession from the Trans-Siberian Railway for its use as far as the Baltic Sea, from where a new steamship line of his would connect with the United States. Harriman's goal was to more firmly link the United States with Europe and Asia, promoting commercial development and securing American leadership in the process.

Harriman thought the venture possible because of the state of disrepair that the three rail lines had reached, the massive debts Japan and Russia had amassed during their war, and because of prior Russian granting of concessions when foreign expertise and capital had been used for railway development. While Harriman was prepared to offer to Russia the double-tracking of the Trans-Siberian Railway, to Japan he offered financial resources and managerial skills. This appears to have interested some in the Japanese government because not only were many ill-prepared to take over the management of a railway, some also thought a commercial alliance with an American firm like Harriman's might help defend their sphere of influence in Manchuria from a possible war of revenge instigated by Russia. Harriman was frustrated, however, by a number of factors. Japanese public opinion, inflamed by not receiving an indemnity from Russia, was against turning over any war booty to a third country, perhaps especially to the citizen of a country that had brokered the peace. Indeed, Harriman's arrival occurred amid the announcement of the terms of the Treaty of Portsmouth (hurriedly signed on September 5, 1905), and he personally witnessed some of the display of public anger. Moreover, key Japanese officials, perhaps especially Komura Jutaro and Goto Shimpei, opposed Harriman's plan. Some Americans may also have opposed the plan, possibly arranging loans for the Japanese without the kinds of concessions that Harriman sought. Although Harriman gained the support of prominent men like Inoue Kaoru and Shibusawa Eiichi and made a tentative agreement with Prime Minister Katsura Taro on October 12, 1905, the Japanese withdrew from that agreement by the end of the month. Harriman attempted to revive the dream the following spring but failed. Intriguingly, that effort was made on Harriman's behalf by Jacob H. Schiff of Kuhn, Loeb and Company, an ally from the Union Pacific and the Great Northern Railways. Schiff was well known in Japanese financial circles—he had helped cover some two hundred million dollars of Japan's war debt.

This did not end Harriman's dream, however, and he continued to ponder alternative schemes crossing China and Mongolia with Chinese or Russian partners. Financial uncertainties and the Qing imperial succession in 1908 forestalled these efforts, though, and the dream died with him the following year.

See also South Manchurian Railway.

REFERENCES: Richard Chang, "The Failure of the Katsura-Harriman Agreement," *Journal of Asian Studies* (November 1961); Michael H. Hunt, *Frontier Defense and the Open Door: Manchuria in Chinese-American Relations, 1895–1911* (New Haven, CT, 1971); George Kennan, *E. H. Harriman, A Biography* (New York, 1922); Maury Kline, *The Life & Legend of E. H. Harriman* (Chapel Hill, NC, 2000); Yoshihisa Tak Mazusaka, *The Making of Japanese Manchuria, 1904–1932* (Cambridge, MA, 2001).

Bill Sewell

Hatem, George (1910–1988)

George Hatem entered China in 1933 as a young American physician recently graduated from the University of Geneva Medical College. Before his death in 1988 in Beijing, Hatem would take the name Ma Haide, become the first American to join China's Communist Party and the first American to gain Chinese citizenship following the Communist takeover of the country. In the field of medicine, he became world famous for his leadership in campaigns to eradicate venereal disease and leprosy from China.

While operating a clinic in Shanghai with two other young Americans, Hatem met two women who would change the course of his life. The first was Agnes Smedley, the American writer and activist who supported the efforts of the Chinese Red Army against Nationalist leader Jiang Jieshi. Smedley introduced Hatem to Madam Song Qingling, widow of Sun Zhongshan and an advocate for the Chinese Communists. At her encouragement Hatem visited the sweatshops of

Shanghai and worked on behalf of the Communist underground in Shanghai, offering his clinic as a safe haven for meetings. In 1936 Madam Song received a request from Mao Zedong, then just completing the Long March, to send one foreign journalist and one foreign doctor to the Red Army. She chose Edgar Snow, then living in Beijing, as the journalist, and Hatem as the physician. During their trip to join the Red Army they were joined by Huang Hua, then a student leader in Beijing and destined to become China's Foreign Minister, Ambassador to the United Nations and Ambassador to the United States. After joining the Communists in Baoan, Snow gathered material to write his classic *Red Star Over China*. Hatem was asked to visit the limited medical facilities run by the Red Army and write a report to the Communist leadership with his observations and suggestions. When Snow left Baoan after two months, Hatem stayed to work side by side with Chinese doctors and medics. At the encouragement of Zhou Enlai, Snow did not mention Hatem in *Red Star Over China*, and for the next several years Hatem disappeared from public view as he treated battle wounds and illnesses of soldiers and villagers. In 1940, after the army settled in Yanan, Hatem met and married Su Fei, an actress who had entered the Red Base Area a year before. In 1943 their only child, Youma, was born.

The only time Hatem surfaced to the West during the next 30 years was between 1944–1946, when General Joseph W. Stilwell sent a small group of American military personnel to Yanan to judge the military capability of the Communists in fighting the Japanese. During the visit of the "Dixie Mission" Hatem, now known as Dr. Ma Haide, served as host to the Americans on behalf of Mao Zedong and the Communist leadership. In 1946, following the defeat of Japan, Hatem joined the Communist delegation to Beijing in the ill fated negotiations mediated by General George C. Marshall to end the Civil War with the Nationalists. In 1949 Hatem entered Beijing with the army of General Ye Jianying and immediately set about creating a public health program with his medical colleagues in new China. One of his first assignments was to close the brothels of Beijing and begin an all out campaign to eradicate venereal disease. For the next several years he worked on this effort, making long trips to villages around the country, especially in the border area of Inner Mongolia. By the late 1950s mass inoculation and public education had rid venereal disease from much of China and he transferred his efforts to the eradication of leprosy. Like his work on venereal disease, Hatem spent much of his time in the countryside treating patients and educating Chinese medical officials on modern medical care. The political turmoil of the Cultural Revolution (1966–1976) brought Hatem's efforts against leprosy to a halt, as he was assigned duties such as stoking the furnace and repairing machines around the Ministry of Public Health. His wife was detained and threatened at her film studio, but finally released at the insistence of Premier Zhou Enlai. Unlike many of his foreign friends in China, Hatem was never imprisoned or interrogated during this ten-year period and, also unlike many of his foreign friends, he argued that foreigners living in China should not get involved in this movement. It should, he said, be a Chinese affair only. At the end of the Cultural Revolution Hatem was allowed to renew his efforts against leprosy and to travel throughout the world to raise awareness of the medical gains China had experienced since the founding of the People's Republic in 1949. He proved a convincing advocate for his adopted country, as he appeared on national television and in national publications when he visited the United States in 1978. This was his first visit home in almost 50 years. This trip began a series of visits to countries all over the world at the invitation of physicians and governments eager to learn from his public health successes.

Over the final ten years of his life Hatem was awarded several honors, including the Distinguished Service Award from the University of North Carolina Medical School, an honorary doctorate from the University of Missouri at Kansas City, the Leprosy Award of the Damien-Dutton Society of Belgium, and a commendation from the W.K Kellogg Foundation for his contribution to the field of public health. In 1986 he received the prestigious Albert Lasker Medical Research Award in the field of public health and in 1988 the government of India awarded him the Gandhi International Leprosy Award.

George Hatem, known as Ma Haide for the last 50 years of his life, died of complications from cancer on October 3, 1988. He was 78 years old.

REFERENCES: Edgar A. Porter, *The People's Doctor: George Hatem and China's Revolution* (Honolulu, HW, 1997), Edgar Snow, *Red China Today* (New York, 1970), E. Grey Dimond, *Inside China Today: A Western View* (New York, 1983).

Edgar A. Porter

Hay, John Milton (1838–1905)

A poet, journalist, historian, and diplomat, John Milton Hay was born at Salem, Indiana on October 8, 1838, but grew up in Warsaw, Illinois. Hay attended Brown University graduating in 1858. During the next year, he entered a law office. Hay campaigned for Abraham Lincoln in 1860, and was later appointed assistant private secretary to President Lincoln. In 1865 he became first secretary of American Legation in Paris, France. After working as a diplomat in a few countries, he was named Secretary of State in 1898.

Hay was important for shaping America's Open Door Policy toward the Far East. He set guidelines for much of America's diplomacy in the 20th century, involving the United States in maintaining China's territorial integrity. Hay's most notable accomplishment in the Sino-U.S. relationship was the prevention of the dissolution of the Chinese empire in 1900. In the late 19th century, the United States watched European powers and Japan establish their spheres of influence in China with apprehension, fearing that American trade rights might be violated by the new arrangements. In 1899 Hay sent the "Open Door" notes to the six powers asking them to approve a policy guaranteeing that in their spheres of influence the rights of other countries would be respected, that there would be no discriminatory port dues and railroad rates, and that Chinese officials would continue to collect tariffs. The doctrine of the "Open Door," or of equal opportunity, was largely formulated by William W. Rockhill, formerly of the diplomatic service and an expert in Far Eastern affairs. Hay saw the validity of this doctrine and chose to sponsor it. So it went public as a policy associated with Hay's name. It was Hay's diplomatic skills and courage that were responsible for its acceptance by the Western powers and Japan. Although the six powers responded coolly to Hay's dispatches, Hay declared that the Open Door doctrine had been accepted, and the American press hailed the policy as a great success.

In 1900 the Boxer Rebellion broke out in China. There were brutal outrage on the part of the Chinese and violation of international law and courtesy. Hay's policy at this critical moment was to use force when necessary and to punish when practicable but to assume that the revolt was local. He insisted on dealing with the Chinese government in Beijing with a view to preventing the dissolution of China. Hay sent a second set of notes. They stated that U.S. policy in China was one of equal trade rights for all nations and respect for China's territorial and administrative integrity. Instead of protecting U.S. business interests, America now shouldered the overly ambitious task of preserving China's territorial integrity. Under the guise of America's historical mission to support the cause of freedom, this task would lead the United States to ever stronger commitments in the Far East in general and China in particular. From one perspective, the famed Open Door Policy was largely an illusion. In 1900, Hay made attempts to force China into ceding territory on Samsah Bay in Fujian Province as a naval station for the United States. China's agreement with Japan not to cede any land in Fujian prevented Hay from realizing this contradictory goal.

In the early 1900s Russia began to further extend its influence and territory at the expense of China. Hay expressed American opposition to Russian expansionist policy. However, he was hindered by the lack of firmness, courage, and consistency shown by the Chinese and also by his awareness that the United States would not fight a war with the powers to maintain American policies in China. In fact after 1901 Hay did not advance the Open Door Policy with much vigor and enthusiasm as he had before.

See also Open Door Policy; Boxer Rebellion (1900).

REFERENCES: Kenton J. Clymer, *John Hay: The Gentleman as Diplomat* (Michigan, MI, 1975); Robert L. Gale, *John Hay* (Boston, MA, 1978).

Yuwu Song

Henry Liu Incident (1984) *see* Jiang Nan Incident (1984)

H.H. Kung (1881–1967) *see* Kong Xiangxi (1881–1967)

Home by Christmas Offensive (1950)

Lasting from June 1950 to July 1953, the Korean War featured a number of dramatic turns of events. Occupied by Japan since the first Sino-Japanese war in the late 19th century, Korea had been divided at the 38th Parallel into American and Soviet zones of influence after the collapse of the Japanese war effort at the end of World War II. Initially the United Nations hoped to supervise elections that would reunify Korea, but the Soviets were reluctant to permit free elections, especially when the South was more populous than the North. Instead, the Soviets installed Kim Il Sung as Communist dictator of North Korea and provided extensive training and supplies to the substantial military force that Kim's regime rapidly but effectively brought into existence. The creation of this military force was expedited by the repatriation of several divisions of well-trained and combat-hardened Korean volunteers who had fought with the Chinese Communists against the Japanese and then against the Nationalists under Jiang Jieshi. Thus, even though most

Soviet and American forces had been removed from the peninsula by 1950, the Soviets had positioned Kim to make good on his increasingly bellicose threats against the South.

Indeed, when the North Korean army invaded the South, it overwhelmed the smaller South Korean and token U.S. forces both numerically and tactically. Soon the whole peninsula had been seized except for a small pocket around the port of Pusan in the southeastern corner. But, taking advantage of the Soviets' boycott of the United Nations over the decision of that organization not to admit the People's Republic of China, the United States successfully sponsored resolution condemning the invasion of South Korea by the North and authorizing a United Nations force to repel the invasion. Soon American and other UN forces and material were pouring into the Pusan pocket, and in one of the most daring undertakings in military history, the UN commander Douglas MacArthur landed forces at Inchon, the port for Seoul, located on the west coast just below the 38th parallel. The North Korean forces in the South were decisively cut off from their bases of supply in the North, and within weeks, more than 100,000 North Koreans surrendered.

Having cleared the South of the invading forces, MacArthur advocated pursuing the remnants of those forces into the North in order to locate and destroy their bases of supply and to thereby eliminate any subsequent threat of invasion. But the high mountains that ran down the center of North Korea required the bifurcating of the United Nations forces into western and eastern components that would be separated by 50 to 75 miles of almost impassable terrain until they rejoined along the border with China at the Yalu River. Given the reduction in the North Korean forces, MacArthur felt that this risk was worth taking. Likewise, given the demonstration of American firepower, especially overwhelming air power, MacArthur also gambled that the Chinese would not make good on their threats to intervene if the UN forces approached the border. By October, UN forces on both sides of the mountains had covered roughly half the distance to the Yalu River when they were surprised by Chinese attacks. The terrain, the limited road network, and the impediments to communications actually worked to the disadvantage of the much better armed and supported, much more mechanized, and much better supplied UN forces. And these conditions actually provided many advantages to the Chinese troops who were lightly armed and supplied for the most part with only what they could carry on their backs. In fact, UN intelligence had not identified concentrations of

Chinese forces before the October attacks and were unable to locate them following the attacks. MacArthur was now faced with a serious dilemma. Since the Chinese attacks had been repelled without doing serious damage to his forces, he could not justify withdrawing from the North. But simply holding his positions would pass the initiative decisively to the Chinese and create a long-term risk. And continuing with the advance would put his forces at ever-increasing risk as the terrain became more rugged and unfamiliar, the weather became more severe, and their lines of supply and communication became more extended. MacArthur chose to move to the Yalu, hoping to surprise and stymie the Chinese with the rapidity of his advance. He gave this ostensible, final push to the Yalu the hopeful name of the "Home before Christmas Offensive." West of the mountains, the Eighth Army pushed north to the Chongchon River, while to the east of the mountains, the X Corps reached the Chosin Reservoir. Then these forces and those all along their tenuous lines of supply were attacked by nearly 200,000 Chinese "volunteers." By December 15, both UN forces had been driven back to the 38th parallel. The retreat was heroic in the main because it could have easily turned into a rout. Having been much lauded for the execution of his daring landing at Inchon, MacArthur was now widely criticized for having blundered into a nearly catastrophic trap. Denied a mandate to direct air strikes at the Chinese bases across the Yalu, MacArthur vented his frustrations publicly and was shortly thereafter removed from his command by President Harry S. Truman.

Following the reestablishment of the dividing line at the 38th parallel, the UN forces settled into a largely defensive posture. The following year, the North Koreans and the Chinese would launch another major offensive against the South, but despite some initial successes, the concentration of American artillery and air power on the lead units drained the momentum from their advance and eventually turned them back. When Dwight D. Eisenhower was elected U.S. president, he convinced the Communists to conclude an armistice by threatening to escalate the U.S. effort and, if necessary, to employ atomic weapons.

REFERENCES: Chen Jian, *China's Toad to the Korean War: The Making of the Sino-American Confrontation* (New York, 1994); Edwin Palmer Hoyt, *The Day the Chinese Attacked: Korea 1950: The Story of the Failure of America's China Policy* (New York, 1990); Patrick C. Roe, *The Dragon Strikes: China and the Korean War: June-December 1950* (Novato, CA, 2000); Dennis D. Wainstock, *Truman, MacArthur, and the Korean War* (Westport, CT, 1999); Allen Seuss Whiting, *China Crosses the Yalu: The Decision to Enter the Korean War* (New York, 1960); Zhang Shuguang, *Mao's Military Romanticism: China and the Korean War, 1950–1953* (Lawrence, KS, 1995).

Martin Kich

Hong Kong

Located close to the biggest city of Guangzhou in southern China, Hong Kong is composed of three parts: the island ceded to Britain after the Opium War of 1840; the Jiulong (Kowloon) peninsula, ceded to Britain in 1860; and the New Territories, leased by the British in 1898 for ninety-nine years.

In early 1980s, the Chinese government announced its intention to get back all the three parts of Hong Kong. After lengthy negotiations, British Prime Minister Margaret Thatcher and Chinese Premier Zhao Ziyang signed an agreement in September 1984. Under the agreement, the British would return Hong Kong to China on July 1, 1997. Hong Kong would retain a capitalist economy for fifty years after that date and would become a "special administrative region." This arrangement was called "one country, two systems." From 1997 to 2047, the Chinese government in the mainland would handle Hong Kong's foreign and military affairs, while allowing the residents to pursue their own economic and social activities. Also during that period, the Hong Kong people would not pay taxes to the central government of China. Even though Hong Kong residents had suspicion about this agreement, especially after the Tiananmen Square Massacre in 1989, the transfer of sovereignty to China went smoothly in July 1997. Similar arrangements were negotiated between China and Portugal in mid 1980s for the return of Macao, a small island near Hong Kong, to China in December 1999. Beijing has always wanted to use Hong Kong under the formula of "one country, two systems" for Taiwan. However, the case is much more complicated. Before the pro-independence party, the Democratic Progressive Party came to power in Taiwan in 2000, both Beijing and Taibei claim, as the United States recognized in the Shanghai Communique of 1972, that, "there is one China and Taiwan is a part of China." The U.S. policy of letting Beijing and Taibei settle their relationship peacefully by themselves denotes that the United States views the Hong Kong model as an option for reunification. The application of the Hong Kong model to Taiwan, however, will remain debatable for years to come.

In the 19th century, U.S. naval forces used Hong Kong as a port to gain concessions from China and Japan. The American navy also used Hong Kong against the Spanish navy in the Spanish-American War. During World War II, along the lines of traditional American anti-colonial foreign policies, President Franklin D. Roosevelt urged British Prime Minister Winston Churchill to return Hong Kong to China. But the British refused. In 1949 the Chinese Communists took over mainland China. Concerns of Red China's attacks on Hong Kong led the British government to request for American military assistance if such attacks occurred. Determined that America would not get involved in a war defending the British colonial empire, Washington turned London's request down. With the intensification of the Cold War in East Asia during the 1950s, the American government began to use Hong Kong as a base to gather intelligence about the People's Republic of China. Fearing that the Communists would expand into Southeast Asia, the United States changed its position on Hong Kong in 1960. The U.S. government now decided to provide military assistance to Hong Kong in case the territory was invaded by China. The U.S. interests, especially business interests in Hong Kong increased greatly after President Richard Nixon's visit to Beijing in 1972. American companies used Hong Kong as a bridge to reach the huge Chinese market. They invested more than $7 billion in Hong Kong by the early 1990s. The American government and private individuals showed great concerns over the future of Hong Kong after China and Great Britain signed the Sino-British Joint Declaration of 1984. They all hoped that democracy, freedom, and economic prosperity in Hong Kong would continue after Beijing took over the colony. The Tiananmen Square Massacre resulted in the U.S. Congress passing legislation that made the Administration in charge of monitoring conditions in Hong Kong.

See also First Opium War (1839–1842); Second Opium War (1856–1860).

REFERENCES: N. B. Tucker, *Uncertain Friendships: Taiwan, Hong Kong, and the United States, 1945–1992* (New York, 1994); F. Welsh, *A History of Hong Kong* (London, 1997).

Yuwu Song

Hong Xiuquan *see* Taiping Rebellion (1850–1864)

Hoover, Herbert Clark (1878–1964)

Herbert Hoover established an outstanding reputation as an engineer, humanitarian, and administrator, before assuming the Presidency in 1929. As President, however, he was confronted with the Great Depression. His policies of reducing taxes, balancing the budget, and limited public works was no more successful in curtailing the depression than his policy of non-recognition with Japanese expansion in Manchuria.

Hoover was born August 10, 1874 in West Branch, Iowa. Following graduation from Stanford in 1894, he amassed a fortune as an international mining engineer. In June 1900, Hoover and his wife were besieged in Tianjin, China during the Boxer Rebellion. This experience, however, failed to halt his enthusiasm for international business ventures. When World War I broke out in Europe, Hoover served as Chairman of the U.S. Commission for Relief in Belgium, and he was appointed by President Woodrow Wilson as U.S. Food Administrator (1917–1919). As Secretary of Commerce (1921–1928) under Republican Presidents Warren G. Harding and Calvin Coolidge, Hoover presided over the international expansion of American business interests. In the 1928 Presidential election, the popular Hoover defeated Democratic nominee Alfred Smith. Hoover's Presidency, however, was a troubled one as he unsuccessfully grappled with the Great Depression and Japanese expansionism in China. In September 1931, after alleging Chinese provocation with an explosion on the Japanese-owned and operated South Manchurian Railroad, the Japanese invaded Manchuria. The Chinese government of Jiang Jieshi appealed for international and American support, but Hoover was focused upon the American economy and the recovery of European war debts. Although reluctant to assume a leadership role in opposition to the Japanese, Hoover did authorize American participation in the League of Nations debates regarding the situation in China. Recognizing the historical interests of Japan in Manchuria, the Hoover administration was unprepared to exercise military and economic sanctions against the Japanese. Japanese expansion, nevertheless, was viewed as a threat to the international peace system of the Washing Naval Treaty and Kellogg-Briand Pact, which the Republican administrations of the 1920s enacted to keep the United States out of war. Hoover instructed his Secretary of State Henry Stimson to pursue a policy of non-recognition regarding Japanese infringement upon the territorial independence and integrity of China.

Paying little attention to Hoover's moral diplomacy, Japan launched an attack upon Shanghai in the spring of 1932. Hoover responded by sending marines and warships to the city, but Japanese aggression was undeterred. Secretary Stimson announced that Japanese actions in China violated the Nine Power Treaty of 1922, and the United States would no longer be bound by treaty restrictions on naval construction or fortification of Pacific possessions. Meanwhile, the League of Nations adopted the policy of non-recognition. The Japanese rejoinder was withdrawal from the League of Nations and the annexation of the puppet state of "Manchukuo." Hoover's policy of non-recognition and moral diplomacy failed to halt Japanese aggression, and the continuing crisis in East Asia was inherited by the administration of President Franklin D. Roosevelt.

Following his electoral defeat in 1932, Hoover retired to private life where he remained a critic of Roosevelt's New Deal. In 1947, he was appointed by President Harry S. Truman to head the Hoover Commission on reorganizing the executive department. Hoover died on October 20, 1964 in New York City.

See also Mukden Incident; Maucuria; Washington Naval Conference (1921–1922).

REFERENCES: David Burner, *Herbert Hoover: A Public Life* (New York, 1979); George H. Nash, *The Life of Herbert Hoover* (New York, 1983); Armin Rappaport, *Henry L. Stimson and Japan, 1931–33* (Chicago, IL, 1963); Joan Hoff Wilson, *Herbert Hoover, Forgotten Progressive* (Boston, MA, 1975).

Ron Briley

Hornbeck, Stanley Kuhl (1883–1966)

Stanley K. Hornbeck was Chief of the Division of Far Eastern Affairs of the Department of State and one of the architects of American foreign policy in Asia from 1928 to 1944.

He had enormous influence on policy towards Asia from the Woodrow Wilson's Administration through the Franklin D. Roosevelt's Administration but would eventually be remembered for "losing" China to the Communists.

Born on May 4, 1883 Franklin, Massachusetts, he was the only son of Marquis and Lydia Kuhl Hornbeck. Hornbeck grew up in Massachusetts and Illinois before settling in Colorado. He studied at the University of Colorado before graduating from the University of Denver in 1903. The following year he was awarded a Rhodes Scholarship for studying at Oxford University. He would go on to earn his Ph.D. from the University of Wisconsin in 1909 where he would come under the tutelage of noted political scientist Paul Reinsch. Following graduation from the University of Wisconsin, Hornbeck briefly taught in China where he saw the affects of the Chinese Revolution of 1911 on the Chinese people. The time that Hornbeck spent in China would come to color his judgment during his later tenure at the State Department. Following his return from China, Hornbeck taught Far Eastern politics and international law at the University of Wisconsin

from 1913 to 1917 and was on faculty at Harvard University from 1924 to 1928 before being appointed the Chief of the Division of Far Eastern Affairs of the Department of State in 1928. In 1937, Hornbeck was appointed advisor to then Secretary of State Cordell Hull and was the State Department's Special Advisor on Political Affairs from 1937 to 1944. During his tenure as Chief, Hornbeck handled negotiations on relinquishing American extraterritorial rights and dealt with the crisis caused by the Japanese occupation of Manchuria and would have enormous influence on American foreign policy in Northeast Asia. Cultivating contacts within the executive branch, Hornbeck positioned himself as an East Asian expert and used his access to make the case for his pro-Chinese views. Throughout his tenure at the State Department Hornbeck displayed a pro-Chinese bias. Hornbeck failed to understand Sino-Japanese relations before the outbreak of World War II in the Pacific. He miscalculated Japanese intentions, vacillating in his assessment of Japan's territorial expansion. At first, he acquiesced to Japan's invasion of Manchuria and then called for an economic blockade.

In the end, Hornbeck's tenure at the State Department would end with a position as the U.S. Ambassador to the Netherlands from 1944 to 1947. Following his retirement, Hornbeck continued to try to influence America's China policy.

REFERENCES: Russell D. Buhite, "The Open Door in Perspective," in Frank J. Merli and Theodore A. Wilson (eds.), *Makers of American Diplomacy: From Benjamin Franklin to Henry Kissinger* (New York, 1974); Richard Dean Burns, "Stanley R. Hornbeck: The Diplomacy of the Open Door," in Richard Dean Burns and Edward M. Bennett (eds.), *Diplomats in Crisis: United States-Chinese-Japanese Relations, 1919–1941* (Santa Barbara, CA, 1974); Joseph C. Grew, *Ten Years in Japan* (New York, 1944); Stanley K. Hornbeck, *The Diplomacy of Frustration: The Manchurian Crisis of 1931–1933 as Revealed in the Papers of Stanley K. Hornbeck* (Stanford, CA, 1981); Shizhang Hu, *Stanley K. Hornbeck and the Open Door Policy, 1919–1937*: Westport, CT, 1995).

Keith A. Leitich

Hu Jintao (1942-)

Hu Jintao succeeded Jiang Zemin as President of the People's Republic of China (PRC) in March 2003, representing China's fourth generation leadership. Born in Jixi city, Anhui province in China, Hu graduated from Hydraulic Engineering Department, Qinghua University, in 1965. Since his joining the Communist party in April 1964, he held important positions both in the party and government. He became Vice President of China in 1998 and General Secretary of the Communist Party in 2002 by replacing Jiang

Zemin. On March 13, 2005, Hu was elected Chairman of the State Central Military Commission, succeeding Jiang Zemin.

The veteran leader Deng Xiaoping was Hu's mentor and guide whose political blessings facilitated his getting elected as member of the Standing Committee of the Politburo of the Chinese Communist Party (CCP) Central Committee in 1992. Hu is regarded as a "builder of consensus" and patient negotiator in resolving internal contradictions within the party and government. Although Hu has pressed ahead with China's economic reforms and the modernization drive, he has advocated "studying and building" Marxist theory, with Chinese brand of socialism, in order to deal with new problems thrown up by economic reforms and globalization. There is a broad continuity of Deng's pragmatic foreign policy under the Hu leadership that considers economic, scientific and technological engagement with the United States critically important for China's emergence as a giant economic and technological power. Besides, Hu regards friendly and stable ties between the two countries essential for peace and prosperity in the Asia-Pacific region. At the same time, Hu has spelt out in clear terms that China is staunchly opposed to a "big power hegemony" and the "power politics" in international relations. As such, Hu made his government's intent fairly known to the Bush administration that China would brook no American interference in China's internal affairs, especially on issues like Tibet and Xinjiang under the garb of championing the cause of human rights.

During his meeting with President George W. Bush in Santiago in November 2004, President Hu discussed a wide range of international and regional issues—nuclear crisis in North Korea, reconstruction of Iraq and Afghanistan. Concerning Taiwan, Hu maintained that his government was staunchly opposed to secessionist activities aimed at separating Taiwan from Mainland China. He reaffirmed his government's determination to reunify Taiwan through peaceful means but he stressed that his country would not tolerate Taiwan's independence at any cost. President Bush, while realizing the sensitivity of the issue, reiterated the U.S. commitment to honor the three China-U.S. joint communiques, including the 1972 Shanghai Communique that acknowledged the "one China policy." On the issue of nuclear crisis in the Korean peninsula, Hu pointed out that China would continue to cooperate and coordinate with all parties involved in the multilateral negotiation to ensure that North Korea dismantle its nuclear weapon building programme and push for resumption of the stalled

negotiation to break the nuclear impasse. Given the complexity of the issue, Hu underlined the imperative of "patience, flexibility and sincerity" on the part of all parties while dealing with North Korea. Besides, Hu cautioned America to desist from terming North Korea as an "outpost of tyranny" or a "rogue state" that might further provoke North Korea into becoming more intransigent.

Since China is a key player in a six-party dialogue, "productive engagement" between Washington and Beijing, as President Hu expressed his optimism, would go a long way in establishing enduring peace and stability in the region. He reassured America that China would fully cooperate with it in the field of counter terrorism, law enforcement, environmental protection, and nuclear non-proliferation provided that such cooperation was based on the principles of "reciprocity and mutual benefit," "sovereignty and equality." This, he said, would be helpful in boosting bilateral economic and trade, financial and technological cooperation essential not only for friendly and stable ties between the two countries but also for the emergence of a secure and peaceful world order. Since Hu is neither well-known nor a popular political leader in America, this is yet to be seen how the American leadership develops a better political rapport with Hu and his team to put Sino-U.S. relations on a firm foundation.

REFERENCES: Xinhua (New China) News Agency, *China View, www.chinaview.cn* (March 13, 2005); Chinese Embassy in India, *News From China* (New Delhi, March 2005); Don Ewing, "Reality Check: Getting to know Hu Jintao," *www.nixoncenter.org/publicat.htm* (April 30, 2002).

B.M. Jain

Hu Na Incident

In July 1982, Hu Na, a nineteen-year-old Chinese tennis champion, sought political asylum in America after a tour in the country. Hu Na's major argument was that if she went back to China, she would be coerced to get more involved in political activities than she would like.

Hu soon found that the decision to grant her political asylum involved the turf of a number of American government agencies, and that the bureaucrats in the State Department were not willing to let her stay. Some officials believed that she did not qualify for political asylum because as a teenage athlete she did not have a political thought in her head. They also believed that the decision to permit her to stay in the United States would likely harm Sino-U.S. relations, at least temporarily. This event quickly became a controversial issue for both China and the United States. The Chinese officials urged the American government to return Hu Na to her family in China arguing that she was too young to have made a mature and independent decision. They also maintained that Hu Na's attorney was paid by donations from Taiwanese sources. They made promises that the girl would not be punished for what she had done. The Reagan administration had heated discussions on this issue. President Ronald Reagan gradually came to know about this case. Under great pressure from his conservative supporters, Reagan intervened. He was even quoted as saying: "We're going to give her asylum if I have to adopt her and make her a part of my own family." The State Department caved in. In April 1983, the U.S. government decided to grant Hu Na political asylum despite China's protests.

The Chinese then retaliated by canceling nineteen cultural and sports exchanges between the two nations scheduled for the rest of the year. This incident became the most serious issue in the Sino-American cultural exchange programs in the early 1980s. However, the effect of this incident on the relationship between China and the United States in general was limited. The Chinese continued to attach tremendous importance to acquiring advanced U.S. technology and to sending scholars and students to America. The relationship with Washington was considered sufficiently important by Beijing that the Chinese government exerted great efforts to prevent irritants and minor problems from becoming great disasters.

REFERENCES: *New York Times* (August 4, 1982, March 21, 1983, April 5 and 8, 1983); Peter Hannaford (ed.), *Recollections of Reagan: A Portrait of Ronald Reagan* (New York, 1997).

Yuwu Song

Hu Shi (1891–1962)

Hu Shi is considered one of the most influential Chinese thinkers of the first half of the 20th century. Hu, the son of a minor government official, was born on December 17, 1891, in Anhui Province. After his father died when he was three, his mother and several male relatives raised him. A highly intelligent child, he supposedly had learned over 1,000 Chinese characters by the age of four when he began schooling in the traditional Chinese classics. In 1904, he received a Western education in Shanghai. Six years later, he won a scholarship, provided from the funds returned to China by the United States from their portion of the Boxer Indemnity, to study at Cornell University. Initially studying agriculture, he switched to

philosophy, being inducted in to Phi Beta Kappa, and received his undergraduate degree in 1914. Next he attended Columbia University where he earned a doctorate in philosophy in 1917, studying under John Dewey, a founder of the philosophical school of pragmatism and the progressive education movement, who had an enormous influence on his thinking. While studying in the United States, Hu often defended China against foreign encroachments, but also noted that China itself was to blame for its international standing.

He returned to China in 1917 and became a professor of philosophy at Beijing University, the foremost institution of higher learning in the country. He taught there until 1927, and again from1930 to 1938. He often served as an interpreter for well-known visitors to China like the feminist Margaret Sanger and his mentor John Dewey. He urged the adoption of vernacular Chinese in literature, and in 1919, Hu became associated with the May Fourth Movement that fostered its use. From 1917 until the Communists took power in 1949, Hu advocated the modernization of China by reevaluating China's past. He also opposed revolutionary means to achieve the Westernization of China, instead favoring an evolutionary path through the mass education of the Chinese. He urged the Chinese to avoid "isms," and criticized the Nationalist Party and the Communists, both of which were critical of his ideas. He also opposed fighting the Japanese fearing it would destroy the reforms to modernize China. In the 1920s and 1930s, Hu wrote numerous articles espousing his theories and ideas.

In 1938, due to his American connections and fluency in English, the Nationalist government appointed him as ambassador to the United States. He served in that position until 1942. After 1942, he remained in the United States working for the Chinese war effort against the Japanese. In 1946, he returned to China becoming the chancellor of Beijing University. When the Communists surrounded the city in 1948, Hu flew to Nanjing and then returned to the United States living in semi-retirement in New York City. In 1957, he became Nationalist China's representative to the United Nations. The following year, he moved to Taiwan to become the President of the Academia Sinica. He died in Taiwan on February 24, 1962.

See also May Fourth Movement; Dewey, John (1859–1952).

REFERENCES: Min-chih Chou, *Hu Shih and Intellectual Choice in Modern China* (Ann Arbor, MI, 1992); Jerome B. Grieder, *Hu Shih and the Chinese Renaissance: Liberalism in the Chinese Revolution, 1917–1937* (Cambridge, MA, 1970).

Greg Ference

Hu Shih (1891–1962) *see* Hu Shi (1891–1962).

Hu Yaobang (1915–1989)

Hu Yaobang was born in Hunan, China. At age 14, Hu became a member of the Communist Youth League. In 1933, he joined the Chinese Communist Party in Jiangxi, China. In 1934, Hu was appointed the Secretary-General of the Central Committee of the Youth League. In 1949, Hu became the head of the political department of the 18th Infantry Corps. In 1956, Hu was elected to the Central Committee of the Chinese Communist Party.

During the Cultural Revolution, Hu fell from power. In 1968, Hu was sent to do manual labor at the May 7th Cadre School. After Deng Xiaoping regained power in 1973, Hu came back to office as the Communist Party's secretary of the Academy of Sciences. Hu supported scientific research and encouraged the study of science. In 1977, Hu became the director of the Central Committee's organization department. Hu cleared the names of 500,000 intellectuals who had been accused of being rightists during the Anti-Rightist Campaign of 1957. In 1980, Hu was elected to the Standing Committee of the Politburo. This helped to move Hu into the core of the party. In 1981, Hu became the Chinese Communist Party General Secretary. Hu understood that the United States and some Western capitalist countries had been taking China as an enemy. Hu also saw the United States as a hegemonic power, especially as Washington sold weapons to Taiwan. Hu emphasized establishing friendly relationship with non-Communist countries. He paid a visit to Japan in 1983, Australia and New Zealand in 1985. He also visited Germany, England, Italy and France in 1986. Hu sought to build up connections and cooperation related to economics, trade and technology with other countries in order to change China's status on the international stage. Hu supported political reform and was tolerant of the students' demonstrations calling for freedom of speech and reforms in 1985 and 1986 respectively. He refused to suppress student demonstrations. This upset Deng Xiaoping and the older conservative members in the Communist Party. In 1987, Hu stepped down as the head of the party under the pressure of the conservatives who blamed him for failing to crack down on the student demonstrations.

In April 1989, Hu died of a heart attack. His death brought a period of public mourning, which developed into a mass movement for re-evaluating Hu and his contribution. The mourners, mainly students stayed at Tiananmen Square.

They sent a petition to the government asking for political reform. On June 4, the government cracked down on the protesters. To some extent, Hu's death ignited the Tiananmen Square Massacre.

See also Tiananmen Square Massacre.

REFERENCES: David M. Lampton (ed.), *The Making of Chinese Foreign and Security Policy in the Era of Reform, 1978–2000* (Stanford, CA, 2001); Robert L. Suettinger, *Beyond Tiananmen: The Politics of U.S.-China Relations, 1989–2000* (Washington, DC, 2003); Zhongmei Yang, *Hu Yaobang: A Chinese Biography* (New York, 1988).

Edy Parson

Hua Guofeng (1920-)

A longstanding member of the Chinese Communist Party and veteran of many Red Army campaigns, Hua Guofeng came to the forefront Chinese politics in 1976, as he first succeeded Zhou Enlai as Premier and then also became the Chinese Communist Party (CCP) Chairman after Communist leader Mao Zedong died. He held the posts simultaneously until 1981. As Chinese leader Deng Xiaoping gradually regained control over the CCP, Hua was denounced for promoting the outdated Maoist doctrines and replaced by Zhao Ziyang as Premier in 1980, and by Hu Yaobang as Party Chairman in 1981. During the period of transition after the 1976 deaths of Zhou (January) and Mao (September), he began changing the country's internal and external policies. On October 6, 1976, he directed the arrest and detainment of the Gang of Four, as well as many other Maoist radicals whom he had seemingly supported up to this time.

Hua was recognized early in his career for his ability to write and present the party message with enthusiastic and effective rhetorical expressions. This ability was made more remarkable by the fact that he began life as the son of a poor peasant family from Shanxi Province and worked his way up through military service into the regional provincial leadership. He joined the CCP in 1935, at age 15 and then fought the Japanese and the Nationalists under Communist leader Zhu De, being named party secretary of Jiaocheng county, Shanxi Province. He then moved south to Hunan, Mao's own province, to become another county chair and begin an unbroken political career as a staunch supporter of Mao's policies. These included agricultural reforms, some of which he personally oversaw, and even the Great Leap Forward that was so economically disastrous for the country. By 1958, he was vice governor of Human Province and then party secretary of the Human provincial committee. While he appeared to support the Cultural Revolution, he did not approve of the Red Guards and was attacked in writing and wall posters for this position. His successively more important political positions attest to his increasing reputation as a strategist for the Party. Hua was relatively unknown outside of China until 1976 and has returned to that relative obscurity since 1981. When he took power in October 1976, he was not universally acclaimed. Nevertheless, during his short period of control, he began sweeping changes in governmental, agricultural and industrial policies to emphasize skill, relevant experience and ability over ideological purity and loosened restrictions on the cultural sphere. Under Hua the rapprochement between the United States and China went smoothly, culminating in the establishment of formal diplomatic relations between the two countries in 1979.

REFERENCES: Hua Guofeng, *Continue the Revolution under the Dictatorship of the Proletariat to the End: a Study of Volume V of the Selected Works of Mao Tsetung* (Beijing, 1977); "Hua Guofeng," *Current Biography* (1977); "Hua Guofeng," *Chambers Biographical Dictionary* (Edinburgh, UK, 1997).

Janice M. Bogstad

Huang Hua (1913–)

Huang Hua was an important diplomat of the People's Republic of China (PRC), eventually rising to the post of Foreign Minister from 1976 to 1982. A critical factor in his diplomatic career was the education he received at Yenching University under American missionary and founder John Leighton Stuart. As one of its first students he developed a close relationship with Stuart.

After joining the Communist party in 1936 Huang began his interaction with foreigners while escaping the Nationalist Government. He served as Edgar Snow's translator in discussions with Mao Zedong in Yanan that culminated in *Red Star Over China*. During his time in Yanan with the Chinese Communist Party (CCP), he was put in charge of looking after the needs of Colonel Davis Barrett's Special Observer Group, known as the Dixie Mission. He was next assigned in 1949 to contact his former teacher, Stuart, who remained in Nanjing after the CCP occupied the city as American ambassador to the Nationalist Government. Despite ideological difference the People's Republic of China hoped to take advantage of the otherwise cordial relationship that existed between the PRC and the United States. However, these diplomatic overtures failed due to the Communist's insistence that Western powers end their relationship with the Nationalist Government in Taiwan. His performance in this role led to a number of other posts in the PRC's diplomatic

corps. Starting in 1950 he served in a variety of diplomatic posts under Foreign Minister Zhou Enlai. These appointments included attending international conferences, such as the Geneva and Bandung, an effort to resolve the Indochina conflict in 1954 and helped launch the Nonaligned Movement in 1955 respectively. He also went to Warsaw in 1958 to participate in the Sino-American talks over the Taiwan Strait crisis. Based on this experience Huang received a number of individual ambassadorial appointments in Africa. From 1960 to 1966 he served in Ghana and attended negotiations in Tanganykia and the Congo. As Ambassador to the short lived United Arab Republic (Egypt & Syria), he remained the only free standing diplomat in the PRC's Foreign Ministry during the Cultural Revolution in 1966. Back in China in July 1971 he drafted the letter, in negotiation with Henry Kissinger, U.S. National Security Advisor that invited President Richard Nixon to visit China in February 1972. Following six months, ending in November 1971, as ambassador to Canada, in another first in Chinese diplomacy, Huang became the permanent representative to the UN. During his four terms as Security Council President he set the tone of consultative Chinese diplomacy, especially within the Non-aligned Movement. Following his five years at the UN, he was appointed as the PRC's Foreign Minister in 1976 where he served until 1982.

From 1982, Huang continued to serve at the highest level of the PRC's foreign relations establishment. He accompanied Deng Xiaoping on important Chinese diplomatic missions to thirty countries in Europe, North America, Asia and Africa. Reflecting his international career, he served as President of China's International Friends Seminar and Association of International Friendly Contact, at ninety-one years of age.

REFERENCES: Samuel Kim, *China, the United Nations and World Order* (Princeton, NJ, 1979); United States Department of States, *Foreign Relations of the United States, 1949, Vol. 8: China* (Washington, DC, 1978); Ministry of Foreign Affairs of the People's Republic of China, "Huang Hua," *www.fmprc.gov.cn/eng/ziliao/wjrw/3606/t44159.htm*.

Lynn Brown

Hughes, Charles Evans (1862–1948)

As Secretary of State under Republican President Warren G. Harding, Charles Evans Hughes played a crucial role in organizing the Washington Naval Conference (1921–1922). The conference brought some stability to relations between Japan and the United States, which had deteriorated during the Woodrow Wilson administration and the Paris Peace Conference. However, the Nine-Power Treaty signed at the conference disappointed proponents of Chinese nationalism.

Hughes was born April 11, 1862 in Glens Fall, New York. Following graduation from Brown University in 1881, he practiced law in New York City. As governor of New York State (1906–1910), his administration was credited with such progressive reform legislation as the establishment of public service commission. In 1910, Hughes was appointed to the Supreme Court by President William Howard Taft. He resigned from the court in order to accept the 1916 Presidential nomination of the Republican Party. He was narrowly defeated by incumbent Democrat Woodrow Wilson. After being appointed as Secretary of State by President Warren Harding in 1921, Hughes was entrusted with organizing the Washington Naval Conference on Naval Limitations. An invitation to the conference was issued to the Chinese government in Beijing, but the rival Guangzhou government headed by Sun Zhongshan refused to participate in a joint conference delegation. Concerned about Japanese expansion in East Asia, Hughes was successful in getting the Anglo-Japanese alliance abrogated and replaced by a four-power non-aggression pact in which Japan, Great Britain, France, and the United States agreed to consultations in the event of conflict in East Asia. Italy joined these nations in the Five Power Treaty placing restrictions on naval construction. In regard to China, Hughes was less interested in the internal power struggle within that nation than he was in stabilizing international competition. In the Nine Power Treaty, conference participants pledged non-interference in the internal affairs of China. Essentially, this agreement would continue the American Open Door Policy of respecting the territorial and administrative integrity of China. While Hughes was pleased with this outcome, the Chinese were less than enthused as the treaty failed to call for an end to extraterritoriality or the withdrawal of foreign troops from China. Hughes believed that China would have to put its internal affairs in order before the United States would consider surrendering its privileged status under the treaty system.

Following Harding's death in 1923, Hughes continued as Secretary of State under President Calvin Coolidge before resigning his position in 1925. He was appointed Chief Justice of the Supreme Court by President Herbert Hoover in 1930. He headed the court until his resignation in 1941. Hughes died on August 27, 1948 in Osterville, Massachusetts.

See also Washington Naval Conference (1921–1922).

REFERENCES: Betty Glad, *Charles Evans Hughes and*

the *Illusions of Innocence: A Study in American Diplomacy* (Urbana, IL, 1966); Dexter Perkins, *Charles Evans Hughes and American Democratic Statesmanship* (Westport, CT, 1956); Merlo John Pusey, *Charles Evans Hughes* (New York, 1951).

Ron Briley

Hull, Cordell (1891–1955)

As Secretary of State under President Franklin D. Roosevelt from 1933 to 1944, Cordell Hull served in the prestigious cabinet position longer than any other diplomat in American history. While his major interest was in tariff reduction and promoting international trade, Hull pursued a more conciliatory policy toward Japanese expansion into China than his Republican predecessor, Secretary of State Henry Stimson. Hull's diplomacy, however, was unable to prevent a Pacific war.

Hull was born in Pickett County, Tennessee on October 2, 1871. Following graduation from Cumberland University Law School in 1891, Hull was admitted to the Tennessee bar. From 1907 to 1931, the Democrat represented the volunteer state in the House of Representatives, with a two-year hiatus from 1921 to 1923 when he served as Chairman of the Democratic National Committee. In 1931, Hull was elected to the Senate, but he served only two years before he was selected by Roosevelt as his Secretary of State. Hull's tenure as head of the State Department was notable for the Secretary's devotion to reciprocal trade agreements. He also improved relations in Latin America with Roosevelt's Good Neighbor policy. But the Japanese incursion into China occupied much of his time. Concentrating on domestic issues with the New Deal and Great Depression, the Roosevelt administration backed away from the Stimson Doctrine of non-recognition of Japanese territorial expansion in China. Expressing reservations regarding the stability of Jiang Jieshi's government, Hull made it clear that the defense of China was in the hands of the Chinese. In addition, passage of the 1934 Silver Purchase Act undermined the Chinese economy and forced the Asian nation off the silver standard.

As the conflict between China and Japan intensified in 1937, Hull continued to follow a policy that would not antagonize the Japanese; refusing to take Japan to task for violating the Nine Power Treaty of 1922. Japanese expansion fostered American sympathy for the Chinese, and in 1939 the United States terminated the Treaty of Commerce and Navigation with Japan. With growing concern over the political situation in Europe, Hull stopped short of advocating sanctions. Nevertheless, in September 1940 when Japan allied with Nazi Germany in the Tripartite Party and moved into Vietnam in the summer of 1941, Hull was in a position to call for freezing of Japanese assets, including oil exports. The ensuing sanctions culminated in the Japanese attack on Pearl Harbor. During World War II, Hull expressed reservations regarding the leadership of Jiang Jieshi, but China was treated as an honorable ally. The Roosevelt administration negotiated a treaty surrendering American territorial rights in China, and the Congress repealed acts excluding Chinese immigration into the United States.

Suffering from failing health, Hull resigned as Secretary of State in 1944. Nevertheless, he continued to serve the Roosevelt administration as a key figure in organizing the United Nations. Honoring his contributions to trade agreements, better hemispheric understanding, and establishing the United Nations, Hull was awarded the Nobel Peace Prize in 1945. He died at Bethesda, Maryland on July 23, 1955.

See also World War II; Stimson Doctrine.

REFERENCES: Michael A. Butler, *Cautious Visionary: Cordell Hull and Trade Reform, 1933–1937* (Kent, OH, 1998); Harold Boaz Hinton, *Cordell Hull: A Biography* (New York, 1942); Jonathan G. Utley, *Going to War with Japan, 1937–1941* (Knoxville, TN, 1985).

Ron Briley

Human Rights

The human rights issue is one that continues to be a problem facing the Chinese and the world as a whole. In most cases, the human rights issue refers to the policies that the Chinese government has in place that do not match Western views of human rights. While there should be a basic, international understanding of human rights, different cultures have different interpretations of these rights. China has made much progress in attaining a Western style view of human rights in recent history, but even these reforms leave many detractors unhappy.

Chinese human rights first became an issue in 1942 when General Joseph W. Stilwell commented on the conscript nature of the Nationalist Army. He commented that conscription was a disaster to the Chinese families in much the same way that natural disasters disrupted their lives. Stories were told of how groups of men would abduct farmers directly from their fields and force them into the national service. When the Communists took over the government, there were no improvements under Chairman Mao Zedong. To understand the slight significance of human rights to the Chinese Communist Party and Chairman Mao Zedong, it is important to understand the Communist view of government. Communism subjugates the individual to the state. Rights normally reserved for the citizen are no longer important if they do little to further the collective good of the nation. In this way, laws that are meant to protect the citizen become tools for the government to use to impose the collective will on the people. While it may seem elementary to believe that a government must protect its citizens, in Communist China this is not the case. It then becomes clearer why there has been a dichotomy of Chinese and world-views on human rights. There are many instances of Chinese human rights abuses; starting with the military and moving through repression of free speech, forced labor and "reeducation camps," forced resettling, and collectivization of personal property.

Following the death of Mao and the gradual liberalization of China as a whole, some progress has been made to correct the human rights violations. The Chinese government slowly allowed more dissent and discussion of political power and centralized control of government. Rights that have been guaranteed in every constitution of China are finally being accepted and enforced. Among these are the rights to free speech, free practice of religion, and freedom of the press. However, as the demonstrations at Tiananmen Square in 1989 showed, the Communist government is slow to change. Many in the government still believe that personal rights and freedoms are second to the needs of the nation. Until China is able to balance the needs of the nation with the natural rights of its people, Western nations will continue to be skeptical of China's human rights dedication.

See also Human Rights in China (HRIC); Wu Hongda (1937-).

REFERENCES: Yuan-il Wu, et. al., *Human Rights in the People's Republic of China.* (Boulder, CO, 1998); Ann Kent, *China, The United Nations, and Human Rights.* (Philadelphia, PA, 1999); Schaller, Michael, *The United States and China: Into the Twenty-First Century* (New York, 2002).

Eric H. Doss

Human Rights in China (HRIC)

Human Rights in China descries itself as "an international non-governmental organization founded by Chinese scientists and scholars in March 1989," but the New York-headquartered group gained most of its leaders and momentum after June of that year. According to its website, "HRIC encourages victims of human rights abuse to seek redress under domestic law and assists them in seeking international intervention as a last resort ... [Its] primary focus ... is to encourage and empower the nascent grassroots human rights movement in China." HRIC's leadership and constituency are comprised of two primary groups—former dissidents like Wang Dan and Liu Binyan, and established China scholars such as Orville Schell—complemented by a few activists for global human rights. Liu Qing, for example, was President as of December 2001 (the HRIC website no longer includes a leadership listing). Liu was a leader in the 1978–1979 Democracy Wall movement and spent 15 years in prison for his dissident activities.

HRIC transmits Chinese-language broadcasts to China through Voice of American and other global radio stations. It also distributes the quarterly *China Rights Forum* (published, separately, in both English and Chinese) to 3,000 individuals and organizations worldwide, including many within China. Additionally, it maintains an activity publicity campaign to dramatize and focus attention on specific and general human rights abuses within China. When Chinese Premier Li Peng visited the United States in August 2000, for example, HRIC circulated a petition asking the Inter-Parliamentary Union to exclude him from that group's United Nations-sponsored conference because of Li's role in ordering the June 1989 crackdown at Tiananmen Square. When the UN group did not exclude Li, HRIC collaborated with the Center for Constitutional Rights to file a publicity-generating lawsuit against him for "crimes against humanity."

In its overtly oppositional stance toward the Chinese government, HRIC differs from most other contemporary U.S.-based Sino-American bilateral relations associations (e.g., The 1990 Institute, the National Committee on United States-China Relations, the Committee of 100, the Center for China-U.S. Cooperation). Whereas these other groups, to the extent they concern themselves with human rights and democracy, emphasize quite diplomacy, HRIC takes a more direct approach. In fact, it criticizes both governments and the non-governmental organizations. In its view, they give such high priority to bilateral trade and cultural exchange with China that they compromise on internationally enforceable human rights standards.

See also Human Rights; Wu Hongda (1937-).

REFERENCES: Norton Wheeler, "Improving Mainland Society and U.S.-China Relations: A Case Study of Four Chinese American-led Transnational Associations," in Peter H. Koehn and Xiao-huang Yin (eds.), *The Expanding Roles of Chinese Americans in U.S.-China Relations: Transnational Networks and Trans-Pacific Interactions* (Armonk, NY, 2002); HRIC Website, *www.hrichina.org*.

Norty Wheeler

The Hump

Once the U.S. entered World War II after Pearl Harbor, her strategic aims embraced China mainly as tying down Japanese forces and providing air bases to attack Japan. Thus China had to be kept in the war with supplies. At first there were routes via the Red River through the Vietnamese port of Haiphong and also from Burma via the Burma Road. Both were cut by early 1942, ceasing all land supply.

At the beginning of World War II the concept of massive air supply was in its infancy and the idea of furnishing the modern components for a whole nation's war effort by air was utopian. Nevertheless, in March 1941, the U.S. had taken the first small step by creating the Air Corps Ferrying Command out of which grew the U.S. Air Transport Command headed by Major General Harold George. This infant organization would be fully tested in the plan to supply the interior of China from India by air alone. The idea was to establish bases in Assam, fly over Burma and the southern Himalayas known as the Hump to Kunming and other locations in Yunnan Province, a distance of 500 miles. The topography and the weather made it the most difficult and dangerous flying assignment in the war. Starting in Assam a sea level, the mountain wall of the Naga Hills quickly rose to 10,000 feet. Flying east out of a valley, one topped the Patkai Range, then passed the Chindwin River valley, then up 14,000 feet over the Kumon Mountains. Then one vaulted 14,000–16,000 foot ridges separating the Irrawaddy, Salween and Mekong Rivers. The true "Hump" was the Santsung Range of the Himalayas between the Salween and Mekong. One had to struggle to get heavily laden planes up quickly. Icing was exacerbated by starting in hot humidity or rain and climbing into chilled air. Assam got 200 inches of rain six months of the year. Freak winds of 250 m.p.h. and turbulence that could flip a plane or plunge it 3,000 feet per minute were daily hazards. Hand-built airfields at both ends were crude, amenities were few and malaria and dysentery were universal. Delivery goals initially were set at 5,000 tons per month. To meet these goals, in the first two years pilots worked sixteen hour shifts and sometimes did three round trips per day. In October 1942, Air Transport Command took control of the whole system from the U.S. to Kunming. Everything from typewriters to bullets to C-rations traveled 12,000 miles via Brazil, the South Atlantic, across Africa and India, then on narrow-gauge trains and barges and then loaded, often by elephant, onto the planes. Even Chinese troops were airlifted for service in Burma. As in Europe, the war in Asia was governed by the bottleneck of logistics. For nearly three years the Hump was China's sole supplier. From Jiang Jieshi came continual demands for more of everything. Planes carried their own return fuel. Three of every five gallons delivered were required by the supply aircraft. The planes used were principally the Douglas C-47 and Curtiss C-46. The latter, called "Dumbo" by pilots, had larger capacity and higher ceiling but was plagued by leaks, iced carburetors and broken fuel lines. Consolidated B-24s in cargo version and, in the last months, Lockheed C-54 four-engine transports were also used. Spare parts were always short and grounded aircraft were routinely cannibalized. In the last six months of 1943 there were 155 accidents with 168 fatalities. Cyrus Smith, President of American Airlines, was brought in to tackle the problem of accidents. Search and rescue was another problem. Under the leadership of ex-stunt pilot John ("Blackie") Porter, more effective methods were developed, including the well-publicized rescue of journalist Eric Severeid in December 1943. Still, so many planes were lost that parts of the route were dubbed "the aluminum trail." It was said to be safer to be bombing Germany.

Under General William Tunner the tonnage rose to 10,000 tons per month by early 1944. The total tonnage delivered by war's end reached 650,000 at a cost of 1,000 men and 600 planes. Overall, the Hump airlift is judged to have helped defeat Japan by sustaining China materially and, more importantly, symbolically during its grimmest peril. American organizational methods used in the China-Burma-India Theater air command certainly set the stage for future mass strategic airlift operations such as the airlift in Berlin in 1949.

See also China-Burma-India (CBI) Theater.

REFERENCES: Bliss K. Thorne, *The Hump* (New York, 1965); Donovan Webster, *The Burma Road* (New York, 2003); Otha Spencer, *Flying the Hump: Memories of an Air War* (College Station, TX, 1992); William Tunner, *Over the Hump* (Washington, DC, 1985); Edwin White, *Ten Thousand Tons by Christmas* (St. Petersburg, FL, 1977).

Dave Egler

Hunter, William C. (1812–1891)

A merchant from New York, William C. Hunter became a resident in Guangzhou and Macao during the "pre-treaty days." Hunter was sent to China in 1825 when he was 13 years old to learn Chinese by the firm of Thomas H. Smith. In 1830 he was employed by Russell & Co. in Guangzhou. He became a partner in the firm in 1837 and retired five years later. Around 1870, he left China and traveled to New York and Paris.

Hunter, who was fluent in Chinese, published two works on the foreign presence in southern China, namely *The "Fan Kwae" at Canton Before the Treaty Days 1825–1844* (1882) and *Bits of Old China* (1885), as well as Chinese translations, poems and prose in the periodicals *The Canton Register*, *The Chinese Repository* and *The Canton Press*. Both of his books are widely used as important source materials by historians studying history and life of Guangzhou and Macao before the Opium Wars. In his books, he described his trip to China, the foreign residents' presence in Macao and Guangzhou, and their business activities and contacts with the local population. His work is therefore a vivid repository of the *modus vivendi* of the Western communities in the south of China before and during the pre-treaty days.

REFERENCES: David Abeel, *Journal of a Residence in China and the Neighboring Countries From 1830 To 1833* (London, 1835); Eliza Jane Gillett Bridgman (ed.), *The Pioneer of American Missions in China: The Life and Labors of Elijah Coleman Bridgman* (New York, 1864); Robert B. Forbes, *Personal Reminiscences* (Boston, MA, 1882); William C. Hunter, *The "Fan Kwae" at Canton Before the Treaty Days: 1825–1844* (London, 1882).

Rogerio Miguel Puga

Hurley, Patrick J. (1883–1963)

Patrick Jay Hurley was born into a poor Irish immigrant's family in the Indian Territory (later Oklahoma) in 1883 and started working in a coal mine with his father when he was eleven. His Indian friends introduced him later to study at Indian University in Bacone and he kept on his studies after that to earn his Bachelor of Law degree from the National University Law School (Washington, D. C.) in 1908. He worked as a successful lawyer, the "National Attorney" for the Choctaw Indian tribe, and served during the Hoover's administration as the Secretary of War (1929–1932). He was famous as the one who helped President Herbert Hoover come to the decision to crack down the March-on-Washington organized by the "Bonus Army" in 1932. Representing an American oil company, Hurley successfully negotiated a deal with the government of Mexico and diverted a crisis in Mexican-American relations in 1938. Though a Republican criticizing President Franklin D. Roosevelt's "New Deal" policies all the time, Hurley kept good personal relations with the President, who appointed him during World War II as a special presidential representative and "fact finder" to visit more than twenty countries.

Hurley's most important mission came in 1944 when he was sent to China to pacify the tense relations between the Chinese leader, Jiang Jeshi and American Army commander General Joseph

W. Stilwell in the war against Japan. Hurley helped Roosevelt come to the final decision to recall General Stilwell. Hurley was also charged with the task to help establish a "coalition government" between the ruling Nationalist Party (GMD) and the Chinese Communist Party (CCP), as part of America's general goals in China and the Far East. Hurley personally flew to Yanan, the Communists' wartime capital, and helped the CCP draft a document for cooperation with the Nationalists. But he soon changed his attitude and urged the CCP to accept the GMD demands. Promoted to serve as American Ambassador to China, Hurley continued his effort to initiate the "coalition," including his effort to bring Communist leader Mao Zedong to Chongqing to negotiate with Jiang and the final approval of the famous "Double Tenth Agreement" in 1945. But his poor understanding and miscalculations of China's situation contributed later to the general misjudgment of America's policy toward China and the fall of the Nationalist government.

While serving as the Ambassador and after his resignation in late 1945, Hurley never stopped accusing that some Americans, civilian or military, had assisted the Chinese Communists in their efforts to take over China. This kind of charges later contributed to the America's second "Red Scare" in late 1940s and early 1950s.

See also Stilwell, Joseph W. (1883–1946); Jiang Jieshi (1887–1975); Civil War (1945–1949); McCarthyism.

REFERENCES: Patrick J. Hurley, *Hurley Papers* (University of Oklahoma Library); Don Lohbeck, *Patrick J. Hurley* (Chicago, IL, 1956); Russell D. Buhite, *Patrick J. Hurley and American Foreign Policy* (Ithaca, NY, 1973).
Xiansheng Tian

Ichigo Offensive (1944)

As the American and British forces conducted offensive operations against the Japanese forces in Burma, the American military and then the American government up to the highest levels pressured the Chinese Nationalists to move against the depleted Japanese forces positioned along the Chinese end of the Burma Road. Finally, the threatened suspension of lend-lease aid moved Jiang Jieshi to order an offensive by his Y-Force under the command of General Wei Li-huang. With American General Frank Dorn serving as a tactical advisor, the Chinese forces had some initial successes, but stiff Japanese resistance at some key points along the battlefront first slowed and then stalled the Chinese advance.

Ironically, as the Chinese were beginning their much-delayed offensive, the Japanese were planning what would be their last major offensive campaign of the war. If unchecked, the increasing deployment of American B-29 bombers at Chinese air bases would mean a steady intensification of the air attacks against the Japanese home islands. Moreover, the American submarine campaign against Japanese shipping threatened to undermine Japanese military operations throughout East and Southeast Asia by severely constricting the supplies available to Japanese forces. The Japanese high command therefore planned to seize Chinese airfields in central and southern China and to seize control of the two major railroads running north and south through eastern China and connecting Korea to Indochina. To bolster the forces available in the theater of operations, Japanese forces were transferred southwards from both Manchuria and Mongolia. To the Ichigo Offensive, the Japanese would commit fifteen divisions totaling more than 800,000 men. The Japanese forces would remain on the offensive from mid-April 1944 through the end of that year. Much to the exasperation of the American military advisors, Jiang failed to commit his forces fully against the Japanese and refused to accommodate the Chinese Communists so that they could relieve the pressure on his own forces by attacking the Japanese on their northern flank. Although there was never a formal falling out between the Americans and the Chinese Nationalists, the American faith in and enthusiasm for Jiang's leadership declined dramatically because of his failure to respond decisively to the Ichigo Offensive.

Although the Japanese achieved both of their main objectives in the Ichigo Offensive, neither turned out to be decisive. The seizure of the Chinese air bases somewhat delayed the American onslaught from the air against Japanese cities. But it turned out that the B-29s could fly from bases farther inside China's interior, and the American campaign in the Pacific soon provided them with island bases even nearer to Japan. Likewise, although the Japanese succeeded in opening an overland supply route along the length of the East Asian territories under its control, the Chinese did finally succeed in opening the Burma Road against the increasingly under-manned and under-supplied Japanese forces facing them in that theater. So any advantage that the Japanese gained in their ability to supply their own troops in China was offset by a long-awaited, major breakthrough in the Allies' ability to supply the Chinese.

See also Burma Road; World War II.

REFERENCES: Donovan Webster, *The Burma Road: The Epic Story of the China-Burma-India Theater in World War II* (New York, 2003).
Martin Kich

Indochina Wars *see* **First Indochina War; Second Indochina War**

Institute of Pacific Relations

The Institute of Pacific Relations, which was accused of Communist subversion during the McCarthy era, was organized in Honolulu in 1925 by a small group of civic-minded internationalists who saw improved ties with Asia as essential for America's future. Among the founders was the President of Stanford University, Ray Lyman Wilbur, who helped formulate the Institute's founding thesis, that non-governmental leaders of Asian and North American countries should explore and resolve their differences. The founders established a permanent secretariat for the Institute, called for national "councils" to be created in participating countries, and agreed to convene general sessions every two or three years. Six national councils attended the 1927 meeting at Honolulu, those from Australia, Canada, the United States, New Zealand, China, and Japan; representatives from Britain, Korea and the Philippines also attended. This meeting adopted a constitution for the Institute, and declared that its mission was to "study the conditions of the Pacific peoples with a view to the improvement of their mutual relations."

The American Council of the Institute was the largest and wealthiest of the member councils, with money coming from individuals and foundations, as well as from regional chapters throughout the United States. The Secretary of the American Council, Edward C. Carter, was instrumental in shifting the secretariat's base from Hawaii to New York City, where it attracted a progressive and idealistic staff. Carter also supported a vigorous research and publication program that included the Institute's journal, *Pacific Affairs*, and the American Council's own publication, *Far Eastern Survey*. Carter hired American academic Owen Lattimore to edit *Pacific Affairs*. With Carter, Lattimore sought Soviet participation in the Institute, and although one article was submitted to *Pacific Affairs* by a Soviet author in 1938, Stalin's purges hindered further cooperation.

At the opening of World War II, several Institute staff members secured diplomatic and intelligence posts in the U.S. government. Beginning in 1944, however, suspicions arose that many such specialists were pro-Soviet and pro-Communist. Suspicions about the Institute personnel gained currency in 1945 following security investigations of the journal *Amerasia*. Its editor and several staff members were arrested for violations of the Espionage Act, and Owen Lattimore, who served on *Amerasia*'s editorial board, also came under suspicion, presumably for his pro-Communist sympathies in the Chinese Civil War of 1945–1949. At the same time one of American Council's largest financial supporters, the Rockefeller Foundation, decided to shift its support to university-based Asian studies centers. It reduced and finally terminated its aid to the American Council and to the Institute, and in the increasingly hostile anti-Communist climate of the early 1950s, new sources of large-scale support were not forthcoming. In early 1951 the Senate Judiciary Committee's Subcommittee on Internal Security issued a subpoena for the internal files of the Institute, which had developed a reputation as a leftwing, pro-Communist organization. The Subcommittee launched hearings aimed at exposing the Institute's links to domestic and foreign Communists as well as its influence upon American foreign policy, particularly in Asia. After the hearings, the Subcommittee produced a report that declared the Institute of Pacific Relations to be a Communist-controlled organization that bore direct blame for the "loss" of China to the Chinese Communist Party in 1949.

With the American Council's funding drastically cut and its reputation publicly destroyed, the local chapters began to dissolve themselves. The Hawaii branch, the first to be organized, severed all ties to the Institute and reorganized in 1953 as the Pacific and Asian Affairs Council. On the basis of the Senate report the Internal Revenue Service revoked the tax-exempt status of the Institute and of the American Council in 1955, citing the organizations' political biases. This move, although eventually reversed, rendered the Institute and the American Council even more unattractive to potential donors. By 1957 the American Council had only 371 members, down from some 2000 in 1945. The University of British Columbia in Vancouver agreed to carry on publication of the Institute's flagship journal, *Pacific Affairs*, but the other major functions of the organization were abandoned. The Institute for Pacific Relations and the American Council were both formally dissolved in 1960.

See also McCarthy, Joseph R. (1908–1957); McCarthyism; Lattimore, Owen (1900–1989); *Amerasia.*

REFERENCES: Paul F. Hooper (ed.), *Remembering the Institute of Pacific Relations: The Memoirs of William L. Holland* (Tokyo, 1995), John N. Thomas, *The Institute of Pacific Relations: Asian Scholars and American Politics* (Seattle, WA, 1974), Lawrence T. Woods, *Asia-Pacific Diplomacy: Nongovernmental Organizations and International Relations* (Vancouver, 1993).

Laura M. Calkins

Intelligence Cooperation in World War II

Before 1941, there had been little intelligence cooperation between the United States and the Chinese government. The U.S. gathered its intelligence in China through a diffused structure with the U.S. Embassy as the hub, from which the personnel of the U.S. Naval Attache and the Military Attache proceeded with the normal, and often inefficient, efforts to collect information for Washington. On the Chinese side, repeated efforts to reach out to Washington for a joint intelligence initiative were rejected primarily due to rampant isolationism within the U.S.

This reality began to change in the spring of 1941 when Congress passed the Lend-Lease Act and President Franklin D. Roosevelt soon qualified China as a recipient nation for the U.S. lend-lease materials. Acting upon the earlier recommendation of Roosevelt's special envoy to China, Lauchlin Currie, the U.S. Army in July 1941 established an official military mission to China headed by Brigadier General John Magruder, an intelligence officer in the U.S. Army. The Magruder Mission, as it was officially named, was sent to China for the open purpose of coordinating with the Chinese on how to use the American lend-lease weapons, but its collateral mission was to establish intelligence cooperation links with the Chinese military, thus marking the beginning of substantial Sino-U.S. intelligence cooperation in wartime China, despite the fact that the U.S. had not yet been at war officially with Japan.

When the Pearl Harbor attacks took place in December 1941, the Magruder Mission in China suddenly became inadequate. The governments of U.S. and China both needed closer military and intelligence cooperation on a much larger scale. Against this background, President Roosevelt authorized the newly established Coordinator of Information (COI, and the Office of Strategic Services or OSS since June 1942) to handle intelligence from China. But the COI was far too fledgling to be able to coordinate various departmentalized U.S. intelligence agencies. As a result, throughout the rest of the war, while the Chinese intelligence apparatus was relatively more consolidated, the U.S. efforts in China were highly diffused and disorganized, which resulted in a pattern of Sino-American wartime intelligence cooperation that was often marked by turf wars and opaque objectives.

The Chinese government tried to put all the intelligence cooperation projects into one joint organization called SACO (Sino-American Special Technical Cooperative Organization). Headed by Major General Dai Li, with his American partner, Commander (later Rear Admiral) Milton Miles, USN, as the deputy, the SACO umbrella scheme had the blessings from the highest authorities of both countries, and was approved by President Roosevelt and Chinese Nationalist leader Jiang Jieshi. But the SACO cooperation did not work out to be effective because of the tense squabbles over operational command, personnel and material distribution. The OSS, initially a junior partner in SACO, wanted to run operations independent of the SACO command in U.S. Army-controlled areas and the Chinese Communist-controlled regions. The U.S. Army intelligence agencies were unhappy with the comprehensiveness of SACO in dominating intelligence operations in China and began to organize their own operations against the wishes of the Chinese government, the most famous of which was the Army intelligence initiative to Communist headquarters in Yanan, the Dixie Mission. In addition, the U.S. embassy had its own sources and methods of gathering intelligence in China, so did the 14th Air Force, the U.S. Treasury department, the Commerce Department, the Board of Economic Warfare headed by Vice President Henry Wallace, and so on.

There were many operational successes, however. The OSS had a good relationship with many Chinese artists and newspapermen in running "Morale Operations" or black propaganda against the Japanese. The 14th Air Force cooperated seamlessly with Chinese intelligence in establishing the best ground-based air-warning system in the region; the U.S. Navy and General Dai Li's Bureau of Statistics and Investigation worked famously well in running coastal watch units, demolition teams, and weather intelligence outposts. When General Joseph W. Stilwell was recalled in October 1944, the Sino-American intelligence cooperation was making a swift turn to the right direction under the efficient leadership of General Albert Wedemeyer. But by then, the war was approaching to its foreseeable ending and the military value of the China Theater was rapidly diminishing due to the phenomenal successes of military campaigns against the Japanese in the Pacific.

See also Office of Strategic Services (OSS); Sino-American Special Technical Cooperative Organization (SACO); Magruder Mission.

REFERENCES: Maochun Yu, *OSS in China-Prelude to Cold War* (New Haven, CT, 1997); Yu Shen, *SACO: An Ambivalent Experience of Sino-American Cooperation During World War II* (Ph.D. Dissertation, University of Illinois at Urbana-Champaign, 1995).

Maochun Yu

International Monetary Fund (IMF)

Created by the Bretton Woods Agreement in 1944, the purpose of the International Monetary Fund (IMF) was to provide for stable monetary and exchange rate conditions in the post-World War II era. The IMF can provide short-term loans to member countries to help them in situations where a shortage of funds has led to balance of payments problems. Leadership in organizing the structure and functions of the IMF came primarily from the United States and Great Britain, and the organization is headquartered in Washington, DC.

China was an original member of the IMF. However, after the Guomindang government moved to Taiwan, the IMF recognized the Republic of China (ROC) in Taiwan as the government of China, which would effectively end the mainland involvement in the IMF for about 30 years. In August 1950, Chinese Foreign Minister Zhou Enlai indicated to the IMF that the government of the People's Republic of China (PRC) in Beijing was China's only government, though he did not request that the PRC be included in the IMF. Rather, he only insisted that the ROC in Taiwan be excluded. As the focus of the PRC was generally more inward during the 1950s and 1960s, there were few strong pushes to obtain IMF membership for the Beijing government, either from China or from the IMF itself. Instead, the goals of the PRC centered more on building a self-reliant national economy. Some Chinese officials and others were concerned that the IMF catered to the needs of the United States and other developed countries at the expense of developing countries, and that China would not benefit from membership. The IMF was also viewed as an institution to promote international capitalism, and thus it created ambivalence in Communist China. After the Cultural Revolution of 1966–1976, China began boosting its attempts to join international economic institutions and open its economy to the outside world. Success with the IMF was achieved in April 1980, when the IMF switched the seat for China from the government in Taiwan to the government in Beijing. China quickly expanded its role in the IMF, contributing enough resources to achieve the eighth highest participation level.

Since joining, China has played an active role in the IMF. After obtaining membership, China worked to improve the conditions of its foreign exchange system. It also received advice and credits to combat cyclical economic problems. Mainly, China was a creditor to the IMF though, and the main benefits to China were recognition in the world community and access to the IMF's information and resources. The IMF has assisted China in developing tools for data collection and for economic evaluation in line with Western practices. The IMF has also sponsored many seminars, training programs, conferences, and studies for Chinese government officials and scholars. During the 1997 financial crisis, China contributed to the IMF's efforts to stabilize the Thai and Indonesian economies. In the coming years, one can expect the relationship between China and the IMF to continue growing.

REFERENCES: James M. Boughton, *Silent Revolution: The International Monetary Fund 1979–1989* (Washington, DC, 2001); Harold K. Jacobson and Michel Oksenberg, *China's Participation in the IMF, the World Bank, and GATT: Toward a Global Economic Order* (Ann Arbor, MI, 1990); David M. Lampton, *Same Bed Different Dreams: Managing U.S.-China Relations 1989–2000* (Berkeley, CA, 2001).

Wade D. Pfau

International Trade Commission

The International Trade Commission of the United States is an independent agency founded in 1916. First titled, the Tariff Commission, the International Trade Commission was so named in 1975. Its agenda is to serve both the U.S. Congress and the President in an advisory role with items such as tariffs, commercial-policy and foreign trade. The powers of the Commission have grown since its inception with the Trade and Competitiveness Act of 1988. The Act allows the Commission to both investigate industries and firms engaging in unfair international trade practices and actually order the exclusion of imports found to be in violation of patent or copyright law. The Commission, of course, cannot exert its jurisdiction over the President. The President may cancel the Commission's changes due to policy concerns, but the Commission holds significant control over international trade issues.

The International Trade Commission is composed of six members who are appointed by the President and are confirmed by the Senate. Each member serves a nine-year term and not more than three members can be from the same political party. In addition, the chairman and the vice-chairman must be of different political party affiliations. An example of the wide-reaching effects of a Trade Commission decision is its 6–0 decision on Chinese trade of foundry coke products. In November of 2000, the Commission found that surges in cheaper imports of foundry coke into the U.S. were negatively impacting U.S. firms. The Commission's investigation found that 133,000 metric tons of foundry coke was being imported into the U.S. from China at $107 per metric ton. The average U.S. price, including production and transportation, was around $177 per metric ton. The $70 discrepancy was significant enough to prompt action by Citizens Gas and Coke of Indianapolis, Erie Coke of Erie, Pennsylvania and Tonawanda Coke of New York to file petitions with the International Trade Commission. In a more advisory decision, the International Trade Commission found in a February of 2004 report that the Chinese textile industry is expected to play a dominant role in the U.S. textile and apparel market. The Commission's action in respect to textiles and apparel is not a sanctioning act. Rather, it is a warning to the U.S. Congress and the President that if left unwatched, the Chinese textile and apparel industry may take too strong of a foothold in the U.S. market.

Since China joined of the World Trade Organization on December 11, 2001, the International Trade Commission's work has been assisted significantly. The WTO allows for more information transparency into international trade dilemmas, thereby giving the Commission more of an ability to make informed judgments.

See also **World Trade Organization (WTO).**

REFERENCES: Donald K Duvall, *Unfair Competition and the ITC: Actions Before the International Trade Commission Under Section 337 of the Tariff Act 1930* (Eagan, MN, 1993); U.S. Government, *21st Century Complete Guide to the U.S. International Trade Commission and the Trade and Development Agency (TDA) Promoting American Trade and Exports (CD-ROM)* (Washington, DC, 2003); Michael Hiscox, *International Trade and Political Conflict: Commerce, Coalitions, and Mobility* (Princeton, NJ, 2001).

Arthur Holst

Isaacs, Harold Robert (1910–1986)

Harold Robert Isaacs, better known in China as Yi Luosheng, was a noted journalist, writer, and political scientist. A one-time Chinese Communist sympathizer, he played a significant role in the Chinese Revolution of the 1930s.

Of Jewish descent, Isaacs was the son of a wealthy New York realtor in Upper Manhattan. He went to Shanghai in 1930 as a journalist shortly after he graduated from Columbia University. After his arrival, he worked briefly on the *Shanghai Evening Post and Mercury* and *The China Press*. Influenced by two radical journalists, Agnes Smedley, an American female, and C. Frank Glass, an Englishman from South Africa, he soon developed his sympathy to the Chinese Communist movement. In Shanghai, he established his friendship with Song Qingling (Mme. Sun Zhongshan), Lu Xun, the greatest of modern Chinese writers, Mao Dun, another renowned writer, and Cai Yuanpei, President of the Academia Sinica. Together with a group of Chinese liberals, he helped found the China League for Civil Rights in 1932 to expose the Guomindang terror and to rescue political prisoners. Encouraged by his Communist friends, Isaacs started the *China Forum,* a weekly journal. From 1932 to 1934, the *China Forum* functioned as an important English-language voice for the underground Communist movement in China. However, under the influence of a Trotskyist, Isaacs began to take interest in Trotskyism. In 1934, mounting disagreement between Isaacs and the underground Chinese Communists finally led to the end of the *China Forum.* Isaacs then moved from Shanghai to Beijing. From 1934 to 1935, while associated with the Chinese Trotskyist organization, he devoted most of his time to studying the history of the Chinese Revolution. Helped by Liu Renjing, a founding member of the Chinese Communist Party and then a Trotskyist, he wrote *The Tragedy of the Chinese Revolution* (1938), a book on the Chinese Revolution of 1925–1927, which later became a classic in Chinese studies. Isaacs returned to the United States in 1935. Until the early 1940s, he was an active member of the American Trotskyist movement. After the assassination of Leon Trotsky in 1940, he gradually drifted away from Trotskyism and eventually abandoned his Marxist-Leninist views. In the late 1930s and the early 1940s, Isaacs worked as a news writer first for Agency Havas and then for CBS. In 1944, Isaacs went to China as a war correspondent for *Newsweek.* His reports from Chongqing, the wartime capital of China, clashed with the policies of the Nationalist government. As a result, the Guomindang barred him from reentering China after his short home leave in 1945. Isaacs continued to write on Asian affairs and U.S. Asia policy until 1950. He then taught at Harvard University and the New School for Social Research in New York before joining the Massachusetts Institute of Technology in 1953. At MIT, he was first a research associate at the Center for International Studies. In 1963, he was appointed professor of political science. He retired in 1976. In 1980, invited by Song Qingling, he revisited China. The outcome was his final book, *Re-Encounters in China* (1980).

In his later career, Isaacs studied issues of cultural identity and ethnicity. His *Scratches on Our Minds: American Images of China and India* (1958) pioneered this field. In 1974, he edited and published a collection of Chinese short novels, *Straw Sandals: Chinese Stories 1918–1933*, a long-delayed project initiated by Lu Xun, Mao Dun, and himself in the 1930s. Among his numerous other publications, the books on Asia also include *No Peace for Asia* (1947) and *Two-Thirds of the World* (1950). Harold R. Isaacs died of complication from heart surgery in Boston in 1986.

REFERENCES: Harold R. Isaacs, *Re-Encounters in China: Notes of a Journey in a Time Capsule* (Armonk, NY, 1985); Peter Rand, *China Hands: The Adventures and Ordeals of the Americans Journalists Who Joined Forces with the Great Chinese Revolution* (New York, 1995), Chen Jinxing, "Harold R. Isaacs' Trotskyist Turn in the *China Forum* Years," *Twentieth-Century China* (November 1998).

Jinxing Chen

Jaffe, Philip Jacob (1895–1980)

Philip Jacob Jaffe, a prominent figure in American left-wing political circles in the 1930s and 1940s and editor of the magazines *China Today* and *Amerasia*, earned his controversial fame in the *Amerasia* case in 1945.

Born into a poor Jewish laborer's family in the Ukraine, Jaffe immigrated to New York City in 1906. After graduating from Columbia University with a Masters degree in English literature in 1921, Jaffe began a mail order greeting card company and eventually became a wealthy businessperson. Jaffe's political activities started in 1915 when he joined the American Socialist Party, but grew increasingly dissatisfied with the party. His interest in China and Communist ideas began in 1929 when he met with his Chinese cousin by marriage, Ji Chaoding, a Communist, in New York. In 1933, invited by Ji Chaoding, Jaffe joined the first meeting of the American Friends of the Chinese People (AFCP), a peripheral organization of the Communist Party of the United States, becoming its secretary. From 1933 to 1936 and under the pseudonym of J.W. Phillips, he served as editor of the AFCP's publication, *China Today*, which published numerous reports on the Chinese Communist movement. In 1937, he left *China Today* to start, along with Frederick Fields and others, a new magazine on East Asian affairs, *Amerasia*. Throughout *Amerasia*'s history until 1947 when it ceased its publication, Jaffe served as the editor-in-chief of the magazine, in charge of editing all articles in each issue. As a wealthy man, he was able to help cover the deficit of the magazine. Its small circulation notwithstanding, *Amerasia*'s association with American Communists was well known and its strong tone of anti-Guomindang and pro-Chinese Communists was evident. Toward the end of World War II, it incurred growing suspicions from the authorities and became the first target of an emerging anti-Communist wave in the United States. The agents of the Office of Strategic Services (OSS) raided the *Amerasia* office in March 1945. In June of the same year, the FBI arrested Jaffe and his associates, among them State Department officer John Stewart Service, accusing them of stealing secret government documents. The case never went to trial, and Jaffe in the end received a moderate fine of $2,500. During the peak of McCarthyism in 1951–1952, Joe McCarthy named Jaffe as one of the Russian spies. The "Tydings Hearings" subpoenaed him, and subsequently charged him for contempt of Congress. Yet, Jaffe was able to avoid any further punishment. Although the *Amerasia* case afterward remained a controversy both in the academic world and in politics, Jaffe gradually faded out of public attention.

In addition to editing *China Today* and *Amerasia*, Jaffe was an active member of numerous left-wing organizations in the 1930s and 1940s. He was the author of *New Frontiers in Asia* (1943), *China's Destiny and Chinese Economic Theory* (1947), and *The Rise and Fall of American Communism* (1975). In June 1937, he made a trip to China and visited Yanan together with his wife Agnes Jaffe, Owen Lattimore, and T. A. Bisson. His article about his trip and his interview with Communist leader Mao Zedong, "China's Communists Told Me: A Journey to the Home of the Famous New Eighth Route Army," appeared in *New Masses* on October 12, 1937.

Jaffe severed his relationship with the American Communist movement in 1947. He published *The Amerasia Case: From 1945 to the Present* in 1979 to claim his innocence in the *Amerasia* case. Although he maintained that he was never a member of the Communist Party of the United States, some scholars have suggested that he was more than a simply "ardent fellow traveler." During his latter years, Jaffe became a disillusioned man, as he stated that the results of his involvement with China and American-Chinese relations "ultimately proved catastrophic for me personally and professionally." He died at the age of 85 in New York City in 1980.

See also McCarthyism; *Amerasia*.

REFERENCES: Philip J. Jaffe, *The Amerasia Case: From 1945 to the Present* (New York, 1979); Harvey Klehr and Ronald Radosh, *The Amerasia Spy Case: Prelude to McCarthyism* (Chapel Hill, NC, 1996); John Stewart Services, *The Amerasia Papers: Some Problems in the History of U.S.-China Relations* (Berkeley, CA, 1971).

Jinxing Chen

Ji Chaoding (1903–1963)

Ji Chaoding, an expert in economics, was Secretary General of the China Committee for the Promotion of Foreign Trade from 1952 to 1963. In his early political career, he was a Communist operating first in the United States and then in the Chinese Nationalist government.

Born into a scholar-official family in Fengyang, Shanxi Province, in 1903, Ji graduated from Qinghua University in Beijing in 1924. Ji went to the United States in the same year on a Boxer Indemnity Scholarship. He received a B.A. degree from the University of Chicago in 1926 and his Ph.D. in economics from Columbia University in 1936.

Ji Chaoding's involvement with Communist activities began in 1925 when he became a member of the Anti-Imperialist League in Chicago. In 1926, he joined the American Communist Party. Until 1941, he was a member of the China Bureau of the American Communist Party. From winter 1926 to summer 1929, he was in Europe participating in a series of Communist-sponsored conferences. In February 1927, he, as a representative from the American Sun Zhongshan Society, attended the International Congress Against Colonial Oppression and Imperialism in Brussels. He was a member of the Chinese Communist delegation to the Sixth Congress of the Comintern held in Moscow in 1928. In 1927, when he was in Paris, Ji married his first wife, Harriet Levine, an American. Ji returned to the Unites States in 1929. While enrolled at Columbia University as a graduate student, he was active in Communist-directed work. Under the pseudonym of R. Doonping, he contributed articles to the *Daily Worker* and the *Chinese Student Monthly*. These articles later appeared as a pamphlet in 1931, entitled *Militarist Wars and Revolution: A Marxian Analysis of the New Revolutionary Civil War and Prospects of the Revolution in China*. In 1932, he co-authored with M. James a pamphlet *Soviet China*, which was published in both Moscow and New York. Ji Chaoding was an organizer of the American Friends of the Chinese People, which was formed in 1933. From 1933 to 1936, he was on the editorial board of its publication, *China Today*. Using various pseudonyms such as Hansu Chan, Huang Lowe, and Futien Wang, Ji frequently contributed to *China Today*. According to Philip Jaffe, editor of the magazine, Ji "was our political guide." In American Communist circles, Ji was "recognized as an able Marxist theoretician and an exceptionally able propagandist for the cause of Chinese Communism." In 1936, Ji completed his dissertation, a study of the key economic areas in Chinese history, which won the Seligman Economics Prize and was published in England. In the same year, Ji attended the international conference of the Institute of Pacific Relations (IPR) at Yosemite, California. The following year, he was appointed a member of the research staff of the International Secretariat of the IPR. His study for an IPR project, *Wartime Economic Development of China*, though never published under his own request due to its strong pro-Communist view, was circulated in 1940 in mimeographed form as an anonymous work. Ji was also an editor of the left-wing magazine *Amerasia* from 1937 to early 1941, and wrote numerous articles for *Pacific Affairs*, *Far East Survey*, *Virginia Quarterly*, as well as *Amerasia*. Ji Chaoding's career made a noticeable turn when he joined the staff of the Chinese Nationalist Government's Universal Trading Corporation in New York in 1940, eventually becoming its administrative vice president. In 1941, Ji left the United States for Chongqing, the wartime capital of China. He held various important positions in Guomindang government financial circles during the following years. In 1944, he became confidential secretary to Kong Xiangxi, Minister of Finance and brother-in-law of Jiang Jieshi and was appointed director of the Economic Research Department of the Central Bank of China.

Ji was in Beijing when the Communist forces captured the city in January 1949. Subsequently, he joined the new government. In 1952, he was appointed Secretary General of the China Committee for the Promotion of Foreign Trade, the position he held until his death in 1963. At his funeral, the party's eulogy openly acknowledged that Ji Chaoding had been "engaged in underground work for a considerable period."

See also Institute of Pacific Relations; *Amerasia*.

REFERENCES: Philip J. Jaffe, *The Amerasia Case from 1945 to the Present* (New York, 1979); Howard L. Boorman (ed.), *Biographical Dictionary of Republic China*, *Vol. 1* (New York, 1968).

Jinxing Chen

Jiang Jieshi (1887–1975)

Born in 1887, Jiang Jieshi spent most of his life battling a wide variety of political and military enemies. The son of a salt merchant, Jiang traveled to Japan as a young man to study in a military academy. While there he became committed to the overthrow of the Qing Dynasty. In 1911 the Qing government was toppled and China fell into a state of political fragmentation that lasted for the next several years. Various warlords and idealists, including Sun Zhongshan, sought to unify China under their control. Realizing that Sun's Guomindang (GMD) was powerless without accompanying military might, Jiang volunteered to travel to the USSR for advanced military training. Upon his return in 1924, Sun appointed Jiang commander of the Huangpu Military Academy.

Following the death of Sun in 1925, Jiang became the most powerful figure in the GMD. By 1926 Jiang had enough confidence in his Huangpu troops to launch the Northern Expedition, designed to militarily unify all of China under GMD control. Through force and alliance making, Jiang succeeded in creating a tenuously unified Republic of China. Despite his apparent military successes, one group remained a thorn in Jiang's side — the Communists. Controlling a fairly large region in southern China, the Communists refused to yield to GMD control. In 1934 Jiang drove the Communists from their Jiangxi Soviet, forcing them on the famous Long March across China. Eventually the survivors of this march, including Mao Zedong, settled in the remote northern region around Yanan, beyond the reach of Jiang's troops. At the same time Jiang was facing his Communist enemies, he was dealing with the opportunistic Japanese. In 1931 the Japanese invaded the northern provinces of Manchuria and created a puppet state. Many Chinese nationalists advocated greater resistance to the Japanese, but Jiang insisted that the Japanese were merely a disease of the skin, while the Communists were a disease of the heart. In other words, he would continue to focus his efforts on eradicating the Communists. In late 1936 Jiang was kidnapped by one of his own generals, Zhang Xueliang. Zhang demanded Jiang redirect his military efforts from the Communists toward the Japanese instead. This so-called Xian Incident led to a "united front" consisting of Jiang's GMD troops and Mao's Communist troops. Faced with a seemingly unified enemy, Japan responded with an all out invasion of China in the summer of 1937. With the 1945 defeat of Japan, Jiang's and Mao's forces quickly resumed hostilities toward each other. Though the United States tried to broker a peace between the two, such efforts were doomed to failure. In 1949 Mao's troops swept across the mainland and Jiang responded by moving his military and party apparatus to the offshore island province of Taiwan. In Taiwan Jiang reassembled his government structure, believing that at some future date he would renew hostilities with his Communist adversaries. However, for the rest of Jiang's life, the political situation between Taiwan and the mainland remained basically unchanged. On Taiwan Jiang created a one-party state that allowed no political dissent. He did, nevertheless, foster an environment of economic freedom and stability. The residents of Taiwan responded by creating an industrial powerhouse that soon became one of America's top trading partners.

Despite these economic ties, by the early 1970s the United States began making overtures to Mao's government in Beijing, angering Jiang and his officials. Jiang died in 1975, turning over the reigns of government to his son, Jiang Jingguo. Though he had created a secure and prosperous Taiwan, he no doubt felt that he had failed to defeat most of his life-long adversaries.

See also Civil War (1945–1949); Guomindang; Mao Zedong (1893–1976); Jiang Jingguo (1910–1988).

REFERENCES: Chiang Kai-shek, *China's Destiny: A Political Bible of the New China* (Washington, DC, 1943); Brian Crozier, *The Man Who Lost China: The First Full Biography of Chiang Kai-shek* (New York, 1976); Jonathan Fenby, *Chiang Kai-Shek: China's Generalissimo and the Nation He Lost* (New York, 2004); Owen Lattimore, *China Memoirs: Chiang Kai-Shek and the War against Japan* (Tokyo, 1990).

David Kenley

Jiang Jingguo (1910–1988)

Born on March 18, 1910 to Chinese Nationalist leader Jiang Jieshi and his first wife Mao Fumei in 1910, Jiang Jingguo would eventually succeed his father to become President of the Republic of China on Taiwan and oversee the beginnings of democratization in Taiwan during the last years of his presidency before his death in 1988.

In October of 1925, at the age of fifteen, Jiang entered a university in Moscow specially designated for visiting Chinese students. During his stay at the university, Jiang studied Russian and economics, as well as satisfying his desire to learn more about Communism. After his graduation, Jiang was refused passage back to China due to Jiang Jieshi's anti-Communist movement within the Chinese Nationalist Party (Guomindang). The Soviet Communists believed that the younger Jiang might be a useful tool in future Sino-Soviet relations, and as a result Jiang would not return to China until 1937. During this time, Jiang attended the Russian Military Affairs Research Center and was eventually shipped off to Siberia, where he worked at least part of the time in a steel factory. While in Siberia in 1935, Jiang met and married a native Russian, Fenna Epatcheva Vahaleva (later known as Jiang Fangliang). At the end of the Chinese Civil War in 1949, Jiang accompanied his father to Taiwan, where he became increasingly involved in the government of the Republic of China. In Septemeber of 1953, Jiang visited the United States, meeting with President Dwight D. Eisenhower , former President Harry S. Truman, and touring governement facilities throughout the country. In the late 1950's, Jiang was the central figure in the construction of the Central Cross Island Highway in Taiwan, finished in 1960. In 1964, Jiang became vice-Minister of Defense, a vital post that allowed him access to the military resources of Taiwan and strengthened his viability as a possible successor to his father. He became Minister of Defense the next year. In 1972,

Jiang took the post of Premier and, following Jiang Jieshi's death in 1975, he became President of the Republic of China on Taiwan in 1978, a post which he held until his death.

During his presidency, Jiang Jingguo presided over the gradual democratization of Taiwan that did not become fully realized until after his death. Dedicated to the free-market ideology of capitalism and seeking economic growth, Jiang's presidency encompassed a period of remarkable economic gain for Taiwan. More importantly, in 1987 Jiang repealed the edict of martial law imposed by his father in 1949 and allowed citizens of the Republic of China to visit family members on the mainland. As Jiang relaxed the autocratic rule, which had characterized his family, political opposition parties such as the Democratic Progressive Party were unofficially allowed to operate in competition with the Guomindang. Jiang Jingguo died of heart failure in Taibei at the age of 78. His 1988 death marked the end of a family political dynasty that had lasted six decades.

See also Jiang Jieshi (1887–1975); Guomindang (GMD).

Refererences: Linda Chaoand Ramon Myers, *The First Chinese Democracy: Political Life of the Republic of China on Taiwan* (Baltimore, MD, 1998); Steven J. Hood, *The Kuomintang and the Democratization of Taiwan* (Boulder, CO, 1996); Jay Taylor, *The Generalissimo's Son: Chiang Ching-kuo and the Revolutions in China and Taiwan* (Cambridge, MA, 2000).

Robert Elder

Jiang Nan Incident (1984)

Henry Liu, also known as Jiang Nan, was a prominent Chinese-American journalist. His brutal murder in the United States in 1984 received worldwide attentions. The case became one of the worst public-relations nightmares for the Chinese Nationalist government on Taiwan, and turned out to be an important factor in the democratic reforms on the island.

Born on December 7, 1932 in Jingjiang, Jiangsu Province, Henry Liu grew up amidst the turmoil of the armed conflict with Japan and the Chinese Civil War. At the age of sixteen, he was drafted into the Nationalist army, and was evacuated to Taiwan in 1949. Liu first attended the elite Political Warfare Academy under Jiang Jingguo, the son of Jiang Jieshi who later became President of the Nationalist government on Taiwan. However Liu's clashes with the authority prevented him from graduating. He then became a reporter for the *Taiwan Daily News*, and was named Washington correspondent in 1967. Liu became a naturalized U.S. citizen in 1973, and began to write articles and books on the ruling Jiang family, its social and political history. His writings were so offensive to the regime in Taiwan that he had received numerous warnings from ranking officials and former friends. Unwavering to the threats, Liu published his unauthorized biography of Jiang Jingguo in the U.S. in late 1984. The furious security apparatus in Taiwan decided to "teach him a lesson." On October 15, 1984, Wang Xiling, head of Guomindang military intelligence, dispatched members of the island's criminal "Bamboo" gang to Daly City, California, where they assassinated Henry Liu in his home. Though the ensuing investigation indicated that he might be a triple agent between the United States, Taiwan and mainland China, the fact that the Guomindang government could operate with such impunity in the United States sent a chill through both the Chinese American community and the intelligentsia in Taiwan. Enraged by the "consistent pattern of acts of intimidation and harassment directed against individuals," the U.S. Congress held a hearing on the case in the spring of 1985. Under pressure from the Reagan administration, the Taiwan government also conducted its own investigation of the incident. The query revealed that the murder was committed by three underworld figures from Taiwan on the order of top-officials of the Military Intelligence Bureau of the Ministry of Defense. Furthermore, there were allegations that a link existed between the leader of the criminal gang, Chen Qili, and the second son of President Jiang Jingguo, Jiang Xiaowu. As a result, Vice Admiral Wang Xiling, head of the Defense Ministry's intelligence bureau, was convicted of plotting Liu's death, and given a life sentence along with the two gangsters who carried out the murder.

The case marked for the first time in Taiwan's history that ranking intelligence or military officials were publicly tried. More significantly, the incident convinced people that political liberalization had to be a natural consequence of the island's rapid economic development, and a more visible progress in democratization was essential to boost Taiwan's image abroad during its struggle for international support.

REFERENCES: David E. Kaplan, *Fires of the Dragon: Politics, Murder, and the Kuomintang* (New York, 1992); *The Murder of Henry Liu: Hearings and Markup Before the Committee on Foreign Affairs and Its Subcommittee on Asian and Pacific Affairs, House of Representatives, Ninety-ninth Congress, First Session on H. Con. Res. 49 and 110, February 7; March 21; April 3, 1985* (Washington, DC, 1985).

Wenxian Zhang

Jiang Zemin (1926-)

Jiang Zemin was born on August 17, 1926, in Yangzhou, China. He earned his university degree in electrical engineering. In 1946, he joined the Chinese Communist Party (CCP). Jiang was a member of the Communist student underground after participation in the nationwide student movement in 1947. Jiang received his training at the Stalin Automobile Works in Moscow in the 1950s. Later, he served as Ambassador to Romania and Mayor of Shanghai. In November 1989, he became General Secretary of the CCP and chairman of the Central Military Commission. In March 1993, he became President of the People's Republic of China (PRC).

Under Jiang's leadership, China experienced rapid economic growth. But at the same time, at the political level, China did not achieve much success in political reform, which led the United States and Western democracies to criticize the Chinese government's policy regarding human rights. During Jiang's administration, he helped improve relations with China's neighbors, especially, Russia and India, as well as the United Sates. Also he asserted China's position as the representative of developing countries in the United Nations Security Council and other international organizations. Many analysts consider the peaceful transition of Hong Kong from British to Chinese sovereignty on July 1, 1997 and the summit meeting with U.S. President Bill Clinton in October 1997, as his main diplomatic successes.

Jiang as the head of the CCP and as a member of the standing committee of the politburo at the 16th Chinese Communist Party Congress in 2002, launched a generational shift in the leadership of China, bringing in the so-called fourth generation. Jiang stepped down in 2003 with Hu Jintao succeeding him as the CCP's General Secretary.

See also Chinese Communist Party.

Refrences: Wang Gungwu and Zheng Yongnian, *The Chinese Communist Party in the Jiang Zemin Era* (New York, 2004); Hung-Mao Tien and Yun-Han Chu, *China under Jiang Zemin,* (Boulder, CO, 2000); Willy Wo-lap Lam, *The Era of Jiang Zemin,* (New York, 1999); Bruce Gilley, *Tiger on the Brick: Jiang Zemin and China's New Elite,* (Berkeley, CA, 1998); Robert Lawrence Kuhn, *The Man Who Changed China: The Life and Legacy of Jiang Zemin* (London, 2004).

Nilly Kamal El-Amir

Jinmen and Mazu Crisis

The retreat of the Guomindang to Taiwan in 1949 and the subsequent establishment of the Republic of China (Taiwan), along with the refusal of the People's Republic of China to recognize the island nation as a legitimate government, have perpetuated the Chinese Civil War. During the 1950s Beijing sought to precipitate a military crisis with Taiwan that would result in a unified Communist China. Mao Zedong's government focused its efforts on several islands in the Taiwan Strait claimed by both Beijing and Taibei: Jinmen, Mazu, and the Dachens. The ambiguous nature of the Truman administration's "two China" policy, which neither recognized Beijing nor Taibei but tacitly supported the latter, along with the Eisenhower administration's overt support for Taibei in its effort to contain Beijing's influence in Asia, brought the United States into this rivalry.

Mao precipitated the first crisis in 1954 with the artillery bombardment of the Taiwan-controlled offshore islands of Jinmen and Mazu, along with the Dachens. Eisenhower dispatched units of the U.S. Navy to the Taiwan Strait in support of Jiang Jieshi's Nationalist Chinese government on Taiwan. Jiang agreed to cede control of the Dachens to Beijing but refused to do so with Jinmen and Mazu, which were considered central to Taiwan's defense. As 1955 began the U.S. Congress approved the "Formosa Resolution" and authorized the use of military force to defend Taiwan. Implicit in the resolution and explicit in Eisenhower's remarks was the threat of a nuclear strike against the People's Republic of China. In April Beijing stopped the bombardment of the offshore islands but refused to recognize the legitimacy of the Taibei government.

For the next three years a tense peace existed in the Taiwan Strait and American ties to Taiwan were strengthened through dual auspices of the U.S.-China Mutual Defense Treaty of 1954 and the Formosa Resolution. Beijing's acquiescence, additionally, weakened its influence in the region as it strengthened that of the United States. With the decline of China's influence in the Asian Communist world, Mao looked to reclaim China's preeminence and eclipse the Soviet Union in the region. Thus, in 1955, Beijing sponsored the Bandung Conference, in Indonesia, of the unaligned nations in Africa and Asia, which heightened tensions with Taibei. Difficulties in instituting his domestic agenda, the Great Leap Forward, exacerbated Mao's foreign policy woes for domestic problems would undermine Chinese influence abroad. As a result, he sought a way to unify the nation and distract the populace from the hardships his program caused.

The offshore islands offered a means through which to do so, as well as to reclaim the regional influence Beijing had lost. In October 1958 the People's Liberation Army renewed its shelling of the now heavily-fortified Jinmen. Eisenhower refused to appease Communist aggression and ordered U.S. Air Force, as well as Navy, units to the region. Although the U.S. forces did not engage in combat with the Chinese they did supply Taiwan with much-needed munitions and supplies, including advanced air-to-air missiles. Simultaneously, the U.S. Secretary of State, John Foster Dulles, proposed a draw down of nationalist forces on Jinmen if Beijing ceased hostilities. Both initiatives proved decisive in halting the Communist campaign. Due to the Jinmen-Mazu Crisis, U.S. policy towards China resumed the cautious ambiguity that had characterized it in the Truman administration.

See also Taiwan Strait.

REFERENCES: Stephen E. Ambrose, *Eisenhower, Volume II: The President* (New York, 1983); Rosemary Foot, *The Practice of Power: U.S. Relations with China Since 1949* (Oxford, 1995); John Lewis Gaddis, *Strategies of Containment: A Critical Appraisal of Postwar American National Security Policy* (Oxford, 1982); Akira Iriye, *The Cold War in Asia: A Historical Introduction* (Englewood Cliffs, NJ, 1974); Shu Guang Zhang, *Deterrence and Strategic Culture: Chinese American Confrontations, 1949–1958* (Ithaca, NY, 1992).

Paul D. Gelpi, Jr.

Johnson, Lyndon Baines (1908–1973)

Assuming the Presidency after the assassination of President John Kennedy, Lyndon Johnson pursued no major initiatives in the nation's China policy. Johnson's tenure as President (1963–1969) was marred by the Vietnam War, and his belief that the insurgency of the North Vietnamese and Viet Cong were fostered by Mao's China made it difficult for Johnson to seek better relations with China.

Johnson was born August 27, 1908 near Stonewall, Texas. Johnson experienced rural poverty growing up in West Texas, and he worked his way through Southwest Texas State Teachers College in San Marcos, Texas. Tapped as an administrator for President Franklin D. Roosevelt's Neighborhood Youth Administration, Johnson embraced the New Deal. In 1937, he was elected to the House of Representatives, where the Democrat served six terms. During World War II, Johnson secured an appointment as a Navy lieutenant commander and briefly saw action in the Pacific. In 1948, he was elected to the Senate, and six years later won re-election; assuming the position of Senate Majority Leader. Johnson sought the 1960 Democratic Presidential nomination, which he lost to Kennedy. The proud Texan accepted Kennedy's offer of the Vice Presidential slot, and the Kennedy-Johnson ticket was victorious over Republican challenger Richard Nixon. As President, John pursued civil rights legislation and social programs to eliminate poverty in the United States. Johnson was concerned that conservative critics would accuse him of being a lib-

eral who was soft on Communism. Johnson attempted to protect his domestic programs and demonstrate his anti-Communist credentials by opposing Communist expansions in Southeast Asia. In the long run, Johnson's "war on poverty" was sacrificed on the altar of the Vietnam War. Initially, there seemed some promise of rapprochement between the Johnson administration and China. Roger Hilsman, Assistant Secretary of State for Far Eastern Affairs, suggested in December 1963 that the United States was prepared to coexist with the People's Republic of China, while retaining its commitments to Taiwan. But before any normalization of relation could be pursued, China would have to be convinced of the American resolve to confront Chinese aggression. Thus, Johnson and his Secretary of State Dean Rusk, a holdover from the Kennedy regime, were determined to make a stand against North Vietnam, whom they interpreted as doing the biding of China. Chinese Communist leader Mao Zedong, however, seemed more concerned with the ideological purity of his revolution than American policies in Indochina. In July 1966, with over 400,000 American troops in Vietnam, Mao launched the Great Proletarian Cultural Revolution. As China turned inward, the Johnson administration increased its bombing of North Vietnam; assuming that China would be unable to intervene in the conflict.

As the Johnson administration became increasingly bogged down in Vietnam, there was little time or opportunity for initiatives with China. Following the Tet Offensive and a growing antiwar movement in the United States, Johnson in March 1968 announced that he would not seek re-election. Discontent with Johnson resulted in Republican Richard Nixon's defeat of Vice President Hubert Humphrey in the 1968 Presidential race. Johnson retreated to his Texas ranch, and he died from a heart attack on January 22, 1973 in Johnson City, Texas.

See also Second Indochina War; Cold War.

REFERENCES: H. W. Brands (ed.), *The Foreign Policies of Lyndon Johnson: Beyond Vietnam* (College Station, TX, 1995); Paul K. Conkin, *Big Daddy from the Pedernales: Lyndon Baines Johnson* (Boston, MA, 1986); Robert Dallek, *Flawed Giant: Lyndon Johnson and His Times* (New York, 1998); George Herring, *LBJ and Vietnam: A Different Kind of War* (Austin, TX, 1994); David E. Kaiser, *American Tragedy: Kennedy, Johnson and the Origins of the Vietnam War* (Cambridge, MA, 2000).

Ron Briley

Johnson, Nelson T. (1887–1954)

Nelson Trusler Johnson began his career as a student interpreter in China in 1907. Over the years he served in multiple positions in the consular service (1909–1918) and the State Department (1919–1929), eventually becoming Assistant Secretary of State under Frank B. Kellogg. He also served as U.S. Ambassador to China (1935–1941) and Secretary General of the Far Eastern Commission (1946–1952).

As Chief of the Division of Far Eastern Affairs from 1925–1928, Johnson was the chief architect of American China policy during the Nationalist Revolution. Johnson recast that policy upon a new set of assumptions—namely, that China's sovereign rights superseded rights the powers had obtained for themselves in China through the unequal treaties. Accordingly, the U.S. would no longer attempt to uphold treaties and would make new "equal" ones with China as soon as possible, even if it meant breaking the united front the international powers had agreed to during the Washington Naval Conference of 1921–1922. The capstone of Kellogg-Johnson policy was the new tariff treaty, signed in 1928, granting U.S. recognition of Jiang Jieshi's Nationalist Government. Even more significantly, the treaty marked the beginning of the end of the so-called "unequal treaties" between China and the powers. In the years leading up to 1928, with China in the throes of revolution, Johnson advocated a policy of non-intervention. He accepted as a matter of fact that the revolution was part of a long process that China must inevitably pass in order to develop into a modern state. He asserted that the greatest contribution the U.S. could make to the settlement of China's problems was to leave the Chinese alone — China's problems must have a "Chinese solution." All the foreign powers would have to exercise restraint and tolerance while the social and political upheaval took place. Johnson had no interest in preserving the special privileges Americans enjoyed as a result of the unequal treaties. He believed, moreover, that unless the powers took steps toward treaty revision, it would be only a matter of time before Chinese nationalists unilaterally abrogated the treaties. On the other hand, Johnson believed that the foreign powers were predatory, and that the U.S. alone wished to see the birth of a new China. Thus in at least one respect, Johnson's ideas about China were conventionally American: he subscribed to the notion that China needed the U.S. for protection and leadership. Therefore, when the Nationalists' overtook Beijing in June 1928, Johnson and Kellogg shifted from a policy of nonintervention to one of using American influence to stabilize the situation in China. This new thinking led to the new tariff agreement. Johnson spent his childhood in pioneer communities in the American Midwest and in Washington, DC, where he went to school. He entered the Foreign Service and in 1907 was sent to China as a student interpreter. For the next 13 years he lived in various parts of China and traveled extensively throughout the country. In 1921 he was appointed consul general-at-large, and for two years was responsible for inspecting the U.S. consulates throughout East Asia. By the time he came to the State Department, Johnson had developed very definite ideas about the situation in China and what should be the response of the U.S. to Chinese nationalism.

Johnson became Assistant Secretary of State in 1927. He returned to China in 1929, where he served as U.S. Minister until 1935, and Ambassador from 1935–1941. From 1941–1946 he was the U.S. Minister to Australia, and from 1946–1952 he served as Secretary General of the Far Eastern Commission. He died in Washington, DC.

REFERENCES: Dorothy Borg, *American Policy and the Chinese Revolution, 1925–1928* (New York, 1947); Russell D. Buhite, *Nelson T. Johnson and American Policy Toward China* (East Lansing, MI, 1968); *The Papers of Nelson Trusler Johnson* (Division of Manuscripts, Library of Congress).

Mike Wilson

Joint Commission on Rural Reconstruction (JCRR)

The Joint Commission on Rural Reconstruction grew out of reformer C. Y. "James" Yen's (Yen Yangchu) Mass Education Movement and related efforts to create "model villages" in Hebei Province, and well-established cooperative relationships between Chinese and American agricultural colleges. Yen's effective lobbying of the Truman administration, at the urging of influential American supporters (among them, Justice William Douglas, and members of Congress Walter Judd and Helen Gahagan Douglas) resulted in direct federal assistance. The China Aid Act passed by Congress on April 3, 1948 established the Joint Commission, composed of three Chinese (Yen, T.H. Shen, and Jiang Menglin) and two Americans (Raymond Moyer and John Earl Baker), to "formulate and carry out a program for reconstruction in rural areas of China" with an initial budget of $27.5 million.

After the Nationalist retreat from the mainland, the JCRR continued its work on Taiwan, and is credited in large part for the phenomenal rate of economic growth that took place in the 1950s and 1960s. Its program of rent reductions and land redistribution in the Taiwanese countryside won official support because it supplied Jiang Jieshi with an expedient set of policies, which helped him cement unassailable political authority. On the mainland, large landholders had composed the core of Guomindang (GMD) support, and the Nationalists naturally proved resistant to serious land reform. On Taiwan, the socio-economic fabric had a different weave, and the GMD quickly availed itself of the opportunity to expropriate the land of the native population and the defeated Japanese.

Jiang's regime actively resisted JCRR-sponsored reforms that challenged the Nationalist order or traditional Chinese values. This was initially true with regard to population control, although the JCRR approach proved so successful that it became a model for other nations in the 1960s. For the United States government, which funded the majority of JCRR initiatives, the organization's record of successful social and economic reforms were vital to the Cold War effort to demonstrate viable alternative development models to Communism. The JCRR's activities were substantially reduced after the U.S. ended economic aid to Taiwan in 1965, and the Commission formally dissolved after the Nixon's visit to Beijing in 1972. Captivated by his larger vision of applying JCRR principles to all of rural Asia, James Yen left the JCRR in 1950 for the Philippines, where he founded the International Rural Reconstruction Movement (now the Institute for Rural Reconstruction), which he headed until his death in 1990.

See also Cold War.

REFERENCES: Charles W. Hayford, *To the People: James Yen and Village China* (New York, 1990); Nancy Bernkopf Tucker, *Taiwan, Hong Kong, and the United States, 1945–1972* (New York, 1994); Shen, Tsung-han, *The Sino-American Joint Commission on Rural Reconstruction; Twenty Years of Cooperation for Agricultural Development* (Ithaca, NY, 1970).

Matthew Young

Judd, Walter H. (1898–1994)

Walter H. Judd, who as a U.S. Congressman in the 1940s and 1950s became a recognized authority on China and on American policy in Asia, was born in the small Nebraska village of Rising City on September 25, 1898. As a young man Judd became a convert to evangelical Protestantism, and decided to devote his life to missionary and medical work among non-Christian people in Asia. He followed his older sisters in attending the University of Nebraska at Lincoln, working in the university cafeteria to pay his expenses and becoming active in the band and in the local chapter of the Young Men's Christian Association (YMCA). He was commissioned as a lieutenant in the U.S. Army in January 1919, but because World War I ended a few months earlier he did

not see active duty. He earned a BA from the University of Nebraska in 1920 and an MD from the University's Medical College at Omaha in 1923. He practiced as an intern at the hospital there and became a leader in the Student Volunteer Movement for Foreign Missions, a clearing house that trained and assigned American university graduates to Christian missions overseas, most in Africa and Asia.

In October 1926, Judd, having signed on for mission work with the American Board of Foreign Missions, arrived at Shaowu in Fujian Province in China, where he worked as a medical missionary for five years. In 1927 during the Chinese Nationalist Party's Northern Expedition, a military campaign led by Jiang Jieshi to subdue China's many warlords and unify the country under Nationalist rule, Judd was taken prisoner by rogue Nationalist troops and narrowly avoided execution. By 1930 he was chronically ill with malaria and decided not to enlist for another missionary tour. Upon leaving China in 1931 he briefly studied Asian history and culture at the Imperial University in Tokyo before returning to the United States. In 1931 Judd secured a fellowship at the Mayo Clinic in Rochester, Minnesota, but in 1934 he accepted a mission assignment to head the largest Congregationalist medical facility in China, the Fenchow Hospital in Shanxi Province. He was accompanied by his wife, Miriam Barber Judd. The approach of invading Japanese forces in August 1937 forced Judd's family to flee to the United States via Hong Kong. Judd himself remained behind, treating civilian Chinese casualties until July 1938, when he too returned to America. Judd embarked upon a nationwide speaking tour, during which he highlighted Japanese brutality in China and the role of American trade policy in supplying Japan's expansionist military program in Asia. He testified before Congressional committees, and in 1942 won election to the U.S. Congress as a Republican from Minnesota. Early in his Congressional career Judd backed several anti-isolationist programs, including the formation of the United Nations, the Voice of America radio broadcasting program, and the Marshall Plan. He also worked to repeal federal laws that banned immigration from China and outlawed the naturalization of ethnic Chinese. As the Chinese Civil War continued and the Nationalists' position deteriorated in 1948–1949, Judd advocated for increased U.S. military aid to Jiang Jieshi. Although the Truman administration declined to defend Jiang, Judd emerged as the key Congressional defender of continued U.S. diplomatic and defense relations with Jiang's new redoubt on the island of Taiwan. During the 1950s he was a proponent of the domino theory and of the use of U.S. military force to contain Communism. He also endorsed the continued exclusion of the Chinese Communist government from the United Nations, founding the bipartisan "Committee of One Million" to back the policy. Judd was considered as a potential vice presidential candidate by both the Eisenhower and Nixon campaigns, and he was the keynote speaker at the 1960 Republican National Convention.

Judd was not re-elected to the Congress in 1962, but he remained active as a lecturer and in the American Medical Association. He was awarded the Presidential Medal of Freedom in 1981. Judd died in Mitchellville, Maryland, on February 13, 1994, and was buried in Nebraska.

See also Committee of One Million; China Lobby; Cold War; Domino Theory; Containment.

REFERENCES: Lee Edwards, *Missionary for Freedom: The Life and Times of Walter Judd* (New York, 1990); Ross Y. Koen, *The China Lobby in American Politics* (New York, 1974).

Laura M. Calkins

Kellogg, Frank B. (1856–1937)

Frank D. Kellogg was American Secretary of State from 1924–1928. Under Kellogg, U.S. China policy shifted to an independent approach, away from the 1921–1922 Washington Naval Conference model of cooperation with other foreign powers. Kellogg was sympathetic to Chinese nationalism and believed that the changing circumstances in China called for a new policy. In 1928 the State Department became satisfied that the Nationalist Revolution had succeeded well enough, and on July 25 concluded a new tariff treaty with the government of Jiang Jieshi. The treaty was important to China for two reasons. First, because it was based on the principle that China was entitled to complete national autonomy, it marked the beginning of the end of the so-called unequal treaties. Second, through the treaty the U.S. officially recognized Jiang's government. The U.S. was the first foreign power to recognize the new Chinese government.

Kellogg has been often lauded as a champion of China's sovereignty. Historian Wesley Fishel concluded, "Kellogg had consistently and with marked sincerity pursued a policy of friendliness and sympathy toward Chinese aspirations." Another scholar L. Ethan Ellis, while he did not much admire Kellogg (a mediocre Secretary of State, in Ellis's estimation), agreed: Kellogg acted out of "good will, working to help China attain her goals at the greatest speed." Kellogg was born in New York, but spent most of his boyhood in

pioneering communities in Minnesota. He received little formal education, but through great effort studied law, gaining admittance to the Minnesota bar in 1877. He became counsel for some of the railroads, iron mining companies, and steel firms that developed the rich Mesabi iron range in Minnesota and, consequently, a friend of the great business figures of the day, such as Andrew Carnegie and John D. Rockefeller. Kellogg attained national notoriety after he prosecuted successfully the first anti-trust case of Theodore Roosevelt's famous trust-busting program in 1900. He was elected to the U.S. Senate in 1916, where he came out in support of American participation in World War I. After the war he voted in favor of the League of Nations. In 1923, President Calvin Coolidge appointed Kellogg to be U.S. Ambassador to England, where he later received the President's invitation to succeed Secretary of State Charles Evans Hughes. Kellogg took the oath of office on March 4, 1925. Kellogg brought to the State Department a very different style of leadership than that which was exercised by his predecessor. Hughes, widely regarded as "one of the ablest men who ever held" the office of Secretary of State, often succeeded in by-passing Congress and in shaping foreign policy by his own personal force. Kellogg on the other hand, was much more conscious of the limits imposed upon him by public opinion and by Congress. He was much less disposed to initiate action, instead depending heavily on his advisers. One of Kellogg's biographers has spoken of his "overdependence upon advisers of a similar bent." For China policy, Kellogg depended most heavily on Nelson T. Johnson, Chief of Far Eastern Affairs in the State Department. Kellogg's State Department signed a record-breaking number of treaties, none more famous than the Kellogg-Briand Pact, the multilateral treaty renouncing war as an instrument of national policy. The pact, proclaimed in July 1929, was broken by armed conflict in Manchuria months later.

Kellogg received the Nobel Peace Prize in 1929 and served on the Permanent Court of International Justice in the 1930s. He died on the eve of his eighty-first birthday of pneumonia, following a stroke.

REFERENCES: Dorothy Borg, *American Policy and the Chinese Revolution, 1925–1928* (New York, 1947); L. Ethan Ellis, *Frank B. Kellogg and American Foreign Relations, 1925–1929* (New Brunswick, NJ, 1961); Robert H. Ferrell (ed.), *The American Secretaries of State and Their Diplomacy Vol. XI* (New York, 1963); Wesley R. Fishel, *The End of Extraterritoriality in China* (Berkeley, CA 1952); Frederick W. Haberman (ed.), *Nobel Lectures, Peace 1926–1950* (Amsterdam, 1972); Dexter Perkins, "The Department of State and American Public Opinion," in Gordon A. Craig and Felix Gilbert (eds.), *The Diplomats: 1919–1939, Vol. I: The Twenties* (New York, 1967).

Mike Wilson

Kennan, George F. (1904–)

George Frost Kennan was born on February 16, 1904 in Milwaukee, Wisconsin. He graduated from Princeton in 1925, immediately taking a job with the Foreign Service. In 1929, the State Department sent him to the University of Berlin for immersion study of Russian thought, language, and culture because it wanted a specialist in those areas to work toward closer relations with the Soviet government. When recognition was finally granted in 1933, Kennan accompanied the U.S. delegation to Moscow.

With the onset of World War II, Kennan was posted in Moscow, spent the majority of the war years there, and from this post gained recognition. In February of 1946, he sent what became known as the "Long Telegram" to the State Department. In it, Kennan first articulated a "containment" policy toward Soviet expansion. He argued that Marxist ideology and actual circumstances within that country combined to force an impossibility of permanent and peaceful coexistence between the Soviets and the Western world. Using analogies such as a "fluid stream," Kennan said that Soviet expansion would occur anywhere it could; to contain that expansion, U.S. policy must actively close any opportunities for expansion. Upon return to the United States, he rewrote the telegram in essay form and published it in *Foreign Affairs*, with his superiors' stipulation that he should use a pseudonym. He signed the article with an "X" thereby giving it the name by which the article is commonly known. Kennan had a less aggressive stance with regards to the Chinese Communist Party (CCP). He played an important role in the late 1940s convincing the State Department of the futility of further supporting the Guomindan (GMD) led by Jiang Jieshi, fearing that U.S. policies might drive Mao Zedong closer to Stalin. Kennan worked closely with John Davies, a China Hand, and others to argue that the CCP would be independent of the USSR, and as such did not represent a serious threat to American security. He believed that even if China became a Soviet satellite, it would drain the Soviets and eventually Chinese nationalist elements would cause a split from the Soviet bloc. Davies masterminded their efforts, but Kennan's name carried more weight as they lobbied to shift U.S. support from the GMD to the new Asian ally and pro-United States bulwark, Japan. In 1949, Kennan and others urged President Harry S. Truman to minimize U.S. involvement in the Chinese Civil War using two primary arguments: first, that the United States had insufficient interests there to justify massive, direct intervention which was all that could have changed the outcome; and second, that increased aid to the GMD would poison future relations with the CCP should it prove victorious. Kennan wanted to stop the spread of Communism certainly, but proposed "drawing the line" outside of China. He hoped to retain recognition of the GMD government on Taiwan while keeping the door open with the CCP. Kennan and Davies also encouraged the writing of the 1949 China White Paper, which reviewed recent Sino-American relations, concluding that the United States had done all it could to help Jiang, and had no option but to accept Communist conquest of China. Generally, Kennan believed the Soviet Union would be "extremely cautious" in spreading Marxism around Asia, being "well aware of the fact that if you cannot overshadow a country militarily, ideology is in itself an untrustworthy means with which to hold them." He did not believe Stalin had any real interests in Asia. In the early 1950s, Kennan suggested mainland Asia be omitted from the containment concept since the United States was "overextended" in its beliefs about what could be accomplished there. Instead, he recommended Japan and the Philippines become the "cornerstone of a Pacific security system." Kennan testified at the televised 1966 Senate Foreign Relations Committee hearings. He "warned that the pre-occupation with Vietnam was undermining America's global obligations," "insisted [the containment doctrine] designed for a stable European nation-state context in the 1940s, did not fit Asia," and urged gradual withdrawal from Vietnam. In the 1980s, he supported the antinuclear movement and has continued to write, often critically, about American foreign policy into the 21st century.

See also Containment; Cold War; Civil War (1945–1949); China White Paper.

REFERENCES: George F. Kennan, *Memoirs: 1925–1950* (Boston, MA, 1967) and *Sketches from a Life* (New York, 2000); Wilson D. Miscamble, *George F. Kennan and the Making of American Foreign Policy, 1947–1950* (Princeton, NJ, 1992); George F. Kennan, "The Sources of Soviet Conduct," *Foreign Affairs* (July 1947).

Catherine Forslund

Kennedy-Chen Conference (1961)

The Kennedy-Chen Conference of 1961 refers to a conference held July 31 and August 1, 1961 between the Republic of China (Taiwan) and the United States. The conference was held in

Washington, DC. Chen Cheng, the Vice President and Premier of the Republic of China, visited the United States beginning July 31, 1961 for the purpose of discussing the permanent representation of the Republic of China in the United Nations and the question of admitting Outer Mongolia into the United Nations. The U.S. President John F. Kennedy and Chen also discussed the conditions within Communist China. They both agreed that the Chinese Communist regime on mainland China was failing to provide for the needs for the Chinese people. There was a food shortage in mainland China due to the commune system. Kennedy and Chen agreed that the United States and the Republic of China had to work closely together in order to strengthen their mutual interests and security. President Kennedy made it clear that the Republic of China should not veto the admission of Outer Mongolia to the United Nations, and that the United States would not support the move.

On August 2, 1961, two days after the talks began, President Kennedy and Premier Chen issued a joint communique. Kennedy reaffirmed the United States' support for the representation of the Republic of China in the United Nations and continued to oppose the admission of the Chinese Communist government into the United Nations. Both Kennedy and Chen expressed their concern that the Soviet Union might veto the admission of Mauritania to the United Nations. Chen announced that Republic of China would support the admission of any newly independent states, including Outer Mongolia, to the United Nations.

Before the Kennedy-Chen Conference of 1961, the Republic of China was threatening to veto the admission of Outer Mongolia into the United Nations because Jiang Jieshi of the Republic of China saw Mongolia as Chinese territory and not as an independent country. However, the Kennedy administration wanted Mongolia in the United Nations. Therefore, the Republic of China was persuaded not to veto the United Nations' membership for Outer Mongolia. Kennedy did not want to upset African countries and jeopardize their supporting votes in the United Nations because the Soviet Union might veto the admission of Mauritania if the Republic of China vetoed the admission of Outer Mongolia. The African countries might then support the Chinese Communist regime and its admission into the United Nations if Mauritania's membership was vetoed.

See also Kennedy, John Fitzgerald (1917–1963); United Nations.

Reference: DuPre Jones (ed.), *China: U.S. Policy Since 1945* (Washington, DC, 1980); Noam Kochavi, *A Conflict Perpetuated: China Policy During the Kennedy Years* (Westport, CT, 2002); Ta Jen Liu, *A History of Sino-American Diplomatic Relations, 1840–1974* (Taibei, 1978).

Edy Parsons

Kennedy, John Fitzgerald (1917–1963)

Although often perceived as ushering in an era of change in international relations, the Presidency of John Fitzgerald Kennedy (1961–1963) brought little transformation in American policy regarding China. Kennedy and his Secretary of State Dean Rusk viewed China as the major threat to international stability, and they were determined to halt Chinese aggression in Southeast Asia.

Kennedy was born May 29, 1917 in Brookline, Massachusetts. Following graduation from Harvard in 1940, Kennedy entered the Navy, where he was decorated for saving members of his destroyed PT boat. The World War II hero entered politics after the war, serving as a Democratic Congressman from Massachusetts until his elevation to the Senate in 1953. After failing to secure the Democratic Vice Presidential nomination in 1956, Kennedy successfully campaigned for the 1960 Presidential spot on the Democratic ticket. In the election of 1960, he narrowly defeated Richard Nixon. Rather than calling for major alterations in American foreign policy, Kennedy was a supporter and product of the post World War II consensus. Although cognizant of the growing drift between Mao's China and the Soviet Union, Kennedy did not encourage a reappraisal of Sino-American relations. Instead, Kennedy and Secretary of State Dean Rusk perceived China as a greater threat to international stability than the Kremlin. The Chinese were believed to support wars of national liberation and to be insensitive to the horrors of nuclear war. Accordingly, Kennedy refused to reopen China policy, and in August 1961, the President secretly informed Jiang Jieshi that the United States would veto any effort at the United Nations Security Council to seat the People's Republic of China at the expense of Taiwan. Kennedy also promised to aid Jiang in covert operations aimed at the mainland. The President was also concerned about domestic opposition from the Republican Party and China Lobby if overtures were made to the People's Republic of China. Kennedy's distrust of Mao's China increased during the Cuban Missile Crisis, as Secretary Rusk argued that Khrushchev's reckless international behavior was the result of pressures from the Chinese and hard liners in the Kremlin. Also, China seemed to take advantage of the missile crisis by attacking India in October 1962. While some Kennedy advisers argued that India provoked the attack and Jiang's government also laid claim to the same disputed territory, the incursion into India confirmed Kennedy's perception of Chinese aggression.

Following the missile crisis, Kennedy pursued a policy of detente with the Soviet Union, but the President remained apprehensive regarding Chinese activities in Southeast Asia and the world. In July 1963, Kennedy convened a National Security Council meeting to assess the threat of Chinese nuclear policy. The following month, he publicly expressed his concerns; asserting that China's willingness to use war, and perhaps even nuclear weapons, constituted "a more dangerous situation than any we have faced since the end of the Second World War." Kennedy blamed the Chinese for the growing unrest in Laos and Vietnam. Kennedy's decision to increase military support to South Vietnam was predicated upon his belief that Chinese aggression must be met with force.

While some argue that Kennedy was re-evaluating his commitment to Vietnam when he was assassinated in Dallas on November 22, 1963, during his short Presidency he made no overtures to the People's Republic and essentially followed the policies pursued by the Eisenhower administration during the 1950s.

See also Cold War; Detente; Kennedy-Chen Conference (1961); United Nations; Second Indochina War.

References: Robert Dallek, *An Unfinished Journey: John F. Kennedy, 1917–1963* (Boston, MA, 2003); Lawrence Freedman, *Kennedy's Wars: Berlin, Cuba, Laos, and Vietnam* (New York, 2000); David Halberstram, *The Best and the Brightest* (New York, 1969); David E. Kaiser, *American Tragedy: Kennedy, Johnson and the Origins of the Vietnam War* (Cambridge, MA, 2000).

Ron Briley

Kissinger, Henry A. (1923–)

Henry Kissinger served as National Security Advisor and as Secretary of State during the Nixon and Ford adminstrations. He was unique among Secretaries of State because he had a doctoral degree in a relevant field, Political Science, and was a published scholar of power politics. He disagreed with the strain of moral diplomacy in American history. Late in his scholarly career, he began to doubt America's willingness to bear the costs of leadership and sought to introduce balance of power politics to play off the Soviet Union and to recognize the People's Republic of China.

President Richard Nixon wanted control over foreign affairs, and distrusted career diplomats in the State Department. He used Kissinger, who expanded the budget of the National Security Council, and consequently greatly expanded the staff. The NSC staff would order studies and proposals from various agencies, including the State Department, to present to the President. Kissinger helped Nixon achieve his greatest foreign policy triumphs, including detente with the Soviet Union, the opening to China, and the winding down of the Vietnam conflict. Kissinger elaborated a theory of balance of power politics and given the range of areas—military power, economic power, political power, etc.—tried to introduce uncertainty into Soviet diplomatic calculations; he tried to create five such centers of varying strength—the United States, the Soviet Union, the People's Republic of China, Western Europe, and Japan. He also believed in "linkage" that the United States would expect Soviet agreement on a range of topics before agreeing to Soviet proposals on any specific topic. In a sense, he sought to reward the Soviet Union for good behavior across the globe. One result was the signing in Moscow in 1972 of an agreement, SALT I, limiting offensive missiles and pledging each side not to install defensive missile systems. Kissinger had an even more spectacular accomplishment. In 1971, he eluded reporters on a trip to Pakistan claiming a stomach ailment, and made a secret visit to mainland China where he met Premier Zhou Enlai, and paved the way for Nixon's historic trip in February 1972, ending more than two decades of hostility towards China's Communist regime. He negotiated secretly for many years with North Vietnamese diplomats, and in 1972 shortly before the election announced he had achieved peace although the formal agreement was several months away. Kissinger and North Vietnamese negotiator Le Duc Tho received the Nobel Prize for Peace (although Le would decline the award). Kissinger rejected the simple determinism of John Foster Dulles and "brinksmanship," recognizing the world was more complex than it had been a decade earlier. He was open to discussions with the People's Republic of China. He also recognized the continuing cost of the conflict in Vietnam and the need to end it. Since leaving government, he formed a consulting firm and has continued to write on foreign affairs.

See also Nixon, Richard (1913–1994); Nixon's Visit to China; Second Indochina War; Detente; Cold War.

References: Larry Berman, *No Peace, No Honor: Nixon, Kissinger, and Betrayal in Vietnam* (New York, 2001); Seymour Hersh, *The Price of Power: Kissinger in the Nixon White House* (New York, 1983); Henry Kissinger, *The White House Years* (New York, 1979);

Robert D. Schulzinger, *Henry Kissinger, Doctor of Diplomacy* (New York, 1989); William Shawcross, *Sideshow: Kissinger, Nixon, and the Destruction of Cambodia, Revised Edition* (New York, 1987).

Charles M. Dobbs

Knowland, William Fife (1908–1974)

As a United States Senator from California in the 1950s, William Knowland was a defender of Senator Joseph McCarthy and leader of the China Lobby. His unwavering support for Jiang Jieshi and Nationalist China resulted in Knowland being labeled the "Senator from Formosa."

Knowland was born June 26, 1908 in Alameda, California. His father was Joseph Russell Knowland, a Republican Congressman and newspaper publisher. In 1929, Knowland graduated from the University of California at Berkeley and joined the staff of his father's newspaper, *Tribune*. He also followed his father into politics, serving in the California state legislature. In 1941, he was selected as chairman of the Republican National Committee. He was drafted into the army in 1942, eventually rising to the rank of major. While Knowland was serving abroad in 1945, California Governor Earl Warren, apparently repaying a political debt to Knowland's father, appointed the young man to replace deceased Senator Hiram Johnson. Knowland was released from active duty and returned to the United States, claiming his Senate seat. The following year, Knowland was elected to a full Senate term by the voters of California. In the Senate, Knowland quickly established a reputation for opposing the Truman administration. While he did break with isolationists to support the anti-Communist Truman Doctrine in Greece and Turkey, Knowland voted to pass the 1947 Taft-Hartley Bill over Truman's veto and restrict union activities. Knowland was elected to a second term in 1952, becoming a frequent critic of the moderate Republicanism pursued by President Dwight D. Eisenhower. The California Senator did not believe that Eisenhower was doing enough to restore the Nationalist Chinese government of Jiang Jieshi in Taiwan to power on the Chinese mainland. Knowland was convinced that the 1949 victory of Mao Zedong and the Chinese Communists in the Chinese Civil War was aided by leftwing sympathizers and traitors in the Department of State. Accordingly, Knowland became a leader of the China Lobby, which opposed the Beijing regime and called for measures to help Jiang to regain power on the mainland. The Senator led Congressional opposition to the seating of Communist China in the United Nations.

With the death of Senate Majority Leader Robert Taft in 1953, Knowland was elected to the leadership post. Two years later, however, he was demoted to Minority Leader after Republican setbacks in the 1954 Congressional elections. Knowland was at odds with the Eisenhower White House over his support of Senator Joseph McCarthy, who shared the California Senator's views on the situation in China. Knowland voted against the Senate measure, which censured the controversial McCarthy, following the Wisconsin Senator's ill-conceived investigation of Communist subversion in the armed forces. Knowland considered a Presidential campaign in 1956, but he abandoned his efforts when Eisenhower announced that he would be a candidate for reelection. Rather than seek another Senate term in 1958, Knowland returned to California and mounted a campaign for the governorship, which he assumed would provide a political foundation for a Presidential bid in 1960. His plans were dashed, however, when he lost the gubernatorial contest to Democrat Pat Brown.

Knowland retired to the *Tribune*, continuing to campaign against the recognition of Communist China from the newspaper's editorial pages. On February 23, 1974, Knowland was found dead at his Monte Rio, California home; apparently the victim of a self-inflicted gunshot wound.

See also China Lobby; McCarthyism; United Nations.

REFERENCES: Joseph Keely, *The China Lobby Man: The Story of Alfred Kohlberg* (New York, 1969); Ross Y. Koen, *The China Lobby in American Politics* (New York, 1974); Gayle B. Montgomery, *One Step From the White House: The Rise and Fall of Senator William F. Knowland* (Berkeley, CA, 1999); William S. White, "What Bill Knowland Stands For," *New Republic* (February 27, 1956).

Ron Briley

Knox Neutralization Scheme

Knox Neutralization Scheme was a plan initiated by Secretary of State Philander C. Knox in November 1909. The plan called for the establishment of an international banking group to provide loan for China to purchase Japan's South Manchurian Railway (SMR) and Russia's Chinese Eastern Railway (CER). The loan would also enable China to construct more railways in the virgin but potentially rich Manchurian areas. During the term of the loan, the loan providers would enjoy the privileges of supervising and controlling the railroads in Manchuria. To some extent, the scheme originated in the efforts of American business tycoon E.H. Harriman to buy the South Manchurian Railway from Japan and Chinese Eastern Railway from Russia, then build a transportation system that would girdle the earth. Knox Neutralization Scheme was designed to preserve the Open Door Policy in China by neutralizing both Japanese and Russian attempts to consolidate their control in Manchuria and prevent other powers from gaining a foot in the Manchurian railway business and establishing their own spheres of influence. The aggressive plan reflected the U.S. recommitment of the Open Door Policy, which was downplayed by President Theodore Roosevelt from 1901 to 1908. It also reflected the plan for the implementation of Dollar Diplomacy of Taft's administration, which aimed at obtaining a bigger share of the market pie in China.

Knox's scheme met fierce resistance from Japan and Russia who reacted by declaring that they would recognize each other's de facto sphere of influence in Manchuria and make collaborative efforts to thwart any attempts from outside to challenge their positions. Eventually, the United States gave in by recognizing the special interests of Japan and Russia in Manchuria.

See also Knox, Philander C. (1853–1921); Open Door Policy; Harriman Affair; Dollar Diplomacy.

REFERENCES: Charles Vevier, *The United States and China, 1906–1913; a Study of Finance and Diplomacy* (New Brunswick, NJ, 1955); Paul Hibbert Clyde (ed.), *United States Policy Toward China; Diplomatic and Public Documents, 1839–1939* (New York, 1964).

Yuwu Song

Knox, Philander C. (1853–1921)

Philander C. Knox was important in the history of Sino-American relations because he played an instrumental role in the pursuit of American economic interests in China in late 1900s and early 1910s by promoting Dollar Diplomacy, the use of American capital to expand U.S. business influence abroad. Knox became nationally famous as the leading legal expert who helped establish the U.S. Steel Corporation in the 1890s. Besides a few public offices he held, he served as Secretary of State during the administration of William Howard Taft from 1909 to 1913. Knox was a firm believer of the Open Door Policy and a strong supporter of expanding American business interests in the lucrative China market. During his term, he created the Division of Far Eastern Affairs in the State Department.

As part of the Dollar Diplomacy, Knox formulated his most ambitious plan, Knox Neutralization Scheme in late 1909, which aimed at neutralizing or internationalizing the railroads controlled by Japan and Russia in Manchuria in order to preserve the Open Door Policy in China.

According to this scheme, an international banking syndicate would be organized to lend money to China so that the Chinese government could buy the Manchurian railways from Japan and Russia. For the life of the loan, the lenders would supervise and control the railroads. A backup plan was that the international banking group would construct a rail line to compete with Japan's South Manchurian Railway (SMR). As the mastermind of the scheme, Knox miscalculated the reactions of the foreign powers. He also misjudged Japan and Russia's determination to deflect any challenge to their spheres of influence in Manchuria. The scheme ran into resistance from Japan and Russia and had to be abandoned by the United States in the end. Although Knox Neutralization Scheme was a total failure, Knox's effort sought to keep the door of China open, a goal that the American government pursued for the next few decades.

Knox was more successful in gaining American admittance to the Six Power Consortium, an agreement reached by European bankers and the Chinese government that China would receive a loan from the West for building rail lines in southern China. But the Chinese Revolution of 1911 and the emerging anti-foreign sentiments following the revolution dampened the enthusiasm of American and European investors.

See also Knox Neutralization Scheme; Open Door Policy; Harriman Affair; Dollar Diplomacy.

REFERENCES: Norman A. Graebner (ed.), *An Uncertain Tradition; American Secretaries of State in the Twentieth Century* (New York, 1961); Charles Vevier, *The United States and China, 1906–1913; a Study of Finance and Diplomacy* (New Brunswick, NJ, 1955); Paul Hibbert Clyde (ed.), *United States Policy Toward China; Diplomatic and Public Documents, 1839–1939* (New York, 1964).

Yuwu Song

Kohlberg, Alfred (1887–1960)

Alfred Kohlberg was a New York-based Chinese textile importer during the years of Republican China. He had made his fortune importing Irish linen that was then embroidered in China for slave wages. As a wealthy silk merchant, he had enjoyed close relationship with Nationalist leaders such as Jiang Jieshi and Kong Xiangxi. As a businessman who had much to lose from a Communist take-over of China, Kohlberg had been a staunch supporter of Jiang and his Nationalist government during the Chinese Civil War (1945–1949) and after.

In 1946, Kohlberg began publication of a monthly magazine, *Plain Talk*. It became part of the hard-line strident anti-Communist press, that specialized in the "who lost China" bout of agonizing then taking place among American conservatives. After Jiang Jieshi and his Nationalist troops fled to Taiwan, Kohlberg continued his support for Jiang and his exiled regime. Kolberg also played an active role in the activities of the American China Policy Association (ACPA), which he joined in 1946. While promoting aid for the Nationalists, he led the attacks on American China policy by criticizing U.S. neutrality in the Chinese Civil War between the Communists and the Guomindang. He later served as the head of the organization, which became one of the most active groups that made up the China Lobby. Operating through the American China Policy Association after 1949, Kohlberg worked as a tireless propagandist for the Nationalist cause. He sent masses of anti-Communist materials to a list of 2,000 editors throughout the country. Though Kohlberg was not registered as a Congressional lobbyist, he flooded the Capitol Hill with his pro-Nationalist materials. He also made campaign contributions to pro-Guomindang candidates for the U.S. Senate. During the McCarthy era Kohlberg spent much of his time and energy searching out groups, which he believed to be Communist sympathizers. Kohlberg initiated the pro-Communist charges against the "China Hands," such as American diplomat John Carter Vincent. He accused him of expressing skepticism about Jiang Jieshi's government and showing sympathy to the Chinese Communists. Reviews by State Department Loyalty Boards resulted in the dismissal of Vincent in January 1953. Kohlberg also declared the Institute of Pacific Relations to be a Communist-controlled organization that bore direct blame for the "loss" of China to the Chinese Communist forces in 1949. These charges against the Institute led to its troubles and its eventual collapse. The Kohlberg propaganda outfit seemed to be doing a good business. Kohlberg and his followers had the field very much to themselves until President Richard Nixon visited China in 1972.

See also Civil War (1945–1949); McCarthyism; China Lobby; Vincent, John Carter (1900–1972); American China Policy Association; Institute of Pacific Relations.

REFERENCES: Joseph Charles Keeley, *The China Lobby Man; the Story of Alfred Kohlberg* (New Rochelle, NY, 1969).

Yuwu Song

Kong Xiangxi (1881–1967)

Kong Xiangxi, best known in the West as H.H. Kung (K'ung Hsiang-hsi), was born in Shanxi Province in 1881. His family was widely regarded as lineal descendants of the revered Chinese philosopher Confucius. His father, Kong Qinglin, built a private fortune facilitating remittance payments from overseas Chinese to their relatives on the mainland. Young Kong seemed to have studied the financial networks created by his father, who maintained offices in Shanxi, Guangzhou, and Japan. He learned more as his father's businesses expanded into other commercial areas in the 1890s, when the elder Kong became the sole agent in Shanxi for the British Asiatic Petroleum Company and also developed import-export and shipping finance companies.

As a young man Kong studied at American-run missionary schools in Shanxi and, later, at the North China Union College at Tongzhou near Beijing. By the late 1890s he was fluent in English, was a convert to Christianity, and was an ardent supporter of the anti-imperial revolutionary movement and of its leader, Sun Zhongshan. After the 1911 Revolution Kong went to Japan as a representative of the Young Men's Christian Association for overseas Chinese in Tokyo, where he met his future wife Song Ailing. One of the American-educated daughters of financier Charles Jones Song, she was working as Sun Zhongshan's English secretary. Kong's links to Sun were strengthened when he married Song Ailing in 1914, the same year that Sun married her sister, Song Qingling. Kong became an aide to Sun Zhongshan and a leader in his Nationalist Party, and also oversaw the arrangements for Sun's funeral after his sudden death in March 1925. Kong then aligned himself with another of Sun's protege, Jiang Jieshi, who in 1927 married another of the Song sisters, Song Meiling. While Jiang fought to unite China under Nationalist rule in 1927, Kong's negotiations with key warlords secured their cooperation and thereby aided Jiang's military effort.

When the Nationalist Government was established at Nanjing in 1928, Kong became Jiang's Minister for Industry and Commerce. After a brief hiatus from office in 1931, Kong was commissioned to travel to Italy, Germany, and Czechoslovakia in 1932, to arrange for arms purchases and military advisers for China. In 1922 he was appointed Governor of the Bank of China and also Minister of Finance. From these posts he sponsored several major reforms, including the consolidation of China's fractured system of local taxation, the regulation of bond markets, and the introduction in 1935 of paper currency. These initiatives were widely praised, but the conversion to paper currency made possible China's damaging hyperinflation, which began in the late 1930s.

In 1937, as the Nationalist government confronted the invading armies of Japan, Kong traveled to the United States and Britain to procure war materials, financial aid, and diplomatic support. He also visited Italy and Germany, both of which had supplied military equipment and advisers a few years earlier. Kong's greatest successes came in his contacts with Americans. Beginning in February 1939 the United States provided Kong's Ministry of Finance with favorable trade deals and cash loans to support China's deteriorating currency position. Soon the U.S. was providing military and economic aid to support the Nationalists' anti-Japanese military efforts. In 1942 the U.S. approved a $500 million loan to China, largely because of Kong's influence and negotiating acumen. Kong also maintained a keen interest in the development of Chinese universities modeled on American higher education institutions. He served as a director of Yenching University, both during its wartime exile in Sichuan Province and after the war when it reopened in Beijing.

After World War II Kong retired from public service, and briefly lived in Shanghai. Forced by the military advances of the Chinese Communists' armies to relocate to Taiwan, Kong later settled in New York State, where he died in August 1967.

REFERENCES: Sterling Seagrave, *The Soong Dynasty* (New York, 1985), Arthur N. Young, *China and the Helping Hand, 1937–1945* (Cambridge, MA, 1963), Arthur N. Young, *China's Nation-Building Effort, 1927–1937: The Financial and Economic Record* (Stanford, CA, 1971).

Laura Calkins

Koo, V. K. Wellington (1887–1985) *see* Gu Weijun (1887–1985)

Korean War

On June 25, 1950 the North Korean Peoples' Army (NKPA) launched an invasion of the Republic of Korea. In defending the Korean ally, the United States committed itself to the conflict that defied American expectations. The war fundamentally altered U.S. foreign relations and military affairs in Asia for the remainder of the 20th century.

Prior to the summer of 1950 the nation had maintained a cautious ambiguity towards the Chinese Communist government. After the entry of the People's Republic of China (PRC) into the war the United States sought to contain Communism within the "bamboo curtain." The Korean War, thus, transformed Sino-American relations. Korea had long been a battleground for competing powers and Americans had been involved in the peninsula's affairs for over 75 years by 1950. As World War II drew to a close U.S. intelligence services, diplomats, and politicians warned President Harry S. Truman of a Soviet interest in Korea. Before the Potsdam Conference in July 1945, Truman proposed a four power multi-year trusteeship of Korea. Although the Soviet Union rejected the proposal, Stalin agreed to divide Korea at the 38th Parallel and a joint occupation with the U.S. once the conference had concluded. To secure American interests, Truman sent an Army division to occupy and protect southern Korea until the nation's future was determined. Yet the U.S. policy of containment, as articulated by the Truman Doctrine and NSC-68, did not consider Korea an area of national interest and U.S. military forces were withdrawn after the establishment of a non-Communist government under Syngman Rhee. The phases of the Korean War correspond to the three distinct campaigns fought by the United Nations (UN) forces. The first, from June to November 1950, witnessed the retreat to a perimeter around Pusan in the southeast, the landings at Inchon, and the subsequent drive up the peninsula in fighting against the NKPA. A salient characteristic of the first phase is the suspicion in Washington that Korea was only part of a larger Communist offensive that would be played out in Europe. The second, from November 1950 to July 1951, included the retreat from the Yalu River following the entry of Chinese Communist forces into the war, the stabilizing of the frontline, and the onset of armistice negotiations. The third, from July 1951 to July 1953, was characterized by the lengthy armistice negotiations and the relatively static nature of the ground war. Only after July 1951, when the front lines had stabilized, did the Truman administration recognize that the conflict was a limited war. In response to the North Korean invasion the United States began evacuating American officials and refugees from the peninsula in addition to providing logistical support for the overwhelmed South Korean forces. The U.S. appealed to the UN Security Council, which adopted a resolution that chastised North Korea for their attack and demanded the cessation of military action, along with the immediate withdrawal of their forces. When North Korea failed to comply with the UN demands, the Security Council directed constituent members to assist the Republic of Korea and conferred command authority on the U.S. President. Truman, in turn, designated General Douglas MacArthur Commander in Chief, United Nations Command.

Although the UN allies provided almost 20,000 troops, the United States fielded the vast majority of military personnel in Korea. Initial efforts failed to halt the North Korean advance and UN forces retreated into a perimeter around the city of Pusan, which was within the range of U.S. warplanes based in Japan. Instead of attacking out of the Pusan perimeter MacArthur executed an amphibious assault at Inchon up the Korean coast. His flanking maneuver paved the way for an advance up the peninsula and the liberation of the Republic of Korea by October 1950. Despite warnings from Beijing to continue the advance up the peninsula, in an effort to liberate North Korea from Communist rule, MacArthur's command pushed forward, which brought the PRC forces into the conflict and widened the war before the year was out.

Not until the spring of 1951 would the UN forces halt the Communist offensive. Fighting then stabilized along the 38th parallel, which had divided the peninsula before the war. For the next two years as peace talks continued at Panmunjom the fighting continued in a war of attrition. During the U.S. presidential campaign of 1952 candidate Dwight D. Eisenhower pledged to go to Korea and end the war. Implicit in his speeches was the threat of nuclear force against North Korea and the PRC. In July 1953 the four belligerents agreed to an armistice that left the Korean peninsula divided along the 38th parallel.

See also Truman Doctrine; MacArthur, Douglas (1880–1964); Korean War POW Negotiations; Panmunjom Armistice Talks; Democratic People's Republic of Korea.

REFERENCES: Roy E. Appleman, *South to the Naktong, North to the Yalu: June-November, 1950* (Washington, DC, 1961); Clay Blair, *The Forgotten War: America in Korea, 1950–1953* (New York, 1987); Bruce Cumings, *The Origins of the Korean War: Liberation and the Emergence of the Separate Regimes, 1945–1947* (Princeton, NJ, 1981); Rosemary Foot, *A Substitute for Victory: The Policy of Peacemaking at the Korean Armistice Talks* (Ithaca, NY, 1990); D. Clayton James, *The Years of MacArthur* (New York, 1970–1985); Burton I. Kaufman, *The Korean War: Challenges in Crisis, Credibility, and Command* (New York, 1986); James E. Schnabel, *Policy and Direction, the First Year* (Washington, DC, 1972); Shu Guang Zhang, *Deterrence and Strategic Culture: Chinese American Confrontations, 1949–1958* (Ithaca, NY, 1992).

Paul D. Gelpi, Jr.

Korean War POW Negotiations

As the U.S. 8th Army under the command of General Matthew Ridgeway, along with other United Nations' units, approached the 38th parallel in early 1951, President Truman offered to begin negotiations with Beijing and Pyongyang. When the UN commander in Korea, General Douglas MacArthur, sabotaged Truman's peace initiative with an ultimatum he was relieved of command. The Communist general offensive in April pushed UN forces back once more and any effort to undertake negotiations were postponed until after UN forces drove the Communists north of the 38th parallel and the frontline was stabilized in June 1951. Later in the month when the Chinese and North Korean leadership agreed to open negotiations, the Soviet Union proposed a multi-lateral conference. Negotiations to begin the armistice talks then proceeded with conference protocol and site location the primary obstacles to any agreement. Late July saw all sides agree to an agenda and talks in Panmunjom, which lay between the opposing front lines.

The prisoner of war issue proved the most divisive but UN acquiescence to the Communist demand that final position of the opposing armies be agreed to first meant the negotiations would drag on for over two years as the Communist leadership continually sought to improve their forward line. From late 1951 to mid-1953 the armies in Korea were engaged in combat reminiscent of the First World War, as casualties mounted on both sides. Nevertheless, the Panmunjom talks went forward.

At issue were the large numbers of Communist POWs held by UN forces that the Communist leadership wanted repatriated without exception. An equal concern of the UN command was those POWs held by the Communists and their fate. The POW issue, in turn, would delay any settlement until the summer of 1953. As befitted a war against Communism, the UN command insisted that repatriation remain an individual choice. Both sides leveled accusations of brain washing in an attempt to sway the negotiations. With the talks stalled, the International Committee of the Red Cross intervened and polled POWs held by UN forces. The release of the poll's results surprised all parties concerned, as only 54,000 North Korean and 5,100 Chinese POWs, of the 132,000 interviewed by the Red Cross wished to be repatriated. When the Communists at Panmunjom claimed that the prisoners had been coerced, armistice talks broke down once more. In late 1952 the UN delegation at Panmunjom walked out of the negotiations, which ended the armistice talks for all intents and purposes.

Three events outside of Korea, in late 1952 and early 1953, would result in the resumption of talks and an armistice, however: the election of Dwight D. Eisenhower President in the United States, Eisenhower's decision to threaten the use of nuclear weapons, and the death of Josef Stalin in the Soviet Union. In April 1953 the delegates at Panmunjom agreed to the establishment of a neutral repatriation commission, which would screen all POWs and release them to whatever country they chose. The cease-fire agreement in July marked an end to the Korean War and POWs were returned home afterwards. After the war, the debate over the fate of the POWs continued in Washington, as well as Beijing and Pyongyang, as both sides believed the other had withheld prisoners.

See also Korean War; MacArthur, Douglas (1880–1964); Panmunjom Armistice Talks; Democratic People's Republic of Korea.

REFERENCES: Roy E. Appleman, *Ridgeway Duels for Korea* (College Station, TX, 1990); Clay Blair, *The Forgotten War: America in Korea, 1950–1953* (New York, 1989); Rosemary Foot, *A Substitute for Victory: The Policy of Peacemaking at the Korean Armistice Talks*, (Ithaca, NY, 1990) and *The Practice of Power: U.S. Relations with China Since 1949* (Oxford, 1995); John Lewis Gaddis, *Strategies of Containment: A Critical Appraisal of Postwar American National Security Policy* (Oxford, 1982); Akira Iriye, *The Cold War in Asia: A Historical Introduction* (Englewood Cliffs, NJ, 1974); D. Clayton James, with Anne Sharp Wells, *Refighting the Last War: Command and Crisis in Korea, 1950–1953* (New York, 1993); Burton I. Kaufman, *The Korean War: Challenges in Crisis, Credibility, and Command* (Philadelphia, PA, 1986); Shu Guang Zhang, *Deterrence and Strategic Culture: Chinese American Confrontations, 1949–1958* (Ithaca, NY, 1992).

Paul D. Gelpi, Jr.

Kowtow

The term *kowtow* comes from the Chinese phrase *ke tou*, which means to knock one's head on the ground with respect or reverence. Foreign envoys before the emperor of China performed the kowtow. In an elaborate ritual, envoys would kneel before the emperor and literally touch the forehead to the ground. Typically an envoy would kneel three times and perform as many as nine prostrations before the emperor. This was intended to show not only reverence but also complete subordination to the emperor. The kowtow ritual was an important element of the tributary system of foreign relations. Established as early as the Han and Tang dynasties and revived under the Ming and Manchu dynasties, the tribute system asserted the moral supremacy of the Chinese empire and its emperor.

The tribute system was founded on the hierarchical principles of Confucian teachings. China was the center of the universe, the so-called Middle Kingdom, and the emperor, therefore, the very son of heaven. In order for representatives of other nations to trade with the Chinese, it was important that they formally acknowledge their inferiority and the superiority of Chinese civilization. To do this, a tribute mission would be arranged, whereby envoys from other nations would bring elaborate gifts, take part in entertainment, and perform the kowtow before the emperor, thereby acknowledging the foreign nation's inferior position in the world and dependence on the emperor. In exchange for tribute and kowtow, the "barbarians" would be allowed to trade with the Chinese.

When Westerners began appearing in China in the 18th century, the ritual of the kowtow began to create problems. Although Dutch traders performed the ritual routinely, the English were another story. When England's Lord McCartney, viceroy of India, took a tribute mission to Beijing, he refused to perform the ritual on the grounds that it implied that he was a subject of the Chinese emperor. Just as the English rejected the kowtow, Americans entertained similar notions about the symbolic ritual. In 1843, when the United States Congress debated the practicality of appointing an envoy to negotiate a commercial treaty in the aftermath of the Opium war, some congressmen mentioned the *kowtow* with particular venom. John Quincy Adams, for instance, saw the kowtow as the principal cause of the recent Opium war. "The cause of the war," wrote Adams, "is *kowtow!*—the arrogant and insupportable pretension of China, that she will hold commercial intercourse with the rest of mankind, not on terms of equal reciprocity, but upon the insulting and degrading forms of relation between lord and vassal."

While American officials were worried that the kowtow might be an issue for their representative, Caleb Cushing, such fears were exaggerated. Prior to the Opium War, the Chinese quickly limited interaction with representatives of the West, allowing limited trading privileges at the port of Guangzhou, but no longer requiring tribute missions to Beijing and the Forbidden City. Additionally, when Caleb Cushing arrived in Macao in 1844 to negotiate a treaty, the emperor's representative, imperial commissioner Qiying, quickly agreed to a treaty (the Treaty of Wangxia) that gave American merchants substantially the same rights as the English had procured as a result of the Opium War. A defeated China was forced to open up more ports to foreign commerce as well as granted Western demands for such provision as extraterritoriality. These changes meant that China was no longer in a position of superiority and, thus, the highly ritualized expression of barbarian inferiority and submission, such as kowtow, was becoming obsolete. The tribute system and the kowtow had been replaced by the treaty system of foreign relations.

See also Treaty of Wangxia (1844).

REFERENCES: Warren I. Cohen, *America's Response to China: A History of Sino-American Relations* (New York, 2000); Tyler Dennett, *Americans in East Asia: A Critical Study of United States' Policy in the Far East in the Nineteenth Century* (New York, 1922); William J. Donahue, "The Caleb Cushing Mission," *Modern Asian Studies Vol. 16* (1982); John King Fairbank, *The Great Chinese Revolution, 1800–1985* (New York, 1985); Mark Mancall, *China at the Center: 300 Years of Foreign Policy* (New York, 1984).

Bruce Tap

Kung, H. H. (1881–1967) *see* Kong Xiangxi (1881–1967)

Kuomintang *see* Guomindang

Lamont, Thomas William (1876–1948)

Thomas William Lamont was a banking partner with the J. P. Morgan Company, and he represented the company's Far Eastern investments during the 1920s and 1930s. After becoming the Japanese government's chief international banker, Lamont initially defended Japanese expansion into China, before eventually breaking with his clients.

Lamont was born September 30, 1870 in Claverack, New York. His father was a severe minister, who insisted that his son work his way through school. Lamont graduated from Phillips Exeter Academy in 1888 and completed his studies at Harvard in 1892. He worked for two years as a journalist before borrowing $5,000 to invest in the firm Cushman Brothers, which acted as a New York marketing agent for food manufacturers. In 1903, Lamont joined the Bankers Trust, and in 1911 he became a partner in J. P. Morgan and Company. As a member of the Morgan firm, Lamont organized large loans for the British and French during the First World War. Appointed as a Treasury Department representative to the Paris Peace Conference, Lamont emerged as an advocate for the League of Nations. In the post World War I period, Lamont was involved in the Dawes Plan (1924) and Young Plan (1929) to restructure German reparations. In addition to heading a commission to restructure the Mexican debt, Lamont represented the Morgan Company in an international consortium formed to provide loans for economic development in China. He feared that "we shall see the great region west of the Ural Mountains in the economic grip of Japan and the most valuable market in the world closed to American manufacture and export." Nevertheless, continuing political instability and civil war in China limited investment possibilities in the region.

On the other hand, the J. P. Morgan Company and Lamont found the devastating earthquake, which struck Japan in 1923 an opportunity to finance that nation's reconstruction. By the end of the decade, J. P. Morgan was the chief international banker for the Japanese government. When Japan used an explosion on the Japanese-owned and operated South Manchurian Railroad as an excuse to invade Manchuria in September 1931, Lamont refused to repudiate the actions of his client; going as far as to author the statement by the Japanese Finance Minister Junnosuke Inouye in wake of the Mukden Incident. By the mid-1930s, Lamont believed that Japanese influence in China might only be limited by resurrecting the international banking consortium. The banker, however, made it clear that military action on behalf of China was clearly unwarranted. Lamont concluded that if China lacked "the strength to protect herself from aggression and exploitation, she cannot reasonably expect other nations to do the job for her. Certainly America is not going to court trouble by any quixotic attempt to checkmate Japan in Asia." Nevertheless, by the time of Finance Minister Inouye's assassination in 1934, Lamont was growing increasingly disenchanted with his Japanese client. The economic investment diplomacy of Lamont and the Morgan firm was, in the final analysis, unable to prevent war between Japan and the United States.

In 1943, Lamont became chairman of the board upon the death of J. P. Morgan, Jr. Lamont was well known as an influential figure in World War II finance, politics, and philanthropy from his vantage point at the head of the Morgan Empire. He died on February 2, 1948.

REFERENCES: Ron Chernow, *The House of Morgan: An American Banking Dynasty and the Rise of Modern Finance* (New York, 1990); Warren J. Cohen, *The Chinese Connection: Roger S. Greene, Thomas W. Lamont, George E. Sokolsky and Far East Asian Relations* (New York, 1978); Edward M. Lamont, *The Story of Thomas W. Lamont, J. P. Morgan Chief Executive* (Lanham, MD, 1994).

Ron Briley

Lansing-Ishii Agreement

The Lansing-Ishii Agreement resulted from meetings between Secretary of State Robert Lansing and Viscount Kikujiro Ishii, former Japanese Foreign Minister and head of a special delegation to Washington, DC. To avert conflict between the United States and Japan, both parties hoped to secure frank recognition of their countries' interests in China. Ishii's instructions included obtaining American recognition of Japanese claims in South Manchuria and Inner East Mongolia, and assurances that Washington would not incite China against Japan. Ishii was also instructed to negotiate a treaty providing the Japanese in the United States status equal to other resident aliens, an issue which had brought the United States and Japan to the brink of war in 1912–1913. Lansing pursued two goals during the talks. First, he wanted to clarify America's diplomatic position in the Far East, which had become murky during the Twenty-One Demands crisis in mid-1915. Second, he hoped to secure continued access to Chinese markets— especially those dominated by Japan —for American industry. Only by maintaining a tangible foothold in China, he believed, could America effectively oppose Japanese imperialism under the Open Door Policy. In formulating the agreement, however, Lansing's pragmatism was partially overshadowed by President Woodrow Wilson's insistence that Japan should fully recommit itself to the Open Door principle and relinquish any interests in China.

During the Twenty-One Demands controversy in March 1915, Washington had conceded that Japan enjoyed a "special relationship" with China based upon geographical proximity. Two months later President Wilson had all but repudiated that principle, but the administration struggled to defend China's integrity, partially because internally it was divided over the most effective method of doing so. By 1916 the White House was losing the initiative in fighting Japanese expansion, especially since entry into World War I in April 1917 made the two countries nominal allies and, ultimately, party to a secret Anglo-Japanese agreement offering Japan possession of Shandong and other Pacific German holdings. In June 1917 Tokyo, hoping to strengthen its hold on the continent, asked Lansing for reaffirmation of the March 1915 pronouncement. Lansing, however, asserted that the United States reserved the right to comment on any Japanese expansion in China.

Japan pressed the issue, sending the Ishii delegation to Washington, DC, in September 1917. After an initial tour across the United States celebrating Japanese-American accord, the negotiators struggled in thirteen meetings from September to November 1917 to find a compromise for their disparate goals. In a statement released on November 2, the United States agreed that "territorial propinquity" gave Japan "special interests in China, particularly in that part to which her possessions are contiguous," but that Washington had "every confidence in the repeated assurances of the Imperial Japanese Government that … they have no desire to discriminate against the trade of other nations or to disregard the commercial rights heretofore granted by China in treaties with other Powers."

The agreement's meaning remained vague and, for both sides, contradictory. Japan's "special interests" were never delineated, and Tokyo seemed to construe the agreement as pertaining to the whole of Chinese territory. The American minister to Beijing, Paul S. Reinsch, similarly interpreted the agreement as an about-face for Wilson's China policy. Wilson and Lansing, on the other hand, denied that Japan had gained from the negotiations, with Lansing explaining to his minister that the agreement merely ensured that Japan would not make use of its geographical advantage in East Asia. Nevertheless, using the agreement as justification in 1917–1918 Tokyo consolidated its control of Shandong and bartered loans to Beijing for other dispensations. Because of the war in Europe, Wilson and Lansing were never able to oppose Japan's actions on the basis of the agreement, and Wilson's hope that America's role in China would be restored fully via the League of Nations failed to come to pass. Although agreements resulting from the Washington Naval Conference officially cancelled the Lansing-Ishii Agreement in 1922, Japan would continue to pursue expansionism in East Asia throughout the interwar period.

See also Twenty-One Demands; Open Door Policy; Lansing, Robert (1864–1928).

REFERENCES: Burton F. Beers, *Vain Endeavor: Robert Lansing's Attempts to End the American-Japanese Rivalry* (Durham, NC, 1962); Frederick R. Dickinson, *War and National Reinvention: Japan in the Great War, 1914–1919* (Cambridge, MA, 1999); Robert Lansing, *War Memoirs of Robert Lansing* (Indianapolis, IN, 1935).

Eric A. Cheezum

Lansing, Robert (1864–1928)

Robert Lansing served as President Woodrow Wilson's second Secretary of State, from 1915 until 1920, following the resignation of William Jennings Bryan, in June 1915. Born in Watertown, New York, on October 17, 1864, Lansing graduated from Amherst College in 1886, joining the New York Bar and his father's law practice a few years later. Lansing's retiring nature and interest in the theory of law over its practical application led him often to build cases which his father would take to trial. His marriage to Eleanor Foster in 1890 opened up new professional, as well as personal, opportunities. In 1892 Eleanor's father, then-Assistant Secretary of State John Watson Foster, appointed Lansing as a legal counselor in the Bering Fur Seal negotiations. Work in international law gradually overtook Lansing's career and interest, with further positions on the

Bering Sea Claims Commission (1896–1897) and the Alaskan Boundary Tribunal (1903). He also represented numerous foreign delegations, including China.

In 1908, following his father's death, Lansing and his father-in-law opened a law office in Washington specifically dealing in cases in international law. Lansing's relationship with Foster — a renowned diplomat — informed his view of the Far Eastern situation. In the wake of the Russo-Japanese War (1904–1905) and the rise of Japanese military power, Lansing became concerned with how the United States could expand its markets in the Far East without alienating Japan. From 1908 to 1914 Lansing represented the State Department in numerous cases, before being appointed as its Counselor on March 20, 1914. Initially a legal advisor to Secretary of State Bryan, Lansing's approach to Asia was rarely in accord with that of the administration. While Lansing shared Wilson's support for the Open Door Policy, he believed that China's rights could only be safeguarded by vigorous protection of specific American interests there. When World War I broke out in Europe in August 1914, Lansing opposed Bryan's Pacific neutralization schemes, insisting only upon protection of American property and treaty rights. Later that year and into 1915, during controversy over rates for the South Manchurian Railway, Lansing concluded that diplomacy based upon the Open Door could never be lasting because the policy was not universally accepted by the international community. Thus, during the Twenty-One Demands crisis of mid-1915 Lansing counseled Wilson to avoid breaking with Japan for fear that it would curtail American opportunities in China. Lansing argued that Washington should officially concede Japan's limited expansion in return for which Tokyo would respect the Open Door principle in those areas.

From 1915 to 1917, Lansing turned to investment in China as a means of repelling Japanese advances, although schemes to support railroad, canal, and other public works projects produced few results. As conflict with Japan came to a head in mid-1917, however, Lansing conducted talks with a delegation from Japan, led by Viscount Kikujiro Ishii, which Lansing hoped would provide the basis for a settlement between the United States and Japan regarding China. Although Wilson, who was hostile to any Japanese expansion, supervised the negotiations, the resultant Lansing-Ishii Agreement demonstrated Lansing's view that the Open Door should protect American interests in China, rather than China in the abstract. During 1918, with Japan continuing to colonize East Asia and Washington focused on the war in Europe, Lansing successfully convinced Wilson that joining a new loan consortium might offset Japanese activity in China. Lansing hoped to reach rapprochement with Japan at the Paris Peace Conference in 1919, believing that a strong stand on the Shandong Question would both quell Japanese imperialism and protect American interests in Asia. Lansing viewed Wilson's subsequent acceptance of Japanese control of Shandong in return for Japanese participation in the League of Nations as a tactical error that would damage American rights and prestige in the East. These tensions exacerbated differences in both men's approach to foreign relations that never healed. Lansing was fired in February 1920 after Wilson learned he had held Cabinet meetings during the president's convalescence. He died on October 20, 1928, in Washington, DC.

See also Twenty-One Demands; Open Door Policy; Lansing-Ishii Agreement.

REFERENCES: Burton F. Beers, *Vain Endeavor: Robert Lansing's Attempts to End the American-Japanese Rivalry* (Durham, NC, 1962); Thomas H. Hartig, *Robert Lansing: An Interpretive Biography* (New York, 1982); Robert Lansing, *War Memoirs of Robert Lansing* (Indianapolis, IN, 1935).

Eric A. Cheezum

Laos

At the end of World War II, the United States was primarily responsible for the decision of the Potsdam Conference that forces of the Republic of China would take the surrender of Japanese forces in most of Laos, going as far south as the 16th parallel. For this mission Jiang Jieshi chose troops of a Yunnan warlord only loosely affiliated with the Guomindang; they arrived in Laos in September 1945. Their main interest was plunder, but their hostility to the French temporarily strengthened the position of various Laotian factions maneuvering against the French. They withdrew in 1946.

The People's Republic of China (PRC) was established in 1949, and it gained control of the areas bordering on Laos in 1950. Chinese aid greatly strengthened Communist forces in the First Indochina War from this point onward. By 1954, the Pathet Lao (the Communist movement of Laos) and the much stronger Viet Minh (a Vietnamese nationalist movement under Communist leadership) controlled large portions of Laos. At the Geneva Conference of 1954, Laos was declared a neutral country, under the rule of the Royal Laotian Government that had been associated with the French during the war. Two provinces were temporarily allocated to the Pathet Lao as a regrouping zone; these were re-integrated with the rest of Laos in 1958. The neutralist Souvanna Phouma lost his position as prime minister in 1958, and this began the collapse of Laotian neutrality. By the beginning of 1961 there was an outright war pitting a right-wing government, supported by the United States and Thailand, against a coalition of neutralist and Pathet Lao forces, with support from the Democratic Republic of Vietnam (DRV, usually called North Vietnam), China, and the Soviet Union. The situation was complicated when the DRV began to sending men and supplies from North to South Vietnam through southeastern Laos, along the "Ho Chi Minh Trail." The War in Laos had become one part of the Second Indochina War.

Major escalation was averted temporarily by the Geneva Conference of 1961–1962. This produced a set of agreements in June and July 1962, under which Laos was once more to become a neutral nation, and all foreign military forces were to withdraw. A coalition government was established, with a cabinet made up of eleven neutralists, four rightists, and four Pathet Lao. Souvanna Phouma became both prime minister and minister of defense. The small number of U.S. military personnel in Laos withdrew in compliance with the agreements; the much larger number of DRV troops did not. The contrast between U.S. respect for Laotian neutrality and DRV violation was a major factor in Souvanna Phouma's decision in the months that followed to abandon his alliance with the DRV, and shift to a *de facto* alliance with the United States. DRV use of the Ho Chi Minh Trail increased greatly in 1964 and 1965. U.S. bombing of DRV and Pathet Lao forces in Laos began on a small scale in 1964 and soon became huge; the 2,093,000 tons of bombs dropped on Laos exceeded the tonnage dropped on Germany in World War II. China provided military aid to DRV and Pathet Lao forces in Laos. There were also Chinese troops and military engineers building roads in northern Laos, but their main function was to serve as a buffer, keeping the war away from the Chinese border. The United States did not want to provoke China, so the areas of the road construction were off limits to U.S. bombing. The construction went very slowly, since completion of the roads would have deprived the Chinese of the excuse to keep troops in this buffer zone. U.S. bombing ended in 1973, and ground action subsided to a low level. The Communist forces in Laos (mostly DRV, some Pathet Lao) could have taken full control of the country soon after the end of U.S. bombing if they wished, but they held off until 1975, after the end of the war in South Vietnam.

The Communist government of Laos in the late 1970s and 1980s was closely aligned with Vietnam; there were Vietnamese troops in Laos. When China and Vietnam became enemies, fighting a small border war in 1979, this turned China against Laos, and China cooperated with Thailand in supporting minor guerrilla actions against the Laotian government and the DRV forces in Laos. But this did not become a significant factor in Sino-U.S. relations. The hostility eased, and normal diplomatic relations between China and Laos were restored, in 1988.

See also Second Indochina War.

REFERENCES: Martin Stuart-Fox, *A History of Laos* (Cambridge, UK, 1997); Qiang Zhai, *China and the Vietnam Wars, 1950–1975* (Chapel Hill, NC, 2000).

Edwin Moise

Lattimore, Owen (1900–1989)

Owen Lattimore was born in Washington, DC, on July 29, 1900. Shortly after his birth, he moved to China where his father taught school for the Chinese government. At the age of twelve, he went to study in Switzerland and then three years later transferred to England where he completed his education, but was unable to gain entry into a university. In 1919 he returned to China becoming a journalist in Shanghai and later worked in Beijing for an exporter of goods from China's frontier regions such as Manchuria, Mongolia, and Xinjiang.

He found his experience working with these areas exhilarating so he quit his job. Along with his wife, he began studying, traveling, and writing about them. The Social Science Research Council granted him a fellowship to travel and study in Manchuria in 1929. In 1930 and 1931, he received grants from the Harvard University-Yenching Foundation and the Guggenheim Foundation to study in Beijing and to travel the border regions of China, resulting in the books *Desert Road to Turkestan* (1929), *High Tartary* (1930), *Manchuria: Cradle of Conflict* (1932), and *The Mongols of Manchuria* (1934), and perhaps his most important work *Inner Asian Frontiers of China* (1940). In all, he would write a total of sixteen books and numerous articles. By this time, he had become fluent in Chinese, Mongol, and Russian. From 1934 to 1941, he served as editor of *Pacific Affairs*. When the Japanese occupied Beijing in 1937, Lattimore returned to the United States with a reputation as one of the foremost experts on Mongolia and Central Asia becoming the director of the Page School of International Relations at Johns Hopkins University in 1938, while also teaching at the institution. In 1940, President Franklin D. Roosevelt asked him to serve as a political advisor to Chinese Nationalist Leader, Generalissimo Jiang Jieshi allowing him to see Nationalist corruption first hand. The next year he returned to the United States becoming a deputy director of the Office of War Information responsible for the Pacific theater. In 1944, he accompanied Vice President Henry Wallace on a fact-finding mission to the Soviet Union and China.

After the war, Lattimore served on the U.S. Reparations Committee in Japan and resumed his work at Johns Hopkins. As an advisor to the State Department, he agreed with the unpopular findings of the China Hands that the Chinese Communists had gained wide support and would probably win the civil war against the corrupt Nationalists. In addition, his visit to Mao Zedong in Yanan in 1937, publication of articles sympathetic to Communism in *Pacific Affairs*, and recommendation of probable recognition of the People's Republic of China, gave ammunition to Senator Joseph McCarthy. McCarthy named him as a Soviet agent in 1950 and one of those China Hands in the State Department responsible for the "loss of China" even though he did not work there and only advised that government agency. He appeared before the Tydings Committee that investigated the State Department, which cleared him of any wrongdoing. Yet, McCarthy continued to attack Lattimore resulting in his appearance before more Senate hearings in 1951–1952 where he was indicted for perjury; the Justice Department finally dismissed charges against him in 1955. Lattimore is said to have coined the term "McCarthyism" during this time, and wrote about his experiences in *Ordeal by Slander* (1950).

Due to pressure and the embarrassment, Johns Hopkins abolished the Page School causing Lattimore to be demoted to a mere lecturer. Feeling his academic career limited in the United States by 1963, he left to become the director of Chinese studies at the University of Leeds in England. He retired in 1970, and returned to America where he continued to write and give lectures. He died in Providence, Rhode Island on May 31, 1989, where his son was a professor of Chinese studies at Brown University.

See also McCarthy, Joseph R. (1908–1957); McCarthyism; China Hands.

REFERENCES: Joanne Cavanaugh Simpson, "Seeing Red," *Johns Hopkins Magazine* (September 2000); Robert P. Newman, *Owen Lattimore and the "Loss" of China* (Berkeley, CA, 1992).

Greg Ference

Lea, Homer (1876–1912)

Homer Lea was a turn-of-the-century visionary geopolitical thinker and activist in the Chinese Revolution of 1911. He was born in Den-

ver to Alfred Erskine Lea and Hersa Coberly Lea, who had moved to Denver from Tennessee and would subsequently move on to Los Angeles. One of three children, Homer was born with a congenital curvature of the spine that left him hunchbacked with severe health complications all of his short life. Although withdrawn and introspective in his early life, his brilliant intelligence enabled him to sustain a relatively normal school career and social life even with less than five feet stature, dim eyesight and delicate health. From early childhood he developed a singular enthusiasm for military matters and, especially, for Napoleon. His mastery of military detail was reportedly astounding. He entered Occidental College in 1896 and the next year transferred to Stanford University, where he developed a close relationship with the President David Starr Jordan.

In Los Angeles he had developed an enthusiasm for the mysteries of Chinatown and became familiar with the Chinese emigre community. In the Bay area he furthered this interest by studying Chinese language and history. He also absorbed the prevailing overseas Chinese enthusiasm for reforming the backward Qing monarchy. As a military enthusiast, he presented himself as an "expert" and immersed himself in the reformist cause. The Qing dynastic court at this time had fallen under the reactionary control of the Empress Dowager Cixi, who had the reform-minded emperor kidnapped and forced his reformer minister Kang Youwei out of China. The Chinatowns of California rallied around Kang and Homer Lea took as his cause the mission to mount a military effort to rescue the imprisoned emperor. Lea sailed to China in 1900. He improvised a command of volunteers, claiming a rank of Lieutenant General, but met with disappointing disaster and had to be smuggled out in April 1901. Lea's well-developed sense of self-promotion and audacity permitted him to bask in a kind of hero's adulation within the Chinese community in the U.S. He then advanced a scheme to raise and train Chinese volunteers in the U.S. for revolutionary service in China. He managed to secure the part-time services of U.S. army veterans. By 1905 a nation-wide network of such corps were drilling with arms and uniforms, to the increasing discomfort of U.S. government authorities.

In 1905 Lea published his first book, although he had authored a number of military affairs articles. The novel, *The Vermillion Pencil*, was set in China and featured a strongly moralistic plot line in which oppressed peasants, with leadership from a Westerner, overcome tyranny. It was later made into a play, "The Vermillion Spider." Lea also began work on what was to be his best-known work, *The Valor of Ignorance*, a geopolitical treatise published in 1909. It was comparable to the muscular militaristic ideas of A.T. Mahan and fully in line with the activist Darwinian notions of Theodore Roosevelt. The premise is that Japan takes advantage of a militarily apathetic and unprepared U.S. to defeat them and dictate peace terms. What made the work especially notable was its eerie prescience, since virtually every scenario, which played out in 1941–1942 was foreseen. Even in 1909 the book caused a stir, especially in foreign countries, where it was widely read. It later became the basis for U.S. staff planning for Plan Orange and was highly regarded by General Douglas McArthur. Lea was to publish one more major geopolitical treatise posthumously in 1912. *The Day of the Saxon* postulated that Germany, Russia and Japan would combine to challenge the Anglo-Saxon powers, including the U.S. and Britain.

In 1908 the death of the reform emperor left the overseas Chinese moving to support Sun Zhongshan's movement for a republic. Lea did as well. He spent much of 1908 involved in a pro-republic conspiracy called the Red Dragon scheme. When the Chinese Revolution of 1911 did occur, Sun appointed Lea Army Chief of Staff based on his "expertise and experience." Lea's position in the Chinese Republican government did not last as he suffered a stroke in February 1912, and finally died in November 1912, at the age of 36. Although Homer Lea was given to self-aggrandizement and exaggeration, he was a true intellectual giant and sincere advocate for China. David Starr Jordan, though a pacifist, regarded Lea as "one of the most picturesque personalities of this generation."

See also Chinese Revolution (1911).

REFERENCES: Eugene Anshel, *Homer Lea, Sun Yat-sen and the Chinese Revolution* (New York, 1984); Marius Jansen, *The Japanese and Sun Yat-sen* (Stanford, CA, 1970); Thomas Kennedy, "Homer Lea and the Peace Makers," *The Historian* (August, 1983); Homer Lea, *The Valor of Ignorance* (New York, 1909); Homer Lea, *The Day of the Saxon* (New York, 1912).

Dave Egler

Ledo Road *see* Stilwell Road.

Lee, Bruce (1940–1993)

Martial artist Bruce Lee (Li Xiaolong), was born Lee Jun Fan, in 1940, the Chinese year of the dragon. Lee's iconic status reflected many aspects of both Chinese and American culture and the intertwining of these two cultures. Bruce Lee would redefine the action-adventure film genre in America, yet his familial acting roots originated with his father, Lee Hoi Chuen. The elder Lee's minor stardom and tour with the Hong Kong opera company brought his wife Grace and their three children to San Francisco, where Bruce was born in 1940. When the family returned to Hong Kong, the infant Bruce began his film career as a child just as the Japanese attacked and occupied Hong Kong (1942–1945). Lee's early memory of shaking his fist at a Japanese plane flying overhead in many ways reflected an anger and frustration that would lead to eventual stardom, and it typified the feelings of many Chinese during these early years.

Lee would explain that, like most young Chinese boys in Hong Kong, he had little hope of success due to British political and economic control of the colony. This disillusion led to participation in street gangs and lack of interest in school. When he complained to his parents of being bullied, they allowed him to attend Yip man's school: the great master of *wing chun* (beautiful springtime). From the age of nine to nineteen, the slightly built Lee learned how to develop *qi* or *chi* (inner energy or life force) and to develop the skill of turning his opponent's force against him through sparse, fluid movements. Kung fu originated with the visit of Indian Buddhist monk Bodhidharma from India to China's Songshan Mountains and made its way into print in 550 A.D., evolving into what is now called 18 Hand Movements, the foundation for Chinese Temple Boxing and the Shaolin Arts. While monks began teaching kung fu throughout China, it was Bruce Lee who introduced it to Americans, thus paving the way for the international fame of such artists as Jet Li, Jackie Chan and Chuck Norris. Lee originally brought kung fu to the United States when his family determined that the United States would offer him safety from Hong Kong street gang violence. Enrolling at the University of Washington in 1962 Lee studied philosophy while teaching others the skills he had learned as a cha cha dancer and working as a waiter. Lee also taught a simplified version of kung fu, which he combined with the street fighting punches and kicks, and would later term this *jeet kune do*, or "the way of intercepting fist." Lee opened two branches of his kung fu institute, the first in Seattle Washington and the second in Oakland, California, before being challenged by San Francisco's Chinatown elders to a fight because he'd taught China's martial arts secrets to Westerners. The elders demanded that if he lost he would have to close his school or stop teaching Westerners. Lee won the fight and would, soon after, reach an even larger audience. Soon a Hollywood producer contacted Lee about playing a "Charlie Chan" type character. After demonstrating his innovative style, Lee would eventually win a role as "Kato" in the television series *Green Hornet*. The *Green Hornet* lasted only six months and gave Lee a bitter taste of Hollywood racism; however, this was a stepping point to Lee's international career. By 1970 Lee was a husband, married to the Caucasian Linda Emery, the father of two children, and had become a well-known kung fu instructor to stars like Steve McQueen, James Coburn and Chuck Norris. Injured during a weight-lifting session, but inspired by the positive thinker Noman Vincent Peale, Lee built upon his Hollywood stardom, left for Hong Kong and found astounding success as a film star there. Lee's lightning speed moves, ability to make his enemies look foolish through comedy and evocation of strength allowed Chinese viewers who had often withheld their own anger at exploitation, to project a positive national identity through him on the screen.

Building upon his success in Hong Kong, Lee returned to Hollywood, in 1973 during the filming of *Enter the Dragon*; however, he would sadly succumb to brain swelling and an early death at the age of thirty-two. Bruce Lee's son Brandon emulated his father's success, but oddly, he too met his untimely death during the filming of the movie *The Crow*, at the age of twenty-seven in 1993.

REFERENCES: Jon E. Lewis, *Bruce Lee* (Langhorne, PA, 1997); Jeet Kune Do, *Bruce Lee's Commentaries on the Martial Way* (Boston, MA, 1997); John Little (ed.), *The Celebrated Life of the Golden Dragon* (Boston, MA, 2000).

Cristina Zaccarini

Lee Teng-hui (1923-) *see* Li Denghui (1923-)

Lend-Lease

Prior to the entry of the United States into the Second World War, President Franklin D. Roosevelt recognized that it was in the American national interest to support those nations who were resisting regimes whose militaristic aims were inimical to American values and would inevitably bring them into conflict with the United States. In one of his fireside chats, he made the persuasive analogy to a neighbor whose house was on fire asking to borrow your garden hose. You would immediately permit the use of the hose, without first negotiating a fee or defining liability, if only because the fire might spread to your own house. On March 11, 1941, the lend-lease legislation received congressional approval. The passage of the legislation represented a sea change in American attitudes. In the 1930s, the economic depression and isolationist sentiment had combined in legislation that proscribed American loans to any nation that had failed to repay monies lent to it during the First World War. Since only Finland had repaid its American loans, this legislation effectively eliminated aid to any combatants if and when hostilities would erupt in Europe. The Roosevelt administration had, however, skirted the spirit of the neutrality laws by allowing military sales to Great Britain and France if their ships transported the materials from American ports. Following the dramatic evacuation from Dunkirk, Roosevelt authorized by executive order the transfer of $43 million of "surplus" weapons and munitions to Great Britain since the rescued troops had left most of their weapons and munitions on the French beaches. Then he authorized the "destroyers for bases" deal with Great Britain, selling it to Congress and to the American public as a way of improving the defense of the Western Hemisphere while also helping Great Britain confront the Nazi submarine offensive. He asserted that lend-lease would make the United States "the arsenal of democracy," which to many anxious legislators and voters was preferable to the nation's becoming a combatant.

Lend-lease did require the President to present an annual appropriations request to Congress and to provide reports on how those appropriations had been used. But it gave him tremendous authority and discretion in distributing the monies or the materials they were used to purchase, as well as in determining how much of the monies needed to be repaid and on what schedule. In all, by the time the program was discontinued with the surrender of Japan, over $42 billion in lend-lease appropriations had been spent. Almost half of these monies had been spent on munitions; about a fifth, on industrial machinery; about a seventh, on agricultural products; about a tenth, on services and transportation costs; and about a twentieth, on fuel. About half of the appropriations went to Great Britain, and another quarter to the Soviet Union. DeGaulle's Free French received about $3.5 billion in aid, and China was the fourth largest recipient, at about $2 billion.

For both logistical and strategic reasons, the appropriations to the Chinese were smaller than they might have been. Because of the Japanese control of Chinese ports, the western Pacific shipping lanes, and Southeast Asia, shipments to the Chinese had to be unloaded in Indian ports, which were inadequate to handle the volume of material. Then the materials had to be transported by air over the Himalayas (called "the Hump") or overland along the Burma or Ledo

Roads. The Japanese conquest of Burma and operations in southeast China continually threatened and for extended periods disrupted the overland shipments. In addition to these logistical constraints, there were justifiable concerns about how the Chinese were using the materials provided to them. The Chinese Nationalists under Jiang Jieshi were notoriously corrupt, and they seemed as intent on eliminating the Chinese Communists under Mao Zedong as they were committed to defeating the Japanese. Ultimately, the "island-hopping" strategy in the Pacific succeeded, and the campaigns against islands that were larger and closer to the Japanese home islands demanded increasingly extensive concentrations of troops and materiel. The American high command therefore shifted resources away from the Chinese theater of operations, where decisive action against the Japanese seemed less and less likely.

See also Burma Road; The Hump; World War II.

REFERENCES: Leon Martel, *Lend-Lease, Loans, and the Coming of the Cold War: A Study of the Implementation of Foreign Policy* (Boulder, CO, 1979); "Supplies of China," *The Nation* (January 23, 1943); Donovan Webster, "Blood, Sweat, and Toil along the Burma Road," *National Geographic* (November 2003); Donovan Webster, *The Burma Road: The Epic Story of the China-Burma-India Theater in World War II* (New York, 2004).

Martin Kich

Li Denghui (1923-)

Li Denghui, former President of the Republic of China on Taiwan, is a watershed figure in Taiwan's history. Born in 1923 in Taiwan, Li experienced first-hand the effects of Japanese colonial rule. As a Japanese subject he attended Kyoto Imperial University and later moved to the United States to continue his education at Iowa State and Cornell University, where he earned a Ph.D. in agricultural economics.

After returning to Taiwan, Li used his skills and education to advance up the political ladder. As a young man, Li joined the Guomindang (GMD), the organization of Jiang Jieshi and the sole source of political power in the single party state. In 1957, Li served as a member of the Joint Commission on Rural Reconstruction. The commission met with remarkable success, due in part to Li's managerial aptitude and his common sense. His service on the committee brought him to the attention of party seniors and launched his political career. Throughout the 1960s and 1970s Li continued to fill various roles in the GMD. In 1978, he used his political networks to become mayor of the capital city of Taibei. Four years

later, he became governor of Taiwan province and in 1984 President Jiang Jingguo selected him to be the Vice President for the Republic of China. With the death of Jiang in 1988, Li succeeded to the presidency. Drawing on many of his life experiences, Li continued and enhanced Jiang's democratization policies. After forcing many lifetime politicians from office, Li paved the way for the first general election in December 1991. Though the opposition Democratic Progressive Party made a strong showing, Li's GMD captured 71 percent of the popular vote. As Li advocated greater democracy, he also tried to readjust relations between the Republic of China on Taiwan and the People's Republic of China on the mainland. He advocated increased trade and investment, greater cultural contacts, and travel across the straits. However, Li did not intend for these reforms to draw the two sides politically closer together. Instead, Li advocated Taiwan separateness, much to the consternation of Communist leaders in Beijing. These two trends—democratization and increased Taiwan separateness—came to a fine focus in early 1995. When Cornell University invited Li to speak to its faculty and student body, Li quickly accepted the offer. The Clinton administration knew that such a high-level visit could be construed as official recognition of Taiwan independence. Wary that the visit would offend Beijing, the White House announced that it would not grant Li the requisite visa. The U.S. legislature, however, voted overwhelmingly and across party lines to grant Li the visa. Consequently, in June of that year Li traveled to New York where the international press corps treated him as a celebrity. Beijing reacted to Li's visit by staging intimidating military exercises off the Taiwan coast. While hoping to paint Li as reckless and irresponsible, Beijing's military maneuvers backfired as 54 percent of Taiwan voters chose Li in the first-ever presidential election of 1996. For the next four years Li continued his policies of democratization and Taiwan separateness, frustrating his Beijing counterparts.

At the end of his term in 2000, Li stepped down as President to become the senior statesman of the GMD. However, because the GMD failed to retain the presidency, party leaders expelled him from the organization Li had served throughout his life. Though his political life has come to an effective end, Li Denghui remains immensely popular and has left a political legacy that will influence Taiwan for years to come.

See also Taiwan; Guomindang.

REFERENCES: Bruce J. Dickson and Chao Chien-Min (eds.), *Assessing the Lee Teng-Hui Legacy in Taiwan's Politics* (New York, 2002); Lee Teng-hui, *The Road* to Democracy: Taiwan's Pursuit of Identity (Tokyo, 1999); Wei-Chin Lee, Sayonara to the Lee Teng-Hui Era: Politics in Taiwan, 1988–2000 (Lanham, MD, 2003); Jaushieh Joseph Wu, Taiwan's Democratization: Forces behind the New Momentum (Oxford, 1995).

David Kenley

Li Hongzhang (1823–1901)

Li Hongzhang was a key statesman, diplomat, and reformer during the late Qing (Manchu) Dynasty. Born into a scholar-gentry family in Anhui province, Li received a fine Confucian education and passed the provincial civil service examination in 1844. After receiving the highest jinshi degree in 1847, he was later appointed to the prestigious Hanlin Academy in the imperial capital. His official career began during the Taiping Rebellion (1850–1864), when he joined the staff of Governor Zeng Guofan in 1858. In 1862 Li was appointed acting governor of Jiangsu province, at which time he began his lifelong acquaintance with Westerners in Shanghai and elsewhere in China. During those years Li successfully integrated a small Western mercenary army, known as the Ever Victorious Army, into the Qing imperial army; the first two commanders had been Americans. This first modern-style army was helpful in ridding the Yangzi valley of rebels. After the defeat of the Taipings, Li was appointed governor-general of Hubei and Hunan provinces, and was instrumental in the defeat of the Nian Rebellion in northern China.

Between 1870 and 1895 Li received numerous honors and promotions, including Grand Tutor to the Heir Apparent and Grand Secretary. As High Commissioner of Trade for the Northern Ocean he became involved in nearly every question involving foreign relations, the adoption of Western techniques, and the sending of Chinese students abroad. During his tenure as high commissioner Li became aware of the importance of modernization and industrialization in China as well as the need to employ Western experts, particularly American experts, to help in China's development. During those years Li initiated the building of China's first telegraph lines (1865) and railroad (1876), as well as a modern shipyard (1876), arsenal (1876), and merchant steamship company (1872). Li's first experience as a diplomat came in 1871, when the imperial court called upon him to negotiate a treaty with Japan concerning issues over Taiwan, the Ryukyus, and Korea. Later on after Japan had seized the Ryukyus and had incorporated them into the Japanese empire, Li appealed to General Ulysses S. Grant, who was visiting China a few years later, to intercede on China's behalf. Aware of America's growing in-

dustrial and military strength after the Civil War, Li had hoped to draw the United States into the defense of Chinese tributaries against European and Japanese encroachments. Grant was instrumental, as a private citizen but not a representative of the government, in arranging negotiations between Li and Takezoe Shinichiro, resulting in an agreement in 1879 to divide the Ryukyu Islands between China and Japan. Unfortunately, these negotiations came to naught and tensions continued to mount between China and Japan, leading to a war in 1894–1895. During those years, too, many Americans were less sympathetic to the Chinese cause and instead viewed Japan as an instrument of progress in Asia.

Although considered to be the most experienced diplomat in China, after his signing of the Treaty of Tianjin with France in 1885 and the Treaty of Shimonoseki with Japan in 1895, Li's reputation was shattered. In the French treaty China gave up its suzerainty over Indochina and in the Japanese treaty China lost Taiwan and the Penghus (Pescadores) as well as her dominance over Korea. Although the major problem had not been Li's diplomatic abilities but rather the weakness of the Qing government, nonetheless Li took the blame on both occasions. As a result he was relieved of all government positions and sent into semi-retirement, only to be called back into service as the Chinese emissary at the coronation of Tsar Nicholas II of Russia in 1896. With this Li became the first high-ranking Chinese official to visit a European country; afterwards on his return home he visited the United States. Li's final diplomatic service came during the Boxer Rebellion (1900), when the Empress Dowager Cixi appointed him to represent China in negotiating the Boxer Protocol in 1901. Li died on November 7, 1901, at the age of seventy-eight.

See also Treaty of Tianjin (1858); Boxer Rebellion (1900); Boxer Protocol; Cixi (1835–1908).

REFERENCES: Arthur Hummel, Eminent Chinese of the Qing Period (Washington, DC, 1943); Stanley Spector, Li Hung-chang and the Huai Army (Seattle, WA, 1964); Kwang-ching Liu, "Li Hung-chang in Chili: The Emergence of a Policy, 1870–1875," in Albert Feuerwerker (et al.), Approaches to Modern Chinese History (Berkeley, CA, 1967).

Robert J. Antony

Li Hung-chang (1823–1901) see Li Hongzhang (1823–1901)

Li Peng (1928-)

Though he experienced several hardships as a boy, Li Peng's youth created a strong political foundation upon which he would later be able to build. Li's father was killed by Guomindang agents when he was only seven, leaving him an orphan in the western city of Chongqing. At about this same time, Li met China's future Premier, Zhou Enlai. Zhou protected and supported several young orphans, including Li. Li eventually moved to the northern Yanan Soviet where he continued to benefit from Zhou's kindness.

After the war with Japan, Li traveled to Russia to study at the Moscow Power Institute. Not surprisingly, upon his return to China he quickly rose through the ranks of the energy bureaucracy. Through his competent service, as well as powerful political connections, Li's status in the party quickly rose. Even during the Cultural Revolution, when many party members were purged or persecuted, Li remained relatively untouched. Following Mao Zedong's death and the end of the Cultural Revolution, Li's star continued to rise. In 1979 he was named the deputy minister of the power industry and two years later became the chief minister. By 1982 he was a member of the Communist Party Central Committee, which served as a stepping-stone to join the Politburo in 1985. Nobody was surprised when he was named Premier in November 1987. To all observers, it seemed Li was destined to greatness. Throughout the 1980s, Li earned the reputation of a reformer. He had been a staunch supporter of land-use rights and had even argued that such rights could be privately bought and sold. He also advocated free market reforms for China's tight housing industry. During the economic stagnation of the late 1980s, Li continued to support the "four modernizations" and called for greater economic liberalization. In 1989, intellectuals such as Fang Lizhi clamored for further change. Many called for greater freedom of expression and advocated the development of a "socialist democracy." By early spring of that year, students and Beijing residents began congregating in Tiananmen Square, demanding an audience with Premier Li Peng. Eventually their numbers exceeded one million.

From the beginning of the protests, the central government appeared paralyzed and indecisive. Many began to suspect a division between the party leaders, believing that Premier Li was the leader of the hard-line camp while General Secretary Zhao Ziyang was more willing to consider the students' demands. Both sides, it was believed, were waiting to see where the party's senior statesman, Deng Xiaoping, would lend his support. On June 3, Chinese troops arrived in Beijing and violently cleared the square. With tremendous speed and precision, the troops crushed the protest with unknown numbers of casualties. In the days following the Tiananmen crackdown, the party experienced a shake-up of power. While Zhao Ziyang was dismissed as General Secretary, Li was allowed to maintain his position as Premier. Nevertheless, it seemed as if his political influence had reached an apex. Though he would continue to serve as Premier until his term of office ended in 1998, he would not command the respect — either with the general public or with his party colleagues — as he had prior to 1989. Following his term as Premier, Li served as Chairman of the National People's Congress and retired in 2003.

Recent scholarship has helped to more firmly establish Li Peng's legacy and reputation. Though he was an advocate of reform throughout the 1980s, he will no doubt be remembered as a "hard-liner" that placed the party ahead of the lives of Beijing students and residents.

See also **Tiananmen Square Massacre.**

REFERENCES: Andrew Nathan (ed.), *China's New Rulers: The Secret Files* (New York, 2003); Wang Gungwu and Zheng Yongnian (eds.), *Damage Control: The Chinese Communist Party in the Jiang Zemin Era* (Singapore, 2003); Andrew Nathan and Perry Link (eds.), *The Tiananmen Papers: The Chinese Leadership's Decision to Use Force Against Their Own People — in Their Own Words* (New York, 2001).

David Kenley

Li Tsung-jen (1890–1969) *see* Li Zongren (1890–1969)

Li Zongren (1890–1969)

Li Zongren was the mastermind of the 1938 Chinese victory over Japan at the Battle of Taierzhuang, but secured his place in history by serving briefly in 1949 as China's acting President between Nationalist leader Jiang Jieshi's retreat to Taiwan and Mao's rise to power. Li's life spanned China's imperial, revolutionary, nationalist and Communist periods — and he served in leadership roles in three of them.

Born in 1890 in Xixiang, Guangxi Province, he was the second eldest in a family of five boys and three girls. As a teenager, Li joined Chinese revolutionary Sun Zhongshan's Tongmenghui movement in 1910 and rose through the ranks, serving from 1925–1949 as a leader of the military clique that ruled the Guangxi region. Li led Nationalist forces in central China against the Japanese invaders during the Sino-Japanese War of 1937–1945, including at the Battle of Taierzhuang. That historic battle took place on the eastern banks of the Grand Canal of China at a frontier garrison northeast of Xuzhou, the junction of the Jinpu Railway between Tianjin and Pudong and the Longhai Railway linking Lanzhou and Lianyungang. Xuzhou was also the headquarters of the Guomindang's 5th War Zone. The Japanese advanced on Xuzhou and did not take Li Zongren seriously nor concern themselves with his moves to encircle them. Instead, the Japanese attacked his forces frontally and were repelled by his unexpectedly superior numbers. He succeeded in surrounding the Japanese, forcing them into retreat, but did not pursue them, which has been viewed over the years as a grave tactical mistake that prolonged the war. Nevertheless, the battle became China's first major victory of the conflict. It rallied Chinese morale, proving Japan defeatable. On April 28, 1948, Li was elected Vice President by China's National Assembly, five days after Jiang Jieshi became President. In the process, he wounded himself politically, earning Jiang's deep enmity by defeating Sun Fo, Jiang's handpicked candidate for the job. As a result, Li was never included in Jiang's inner circle of advisors and was excluded from leadership when Jiang retreated to Taiwan as Mao's Communists swept over the mainland. In November 1949, Li traveled to New York City on the pretext of a medical crisis. Chronic stomach problems were treated at Columbia University hospital, where with Jiang's retreat to Taiwan left Li as the acting President of China. From New York, he attempted unsuccessfully to negotiate with the Communists, further infuriating the exiled Jiang. Li remained in the United States for the next 16 years—although officially still China's Vice President for five of those years. His absence prompted Jiang on Taiwan to initiate impeachment proceedings against him in January 1952, but Li was only officially removed as Vice President in March 1954 after two years of debate. Li surprised many by returning to mainland China on July 20, 1965, living in Beijing as an advisor and confidant of Communist insider Zhou Enlai. Li died in Nanjing of stomach cancer at 78.

See also **Chinese Civil War (1945–1949); Jiang Jieshi (1887–1975).**

REFERENCES: Lloyd E. Eastman, *The Nationalist Era in China, 1927–1949* (Cambridge, UK, 1991); John K. Fairbank, *The Cambridge History of China: Volume 13, Republican China 1912–1949, Part 2* (Cambridge, UK, 1986); Li Tsung-jen, *Memoirs of Li Tsung-jen* (New York, 1979); Edgar Snow, *The Battle for Asia* (New York, 1941).
Rob Kerby

Lilley, James (1928-)

An ambassador, clandestine officer, and academic whose career orbited about the twin foci of China and Washington, Lilley was born in 1928 in Qingdao, Shangdong Province, China, where his father worked for Standard Oil. Like many other principal figures in China policy of his generation, he was a Yale graduate, and joined the clandestine service upon graduation in 1951.

After service in Taiwan and Hong Kong during which most American attempts to infiltrate agents into the mainland failed, Lilley served as a declared representative of the operations directorate within the first U.S. liaison office in Beijing, where from 1973 he was first chief of station. He accompanied George H.W. Bush in the latter's travels around China in 1977 as chief of the American Liaison Office, gaining the latter's lifelong confidence. In 1982 to 1984, Lilley served as director of the American Institute in Taiwan, following a tour as national intelligence officer for China from 1975 to 1978. He subsequently returned to the region as United States ambassador to the Republic of Korea from 1986 to 1989 and to China from then until 1991, and also held a number of positions relating to China policy in Washington, Deputy Assistant Secretary of State for East Asian Affairs from 1985 to 1986, and Assistant Secretary of Defense for international affairs from 1991 to 1993. As ambassador to China, Lilly drafted the text of national security advisor Brent Scowcroft's toast to Foreign Minister Qian Qichen and other senior Chinese officials during Scowcroft's secret mission in June 1989 to lay the groundwork for restored relations with China after Tiananmen Square. Lilley later came to regard the mission as a miscalculation, in light of public outrage in the United States against Beijing. As Assistant Secretary of Defense he was a forceful advocate of F-16 sales to Taiwan, against opposition from the Department of State.

When not in government, he held several positions as an academic (at SAIS, Harvard, Claremont McKenna, and the University of Maryland). Since 1993, Lilly has been director of the Asia program at the American Enterprise Institute. His memoirs, written together with his son, a Washington journalist, appeared in 2004 with the title *China Hands: Nine Decades of Adventure, Espionage, and Diplomacy in Asia.*

See also **Scowcroft-Eagleburger Mission; Tiananmen Square Massacre.**

REFERENCES: James R. Lilley and Jeffrey Lilley, *China Hands: Nine Decades of Adventure, Espionage, and Diplomacy in Asia* (New York, 2004); James Mann, *About Face: A History of America's Curious Relationship with China, from Nixon to Clinton* (New York, 2000).
Patrick Belton

Lin Yutang (1895–1976)

Lin Yutang was a prolific, versatile writer and scholar who produced edited anthologies, translations from Chinese to English, criticism, fiction, literary history, and personal reflections. He was most proud of his *Chinese-English Dictionary of Modern Usage (1972)* but English-speakers might consider his major contribution to be in the transmitting both classical and mid 20th century Chinese culture to Western readers through anthologies of story selections which he translated and edited as well as his works on individual luminaries such as *The Wisdom of Confucius, Chuangtzu, The Importance of Understanding*, and *The Gay Genius: The Life and Times of Su Tungpo.*

Born in Changzhou, Fujian Province, China and son of a Chinese-Christian minister, he was educated in China (St. John's College, Shanghai, BA 1916), America (Harvard University, MA, 1920) and Germany (Leipzig, Ph.D., 1923). He studied philology and literature and was at least bi-lingual in English and Chinese but also somewhat fluent in French and German. He credited most of his education, however, to an avid interest in reading "old books" and thinking about them. During a career interrupted by the Japanese invasion and the Chinese Communist movement, he held positions at universities in Beijing and Fujian in the 1940s and in Singapore as Chancellor of Nanyang University from 1954 to 1955. He also worked for the Guomindang government in Wuhan and for UNESCO in Paris. He spent the last twenty years in the United States. In a more popular context, he is responsible for transmitting his understanding of modern Chinese life through novels and novelizations such as *Lady Wu: A True Story, The Secret Name, The Vermillion Gate* and *Moment in Peking.* And for describing it through his 1930s non-fiction works such as *The Little Critic: Essays, Satires and Sketches on China*, and *My Country and My People*, and later *A History of the Press and Public Opinion in China.* He also wrote a very popular novel about a Chinese-American family in 1930s' U.S. called *Chinatown Family.* This latter work was recommended reading for students of China in U.S. universities of the 1950s. Perhaps the most biographical work is *The Importance of Living* in which he sets the tone for later works that comment on Eastern and Western writers from a very personal context. He describes it thus: "This is a personal testimony, a testimony of my own experience throughout life." He was nominated several times for a Nobel Prize in Literature. While some of his writing was done in Chinese, the majority, written in English, was directed at a Western audience, and he had many friends in the literary community of the U.S. in the 1940s and 1950s. The majority of the fictional and philosophical works are written in a conversational tone, which can be appreciated by the ca-

sual reader, such as one who might pick up *Walden Pond* of an evening. For example, in Chapter Two of *Importance*, he contracts Christian, Greek and Chinese views of mankind, but for the Chinese he concentrates on Confucianism and Taoism as he considers Buddhism to be "depressing." His other popular work, *On the Wisdom of America*, presents his own selection of short pieces from major American writers such as Olive Wendell Holmes, William James, Alfred North Whitehead, but also James Thurber and E. L. Sandburg. His particular charm was in giving Western readers the sense that they were seeing their own cultural heritage from an outside perspective, and then adding to it bits of information about traditional Chinese culture and its relationship to the China of his day. Part of his immense popularity, especially with the earlier books, arose out of this ability to education without openly challenging, no mean feat in decades just before and just after World War II when fear of the East, Communism, and the atomic bomb dominated the American consciousness.

REFERENCES: Lin Yutang, *Chinese-English Dictionary of Modern Usage* (Hong Kong, 1971); Lin Yutang, *The Importance of Living* (New York, 1937); Lin Yutang, *Chinatown Family* (New York, 1948); Lin Yutang, *A History of the Press and Public Opinion in Chin* (Chicago, IL, 1936); Deborah A. Straub, "Yutang Lin," *Contemporary Authors Online* (New York, 2003).

Janice M. Bogstad

Lodge, Henry Cabot (1850–1924)

Born into a Brahmin family in Boston, Massachusetts, Henry Cabot Lodge received his baccalaureate, law, and doctoral degrees from Harvard University. Around a three-year stint as a history professor at Harvard, he served as an assistant editor at the *North American Review* and a co-editor of the *International Review.* In 1880, he was elected to the Massachusetts state legislature. After one unsuccessful bid, he was elected to the U.S. House of Representatives in 1887, where he served until 1893. In that year, he was elected to the U.S. Senate, where he would serve until his death in 1924. During the early years of his political career, Lodge continued to produce scholarly historical studies such as *Alexander Hamilton* (1882), *Daniel Webster* (1883), *George Washington* (1889), and *The Story of the Revolution* (1898, 2 vols.). In addition, he edited the nine volumes of Hamilton's collected writings (1885).

Lodge is probably most remembered for his great personal and political antipathy towards President Woodrow Wilson and his leadership of the opposition to the United States' membership in the League of Nations that Wilson had championed. The American rejection of the League and the election to the presidency of Warren G. Harding, whose nomination Lodge strongly supported, initiated almost two decades of strong isolationist sentiment within the United States. But Lodge was actually anything but an isolationist, and his attitude toward U.S. relations with China is illustrative of his imperialistic view of how American foreign policy ought to be conducted.

A great admirer of President Theodore Roosevelt, Lodge believed that the projection of U.S. economic and military power overseas would result in a stronger sense of national identity and purpose and would inevitably improve the conditions under which other peoples lived. Like Roosevelt, Lodge advocated the Open Door Policy in China. Ostensibly, the policy would accelerate the modernization of China to the great benefit of its people and would circumvent conflicts among the Western powers over China. But the policy violated Chinese sovereignty by demanding that it accede to its open-ended economic exploitation by Western powers. More specifically, Lodge supported the establishment of a banking consortium in China through which the United States and the European powers with economic interests in China could manage aspects of the Chinese economy to insure the continuing profitability of their investments. Wilson's decision, shortly after his election, to discontinue U.S. participation in this banking consortium was an early point of contention between him and Lodge. Moreover, Lodge had strongly supported Roosevelt's decision to send the Great White Fleet across the Pacific to exhibit American military might to its potential rivals in the region. Indeed, proving himself even more imperialistic than Roosevelt, Lodge had advocated the establishment of American military bases in China not only to insure that American economic interests could be protected but also to facilitate the expansion of those interests, if necessary through force.

REFERENCES: John A. Garraty, Henry Cabot Lodge: A Biography (New York, 1968); Karl Schriftgiesser, The Gentleman from Massachusetts: Henry Cabot Lodge (Boston, MA, 1944); William C. Widenor, Henry Cabot Lodge and the Search for an American Foreign Policy (Berkeley, CA, 1980); William C. Widenor, "Henry Cabot Lodge: The Astute Paliamentarian," in Richard A. Baker and Roger H. Davidson (eds.), First among Equals: Outstanding Senate Leaders of the Twentieth Century (Washington, DC, 1991).

Martin Kich

Lord, Winston (1937–)

A native of New York City and 1959 graduate of Yale College, Lord came from a family of diplomats; his mother, Mary Pillsbury Lord, served as United States delegate to the United Nations General Assembly and as representative to the Human Rights Commission.

As staff member of the National Security Council from 1969 to 1973, he accompanied Henry Kissinger on his secret trip to Beijing in 1971, and joined the American delegation during Nixon's visit to China the following year. He subsequently served as the State Department's director of policy planning, from 1973 to 1977, U.S. ambassador to China, from November 1985 to April 1989, and Assistant Secretary of State for East Asian and Pacific affairs, from April 1993 to February 1997. After leaving the embassy in Beijing, Lord contributed an op-ed piece with the title "Misguided Mission" to the *Washington Post* of December 19, 1989, criticizing the secret June Scowcroft mission, which had only recently been disclosed. Also, writing in *Foreign Affairs* at the same time, he registered harsh condemnation and profound sadness for the "dimming of Deng Xiaoping's vision in the twilight of his remarkable odyssey," though he nonetheless urged against attempting to confront or attempt to change a Chinese leadership not likely to survive anyway. Testifying before the Senate Judiciary Committee in January 1990, he predicted that within three years there would be a "more moderate, human government in Beijing." He nonetheless supported conditionality on renewing China's most-favored-nation trading status, both in a 1991 *New York Times* piece and privately to Senators in early February 1993. In this vein, he endorsed the Solarz proposal at the start of the Clinton administration calling for a one-year MFN renewal with further normal trade relations dependent upon Chinese progress in human rights. He also argued passionately within the State Department that the administration should accurately record Chinese political repression. In July 1993, Lord warned Secretary of State Warren Christopher in a classified letter that relations were "spiraling downward," urging a strategy of intensive engagement in which incentives would substitute for threats. Together with Assistant Secretary of Defense Charles Freeman, he prepared a China policy review at the end of August. He was thus an author of the "comprehensive engagement" strategy which Clinton adopted beginning with an action memorandum of September; with national security advisor Anthony Lake, he was charged with briefing Chinese ambassador Li Daoyu with the results of the review on September 5. This new strategy attracted great opposition from Congress, with Senators besieging Lord at a September 27 hearing of the Committee on Foreign Relations East Asia subcommittee for not having included increased aid to Taiwan, including submarines. He opposed in May 1995 the successful congressional drive to invite Taiwanese President Li Denghui to visit the United States, as introducing an important element of "officiality" to that relationship.

Lord's non-governmental service in foreign affairs has been equally wide-ranging, including service as chair of the National Endowment for Democracy, as vice-chair and later co-chair of the International Rescue Committee, and perhaps most notably as President of the Council on Foreign Relations from 1977 to 1985. He is married, since 1963, to Bette Bao Lord, an acclaimed novelist.

REFERENCES: Winston Lord, "China and America: Beyond the Big Chill," *Foreign Affairs* (Autumn 1989), "Misguided Mission," *Washington Post* (December 19, 1989); James Mann, *About Face: A History of America's Curious Relationship with China, from Nixon to Clinton* (New York, 2000).

Patrick Belton

Low, Frederick Ferdinand (1828–1894)

Frederick Low was a businessman, politician, and diplomat. He was born on June 30, 1828 in Frankfort, Maine and at age fifteen became an apprentice to Russell, Sturgis and Company, a shipping firm closely linked to the China trade. In the Gold Rush of 1849 he set out for California and after making a modest claim moved to San Francisco. He formed a shipping partnership in 1850, and later a steamship line along the Sacramento River, as well as a banking business. In 1862, Low was elected to the Congress as a Republican. He was subsequently appointed as collector of the Port of San Francisco. In 1863, Low became Governor of California, resisting secessionist movements in the state and sending money and 16,000 volunteers. As governor, he also opposed state laws that were discriminatory to Chinese and helped to establish the University of California.

Because of his outspoken defense of Chinese rights in California, President Ulysses S. Grant appointed Low minister to China in 1869. Continuing diplomatic practice established by U.S. diplomat Anson Burlingame, Low initially supported a policy of cooperation with the Chinese. In June 1870 French missionaries were massacred by the Chinese in Tianjin, and Low's support for cooperation was challenged. He called for punishment of the perpetrators, but condemned French actions that had caused Chinese anti-foreign sentiment. In 1871, acting on inaccurate information that Korea would be receptive to opening relations with the United States, Low reluctantly attempted an expedition to Korea on the same lines as Commodore Matthew Perry's entrance into Japan. Known as the Low-Rogers Expedition, Low along with Admiral John Rogers steamed near Seoul with five American ships. The Koreans fired upon surveyors from the expedition and the Americans retaliated by invading the coast, destroying five Korean forts, and killing about 300. The Americans withdrew and the expedition was considered an embarrassing example of American diplomacy, especially to the Chinese who began to consider the United States no better than the European nations active in China. Low redeemed his reputation, both in the United States and in China, in the audience question controversy of 1873. Westerners had chafed at the kowtow ceremonial requirements, which symbolized the superiority of the Chinese emperor. Low successfully negotiated the right of foreign petitioners to have an audience with the emperor without the kowtow ceremony. A symbolic victory, Low did not think that resolving the audience question issue would promote any real cultural or diplomatic change. Although he was not a "gunboat" diplomat when it came to Chinese relations, Low was not optimistic about the future of cooperation between China and the West.

Low returned to California in 1874 and resumed his businesses, becoming a manager of the Anglo-California Bank and involving himself in a variety of other enterprises. He died on July 21, 1894 in San Francisco, California.

See also Kowtow.

REFERENCES: David L. Anderson, *Imperialism and Idealism: American Diplomats in China, 1861–1898* (Bloomington, ID, 1985); David L. Anderson, "Between Two Cultures: Frederick Low in China," *California History Vol.* 59 (1980); Paul H. Clyde, "Frederick F. Low and the Tianjin Massacre," *Pacific Historical Review Vol.* 2 (1933).

Linus Kafka

Luce, Clare Boothe (1903–1987)

Clare Boothe Luce was an American playwright, magazine editor for *Vanity Fair* (1931–1934) and *Vogue* (1939). She was also a feature writer for several publications, including *Life*, for which she worked as a war correspondent in 1942, notably in China. She became a prominent member of the social life in New York, saw her plays produced and made into movies, acted, held a congressional office, and was known to most Americans in the 1940s through 1960s in these several capacities. Through all these years, she kept letters and diaries that both she and her biographers have used to document her extraordinary life.

Born Clare Boothe, she had very humble beginnings but was nevertheless educated, sometimes as a day student, at some of the better schools in Nashville (Ward Seminary), and New York (St. Mary's and, later, Castle School) where she made lasting connections with some of America's elite families. Clare was very bright and ambitious even as a young girl. She was able to use her intelligence, along with her beauty, to rise to positions of prominence in American society, as a writer, and eventually as member of the House of Representatives from Connecticut (1943–1947) and American Ambassador to Italy (1953–1957). She served on the board of directors of several charitable and service organizations, including press clubs, and, by the end of her life received many honorary degrees from universities such as Georgetown, Temple, and University of Notre Dame. Luce married twice, first George Tuttle Brokaw, who was 43 to her twenty years of age when they met. They had a daughter Ann (1926), but divorced in 1929. Her marriage to Henry Luce (1935), wealthy publisher of *Time* and *Fortune*, and later *Life* lasted until his death in 1967. Henry Luce was born in China in 1898, the son of Presbyterian missionaries. He lived most of his first 14 years in China. Thus, when the opportunity came to travel in China and report back to the U.S. on the Chinese efforts against the Japanese in 1941, both he and Clare (partly as his photographer), went first to Chongqing, China's wartime capital, in May 1941, under intermittent attacks by Japanese air raids, and then to the front through the city of Xian. They both sent back stories about the Generalissimo and Madame Jiang Jieshi, as well as the desperate condition of the Chinese war effort. They also met with Communist leader Zhou Enlai and Clare included his views of the war in her articles. Clare was planning a book on China to parallel her popular one about Europe on the eve of war (*Europe in the Spring*) but "Wings over China," a feature for *Life*, was the only result. During her China trip in 1942, she also spoke with General Joseph W. Stilwell, who became part of her articles on the necessity of U.S. continuing support for China during the war. She also proposed a book on General Douglas MacArthur, which, like the prospective China book, was never published. During 1941–1942, she also wrote for *Time* and *Fortune,* and contributed articles and fiction to *Jubilee, Sports Illustrated* and *National Review,* among others.

Clare Boothe Luce's now-prominent position in American society, as well as her access to the public through her husband's several magazines, ensured that her opinions reached a wide, if not always credulous, audience. She lectured in support of Nationalist China and Jiang Jieshi, wrote reports for conservative organizations and

continued to keep China's problems in the public eye, based largely on the reputation as a China expert she had gained in the early 1940s. For example, her address "The Mystery of American Policy in China," was published in *Plain Talk* in 1949. As late as 1964, she published a pamphlet on Sino-Soviet relations. In late 1940s and earlier 1950s, as members of the China Lobby she and her husband played an important role in the "Who lost China" fight.

Clare Boothe Luce continued to fascinate audiences until her death of cancer in 1987, inspiring multiple biographies even up to ten years later (1997). Her writing was known for its color and conservative perspective more than for its accuracy, but it reached a wide audience and influenced the thinking of both the public and government decision-makers.

See also Luce, Henry (1898–1967); China Lobby; Jiang Jieshi (1887–1975); Song Meiling (1897–2003).

REFERENCES: Clare Boothe Luce, *Europe in the Spring* (New York, 1941); Clare Boothe Luce, *Kiss the Boys Good-bye* (New York, 1939); Clare Boothe Luce, "The Crisis in Soviet-Chinese Relations (pamphlet)," (New York, 1964); "Clare Boothe Luce," *Contemporary Authors Online* (2004); Alden Hatch, *Ambassador Extraordinary: Clare Boothe Luce* (New York, 1955); Sylvia Jukes Morris, *Rage For Fame* (New York, 1997); Wilfred Sheed, *Clare Boothe Luce* (New York, 1982); Stephen Sladegg, *Clare Boothe Luce* (New York, 1970).

Janice M. Bogstad

Luce, Henry (1898–1967)

Born to American missionaries in Penglai, Shandong Province, China, on April 3, 1898, Henry Robinson Luce would remain involved in Sino-American relations throughout his long career as the influential founder, editor, and publisher of *Time, Life*, and *Fortune* magazines. Luce spent nearly all of his childhood in China. He received his secondary and higher education in the United States, on a scholarship at Hotchkiss School and then at Yale, where he served as managing editor of the *Yale Daily News*, was elected to Phi Beta Kappa, and became a member of the elite secret society Skull and Bones. Intensely patriotic, he enlisted in the Army upon graduation to serve in World War I, though combat ended before he was sent overseas.

In 1922, after a year studying at Oxford and some months working for the *Chicago Daily News,* Luce moved to New York to found *Time* magazine with Briton Hadden, an acquaintance from Hotchkiss and Yale. Seeking to distinguish their news weekly from daily newspapers and from the extant *Literary Digest,* they wrote that *Time* would contain no editorial page and no bias, except for a respect for old manners, an interest in new ideas, and a suspicion of large government. Luce nursed *Time* through its early years with bold confidence in its eventual success (Hadden died within a decade of its inception). Luce also founded *Fortune* magazine immediately before the stock market crash of 1929 and published the first issue of *Life* magazine in 1936. He married playwright Clare Boothe Brokaw in 1935; his first marriage, to Lila Hotz, had lasted from 1923–1935 and resulted in his only two children, Henry III and Peter Paul. During World War II, Luce advocated sending more support to China, rather than diverting additional resources to the war in Europe. He also helped to found United China Relief, an agency that brought together eight organizations supplying various forms of humanitarian aid to China. After the war, during the struggle for the government of China, Luce strongly supported the Nationalist Jiang Jieshi over Communist Mao Zedong. Featuring Jiang and Madame Jiang several times on the cover of *Time* and in many photographs in *Life*, Luce's magazine empire helped to create American support for a government headed by the exiled Jiang. For Luce, the son of devout Presbyterian missionaries and a committed patriot, Communism represented a dual threat against religious freedom in China and against a culture of liberty. During the Truman administration, *Time*, *Life*, and *Fortune* magazines criticized the policies of the Democratic Party, believing them to be conciliatory towards Communism. Luce also coordinated the advocacy conducted by the loosely organized "China Lobby," as it came to be called, in support of Jiang. Luce was criticized for his control of the editorial stance of *Time* magazine (his own Chongqing correspondent, Theodore H. White, was dismissed for an increasingly strident opposition to Jiang's government), but he would continue unapologetically to oppose Communism in China throughout his life.

Until his death, Luce was an active philanthropist, founding, expanding, and financing several Christian universities in China. The Henry Luce Foundation, which he established in 1936, continues to fund scholarship on Asia, art, religion, theology, environmental science, and public policy, as well as supporting opportunities for women in science.

See also China Lobby; Jiang Jieshi (1887–1975); Song Meiling (1897–2003); Luce, Clare Boothe (1903–1987).

References: *Henry Luce Foundation Profile* (New York, 2004); John K. Jessup (ed.), *The Ideas of Henry Luce* (New York, 1969); Patricia Neils, *China Images in the Life and Times of Henry Luce* (Savage, MD, 1990); W. A. Swanberg, *Luce and His Empire* (New York, 1972).

Tara Robbins

Lytton Report

The Lytton Commission of Inquiry was formed by the League of Nations to investigate the charges of Japanese aggression brought to the attention of the League by China following the Mukden Incident of September 18, 1931. The League Council voted 13–1 (Japan) for a negotiated settlement. China relied on Britain and the U.S. to restrain Japanese actions, and hoped that the Russians would also act in this regard. The Commission was headed by the Earl of Lytton, a British official with Indian experience, to investigate and propose remedial steps to settle the crisis. Serving on the commission were General Henri Claudel of France, familiar with Asian colonial affairs, Count Luigi Aldovandi-Marescotti , an Italian diplomat, Albert Schnee, a German expert on East African colonial affairs, and the American Major General Frank R. McCoy, who also had had diplomatic experience.

The Commission arrived in Japan on February 29, 1932 and spent a week interviewing civil and military officials. The Japanese tried to emphasize the local nature of the events in Manchuria, thus not a matter for international concern. Domestic Japanese events prevented a change in attitude by the government: they announced the creation of the independent state of Manchukuo in Manchuria. The former Manchu Emperor of China, Puyi was placed on the throne of this new state by the Japanese. The commission then traveled to Shanghai, Nanjing and Beijing to consult with Chinese officials, and then to Shenyang (Mukden) seven months after the event. Gu Weijun, who had been Acting Foreign Minister, accompanied the Commission as the Chinese official assessor. He feared that the Russians and the Japanese would make a deal dividing Manchuria between them. The Japanese continually obstructed the Commission during their six-week stay there, under the guise of protecting them from bandits.

The report of this investigation was finished on September 4, 1932, in which, the Commission recognized the economic importance of Manchuria to the Japanese, and the need for stable conditions there. But they concluded that the actions of the Japanese Kwantung Army in Manchuria, particularly in the occupation of Shenyang, were not those of self- defense, as claimed. The Commission believed that the interests of the Chinese and the Japanese in Manchuria were not irreconcilable, and that negotiations should begin on issues of mutual concern. On February 24, 1933 the League Assembly met in special session; the Lytton Report was adopted 42–1 (Japan), with Thailand abstaining, and twelve members absent.

The Japanese disagreed with the finding that Manchuria would be autonomous under Chinese control, and that the Kwantung Army should pull back to the confines of its railroad zone. When the League refused recognize the legality of Manchukuo, the Japanese delegates walked out of the meeting, although the League had not placed sanctions on Japan. The Japanese government formally announced withdrawal from the League on March 27, 1933. This action negated much of the League's collective security base, which the Japanese had helped found. The Chinese did not regain control of Manchuria until the end of World War II in 1945. This report is the epitome of ambiguity, reflecting the uncertain role, which the League pursued. It named Japan as the aggressor, but identified legitimate interests of the Japanese in Manchuria. The Chinese by themselves were unwilling or unable to halt the aggression due to internal constraints.

See also Mukden Incident; Manchukuo; Machuria; Puyi (1906–1967).

REFERENCES: Immanuel C. Y. Hsu, *The Rise of Modern China* (Oxford, 2000); Youli Sun, *China and the Origins of the Pacific War, 1931–1941* (New York, 1993); Parks M. Coble, *Facing Japan: Chinese Politics and Japanese Imperialism, 1931–1937*, (Cambridge, MA, 1991).

Katherine Reist

MacArthur, Douglas (1880–1964)

General Douglas MacArthur is best known as a great military commander during and after World War II. He is also remembered for his insubordination and removal by President Harry S. Truman for advocating the escalation of the Korean War and the use of nuclear weapons against North Korea and the People's Republic of China (PRC) in early 1950s. Whatever the popular memories of MacArthur, he represents an important part of the United State's involvement in Asia.

After World War II, MacArthur was charged with administrating and rebuilding the destroyed Japanese nation. He also became very involved with politics regarding China in 1949 and 1950 when Jiang Jieshi and his Nationalist government fled to Taiwan after being defeated in the Chinese Civil War by the Communists. He advised the United States as to the strategic value of Taiwan and lobbied in the American government for a defense commitment to the Republic of China against the Chinese Communists. MacArthur took the stand that while Jiang Jieshi was not the ideal ally; his government was an ally none the less and deserved support. As the Cold War began in earnest, American interest began to focus on the Korean peninsula as a stand against the spread of Communism. When the North Korean military invaded across the 38th parallel in the summer of 1950, the need for action was immediate. The only person considered to command the UN forces in the region was MacArthur. He was given command and forced the North Korean Communists to retreat almost to the border of China. MacArthur was not prepared for the Chinese Communist troops to counterattack and force his offensive below the 38th parallel in late 1950. This led to a stalemate on the peninsula for the continuation of the conflict. In March 1951, MacArthur demanded that the Chinese forces surrender immediately or risk attacks on China. This action sabotaged Truman administration's initiative for a ceasefire. Although shocked and angry, President Truman showed restraints. The last disagreement that Truman would allow came when MacArthur sent a letter on April 5, 1951 to House Republican Minority Leader Joseph W. Martin criticizing the administration for its restrictions against launching attacks on mainland China. MacArthur was convinced that Truman's policy in Korea was a policy of appeasement and that he could win the conflict if control of the nuclear arsenal would be turned over to the military. Truman had enough of his insubordination and announced the change of command on April 10, 1951, even before MacArthur had been notified.

History will tell many stories about General Douglas MacArthur. It will tell of his egotism and his disagreements with Truman, of his insubordination and his belief in only his own capabilities of leadership. History will also tell of Japan's admiration and love of him, of his foresight in international conflicts. It will tell of his unique ability to command men and lead armies. Whatever the role he played, MacArthur remains one of the most popular and important names in the history of relations between Asia, China, and the United States.

See also Korean War.

REFERENCES: Charles Willoughby, *MacArthur 1941–1951* (New York, 1954); Michael Schaller, *Douglas MacArthur: The Far Eastern General* (New York, 1989); William Manchester, *American Caesar: Douglas MacArthur 1880–1964* (Boston, MA, 1978).

Eric H. Doss

MacMurray, John Van Antwerp (1881–1960)

John Van Antwerp MacMurray, U.S. Minister to China from 1925 to 1929, was a conservative voice during a transitional time for American policy that was supervised by Secretary of State Frank B. Kellogg. Under Kellogg, U.S. China policy shifted to an independent approach, away from the 1921–1922 Washington Naval Conference model of cooperation with other foreign powers. Kellogg was sympathetic to Chinese nationalism and wanted to revise Sino-American treaties with the aim of restoring China's tariff autonomy and ending extraterritoriality. On the other hand, MacMurray, who had participated in the Washington Conference, believed that China was too disordered, and that offering to renegotiate treaties would signal weakness and encourage the destabilizing force of Chinese nationalism. As he took his ministerial post in Beijing, MacMurray became alarmed by the nationalistic zeal flaring up in China. He referred to the "fanaticism" of the anti-foreign movement in Shanghai in 1925, and saw it as an outburst of only a small portion of the Chinese population, that was nevertheless awakening "instincts and passions hitherto dormant" in the Chinese people. He therefore recommended a policy of firmness. He wanted the U.S. to strictly adhere to the united front with Britain and Japan, forged at the Washington Conference, against Chinese nationalist attempts to unravel the "unequal treaties." MacMurray did not waver from this position, and only reluctantly helped implement the new U.S. policy, which culminated in recognition of the Nationalist Government of Jiang Jieshi in 1928.

MacMurray's experience in Asia was rich. He served as Assistant Chief and then Chief of the Division of Near Eastern Affairs at the State Department (1911–1913). He began specializing in Far Eastern affairs as Secretary of the Beijing Legation (1913–1917), Counselor of the American embassy in Tokyo (1917–1919), and, back at the State Department, Chief of the Division of Far Eastern Affairs (1919–1924). In 1921 he published "Treaties and Agreements with and Concerning China." In the same year he served as expert assistant on Pacific and Far Eastern affairs to American Commissioners at the Washington Conference. He also was an observer for the U.S. government at the Chinese-Japanese negotiations for the settlement of the Shandong question (1921–1922). In 1924 he became Assistant Secretary of State, but one year later he was back in his area of specialization as Minister to China. In this capacity he chaired the American delegation to the Special Conference on the Chinese Customs Tariff (1925–1926).

MacMurray was born in Schenectady, New York in 1881. He attended Princeton University (1898–1902), Columbia Law School in 1903, and was admitted to the New York Bar in 1906. He married Lois R. Goodnow in 1916 and had three children. He died at his home in Norfolk, Connecticut on September 25, 1960.

See also Kellogg, Frank B. (1856–1937).

REFERENCES: Dorothy Borg, *American Policy and the Chinese Revolution, 1925–1928* (New York, 1947); *John Van Antwerp MacMurray Papers* (Seely G. Mudd Manuscript Library, Princeton University); United States Department of State, *Papers Relating to the Foreign Relations of the United States 1925, I* (Washington, DC, 1940).

Mike Wilson

Magruder Mission

The Magruder Mission is the common name of a military mission to China that began in July 1941 and was officially called The American Military Mission to China, or AMMISCA. Brigadier General John Magruder, former military attache in China was chosen to lead the mission.

The purpose of the mission was to ensure the delivery and proper use of Lend-Lease equipment that was being directed to China. Starting with an appeal for aid on March 31, 1941, the United States began to approve weapon shipments to China to help stave off the Japanese invasion. One of the main problems that the United States Army saw with the equipment was that it was destined for untrained military units. In addition to the inherent problems with placing expensive weaponry in untrained hands, the supply lines being used by the Chinese were very primitive and could not support the influx of materiel promised by the United States. The decision was made to send Magruder to China to help equip and train the military and ensure the orderly transport of the equipment. U.S. Additionally, Magruder was charged with acting as a liaison for strategic planning and co-operation with China. When Magruder arrived in October, the operation began in earnest. In addition to helping distribute the newly arrived equipment, he also served the Army by overseeing any other requests for military supplies. This allowed the Army greater control and discretion in approving aid requests. The General's first impression of the Chinese military was apprehensive. He believed the Chinese to possess great potential, but still needed much training and support before they would become a viable force against the Japanese aggression. However, this centered on being able to distribute the supplies that were arriving. The transportation system depended on antiquated railroads and unimproved roads. He urged the War Department to help the Chinese improve the Burma Road, the main supply route used to bring the equipment in. While supplying basic military equipment and road building materiel, Magruder had to prevent the use of high-powered offensive weapons. He understood that if the Chinese attacked with such weapons, the action might prompt the Japanese to attack American interests in the region.

As the infrastructure in China began to improve, more materiel was able to enter the free sections of the country. However, with the war situation getting worse, Magruder decided it was time for him and his contingent to escape. He pulled out of China in June of 1942, ending the AMMISCA.

See also Burma Road.

REFERENCES: Michael Schaller, *The U.S. Crusade in China, 1938–1945* (New York, 1979); D.C. Gupta, *United States Attitude Towards China* (New Delhi, 1969).

Eric H. Doss

Ma Haide (1910–1988) *see* Hatem, George (1910–1988)

Manchukuo

Manchukuo (land of the Manchus) was the name given to the nominally independent state created by action of the Japanese military after the Mukden Insident in September 1931. Textbooks invariably refer to the dubious legality and limited independence of Manchukuo by use of the term "puppet state." It comprised the three current northeast provinces of China — Liaoning, Jilin and Heilongjiang plus Rehe (Jehol) and part of what is now Inner Mongolia. It is bounded on the north and east by the Amur River and Ussuri River, dividing it from Russian trans-Baikal Siberia on the north and Maritime Province on the east. To the west lay Inner and Outer Mongolia and to the south the Gulf of Chihli and Great Wall. It encompassed 550,000 square miles, approximately the area of Alaska. The geographic entity of Manchuria had been the ancestral home of Manchu and Mongol tribes. When the united Manchus conquered China in 1644 to constitute the last imperial dynasty, Qing, the rulers determined that Manchuria was to remain tribal and forbade ethnic Chinese immigration. However, with the weakening of Qing rule in the late 19th Century, Chinese settlers poured into frontier Manchuria. By 1931 the population of 30 million was more than 85% ethnic Chinese with the remainder Manchus, Mongols, ethnic Turks, White Russians, Koreans and Japanese.

In late 19th century, with weakening Chinese control and attractive resources, including warm water ports, Manchuria drew the attention of various outside nations. The Russians were most active on the scene until their defeat in the Russo-Japanese War in 1905. By their victory Japan obtained leaseholds from China on certain key areas — the southern peninsula, Liaodong, and a strip paralleling a rail connection to the interior called the South Manchurian Railway. Within the leased areas the Japanese colonial bureaucracy and South Manchurian Railway Company soon formed an interlocking network that integrated transportation, marketing, banking, travel, and all public services so completely that it was compared to the U.S. Panama Canal Company in its comprehensive management of the area. Protecting the leased areas was an increasingly sophisticated force known as the Kwantung Army, which began to take on an increasingly independent and conspiratorial attitude. Outside the leased areas was Chinese, but increasingly dominated by a powerful warlord, Zhang Zuolin. By 1928 the Japanese position based on leaseholds was under tremendous pressure from a resurgent nationalist movement in China that targeted foreign imperialism. Kwantung Army conspirators assassinated Zhang Zuolin and Japanese settlers formed pressure groups pushing for separating Manchuria from China. Kwantung Army activists began formulating plans for a military coup against the warlord forces of Zhang's son, Zhang Xueliang. It also became apparent that China's leader, Jiang Jieshi, would probably not defend Manchuria, being preoccupied with suppressing the Communist movement in China. On September 18, 1931, the Kwantung Army struck the large but disorganized warlord forces. Scattered fighting continued well into 1932 and a low-level insurgency was never suppressed. Nonetheless, the Kwantung Army blitzkrieg was remarkably successful. The last emperor of the Qing, Aisin Gioro Puyi, of impeccable Manchu lineage, was plucked out of retirement in Tianjin by Kwantung Army agents and was formally installed, with great pomp and ceremony, as "regent" of Manchukuo in March 1932. The city of Changchun in central Manchuria was designated as the capital and renamed Hsinking ("new capital"). The United States adopted a policy of non-recognition of Manchukuo and the League of Nations' Lytton Commission condemned the aggression, causing Japan to withdraw from the League. Manchukuo was recognized by only a handful of fascist regimes. Even in Japan the government was reluctant to embrace the fruits of freelance conspiracy but it was soon apparent that the military could force such recognition, especially with broad public support.

Within Manchukuo, the South Manchurian Railway Company, Japanese colonial apparatus and diplomatic corps, as well as the Kwantung Army, exercised most policymaking functions. The Japanese government made great efforts to settle the Japanese in rural Manchukuo, although never exceeding 25,000. About two million Korean settlers went. Border clashes with the Soviet Union in 1938 and 1939 ended Kwantung Army ambitions to use Manchukuo as a springboard for northward expansion. During the Pacific War there was pressure on Manchukuo to supply raw materials and manufactures for the war. On August 9, 1945, with the Kwantung Army drained of manpower, the Soviets completely overran Manchukuo and stripped it of industrial apparatus. With Japan's surrender, the area was returned to China.

See also Manchuria; Puyi (1906–1967); South Manchurian Railway; World War II.

REFERENCES: Louise Young, *Japan's Total Empire: Manchuria and the Culture of Wartime Imperialism* (Berkeley, CA, 1998); Peter Duus, Ramon Myers and Mark Peattie (eds.), *The Japanese Informal Empire in China, 1895–1937* (Princeton, NJ, 1989); Peter Duus, Ramon Myers and Mark Peattie (eds.), *The Japanese Colonial Empire, 1895–1945* (Princeton, NJ, 1984); Prasenjit Duara, *Sovereignty and Authenticity: Manchukuo and the East Asian Modern* (Lanham, MD, 2003); Takeo Ito, *Life Along the South Manchurian Railway: The Memoirs of Ito Takeo* (New York, 1988).

Dave Egler

Manchuria

The term "Manchuria" is a troublesome imperialist leftover. Intended to refer to the homeland of the Manchus—the ethnic group that produced China's final dynasty, the Qing—the term was improperly assigned initially, never defined exactly, yet gradually reified. Traditionally, the Manchus inhabited only sections of eastern Manchuria, while Mongols, Koreans, Chinese, and other peoples occupied other regions. Geographic realities, however, contributed to Manchuria's functioning in some ways as a coherent region, contributing to the perception that Manchuria was a separable territory. This line of thinking, however, is anathema in the People's Republic of China—today Chinese refer to Manchuria simply as *Dongbei*, meaning the "northeast." (It is worth noting, however, that Koreans also lay claim to parts of Manchuria, as there is a large resident Korean population in the Yanbian Korean Autonomous Region and the ancient Korean kingdom of Koguryo included much of eastern Manchuria.)

Manchuria became the object of 20th century imperialist rivalries, especially between China, Russia, and Japan. The Sino-Japanese War (1894–1895) and the Russo-Japanese War (1904–1905), fought primarily in Manchuria, resulted in the gradual diminution of Chinese authority in favor of Russian in the north and Japanese in the south. Japanese military successes impressed many in the United States and elsewhere, likely encouraging President Theodore Roosevelt to acquiesce in Japanese expansion there and in Korea. Historians usually describe the Russian and Japanese spheres of influence as instances of "informal empire," meaning imperialists held sway indirectly through local allies and semi-governmental organizations, in this case the Russian China Eastern Railway and the Japanese South Manchuria Railway. This proved initially effective, despite Chinese protests, though by the late 1920s Manchuria was increasingly unstable. While a 1929 military incursion demonstrated a Soviet willingness to use force to secure northern Manchuria, a cabal of Japanese responded by effecting the September 18, 1931 Mukden Incident, creating the "puppet-state" of Manchukuo the following year. Rather than confront this more militant and "formal" form of Japanese imperialism, the Soviet Union withdrew, selling the China Eastern Railway to the new "state," and leaving China to confront Japan alone in Manchuria. The U.S., however, quickly stepped forward, in the form of Henry Stimson's doctrine of "non-recognition." China and Japan eventually recognized Japanese control of Manchuria in the Tanggu Truce of May 1933, but the diplomatic confrontation over Manchuria troubled Japanese-American relations through the fall of 1941. After Japan's surrender, the U.S. helped the Nationalists occupy Manchurian cities. This was against the advice of Albert Wedemeyer, however, for there Nationalist troops became encircled, the first casualties of the Chinese Civil War of 1945–1949. This was because Manchuria was becoming, partly with Soviet assistance, the main base area for the Chinese Communist Party. The showdown there, ending in the fall of 1948, foretold much of the civil war to come—an acceleration of the revolution, larger deployments of Communist forces, and a rapid Nationalist collapse.

Manchuria subsequently played key roles in the new state, as Manchurian industries, rebuilt with Soviet aid, were initially China's most developed. They were soon threatened, however, when American troops drew close to the border during the Korean War and General Douglas

MacArthur considered destroying Manchuria's industrial and transportation infrastructure. Not all threats, however, were external, as Gao Gang (1905–1954)—who ruled Manchuria from 1949 to 1954—appeared to have gained a measure of regional autonomy. Gao's purge was the first major purge of the new state, targeting not only Gao but also the Soviet presence — Soviet troops occupied Dalian and Lushun until 1955. Anti-Soviet feelings did not emerge publicly though until the Sino-Soviet split and military confrontations on Manchuria's borders.

See also Manchukuo; Puyi (1906–1967); South Manchuria Railway; Stimson Doctrine; World War II; Civil War (1945–1949).

REFERENCES: Thomas Lahusen (ed.), *Harbin and Manchuria: Place, Space, and Identity* (Durham, NC, 2001); Chong-Sik Lee, *Revolutionary Struggle in Manchuria: Chinese Communism and Soviet Interest, 1922–1945* (Berkeley, CA, 1983); Robert H. G. Lee, *The Manchurian Frontier in Qing History* (Cambridge, MA, 1970); Gavan McCormack, *Zhang Zuolin in Northeast China, 1911–1928: China, Japan, and the Manchurian Idea* (Stanford, CA, 1977); Felix Patrikeeff, *Russian Politics in Exile: The Northeast Asian Balance of Power, 1924–1931* (Oxford, 2002); Bill Sewell, "Postwar Japan and Manchuria," in David W. Edgington (ed.), *Japan at the Millennium: Joining Past and Future* (Vancouver, 2003).

Bill Sewell

Manchurian Incident *see* Mukden Incident

Mansfield, Mike (1903–2001)

Mike Mansfield rose from the coalmines of Montana to become one of the most powerful members of the U.S. Senate. Mansfield was born in New York City in 1903 but grew up in Montana with his aunt. He served in the U.S. military from 1917 to 1922 and developed a lifelong interest in China during that time. He returned to Montana and worked in the mines, then enrolled in a special high school completion/college degree program at the University of Montana. He wished to teach school but was told his Catholic faith made that impossible, so he returned to school, earned a master's degree and taught on the faculty from 1934 to 1942. From 1942 to 1952, he represented Montana in the House of Representatives, and from 1952 to 1976 he was a U.S. Senator from Montana. From 1977 to 1989, he was the American Ambassador to Japan.

Mansfield supported American policy toward China from 1942 to 1964; the only exception was his public denunciation of the Eisenhower administration for threatening criminal action against a journalist who had visited China in violation of the American travel ban. For the most part, Mansfield focused on domestic programs and downplayed Asian affairs. As the American military commitment in South Vietnam escalated in the 1960s, Mansfield concluded that an end to American non-recognition of Communist China would be a key to resolving the conflict. Mansfield decided to send a message to the Communist Chinese Premier Zhou Enlai using Prince Sihanouk of Cambodia as a go-between. President Lyndon B. Johnson supported the effort. Secretary of State Dean Rusk did not oppose it, but he told Mansfield that he had a hunch the overture would be futile. Rusk was correct; no reply ever came from the Chinese. Mansfield tried again during the Nixon administration, and eventually heard from the Chinese that they wanted Mansfield to visit Beijing. Before any arrangements could be made, Richard Nixon announced his famous visit to Beijing that took place in 1972. The visit was full of glowing pronouncements that glossed over the festering difference between the two nations. Mansfield would travel to China three times from 1973 to 1976 to assist in the thorny work needed to normalize Sino-American relations.

Mansfield was a rare example of a senator who worked hard to master the complex international issues that the U.S. confronted as a superpower. Although overshadowed by Nixon and Kissinger, his role in the normalization of Sino-American relations was substantial and commendable.

REFERENCES: Francis R. Valeo, *Mike Mansfield* (Armonk, NY, 1999); Gregory A. Olson, *Mike Mansfield and Vietnam* (East Lansing, MI, 1995).

Michael J. Polley

Mao Tse-tung (1893–1976) *see* Mao Zedong (1893–1976)

Mao Zedong (1893–1976)

Mao Zedong, the most important Chinese Communist leader in the 20th century, attended the first national meeting of the Chinese Communist Party (CCP) in 1921 as one of its twelve founders. Believing that peasantry was a major societal force and that a violent revolution was the right course for China's Communist movement, he organized rural-centered armed revolts in Hunan in 1927. After the first CCP-Guomindang (GMD) coalition collapsed, he established the first revolutionary base in 1928 in Jinggangshan, where he became chairman of the Executive Committee of the Chinese Soviet Republic in 1931. He led the 9,600-km Long March in 1934–1935 to save the Red Army and find a new base away from Nationalist leader Jiang Jieshi's campaigns, emerging as the unquestionable man at the top of the leadership. In World War II, his successful strategy of cooperating with Jiang and mobilizing guerrilla warfare behind Japanese lines increased CCP membership from 40,000 in 1937 to 1.2 million in 1945 with nearly 1 million regular troops and 2 million militia. He became chairman of the Central Military Commission (CMC) in 1937, chairman of both the Politburo and Secretariat in 1943, and chairman of the Central Committee in 1945. Unwilling to cooperate with each other after World War II, Mao and Jiang ended their second united front and resumed the civil war in 1945–1949.

After Jiang lost the war and relocated the seat of the GMD government from the mainland to Taiwan, Mao established the People's Republic of China (PRC) in 1949 and became its first president. He declared that the new China would favor the Soviet Union and signed the Sino-Soviet Treaty of Friendship and Alliance with Soviet leader Joseph Stalin in Moscow in February 1950. The Truman administration refused to recognize the new Communist state and maintained its diplomatic relations with Jiang in Taiwan. In October 1950, Mao decided to dispatch Chinese troops to the Korean War when Stalin asked him to rescue the North Korean regime after the UN forces crossed the 38th Parallel and pressed northward. He mobilized the one-year-old Chinese republic to fight the "War to Resist America and Aid Korea" against the most powerful army in the world. More than 3 million Chinese troops were confronted by U.S. air and naval superiority and suffered heavy casualties. Having noted that the UN forces could not be driven out of Korea by force, Mao began negotiations with the U.S. and South Korea in 1951. The truce agreement was signed in July 1953. China's intervention in the Korean War led the PRC and U.S. into their most hostile period in history.

Mao's commitments to Vietnam, Indochina, and Communist movements elsewhere reflected his ideology and world-view. His attacks on GMD-held offshore islands in the Taiwan Strait caused serious crises when President Dwight D. Eisenhower ordered the U.S. Seventh Fleet to protect Taiwan. Presidents John F. Kennedy and Lyndon B. Johnson continued America's trade embargo against the PRC and excluded it from the UN and most international organizations. To overcome domestic problems, Mao launched radical campaigns one after another, such as the Great Leap Forward in 1958–1960 and the Great Proletarian Cultural Revolution in 1966–1976, which caused deaths in the tens of millions. After

the Sino-Soviet split in the 1960s, Mao criticized Moscow as "socialist imperialist." He tried to form a world alliance to stop "Soviet expansion" through an improvement of China's relations with the major Western powers. The PRC became a UN member and resumed its seat in the Security Council in 1971. Mao normalized China's relationship with the U.S. by inviting President Richard Nixon to Beijing in February 1972 and issuing the Shanghai Communique. In 1973, China and America opened liaison offices in each other's capitals, and George Bush became the chief representative from Washington in 1974. President Gerald Ford visited Beijing to negotiate with Mao and cut off official relations with Taiwan.

Mao's new policy eased Cold War tensions in Asia and helped bring certain hostilities in Asia to an end, including the Vietnam peace agreement and normalization of Sino-Japanese relations. Since 1974 he suffered from Parkinson's disease. Mao died in Beijing on September 9, 1976.

See also Maoism.

REFERENCES: Chen Jian, *Mao's China and the Cold War* (Chapel Hill, NC, 2001); Philip Short, *Mao: A Life* (London, 1999); Xiaobing Li and Hongshan Li (eds.), *China and the United States* (Lanham, MD, 1998).

Xiaobing Li

Maoism

China's losses during World War I created a wave of nationalism and intellectual exploration amongst Chinese students, including Mao Zedong. Mao was influenced by the successful antimonarchical movements in Russia and Japan, and after the Russian Revolution in 1917–1918, Mao became an adherent of Marxism and Leninism. He began to synthesize a series of political precepts through which he could apply the Western and Bolshevik ideals of political and economic egalitarianism to China's highly stratified and agrarian-based society.

Mao's analysis of China's political and social conditions and his prescriptions for change developed over a period of approximately 40 years, between 1925 and 1965. In his earliest treatise, *Report on the Peasant Movement in Hunan* (1926), Mao emphasized the revolutionary potential of the agricultural peasantry, thereby contradicting Marx and Engels who had characterized European peasants as ultra-conformists incapable of radical political action. To guide a peasant-based revolution, Mao realized that a political party would be needed, and he adopted Leninist party-building tactics as a model for the Chinese Communist Party (CCP). Uniquely, however, Mao insisted that the Party observe the peasants' wishes in policy-making, utilizing the "mass line" approach. As head of the Party in the 1930s, Mao ordered that land, tax, and debt redistribution campaigns benefiting peasants be given priority. Mao believed that a violent struggle against the landowners was inevitable, and declared that "political power grows out of the barrel of a gun." He organized an army under the Party's control, but after Japan's invasion of China in 1937 he ordered that the Communists embrace temporary coalitions with class enemies against the greater evil of foreign occupation. Simultaneously, Mao devised a complex theory of guerrilla combat tactics, which emphasized flexibility, "strategic retreat" to conserve strength, and hit-and-run insurgency operations that demoralized the enemy. After Japan's defeat in 1945 the Communists combined land reform campaigns with rural-based guerrilla operations against the pro-Western Chinese Nationalists. By late 1949 Mao's Communists had prevailed in China's civil war, and the formation of Mao's People's Republic of China was declared on October 1, 1949.

In developing new theories of governance Mao prioritized the resolution of "contradictions" in society, emphasizing the transcendence of mutual obstacles to achieve mutual benefits. For example, in the new People's Republic the needs of the central government for control over agricultural output and the needs of local Party personnel to enlist people in the new Communist system were met through the creation of "people's communes." These large-scale agricultural collectives combined farming with communal living under the active tutelage of Party cadres. Mao later used the communes to implement his 1958–1959 "Great Leap Forward" campaign to rapidly increase China's agricultural and industrial output.

The failure of the "Great Leap" compelled Mao to expand his theoretical conception of revolution. He claimed that all governments were subject to complacency and corruption, and that the people would occasionally have to rebel against their leaders. Mao's ideas of "continuous revolution" were introduced in China in mid 1960s through the Chinese Great Proletarian Cultural Revolution, in which virtually every symbol of tradition and authority, including the Communist Party itself, came under attack. In the anarchic conditions that resulted, Mao himself was nearly driven from power. Eventually the military was deployed to restore order. The excesses of the Cultural Revolution exposed Mao's fallibility, and after his death in 1976, a new party leadership coalesced around Deng Xiaoping, who promised to moderate Maoism with practicality

and greater economic autonomy for individual Chinese.

See also Mao Zedong (1893–1976); Deng Xiaoping (1904–1997); Cultural Revolution.

REFERENCES: Jerome Chen, *Mao and the Chinese Revolution* (London, 1965), Jack Gray. *Mao Tse-tung* (Valley Forge, PA, 1974), Stuart Schram, *The Political Thought of Mao Tse-tung* (New York, 1969).

Laura M. Calkins

Marco Polo Bridge Incident (1937)

The Marco Polo Bridge Incident of July 1937, also known as the China Incident, ignited World War II in East Asia between China and Japan. During the 1930s, few Chinese had any illusions about Japanese imperialist designs on their nation. Hungry for raw materials and pressed by the problem of overpopulation, the Japanese militarists initiated the seizure of China's Manchuria after the Mukden Incident in September 18, 1931. Japan then established Puyi, ex-emperor of the Qing Dynasty, as head of the puppet regime of Manchukuo in 1932. The loss of Manchuria, the industrial base of China, worsened the existing depression in China's economy. The League of Nations reacted to the occupation of Manchuria with an investigation resulting in the Lytton Report. In defiance, the Japanese withdrew from the League and began to push from Manchuria into northern China. Chinese resistance to Japanese encroachments finally stiffened on July 7, 1937, when a skirmish between Chinese and Japanese troops took place outside Beijing near the Marco Polo Bridge (Lu Gou Qiao). This clash not only marked the beginning of open, but undeclared, war between China and Japan, but also hastened the formal announcement of the second United Front between the Guomindang (Nationalists) and the Chinese Communist Party against Japan.

On the night of July 7, 1937, Chinese troops fired on Japanese troops conducting field exercises at the Marco Polo Bridge. After an exchange of fire, the Japanese commander found that one of his soldiers was missing. The Japanese approached the nearby city Wanping and asked the Chinese authorities for permission to enter the city to search for the missing man. Upon refusal, the Japanese attacked and occupied the city of Wanping on July 8. Konoe Fumimaro, the new Japanese prime minister, then allowed Japanese army to punish China. Ten days after the Marco Polo Bridge incident, Jiang Jieshi, leaders of the Republic of China, sent troops to the north into the demilitarized areas in accordance with the He-Umezu Truce Agreement of 1935. Jiang then called on Chinese people to resist Japan, receiving encouragement from his German advisor General Alexander von Falkenhausen who predicted that Chinese forces would drive the Japanese "over the Great Wall." Although his optimism was unjustified, Jiang had no other choice but to fight while hoping for assistance from the United States and other Western powers. On July 28, Japanese bombers attacked three cities. On August 13, Japan began terror bombing of Shanghai. By 1938, Japan controlled most of northern China and most of its coast, forcing Jiang to retreat from Nanjing to the western city of Chongqing. Japan now fought a protracted war.

See also World War II.

REFERENCES: F. F. Liu, *A Military History of Modern China* (Princeton, NJ, 1956); David Lu, *From Marco Polo Bridge to Pearl Harbor* (Washington, DC, 1961); James Morley, *The China Quagmire* (New York, 1983).
Yuwu Song

Marshall, George C. (1880–1959)3

George C. Marshall was one of World War II's greatest heroes, and his reputation was further enhanced by his role in the recovery of postwar Europe. After graduation from the Virginia Military Institute in 1901, Marshall served in various military posts in Asia, Europe, and in the homeland. During the First World War, he won high praise for his military planning and obtained recognition and friendship from General John J. Pershing whom he served as Aide-de-Camp. In 1938 he took the post of Assistant Chief of Staff of the Army. On September 1, 1939, Marshall was appointed as army chief of staff with the rank of Major General. Afterward he became heavily involved in the preparation for war. Over the next four years, the U.S. Army expanded from 175,000 to more than 8 million. He became a key figure in the making of allied military strategy in World War II and served as a member of the Joint Chiefs of Staff and of the Combined Chiefs of Staff. Marshall enjoyed the great confidence of President Franklin D. Roosevelt and accompanied the President to attend many war conferences. He won praise from Winston Churchill, the British Prime Minister, who called Marshall "the true organizer of victory." Marshall was promoted to General of the Army in December 1944 and retired from his post next November.

Marshall's first contact with China occurred earlier in his career when he observed the Russo-Japanese War, and received permission from the Japanese to visit battlegrounds in Korea and Manchuria. He returned to China in 1924 when he was assigned as the executive commander and later the commander of the 15th U.S. Infantry stationed in Tianjin where he befriended Joseph W. Stilwell. When Marshall became Commandant of Fort Benning, he asked Stilwell to be the Director of Combat Training. Since Marshall recognized Stilwell's training and his good knowledge of China, he recommended General Stilwell for the post of the Chief of Staff of the China Theater in January 1942. In the tension and friction between Stilwell and the Nationalist Government, Marshall gave Stilwell his full support. Marshall was further involved in the Chinese affairs when he was sent by President Harry S. Truman as special envoy to mediate the Chinese Civil War in December 1945. Though his mission did bring about peace for a short time in early 1946, the civil war broke out again. In January 1947, Marshall returned to the United States to become Secretary of State. The most notable achievement of his secretaryship was the execution of the European Recovery Plan or what became known as the "Marshall Plan." With regard to the civil war in China, Marshall believed that peace was impossible, and over the next two years, did his best to disentangle the United States with China's civil war. From September 1950 to September 1951, Marshall served as Secretary of Defense. During this period, he assisted Truman in preventing the escalation of the Korean War.

Because of his contributions to world peace, George C. Marshall was awarded the Nobel Peace Price in 1953. Marshall died at Walter Reed Hospital at Washington, D.C. on October 16, 1959.

See also Civil War (1945–1949); Truman, Harry S. (1884–1972); Acheson, Dean (1873–1971); China White Paper; Marshall Mission.

REFERENCES: Larry I. Bland (ed.), *George C. Marshall Interviews and Reminiscences for Forrest C. Pogue* (Lexington, VA, 1991); Larry I. Bland and Sharon Ritenour Stevens (eds.), *The Papers of George Catlett Marshall* (Baltimore, MD, 1981–2003); Forrest C. Pogue, *George C. Marshall* (New York, 1963–1987).
Chen-mian Wang

Marshall Mission

George C. Marshall was one of the greatest figures in America during the 1930s and 1940s. He served as Chief of Staff of the U.S. Army beginning in 1939, and many credited him as the architect of America's victory in the Second World War. He retired from the U.S. Army in November 1945, but accepted a request from President Harry S. Truman to lead a mission to China to find a way to prevent the seemingly inevitable war between Jiang Jieshi's Nationalist government and the Communist movement of Mao Zedong.

General Patrick Hurley had been the U.S. Ambassador to China, but he resigned in November 1945. Failure of the negotiations between Jiang and Mao frustrated him and Hurley claimed that

State Department officials supported Mao when, to the contrary, they were only predicting an ultimate Communist victory given their analysis of the situation in China. Truman wanted Marshall to go to China to arrange a truce in the civil war, help the Nationalist regime regain control of China, establish a coalition government, but not involve the United States militarily. Marshall arrived in China in January 1946, and he set about meeting Jiang and Mao. He needed to bring the Communists into the central government with a share of power, and to reduce the size of the contending military forces. For a while, there was a halt in the fighting and in the jockeying for position as both sides waited to see the outcome of Marshall's mission and recommendations to Truman. That is, the Communists did agree to a truce in January 1946, and they acted interested in Marshall's goal of a coalition government, participating in the Political Consultative Conference, which he established. However, the real issue was which contending group, Nationalists or Communists, best represented the nationalist movement begun by Sun Zhongshan and broadened by the May 4th Movement. Thus, the negotiations in Chongqing were a sideshow; the main drama was unfolding on the plains of North China and in Manchuria, where the Communists felt they could win a great victory. Marshall returned to Washington in March 1946 to help with U.S. financial assistance; while he was away, the fighting resumed in April. At first, the Communists won in Manchuria, and then Jiang began committing more and more of his army. From July to September 1946, the Nationalists won a series of victories, confident of their five-to-one superiority in manpower. Meanwhile, Mao and his supporters felt Jiang and his regime were "paper tigers" they could blow away with well-timed, well-aimed blows. And so the short-lived effort at negotiation failed before this military contest of strength.

Marshall ultimately failed, and likely no one could have succeeded in bringing Jiang and Mao to any agreement short of a military contest. He returned to the United States in December 1946, and blamed the deteriorating situation on "extremist elements on both sides." Later, Marshall would denounce the Chinese Communists as "irreconcilable," and the Nationalists as "reactionary," and thus a pox on both of their houses. Soon thereafter, in summer 1947, President Truman would send yet another military man, U.S. Army General Albert C. Wedemeyer, to secure a peace. But there was little that America could do in the 1940s to enforce a peace or prevent a Communist conquest of China. The answer to the future of China rested with the Chinese people.

See also Civil War (1945–1949); Truman, Harry S. (1884–1972); China White Paper; Marshall, George C. (1880–1959).

REFERENCES: Larry I. Bland (ed.), *George C. Marshall's Mediation Mission to China, December 1945-January 1947* (Lexington, VA, 1998); Peng Deng, *China's Crisis and Revolution Through American Lenses, 1944–1949* (Lanham, MD, 1994); Margaret B. Denning, *The Sino-American Alliance in World War II: Cooperation and Dispute Among Nationalists, Communists, and Americans* (New York, 1986); Suzanne Pepper, *Civil War in China: The Political Struggle, 1945–1949* (Lanham, MD, 1999); Chonghai Petey Shaw, *The Role of the United States in Chinese Civil Conflicts, 1944–1949* (Salt Lake City, UT, 1991).

Charles M. Dobbs

May Fourth Movement (1919)

The term refers to both the student political demonstrations of May 4, 1919 in Tiananmen Square, Beijing, as well as a much broader and complex cultural, emotional, and political movement that preceded and followed the May Fourth Incident. Together they are presumed to represent the birth of modern China. The incident involved about 3,000 students from thirteen colleges and universities meeting in Beijing to protest the Versailles Treaty terms for China and to awaken the masses all over the country to an awareness of China's plight. Ignoring police orders to desist, the students assembled in Tiananmen Square and marched toward the foreign legation quarter, calling on Chinese of all classes to rally against foreign imperialism as well as the passivity of the warlord regime in Beijing. Despite only one fatality and thirty-two arrests in clashes with police, support for the students' cause was spontaneous among both businessmen and workers in the major cities of China. As a consequence, both Chinese delegations (Beijing and Guangzhou) at the Paris Peace Conference refused to sign the Versailles Treaty and withdrew. It also marked the beginning of a profound questioning of the nature of Chinese culture and society as well as an effort to understand why the Revolution of 1911 had been so superficial.

The roots of the May Fourth Movement were to be found in the New Culture Movement most notably represented by the journal *New Youth*, founded by Chen Duxiu in 1915 and devoted to a full-scale attack on traditional Confucian culture. Chen urged the building of a modern society based on the independence of individuals committed to Mr. Democracy and Mr. Science. Centered in Beijing University, the movement represented a heady period in Chinese cultural history when everything seemed possible. Intellectuals such as Cai Yuanpei, Lu Xun, Hu Shi, and Chen

Duxiu enthusiastically explored the ideas of Lenin, John Dewey, Margaret Sanger, Rabindranath Tagore, Henrik Ibsen, and Bertrand Russell in the search for a new China. Hu Shi referred to the movement as an effort to reorganize the national heritage. The short-term consequence of the May Fourth Movement was youthful enthusiasm for the revitalized Guomindang (GMD) and the new Chinese Communist Party (CCP) founded in 1921 by Chen Duxiu and Li Dazhao, dean and librarian, respectively of Beijing University.

See also Dewey, John (1859–1952); Paris Peace Conference; Treaty of Versailles (1919); Chinese Revolution (1911).

REFERENCES: Cezong Zhou, *The May Fourth Movement: Intellectual Revolution in Modern China* (Cambridge, MA, 1960); Vera Schwarcz, *The Chinese Enlightenment: Intellectuals and the Legacy of the May Fourth Movement of 1919* (Berkeley, CA, 1986); Yusheng Lin, *The Crisis of Chinese Consciousness: Radical Antitraditionalism in the May Fourth Era* (Madison, WI, 1979).

Errol M. Clauss

May Thirtieth Movement (1925)

The May Thirtieth Movement was sparked when British and Japanese policemen of the Shanghai International Settlement fired into a crowd of Chinese students and workers. The demonstrators demanded the release of several students arrested in earlier labor disputes and protested against the militarism of the Beijing "warlord" regime as well as the foreign imperialism, which it seemed to accept. After a mere ten second warning to disperse, the police killed eleven of the demonstrators and left twenty more wounded.

The outrage at the massacre was immediate and quickly spread across China, with demonstration after demonstration in support of the "May Thirtieth Martyrs," some of them involving violent clashes with British and Japanese forces. The unrest that had began with the May 30 demonstrations was never contained and led directly to the National Revolution of 1926–1928, which overthrew the Beijing government and brought to power the Guomindang (GMD) regime of Jiang Jieshi. Within days the GMD challenged the faltering Beijing regime by announcing a new repudiationist national government of the Republic of China in Guangzhou. By the end of the month the massive Hong Kong strike and boycott had begun, rallying both radical and middle class support for an awakened China.

The roots of the May Thirtieth Movement are to be found in the echoes of the May Fourth Movement of 1919, the Soviet-sponsored United Front (GMD-CCP) of 1924 and the economically devastating warlord conflicts of the same year. To a British diplomat, May 30 was "like the fall of the Bastille" in European history. Many foreigners in China, including diplomats, sensed immediately that significant and enduring change was at hand. Like May Fourth, May Thirtieth had a significant cultural context. Shanghai intellectual Cheng Fangwu proclaimed that the Chinese literature moved from "literary revolution" to "revolutionary literature." On the whole, nationalism remained a permanent part of modern Chinese politics for all classes.

REFERENCES: N. Clifford, *Spoilt Children of Empire: Westerners in Shanghai and the Chinese Revolution of the 1920s* (Hanover, NH, 1991); A. Waldron, *From War to Nationalism: China's Turning Point, 1924–1925* (Cambridge, UK, 1995); C. M. Wilbur, *The Nationalist Revolution in China, 1923–1928* (Cambridge, UK, 1984); R. Rigby, *The May 30 Movement* (Canberra, 1980); D. Borg, *American Policy and the Chinese Revolution, 1925–1928* (New York, 1968).

Errol M. Clauss

McCarthy, Joseph R. (1908–1957)

Republican Senator Joseph R. McCarthy led a campaign of fear that Communists infiltrated the U.S. government in the early 1950s. McCarthy was an intelligent but intellectually lazy man who understood that details, no matter how dubious their source, led credibility to any argument. He was nicknamed "Tailgunner Joe" because he had claimed to have served as a tailgunner on bombing raids during World War II, although such claims were false. McCarthy entered the Senate in 1947. An ambitious man, he found in anti-Communism the cause he sought to propel him into the national spotlight.

Following the Communist victory in China in 1949, McCarthy convinced many Americans that the Communist menace came not only from outside the U.S., but also from within. Beginning with a speech in February 1950 in Wheeling, West Virginia, in which he claimed that he had a list of 205 Communists who were then working for the State Department, McCarthy rocketed to national prominence with his claims of widespread Communist infiltration in the United States government. The "loss" of China to the Communists was blamed on American Communists and Communist sympathizers working in the State Department. While McCarthy seldom offered specifics, the China Hands were the obvious targets of his claim. He convinced the nation that thousands of Americans who were secretly committed to the overthrow of democratic government were working in that very government. Although never able to prove his claims, he spread fear across the nation. He responded to questions about his "facts" by making louder and more spectacular charges. He went so far as to accuse one of the nation's top experts on the Far East, Owen Lattimore, of being the "top Soviet espionage agent" in the country. No one in the nation was immune to his unfounded and usually baseless charges. McCarthy accused no less a respected figure as General George C. Marshall, head of the Army during World War II and a post-war Secretary of State, as a "member of the largest conspiracy the world had ever known," insinuating that the fall of China to Communism had been assisted by if not actually orchestrated by Marshall.

McCarthy's height of power lasted roughly 1950 to 1954. His downfall came when he overreached himself. The election of Republican Dwight D. Eisenhower as President in 1952 had led many in the federal government to expect a diminishing of the hysteria. Instead McCarthy increased his rhetoric, leading him in 1954 to accuse the Army itself of being soft on Communism. The resulting Army-McCarthy Hearings, carried across the nation on the relatively new medium of television, laid the Senator's tactics open. Against the gentlemanly demeanor of the Army's counsel, Joseph Welch, McCarthy appeared a bully and a bungler.

Following the negative reaction to his behavior at the televised hearings, McCarthy turned increasingly on his senatorial colleagues. Sensing that the tide had turned, the Senate voted to condemn McCarthy by a vote of 67 to 22 for Contempt of the Senate. Eisenhower later claimed to have allowed McCarthy to continue his rants in the belief that McCarthy's own excesses would eventually be his undoing. Three years after his censure by the Senate, following years of heavy alcohol abuse that had ruined his health, he died at the age of 48. To his death McCarthy never wavered from his stated belief that a well-organized Communist conspiracy had infiltrated the United States government.

See also Cold War; McCarthyism.

REFERENCES: Robert C. Goldston, *The American Nightmare: Senator Joseph R. McCarthy and Politics of Hate* (Indianapolis, IN, 1974); Joseph Esherick, *Lost Chance in China: The World War II Dispatches of John S. Service* (New York, 1974); E. J. Kahn, *The China Hands: America's Foreign Service Officers and What Befell Them* (New York, 1975).

Barry Stentiford

McCarthyism

The term "McCarthyism" came from the tactics used by Senator Joseph McCarthy, Republican senator from Minnesota, during his crusade against alleged Communists in the U.S. government in the early 1950s. The Communist victory in the Chinese civil war led to charges that sympathetic State Department employees had betrayed Jiang Jieshi and his Nationalist government and allowed the Communists to win the civil war. McCarthy's tactics were to use loud public attacks against prominent people and entire sections of the United States government. The larger the target and the more outrageous the allegation, the better the tactic worked. As a result of his attacks, the State Department's "China Hands," specialists with long experience in China who had predicted the Communist victory, were shuffled into obscure assignments and their expertise wasted. Men such as John P. Davies, Oliver E. Clubb, John C. Vincent, and John Stewart fell under suspicion and were relegated to humiliating and unimportant positions at a time when the United States had little idea of what was happening in China.

McCarthy was an intelligent man and a talented performer. When facts were not available, he was able to make up specific "facts" to add credibility to his charges. He was not, however, a disciplined man, and was unable to be consistent with his fabricated statistics and accusations. The term "McCarthyism" to describe the tactics used by Senator McCarthy was coined by political cartoonist Herbert Block, who used the pen name "Herblock." The tactic was not new with McCarthy, being a favorite tool of demagogues and petty despots since the involvement of mass participation in society. However, with a public that followed newspapers carefully, and the exposure that a national media gave him, McCarthy was ably to bluff and bully his way to becoming the most feared man in America for a few years. Politicians from both major American political parties feared being labeled a Communist by McCarthy and thus avoided attacking him or his methods until he was discredited during the Army-McCarthy hearings. However the right wing of the Republican Party had used and aided McCarthy to win elections. Richard M. Nixon, an early supporter of McCarthy, was nominated as the Vice Presidential candidate under Dwight D. Eisenhower for the 1952 election largely to appease the McCarthyites. The tactic worked as Eisenhower was not attacked by the McCarthyites and Nixon became a nationally known politician who eventually won the Presidency in 1968.

McCarthy was censured by the Senate in December 1954, following the lessening of the fear of Communism after the end of fighting in Korea and the death of Stalin. The downfall of McCarthy and the discrediting of his tactics led politicians who had risen on his coattails to disassociate themselves from McCarthy and his tactics. Although both the Republican and Democratic parties remained staunchly anti-Communist, the excesses of McCarthy led to a backing away from publicly labeling of political opponents as Communists. Instead, politicians increasingly used the charge of an opponent being "soft on Communism," rather than being agents of a world wide Communist conspiracy.

McCarthyism affected much of the United States government, and society at large, but its greatest and most damaging impact was on the Far East section of the State Department. The destruction of the careers of top experts on China from allegations of being sympathetic to the Communists, if not Communists themselves, crippled the State Department's ability to provide realistic appraisals of the intentions of the Chinese government to the executive branch. The resulting inept handling of the Far East had a serious impact on the conduct of the Korean War, as well as the blundering path that led to American involvement in the Vietnam War. Although most specifically applied to politicians who use anti-Communism and public fears of Communist influence in America as a vehicle to gain political advantage, the term is also used to describe many public crusades not connected with Communism. Any public crusade where the mere accusation of association can end a career has the potential to revive the type of fear and attack on freedom that was McCarthyism.

See also McCarthy, Joseph R. (1908–1957); Cold War.

REFERENCES: Thomas C. Reeves (ed.), *McCarthyism* (Malabar, FL, 1985); Earls Lathami, *The Meaning of McCarthyism* (Boston, MA, 1973); Ellen Schnecken, *The Age of McCarthyism* (Boston, MA, 1994).

Barry Stentiford

McKinley, William (1943–1901)

As President of the United States from 1877 to 1901, William McKinley presided over an administration that increased the American presence in the Pacific by annexing the Philippines and Hawaii following the Spanish-American War of 1898. This territorial expansion furthered American economic and strategic interest in China; culminating in the Open Door notes of Secretary of State John Hay and military intervention to suppress the Chinese Boxer insurgency.

McKinley was born in Niles, Ohio. After serving in the Civil War, he practiced law in Canton, Ohio. Entering politics, he served as a Republican Congressman from 1876 until 1891. He gained the support of the business community with his support of protectionism in the McKinley Tariff (1890). With the patronage of industri-

alist Mark Hanna, McKinley secured the governorship of Ohio (1892–1896). In 1896, he narrowly defeated the Democratic candidate William Jennings Bryan for the Presidency. McKinley was soon embroiled in the Cuban insurgency against Spain, which was encouraged by newspaper editors such as William Randolph Hearst and Joseph Pulitzer. Following the sinking of the battleship *Maine* in Havana Harbor on February 15, 1898, the United States declared war on Spain. With the acquisition of the Philippines and the island of Guam in the peace negotiations, the United States became a Pacific power. Secretary of State Hay turned to William Rockhill, the State Department's China expert, to formulate a Far Eastern policy. Rockhill asserted that a stable and viable Chinese state was essential for the United States to further its economic and strategic position in the region. To bolster the deteriorating Manchu Dynasty, Hay dispatched diplomatic notes to the major powers that had acquired spheres of influence in China. Hay's notes called for these powers to not discriminate against the trade of other nations and to not interfere with Chinese customs service collection of tariff duties. The later provision would support the integrity of the Chinese state. Although the replies to John Hay were ambiguous, no nation was prepared to directly challenge the American position, and the McKinley administration was able to announce that American interests in China were preserved.

Nevertheless, relations between the United States and China were strained by American discriminatory practices against Chinese immigrants, as well as growing Chinese violence against American missionaries. To protect Westerners besieged by the Boxers, a Chinese nationalist society, the McKinley administration proposed that military action be limited to northern China and that the territorial integrity of China be preserved. The American policy was implemented in the September 1901 protocol ending the conflict. The Chinese government agreed to pay more than $300 million in indemnities to the major powers, but the territorial integrity of China was preserved by the McKinley administration.

In 1900, the expansionist policies of the McKinley administration were seemingly endorsed by the American electorate as the incumbent once again defeated Bryan, who this time waged an anti-imperialist campaign. Shortly after beginning his second term, McKinley was shot on September 6, 1901 while attending the Pan-American Exposition in Buffalo and died nine days later. The McKinley policies of furthering American interests by fostering stability in China were continued by his successor Theodore Roosevelt.

See also Boxer Rebellion (1900); Boxer Protocol; Open Door Policy.

REFERENCES: Brian P. Damiani, *Advocates of Empire: William McKinley, the Senate, and American Expansion* (New York, 1987); John M. Dobson, *Reticent Expansionism: The Foreign Policy of William McKinley* (Pittsburgh, PE, 1988); Kevin Phillips, *William McKinley* (New York, 2003).

Ron Briley

Military Assistance Advisory Group in Taiwan (MAAG)

Impending defeat in the Chinese Civil War in 1948–1949 forced the pro-Western Nationalist Chinese government, led by Jiang Jieshi, to flee from the mainland of China for the offshore island of Taiwan (Formosa). Some 2 million servicemen, officials, and political refugees from the Chinese Communists on the mainland resettled on the island, which became the home of the exiled Nationalist government.

Since its founding in October 1949, the Communist-led People's Republic of China had regularly declared that Taiwan must be re-integrated with the mainland. Senator Pat McCarran of Nevada proposed deploying American military personnel to train Nationalist troops and lead them in the field, if necessary. After the outbreak of war on the Korean peninsula in June 1950, President Harry S. Truman agreed that Taiwan's defense was essential to the containment of Communism. He announced that the U.S. would defend a "strategic perimeter" in East Asia, including the island of Taiwan. Communist violations of this perimeter, he suggested, would spark American military reprisals. In early 1951 an American survey evaluated the Nationalists' war preparedness and found serious deficiencies in both training and equipment. The Truman administration decided to open a supply and training headquarters on Taiwan to coordinate and deliver aid to the Nationalist military. The creation of a "military assistance advisory group," or MAAG, for Taiwan was announced on April 21, 1951, and on May 1, U.S. Army Major General William C. Chase arrived in Taibei to take up duty as the MAAG Chief in Taiwan. The MAAG office, with its broad military training programs and amply financed weapons and equipment transfer operations, soon came to dominate the American presence on Taiwan. Even American diplomatic representatives based at the U.S. Embassy in Taibei regularly deferred to MAAG protocols and policies. Under MAAG's influence, the Nationalist military was transformed from a disheveled army with outdated weaponry into a well-armed modern force modeled on the United States' own three-pronged service structure, with distinct air, naval, and land forces. During the early 1950s the Nationalist Air Force, in particular, received state-of-the-art communications and electronics equipment, as well as recent models of U.S. fighter aircraft, through the MAAG office in Taiwan. The costly Korean conflict, combined with land reform difficulties, left China's Communist leadership unwilling to attempt a military conquest of Taiwan. The MAAG-sponsored build-up of Nationalist forces functioned as a deterrent, as did the 1954 U.S.-China Mutual Defense Treaty, which allowed the U.S. to place its own land, sea, and air forces in and around Taiwan. Nonetheless, in January 1955 the Communists seized a small islet north of Taiwan and starting shelling Nationalist defenses on Jinmen and Mazu, two strategically located islands in the Taiwan Strait. The U.S. Congress passed a resolution pledging to defend Taiwan, and MAAG headquarters began contingency planning for a wider conflict, but diplomacy averted further military confrontations. MAAG continued to facilitate deliveries of high-tech weaponry on the island. Under a 1957 bilateral agreement, the U.S. provided nuclear-capable surface-to-surface Matador guided missiles, which had an effective range of 600 miles. In 1958 the Communists responded with renewed shelling of Jinmen and Mazu and with threats of invasion. MAAG coordinated a major naval re-supply program that brought weapons, equipment, food and fuel stocks to Taiwan. The crisis ended when the Chinese Communists, assured of Soviet support, suspended the bombardment.

MAAG continued to oversee American military aid to the Nationalist government during the 1960s while arranging the trans-shipment of building materials, ammunition, and other equipment through Taiwan to American military forces in Vietnam. As part of the American decision to seek a normalization of relations with the People's Republic of China in the early 1970s, however, the U.S. downgraded its ties with the Nationalists. The MAAG office was closed in 1973 when the U.S. suspended military aid to Taiwan.

See also Cold War; Taiwan; U.S.-China Mutual Defense Treaty of 1954; Taiwan Strait.

REFERENCES: Karl Lott Rankin, *China Assignment* (Seattle, WA, 1964), Steve Tsang, "Chiang Kai-shek and the Kuomintang's Policy to Reconquer the Chinese Mainland, 1949–1958," in Steve Tsang (ed.), *In the Shadow of China: Political Developments in Taiwan Since 1949* (Honolulu, HW, 1993).

Laura M. Calkins

Missionaries (American) in China

As noted Sinologist John K. Fairbanks states, it is extremely difficult to get a clear picture of the effects of Western missionary work in China. While there is voluminous writing by the missionaries, in the form of letters and diaries, as well as more official publications, it is not as objective as historians might wish. Also, as noted by Hunter, the missionaries had evangelical goals while their government and merchant supporters had others. Christian missions to China began in the 13th century Franciscan Catholics, but the majority of American missionaries in China were Protestant and worked from the 1930s to the end of the Republican period (1949) when most Christian missionaries were expelled and some were jailed or killed.

The first known Protestant missionary to China was Robert Morrison, from the London Missionary Society. He worked in Guangzhou starting in 1907. The first American Protestant missionary was Elijah Coleman Bridgman, who began work in Guangzhou in 1830, and was followed soon after by Episcopal, Baptist and Presbyterian representatives. Dr. Peter Parker was a younger son from a farm family in Framingham, Massachusetts. He is distinguished for founding a missionary hospital in Guangzhou in 1835. While each of these men is remembered in China and America for ministering to both body and soul of the Chinese people, their individual accomplishments were offset on the negative side by the fact that they were often supported by the very merchants who profited from the opium trade, a trade that led to the debilitation of many poor Chinese. In fact, missionary access to the Chinese increased greatly after the First Opium War (1839–1842) opened five more port cities to Western powers. Increasing numbers of missionary societies were founded and sent their Protestant adherents abroad, and raised funds for their efforts in America.

As time passed, the three main goals of Protestant missions, evangelism, medical care, and education changed in importance. The first missionaries put an emphasis on evangelism but education, especially in the emerging Western sciences, took on more importance as the world approached a new century. Nevertheless, this was possible because early missionaries concentrated on learning Chinese so that they could preach to the common people, translate religious texts for their use, and understand Chinese culture so they could represent it to their supporters in America. Since missionaries were often in direct contact with Chinese people, they were viewed as information sources in the West and asked for information about the West by interested Chinese. So societies like SDK (Society for the Diffusion of Useful Knowledge in China, founded 1834) and publications such as the *Chinese Monthly Magazine* (1933), which published on a broad range of topics, and Bridgman's *Short Account of the USA*, influenced not only the Chinese picture of the United States, but also of the importance of Western-style knowledge in forming a strong country. Another work, Arthur Henderson Smith's *Chinese Characteristics* (1890) had the negative affect of causing Western readers to vastly underestimate Chinese cultural heritage. Paradoxically, the U.S. Civil War prepared many more women to join Chinese missionary work, with a degree of success that soon eclipsed that of American men. There had been a rapid increase from just a few women like Henrietta Shuck (Macao, 1860s) and Luella Miner (1880s), to over 60% of missionary volunteers by 1890. While societies at home tried to limit both their fundraising and the scope of their activities, American female missionaries were successful in China because, in a sex-segregated society, they could reach Chinese women and children and act as role models for Chinese women. They succeeded to the extent that they were able to set up schools and hospitals for women and were enlisted by the Chinese to combat foot-binding as early as 1902. While they were not as popular or prolific in China during the Republican period from 1911–1949, many missionaries attempted to continue their religious and secular work, gaining both criticism and fame. For example, Minnie Vautrin, from a small town in Illinois saved many Chinese women from death or violation during the Japanese invasion and destruction of Nanjing in 1937.

While few Christian missionaries remained in China after the beginnings of the Communist rule, it is important to point out that Buddhist and other religious communities also suffered greatly up until the 1980s. It should also be noted that American missionaries were unquestionably the mediators and informants for those engaged in statecraft as well as the common person in both the West and China and their many efforts to convert the Chinese people left a much greater legacy in dictionaries, translations, and other means of conveying the basics of these two very different cultures to one another. While their goals and their methods may not have been either realistic or unbiased, the overall effect was an interaction of cultures that badly needed to understand each other, and often in situations where little other information was available.

See also Parker, Peter (1804–1888).

REFERENCES: Suzanne Wilson Barnet and John

King Fairbank (eds.), *Christianity in China: Early Protestant Missionary Writers* (Cambridge, MA, 1985); Edward V. Gulik, *Peter Parker and the Opening of China* (Cambridge, MA, 1973); Hua-ling Hu, *American Goddess at the Rape of Nanking: The Courage of Minnie Vautrin* (Carbondale, IL, 2000); Jane Hunter, *The Gospel of Gentility: American Women Missionaries in Turn-of-the-Century China* (New Haven, CT, 1984); John Theodore Mueller, *Great Missionaries to China* (Freeport, NY, 1972); Paul Varg, *Missionaries, Chinese, and Diplomats; the American Protestant Missionary Movement in China, 1890–1952* (Princeton, NJ, 1958).

Janice M. Bogstad

Most Favored Nation (MFN)

"Most Favored Nation" is a concept whereby when a country concedes or grants an advantage or right to one nation, it has to grant or concede that advantage or right to any other nation enjoying "most favored nation" status. Thus, if in a series of nations, each of which enjoys MFN, each gains a new right, all of the nations gain each and every one of these rights.

In the Treaty of the Bogue ending the first Opium War, Great Britain secured the idea of most favored nation (see Article VII). Thereafter, the United States wanted to share in the benefits of the British victory. President John Tyler sent a trade mission led by U.S. Representative Caleb Cushing of Massachusetts. Although the Qing rulers had extended the most favored nation status to the other seafaring powers, they had not written it into treaty. When Cushing arrived, local authorities in typical fashion stalled Cushing in Macao so that he could not proceed to Beijing to meet with the Emperor and present the president's letter on trade and relations. The Qing did send the same mandarin official, Qi Ying, who had negotiated with the British, to Macao and Cushing engaged in talks with him. The result was the Treaty of Wangxia, signed on July 3, 1844. The Chinese opened the same five ports to American trade and for American consuls to work; they gave the United States "most-favored-nation" status, so that America would automatically receive any future rights or concessions that foreign powers wrested from China, and they also gave the United States the right of "extraterritoriality" in civil cases (having conceded to Great Britain this principle in criminal cases) which also was very important. And so this right first given to the British would now become standard in every treaty and in all dealings with foreign powers. Throughout the 19th century and until the Second World War in the 20th century, most favored nation status was a tool that imperialist nations used to extend their informal empires in China, and so were part of China's "sorrow."

After Cushing negotiated the Treaty of Wangxia, other diplomats sought the same concession for treaties of recognition and trade for their governments. In the aftermath of the Second World War and the onset of the postwar international trading system, most favored nation status has changed. MFN goes along with the General Agreement on Trade and Tariffs (GATT), and helps foster bilateral trade relations between countries. In 1948, when the United States joined GATT, it extended MFN to every GATT member. However, in 1951, with the Chinese intervention in the Korean conflict and the spread of the McCarthy-inspired Red Scare domestically, the U.S. government revoked this right for the Soviet Union and most Communist countries, Yugoslavia being a notable exception. And the Jackson-Vanik Amendment (1974) linked MFN status to the willingness of Communist governments to let their people emigrate freely.

Later, in the 1990s, when most Communist countries had gained MFN status, there were very real issues in the bilateral trade between the United States and the People's Republic of China. On the one hand, there was the prospect of opportunities for American businesses in China, although the prospect rarely was fulfilled. On the other hand, Chinese goods seemed to be flooding the U.S. market, creating a huge trade deficit, spurred, in part, by the refusal of the government in Beijing to readjust its very favorable international exchange rates. And there were some politically liberal and conservative groups that questioned MFN status for the PRC given sale of sensitive military technology and allegations about China's use of prison labor for goods being sold in America. Indeed, President George H.W. Bush resisted great internal pressure after the Tiananmen Square uprising in early June 1989 to rescind MFN status for China. While the countries emerging from the former Soviet Union gained MFN status in 1992, the PRC did not achieve this until 2000.

Prior to 2000, the U.S. President had to grant a waiver annually for the PRC to retain its most favored nation status. And, each year there was a debate in Congress whether China had met various conditions to retain its status. While these annual debates failed to deter the waivers throughout the 1990s, they were a sign of challenges in the Sino-American relationship and how important albeit different the most favored nation clause continued to be.

See also General Agreement on Trade and Tariffs (GATT); World Trade Organization (WTO).

REFERENCES: Nicholas R. Lardy, *Integrating China*

into the Global Economy (Washington, DC, 2002); James R. Lilley, and Wendell L. Willkie II (eds.), *Beyond MFN: Trade with China and American Interests* (Washington, DC, 1994); Gungwu Wang, *Anglo-Chinese Encounters Since 1800: War, Trade, Science, and Governance* (New York, 2003); Shu Guang Zhang, *Economic Cold War: America's Embargo Against China and the Sino-Soviet Alliance, 1949–1963* (Washington, DC, 2001).

Charles M. Dobbs

Mott, John R. (1865–1955)

John Raleigh Mott was a major leader of the international Christian movements that lasted from the late 19th century to the mid-1950s. He was born in the state of New York and grew up in Iowa. He first enrolled at Upper Iowa University and later moved to Cornell University to receive his Bachelor of Philosophy and Bachelor of History and Political Science in 1888. Mott served as the President of the YMCA of Cornell for two years. In 1886, while still a student of Cornell, he attended the Northfield Student Conference led by Dwight Moody and was inspired to become one of the 100 men who pledged themselves for foreign missions—the origin of the Student Volunteer Movement for Foreign Missions (SVM).

After graduating from Cornell, Mott accepted the post of national secretary of the Intercollegiate YMCA of the USA and Canada, which required him to visit campuses to promote Christian activities and movements over the next 27 years. During this period, Mott was also chairman of the executive committee of the SVM. Mott began to imagine an international student Christian organization when he went to Amsterdam to attend a conference of the World's Alliance of YMCA in 1891. Through his efforts and wide contacts, the World's Student Christian Federation was formed in 1895. This Federation increased its members to more than twenty after Mott, then its general secretary, finished a two-year world tour to promote its ideal. Another ambitious project was the World Missionary Conference in Edinburgh, held in 1910, which promoted an ecumenical cooperation in worldwide evangelism. Mott was the leader of this Conference and went on to become the Chairman of the International Missionary Council. During World War I, Mott became general secretary of the National War Work Council. Mott had numerous contacts with China during his lifetime. As early as being a college student in Iowa, the title of his prize-winning oration was "The Chinese Should Not Be Prohibited From Immigrating To The United States of America." His first trip to China was in the early autumn of 1896 to form student Christian organizations. Because of his visit, the YMCA membership increased several times together with

the devotion of 76 Chinese students to the service of Christ. After the Edinburgh conference, Mott went to China in early 1913 to help establish the China Continuation Committee. His devotion to the church made him decline President Woodrow Wilson's offer to be the top United States diplomat to China.

Mott kept close contacts with Chinese Christians through various Christian organizations. He generously offered financial support to many Christian organizations and movements in China. For example, the majority of the volunteers from the Student Voluntary Movement, when Mott served as chair of the executive committee, went to China. The National Christian Literature Association of China, the major agency to advocate the indigenization of Christianity in China in the 1920s, relied on financial support from the Institute of Social Science Research when Mott headed the Institute. Many other channels, such as Institute of Pacific Relations, the YMCA, and the International Missionary Council, constituted an intimate relationship between Mott and China. Furthermore, Mott kept frequent contacts with Christian leaders in China and visited China numerous times. Just before the fall of Shanghai to the hands of the Chinese Communists in 1949, Mott flew to Shanghai to offer encouragements to his fellow Christians. Though he was later criticized by the Chinese Communists as an agent of American imperialism, Mott had not lost his hope in China and continued to give his help to overseas Chinese.

In 1946, Mott received the Nobel Peace Prize for his work in establishing and strengthening international Christian student organizations that worked to promote peace.

Mott died in 1955 at the age of 89.

See also Young Men's Christian Association (YMCA).

REFERENCES: Charles Howard Hopkins, *John R. Mott, 1865–1955: A Biography* (Grand Rapids, MI, 1979); Robert C. Mackie, *Layman Extraordinary: John R. Mott, 1865–1955* (London, 1965); John Raleigh Mott, *Addresses and Papers of John R. Mott* (New York, 1946–1947); Martha Lund Smalley, *Legacy of John R. Mott* (New Haven, CT, 1993).

Chen-main Wang

Mu Ouchu (1876–1943)

Mu Ouchu, also named Mu Xiangyue, was a native of Shanghai, China. He was educated at home in the traditional manner, but learned English when he was almost twenty. In 1900, he joined the Yangzi Customs Office. In 1906, he became an English teacher in a Shanghai teachers' training college. Aspiring to study abroad, Mu went to the U.S. to study agriculture at University of Wisconsin in 1909. Later on, he transferred to the University of Illinois and received his Bachelor degree in Agriculture in1913. He pursued a Master's degree in agronomy with a focus on soap manufacturing, cotton planting and weaving from the Texas Agriculture and Mechanical College in 1914.

After his return to Shanghai, he introduced and promoted the American method of cotton growing and set up a large-scale cotton mill factory, De Da in 1915. This Mill had an obvious competitive advantage over its competitors because of Mu's scientific management. In 1916, he opened a new textile factory, Hou Shen in Shanghai. Later in 1919, he set up another large cotton mill, Yu Feng in Zhengzhou, capital of today's Henan Province in China. He applied what he had learned in agriculture and business management in America to his work and quickly became a successful tycoon in China's business circles. Mu's initiatives enhanced the managerial level of the Chinese weaving industry. Soon he was acknowledged as the leader in the cotton business field and was called "The Cotton King of China." Mu Ouchu not only excelled at business and entrepreneurship, but he was also very keen on *kunqu*, an ancient traditional Chinese opera based upon *kunqian* melodies. Mu, an established industrialist, made stupendous efforts in reviving and promoting the performing art of Kunqu. Mu participated in the performances for fund-raising. Finally, in 1921, sponsored by Mu, the Kunqu Teaching and Learning Institute was opened in Suzhou, Jiangsu Province. In late 1928 Mu was invited to join the Nationalist government. He first served as a deputy minister in the Ministry of Commerce. In next year, Mu was appointed as director of the Preparatory Committee of Chinese Central Agriculture Lab. Mu was also quite active in social affairs. While living a simple and frugal life, he donated huge sums of money to education. In 1920, Mu gave 50,000 taels of silver to Cai Yuanpei, then President of Beijing University, to select brilliant students for studying in the United States and other countries. Among those who directly or indirectly benefited from Mu's financial assistance was the 1957 Nobel Prize Winner Yang Zhenning of New York State University at Stony Brook. During his life time, Mu wrote numerous articles introducing American management to the Chinese.

Mu died in Chongqing in 1943. His writings include an autobiography *Ouchu Wu Shi Zi Shu* and some books on improving the cotton plant and the textile industry in China.

REFERENCES: Zhu Xinliang, *Zhongguo da bai ke quan shu/Zhongguo li shi [Chinese History, Encyclopedia of China]* (Beijing, 1992); Lin Zhongjie, *Zhongguo xian dai shi ci dian [A Historical Dictionary of Contempary Chinese History]* (Taibei, 1985); Shao Da, "The Tales of Kunqu and Its Supporter Mu Ouchu," *www.china.org.cn*.

Fu Zhuo

Mukden Incident (1931)

Also known as the Manchurian Incident, this event can be traced back to the late 1890s when the Japanese had expansionist designs on the Asian mainland including Manchuria, which had abundant natural resources.

As a result of their defeat in the Russo-Japanese War, 1904–1905, the Russians surrendered their rights in Manchuria to the Japanese who were permitted to station troops supposedly to guard the South Manchurian Railway. Mukden (Shenyang), the largest and most important city in the region, became the center for Japanese activity in Manchuria. The fall of the Qing Dynasty in 1911 plunged China into chaos and the Japanese permitted several warlords to use the city as their base, the most powerful being Zhang Zuolin who ran Manchuria from 1919 until 1928 with Japanese support. The Nationalist Northern Expedition to unify China, led by Jiang Jieshi, threw Zhang Zuolin out of northern China back into Manchuria in 1928. Fearing that Jiang would march into and take control of Manchuria, the Japanese Kwantung army assassinated Zhang Zuolin in Mukden in June 1928, hoping to use his death as a pretext for seizing Manchuria. Japanese, as well as world opinion, including American, condemned the assassination temporarily preventing the Kwantung army from further action. Zhang Xueliang, who succeeded his father, swore loyalty to the Jiang's Nationalist government to counter growing Soviet and Japanese influence in Manchuria. With Nationalist support, Zhang was able to limit the Soviets and increase Nationalist presence in Manchuria much to the dismay of the Kwantung army especially its junior officers. They plotted, unbeknownst to their senior officers and officials in Tokyo, to end Nationalist influence and expel Zhang Xuelian from Manchuria. In May 1931, they orchestrated an incident between Chinese and Korean farmers over water rights on the Sino-Korean border that produced to anti-Chinese riots in Korea and Japan. In June, they used the killing by local Chinese of a Japanese army captain on a spy mission in northwest Manchuria to increase their hold on the region. Finally, on the night of September 18, 1931, the Mukden Incident took place. Japanese troops blew up the tracks of the South Manchurian Railway outside Mukden, claiming Chinese sabotage. The Kwantung army then moved quickly seizing the city to "protect" it, Japanese property and citizens. Without permission from Tokyo, the army expanded its hold occupying the entire region by the end of the year establishing the puppet state of Manchukuo in 1932. Zhang Xueliang's forces offered little resistance and retreated into China proper. The Chinese consider the incident the beginning of the Second World War in Asia.

The Nationalist government appealed for help from the United States and the League of Nations. The League of Nations sent a commission headed by British Lord Lytton that included representatives from France, Germany, Italy and the United States, and found Japan to be the aggressor in Manchuria and refused to recognize Manchukuo, causing Japan to leave the League. In the throes of the Great Depression, the United States refused military intervention, instead urging other countries to take action against Japan. The United States adopted the Stimson Doctrine in January 1932. This policy formulated by Secretary of State Henry Stimson refused to recognize the political situation in Manchuria or the state of Manchukuo. It remained in effect until the end of the Second World War.

See also Lytton Report; Manchuria; World War II; Stimson Doctrine.

REFERENCES: Alvin Coox and Hilary Convoy (eds.), *China and Japan: A Search for Balance Since World War I* (Santa Barbara, CA, 1978); Sadako Ogata, *Defiances in Manchuria: The Making of Japanese Foreign Policy* (Berkeley, CA, 1966); Takehiko Yoshihasi, *Conspiracy at Mukden* (New Haven, CT, 1963).

Greg Ference

The 1990 Institute

The 1990 Institute was founded in April 1990 as a policy research association, committed to an active dialogue with China's government and civil society institutions, toward the end of helping China sustain the reform and modernization process that appeared to be threatened by reaction at home and ostracization abroad.

The more specific occasion for its birth was the fortuitous meeting of a Chinese American business executive (C.B. Sung), whose social fraternity was looking for a service project, and a Chinese American economist (Hang-Sheng Cheng), who was trying to match American and Chinese economists for a joint research project on China's economic reforms. Both lived and worked in the San Francisco Bay Area, home to a large Chinese-American population. In the aftermath of the Tiananmen tragedy, thousands of these anguished Bay Area residents formed at least a dozen organizations committed to circulating angry petitions, raising money, and otherwise providing immediate support to the protesters in whatever way they could. While no less sympathetic to the democratic aspirations of the students and workers who fell victim to violent repression in the streets of Beijing, the founders of The 1990 Institute took what they saw as a more pragmatic, long-range approach. One of their key premises was that sustaining momentum for economic reform would eventually bring about a more general liberalization of Chinese society.

Within its first year, the Institute drew respected non-Chinese Americans into its leadership and constituency. In 1993, it published a contributed volume that provided an overview of the economic reforms of the 1980s. In one of the dramatic highlights of the Institute's history, its Chairman (C.B. Sung) publicly presented a copy of the Chinese translation of *China's Economic Reform* to Chinese President Jiang Zemin. The presentation took place in October 1993 in Beijing, at the 80th anniversary of the Western Returned Scholars Association. Throughout the 1990s, the Institute published monographs and policy papers on fiscal, monetary, agricultural, enterprise, and labor market reform. To varying degrees, the scholars it commissioned and sponsored collaborated with and presented findings to policy research institutions in China. The 1990 Institute has also organized binational conferences on legal and enterprise reform, and several of its members contributed to 1996 Congressional Hearings on China's economic reform. In 1999, the director of China's State Administration of Taxation (SAT) wrote a new introduction to the Institute's book on fiscal reform, published the book in Chinese translation, and distributed it to SAT branches nationwide as required reading.

In the late 1990s, the Institute expanded its agenda by adding a series of cultural, environmental, and educational programs to its initial agenda of policy research. Partnering with a variety of government-sponsored and independent Chinese NGOs, it has help organize an essay contest on social ethics, a binational conference on "Women, Leadership, and Sustainability," a Children's Environmental Art Competition, and a Dragon Fund charity to improve educational opportunities for girls in two of China's poorer provinces.

REFERENCES: Norton Wheeler, *Bridging the Pacific: The 1990 Institute and Transnationalism in Late-20th Century U.S.-China Relations* (Masters Thesis, University of Kansas, 2002); Norton Wheeler, "Improving Mainland Society and U.S.-China Relations: A Case Study of Four Chinese American-led Transnational Associations," in Peter H. Koehn and Xiao-huang Yin (eds.), *The Expanding Roles of Chinese Americans in U.S.-China Relations: Transnational Networks and Trans-Pacific Interactions* (Armonk, NY, 2002).

Norty Wheeler

Nanjing Incident (Nanking Incident) *see* Rape of Nanjing

National Council for U.S.-China Trade *see* U.S.-China Business Council

National Committee on United States-China Relations (NCUSCR)

The National Committee on United States-China Relations (NCUSCR) was founded in 1966 by leading figures in American politics, business, labor, and academia, who sought to improve understanding between the two countries that had no official relations and few unofficial channels of communication. In the years before the establishment of relations in 1979, the National Committee was a favored destination of funding by the State Department and other agencies of the U.S. government. Later, it had to compete for funding with other bilateral organizations that proliferated after normalization. NCUSCR has always raised additional funds from corporate, philanthropic, and individual donors. It defines its own agenda and, in fact, has rarely even been asked to hew its programs to official U.S. government policies. The ping-pong matches and Nixon's 1972 visit to China were the National Committee's first high-profile activities. Three decades later, it remains the most active bilateral relations organization.

NCUSCR's main emphasis from 1966 through 1974 was educational outreach, *per force* addressed primarily to an American audience. After normalization in 1972, athletic and artistic exchanges were added to the programming. In the 1980s and into the 1990s (with only slight disruption by the Tiananmen Square events of 1989), exchange programs expanded to encompass education, communications, governance, international relations, and global issues like the environment. There was a balance in emphasis, varying from program to program, between improving Americans' understanding of China and vice versa. The National Committee has, for example, brought a delegation of foundations executives to China to learn about the emerging non-governmental sector here and a delegation of Chinese NGO leaders to the United States to learn about that sector in American society. For over two decades, the National Committee has taken groups of 13 visiting Chinese students and scholars on a two-week tour of American public and private institutions.

Beginning in the mid-1990s, the National Committee added a few longer-term programs to its portfolio of educational and exchange programs. For example, it facilitated a multi-year environmental conservation study of the Ussuri River Basin along the Chinese-Russian border. In so doing, it brought together Russian and Chinese scientists and officials, along with funders and environmentalists from the United States. In another example, the National Committee assisted Chinese organizations that were developing a private educational system in Guizhou Province. In 2002, NCUSCR was awarded a United States Labor Department grant to assist Chinese agencies in the development of labor laws, as a component of the nation's general emphasis on promoting "rule of law."

REFERENCES: National Committee on United States-China Relations, *www.ncuscr.org*.

Norty Wheeler

National Products Movement (*guo huo yun dong*)

In the first half of the 20th century, Chinese efforts to eliminate foreign imperialism and create a powerful nation-state had innumerable social manifestations. A broad array of political, economic, and social forces placed cultural constraints on consumption through a massive but diffuse social movement. The National Products Movement (*guohuo yundong*), as it was known at the time, popularized the meaning of material culture around the duality of "national products" (*guohuo*) and "foreign products" (*yanghuo*). Above all, this movement attempted to make the consumption of national products and the avoidance of imports a fundamental part of Chinese citizenship.

There was never one centrally controlled movement. Silk manufacturers, student protestors, women's organizations, business enterprises, government officials, and ordinary citizens alike invoked the term "National Products Movement." Moreover, as the movement grew, its name, its slogans, and the categories of nationalistic consumption it created became ubiquitous in cities and even appeared in the countryside. Its manifestations included the Clothing Law of 1912, the *National Product Monthly* and many other magazines, frequent anti-imperialist boycotts, the Nationalist government-sponsored "National Products" campaign of the late 1920s, official "National

Products Years" in the 1930s (Women's in 1934, Children's in 1935, and Citizens' in 1936), weekly supplements published in a major national newspaper, *Shenbao* in the mid-1930s, thousands of advertisements, regular national-product fashion shows, and specially organized venues—visited by millions—for displaying and selling national products, including museums, fixed and traveling exhibitions, and a chain of retail stores.

Prominent commercial and industrial leaders, individuals with clear economic interests at stake, formed the backbone of the movement throughout China. Throughout this period, Chinese enterprises struggled to maintain market share and gain acceptance for manufactures that competed directly with imports. The "unequal treaties" imposed by the imperialist powers intensified this competition by, among other methods, denying China the ability to restrict imports by raising tariffs. Entrepreneurs such as Zhang Jian, Song Zejiu, Rong Desheng, Liu Hongsheng, Wu Yunchu, and countless others became living examples of two common expressions of the day: "Business enterprises rescue the nation" and "Establish factories for national self-preservation." They established the businesses that formed the foundation of a nascent consumer culture, manufacturing personal hygiene articles such as toothpaste and soap, textile products like towels and silk dresses, and household goods such as light bulbs and electric fans. Thus, before the re-emergence of a relatively strong state in 1927–1928, much of the organizational and financial strength of the movement came from economic interest groups formed by business leaders who owned consumer goods industries. Local chambers of commerce, native-place associations, and newer ad hoc organizations specifically devoted to the movement had a huge financial stake in linking consumerism and nationalism to protect what they had come to consider their home market.

Many other Chinese became involved in the movement, sometimes unwittingly and often unwillingly. During the frequent anti-imperialist boycotts from 1905 to 1937, students of all ages joined in the movement. The more extreme among them vowed not to consume imports, forced merchants to adhere to boycotts, and even made and sold national products. Nor did all the participants share the same motivation. Zealous students and opportunistic hooligans often appropriated these categories of national and foreign products to justify violence against anyone refusing to boycott foreign goods or to "donate" to "patriotic organizations." Throughout China, merchants who refused to stop selling Japanese products were murdered. Such activities discredited the movement but reinforced the hegemony of the notion that products had nationalities and that citizens within a nation owed their allegiance to its products.

See also China Tariff Autonomy.

REFERENCES: Karl Gerth, *China Made: Consumer Culture and the Creation of the Nation* (Cambridge, MA, 2003); Kikuchi Takaharu. *Chūgoku minzoku undō no kihon kōzō: Taigai boikotto no kenkyū [The Historical Background of the Chinese National Movement: a Study of Anti-foreign Boycotts]* (Tokyo, 1974); Pan Junxiang, *Jindai Zhongguo guohuo yundong yanjiu [A Study of Modern China's National Products Movement]* (Shanghai, 1998).

Karl Gerth

Nationalist Party *see* Guomindang

Nationalists *see* Guomindang

Neutralization of Taiwan

President Harry S. Truman's decision on June 27, 1950 to order the U.S. Seventh Fleet to protect Taiwan against invasion from the People's Republic of China (PRC) and to prevent Guomindang (Nationalist) attacks against the mainland prevented an end to the Chinese Civil War. Coming two days after the Korean War started, this "neutralization" of Taiwan extended U.S. protection to the exiled Republic of China (ROC) under Jiang Jieshi, reversing the policy Truman had declared less than six months earlier. His actions infuriated leaders of the Chinese Communist Party in Beijing, who viewed the Nationalist government on Taiwan was the last remaining barrier to China's reunification. Although Truman had wanted to avoid linking the United States to Jiang's regime, U.S. protection for Taiwan would become a long-term commitment, formalized in the U.S.-China Mutual Defense Treaty of 1954. Until President Richard M. Nixon visited China in 1972, it was the major obstacle to reconciliation between the United States and the PRC.

By late 1949, Truman and Secretary of State Dean Acheson had decided that the PRC would invade Taiwan in the near future and destroy the rival ROC. Accordingly, on January 5, 1950, the President announced publicly his determination to remain uninvolved in China's civil war, explaining that while the United States would continue economic aid to Taiwan, U.S. military assistance and advice would cease. Few thought that Nationalist forces, after collapsing on the mainland, could defend the island effectively in the face of a determined Communist assault. The U.S. Joint Chiefs of Staff did not want the island to fall into Communist hands because of its strategic position, but they also were against a U.S. commitment of direct defense of Taiwan. Instead, they recommended a military survey, which would lead to renewed U.S. military aid. Acheson dissented, arguing that further U.S. involvement in the Chinese Civil War would force the Chinese into the arms of the Soviets. As the debate continued in the early months of 1950, Assistant Secretary of State for Far Eastern Affairs Dean Rusk recommended neutralizing Taiwan. By early June, Washington was urging privately Jiang's removal prior to a policy reversal.

North Korea's invasion of South Korea provided the impetus for action. When Truman and his major advisors met at Blair House on the evening of June 25 to address the crisis, Acheson proposed that Truman order the Seventh Fleet to "neutralize" Taiwan. He still wanted to avoid alignment with Jiang, suggesting that the United Nations might determine the future status of Taiwan. At the Blair House meeting the next evening, the President approved Acheson's recommendation. In a June 27 public statement, Truman announced that he had ordered the Seventh Fleet "to prevent any attack on Formosa." In addition, he was informing the Nationalists to cease all air and sea operations against the mainland and ordering the Seventh Fleet to "see that this is done." Determination of the future status of Taiwan, he advised, would have to await the restoration of peace in the Pacific, a peace settlement with Japan, or consideration at the United Nations.

There was no debate about neutralization of Taiwan at the Blair House meetings because U.S. military and diplomatic officials already had laid the groundwork for the decision. The Communist attack on South Korea put a premium on military and strategic considerations, but it also gave force to the argument for action to register U.S. resolve. Domestic political considerations were another priority, since both Truman and Acheson needed to protect against revived criticism for the "loss of China" as the administration intervened to save Korea. While the Truman's decision was popular at first in the United States, following Chinese intervention in Korea during November 1950, his order that the Seventh Fleet should prevent Nationalist attacks against the mainland became the target of increasing criticism. In January 1953, Republican Dwight D. Eisenhower assumed the presidency and one of his first acts was to reverse that policy. Soon, however, he secured a secret promise from Jiang to consult with Washington before launching any offensive operations against the mainland larger than the small-scale raids Truman had allowed.

See also De-neutralization of the Taiwan Strait; Korean War; Truman, Harry S. (1884–1972); Acheson, Dean (1873–1971); U.S.-China Mutual Defense Treaty (1954).

REFERENCES: Robert D. Accinelli, *Crisis and Commitment: United States Policy toward Taiwan, 1950–1955* (Chapel Hill, NC, 1996); Thomas J. Christensen, *Useful Adversaries: Grand Strategy, Domestic Mobilization, and Sino-American Conflict, 1947–1958* (Princeton, NJ, 1996); Bruce Cumings, *The Origins of the Korean War, Vol. II: The Roaring of the Cataract, 1947–1950* (Princeton, NJ, 1990); William Stueck, *The Korean War: An International History* (Princeton, NJ, 1995).

James I. Matray

Nine Power Treaty (1922)

The Nine Power Treaty of 1922 was one of the three treaties that resulted from the Washington Naval Conference of 1921–1922. The United States, Great Britain, Japan, France, Italy, China, Belgium, the Netherlands, and Portugal signed a treaty on February 6, 1922 that affirmed China's sovereignty, independence, and territorial integrity and that affirmed the signatories' commitment to giving merchants and industrialists of all nations, especially the signatories, equal rights to do business in China. It was a repudiation of the movement to more formal empire that began in the decade before the First World War and the recognition of the cherished American principle of "the Open Door" and decades of American diplomacy to broaden economic opportunities for American merchants and industries.

The pact reflected the relative power of the United States, in that the signatories all pledged to "use their influence for the purpose of effectually establishing and maintaining the principle of equal opportunity for the commerce and trade of all nations throughout the territory of China." The signatories also pledged to refrain from "taking advantage of China," and from seeking "special rights or privileges," and they further agreed "not to enter into any treaty, agreement, arrangements or understanding ... which would infringe or impair the(se) principles." The treaty drew particular attention to railroad rights, rights of passage, and any impairment on the free and easy movement of trade and goods. While the pact preserved the rights of foreign nationals to conduct business in China, the signatories did not accept China's demand for immediate restoration of tariff autonomy and ending of extraterritoriality. The nine treaty signatories did agree to establish an international commission to study Chinese tariff policies, and they did agree to a small increase in the 80-year old 5% ad valorem tariff.

Put simply, the Nine Power Treaty expressed good intentions towards China but had no enforcement obligations. It neither proposed a hard schedule for ending foreign rights gained from the unequal treaty system nor for guaranteeing China's independence. Indeed, life in China, humiliating for the Chinese and privileged for foreigners in the concessions areas, continued pretty much as it had before. The Nine Power Treaty proved to be the weakest part of the Washington Naval Conference treaties, and, perhaps, a stronger treaty with real enforcement provisions might have helped control the turn to aggressive forms of Japanese and Chinese nationalism that followed in the next several years and that broadened into the Pacific War.

In leading the fight for the Nine Power Treaty, and in securing support for the Open Door principles, did the United States regain the moral leadership in diplomacy that it conceded when it failed to join the League of Nations? At least for the moment, this pact indicated American primacy in the postwar power vacuum in East Asia, which America soon would concede.

See also Washington Naval Conference (1921–1922); Open Door Policy.

REFERENCES: Thomas H. Buckley, *The United States and The Washington Conference, 1921–1922* (Knoxville, TN, 1970); Akira Iriye, *After Imperialism: The Search for a New Order in the Far East, 1921–1931* (Cambridge, MA, 1965); Westel W. Willoughby, *China at the Conference, A Report* (Baltimore, MD, 1922).

Charles M. Dobbs

Nixon Doctrine

The Nixon Doctrine marked a retreat from America's troubled involvement in the Vietnam War and signified a more pessimistic statement about the American people's willingness to bear the burdens of being a superpower in the future. During a stop in Guam on July 25, 1969 on a trip to Asia and Europe, President Richard Nixon noted the need for a change in American foreign policy. If this was the "macro" statement, then his three-fold announcement on the Vietnam War were the "micro" statements that fleshed out this new Nixon Doctrine.

Nixon's three-fold policy was designed to diffuse opposition to the war at home while helping South Vietnam defend itself from North Vietnam. Nixon announced a reduction in U.S. troops in Vietnam, and because of this troop withdrawal the Nixon administration also announced a draft lottery, to begin in fall 1969, which would draft fewer young men as U.S. manpower needs for Vietnam declined. To balance this reduction in U.S. ground forces, Nixon called for Vietnamization, that is, for the South Vietnamese people to assume a greater share of the burden of defending

themselves. To help South Vietnam, Nixon guaranteed increased military and economic aid, and, where appropriate, support of U.S. airpower, but never again a massive involvement of U.S. ground forces. This narrowly focused policy became, in a broader and more global sense, the Nixon Doctrine. The United States would honor all of its international treaty obligations; it would use its nuclear deterrent to protect its allies from nuclear blackmail and from the threat of attack; and it would help its allies defend themselves from Communist aggression with U.S. military assistance and advice. It was a clear step back from the commitment of more than 500,000 ground troops in Vietnam. The United States would only commit ground troops when another major power intervened. Indeed, the Nixon administration expected U.S. allies to provide for their own basic defense.

The Nixon Doctrine developed from a pessimistic world-view that President Nixon and his National Security Advisor, Henry Kissinger, held about the world and about the American people. They accepted increasing Soviet military power; they recognized the rising economic power of Japan and the countries of Western Europe. They believed the American people were no longer willing to bear the burdens of being a true superpower. And so they tried to create a degree of uncertainty in international relations, to establish five power centers—the United States and the Soviet Union, the People's Republic of China, and at least economically Western Europe and Japan. Indeed, they sought a way to keep America a superpower in influence without having to pay the cost.

Equally importantly, the United States began to look for regional allies, since it would no longer serve as the world's policeman. This would lead to increased arms sales, as opposed to grants of arms, to governments in Iran, South Africa, and elsewhere, and very real problems for American diplomacy and America's national interests outside the scope of this essay. It would also undergird the developing relationship with the People's Republic of China to balance the Soviet Union and thus help bring about an end to the Bamboo Curtain and the rise of the U.S.-PRC-USSR strategic triangle.

See also Nixon, Richard (1913–1994); Bamboo Curtain; Nixon's Visit to China; Strategic Triangle of U.S.-Soviet-China Relations; Detente.

REFERENCES: Tsuyoshi Ito, *Alliance in Anxiety: Detente and the Sino-American-Japanese Triangle* (New York, 2003); Robert S. Litwak, *Detente and the Nixon Doctrine: American Foreign Policy and the Pursuit of Stability, 1969–1976* (New York, 1984); Joo-Hong Nam, *America's Commitment to South Korea: The First Decade*

of the Nixon Doctrine (New York, 1986); Franz Schurmann, The Foreign Politics of Richard Nixon: The Grand
Design (Berkeley, CA, 1987); Richard C. Thornton, The
Nixon-Kissinger Years: Reshaping America's Foreign Policy (St. Paul, MN, 2001).

                                    Charles M. Dobbs

Nixon, Richard Milhous (1913–1994)

Born in Yorba Linda, California, in 1913 into
a working-class Quaker family, Richard Milhous
Nixon had served in the U.S. House of Representatives as a Republican from California. A member of the House Un-American Activities Committee, he rose to national prominence for his role
in the Alger Hiss espionage case, establishing his
reputation as a hard-line anti-Communist. He
vehemently accused the Truman administration
of "losing" China to the Communists in 1949.
Nixon served as Vice President during the Eisenhower administration and became President in
1969. Like his arch-rival President John F.
Kennedy, Nixon was far more interested in foreign
policy than in domestic affairs. It was in this arena
that Nixon wished to make his mark. Nixon was
a master of realpolitik. Politically, he hoped to get
credit for reducing Cold War tensions; geopolit-
ically, he wished to use the strengthened relations
with the Soviet Union and the People's Republic
of China as leverage to force North Vietnam to
end the war with a settlement. Nixon would play
Beijing against Moscow, Moscow against Beijing,
and both against Hanoi. And he was very successful in this arena.

Nixon began to have his eye on China in mid
1960s. In 1967, writing in Foreign Affairs, he cautioned that continuing to ignore mainland China
was both unrealistic and unwise, "… we simply
cannot afford to leave China forever outside the
family of nations, there to nurture its fantasies,
cherish its hates, and threaten its neighbors." Bilateral relations between the Soviet Union and
China had been deteriorating since the 1950s and
open conflict with border clashes had taken place
during Nixon's first year in office. The President
sensed opportunity and began to send out tentative diplomatic feelers to China. Nixon was perhaps the most unlikely American leader to court
the Chinese Communists. As one America's
staunchest anti-Communist politician of the Cold
War, Nixon was in a unique position to launch a
diplomatic opening to Red China, leading to the
birth of a new political maxim: "Only Nixon
could go to China." Nixon's reputation as a hard-
line Cold Warrior gave him political cover. Who
could accuse Nixon of being "soft on Communism?"

Upon assuming office, Nixon initiated a

thaw in U.S. attitudes toward China. He had Secretary of State William Rogers loosen trade and
visa restrictions, and pull U.S. troops out of military bases near China. Overtures were relayed
via third party nations such as Romania and Pakistan. Then Nixon sent National Security Advisor Henry Kissinger on a secret July 1971 meeting
with Chinese Premier Zhou Enlai. What followed
was Nixon's highly televised meeting with Chinese Communist leader Chairman Mao Zedong in
February 1972. Historian Patrick Tyler reflected,
"It was as if God had stretched out his hand and
conferred celestial meaning on the event." Mao
reached over and took Nixon's hand and held it for
a long minute. Pointing at Kissinger, Mao said to
Zhou, "Seize the hour and seize the day." And the
world balance of power shifted.

Nixon's most lasting success, reopening the
long-closed door to mainland China, was only a
first step, but a decisive one, in the budding rapprochement between the United States and the
PRC. Although Nixon's political career and reputation in the United States was ruined by the
Watergate scandal in 1974, he had remained extremely popular in China. In a rare case, Mao invited Nixon's daughter Julie Nixon and her husband to see him when they first visited China over
New Year's in 1975–1976. And they were the second to the last American party to visit Mao before
his death.

**See also Nixon Doctrine; Nixon's Visit to
China.**

REFERENCES: William Bundy, A Tangled Web: The
Making of Foreign Policy in the Nixon Presidency (New
York, 1998); Henry A Kissinger, The Kissinger Tran-
scripts: The Top Secret Talks with Beijing and Moscow, A
National Security Archive Document Reader (New York,
1999); Henry A. Kissinger, White House Years (New
York, 1979); Richard Nixon, RN: The Memoirs of
Richard Nixon (New York, 1978); Patrick Tyler, A Great
Wall: Six Presidents and China: an Investigative History
(New York, 1999).

                                         Rob Kerby

Nixon's Visit to China

On July 15, 1971, U.S. President Richard
Nixon stunned the world with the announcement
that in February 1972 he would travel to the People's Republic of China. Nixon had been one of
the coldest of America's Cold Warriors when he
began his political career, and it seemed absolutely inconceivable that such an individual
could reverse more than two decades of U.S. policy and reach out to the Communist rulers of
China.

For some months there had been a quiet,
scarcely noticed effort by the governments in
Washington and Beijing to open a dialogue. The

U.S. Ambassador in Poland actually greeted his PRC counterpart at a reception. In November 1970, Chinese Premier Zhou Enlai told visiting journalist (and longtime friend of the Communist leadership) Edgar Snow that the PRC would welcome talks, and Mao Zedong the next month said to Snow that Nixon "was welcome either as tourist or president." Meanwhile, in a February 25, 1971 speech to the Congress, President Nixon referred to the mainland as the People's Republic of China, the first time a U.S. official publicly described the Communist government by its chosen name. He then ended the 21-year old trade and travel restrictions with the mainland. The Chinese signaled their interest when they invited an American ping pong team competing in Japan to visit the mainland. And a growing stream of Chinese goods—newspapers and magazines, beer, textiles, and jade among others—began entering the United States without the once-required Treasury Department licenses. In July 1971, National Security Advisor Henry Kissinger finalized the deal. He was visiting Pakistan when, allegedly, he took ill, and reporters learned he was resting. Meanwhile, he secretly flew to China, met with Zhou and they agreed on many issues and agreed to disagree on the status of Taiwan and the Republic of China government headquartered there.

Nixon's visit to China from February 21 to 28, 1972 transformed world politics. It took the presidential party four days to travel from Washington, DC to the Asian mainland to help mitigate the worst affects of "jet lag." Nixon landed in Beijing, and shook hands with Premier Zhou at the airport, to atone for Secretary of State John Foster Dulles' discourtesy at Geneva in 1954. Nixon then had a series of public relations visits—to the Great Wall for example—and then meetings with Zhou and—privately—with Chairman Mao Zedong. The United States gave China two American musk oxen and China gave America two Chinese pandas, thereafter housed at the National Zoo in Washington, DC.

Behind the pageantry, there were serious negotiations. The resulting Shanghai Communique released on February 27 noted both nations' respect for differing social, economic, and political systems, but admitted that Taiwan remained a problem, a "murderously tough problem" according to Kissinger. The two parties produced a document in which the PRC stated that Taiwan was an internal matter, the "crucial question obstructing the normalization of relations between China and the United States," while the United States accepted the idea of "one China," called for a "peaceful settlement of the Taiwan question by the Chinese themselves," and promised to reduce its military presence on the island. As Kissinger later noted, the two sides agreed diplomatically to disagree.

Of course the symbolism of the visit mattered more than the substance of the talks. Surely governments across the world, but especially in Moscow, Pyongyang, and Hanoi, must have carefully reconsidered their respective positions on the Cold War in East Asia. Nixon's visit helped bring an end to the so-called Bamboo Curtain, and along with announcements on trade, the gold standard, and currency valuation, caused the so-called Nixon shocks in Japan, and a schism in the once extremely warm relations between the two postwar allies on either side of the Pacific.

See also Nixon Doctrine; Nixon, Richard (1913–1994); Bamboo Curtain; Strategic Triangle of U.S.-Soviet-China Relations; Detente.

REFERENCES: Claude A. Buss, *China: The People's Republic of China and Richard Nixon* (San Francisco, CA, 1974); John W. Garver, *China's Decision for Rapprochement with the United States, 1968–1971* (Boulder, CO, 1982); Ronald Keith, *The Diplomacy of Zhou Enlai* (New York, 1989); Robert Litwak, *Detente and the Nixon Doctrine: American Foreign Policy and the Pursuit of Stability* (New York, 1984); Richard C. Thornton, *The Nixon-Kissinger Years: Reshaping America's Foreign Policy* (St. Paul, MN, 2001).

Charles M. Dobbs

Non-recognition *see* Stimson Doctrine.

Normalization

After the founding of the Communist China in October 1949, relations between the People's Republic of China (PRC) and the United States were marked by deep hostility, beginning from the PRC's expulsion of U.S. consular officials from the mainland in early 1950. The major reason for the estrangement was rooted in the ideological cleavage between the two countries. China's Marxist-Leninist-Maoist ideology was a complete antithesis of the U.S. capitalist democracy. Mao Zedong advocated "lean to one side" policy, that is, the side of socialism. He abhorred capitalism and looked upon the U.S. as an imperialist power. Whereas, America pursued the policy of containment towards China in order to check the spread of Communism in the Third World. The Korean War of 1950–1953 was a classic case of an open ideological warfare that ended all possibility of normal relations between the PRC and the United States. During the Korean War China and America found themselves at the opposite sides, with China defeating U.S.-UN forces in November-December 1950. In response, America imposed a complete embargo on trade with China. In essence, the bitter hostility in Sino-American relations was reflected in a series of steps taken up by the United States, including non-recognition of China, establishment of diplomatic ties with Taiwan, and signing of the Mutual Defense Treaty with Taiwan in 1954, and blocking of the PRC's entry into the United Nations till 1971.

The era of normalization of Sino-American relations dawned during the presidency of Richard Nixon who initiated the policy of rapprochement with China. As part of this policy, U.S. National Security Advisor Henry Kissinger undertook secret trips to Beijing in July and October 1971. Kissinger conveyed to Chinese leader Mao Zedong that America was keen on improving ties with China and on seeking latter's cooperation in maintaining peace and stability around the world. Kissinger attempted to convince Mao that it was the Soviet Union rather than the United States that posed security threat to China. Later, during President Nixon's historic visit to China in February 1972, Joint Shanghai Communique was issued on February 28, 1972. The U.S. side declared, "The United States acknowledges that all Chinese on either side of the Taiwan Strait maintain there is but one China and that Taiwan is a part of China." Adoption of "one China" policy represented a major shift in the U.S. China policy, which was partly rooted in the American belief that Chinese cooperation was essential in ending the Vietnam imbroglio. Furthermore, the deterioration in Sino-Soviet relations, notably the border clashes along the Ussuri River in 1969, afforded America a great opportunity to come closer to China and forge strategic ties with it against the Soviet Union. China too was keen to improve ties with the U.S. in order to ensure its security against Soviet aggression. During the Carter administration, full diplomatic relations were established between China and the United States in January 1979 under the 1978 Joint Communique on Normalization of Relations. Taiwan was de-recognized and the U.S.-China Mutual Defense Treaty of 1954 abrogated. Further, the Reagan administration undertook to reduce gradually arms sales to Taiwan under the August 1982 Communique on U.S. arms sales to Taiwan. These three communiques are considered the cornerstone of the normalization of Sino-American relations.

See also Korean War; Nixon's Visit to China; One China Policy; Ping Pong Diplomacy; Cold War; United Nations; Strategic Triangle of U.S.-Soviet-China Relations; Detente.

REFERENCES: U.S. Department of State, *Shanghai Communique of 1972* (Washington, DC, 1997); United States Information Service, *Joint Communique on Establishment of Diplomatic Relations* (Washington, DC, 1978); United States Information Service, *Communique on U.S. Arms Sales to Taiwan* (Washington, DC, 1982); Harry Harding, *A Fragile Relationship: The United States and China Since 1972* (Washington, DC, 1992); David M. Lampton, *Same Bed, Different Dreams: Managing U.S.-China Relations, 1989–2000* (Berkeley, CA, 2001); Henry A. Kissinger, *The White House Years* (Boston, MA, 1979).

Romi Jain

North Korea *see* Democratic People's Republic of Korea.

North Korean Nuclear Controversy

The North Korean nuclear controversy was precipitated by North Korea's announcement to withdraw from the Nuclear Non-Proliferation Treaty (NPT) on March 12, 1993. The decision to withdraw from the NPT was a calculated game of nuclear brinksmanship by North Korean President Kim Il Sung to halt North Korea's acute economic crisis by using North Korea's alleged nuclear arsenal as a bargaining chip to secure economic and political concessions from the United States, as North Korea remained in a technical state of war with South Korea, which refused to sign the armistice that ended the Korean War.

Fearful of threat of destabilizing change both the United States and the People's Republic of China (PRC) shared a common interest in preserving stability on the Korean Peninsula as well as maintaining nuclear non-proliferation. Concerned that the nuclear controversy would undermine its long-term political and security interests on the Korean Peninsula; China sought to intervene in support of its nominal ally, North Korea. Even though Beijing consulted with Washington the Chinese pursued their own political and security interests, namely shoring up the ailing North Korean regime as a buffer against American suzerainty in Northeast Asia. China opposed any sanctions or boycott against North Korea and steadfastly refused direct participation in international negotiations favoring flexible discussions between North Korea, South Korea, the United States, and the International Atomic Energy Agency (IAEA). From the onset of the North Korean nuclear controversy the United States sought to internationalize the confrontation with North Korea as the possibility of destabilizing change on the Korean Peninsula was of increasing concern to the other regional powers (i.e. China, Japan and Russia) with strategic interests on the Korean Peninsula. Between October 1993 and April 1994, the international nuclear crisis reached its height as North Korea impeded the work of

IAEA nuclear inspectors. This prompted the UN General Assembly to adopt a special resolution on November 4, 1993 calling for North Korea to arrange close cooperation with the IAEA. Following protracted negotiations, the IAEA was allowed to resume inspections on March 16, 1994. Following intensive diplomatic discussions, the end of the North Korean nuclear controversy culminated on October 21, 1994, with the signing of the 1994 Agreed Framework Accords in Geneva, Switzerland with the United States brokering a follow-on arrangement called the Kuala Lumpur Joint Declaration for the provision of two light water reactors under terms of the Korean Peninsula Energy Development Organization Agreement (KEDO) on June 12, 1995, with the cost of the reactors being paid for by South Korea, Japan, and a consortium of other countries. The Light Water Supply contract was signed on December 15, 1995.

The North Korean nuclear controversy of 1993–1994 provided the opportunity to move the Korean Peninsula onto the agenda of the U.S.-PRC dialogue regarding nuclear weapons on the Korean Peninsula. Even though United States and the People's Republic of China shared a common interest in preserving stability on the Korean Peninsula, this did not preclude cooperation in as much as their strategic interests coincided.

See also Korean War; Democratic People's Republic of Korea (DPRK); Republic of Korea (ROK); Nuclear Non-Proliferation Treaty (NPT).

REFERENCES: Nathan E. Busch, *No End in Sight: The Continuing Menace of Nuclear Proliferation* (Lexington, KY, 2004); Victor D. Cha *Nuclear North Korea: A Debate on Engagement Strategies* (New York, 2003); K. D. Kapur, *Nuclear Policy in East Asia: U.S. and the Korean Nuclear Crisis Management* (New Delhi, 1995); James Clay Moltz and Alexandre Y. Mansourov, *The North Korean Nuclear Program: Security, Strategy, and New Perspectives from Russia* (New York, 2000).

Keith Leitich

Nuclear Non-Proliferation Treaty (NPT)

Nuclear Non-Proliferation Treaty (NPT) is an international treaty designed to halt the spread of nuclear weapons or transfer of nuclear weapon technology to non-nuclear states to achieve the goal of global nuclear disarmament. The NPT was signed on July 1, 1968 by the United States, the Soviet Union, the United Kingdom, and other 59 countries. China at that time did not sign the NPT, describing it as a "conspiracy" hatched by the United States and the USSR to maintain their "nuclear monopoly." China had joined the nuclear club in 1964, and developed itself into the third largest nuclear power following America and the Soviet Union. Throughout the 1970s,

China remained engaged in upgrading its nuclear and missile building program, and kept itself isolated from international nuclear weapon control and disarmament mechanisms.

In the 1980s, China's transfer of sensitive nuclear technology to volatile regions such as the Middle East, South Asia, and the Gulf caused a grave concern to the United States. As a result, "China threat" occupied a central place in the American political discourse. This apart, America used several policy instruments to pressure China to accede to the NPT, which included suspension of technology transfer and imposition of economic blockade against China's commercial firms. In effect, China ultimately realized that antagonizing America on the non-proliferation issue might prove counterproductive to its long-term national interests. Consequent upon, China signed the NPT in March 1992. In 1993, China signed the Chemical Weapons Convention (CWC), endorsed an indefinite extension of the NPT in1995, and signed the Comprehensive Test Ban Treaty (CTBT) in 1996, in addition to its commitment to abide by the Missile Technology Control Regime (MTCR).

Despite that America suspected that China was secretly engaged in transferring nuclear technologies and equipments including missiles to Pakistan, inducing the White House to slap sanctions against China and stop supply of U.S. satellite hardware to China. Whereas, Chinese President Jiang Zemin while charging the United States with adopting double standard on the non-proliferation issue by withdrawing itself from the 1972 ABM Treaty, reaffirmed China's commitment to the international arms control and disarmament regime. Furthermore, Chinese leaders entertained the belief that America was trying to weaken China by falsely implicating it in nuclear proliferation issue.

The 9/11 tragic events brought about a radical transformation in the strategic environment. The administration of President George W. Bush, although reiterating its commitment to non-proliferation goals in a cavalier fashion, did publicly acknowledge that following the terrorist attacks on America, conventional methods of arms control like NPT, had outlived their utility. President Bush made it abundantly clear that his administration's top priority was to ensure that weapons of mass destruction did not fall into the hands of terrorist organizations. Towards this goal, both China and the United States are engaged in cooperative efforts to root out "nuclear terrorism" as well as to strengthen the non-proliferation regime.

REFERENCES: Michael D. Swaine, *Interpreting China's Grand Strategy: Past, Present, and Future* (Santa

Monica, CA, 2000); Jonathan D. Pollack (ed.), *Sino-American Strategic Dynamics in the Early 21st Century: Prospects, Scenarios, and Implications* (Newport, RI, 2003); Suisheng Zhao (ed.), *Chinese Foreign Policy: Pragmatism and Strategic Behavior* (Armonk, NY, 2003).

B. M. Jain

Office of Strategic Services (OSS)

Office of Strategic Services (OSS) was the American intelligence organization created on July 11, 1941 by President Franklin D. Roosevelt. It was headed throughout World War II by the New York lawyer William Joseph Donovan, a luminary in the Republican Party, until its demise in October 1945 when President Harry S. Truman abruptly dismantled it.

Inspired by the British model of centralizing overseas intelligence gathering, the Roosevelt administration decided to experiment on a first-ever national intelligence organization to replace the existing highly departmentalized intelligence establishment. Initially known as the Coordinator of Information, the OSS began its global operations in earnest in mid-1942, with a comprehensive internal structure that laid the foundation for today's intelligence community in the United States. Broadly speaking, the OSS involved three major sections that oversaw various specialized branches: intelligence gathering, intelligence analysis, and special operations. The OSS was revolutionary in concept and practice. It was the first American national intelligence organization created to be responsible to one single command. For the first time, a large number of area specialists in colleges and universities were recruited as intelligence analysts. The marriage of intelligence and intellect became the most valuable asset of the OSS and it distinguished the OSS as the most productive source of wartime intelligence analysis. The special operations of the OSS forged a strong tie between the U.S. military and the U.S. intelligence activities. But the most influential and long-lasting impact of the OSS is perhaps the comprehensive re-interpretation of what constituted legitimate wartime intelligence operations, for it greatly expanded the concept of psychological warfare to include virtually any means available — black propaganda, disinformation, assassinations, etc. By doing so, it also generated one of the liveliest debates within the American society as to the legal and moral boundary of intelligence operations that would be echoed in the post-Vietnam and post-Watergate era in the U.S.

The OSS had a robust China program. As a fledgling organization, the OSS met with suspicion and guarded reception by most theater commanders. The extraordinary disunity of command and tense squabbles on strategy in the China Theater gave the OSS a good opportunity to prove its worth to the U.S. national leadership and to gain strength in the fields. Consequently, William Donavan regarded China as one of his main areas of interests. At peak time, the OSS had two thousands agents of various specialties operating in China. Yet overall, the saga of the OSS in wartime China was not completely a sanguine one. The chief theme of the OSS story in China was its deep involvement in a command fight with the largest Chinese intelligence organization, the Bureau of Investigation and Statistics (BIS or *Juntong*), headed by Major General Dai Li. The OSS wanted to have complete independence of command and operations while Dai Li wanted to restrict the OSS within the confine of the Sino-American Special Technical Cooperative Organization, or SACO, which was a massive Sino-American intelligence initiative, of which the OSS was an original signer. When the U.S. Navy teamed up with Dai Li as the primary U.S. partner in the SACO, the OSS's plan to gain freedom of operation independent of the Chinese and theater control through the SACO project backfired as the U.S. Navy decidedly went over to the Chinese side in this dispute. Eventually, the OSS proceeded to establish several unofficial units attached to various U.S. wartime organizations in China, without independent command authority, and without Chinese endorsement. The most famous of these unofficial OSS units were the AGFRT with General Claire Lee Chennault's 14th Air Force based in Kunming, and a small but significant contingent within the Army-controlled Dixie Mission to the Communist controlled North China.

Emboldened by its cooperation with the Yugoslav Communist guerrilla forces in the Balkans, the OSS tried to join forces with the Chinese Communist forces, much to the chagrin of the Chinese Nationalist Central Government. When secret deals between the OSS and the Chinese Communist authorities in Yanan were uncovered by President Roosevelt's special envoy to China, General Patrick Hurley, the OSS became a crucial player in the ensuing debate on U.S. policy toward the Chinese Communists and the Chinese Nationalists, a debate that would culminate in the fierce partisan argument over "Who Lost China?" in the 1950s.

See also Sino-American Special Technical Cooperative Organization (SACO); Intelligence Cooperation in World War II.

REFERENCES: Maochun Yu, *OSS in China-Prelude to Cold War* (New Haven, CT, 1997); Milton E. Miles,

A Different Kind of War: The Little-Known Story of the Combined Guerrilla Forces Created in China by the U.S. Navy and the Chinese During WW II (Garden City, NY, 1967).

Maochun Yu

Olympics

The second half of 1993 proved to be a low point for Sino-American relations for a number of reasons. In one particular case, the U.S. Congress applied strong pressures in opposition to Beijing's bid to host the 2000 Olympic Games. This badly damaged Chinese popular opinion toward the United States, especially after the bid for the 2000 Olympic Games was subsequently awarded to Sydney. Chinese aspirations to host the Olympics were very strong, and the loss of the bid was viewed as a national insult to be blamed on meddling by the United States.

China began its campaign for the 2000 Olympics in January 1993. Plans were made for infrastructure and environmental improvements, and to provide excellent facilities and conditions for the Olympic athletes. The push for the Olympics received widespread popular support across China, and Chinese officials promised that no opposition would develop. Supporters of bringing the Olympics to China argued that it would help China to showcase itself to the world community and become a more integrated global member. Outside China, contention developed to China's Olympic bid. Groups, such as the Human Rights Watch in the United States and the Australia Tibet Council, argued that the human rights record of China made it ineligible to host an Olympic Games. Memories of Tiananmen Square also lingered with the appointment of Beijing mayor Chen Xitong as the chairman of China's Olympic Bid Committee. U.S. Senator Bill Bradley of New Jersey even wrote a letter to the International Olympic Committee arguing, "Holding the Games in China, while its Government routinely imprisons and tortures peaceful political dissidents, would confer upon China's leaders a stamp of approval they clearly do not deserve." These sentiments culminated in the U.S. House of Representatives passing a resolution on July 26, 1993, against China's bid, while 60 members of the U.S. Senate signed a letter sent directly to the International Olympic Committee Selection Committee's opposing the bid.

On September 23, 1993, Sydney won the vote to host the 2000 Olympics in the third round of balloting. However, due to a misunderstanding during the presentation ceremony, many Chinese citizens spent a five-minute period of time with the mistaken impression that Beijing had won.

For a number of Chinese, interference by the United States was seen as the primary cause of Beijing's loss, and feelings of national insult and loss of face were strong. The Chinese were not interested in American views of their human rights record, and they condemned the United States for mixing politics with sports.

In 2001, Beijing would succeed in winning the bid for the 2008 Olympic Games. For China's second effort, the United States maintained a more neutral approach.

See also Tiananmen Square Massacre; Human Rights in China (HRIC); Human Rights.

REFERENCES: David M. Lampton, *Same Bed Different Dreams: Managing U.S.-China Relations 1989–2000* (Berkeley, CA, 2001); Robert L. Suettlinger, *Beyond Tiananmen: The Politics of U.S. China Relations 1989–2000* (Washington, DC, 2003).

Wade D. Pfau

One China Policy

For more than fifty years, the United States has adhered to a "One China Policy" in regards to the competing Chinese regimes located in Beijing and Taibei. It is interesting to note that the reasons for this adherence changed over time.

In the aftermath of the crushing defeat in the Chinese Civil War of 1945–1949, Nationalist leader Jiang Jieshi and his Guomindang supporters in late 1949 fled to Taiwan, an island one hundred miles from the Chinese coast. For the next twenty-five years, U.S. foreign policy officially regarded the Nationalist regime in Taibei, Taiwan as the government of all China and equally officially refused to recognize the Communist regime in Beijing, China as the effective rulers of the mainland. This played out in various ways, most notably in the continuing U.S. effort to recognize the Republic of China on Taiwan and not the People's Republic of China on the mainland as the government recognized for China's permanent seat on the UN Security Council. Over these twenty-five years a distinct Chinese society began to emerge on Taiwan, and, equally importantly, a distinct political system and political issues also began to emerge. After Jiang and his son and successor, Jiang Jingguo, died, native Taiwanese assumed leadership positions, and the politics of the "One China Policy" became considerably more complicated. When President Richard Nixon traveled to China in February 1972, the most difficult part of the negotiation with his Chinese hosts concerned the status of Taiwan. The government in Beijing insisted that there was only one China, that Taiwan was a part of China, and that eventually the mainland had to bring Taiwan back into China. The U.S. government officially agreed to disagree.

Beginning in the 1990s, Taiwan political leaders began considering the idea of Taiwan as a country separate from but friendly with China. They were quite willing to give up any dream of reuniting China under their control, but they also wished to be free of the mainland to pursue their own political, social, and economic future. After the British returned Hong Kong, Jiulong (Kowloon), and the New Territories to China, China's sometimes heavy-handed approach to Hong Kong helped strengthen the attractiveness of independence to many Taiwanese. Thus, in 1999 President Li Denghui of the Republic of China suggested that People's Republic of China and Taiwan were separate countries, and the Communist government in Beijing cut off the dialogue in anger. Chen Shuibian became President of the Republic of China in 2000, and appeared sympathetic to Li's view of Taiwan and China as separate countries. Indeed, in early August 2002, he noted, "It is clear that both sides of the straits are separate countries." Both Chinese Communists and surviving remnants of the Guomindang on Taiwan rejected this Two China Policy but for obviously different reasons. As Taiwan moved closer to elections in 2004, Chen publicly rejected the One China Policy, while his principal opponent, Lian Zhan (Lien Chan), continued to support the older formulation of "one China, different interpretation," which suggests after some period of negotiations, Taiwan might reunite with the mainland. Chen won a razor thin election victory, but Lian has challenged the results.

The future of this policy may well determine whether there will be war between the mainland and the island. The People's Republic of China makes any government seeking relations to accept its One China Policy. Taiwan is undergoing a lively political discussion, and several times, when it has appeared that Taiwan might officially proclaim its independence of the mainland, Beijing has threatened to use its military might, which potentially embroils the United States in the conflict.

See also Taiwan; Two China Policy; United Nations; Cold War; Shanghai Communique.

REFERENCES: John F. Copper, *China Diplomacy: The Washington-Taibei-Beijing Triangle* (Boulder, CO, 1992); Elizabeth Van Wie Davis (ed.), *Chinese Perspectives on Sino-American Relations, 1950–2000* (Lewiston, NY, 2000); Rosemary Foot, *The Practice of Power: U.S. Relations with China Since 1949* (New York, 1995); Gerrit Gong (ed.), *Taiwan Strait Dilemmas: China-Taiwan-U.S. Policies in the New Century* (Washington, DC, 2000); June M. Grasso, *Truman's Two-China Policy: 1948–1950* (Armonk, NY, 1987); Shu Guang Zhang, *Deterrence and Strategic Culture: Chinese-American Confrontations, 1949–1958* (Ithaca, NY, 1992).

Charles M. Dobbs

Open Door Policy

The Open Door is a historical principal, often agreed upon according to international law, giving several states and their subjects equal access to a country or region for the purpose of trade or other economic activities. It was frequently used by the European colonial powers during the 19th century and connected with the concept of free trade. The United States advanced the principle of Open Door as early as the 1840s, e.g. after the Dutch takeover of Sumatra in 1846, when it became clear, that without an Open Door Policy, U.S. traders were threatened to be locked out of the local markets by other powers. In China, the Open Door was de facto established in an agreement between China and England 1843 supplementary to the Treaty of Nanjing, in which the most-favored-nation clause was agreed upon. England adhered to the system of free trade because of her dominant role in the China trade, when the Open Door granted almost a monopoly to British trade without the further efforts connected with approaches to direct control.

Most commonly, the Open Door Policy is connected with two notes sent by the U.S. Secretary of State, John Hay, to England, France, Germany, Italy, Japan and Russia in 1899 and 1900. Background of Hay's initiative were two new developments of the 1890s: China's defeat against Japan 1894–1895 led to a "scramble for China," which first concentrated on economical gains. The German seizure of Jiaozhou Bay in November 1897 led to similar acquisitions by France, Russia and England. In addition, after the Spanish-American War of 1898 and the acquisition of the Philippines, the U.S. had become a colonial power in Asia and thus even more interested in the developments in neighboring China. When it seemed possible that China would be carved up into colonies, Hay intervened. In his first note, he drew the outlines of the U.S. concept of the Open Door, developed by the U.S. diplomat William Woodville Rockhill (1854–1914). Hay demanded formal declarations by the other powers to uphold China's territorial and administrative integrity and not to interfere with the use of treaty ports within their spheres of interest. Although replies from the powers were evasive, in March 1900 Hay claimed success. Indeed, only Japan openly disagreed and the Open Door became the Western policy in China, further confirmed by the Anglo-German treaty in October 1900. Although the U.S. initiated the Open

Door Policy and helped to preserve China from being carved up, American respect for Chinese sovereignty was far from absolute, considering American plans for an occupation of a Chinese port as a naval station for the United States and the continued presence of U.S. gunboats on Chinese rivers.

The U.S. kept guarding the Open Door, protested against Russian domination in Manchuria in 1902 and after Japan's victory in the Russo-Japanese War of 1904–1905 urged the Japanese government to maintain a policy of equality in China's Northeast. Japan again threatened the Open Door with her Twenty-One demands in 1915. After U.S. intervention, Japan assured respect for the Open Door but the U.S. had to recognize that Japan had special interests in China. The Open Door was further weakened by treaties between Japan and the European allies in World War I, granting Japan the German possessions and rights in China.

The Open Door principle in China was for the first time officially codified in international law through the Nine Power Treaty of 1922 as a result of Washington Naval Conference or the Conference on the Limitation of Armaments in Washington, D.C. in 1921–1922. Japan started to shut the Open Door in 1931 with the occupation of Manchuria and the policy came to an end after the outbreak of World War II in the Pacific when the Japanese attacked Pearl Harbor in December 1941. After a short revival in 1945–1949, Western gunboats returned to China along with the principles of the prewar era in spite of recognizing China as sovereign state. With the victory of the Communist Party in the Chinese Civil War in 1949, the door was shut and foreigners were expelled from China. The reform policy since the late 1970s marked a careful revival of trade principals according to international law, but the term Open Door is almost out of use today.

REFERENCES: Kevin B. Bucknall, *China and the Open Door Policy* (Sydney, 1989); Paul A. Varg, *Open Door Diplomat, The Life of W.W. Rockhill* (Urbana, IL, 1952); Mary H. Wilgus, *Sir Claude MacDonald, the Open Door, and British Informal Empire in China* (New York, 1987).

Cord Eberspaecher

Operation Oracle

Operation Oracle refers to the code name of an aborted U.S. plan to end the first Taiwan Strait crisis through a United Nations Security Council cease-fire resolution. After the Chinese Communist troops bombarded the Nationalist-held offshore island Jinmen and started the crisis on September 3, 1954, the United States faced the "horrible dilemma" of whether to defend the offshore islands or not. As a solution, Secretary of State John Foster Dulles proposed a plan to freeze the status quo in the Chinese offshore islands through a resolution by the UN Security Council. President Dwight D, Eisenhower approved the plan. To implement the plan, the United States sought help from Britain. Both agreed that New Zealand should introduce to the Security Council the resolution, as the island country was a Council member and one U.S. Pacific ally.

After the negotiations started, however, Oracle encountered difficulties. Britain and New Zealand pursued different goals from the United States in proceeding with Oracle. Britain and New Zealand hoped that the UN resolution would not only lead to the cease-fire in the Strait area but also facilitate the settlement of a broader series of China-related issue, while the United States only expected the introduction of a UN cease-fire resolution, which would pave the way for the future two-Chinas. Only with Dulles's firm resistance did Britain and New Zealand accept the U.S. plan limiting the UN resolution strictly to the cease-fire in Jinmen. At the same time, Oracle faced the opposition from the Nationalists, as the resolution to them implied a two-China arrangement and would lead to a UN trusteeship of Taiwan and a Chinese Communist membership in UN. After Washington offered negotiation of a mutual defense treaty with Taiwan, the Nationalist government agreed not to announce the opposition in the UN but to reserve its position waiting for reactions from the Communist side. However, the U.S. treaty negotiations with Taiwan made the British hold Oracle in abeyance until they made sure the treaty was strictly defensive. Besides, the Chinese Communists, outraged by the U.S.-Taiwan alliance treaty negotiations, in late November sentenced two U.S. civilians and eleven airmen to various prison terms on espionage charges, further reducing the possibility for Beijing to accept the UN resolution.

After the U.S.-Taiwan mutual defense treaty was signed in December 1954, the United States, Britain, and New Zealand finally activated their Oracle plan. On January 28, 1955, New Zealand submitted to the UN Security Council a letter requesting a meeting of the Council to consider the conditions in the Strait area, which were "likely to endanger the maintenance of international peace and security." Two days later, the Soviet Union joined the UN diplomatic maneuvering and requested that the Council meet to consider U.S. "aggression" against the People's Republic of China (PRC). On January 31, the Security Council put both the New Zealand and Soviet proposals on its agenda and invited the PRC to participate in the discussion of the New Zealand proposal. Three days later, the PRC categorically rejected the invitation, denouncing that the purpose of the New Zealand resolution was to legitimate the existence of two Chinas. Because of Beijing's refusal, London immediately lost interest in moving forward Oracle. Dulles had to agree to put the plan on hold. From the Oracle plan, the United States for the first time proceeded toward de facto two Chinas. However, facing the oppositions from both allies and enemies, Operation Oracle was doomed.

See also Taiwan Strait Crises; U.S.-China Mutual Defense Treaty (1954); One China Policy; Two China Policy.

REFERENCES: Chang Su-ya, " 'An Li Hui Ting Huo An': Mei Guo Ying Fu Di Yi Ci Tai Hai Ce Lue Zhi Yi," [" 'Security Council Cease-fire Case': One of U.S. Strategies Handling the First Taiwan Strait Crisis"] in *Jin Dai Shi Yan Jiu Suo Ji Kan [Collected Papers of Modern History Research Institute] Vol. 22* (1993); Rosemary Foot, "Search for a Modus Vivendi: Anglo-American Relations and China Policy," in Warren Cohen and Akira Iriye (eds.), *The Great Powers in East Asia, 1953–1960* (New York, 1990); Robert Accinelli, *Crisis and Commitment: United States Policy toward Taiwan, 1950–1955* (Chapel Hill, NC, 1996); John W. Garver, *The Sino-American Alliance: Nationalist China and American Cold War Strategy in Asia* (New York, 1997).

Tao Peng

Opium Trade

The roots of the opium trade between the United States and Manchu China began in the late 1700s, when both nations shared a desired policy of isolation. The Manchu limited eager European traders to hongs (warehouses), supervised by the Co-hong, a merchant monopoly. They demonstrated their penchant for isolation and superiority by having a variety of bureaus and agencies to conduct relations with non-Chinese peoples rather than a Ministry of Foreign Affairs: this was known as the Guangzhou trading system (1760–1840). The U.S. government admired the policy of the Manchus, because it hoped to curtail U.S. ties with Europe, and in the case of men like Thomas Jefferson, shared the Chinese disdain for the British. Conversely, congressionally supported American economic interests worked in opposition to the goals of the Chinese, as merchants were eager to replace the British West Indies trade that had been lost by the American Revolution and looked toward China to do so.

In the 1780s, New York bankers began sending ginseng-laden ships to China, and delighted merchants earned high profits importing Chinese teas, chinaware, silks, handicrafts, carpets, spices, and porcelain to Americans. Despite the initially encouraging profits, the growing economic relationship between the reluctant Chinese and the West, was fraught with tension. While Chinese products met the needs of Americans, there was a limited market for American goods in China. Western exports such as lead, tin, cotton, furs, woolens, clocks and other mechanical items did not elicit the demand that the Americans or the British evinced for Chinese goods. This was exemplified in the late 1700s when British emissary to China Lord George Macartney asked for an end to Chinese trade restrictions relegating Westerners to Guangzhou, and the Manchu Emperor Qianlong held steadfast, sending an edict to George III explaining that: "We have never valued ingenious articles, nor do we have the slightest need of your country's manufactures." As a result of the continued trade imbalance, Westerners, including Americans, were forced to pay for Chinese goods in silver. This greatly alarmed the British, who sought to rectify the imbalance by selling Indian opium to the Chinese. When American traders became aware that the British were profiting from this illegal drug, American opium from Turkey began competing with British opium: by 1805, respected Bostonian families sold Turkish opium to an increasingly diverse and addicted Chinese populace. In response, the Chinese Emperor prohibited the smoking and importation of opium; however, disastrously, Western importers and Chinese merchants' and mandarins' flouted his orders.

When the emperor appointed Commissioner Lin Zexu to stop the opium trade, British aggression resulted in the Opium War of 1840, culminating in British victory with the Treaty of Nanjing in 1842. This treaty aimed to accomplish what MacArtney had asked for decades earlier: to open China up to the West, as well as to halt Chinese attempts to apply Chinese rule of law against Americans and the British. The treaty would not be fully established until the British defeated the Chinese a second time, obtaining a treaty in Tianjin in 1858. While Americans did not fight in the Opium Wars, they would profit from them: with the 1844 Treaty of Wangxia, signed by Massachusetts Congressman Caleb Cushing, whose family had grown rich from the opium trade, the Chinese were forced to grant American Protestant missionaries the right to learn the Chinese language fluently (this had previously been prohibited), and build "hospitals, churches and cemeteries" in the five treaty ports now open. Opium trade increased dramatically after the Opium Wars, thus Americans reaped the fruits of the empire on the coattails of the British, while the Chinese were diplomatically and militarily unable to halt the infiltration they had so vehemently opposed.

The treaties established as a result of the illegal trade that precipitated the Opium wars were a source of humiliation for the Chinese and would not be rescinded until the 1940s. As such, the opium trade is a reflection of the growing Western commercial imperialism that grew out of the 18th century mercantilism and the Guangzhou trading system.

See also Treaty of Nanjing (1842); Treaty of Wangxia (1844); First Opium War (1839–1842); Second Opium War (1856–1859).

REFERENCES: Kathleen Lodwick, *Crusaders Against Opium: Protestant Missionaries in China 1874–1917* (Stanislaus, CA, 1997); Charles C. Stelle, "American and British Trade in Opium to China, 1821–39," *Pacific Historical Review Vol. 10* (1941).

Cristina Zaccarini

Opium Wars *see* First Opium War; Second Opium War

Overseas Chinese

The term Overseas Chinese, or *huaqiao*, refers to the Chinese diaspora abroad. Although 95% of overseas Chinese live in Southeast Asia, Chinese are scattered across the world. Most overseas Chinese traditionally come from villages in Guangdong and Fujian provinces where migration abroad is a family strategy to deal with limited economic opportunities. In Imperial China, migration abroad was technically illegal, so Chinese living abroad risked punishment upon return. After emigration laws were forcibly liberalized by the British government's victories in the Opium wars, labor migration and the coolie trade caused large increases in the numbers of Chinese living abroad.

No matter what the destination was, the Chinese generally were not well received by the local communities. In some cases, as in the Americas, Chinese laborers were seen as creating unfair competition for workers, and local governments responded to labor concerns with harsh and restrictive immigration regulations. In other cases, as in much of Southeast Asia, it was not the poor migrant Chinese laborer that was most feared, but the wealthier merchant. Either way, the Chinese were seen as either unable or unwilling to assimilate into the local culture and were therefore subject to suspicion. Throughout the 19th century and into the 20th, events proved to overseas Chinese that a weak Chinese government

meant poor treatment of Chinese nationals abroad, so many began to take an active interest in practical activities to strengthen the homeland. At the time of the 1911 revolution, Sun Zhongshan toured Chinese colonies abroad soliciting financial support for his rebellion against the dying Qing Dynasty; he would call the overseas Chinese "The Mother of the Republican Revolution." Similarly, in the era of the war of resistance against Japan from 1931 to 1945, overseas Chinese were once again called upon to provide funds to defend China. After World War II, many overseas Chinese took an interest in the establishment of the People's Republic of China (PRC) because they felt a strong and independent China would help improve their status abroad.

As the Cold War set in, the Nationalist Party (Guomindang) that relocated to Taiwan already had a long tradition of looking overseas for support and, in turn, providing overseas Chinese with services through its Overseas Chinese Affairs Commission (OCAC) such as assistance in setting up Chinese schools and newspapers, travel to see the progress of development in Taiwan, and new investment opportunities. The Chinese Communist Party (CCP) had no such groundwork, though it also established an OCAC to manage overseas Chinese affairs. Although many governments including the Republic of China (ROC), the United States, and Great Britain expressed concerns in the 1950s that the PRC might try to make use of the overseas Chinese of Southeast Asia as a "fifth column" to initiate Communist revolutions in those countries, the CCP came to see the overseas Chinese as a political liability interfering with their relations with the Southeast Asian nations. Traditionally, all Chinese governments have followed a law of nationality that said Chinese born anywhere in the world of a Chinese father were Chinese citizens; moreover, there was no provision for the divestment of citizenship. In 1957, however, the PRC renounced dual citizenship and began to encourage the Chinese to become citizens in their countries of residence. In contrast, throughout the Cold War the ROC was very active in courting and claiming the loyalty of Chinese living around the world

Today two kinds of services are still provided to overseas Chinese: investment and education. Harnessing the impressive financial power of the overseas Chinese to benefit the development of either the mainland or Taiwan is still a major goal for both governments. Similarly, overseas Chinese youth are encouraged to acquire a Chinese education through Chinese language textbooks published in China or Taiwan and special programs to encourage overseas Chinese youth to "return" to China or Taiwan for their high school or university level studies. These programs ensure that overseas Chinese maintain financial and cultural links to their ancestral land, though their political loyalties now rightfully belong to their countries of nationality.

See also Chinese Americans.

REFERENCES: Stephen Fitzgerald, *China and the Overseas Chinese: A Study of Peking's Changing Policy, 1949–1970* (Cambridge, UK, 1972); Wang Gungwu, *China and the Chinese Overseas* (Singapore, 1991); Lynn Pan (ed.), *The Encyclopedia of the Chinese Overseas* (Cambridge, MA, 1999).

Meredith Oyen

Panay Incident

Commissioned into the U.S. Navy's Asiatic Fleet in late 1928 the USS *Panay* was one of the Yangzi River gunboats that provided the bulwark of the American presence in China. Like her sister ships on the China Station, the *Panay* was built in a Chinese shipyard and was not an ocean-going vessel. Designed for service on the Yangzi River the ship was armed accordingly and boasted two three-inch naval guns, in addition to several rifle-caliber machine guns. Against any vessel she was likely to meet along the river, the *Panay* could hold her own, as well as provide shore bombardment in support of U.S. operations on the river's banks.

Along with the other gunboats of the Asiatic Fleet, the *Panay*, therefore, embodied the U.S. mission in China, gunboat diplomacy in support of American commercial interests. For the boats and their crews this meant a mission wrought with danger, as it was common for both sides in the Chinese civil wars in 1920s and 1930s to fire upon them. The onset of the Sino-Japanese War in 1931 resulted in a more precarious position for the gunboats because the United States maintained its official neutrality while it supported the Guomindang. With the Japanese attack on Shanghai in 1937 and the subsequent offensive inland by the Imperial Japanese Army, the Yangzi River gunboats operated in a war zone.

After the Japanese attacked Nanjing in late 1937, the *Panay* was one of the gunboats used to evacuate Americans from the city. To avert a Japanese air attack the commander of the *Panay* had two large American flags laid out on the vessel's upper deck. Yet the ship came under Japanese attack and was sunk on December 12, 1937. Subsequent Japanese claims that the pilots were unable to identify the vessel's markings because of their altitude were exposed as false when newsreel footage showed that the planes attacked at low-level and then strafed survivors in the water. Two

Americans died and thirty more were wounded in the attack. Despite the loss of life, the incident did not provoke war between the two nations, as most Americans favored withdrawal from China to avoid further provocations. Shortly thereafter Tokyo apologized to Washington and paid a $2 million indemnity. As a result, the crisis subsided.

REFERENCES: George W. Baer, *One Hundred Years of Sea Power: The U.S. Navy, 1890–1990* (Stanford, CA, 1994); Thomas H. Buckley, *The United States Navy and the Washington Naval Conference, 1921–1922* (Knoxville, TN, 1970); William R. Braisted, *The United States Navy in the Pacific, 1897–1909* (Austin, TX, 1958) and *The United States Navy in the Pacific, 1909–1922* (Austin, TX, 1971); Kenneth J. Hagan, ed., *In Peace and War: Interpretations of American Naval History, 1775–1984* (Westport, CT, 1984); David M. Kennedy, *Freedom from Fear: The American People in Depression and War, 1929–1945* (New York, 1999); Allan R. Millett and Peter Maslowski, *For the Common Defense: A Military History of the United States of America* (New York, 1994); Naval History Division, Office of the Chief of Naval Operations, *Dictionary of American Naval Fighting Ships* (Washington, DC, 1959–1981); Gerald E. Wheeler, *Prelude to Pearl Harbor: The United States Navy and the Far East, 1921–1931* (Columbia, MO, 1963).

Paul D. Gelpi, Jr.

Panmunjom Armistice Talks

The negotiations at the village of Panmunjom between the various factions fighting in Korea failed to create a peace treaty but did establish a ceasefire that held into the 21st century. Talks originally began in the old capital city of Kaesong on July 10, 1951. However, these early talks soon faltered and on August 25, the Communists walked out. Talks resumed on October 25, 1951, in the village of Panmunjom. Panmunjom sits about 5 miles south of the 38th parallel, on the front line.

The United Nations team was led by American Admiral C. Turner Joy, Commander of Naval Forces, Far East. The Communist mission was led by General Nam Il, Chief of Staff of the North Korean Army and Vice Premier of North Korea. The Chinese were represented by General Deng Hua, commander of the 15th Army Group, and General Xie Fang, Chief of Propaganda for the Northeast China Military District. The Communist negotiators had long military-political experience, and were revolutionaries. The UN side was represented by men with more limited military backgrounds. As such, the UN negotiators were frustrated by what they saw as Communists tricks. The UN was further pressured by public opinion, which saw the start of the talks as the beginning of the end of the war and quickly grew impatient with continued combat and casualties.

When the talks began, the UN believed that

a ceasefire might be a few weeks away. Instead, the talks continued for two bloody years. The talks stuck on a myriad of issues. The North Koreans originally tried to portray the negotiations as a UN surrender. Under Joy's direction, the UN continued military actions during the talks, fearing that the Communists planned to use the talks to build up their supplies in Korea. In essence, the Communists wanted the ceasefire line to follow the former dividing line of the 38th parallel, while the UN wanted the line to follow the current front line. Another major sticking point was the question of whether non-Korean troops would remain on the peninsular following an armistice. Linked to the last point were questions of repairing or building airfields and stockpiling supplies. Then negotiations bogged down over the problem of which countries should serve as neutral observers. While the UN wanted Switzerland, Sweden, and India, the Communists insisted that Bulgaria, Poland, and Czechoslovakia serve as the neutral observers. By the spring of 1952, three major issues remained unresolved: The rebuilding of airfields, the role of the Soviet Union as a neutral observer, and the repatriation of prisoners of war. The prisoner issue became a tough problem to surmount. Both sides assumed that the vast majority of the prisoners would want repatriation. However, under questioning less than half the prisoners held by the UN wanted to be returned to North Korea or the Peoples Republic of China. Many prisoners had served in the North Korean or Communist Chinese armies only a short time, and hoped to use their status as prisoners to escape to South Korea, Taiwan, or even the West. Of approximately 170,000 POW's, only 70,000 wanted to return to Communist control. The break came in the spring of 1953, when both sides agreed to a separate exchange of sick and wounded poisoners. The exchange occurred between April 20 and May 3. On May 25, the UN proposed turning the POW matter over to a group of five nations, with India providing the bulk of support. The Communists accepted this on June 8. With POW issue behind them, a full truce was reachable. The six weeks following saw some of the heaviest fighting of the war. Both sides sought to end with their lines in an advantageous position. Syngman Rhee, President of South Korea, opposed the ending of the war short of unification under his regime, and sought to break any agreements between the UN and the Communists.

Beginning July 13, the Communists opened their largest offensive in two years, but within a week, the offensive had been contained. The signing came on July 27, 1953, at 10 AM. The simple ceremony lasted under 15 minutes. Both sides fired artillery for the next twelve hours, and then stopped when the armistice went into effect. As no peace treaty had been negotiated through the end of the 20th century, the armistice hammered out during the last two years of the war served to maintain the uneasy peace on the Korean peninsular into the 21st century.

See also Korean War; Korean War POW Negotiations.

REFERENCES: Edwin P. Hoyt, *The Bloody Road to Panmunjom* (New York, 1985); C. Turner Joy, *How Communists Negotiate* (New York, 1955); Allan E. Goodman (ed.), *Negotiating While Fighting: The Diary of Admiral C. Turner Joy at the Korean Armistice Conference* (Stanford, CA, 1978); William W. Vatcher, *Panmunjom: The Story of the Korean Military Armistice Negotiations* (New York, 1958).

Barry Stentiford

Paper Tiger

This term was coined by Mao Zedong (1893–1976), leader of the Chinese Communist Party, in an interview with Anna Louise Strong, American journalist, in Yanan on August 6, 1946.

After World War II, the Truman administration's effort to mediate for a political settlement between the Nationalists and the Communists failed. At the time, the civil war between the two sides just broke out and the Nationalists, with the U.S. aid, were on the upper hand. At the same time, the tension between the U.S. and the Soviet Union was also mounting. In the interview, Mao blamed Jiang Jieshi, leader of the Nationalist government, and its ally, the U.S. government, for China's civil war; and accused the latter for preparing a war against the Soviet Union. When asked about the possibility of U.S. using atom bombs against the Soviet Union, Mao responded with his famous populist remarks: "The atom bomb is a *paper tiger* which the U.S. reactionaries use to scare people. It looks terrible, but in fact it isn't. Of course, the atom bomb is a weapon of mass slaughter, but the outcome of the war is decided by the people, not by one or two new types of weapon. All reactionaries are *paper tigers*. In appearance, the reactionaries are terrifying, but in reality they are not so powerful. From a long-term point of view, it is not the reactionaries but the people who are really powerful." On learning that his characterization of all reactionaries as "*zhi laohu*" was interpreted as "scarecrows," Mao corrected it with the literal translation "paper tigers."

Since then "paper tiger" had become part of his and the official rhetoric of the People's Republic of China in referring to the feeble nature of their frightful and powerful enemies. During the Cold War, it was used most frequently for "the

U.S. imperialists," and, after the Sino-Soviet split in 1960, increasingly for "the Soviet social-imperialists." Today the term is used in referring to any individual or regime that looks powerful but is actually weak.

REFERENCES: Mao Zedong, "Talk with the American Correspondent Anna Louise Strong (August 6, 1946)," *Selected Works of Mao Zedong, Vol. IV* (Beijing, 1992).

Yusheng Yao

Paris Peace Conference

The Paris Peace Conference and the resulting Treaty of Versailles and the companion treaties ended the First World War (signed in nearby Paris suburbs), extracting a relatively harsh and punitive peace on the defeated Central Powers, and also establishing the League of Nations to help prevent future conflict.

One of the key issues for the peace talks was the disposition of Germany's overseas empire. Despite the hopes caused by the rhetoric of U.S. President Woodrow Wilson for a lenient peace and for national self-determination, the resulting treaties were harsh and signaled a victors' peace. Germany conceded German East Africa to Great Britain, German Southwest Africa to South Africa, and Cameroon to France. Perhaps the most controversial provision was an acceptance of Germany's guilt in causing the war. The other defeated Central Powers also suffered in the resulting peace treaties. And then there was the matter of Germany's empire in the Pacific and its "concession" on the Shandong peninsula of China. Japan prepared very well for the Paris Peace Conference, and had three demands in return for its brief work in seizing Germany's Pacific empire and its Pacific fleet. The Japanese delegation demanded Germany's Pacific islands holdings, Germany's concession in Shandong, China, especially its railroad and mining rights, and finally a statement of racial equality among nations as a basis for Wilson's cherished League of Nations. While Japan's claim to Germany's concession in China rested on a somewhat shaky legal foundation, its demand for a declaration of racial equality of nations was reasonable and caused problems for other countries. Chinese diplomats had argued that the language of Germany's original concession and China's 1917 declaration of war voided Japan's claim but Great Britain and France felt bound by secret agreements with Japan. Moreover, Australia and other British Dominions would not agree to the clause on racial equality, and to assuage Japan, the other participants pressed Wilson to concede Japan's territorial demands, which, ultimately, he did. Wilson

was able to make Japan agree it would return Shandong eventually to Chinese control maintaining only Germany's former economic rights.

When news of the conference's approval of Japan's takeover of Germany's Shandong peninsula concession reached China, the result was the so-called May Fourth Movement and the birth of modern Chinese nationalism. Students from Beijing area universities struck in protest on May 4, 1919, and merchants and other workers soon joined them. Chinese students in France helped surround the quarters of the lead Chinese delegate at the Paris Peace talks, Gu Weijun, and prevented him from attending the signing ceremony — better to suffer such shame without participating in it.

Thus, the Paris Peace Conference created a sense of unfairness in Germany at the harsh treaty terms, and created competing Chinese and Japanese nationalism on a collision course both leading to the Second World War, which the conference was designed to prevent. Chinese nationalists would doubt the supposed good intentions of American diplomacy, while Japanese nationalists would become increasingly frustrated by China's resistance and eventually look to military action to secure its empire in Asia.

See also Gu Weijun (1888–1985); May Fourth Movement (1919); Treaty of Versailles (1919).

REFERENCES: Manfred F. Boemeke, Gerald D. Feldman, and Elisabeth Glaser (eds.), *The Treaty of Versailles: A Reassessment after 75 Years* (New York, 1998); Chin Wen-ssu, *China at the Paris Peace Conference in 1919* (Jamaica, NY, 1961); Michael L. Dockrill and John Fisher (eds.), *The Paris Peace Conference 1919: Peace Without Victory* (New York, 2001); Erik Goldstein, *The First World War Peace Settlements, 1919–1925* (New York, 2002); William R. Keylor (eds.), *The Legacy of the Great War: Peacemaking, 1919* (Boston, MA, 1998); Margaret Olwen MacMillan, *Paris 1919: Six Months That Changed the World* (New York, 2002); Alan Sharp, *The Versailles Settlement: Peacemaking in Paris, 1919* (New York, 1991).

Charles M. Dobbs

Parker, Peter (1804–1888)

While it would be decades before American merchants were as numerically prevalent as their British counterparts in 19th century China, the American missionary presence rivaled that of the British beginning with the arrival of the first medical missionary to China, Massachusetts-born Peter Parker. The thirty-year-old Parker arrived in Guangzhou in 1834, the year that he was ordained to the Presbyterian ministry and awarded a medical degree from New Haven. His goal was to replace Chinese superstitions with the Christian gospel and European knowledge, and he sought to do this by providing free medical treatment to Chinese patients. In 1835 both American and British supporters funded the opening of the first Ophthalmic Hospital, which later became a general hospital, at Guangzhou, and due to this support, Parker could fulfill his goal of providing free treatments. Above the hospital entrance a sign read: *Pu Ai Yi Yuan* (Hospital of Universal Love), and there Parker treated male and female Chinese of all classes and ages from many parts of China.

Parker is most known for introducing anesthesia to China in the form of sulphuric ether, however, at the time of his arrival, he brought with him a knowledge of European pharmacology that did not offer the Chinese anything significantly more beneficial than their traditional healing methods. Initially the Chinese were so distrustful of Parker that they employed a spy, a linguist, to oversee his work at the hospital; however, Parker would impress them with his ability to remove external tumors and especially perform cataract operations. While opthalmological surgery had initially been introduced to the Chinese from India between the 7th and 9th century, and was practiced in China in the 9th century, it had not become integrated into the medical knowledge and skills of the Chinese, and was therefore impressive enough to make Parker famous: thus, he was able to treat thousands of Chinese patients within a span of a few years. These successes would not impress his sponsoring organization, the American Board of Commissioners for Foreign Missions (ABCFM), who had funded him primarily for his ability to win Chinese souls through medicine, and the ABCFM would eventually withdraw their support. In part to raise money for his hospital, Parker left China for America during the Opium War of 1839–1842. During at least one fund-raising endeavor, Parker showed potential donors portraits of Chinese patients treated by Parker for very large tumors, drawn by Chinese artist Lam Qua. These paintings have inspired much interesting scholarly debate regarding the cultural context of 19th century Sino-American relations. Upon his return to China in 1842, Parker continued his medical work and also engaged in diplomacy. Like most missionaries Parker opposed the U.S. government's neutrality in the Opium War, believing that the British victory over the Chinese would mean an end to the ban on Christianity and missionary travel to the interior. When the Treaty of Wangxia was signed between the U.S. and China, Peter served under Caleb Cushing as his chief secretary and interpreter.

Parker was one of several Christians to initially support a Christian-led attempt at leadership change in China in 1850. The impact of the Opium War and increased Western influence led to a weakening of the Manchu emperor from within: a popular, religious movement turned into an attempt to replace the Manchu Emperor Xian Feng with a fanatical self-baptized Christian Hong Xiuquan (Hung Hsiu-ch'uan). By 1853, when Hong had 500,000 followers and succeeded at capturing Nanjing, Parker secretly made contact with him with the hope that the Taiping rebels could continue their efforts and bring Christianity to Guangzhou. When in 1855 Parker was named American Commissioner and Minister to China, he pursued an aggressive policy in order to abolish all Chinese commercial restrictions against the United States. As a consequence of these problematic endeavors, Parker was recalled as commissioner in 1857, replaced by William B. Reed.

See also Missionaries (American) in China.

REFERENCES: Edward V. Gulick, *Peter Parker and the Opening of China* (Cambridge, MA, 1973); Elizabeth H. Thomson, "Peter Parker: Physician-Missionary-Diplomat," *Yale Medicine* (Summer 1979); Paul U. Unschuld, *Medicine in China: A History of Ideas* (Berkeley, CA, 1985).

Cristina Zaccarini

Pauley Mission (1946)

In the spring of 1948, the American government learnt that the Soviet Red Army was taking away Japanese property in Manchuria back to Russia as reparations. Concerned about the Russian action of robbing China of industrial plants, the Truman administration sent American businessman Edwin W. Pauley on a mission to survey what was going on in Manchuria. With a team of industrial engineers, Pauley toured around Manchuria investigating the major factories. Soon they met difficulties. The Russians and the Chinese Communist authorities refused Pauley's request to get into Dalian (Dairen), an important industrial port city in Manchuria. A similar request to enter Andong was turned down by the local Chinese Communist authorities. However, Pauley and his men continued their work in other places. The Pauley mission compared the records of the Manchurian industry at the end of the war with the findings at the time of the investigation. They discovered that the discrepancy was huge. They also found that the Soviet removals of factory equipments and other properties resulted in terrible destructions and damages to the industry in that area. The estimates of the replacement value of the removals and destructions reached more than $2 billion. The mission's report pointed out that the Russians could not justify their removals of all Japanese assets in Manchuria because the Red Army entered the war only a few days before the Japanese surrender and they did not contribute as much to the final victory as they had claimed. The report concluded, "the damage which Manchurian industry has sustained since V-J Day has set back China's industrial progress for a generation."

See also Civil War (1945–1949).

REFERENCES: U.S. Department of State, *United States Relations With China* (Washington, DC, 1949).

Yuwu Song

Peiping

The capital of China under the Qing Dynasty had been Beijing; the name meant "northern capital." In 1928, it was renamed Beiping ("northern peace") to indicate that it was no longer the capital; the new Guomindang government had established itself in Nanjing.

In 1949, the victorious Communists made the city the capital of China once more, and restored it to its traditional name of Beijing (for which the standard spelling in the United States at the time was Peking). Britain and most other nations accepted the name change. But the Guomindang withdrew to Taiwan, where they declared that Taibei had become the new capital of China. They refused to recognize that Beijing had become the capital of China, and therefore refused to call it by a name that implied it was the capital. They continued to call it Beiping (for which the standard spelling in the United States was Peiping). The United States government, going along with the Guomindang theory that the capital of China was Taibei, also went along with the Guomindang's linguistic symbolism. Both public statements of U.S. officials and the internal documents of the State Department used "Peiping" much more often than "Peking" up until 1965.

Most of the American media had already abandoned the use of "Peiping," embodying as it did a deliberate insult to the People's Republic of China. *The New York Times*, for example, had shifted from "Peiping" to "Peking" in 1962.

REFERENCES: Ural Alexis Johnson, *The Right Hand of Power: The Memoirs of an American Diplomat* (Englewood Cliffs, NJ, 1984).

Edwin Moise

Peking Union Medical College (PUMC)

The present day Peking Union Medical College (PUMC), located in downtown Beijing (Peking), began in 1906 as Union Medical College, with the support of the Qing Dynasty and American and British missionary societies. In 1915 the Rockefeller Foundation began to support this medical school, which represented the "Johns Hopkins Model," combining laboratory research with clinical practice. Peking Union Medical College became China's center for the teaching of Western medicine, particularly the modern scientific public health methods and the treatment of diseases that were prevalent in China. The PUMC's leadership in China was solidified in 1928 when the Rockefeller Foundation granted it $12 million.

PUMC had one of the highest tuition fees of all missionary and non-missionary schools and imposed strict standards upon students, which were mostly upper class. Missionary schools were the training grounds of most PUMC students, since English was the language used in both entrance exams and coursework. Students did their course work and were required to take clinical clerkships in their fourth years and internships in their fifth years. PUMC faculty were both researchers and instructors, and graduates of the most prestigious universities in the world. By 1927 the total number of Chinese faculty was fifty-eight while there were thirty-seven foreigners, however, half of the foreign faculty were either professors or associate professors while the Chinese were mostly all either assistant or associate professors. Faculty and student research led to significant findings in the understanding of such diseases as schistosomiasis, hookworm, and kala-azar. For example, by 1940, the reservoir host for kala-azar, a parasitic disease causing anemia, and enlarged spleens or livers, was identified as the dog and the vector host, the sandfly. The PUMC, under Dr. John Grant, pioneered public-health education in China in 1925 with the help of the Beijing municipal government. Students who worked for Grant's department of public health would become Nationalist government officials in its health bureaucracy and spread the influence of PUMC through the national health system. PUMC's School of Nursing helped spread public-health education by training nurses in school and industrial health and maternal care while promoting nursing as a respectable profession. With the onset of Nationalist attempts to improve China's healthcare, and its obstacles stemming from lack of resources and political control, the Rockefeller Foundation reevaluated its work in China, singling out PUMC as especially old-fashioned in its endeavors. The Foundation incorporated the ideas of public-health expert Selskar M. Gunn, who had visited China in 1931–1932, and learned of the rural reconstruction work of men like James Yen, C.C. Chen and J. Heng Liu. With a three-year grant of one million dollars the Foundation launched "The China Program," initiating social medicine at PUMC. Graduates of the PUMC dominated health bureaucracies and medical schools after the Communist victory in 1949, with twelve PUMC graduates directing Chinese medical colleges from 1949–1950 and in 1957, six PUMC graduates of eight directors of institutes of Chinese Academy of Medical Sciences. The editorial board of the Chinese Medical Association and the organization itself were dominated by PUMC graduates or faculty.

Today Peking Union Medical College, which is affiliated with the Chinese Academy of Medical Sciences (est. 1956) remains the most prestigious, elite medical school in the People's Republic of China. It has an eight-year-old medical program for which it picks the top sixty students per year from the nation's middle schools.

REFERENCES: Mary B. Bullock, *An American Transplant: The Rockefeller Foundation and Peking Union Medical College* (Berkeley, CA, 1980). James C. Thomson Jr., *While China Faced West, American Reformers in Nationalist China, 1928–1937* (Cambridge, MA, 1969); Ka-che Yip, *Health and National Reconstruction in Nationalist China, The Development of Modern Health Services, 1928–1937* (Ann Arbor, MI, 1995); William H. Schneider (ed.), *Rockefeller Philanthropy and Modern Biomedicine: International Initiatives from World War I to the Cold War* (Bloomington, IN, 2002).

Cristina Zaccarini

Peng Dehuai (1898–1974)

Peng Dehuai (Peng Te-huai) was one of the most powerful and revered military leaders of the Chinese revolution. As a former Guomindang (GMD) army officer, he led his troops' insurrection and joined the Chinese Communist Party (CCP) in 1928. He became the commander of the Thirteenth Division of the Red Army, vice chairman of the Central Military Commission (CMC) in 1932, and commander of the Shan-Gan Army Group while Mao was his political commissar in 1935. Peng was deputy commander of the Eighth Route Army in World War II . After the CCP-GMD coalition collapsed and the Eighth Route Army became the People's Liberation Army (PLA), he served as PLA chief of the general staff, commander and political commissar of the Northwest Field Army Group, and commander of the First Field Army Group during the civil war. When the PRC was founded, he was appointed chairman of the Northwest Military and Political Committee, commander of the Northwest Military District, and deputy commander-in-chief of the PLA in 1949.

Peng supported Mao's decision to send Chinese troops to the Korean War during an enlarged Politburo meeting on October 4–5, 1950, after the UN forces crossed the 38th parallel and reached the Chinese-Korean border. He was appointed the commander-in-chief and political commissar of the Chinese People's Volunteer Forces (CPVF) in Korea and later the commander-in-chief and political commissar of the Chinese-North Korean Allied Forces. From 1950 to 1953, he commanded more than 3 million Chinese troops in the Korean War, or the "War to Resist U.S. and Aid Korea," as it was called in China.

Peng planned and conducted all major operations, made most of the important decisions on the front, communicated with Mao daily, and worked closely with Kim Il Sung and other North Korean leaders. During the early offensive campaigns in 1950–1951, he employed traditional combat tactics: surprise attacks, numerical superiority, and mobile operations. When these tactics began to lose effectiveness, he adopted a more cautious strategy, shifting from a mobile war to trench war in 1951–1953. Though there were different opinions on how to fight China's first foreign war against the most powerful army in the world, Peng loyally followed Mao's instructions and did his utmost to carry out Mao's plans. He represented China and North Korea in the peace talks with the U.S. and South Korea, and signed the Korean truce agreement in July 1953. He agreed with Mao that China achieved its victory in the war by saving the Communist regime in North Korea, preventing a possible U.S. invasion of China, receiving more military and economic aid from the Soviet Union, and making the new republic an influential Communist power in the world. After the Korean War, Peng became the defense minister, deputy Premier, and a PLA marshal. He launched the PRC's first military reform which extensively copied the Soviet military model and resulted in the Soviets' providing massive amounts of weapon systems, training all the services, organizing China's defense industry, and transferring nuclear technology to China.

Outspoken and critical of Mao's radical domestic programs like the Great Leap Forward in 1958, Peng was accused by Mao of forming a "right opportunist clique" and conducting "unprincipled factional activity," charges that often represented pro-Soviet political positions, and thus removed from all his posts in 1959. He lived thereafter in virtual house arrest. He wrote many letters to Mao and the Central Committee appealing for suspension of his disgrace. These letters brought more critiques against him. In 1965, he had a chance to prove his innocence and loyalty by serving as the deputy director of the "remote regional reconstruction" in Sichuan Province. But he did not survive the Cultural Revolution. He was arrested again in 1966 and sent back to Beijing where he was criticized, denounced, and tortured through the rest of the 1960s and early 1970s.

Peng died in jail on November 29, 1974. After Mao's death in 1976, the CCP Central Committee announced Peng's rehabilitation in 1978, and his funeral was held in Beijing later that year.

See also Korean War.

REFERENCES: Richard Peters and Xiaobing Li, *Voices from the Korean War: Personal Stories of American, Korean, and Chinese Soldiers* (Lexington, KY, 2004); Chen Jian, *China's Road to the Korean War* (New York, 1994); Jurgen Domes, *Peng Te-huai: the Man and the Image* (London, 1985).

Xiaobing Li

Peng Te-huai (1898–1974) *see* Peng De-huai (1898–1974)

People's Republic of China (PRC)

During the Second World War, the United States sent envoys to the Chinese Communists to encourage cooperative arrangements with the Chinese Nationalists against the Japanese. But neither the Communists nor the Nationalists trusted each other, and each force was trying to position itself to dominate China after the eventual Japanese defeat. In fact, the Communists and the Nationalists had been fighting each other for almost a decade longer than they had been fighting the Japanese, and when Japan surrendered, the conflict between the two Chinese factions did not so much begin as escalate. The battle for China coincided with the beginnings of the Cold War, and so, almost by default, the United States backed the Nationalists. Ironically, the Nationalist cause had become so undermined by corruption and defeatism that many American-provided weapons and munitions were abandoned or sold to the Communists before they had been used by the Nationalists themselves. Yet, even after the Nationalists were forced off the mainland and withdrew to Taiwan, the United States continued to treat them as the legitimate government of all of China and refused to extend any formal recognition to the Communist regime, the People's Republic of China (PRC) under Mao Zedong, founded on October 1, 1949.

In the early 1950s, American and Chinese Communist forces came into direct conflict when the UN forces in Korea had driven northward almost to the Yalu River, which provides the border between China and Korea. Some 200,000 Chinese troops swept the UN forces back below the 38th Parallel that had been and became again the dividing line between North and South Korea, and only an overwhelming demonstration of American air power, in conjunction with concentrated artillery fire, stopped the Chinese advance. Then, in the 1960 presidential election, the issue of American guarantees to Taiwan resurfaced as the Communists threatened two small islands, Jinmen and Mazu, held by the Nationalists.

But for most of the next two decades following the Korean War, the PRC was absorbed with internal economic and political convulsions. After several five-year plans for industrializing China had failed to meet their goals, Mao proclaimed the necessity of a national effort that came to be known as the "Great Leap Forward." Initiated in 1958, it demonstrated that political ideology, regardless of how fervent it is (or perhaps in an inverse proportion to how fervent it is), does not produce industrial efficiencies and innovations. Because of the tremendous dislocation and disillusionment that had resulted from the failure of this economic effort, Mao felt politically vulnerable. He therefore endorsed a "cultural revolution" to be accomplished primarily by the generation just coming of age, who had been indoctrinated in Maoism since birth. In effect, from 1965 to 1969, the nation was subjected to an extended reign of terror in which even highly positioned government and party officials were vulnerable to denouncement by groups with no formal status within the state but, temporarily, with more power than the formal institutions of the state. To outside observers, Communist China remained a very enigmatic and volatile state.

Ironically, just three years after the "cultural revolution" had exhausted itself, President Richard Nixon, previously an arch anti-communist, visited China and began to reverse three decades of deepening hostility and suspicion between the two nations. Ultimately, the United States would establish formal relations with Communist China and even endorse its admission to the UN Security Council, while still continuing to guarantee the sovereignty of Taiwan. Mao's death in 1976 and the ascension of the reformer Deng Xiaoping to the leadership of the party and government accelerated the Westernization of segments of the Chinese economy. By the 1990s, the PRC was experiencing dramatic annual increases in its GDP largely from its ballooning trade surpluses with the United States and other Western nations. Yet, in addition to the trade imbalance, the violent suppression of student demonstrations in Tiananmen Square and recurring allegations that a Chinese version of the Soviet gulag has provided slave labor to China's new entrepreneurs have strained the relationship between China and the United States. The debate keeps resurfacing within the United States over the best way to insure political as well as economic reforms within China. Some have argued that the United States should use its deepening economic relationship with the PRC as leverage to force political reforms. But others have asserted that political reforms are inevitable if the economic reforms continue and that trying to force political reforms on China may prove counter-productive.

REFERENCES: Warren I. Cohen, *America's Response to China: A History of Sino-American Relations* (New York, 1990); Akira Iriye, *The Cold War in Asia: A Historical Introduction* (Upper Saddle River, NJ, 1974); E. J. Kahn, Jr., *The China Hands* (New York, 1975); Robert MacFarquhar, *Sino-American Relations, 1949–1971* (Westport, CT, 1972); Edwin W. Martin, *Divided Counsel: The Anglo-American Response to Communist Victory in China* (Lexington, KY, 1986); Robert G. Sutter, *China Watch: Toward Sino-American Reconciliation* (Baltimore, MD, 1978); James C. Thomson, Peter W. Stanley, and John Curtis Perry, *Sentimental Imperialists: The American Experience in East Asia* (New York, 1981).

Martin Kich

Permanent Normal Trade Relations

Permanent Normal Trade Relations (PNTR) in U.S. trade law, previously called most favored nation trade status, refers to the legislation granting a country normal trade status. Permanent Normal Trade Relations with China was voted on in the U.S. Congress and was signed by U.S. President William J. Clinton on October 10, 2000. PNTR put China on an equal footing with other U.S. trading partners.

After 14 years of negotiations, China was poised to enter the World Trade Organization (WTO) in 2001. A cornerstone principle of the WTO is that members must grant each other trade privileges as favorable as they give to any other WTO member. Under U.S. trade law, however, Title IV of the Trade Act of 1974 required the President to deny PNTR to certain designated countries, including China. Section 402 of the Act, better known as the "Jackson-Vanik amendment," permitted 1-year waivers if the President could determine that China substantially complied with certain freedom of emigration objectives. China first received a waiver in 1980, and U.S. presidents renewed the waiver annually from 1981 to 1999 after vigorous debates in the U.S. Congress focusing on China's human rights record.

China's prospective WTO membership raised a critical issue about how the United States could handle China's normal trade status under U.S. law. For both legal and policy reasons, the Clinton administration asked Congress to grant China permanent normal trade relations before China joined the World Trade Organization to avoid a conflict between the U.S. law requiring annual approval of China's normal trade relations status, and the U.S. obligation as a WTO member to provide unconditional trade privileges as favorable as for any other WTO member. Much of the congressional debate over PNTR for China continued to focus on political concerns for human rights and on the business community's desire to trade and invest in China. Now that China has PNTR with the U.S. and is a member of the World Trade Organization, future trade disputes will be largely handled under the WTO without reference to political issues.

See also World Trade Organization (WTO).

REFERENCES: *Permanent Normal Trade Relations for China (PNTR): Committee Hearings, U.S. House of Representatives, 2000* (Washington, DC, 2000); Long Yungtu, Carlos A. Magarinos, and Francisco Sercovich (eds.), *China in the WTO* (New York, 1971); Joseph Fewsmith and William Kirby (eds.), *China Since Tiananmen* (New York, 2001); David M. Lampton (ed.), *The Making of Chinese Foreign and Security Policy in the Era of Reform* (Stanford, CA, 2001).

Elizabeth Van Wie Davis

Phillips, William (1878–1968)

William Phillips was born on May 30, 1878 into a well-to-do New England family. He graduated from Harvard University and Harvard Law School. He entered the foreign services in 1905. In 1908 he was appointed the first chief of the Far Eastern Division of the U.S. State Department. Later he became Assistant Secretary of State. Phillips was instrumental in formulating American foreign policies in East Asia during the early 1900s.

In late 1910s, Imperial Russia gained control over the North Manchuria Railway and its administrative center, the city of Harbin. The Russians living in that area wanted to set up a Russian-controlled local government. Phillips warned the American government about the potential dangers of U.S. recognizing the Russian sovereignty in that region. He argued that it would lead to losing the American extraterritorial rights to the Russians, wearing away Chinese territorial integrity, and setting precedents for other powers, especially, Japan, to follow. Secretary of State Elihu Root took Phillips's advice in opposing acknowledging Russian sovereignty over that area. But Root later changed his position during the meeting with the Japanese Ambassador Takahira Kogoro in Washington in November 1908. Root compromised the doctrine of the Open Door by acknowledging Japan's control in

Manchuria and backing away from opposing the Russians. At this time Root and President Theodore Roosevelt began to regard China as a weak, hopeless, and helpless nation, whose very survival depended on the restraints of the powers. Like Secretary of State John Hay, the architect of the Open Door Policy, they were both handicapped by the knowledge that the United States would not go to a war with either Russia or Japan over Manchuria.

With the election of William Howard Taft as U.S. President and the appointment of Philander C. Knox as Secretary of State, the pro–Open-Door forces gained ground in the capital. In the spring of 1909, Phillips wrote a memo outlining the main features of the American foreign policy of the Taft administration. His memo emphasized the need to abide by the Open Door Policy and preserve the Chinese territorial integrity. Phillips's position served as the basis of the assumption among the American diplomats that U.S. business interests in China would exceed those of the European powers and Japan, so it was necessary for the United States to always maintain business and commercial access to China. This view helped lay the foundation for the emergence of Dollar Diplomacy and Knox Neutralization Scheme in the future.

See also **Open Door Policy; Dollar Diplomacy; Knox Neutralization Scheme.**

REFERENCES: William Phillips, *Ventures in Diplomacy* (Boston, MA, 1952); A. W. Griswold, *Far Eastern Policy of the United States* (New Haven, CT, 1966).

Yuwu Song

Ping-Pong Diplomacy

"Ping-Pong Diplomacy" refers to the use of sporting competition to improve relations between nations. The phrase derives from an exchange of visits between the table tennis teams of the United States and the People's Republic of China in the early 1970s.

During the World Table Tennis Championships held in Nagoya, Japan in 1971, the American team was invited to visit the People's Republic of China before returning to the United States. No group from the U.S. had visited mainland China since the Communist revolution in 1949. Because diplomatic relations did not exist between the two countries at that time, the American team had to seek a waiver from their government permitting them to make the trip. President Richard M. Nixon agreed to lift the travel restriction for the team, provided that there was to be no official U.S. government participation with the trip. Four days after receiving their invitation, the U.S. Table Tennis Team crossed the border from Hong Kong into the People's Republic of China. The Americans were treated to demonstrations of Chinese revolutionary culture and played in matches with the Chinese national team. During the visit, the world champion Chinese team was careful not to embarrass the visiting Americans, who were ranked 28th in the world at the time. Highlights of the trip included a visit to the Great Wall and dinner with Premier Zhou Enlai in the Great Hall of the People near Tiananmen Square. The Premier told the visiting Americans that their visit signaled a beginning of a new era of relations between their two countries. Graham Steenhoven, President of the U.S. Table Tennis Association, issues an invitation for a reciprocal visit by the Chinese team to the United States. Steenhoven had enlisted the assistance of Alexander Eckstein, the chairman of the National Committee on United States-China Relations, for his organization to fund the visit by the Chinese. The following year, the Chinese Team visited the United States and met with President Richard Nixon at the White House.

The true significance of Ping-Pong Diplomacy for Sino-American relations is the opportunity it gave President Nixon and Chairman Mao Zedong to initiate a new era of relations between the two countries. Within days of the U.S. team's arrival in the People's Republic, Nixon announced several new policies regarding China. The travel ban was ended and several trade restrictions were lifted. President Nixon then sent his National Security Advisor, Henry Kissinger, on a secret mission to meet with Zhou Enlai in preparation for a presidential visit to the country. A vote in the United Nations on October 25, 1971 admitted the People's Republic of China in place of the Republic of China and the Chinese government opened its UN mission in New York. Finally, in February 1972, President Nixon made his historic trip to Beijing. The Chinese Table Tennis team visited the United States several months later.

See also **Nixon's Visit to China.**

REFERENCES: O. Edmund Clubb, "China and the United States: Beyond Ping-Pong," *Current History* (September 1971); David A. Devoss, "Ping-Pong Diplomacy," *Smithsonian* (April 2002); Ruth Eckstein, "Ping Pong Diplomacy: A View From Behind the Scenes," *Journal of American-East Asian Relations* (Fall 1993).

Anne M. Platoff

Potsdam Declaration (1945)

Emerging out of the Potsdam Conference held in Berlin July 17 to August 2, 1945, the Potsdam Declaration issued on July 26, 1945 is the thirteen-point document, which formally warned

Japan to surrender to the Allies. As stated, unless Japan surrendered unconditionally and accept the Declaration's terms its military and country would be obliterated by the Allied forces. Three Allied leaders, President Harry S. Truman, British Prime Minister Clement Atlee and Jiang Jieshi, President of the Republic of China were co-signers of the Declaration which permitted Japan an opportunity to surrender on specific terms.

In addition to serving as a grave warning, the Potsdam Declaration stipulated the specific steps that the Japanese government had to take to eliminate militarism, which was considered as the root of Japanese expansionism. For Japan to comply they would be required to take numerous actions: disarming of the military, dismantling war-producing capacity, establishing democratic political institutions and a new constitution, conducting war criminal trials and recognizing occupation forces as the supreme authority in monitoring Japan's transition to a peaceful country. In a convergence of events, The Manhattan Project was nearing completion during the Potsdam meetings in Berlin. This secret American project involved an accelerated program to develop nuclear weapons, partly out of fear that Germany or the Soviets may have secret programs themselves and partly out of American intentions to expedite the surrender of Japan. President Truman was informed of the readiness of the weapon during the conference and allowed him an opportunity to pre-empt Soviet Josef Stalin's intentions of invading Manchuria and Korea. Truman informed British Prime Minister Winston Churchill of the development of powerful nuclear weapons. Churchill supported Truman's plan to use them against Japan. Truman was vague in informing Stalin of the type of this new weapon, however, Stalin also supported its use.

Four days after the official issuance of the Potsdam Declaration, on July 30 the Japanese sent an indifferent reply, "the Japanese Government has found nothing important or interesting in the Allied declaration and anticipated no action than to ignore it completely." At this juncture Truman considered his options, one being to invade Japan or second to use atomic weapons. The Joint Chiefs of Staff had prepared for the possible invasion of Japan in several stages: Operation Olympic and Operation Coronet. One estimate placed the casualty rate at a quarter million in stage one and potentially a million casualties total out of the planned five million invasion troops. For Truman apparently the use of the atomic weapons outweighed the alternatives and in early August sent the order to use atomic weapons.

On August 6, 1945 the bomber Enola Gay released the first atomic bomb on Hiroshima, eventually killing over 80 per cent of the population. Although Japanese Prime Minister Suzuki and Foreign Minister Tojo attempted to negotiate a qualified peace by way of the Soviets, their overtures were spurned by Moscow. Instead the Soviets declared war on Japan and invaded Manchuria and Korea. Following the detonation of the second weapon on August 9, 1945 on Nagasaki, Japan's cabinet voted to accept the Declaration by a slim margin. With the cost of the devastation exceedingly high, the Japanese Cabinet had consented to an unconditional surrender and placing themselves in an uncertain future.

With the war over, Japanese officials signed the Instrument of Surrender on September 2, 1945 on the *USS Missouri*. The American military assigned General Douglas McArthur to serve as Supreme Commander Allied Powers to oversee a largely American occupation force steer Japan on a course of transition toward a more democratically-based society. During the occupation McArthur was careful to insist that Japan would adhere to the points in the Declaration. This is illustrated by McArthur's rejection of Japanese attempts at writing a satisfactory constitution, and decision to organize an American military and civilian committee to draft a democratic constitution.

See also World War II.

REFERENCES: James L. Gormly, *From Potsdam to the Cold War: Big Three Diplomacy 1945–1947* (Wilmington, DE, 1990); John Dower, *Embracing Defeat: Japan in the Wake of World War II.* (New York, 1999); Robert James Maddox, *The United States and World War II* (Boulder, CO, 1992).

Jim Steinberg

Powell, John Benjamin (1886–1947)

John Benjamin Powell was a renowned editor, correspondent, and writer on Asia, in particular on China. Born on a Missouri farm in Marion County, Powell worked first as a newspaper carrier and then a local newspaper reporter to earn his money for high school and college. After graduating from the University of Missouri School of Journalism at Columbia in 1910, he was on staff of the *Courier-Post*, a newspaper in Hannibal, for two years before becoming a member of the University of Missouri faculty, teaching journalism.

The turning point for his career occurred in 1916 when Thomas Franklin Fairfax Milliard, a well-known Far East correspondent and an alumnus of the University of Missouri, invited him to assist in publishing a new journal in Shanghai. Powell arrived in Shanghai in February 1917, and the first weekly issue of *Millard's Review of the Far East* appeared in June. In late 1917, Millard left Shanghai for New York and then decided to withdraw from the *Review*. In 1922, Powell purchased Millard's share of the paper and changed the name of the paper to *The Weekly Review of the Far East*, and once again the following year, to *The China Weekly Review*. From 1923 to 1925, he was also editor of an English-language daily in Shanghai, *The China Press*. A reputable man among foreign journalists in Shanghai, Powell enjoyed respect from his colleagues regardless of their divergent viewpoints. At various times, he represented other news organizations in Shanghai, including the *Chicago Tribune*, the *Manchester Guardian*, and the *London Daily Herald*. In addition, his writings appeared in many other American, European, and Chinese newspapers and magazines. Powell modeled the *Review* on Walter Lippman's *New Republic*, a distinctive physical format of the time. However, more appealing was the journal's extensive and in-depth coverage of Chinese politics and foreign affairs that made it the most popular English-language paper in Shanghai. Powell was a sympathizer of Dr. Sun Zhongshan and the Nationalist Revolution. Consequently, he supported Jiang Jieshi's Nanjing government. He was a strong advocate for close relations between China and the Unites States. He was among the first group of foreign correspondents who warned about Japan's increasing ambition towards China.

A man of bravery, Powell covered news at the risk of his life. In 1923, he was captured by Chinese bandits and was held for five weeks. After Pearl Harbor, he made a courageous decision to stay in Shanghai to report the war. On December 20, 1941, he was arrested by the Japanese. In the Japanese prisons, Powell's feet were infected, and finally the entire foreparts of both feet had to be removed. Released as part of a prisoner exchange on May 23, 1942, Powell left Shanghai and returned to the United States in August. After his return, Powell was hospitalized for almost three years. Despite his failing health, he continued to write. His book *My Twenty-Five Years in China* was published in 1945. He delivered speeches at public rallies and on the radio. In August 1946, he testified at the trials for war crimes in Tokyo. Powell remained a strong supporter of Jiang Jieshi and the Guomindang government, and continued to campaign for the awareness of the importance of Asia and China in the United States. On February 27, 1947, after delivering a speech to a group of Missouri alumni in Washington, Powell collapsed and died of a heart attack.

Most of Powell's files and records were presumably destroyed by the Japanese when they raided his office and residence in Shanghai in December 1941. *The China Weekly Review* resumed publication under the editorship of Powell's son, John William Powell, in December 1945, and continued until July 1953.

REFERENCES: John B. Powell, *My Twenty-Five Years in China* (New York, 1945); John A. Garraty and Edward T. James (eds.), *Dictionary of American Biography, Supplement Four, 1946–1950* (New York, 1974); The University Missouri Bulletin, *The Yun Gee Portrait of John B. Powell* (New York, 1944).

Jinxing Chen

Price, Frank (1895–1974)

Francis Wilson Price served for numerous years as an American missionary to China where he was born and raised by parents affiliated with the Southern Presbyterian Church. In 1915, Price graduated from Davidson College. After the United States entered World War I in 1917, Price enlisted in the U.S. Army. The Armistice of November 1918 prevented Price from participating militarily in the conflict. Nevertheless, he remained in France for one year assisting the Young Men's Christian Association in tending to the spiritual and physical needs of thousands of Chinese brought to France during the war to perform menial labor.

In 1922, Price graduated from Yale Divinity School and became a professor at both Nanjing Theological Seminary and Hangzhou Christian University. Over the next decade, he participated in a rural reform movement that sought to improve the health, sanitation and agricultural methods of numerous Chinese villages. And Price hoped to help bring about an indigenous Chinese church not dominated and dependent upon foreigners. Price developed a keenness for Chinese politics. His fondness for Sun Zhongshan, the so-called father of modern China and a longtime revolutionary, led Price to translate Sun's *San Min Zhu Yi* or the Three Principles of the People into English. When Sun's body was reinterred in Nanjing in 1929, Price met Sun's successor, Generalissimo Jiang Jieshi, for the first time. Because Jiang's Nationalist government resided in the capital of Nanjing and because he converted to Christianity in 1930, Frank Price developed a friendship with the Generalissimo. At times, the American missionary preached at special prayer meetings and Bible studies that Jiang attended. When Jiang was held captive during the Xian Incident of 1936, Price prayed with Madame Jiang. In 1937, Price returned to the United States to pursue a doctorate at the Yale Divinity School. After the Sino-Japanese War broke out in July, Price and other missionaries formed the China Information Service. The next year, he and his brother Harry established the American Committee for Non-Participation in Japanese Aggression that called on the U.S. to impose an embargo on war materials being sold to Japan. That same year, he returned to China to become director of the West China Unit of Nanjing Theological Seminary in Chengdu.

In 1941, Price served as an interpreter during conversations between Jiang Jieshi and Lauchlin Currie, an economic adviser to President Franklin D. Roosevelt. His friendship with the Jiangs and his propaganda skills led Jiang Jieshi to ask Price to become an official political advisor. Price's mission board turned down the request, but throughout the war, Price served as an unofficial advisor for both political and spiritual matters as well as a translator of Jiang's speeches and writings. Throughout the war, he advised Jiang to implement political, economic and military reforms as well as tried to keep the Chinese leader informed of problems in Nationalist-controlled China. In 1945, Price advised the Chinese delegation to the San Francisco Conference. After World War II, Price continued to advise Jiang of the need for reform, and opposed the use of force against the Chinese Communists. In 1946, Price returned to the U.S. on furlough for two years. There, he defended Jiang against criticisms of his rule by journalists and academics, and lobbied for U.S. aid to Jiang. By 1948, however, Price lost faith in Jiang Jieshi, and soon called on the U.S. to accord official diplomatic recognition to the People's Republic of China.

Price remained in the PRC, but after the Korean War, he found himself and others like him increasingly denounced by the government. In 1952, the authorities permitted Price and his wife to return to the U.S. He spent many years teaching at Union Theological Seminary in New York, and writing about China and Communism. He died in Lexington, Virginia in 1974.

See also Young Men's Christian Association (YMCA).

REFERENCES: Samuel Hsueh-hsin Chow, *Religious Education and Reform In Chinese Missions: The Life and Work of Francis Wilson Price: 1895–1974* (Ph. D. Dissertation, St. Louis University, 1988); Stephen G. Craft, "American Isaiah In China: Frank W. Price, Chiang Kai-Shek And Reforming China, 1941–49," *Journal of Presbyterian History* (Fall 2004).

Stephen Craft

Price, Harry (1905–2002)

Harry Price's long affiliation with China began at birth in Zhejiang Province, China to Presbyterian missionaries. Entering Davidson College at the age of 16, Price graduated in 1925 with a Bachelor's degree. Over the next two years, he did graduate work at the University of Missouri and assisted a Presbyterian campus minister. In 1929, Price traveled to Shanghai, China as an assistant to the American Commission of Financial Experts to the Government of China, or the Kemmerer Commission, led by Prof. Edwin Kemmerer of Princeton University. The purpose of the Kemmerer Commission was to assist the new Nationalist government to reorganize its finances. Price returned to the United States where he did graduate work at Columbia and Princeton before receiving a M.A. in Economics from Yale in 1932.

In 1932, Price moved to China to become a professor at Yenching University in Beijing where he taught economics, served as Dean of the College of Public Affairs, and worked as an assistant to John Leighton Stuart, the university president. Two weeks before the outbreak of the Sino-Japanese War in 1937, Price traveled to the United States on furlough. Influenced by articles describing the percentage of various war materials sold to Japan by the United States, he and his brother Frank invited a diverse group of Americans to form the American Committee for Non-Participation in Japanese Aggression. Harry Price became the director of the national headquarters located in New York City. Price, his brother Frank, and others established the American Committee in order to inform Americans of the impact of the war on China and to use public opinion to pressure the United States government to impose an embargo on raw materials sold to Japan. After Pearl Harbor, Price worked for the US's Lend-Lease program which provided war material to Nationalist China. At the end of World War II, Price went to Shanghai as Deputy Director for the United Nations Relief and Rehabilitation Administration-China to provide relief to people trying to recover from eight years of war. Later, he went to work in Europe under the auspices of the European Recovery Plan (ERP) or Marshall Plan. In 1955, Price wrote the official history of the ERP under the title *The Marshall Plan and Its Meaning*.

From 1957–1962, Price returned to Asia as UN representative to Nepal. Then he traveled to the Philippines to work with James Y.C. Yen, a longtime family friend who for many years led a rural education movement in China. Yen headed the Philippine branch of the International Institute of Rural Reconstruction, which sought to better the lives of poor peasants throughout Asia now that Communist China was closed to such endeavors. Price, Yen and Greg Feliciano joined together in writing *Rural Reconstruction and De-*

velopment: A Field Manuel for Workers. In 1970, Price left Asia to become a professor economics and head of the department at Maryville College in Tennessee.

REFERENCES: Donald Friedman, *Road to Isolation: The American Committee for Non-Participation In Japanese Aggression* (Cambridge, MA, 1968).

Stephen Craft

Pruitt, Ida (1888–1985)

Ida Pruitt was an American who spent over thirty years of her long life in China, first as a child of Southern Baptist missionary parents and then as a Medical Social Worker in Beijing. Her life and her work among Western and Chinese peoples gave her a perspective on Chinese culture before World War II that she tried to convey in articles and a few books. These were principally published after she finally left China with the advent of the Japanese invasion of 1939.

Pruitt was born in Penglai, Shantong and lived her first twelve years in her parents' missionary compound where she still had frequent contact with Chinese neighbors. It was in this period that Pruitt developed her "dual heritage" in Chinese and Western cultures. She thus was later able to join a small number of writers who communicated about China to the West and who took up the cause of China's social and economic development, which dominated the rest of her life. Pruit, as was usual for missionary children, was sent home to school, first to Philadelphia and finally to attend Columbia University's Teachers College. Before returning to China, she worked for the Philadelphia Society of Organizing Charities doing war-relief work in 1918–1919. She returned to China in 1921 to found and head the Social Services Department of the Union Medical College in Beijing. This work put her in touch with Chinese women and was described in her most famous books. She came to the attention of the larger public in the United States soon after the publication of *A Daughter of Han* which narrates the story of Ning tai-tai, a working-class woman Pruitt met in Beijing near the end of Ning's difficult life. Over the course of two years, the elderly Ning visited three times a week and described her life as an poor child, impoverished wife and struggling mother in pre-revolutionary China. Pruitt's tale ends when she left China in 1938 but a section on Ning's revolutionary granddaughter, making an excellent contrast with the options Ning saw for herself as a young woman. The story is told in Ning's voice and labeled an autobiography but the author's perspective as a Western woman is also evident in her choice of incidents. While she never claimed to "think like a Chinese" and confined her writing largely to translations and the stories of the women she encountered in her work, Pruitt had a great respect for the struggles of China as a whole. Much later, Pruitt's book on an upper-class woman, Yin tai-tai (*Old Madam Yin*) was published. Matriarch of a large, prosperous family, Yin's story is told in vignettes of their frequent meetings and through in Pruitt's third-person authorial voice. This portrait of a traditional Chinese woman in 1930s China is supplemented with a history transmitted to Pruitt largely through a young servant woman, Ho Chieh (Ho Jieh), whom Yin brings to Pruitt's new household in Beijing. This work reveals the talent, strength and skill that allowed generations of Chinese women to survive a family and social system that was often inimical to them. That Pruitt was 91 years old when it was published and had been out of China for almost forty years may have given her the distance to foreground her relationship to the story of Yin and also her earlier subject, Ning. While Pruitt wrote principally about Chinese women, she continued to work for the Chinese as they tried to build a modern, industrial country. After moving back to Philadelphia in 1938, she lectured on China in the U.S. and raised money for Chinese Industrial Cooperatives, for which she was the executive secretary of the American Committee in the 1940s and 1950s. She also continued her efforts in advocating diplomatic recognition of the People's Republic of China for thirty years after the Communist government was installed.

Unlike her contemporary, Agnes Smedley, she had the protection of church organizations and kept sufficiently within conventional roles so that this support of the mainland Chinese did not seem to have hurt her reputation as either an social reformer or a writer. *Daughter of Han* was, for many years, part of curricular reading for American students of China.

REFERENCES: *Contemporary Authors Online*, (New York, 2003); Ida Pruitt, *A China Childhood* (San Francisco, CA, 1978); Ida Pruitt, *A Daughter of Han: The Autobiography of a Chinese Working Woman* (New Haven, CT, 1945); Ida Pruitt, *Old Madam Yin: A Memoir of Peking Life, 1926–1938* (Stanford, CA, 1979).

Janice M. Bogstad

Puyi (1906–1967)

Also known as Henry Puyi, he was born in Beijing on February 7, 1906, a nephew of the emperor. The Empress Dowager Cixi, hoping to remain the power behind the throne through yet another regency, named the three-year-old boy emperor, taking the reign name Xuantong, upon the death of his uncle on November 14, 1908. Unfortunately for Cixi she died the next day. The emperor's father Prince Chun then became regent but was unable to stem the tide of dissatisfaction against the Qing dynasty, which fell in 1911 leaving China in chaos. Puyi abdicated but was permitted to keep his title, to receive an annual sum of about three million dollars, and to reside in the Forbidden City the imperial palace complex in Beijing where he lived in seclusion. He very briefly returned to the throne in 1917 when a warlord unsuccessfully attempted to restore the Qing dynasty.

In 1924 another warlord seized Beijing and expelled Puyi who fled to his father's home in the port city of Tianjin. According to Puyi, the philosopher and educator Hu Shi urged him to study in the United States or Britain. Instead, in February 1925, Puyi took refuge in the Japanese concession in Tianjin where he lived until November 1931. During his time in Tianjin, Puyi claimed he often visited the foreign consulates, including the American, where he was addressed as "Your Majesty." In November 1931, Puyi sailed on a Japanese ship to Manchuria, which the Japanese had seized after the Mukden Incident in September. They established the puppet state of Manchukuo and asked Puyi to serve as its chief executive, elevating him to emperor two years later. As head of state, Puyi unsuccessfully asked the United States for diplomatic recognition which was refused on the basis of the Stimson Doctrine. Until 1945, Puyi, now Emperor Kangde, technically ran the government, which, in actuality, was under the complete control of the Japanese Guangdong army. On December 8, 1941, shortly after learning of the Japanese attack on Pearl Harbor, Puyi issued an imperial decree, broadcast personally on radio stating his total support for Japan. In the summer 1944, American bombers started attacking Manchukuo. Puyi protested these actions noting that no state of war existed between the two countries. The United States rejected these protests considering Manchuria territory of its ally China thus viewing Puyi and Manchukuo as illegitimate. When Japan surrendered in August 1945, Puyi abdicated again and attempted to flee to Japan when the Soviets captured him and held him prisoner for the next five years. Puyi mistakenly hoped that the USSR would allow him to seek refuge in one of the Soviet's allies of Britain or the United States. In August 1946, the Soviets, ignoring American disapproval, flew Puyi to Tokyo to serve as a witness for the prosecution in the war crime trial. The Americans feared that Puyi's presence would renew demands for an war crimes indictment of Japanese Emperor Hirohito or the calling of him as a witness in the trial. During his time in Tokyo, Puyi gave his only newspaper interview to the United Press.

The Soviets handed Puyi over to Communist China as a war criminal in August 1950 where for the next nine years he served in a re-education camp. During the Korean War as American troops approached the Yalu River almost unhampered, Puyi expected the Communists would execute him to keep him from falling into enemy hands. After his release in 1959, he moved to Beijing working as a gardener and librarian. He died in the early days of the Cultural Revolution on October 17, 1967. A very successful film about his tragic life, *The Last Emperor*, was released in 1987 and won nine academy awards.

See also Manchukuo; Manchuria; South Manchurian Railway.

REFERENCES: Puyi, *From Emperor to Citizen: The Autobiography of Aisin-Gioro Puyi*, translated by W.J. F. Jenner (New York, 1987); Edward Behr, *The Last Emperor* (London, 1987); Brian Power, *The Puppet Emperor: The Life of Puyi, the Last Emperor of China* (New York, 1986).

Greg Ference

Qian Qichen (1928-)

Qian Qichen, a leading Chinese diplomat with keen negotiating skills, is the former Vice Premier of the State Council and the minister of Foreign Affairs from 1988 to 1998. Qian was born in 1928 in Jiading, Shanghai. While a student at a secondary school attached to Datong University in Japanese-occupied Shanghai, Qian became an underground activist and a local leader for the Chinese Communist Party (CCP), which he joined in 1942. From 1945 to 1949, Qian worked as a journalist at *Da Gong Bao*, a Shanghai newspaper. After the establishment of the People's Republic of China, he first worked at several district offices of the Communist Youth League in Shanghai, and then at the central committee in Beijing. In 1954, Qian went to Moscow to study in the Central Communist Youth League School. After leaving school in 1955, Qian worked in the Chinese embassy in Moscow, serving as second secretary, deputy section chief and director of the research office. In 1963, Qian returned to China and worked in the Ministry of Higher Education as section chief in charge of Chinese students studying abroad, and then deputy director of the Department of External Relations. In 1972, Qian went back to Moscow, serving as a consul in the Chinese embassy. Two years later, he was named Chinese ambassador to Guinea. From 1977 to 1982, Qian was director of Information Department of the Ministry of Foreign Affairs. While serving as the first spokesperson of the Ministry, he was appointed vice minister of Foreign Affairs in 1982. With fluent English and Russian, he led the Chinese delegation in negotiations with the Soviet Union on issues regarding Sino-Soviet borders and other political issues in the 1980s. He was also in charge of United Nations affairs before his promotion to be minister of Foreign Affairs in 1988, a position he held until 1998. In addition, Qian was appointed state councilor in 1991, elected a member of the Politburo of the CCP Central Committee the following year, and named Vice Premier of the State Council in 1993.

Qian received wide recognition for voicing China's policies towards its neighbor countries, and presenting China's position on human rights and economic development to the rest of the world. Since the early 1980s, he has actively contributed to and advanced China's foreign policies regarding Hong Kong, Macao, Russia, Taiwan and the United States. A proponent of mutually beneficial exchange, Qian supported the improvement of relationship with the U.S., believing that bilateral economic and trade relations will help both the Chinese and American peoples. According to Qian: "China has always attached much importance to its relations with the United States…. It does not mean there are no differences between the two sides. It means that the two sides can find where their common interests lie despite their differences. To develop Sino-U.S. relations, both sides should strictly observe every basic principle contained in the three Sino-U.S. joint communiques and the principle of non-interference in each other's internal affairs."

In his capacity as the Chinese minister of Foreign Affairs, Qian worked with his U.S. counterparts on various issues ranging form trade and arms sales, China's Most Favored Nation status, Taiwan, Tibet, to Chinese dissidents and human right concerns. During his tenure, the Sino-U.S. relations improved gradually from the low point after the Tiananmen Square Massacre in 1989 to a constructive strategic partnership under the Clinton administration. Even in his retirement, Qian is still an influential figure in Chinese foreign policies today, who believes a healthy and stable Sino-U.S. relationship not only conforms to the fundamental interests of peoples in the two countries, but also is significant to promoting the world peace and prosperity in the 21st century.

REFERENCES: Pak-wah Leung, *Political Leaders of Modern China: A Biographical Dictionary* (Westport, CT, 2002); "Profiles of Newly Elected Chinese Leaders," *Beijing Review* (April 6 1998).

Wenxian Zhang

Qiao Guanhua (1913–1983)

Guanhua Qiao was born in Yancheng in China's Jiangsu Province on March 3, 1913. He studied in Germany where he earned a Ph. D. He worked as a journalist before returning to China in 1937.

During the War with Japan Qiao wrote commentaries on international affairs. In the autumn of 1942 he began work with the *New China Daily News*, which was operating at Chongqing (1937–1945). He edited a column on international affairs until the end of World War II. In 1946 Qiao went to Shanghai with Zhou Enlai as a member of the Delegation of the Chinese Communist Party. At the end of 1946 he was sent to Hong Kong to be the Director of the Hong Kong Branch of the (Xinhua) New China News Agency. In 1949 the Chinese Communist Party took control of China and Qiao became the Deputy Director-General of the Foreign Policy Committee in the Ministry of Foreign Affairs in the new People's Republic of China under Chen Yi. Later he was appointed Assistant Foreign Minister. In October of 1950 he went as an advisor with Wu Xiuquan, the Special Representative of the People's Republic to the United Nations. There he attended a UN Security Council meeting in which he attacked the United States for its support of the Republic of China on Taiwan. Beginning in July 1951 Qiao attended the Korean armistice talks in Panmunjom as the chief deputy to Li Kenong who was head of the Chinese Communist delegation. In April 1954 Qiao served with Zhou Enlai at the Geneva Conference. From October 1961 to August 1962 he worked with Foreign Minister Chen Yi at the second Geneva Conference. In March of 1964 he became Vice-Foreign Minister. He served in this post until November of 1974. Qiao's work as a diplomat included responsibilities such as preparing drafts for speeches, or for diplomatic papers. These included Premier Zhou Enlai's Letter to Asian and African Heads of State on the question of the Sino-Indian Boundary (November 1962); and Chairman Mao Zedong's Statement of May 2, 1970 urging the Cambodians to accept Communist rule and to fight against the United States.

Beginning in the 1970s Qiao was Vice-Foreign Minister in charge of American relations. After he became Foreign Minister he assisted Zhou Enlai in developing diplomacy that led to the opening of relations with the United States. When President Richard Nixon visited China in 1972 he held talks with Secretary of State Henry Kissinger and helped to draft the Sino-U.S. Joint Communique. When the Chinese seat in the United Nations was transferred to Communist China in November 1971 Qiao headed the Chinese Delegation to the 26th Session of United Nations General Assembly. Qiao delivered a speech to the Assembly expounding Communist China's foreign policies. He headed Communist China's UN delegation until 1976. In May of 1973 he accompanied Deng Xiaoping during a state visit to France. In October of 1976 he returned to France as the Foreign Minister of the People's Republic of China. That same year he also served as an advisor to the Chinese People's Association for Friendship with Foreign Countries. In December of 1976 Qiao was removed from his post. Thereafter he was frequently attacked in the news media for an alleged association with the radicals—"Gang of Four"—during the Cultural Revolution. Actually while Qiao was a protege of Zhou Enlai, it was his wife Zhang Hanzhi who was a close friend of Madame Mao, Jiang Qing, one of the radicals. In February 1978 Qiao was reported to be under detention. Qiao Guanhua died September 22, 1983.

Among his writings are "Selected Commentaries on International Affairs" and "From Munich to Dunkirk." Zhang Hanzhi was the Director, Department of North American and Oceanic Affairs, Ministry of Foreign Affairs. Their son, Qiao Zonghuai became Vice-Minister, Ministry of Foreign Affairs, and their daughter, Hong Huang, is a publisher.

See also United Nations.

REFERENCES: Ministry of Foreign Affairs, *Qiao Guanhua: Minister of Foreign Affairs of the People's Republic of China* (Beijing, 2003); "Chinese Deputy Foreign Minister Qiao Guanhua and Vietnamese Ambassador Ngo Minh Loan," *Cold War International History Project Virtual Archive No. 29* (Beijing, May 13, 1967); Zhang Hanzhi, *Kua Guo Hou Hou De Da Hong Men [Stride Through the Thick Red Gate]* (Shanghai, 2002).
Jack Waskey

Quarantine Speech (1937)

By the time President Franklin D. Roosevelt was re-elected in 1936, events had transpired around the world that would soon shift focus away from domestic programs. In July 1937, Japan launched its attacks on China. In response, Roosevelt delivered "The Quarantine Speech" in Chicago in October. In the speech the President compared the outbreak of international violence to that of a communicable disease needing to be quarantined. He argued that these aggressors were spreading the "epidemic of world lawlessness." The Quarantine Speech displayed Roosevelt's long-held belief in a system of collective security and his belief in quarantine as an alternative to the political environment of American neutrality and isolationism that was prevalent in the 1920s and 1930s. Due to the lack of enthusiasm of Sec-

retary of State Cordell Hull and the British, nothing came out of this proposal directly.

However, this speech began debates over just how much America should be concerned with international diplomacy. To some Roosevelt's speech was a further erosion of the isolationist attitudes. The Quarantine Speech intensified U.S. isolationist mood, causing protest by isolationists and foes to intervention. Even though the news media responded critically that the speech had represented "an attitude and not a program," The President sensed that American people were not ready for involvement in international affairs. As a result, he refrained from advocating any "Quarantine" measures against Japan including economic sanctions.

See also Brussels Conference (1937).

REFERENCES: Kenneth Sydney Davis, *FDR, Into the Storm, 1937–1940: A History* (New York, 1993); Ted Morgan, *FDR: A Biography* (New York, 1985).
Yuwu Song

Radio Free Asia (RFA)

The International Broadcasting Act of 1994 was passed by the 103rd Congress and signed into law on April 30, 1994. Subsequently, in March 1996, the Asia Pacific Network, Inc. was incorporated and began broadcasting six and a half months later. Despite the formal name, Congress and nearly everyone knows it as Radio Free Asia.

During the Chinese government's 1989 crackdown on the pro-democracy movement in Tiananmen Square, some American political leaders felt that an expansion of the existing services offered by Voice of America (VOA) would suffice to support the apparent growing Chinese democracy movement. However, proponents of a separate surrogate broadcasting company (one that provided "independent, uncensored, and accurate news, events" and cultural programs about the targeted country) argued instead that something akin to Radio Free Europe/Radio Liberty was needed to promote democracy and freedom in areas where political repression and governmental control of news was practiced. Congressional debate was extensive over "whether, and how to broadcast into Asia." Proponents of "surrogate" broadcasting argued that it would help promote democracy; that more Asian freedom aided U.S.-Asian relations. Moreover, they believed that the United States needed to broaden its Eurocentric focus while it promoted freedom beyond its borders. Opponents considered China to be more open (with more information sources) than Eastern Europe was when VOA started broadcasting there during World War II and in the subsequent Cold War years. Thus, the VOA could adequately cover the needs there. Additionally, expanding existing operations would be less expensive and less "confrontational" to Asian governments, they argued. The proponents eventually won out and, after two years of planning and preparing, the first one-hour broadcast was beamed into China in Mandarin on September 29, 1996.

The Chinese Government initially reacted to RFA broadcasts with letters of opposition to top-level U.S. government officials and within a year it was jamming RFA frequencies. They also attacked the credibility of the station by editorializing in major Chinese newspapers that the CIA was behind the operation. Within a year of its inception, RFA had expanded its broadcasting in Mandarin to five hours daily. It also began a few hours a day in other congressionally mandated languages: Cantonese, Tibetan, and Korean, to name a few. Other targeted Asian countries—Vietnam and North Korea—began jamming RFA broadcasts, too. Attempts at jamming have been continual, but with varying degrees of effectiveness. It is more often effective in major cities than in rural areas, however, in urban areas there is the possibility of access to programming over the Internet. Richard Richter, the President of RFA, explained that its job is "to bring news and information about their own country to populations denied the benefit of freedom of information by their governments." The call-in programs in multiple languages are perhaps the most important part of RFA's work. Listeners can call a toll-free number, talk directly with the program host, and report news and/or voice their views. When Chinese dissident Zhang Shanguang was convicted in 1998 for "providing intelligence" (of labor unrest) to hostile foreign organizations, a telephone interview with RFA was cited in the indictment.

RFA and VOA ensure that one or the other service is offered in Mandarin at all times. During each day, they act as competitors, offering different programming at overlapping hours. It remains to be seen how the Broadcasting Board of Governors will organize the two services in the future. Some have speculated that decreases in Chinese media censorship in recent years are attributable to the efforts of services like BBC, VOA, and RFA. As long as broadcasting into other nations continues to serve U.S. foreign policy purposes, proponents will continue to support the practice, ideologically and financially.

See also Cold War; Voice of America.

REFERENCES: Susan B. Epstein, "Radio Free Asia," *CRS Report for Congress* (Washington, DC, 1997); Radio Free Asia, *www.rfa.org*; James Wood, *History of International Broadcasting* (London, 2000); Erik Eckholm, "In

Drive on Dissidents, China Gives 4th Severe Sentence in Week," *New York Times* (December 28, 1998).

Catherine Forslund

Rankin, Karl Lott (1898–1991)

Karl Lott Rankin was the son of a Congregationalist minister. He was born in Manitowoc, Wisconsin and spent much of his childhood in Topeka, Kansas. He was a civil engineer, having studied at the California Institute of Technology from 1917 to 1919, Federal Polytechnic, Zurich, Switzerland, from 1920 to 1921; and Princeton University where he completed his Civil Engineering degree in 1922. He began his work outside of the United States after serving in the Navy in World War I, working for Near East Relief as a field engineer in Turkey and the USSS (Caucasus region) in the 1920s and other assignments of a similar nature followed in Prague, Athens, Tirana, Albania, and Brussels. Briefly interned by the Japanese in 1941 on his way to Egypt, he went back on the civil engineering circuit of the Near East until assigned a diplomatic post in China.

Rankin, on home-leave from his postings with the Department of State, was expecting to go to Jerusalem when he was abruptly reassigned to replace Jack Cabot as consul general in Shanghai. When Shanghai was taken over in late 1949 to become part the People's Republic of China, an event hardly expected by the United States government, Rankin was quickly reassigned to be charges d'affaires in Taibei (1950–1953) and then Ambassador to the Republic of China on Taiwan (1953–1957). In this turbulent period, containment of Communism dominated Western thinking. The Korean War was fought and the Truman administration and General Douglas MacArthur opposed each other over the United States policy on relations with mainland China and it was the height of the McCarthy era back in the United States. While in Taiwan, Rankin argued forcibly against the "Two China" and the "appeasement" policies that were forwarded in the 1950s and in favor of the protection of Taiwan from mainland China as a bastion against Communism. His belief in the legitimacy of the Guomindang as China's rightful government was preserved later in life when composing his one notable book, *China Assignment*. In the book, he carefully skirts the issue of whether or not the U.S. should support the Republic of China on Taiwan with enough funds and military aids to carry on the "hot war" with the People's Republic advocated by General MacArthur. Throughout the book, he calls the capital of the People's Republic of China "Peiping" indicating that he does not recognize it as a legitimate capital. The book is a compilation of selections from his official correspondence as ambassador and his commentary on the letters, official embassy communiques to Washington and telegrams plus his later interpretation of their context and meanings. Rankin's book, written after the end of his diplomatic career as Ambassador to Yugoslavia (1957–1961), was influential on American policy towards China in the 1960s but it gradually became irrelevant after the recognition of the People's Republic of China by the United States. It is nevertheless a solid representation of general attitudes in the United States in the 1950s.

See also Cold War; Jiang Jieshi (1887–1975); MacArthur, Douglas (1880–1964).

REFERENCES: Karl Lott Rankin, *China Assignment* (Seattle, WA, 1964); *Karl L. Rankin Papers, 1916–1971* (Princeton University Library, *http://infoshare1.princeton.edu/libraries/firestone/rbsc/finding_aids/rankin.html*); *Contemporary Authors Online* (New York, 2002).

Janice M. Bogstad

Rape of Nanjing

The Rape of Nanjing was an act of cruelty perpetrated on the civilians of Nanjing by the Imperial Japanese Army in late 1937. The Rape came to symbolize the suffering of the Chinese civilians during the war and the cruelty of the Japanese army. The Rape continues to poison Sino-Japanese relations.

In August 1937, Japanese armies attacked the city of Shanghai as part of their war against China. The battle for that city took three months and cost both the Japanese and Chinese armies greatly in dead and wounded. After consolidating their hold on Shanghai, the Japanese turned inland and advanced on the former Chinese capital of Nanjing. The Japanese had dropped leaflets on the city prior to commencing military operations promising to restore order, respect private property, and treat civilians well. City leaders hoped to avoid bloodshed and the destruction of their city as had occurred in other Chinese cities, and declared the city open in December 1937. Under internationally accepted practices, an open city agrees to put up no defense against invaders in return for the invaders agreeing to take over the city with minimal destruction. However, once in Nanjing, the Japanese army instead began a period of seven weeks of wanton cruelty against the civilians of the city. Rape and murder became the most common of the war crimes practiced by the invading army, with later Chinese estimates reckoning that the entire female population of the city had been raped, usually multiple times. However, rape was just one of the horrors perpetrated on the residents of Nanjing, with torture, murder,

vandalism, and theft common. Japanese newspapers reported on a "friendly" competition between two lieutenants to see who could behead the most Chinese in a day. Estimates of the number of dead Chinese civilians from the Rape range from 52,000 to 300,000. Looting and arson left most areas ruined.

The Japanese army apparently believed that the example of Nanjing would cow the Chinese population and end all resistance to the Japanese. Instead, as a result of the reputation of the Japanese army following the surrender of Nanjing, few Chinese towns or cities surrendered without resistance. Japanese officials have long claimed that the Rape was not a planned or even condoned campaign but instead caused by the breakdown of strict discipline within the army as a result of hard campaigning and the anger of army reservists after not being allowed to return home after the Shanghai campaign. Some Japanese have gone as far as to claim that the Rape was a creation of anti-Japanese propaganda in the West and never actually occurred, although further research in the 1990s has proven the event occurred. Most historians believe the Rape resulted from an intentional policy of the Japanese army leadership. Such sanctioned barbarity would psychologically harden the Japanese soldiers to the brutality of war, and attempted to instill total fear of the Japanese army in the Chinese. The emphasis on rape in the Japanese army stemmed perhaps from a long standing feeling of cultural inferiority of the Japanese vis-a-vis the Chinese, combined with the relaxation of normal society pressures created by war.

Reaction to the Rape in the United States was muted. The U.S. had opposed Japan's war in China, and Japan was already suffering under a ban on the sale of scrap metal that the U.S. had earlier imposed. Japanese censures were able to prevent most early reporting of the atrocity from reaching the outside during the Rape. Several months after the Rape, *Life* magazine ran a famous photograph of a wounded, abandoned baby screaming in a Nanjing railroad station that had been destroyed by Japanese bombs, but the horrors of the Rape blended with the general image of Japanese aggression and atrocities committed against the Chinese. Americans were far more outraged by the sinking of the gunboat the USS *Panay*, and the strafing of its survivors, on the Yangzi River by Japanese warplanes on December 12, 1937. The concept of the Rape as a historic event did not really enter public discourse in the United States until the Chinese-American author Iris Chang published her book on the topic in English in 1998.

See also World War II.

REFERENCES: Iris Chang, *The Rape of Nanjing: The Forgotten Holocaust of World War II* (New York, 1998); Masahiro Yamamoto, *The Rape of Nanjing: Anatomy of an Atrocity* (Westport, CT, 2002); Xu Zhigen, *Lest We Forget: Nanjing Massacre 1937* (New York, 1975).

Barry Stentiford

Reagan, Ronald (1911–2004)

Ronald Wilson Reagan served as U.S. President from 1981 to 1989 and paid an official visit to China in 1984, meeting with China's leadership and speaking to the Chinese people. Reagan looked to China as he mobilized all the resources he could muster to bankrupt the Soviet Union in the 1980s. He engaged China to work together closely to stop the Soviet aggression in Afghanistan by sharing intelligence and providing arms to the Afghanistan freedom fighters.

But Reagan had played an important role long before that. In 1972, it was then-Governor of California Reagan that President Richard Nixon had to win over before Nixon dared to embark on his historic trip to Beijing. Reagan spoke for the staunchly conservative wing of the Republican Party — and he had to be won over if Nixon was going to survive politically. As Taiwan's champion, it was Reagan who crafted the American policy of building a practical relationship with the mainland People's Republic, but to "in no way retreat from our alliance with the Chinese on Taiwan." And while Reagan is credited by many with winning the Cold War, his role in the changing face of China today is worth reflection. At Chinese Foreign Ministry press briefings on the week of Reagan's death in 2004, spokesman Liu Jianchao cited three joint communiques issued during the Reagan administration that 22 years later continued to form the basis for U.S.-Chinese relations. In particular, Liu cited the joint communique issued on August 17, 1982 "which set forth the principles for the solution of U.S. arms sales to Taiwan." It had resulted from demands by Chinese leader Deng Xiaoping that the United States set a definite timetable for the end of arms sales to Taiwan. Deng was testing to see how far the newly elected Reagan could be pushed. After intense negotiations, China agreed to tolerate periodic American sales to the island while the U.S. agreed to limit the quality of weapons and to slowly reduce their quantity. China would be the first Communist country Reagan ever visited. His trip was long on symbolism, played well on television, and gave him an excellent opportunity to take up one of his greatest and most beloved roles, that of the Great Communicator. Reagan's speeches in China emphasized American values of freedom and democracy and highlighted common interests in trade and anti-Soviet strategy. Authorities in Beijing censored the Chinese translation of his addresses at the Great Hall of the People and China Central Television. However, Reagan was able to get his message across uncensored when he spoke at Fudan University in Shanghai. There, he won the hearts of many — and nurtured hopes that some would say were expressed in Tiananmen Square during the student democracy movement of 1989.

REFERENCES: David Boaz, "Remembering Ronald Reagan," *Cato Institute Daily Dispatch*, www.cato.org/dailys/06–07–04.html (Washington, DC, 2004); Lou Cannon, *The Role of a Lifetime* (New York, 1991); "Chinese Remember Reagan's Efforts to Improve Sino-U.S. Friendship," *People's Daily Online* (Beijing, June 7, 2004); Edward Lanfranco, "Reagan's legacy in Sino-U.S. Relations," *The Washington Times* (Washington, DC, June 11, 2004); Peggy Noonan, "Ronald Reagan," *The Time 100* (New York, 2004).

Rob Kerby

Reed Treaty *see* Treaty of Tianjin (1858)

Reinsch, Paul Samuel (1869–1923)

Paul S. Reinsch was United States Minister to China during the Woodrow Wilson Presidency, from 1913 to 1919; from 1919 until his death he served as special advisor to Chinese policymakers. As American minister in the aftermath of the Chinese Revolution, Reinsch argued vociferously for principled support of Chinese territorial and administrative integrity against European and Japanese imperialism. By the 1920s he had become an outspoken critic of the Harding Administration's treatment of China, particularly with regard to the Shandong settlement.

Born on June 10, 1869 in Milwaukee, Wisconsin, Reinsch graduated from the University of Wisconsin, Madison, in 1892, and remained there to study with historian Frederick Jackson Turner. Reinsch received his doctorate in 1898 and two years later published *World Politics at the End of the Nineteenth Century as Influenced by the Oriental Situation* (1900), which analyzed world relations with East Asia and set out Reinsch's anti-imperialism and support for the Open Door Policy. A nationally-known expert on colonial studies and international relations, Reinsch taught at Madison until his appointment to Beijing in 1913, and was an active internationalist, participating in Pan American conferences in 1909 and 1910.

Appointed minister on August 15, 1913 on the strength of his work at Madison, Reinsch's advocacy of the Open Door convinced President Wilson that he would promote the administration's new policy of independent action in China.

Left largely on his own in shaping day-to-day policy, Reinsch concentrated on enhancing American business opportunities there and on helping to modernize China's political and economic infrastructure. Reinsch never saw the completion of either goal. Efforts in his first three years in office to help American businesses like Standard Oil and Bethlehem Steel to invest in China fell afoul of both Chinese and international politics. Similar fates met Reinsch's negotiations for the Huai River Conservancy and railroad expansion. Reinsch soon discovered that the Wilson administration encouraged investors but would not officially back them. Wilson's seeming ambivalence about China's fate was a source of constant frustration to Reinsch. When Washington seemed to bend to the will of Japan in early 1915, during the Twenty-One Demands crisis, Reinsch feared a rapprochement between the two countries that would ultimately endanger China. The collapse of Yuan Shikai's regime, which Reinsch had supported because of its stabilizing influence, in late 1915-early 1916, and Yuan's death and replacement by Li Yuanhong, further convinced Reinsch that American aid was needed before chaos overtook the country. By October 1916 Reinsch told Wilson plainly that without American aid American interests could be lost. After further development loan negotiations in 1916–1917 failed to pan out, Reinsch turned to Chinese participation in World War I as a solution to its problems. Reinsch believed that belligerent status would enable the United States more directly to offer aid, and would guarantee China restitution of Shandong during peace talks. Chinese participation elicited vitriolic debate in Beijing, and China's eventual entry into the war in August 1917 left Reinsch despondent about the self-destructive nature of Chinese internal politics. The publication of the Lansing-Ishii Agreement in November 1917 heightened Reinsch's belief that even if he could convince American investors to look past Chinese political corruption, it was too late to oppose Japanese expansion.

Reinsch spent a frustrating last year in Beijing. His scheme to internationalize China's finances was rejected and his argument for the unfettered return of Shandong at the Versailles Conference ignored. His policies seemingly out of sync with Wilson's, Reinsch resigned on June 7, 1919. Before departing China, Reinsch negotiated for himself the role of "counselor" to the Chinese government, remaining in that capacity until his death. His health declining rapidly, Reinsch reluctantly, and unsuccessfully, ran for the Senate in 1920. Although frequently ignored by Chinese leaders, Reinsch's criticism of the Nine Power Treaty proved an irritant to the State Department during the Washington Naval Conference negotiations in 1921–1922. His efforts to shape America's China policy largely ignored, Reinsch died in China of a brain tumor on January 22, 1923.

See also **Twenty-One Demands; Open Door Policy; Nine Power Treaty (1922).**

REFERENCES: Noel H. Pugach, *Paul S. Reinsch: Open Door Diplomat in Action* (Millwood, NY, 1979); Paul S. Reinsch, *An American Diplomat in China* (Garden City, NY, 1922).

Eric A. Cheezum

Religion

Religion in the United States is characterized by its complex and constantly morphing nature. One of the components of American religion is the diversity that is found there. The influx into America of Chinese religious thought within the last two centuries has contributed significantly to that diversity. Whether one looks at the complex nature of the Chinese American existence or at the influence that Chinese religious thought has had on non-Chinese converts or observers, Chinese religion(s) have been an important factor in the history of Sino-American relations.

For many Chinese people religion is a multivalent entity. There are three classical religions that have roots in China: Confucianism, Taoism and Zen (Chan) Buddhism. These systems of thought and belief have often intermingled so much that it is at times difficult to distinguish where the lines can be drawn between them. Zen is itself the result of the confluence of indigenous Taoism and immigrant Buddhism. This nature is evident often in the Chinese temples and home shrines found in the United States, which employ symbolism from all three of the traditions. Confucianism, Taoism and Buddhism have exploded in the amount of impact they have had on America from the small beginnings at the opening of trade with China in 1784 to the blossoming population of Chinese immigrants from Hong Kong, Taiwan and mainland China and the burgeoning popular influence of Chinese religion. This new popularity can be seen in such books as *The Tao of Pooh* with its typical mix of American consumerism and popular spirituality. As early as the 1840s, there were sizable numbers of Chinese immigrants arriving on the Western coast of North America and in 1852 the first contract workers arrived in Hawai'i. They were coming as laborers and brought their Buddhist, Confucian and Taoist ideas along with them, e.g., the importance of the *sangha* (Buddhist community), the unique respect of elders and ordered society from Confucianism, and the Taoist *yin-yang*. By 1853, the first Chinese temples were being built in San Francisco's Chinatown and by the end of the century there were approximately 400 temples in the western states. Matching the confluence of religious ideas among the people, these sacred spaces provided room for the symbols and the practices of each of the Chinese systems.

The experience of the Chinese in North America has been disconcerting at times. While they were living in the land that professed freedom of religion and in May 1859, the California Supreme Court ruled that the practice of Buddhism could not be limited by the state, they also experienced a great amount of religious discrimination. Early on, Protestant ministers had been the greatest defenders of the Chinese immigrants, arguing that the protection of their freedom would lead to their inevitable conversion. Yet rather than conversion, for many Chinese, there was a revival of interest in their ancient faiths. In May 1876, Chinese-American businessmen brought Confucian scholar Fung Chee Pang to San Francisco to speak on the teachings of the ancient faith. His meetings and the news coverage that they generated brought about much interest in Chinese religion, primarily in the Chinese but also in a few of those who were not. The unexpected response began a reversal in the trend towards protection. A growing animosity towards the Chinese, ostensibly for labor reasons, led in 1882 to the Chinese Exclusion Act.

The years following the Exclusion Act saw a decline in the proportion of Chinese residents in the United States as no new Chinese immigration was allowed, but the practice of Taoism, Confucianism and Chinese Buddhism continued. When, in the 1960's, many of the restrictions were lifted, the new immigrants from Hong Kong, Taiwan and political refugees from mainland China found existing religious structures, which were being given new life with their arrival. Not only did they find a much different political environment in the second half of the 20th century, they found a much more diverse and open religious environment. There are still groups in the United States who are closed-minded to the religious perspective of the ethnic Chinese. Nevertheless, there is largely a climate of an appreciation of diversity, which can be attributed to the efforts immigrants and emissaries from around the world.

See also Chinese Americans; Chinatowns; Chinese Exclusion Act of 1882.

REFERENCES: Thomas A. Tweed and Stephen Prothero (eds.), *Asian Religions in America: A Documentary History* (New York, 1999); Thomas A. Tweed, *The American Encounter with Buddhism, 1844–1912: Victorian Culture and the Limits of Dissent* (Chapel Hill, NC, 2000); David K. Yoo (ed.), *New Spiritual Homes: Religion and Asian Americans* (Honolulu, HW, 1999); Tony Carnes and Fenggang Yang (eds.), *Asian American Religions: The Making and Remaking of Borders and Boundaries* (New York, 2004).

Gene Mills, Jr.

Republic of China (ROC)

The Sino-Japanese War of 1894–1895 and the Russo-Japanese War of 1904–1905 served to erode the last vestiges of Manchu power in China. The resolution of these conflicts served to formalize the Japanese occupation of Korea and to legitimize Japanese claims of interest in adjacent regions of China. In addition, the dissolution of imperial authority left China completely open to Western economic incursions and cultural influences. The United States had a major part in these developments. In 1900, American military units played a pivotal role in the suppression of the Boxer Rebellion. A popular uprising implicitly supported by the Manchu leadership, the Boxer Rebellion was a partly mystical, last-gasp attempt to expel foreigners from China and thereby preserve its traditional institutions. In 1905, President Theodore Roosevelt brokered the treaty that resolved the Russo-Japanese War, which essentially divided Manchuria into Japanese and Russian spheres of influence. Subsequently, Roosevelt articulated the "Open Door Policy" toward China. Under the guise of reducing potential conflicts among the Western powers in China and of accelerating the modernization of China, this policy effectively opened all of China to the virtually unrestricted exploitation by Western business interests.

In late 1890s and early 1900s, Dr. Sun Zhongshan, founder of the Guomindang, the Nationalist Party, emerged as the leader of the republican revolutionary movement in China. In October 1911, the revolutionaries overthrew the Machu Dynasty and established the Republic of China (ROC). Despite its success in eliminating the Manchus, the Guomindang actually controlled only a small portion of China, for strong warlords, or, in several instances, coalitions of warlords, had established control over almost all of China beyond the Guomindang's base in the south. Moreover, the provisional government established by the Guomindang was initially headed by the autocratic Yuan Shikai, and Sun Zhongshan's vision of a Chinese republic never really had an opportunity to take hold. After successfully suppressing a cessation movement in seven nearby provinces, Yuan declared himself emperor. Although he died shortly afterwards, his actions blurred any distinctions between the leadership of the Guomindang and the war lords, especially to outside observers. In any case, the outbreak of the First World War focused Western attention on Europe and the Atlantic. The Western powers acquiesced to the Japanese occupation of German colonial possessions in the Pacific, and China devolved into an almost constant state of civil strife that periodically erupted into civil wars. Jiang Jieshi eventually rose into the leadership of the Guomindang in the mid-1920s. Initially aligning himself with the aggressive Chinese Communists and accepting military aid from the Soviet Union, Jiang initiated an extended campaign against the warlords in 1928. Over the next six years, he established Guomindang control over most of the provinces of eastern China, from Guangzhou to Beijing. Early in the campaign, however, he purged his forces and territories of Communists. Under Mao Zedong, the surviving Communists undertook the 6,000-mile Long March into what became their strongholds in north central China. Along the way, the Communists lost 70% of the 100,000 people who set out to escape Jiang's forces.

When the Japanese formally occupied Manchuria in 1931 and established the puppet-state of Manchukuo, installing the last Manchu emperor as their surrogate, the international protests were muted by Jiang's own reluctance to challenge this outright seizure of Chinese territory. Jiang was preoccupied by his continuing efforts against the warlords still in control of China's western provinces and by his efforts to check the Communists' increasing appeal to the rural population. From the start of the conflict with Japan, he demonstrated an unwillingness to commit his forces fully against them, a pattern that would continue throughout the duration of the war to the greatly exasperation of his American and British allies. But when the Japanese invaded China proper in 1937, there was a great deal of international outrage, fueled by the Japanese terror bombing of cities such as Shanghai and culminating in the shock at the rampage through the ROC capital that became known as the "Rape of Nanjing." In response to these "outrages," the United States imposed a boycott against Japan, denying it American steel, rubber, and oil at a time when the United States was the major exporter of those resources to Japan. This boycott provoked Japan to look militaristically toward Southeast Asia as another source of those raw materials. Once it entered the war, the United States would materially and militarily support the Chinese Nationalists under Jiang against the Japanese and, afterwards, against the Chinese Communists. That support would continue even after the Nationalists were defeated by the Communists in the Chinese Civil War of 1945–1949 and driven from the mainland and took refuge on Taiwan. Indeed, for several decades the United States refused to recognize the People's Republic of China (PRC), the Communist regime, established on the mainland in October 1949 and officially maintained that the government of the Republic of China on Taiwan was the legitimate government of all of China. But, throughout this period, the United States was less enamored of the Nationalists—in particular, of Jiang's leadership—than it was determined to check the enemies it had in common with the Nationalists.

See also Sun Zhongshan (1866–1925); Jiang Jieshi (1887–1975); People's Republic of China (PRC).

REFERENCES: Howard L. Borman and Richard C. Howard, *Biographical Dictionary of Republican China* (New York, 1967); E. L. Dyer, *China at War, 1901–1949* (New York, 1995); Shinkichi Eto and Harold Schiffrin (eds.), *The 1911 Revolution: Interpretive Essays* (Tokyo, 1984); Mary Clabaugh Wright, *China in Revolution: The First Phase, 1900–1913* (New Haven, CT, 1968); Ernest Young, *The Presidency of Yuan Shih-k'ai: Liberalism and Dictatorship in Early Republican China* (Ann Arbor, MI, 1977).

Martin Kich

Republic of Korea (ROK)

There has always been competition on the Korean Peninsula between China and the United States, but it was the Korean War that was responsible for setting relations between China and the United States for the second half of the 20th century. In the aftermath of the Korean War, the United States and China recognized rival regimes —the United States recognizing Republic of Korea (ROK) or South Korea, while the People's Republic of China preferred to recognize its Cold War ally, the Democratic People's Republic of Korea or North Korea. It has only been since the end of the Cold War that South Korean-Chinese have established political, economic, and cultural relations.

The U.S.-ROK alliance was the cornerstone of East Asian security and international relations since the end of the Korean War. The national security of South Korea was based on a defense relationship with the United States. Over time, South Korea became structurally tied to the U.S. through an alliance framework as economic and strategic ties came to bind the two countries. In recent years, South Korea's political liberalization expanded the basis for stronger and more comprehensive relationship with the United States based on mutual interests.

The end of the Cold War signaled a shift in the geopolitics of Northeast Asia as the collapse of the Soviet Union brought about new political and trade dynamics to the region. Sensing a strategic shift in the global trading system, Seoul signaled its intent to increase and diversify its trade relations with the hitherto untapped markets of the Socialist-bloc countries as well as the People's Republic of China while still engaging North Korea diplomatically. The successful culmination Seoul's *Nordpolitik* policy (Northern Policy) saw the normalization of Sino-Korean relations in 1992.

Since the normalization of the Sino-South Korean relations in 1992, South Korea has again become the focal point of Sino-America relations in East Asia as the rise of China has become increasingly important in South Korea's strategic calculations. Seoul has maintained its friendly and mutually beneficial relationship with the United States while strengthening economic, diplomatic, cultural and military ties with China. These increasing ties with Beijing will inevitably impact the U.S.-ROK security relationship as cultural complementarity will influence South Korean views on political and security issues in Northeast Asia.

China's expanding relationship with South Korea provides a balance to Seoul's dependence on the United States. The tug-of-war between the United States and China over South Korea will continue as China seeks to indirectly challenge the long-standing framework of U.S.-centered alliances that provide the basis for security in Northeast Asia.

See also Korean War; Democratic People's Republic of Korea (DPRK); North Korean Nuclear Controversy.

REFERENCES: Scott Snyder, "Sino-Korean Relations and the Future of the U.S.-ROK Alliance," in National Bureau of Asian Research (ed.), *Perspectives on the Future of the Korean Peninsula* (Seattle, WA, 2003); Robert G. Sutter, *Korea: Improved South Korean-China Relations: Motives and Implications* (Washington, DC, 1997); Ahn Choong Yong, "Economic Relations Between Korea and China," *The Korean Journal of International Studies* (Spring/Summer 2002).

Keith Leitich

Resist America, Aid Korea (*kang mei, yuan chao*)

The term Resist America, Aid Korea is both the Chinese name for their participation in the Korean War (1950–1953) as well as a domestic Chinese campaign to generate support for the war and consolidate Chinese Communist Party's (CCP) political power.

Tension between the Soviet Union-supported North Korean government and U.S.-backed South erupted into a full-scale war on June 25, 1950. Initially, South Korean and UN forces (largely comprised of U.S. troops) had the upper hand. By September, the South had captured most of North Korea. Beijing regarded UN troops crossing the 38th parallel as a provocation and threat to China's industrial heartland in its Northeast. Mao also viewed the war with the U.S. as an opportunity to expand the Chinese revolution and "beat American arrogance." After Washington ignored its repeated warnings, China sent upwards of 200,000–300,000 "People's Volunteers," a term adopted to avoid the formal status as a belligerent, in October 1950. The worst of the fighting took place between November 1950 and July 1951. After initial defeats, the Chinese forces commanded by General Peng Dehuai fought the UN forces to stalemate at the 38th parallel. Chinese troops remained in Korea after the signing of an armistice at Panmunjom in July 1953, finally withdrawing only in late 1958.

The war was costly and announced arrival of full-scale Cold War in East Asia. Estimates of Chinese losses range from a half a million to one million men, including Mao Zedong's son, Mao Anying, killed during a U.S. air raid. Chinese People's Volunteers killed, wounded, or captured over a million UN troops. Likewise, the war came at a terrible time for China, then just beginning to recover from eight years of war against Japan and the Civil War with Jiang Jieshi's Nationalists. As a result of the war, Taiwan and South Korea became part of the U.S. defense perimeter, forcing Beijing to cancel its plans to invade Taiwan. Likewise, the war set the stage for twenty years of confrontation between China and the U.S. and pushed China into closer ties with Moscow. In China, the war led to the acceleration of CCP attempts to consolidate control. Rumors of American-sponsored invasion by Jiang Jieshi and fears of a counter-revolution led the Communists to crack down on domestic opposition by intensifying land reform, insisting on ideological compliance from intellectuals, and waging a brutal campaign against business leaders. The domestic campaign to support the war included the popular dissemination of reports on U.S. germ warfare and U.S. policies of rearming Japan, and led to the elimination of U.S. cultural influence in China.

See also Korean War.

REFERENCES: Chen Jian, *China's Road to the Korean War: The Making of the Sino-American Confrontation* (Chapel Hill, NC, 1994); William Stueck, *The Korean War: An International History* (Princeton, NJ, 1995); Bruce Cumings, *The Origins of the Korean War*

(Princeton, NJ, 1990); Allen S. Whiting, *China Crosses the Yalu: The Decision to Enter the Korean War* (New York, 1960).

Karl Gerth

Reston, James "Scotty" (1909–1995)

Born in Scotland, he attended public schools in Dayton, Ohio and graduated from the University of Illinois. Beginning his newspaper career in Dayton, Reston rose to the highest level of American journalism, becoming executive editor of the *New York Times* in 1968, winning several major awards, including two Pulitzer Prizes. The first in 1944 for foreign affairs came from his reports on the Dumbarton Oaks Conference held that same year in suburban Washington, DC. His newspaper revealed the documents he received from the Nationalist Chinese delegation proposing the structure of the United Nations and the post-World War II plans of the Allies.

Continuing Reston's interest in Sino-American affairs he wrote in his autobiography, *Deadline*, that United Nations forces, led by the United States in October 1950, failed to heed the People's Republic of China's warning not to cross the 38th parallel in Korea and approach the Yalu River or risk Communist intervention. President Harry S. Truman and General Douglas MacArthur ignored the warnings, thus escalating the Korean War to a superpower conventional weapon showdown lasting three more years.

Following the Korean War, Reston was next reported on Indochina. During a visit to Vietnam in 1953 he reported on a large Communist army that was well supplied by the Chinese. But he also characterized the conflict, of the nationalist Vietminh against France as largely a civil war. During a subsequent visit in 1963, with U.S. troop levels now over 200,000, he reported his suspicions that American government briefings on the war were not completely accurate. An outgrowth of this situation was the *New York Times* publication of Pentagon papers copied illegally by Daniel Ellsberg, a former Pentagon employee and opponent of the war, describing mistakes made by the United States. Teston and the paper refused a request from then U.S. Attorney General John Mitchell to stop publication of the documents and return them to the Pentagon. After losing an initial court ruling, the papers were subsequently printed in 1971 after the U.S. Supreme Court ruled against the government's effort to prohibit their disclosure. In the summer of 1971 Reston managed to procure visas for himself and his wife Sally to visit China, coincidentally within days of U.S. Secretary of State's Henry Kissinger's secret mission to Beijing, arranging President Richard's Nixon's breakthrough visit. After a memorable story of having his appendicitis cured in China by acupuncture, he had a wide-ranging five-hour interview with Chinese Premier Zhou Enlai. It was one of the first interviews given by a high Chinese official to a Western journalist for many years. Zhou was critical of U.S. policy in Vietnam while at the same time praising George Washington. The Chinese Premier also was candid in admitting to problems that the PRC faced: overpopulation, Taiwan, and the Soviet Union, including a possible nuclear attack by the USSR.

James "Scotty" Reston was one of the most prominent American journalists of his generation, with wide ranging contacts inside the U.S. and out. His columns in the *New York Times* were very influential and many times reflected the natural antagonism between the government and a free press. He died at his house outside of Washington, D.C. on December 6, 1995 at the age of 86.

See also Korean War; Nixon's Visit to China; Zhou Enlai (1898–1976).

REFERENCES: R. W. Apple, "James Reston, a Journalist Nonpareil, Dies at 86," *New York Times Biographical Service* (December 1995); James Reston, *Deadline* (New York, 1991).

Lynn Brown

Ridgway, Matthew B. (1895–1993)

Born to a professional army officer on March 3, 1895, at Fort Monroe, Virginia, Ridgway up on several army bases. He graduated from West Point in 1917 as a second lieutenant. He spent World War One as a company commander in Texas, and shortly before the war ended, he was transferred to West Point where he served as an instructor until 1924. In 1925, Ridgway, now a captain, Ridgway commanded a company of the Fifteenth Infantry regiment in Tianjin, his first overseas assignment, where he met another American officer George C. Marshall. During the remaining inter-war years, Ridgway studied at Fort Benning Infantry School and the Army War College, and served in staff positions in the United States, Brazil, Nicaragua, the Panama Canal Zone, and the Philippines attaining the rank of colonel.

In January 1942 he was given command of the Eighty-Second Infantry Division changing it into an airborne unit. He planned the invasion of and parachuted with his troops into Sicily in July 1942, and took part in the landings at Saleno, Italy, in September before his division was transferred to England. He again parachuted with his forces into Normandy on D-Day, June 6, 1944, after which he became commander of the XVIII Corps, which fought in Belgium, the Netherlands, and the Battle of the Bulge before meeting Soviet forces at the Elbe River in Germany in May 1945. One month later, Ridgway was promoted to lieutenant general. After the war, he served in command posts in the Mediterranean and the Philippines, and became the senior American army representative on the United Nations Military Staff Committee. In December 1950 President Harry S. Truman appointed Ridgway commander of the U.S. 8th Army in Korea, under General Douglas MacArthur, who gave him total control. Starting in late October 1949, the invading Communist Chinese "volunteers," with their North Korean allies, inflicted heavy causalities on this army, along with its United Nations allies, as they approached the Yalu River, the border between North Korea and China. The UN Forces fled in chaos south from the onslaught with some military leaders thinking that they should be evacuated from Korea. Upon taking command, Ridgway directed an orderly retreat to take up defensive positions south of Seoul. To raise morale, he relieved incompetent officers of command and visited his troops at the front. In a short time, the Chinese advance was halted, Seoul was retaken, and UN Forces moved up again to the 38th parallel, the demarcation line between North and South Korea. When General MacArthur urged total invasion of North Korea, President Truman relieved him as Allied commander and head of the occupation forces in Japan and replaced him with Ridgway. With the rank of general, Ridgway fought a stalemated war on the Korean peninsula, and sent out the first peace feelers for negotiations with the Chinese and North Koreans in early summer 1951.

In 1952 Ridgway oversaw the end of the American occupation of Japan and replaced Dwight D. Eisenhower as NATO Supreme Commander. In October 1953 he became the army chief of staff where he successfully argued with Eisenhower administration officials against American intervention to help the French in Indochina in 1954 by pointing out such aid would require large amounts of American forces and possible invasion of China. He retired from the army in June 1955 over differences with the Eisenhower administration's plans for the army. He became the chair of the Mellon Foundation in Pittsburgh until 1960. He was an early critic of the Vietnam War in the 1960s and one of the "wise men" who successfully urged President Lyndon B. Johnson to halt the escalation of the American war effort in Vietnam. He died in Fox Chapel, near Pittsburgh, on July 26, 1993.

See also Korean War.

REFERENCES: Roy E. Appleman, *Ridgway Duels for Korea* (College Station, TX, 1990); Matthew B. Ridgway, *Soldier: The Memoirs of Matthew Ridgway as Told to Harold H. Martin* (New York, 1956).

Greg Ference

Roberts, Issachar Jacox (1802–1871)

Issachar Jacox Roberts, American Baptist missionary in 19th century China, was born in Sumner County, Tennessee in 1802. Although orthodox in his Christian beliefs, Roberts is known for influencing Hong Xiuquan who led the Taiping Rebellion (1850–1864) against the Qing Dynasty.

Roberts completed ministerial training at a theological school in 1828 and was ordained a Baptist minister. In 1837 he went to China as a Baptist missionary. In 1847 Roberts met a thirty-three-year-old Chinese male, Hong Xiuquan, the future leader of the Taiping Rebellion. Hong asked Roberts to explain a series of dreams in which he had envisioned himself as being the second son of the Judeo-Christian God. Roberts dismissed the dreams. He gave Hong his first fully translated version of the Bible. Studying the Bible under the guidance of Roberts for two months, Hong left a deep impression on Roberts, who described him as the most earnest and deeply interested student of Christianity he had ever found in China; but strongly tinctured with fanaticism. Two months' study of the Bible, even as intensive as it was, would not have been sufficient for Roberts to impart more than a superficial understanding of Christianity, but what Hong did learn proved to have tremendous consequences. The moral rigidity of the Ten Commandments and wrathful retribution of the God in the Old Testament overwhelmed any attraction the traditional Confucian philosophy and ethic had for Hong. A few years later Hong led a small uprising of Chinese Christians in Guangxi Province, which later turned into a massive rebellion lasting for 14 years, during which, Hong established the government of the Heavenly Kingdom of Great Peace and his own capital in Nanjing. Controlling several richest provinces in southern China, he posed a serious challenge to the Qing government.

Certain teachings and practices of Hong's regime reflected the knowledge of the Christian religion that Hong had learned from Roberts. The rebels accepted God as Creator of the universe and the Ten Commandments as guiding moral principles. They also practiced baptism. The constitution of the Taipings was similar to the constitution that Roberts had drawn for his church in Guangzhou, and the Taiping churches were organized in the pattern of Roberts' church. The Taipings also adopted Christian practices of grace before meals and observance of the Sabbath by study and worship. The legal code, which reflected Roberts' moral philosophy, included forbidding of prostitution, gambling, witchcraft, adultery, slavery, and the use of opium, tobacco, and alcoholic beverages. Foot binding was banned. The land system was communal in nature. The citizens of the Kingdom were supposed to share things. Their slogans were, "There being fields, let all cultivate them; there being food, let all eat; there being clothes, let all be dressed; there being money, let all use it, so that nowhere does inequality exist, and no man is not well fed and clothed." But some of the core Christian teachings such as peace, love, humility, forgiveness, and service to others were ignored.

On October 13, 1860, Issachar Roberts arrived in Nanjing thirteen years after Hong had studied under him in Guangzhou. Hong now became the "Heavenly King" of the Taipings at Nanjing. Hong welcomed Roberts, provided him with free room and board, and even encouraged his former tutor to dress in Taiping clothing. Yet, at their only meeting Roberts was shocked to find that he was expected to kneel in the presence of his former student. Roberts was also infuriated that Hong now seriously believed himself to be the brother of Jesus. Roberts attempted in vain to turn his former student toward orthodox Christianity. He was told that he could only preach the Taiping version of Christianity. Hong tried to win Roberts' favor by conferring a title upon him, similar in rank to that of a British marquis. He also offered him three wives, but Roberts declined. On February 26, 1861, Hong commissioned Roberts as Director of Foreign Affairs for the government of the Heavenly Kingdom of Great Peace. The American missionary turned it down, but offered help to the rebel government in foreign policy matters for the next twelve months. In Hong's inner circle, Roberts was the only Caucasian. It was during this period that he was able to win Hong's agreement to permit foreign Christian missionaries free access to all Taiping territory. Roberts also negotiated with Hong that the "Chinese Soldiers of Christ" would construct at least eighteen church buildings in every major city. Roberts finally became disillusioned with Hong's interpretation of Christianity. He gave up all hope of bridging the gap between orthodox Protestant Christianity and the Taipings' version of Christianity with Hong as part of the Holy Trinity. After lecturing Hong's lieutenants so severely that he was threatened with arrest, he fled Nanjing on January 20, 1862. Roberts later wrote of his pupil, "His religious toleration, and multiplicity of chapels, turns out to be a farce, of no avail in the spread of Christianity — worse than useless."

With Hong's suicide in 1864, the Taiping Rebellion came to an end. Roberts returned to the United States in 1866. He died of leprosy in 1871 at Upper Alton, Illinois.

See also Taiping Rebellion (1850–1864).

REFERENCES: Eugene Powers Boardman, *Christian Influence Upon the Ideology of the Taiping Rebellion, 1851–1864* (Madison, WI, 1952); Teng Yuan Chung, "Reverend Issachar Jacox Roberts and the Taiping Rebellion," *Journal of Asian Studies, Vol. 23, No. 1* (1963).

Yuwu Song

Roberts Missions

Edmund Roberts (1784–1836), merchant and special diplomatic agent of the United States in Asia, was born in Portsmouth, New Hampshire. In 1827 he sailed to Bombay and Zanzibar, then ruled by the Sultan of Muscat, whom he befriended. Upon his return he urged New Hampshire Senator Levi Woodbury to request that commercial treaties be negotiated with Asian countries. Through the influence of Woodbury, who became President Andrew Jackson's Secretary of the Navy, Roberts was appointed in 1832 as "special agent of the United States." Roberts was empowered to negotiate treaties with the Birman Empire (Burma/Myanmar), Cochin China (the southern third of Vietnam), Japan, Muscat, Siam, and the Sultanate of Atjeh (also referred to as "Achin" or "Acheen") in Sumatra. He was given blank letters of credence, signed by Andrew Jackson, for states not mentioned in his instructions. To lessen the risk of interference from other powers, Roberts traveled incognito and was given the position of "clerk to the commander of the United States sloop '*Peacock*'" at a salary of $1,500 per year.

In November 1832 Roberts arrived in Guangzhou en route to other ports. The Chinese were unhappy at the presence of an American warship and the *Peacock* was ordered to leave at the earliest possible moment. Neither in Robert's writings nor those of John Shellabar, U.S. Consul in Batavia and an enthusiastic supporter of the mission, is there even a suggestion of a treaty with China. However, both men strongly urged treaties with Japan, Muscat, and Siam. American reluctance to negotiate with China at this early stage may have derived from mercantile fears that the Chinese might insist on American abstinence from the lucrative, but illegal, importation of opium. The Roberts mission never reached Burma. In Sumatra he presented the Rajah of Bencoolen a gift of tobacco and received a thank you note. He could not finalize a treaty in Cochin

China due to "vexatious requisitions of etiquette." However, on March 20, 1833, at the court of Rama III in Bangkok, Roberts concluded his first treaty of amity and commerce. The Siamese agreement exempted Americans from governmental monopoly controls and all export and import duties. In Muscat Roberts renewed his friendship with the Sultan and, on September 21, 1833, signed another treaty of amity and commerce. It guaranteed the American consul extraterritorial powers, fixed duties at five per cent, and contained a most-favored-nation clause. At this point Roberts thought it prudent to return to the United States and secure ratification of his treaties. He returned to Portsmouth in April 1834. The Senate ratified his treaties in June 1834.

In March 1835 Secretary of State John Forsyth authorized Roberts to return to Muscat and Siam to exchange ratifications of the treaties he had negotiated and attempt further contacts with Cochin China and Japan. After successful visits to Muscat and Siam, Roberts became seriously ill. He died in Macao on June 12, 1836. He is buried in the East India Company cemetery, where American merchants erected a monument to the first American diplomat in East Asia. Roberts's Japan mission was picked up by Commodore James Biddle ten years later.

See also Opium Trade; Biddle, James (1783–1848).

REFERENCES: Jonathan Goldstein, "For Gold, Glory, and Knowledge: The Andrew Jackson Administration and the Orient, 1829–1837," *International Journal of Maritime History* (December 2001).

Jonathan Goldstein

Robertson, Walter S. (1893–1970)

From 1953 to 1959, Walter S. Robertson was Assistant Secretary of State for Far Eastern affairs, playing an influential role in formulating and implementing U.S. policy in Asia.

Born in Nottoway, Virginia, he studied at William and Mary College and Davidson College until 1912 when he began a banking career. During World War I, he served as a pursuit pilot in the U.S. Army Air Corps. Postwar success as an investment banker in a Richmond banking and brokerage firm led to his becoming a partner in 1925. Robertson began to serve in the U.S. government during World War II, first in 1943 as Lend Lease administrator in Australia. The next year, the State Department assigned him to the U.S. embassy at Chongqing, China, where he was economic counselor and then charge. When General Patrick J. Hurley resigned as ambassador in 1945, he took charge of the embassy until Ambassador J. Leighton Stuart arrived several months later. During this interlude, Robertson assisted General George C. Marshall during his unsuccessful mission to China. Marshall's negotiations convinced him that compromise between the Chinese Communist Party (CCP) and the Guomindang (Nationalists) was impossible. He saw no prospect for normal relations with a CCP regime. A staunch defender of the Nationalists, Robertson believed that the U.S. government contributed to the defeat of Jiang Jieshi in the Chinese Civil War, acting on the advice of allegedly pro-Communist U.S. diplomats known as the China Hands and withholding economic and military assistance to the Guomindang.

Returning to private life in 1946, Robertson, a Democrat, soon became involved in the angry political controversy surrounding the "loss" of China to Communism. When he voiced strident criticism of U.S. China policy in testimony before Congress in 1948, he attracted the notice of the Truman administration's conservative critics. Following his election as President in November 1952, Republican Dwight D. Eisenhower named John Foster Dulles Secretary of State, who then asked Robertson to be Assistant Secretary of Far Eastern Affairs to preempt right-wing attacks on the administration. Robertson worked closely with Dulles and maintained good relations with Congressional leaders. Although few men in public life were as conservative or fervently anti-Communist as Robertson, his personal integrity and gracious manner set him apart from other like-minded leaders.

Assistant Secretary Robertson dealt effectively with problems concerning relations with allies in East Asia. Traveling personally to the Republic of Korea, he conducted difficult negotiations with President Syngman Rhee and won his assent to the Korean Armistice Agreement of 1953. Robertson also made effective use of his capable subordinates. For example, he relied on Ambassador John M. Allison to handle Japanese affairs regarding trade, rearmament, and popular unhappiness with the U.S. military presence. Robertson was a stubborn supporter of the Republic of China (ROC) after it fled to Taiwan late in 1949, pressing hard for non-recognition of the People's Republic of China (PRC). He was a vigorous advocate of the U.S.-China Mutual Defense Pact of 1954. Robertson never wavered in his insistence that the ROC, rather than the PRC, was the legitimate Chinese government. During the April 1954 crisis in French Indochina at Dien Bien Phu, he urged the Eisenhower administration to adopt a confrontational stance toward Beijing. Later that year and again in 1958, Robertson advocated the same course when the PRC bombarded offshore islands in the Taiwan Strait. His hostility toward the PRC derived not only from his anti-Communism, but his friendship with Jiang and great admiration for the Nationalist leader.

Research on the first decade of the PRC suggests, however, that Robertson's understanding of Beijing's challenge to U.S. policy objectives was more shrewd than his numerous critics have allowed. But his tendency to identify any opposition to an anti-Communist stance as unwitting support for world Communism carried high risks and brought great costs, resulting in the pursuit for ill-advised policies, such as U.S. intervention in Indonesia in the 1950s. His role in replacing independently minded diplomats critical of either the Guomindang or containing the PRC also created a deep void of expertise in the State Department. He resigned for health reasons in 1959.

REFERENCES: William Stueck, *The Korean War: An International History* (Princeton, NJ, 1995); James C. Thomson, Jr., Peter W. Stanley, and John C. Perry, *Sentimental Imperialist: The American Experience in East Asia* (New York, 1981); Nancy B. Tucker, *Uncertain Friendships: Taiwan, Hong Kong, and the United States, 1945–1992* (New York, 1992); Shu Guang Zhang, *Deterrence and Strategic Culture: Chinese-American Confrontations, 1949–1958* (Ithaca, NY, 1992).

James I. Matray

Rock Springs Massacre (1885)

Taking place in Rock Springs, Wyoming, on September 2, 1885, the Rock Springs Massacre occurred as part of a spate of similar violent outbreaks targeting Chinese immigrants in the Pacific Northwestern United States during the mid 1880s.

In the years before the massacre, Rock Springs was an important source of coal for the Union Pacific Railroad as it extended west across the United States; the mine in Rock Springs was run by the Union Pacific Coal Company. In the decade before the massacre, the company cut miners' wages by twenty percent and increased working hours. Many of the Welsh and Swedish miners in Rock Springs responded with strikes, organized primarily by the Knights of Labor organization. Employers responded by hiring Chinese immigrants as strikebreakers, and by the time of the massacre in 1885, a majority of the workers at the Rock Springs mine were of Chinese origin.

Driven by images of "Heathen John," intense competition for jobs, and a depressed economy, a mob of white miners attacked the Chinese settlement in Rock Springs on September 2, 1885, shortly after a similar uprising in Tacoma, Washington. Killing at least 28 and wounding at least 15, the mob drove the Chinese laborers into the surrounding hills or to surrounding towns such as Green River. The mob burned the Chinatown of Rock Springs, and the swiftness of the attack is evidenced by the fact that several of the Chinese killed were found partially burned in their homes according to the report sent to the Chinese consul in New York by a survivor of the attack. In the days following the incident, Wyoming Governor Frances Warren requested aid from Washington, DC, and Federal troops were sent in by U.S. President Grover Cleveland to restore order and guard the Chinese workers' return to Rock Springs. An article in the Rock Springs newspaper on September 3, the day after the attack, chronicles the fearful reentry of Chinese workers on railroad cars guarded by Federal troops. Federal troops remained in Rock Springs for over a decade.

The Rock Springs Massacre is also significant in that it took place at a time when the Chinese Qing government was attempting to protect its emigrants abroad. After the Rock Springs Massacre and the consequent report to the Chinese consul in New York, the Chinese government protested to U.S. President Grover Cleveland. Cleveland requested the U.S. Congress to make reparations to the Chinese in Rock Springs, and Congress complied, awarding the Chinese workers $150,000 in compensation.

See also Chinese Americans.

REFERENCES: Dudley Gardner and Verla Flores, *Forgotten Frontier: A History of Wyoming Coal Mining* (Boulder, CO, 1989); Carlos Schwantes, "Protest in a Promised Land: Unemployment, Disinheritance, and the Origins of Labor Militancy in the Pacific Northwest, 1885–1886," *The Western Historical Quarterly* (October 1982); Craig Storti, *Incident at Bitter Creek: the Story of the Rock Springs Chinese Massacre* (Ames, IA, 1991).

Robert Elder

Rockefeller Foundation

The Rockefeller Foundation was established formally on May 14, 1913. New York Governor William Sulzer approved John D. Rockefeller's plan to begin a charitable organization in New York City. The Foundation's mission is to "promote the well-being of mankind throughout the world." The initial endowments installed to the Foundation were approximately $250 million. In 2001, the Foundation's endowment approaches $3.1 billion on the open market.

Since 1913, the Foundation has been involved in a multitude of philanthropic endeavors. Early on, John D. Rockefeller, Jr., assisted his father in the foundation's activities, along with Frederick T. Gates, who was the leading figure in bringing the foundation's work towards medical research, education and public health. The Foundation made significant contributions in the fights against hookworm, malaria, yellow fever and other debilitating diseases all over the world. The Rockefeller foundation was so wide ranging in its activities, it even played a large role in financial relief measures after World War I. Recently, the Rockefeller Foundation has distributed its work into four primary categories: Creativity and Culture, Food Security, Health Equity and Working Communities. The over-arching category of Global Inclusion encompasses and dovetails with all four categories.

Shortly after the Rockefeller Foundation's inception in 1913, the China Medical Board was created as a division of the greater Foundation. One of the first missions of the China Medical Board was to assist with the funding and resource management of Peking Union Medical College. In 1951, Peking Union Medical College was nationalized due to the ongoing Korean War. The China Medical Board withdrew its funding then, but reinstituted it in 1980, when it began again funding healthcare professionals in the People's Republic of China. Since the Rockefeller Foundation and the China Medical Board (integrated as an independent entity in 1928) are grant-based organizations, individuals and organizations must apply in order to receive funding for their own projects. An example is the University of Washington's Department of Medical Education's partnership with Sichuan University in Chengdu, which is funded entirely through the China Medical Board and the Rockefeller Foundation.

Through its continued philanthropic work with nations and peoples throughout the world, the Rockefeller Foundation is a vital component of international humanitarian funding. Its long history of success in funding research and assisting in the foundation of institutions for medical progress has played an important role in the health and well being of humanity worldwide.

See also Peking Union Medical College.

REFERENCES: Frank Ninkovich, *The Rockefeller Foundation, China and Cultural Change: Frank Ninkovich* (Bloomington, IN, 1984); John Farley, *To Cast out Disease: A History of the International Health Division of Rockefeller Foundation: 1913–1915* (Oxford, UK, 2003); Mary Bullock, *An American Transplant: The Rockefeller Foundation and Peking Union Medical College* (Berkeley, CA, 1980).

Arthur Holst

Rong Hong (1828–1912)

Rong Hong, better known as Yung Wing, was a pioneer and leader in China's studying abroad movement. Born to a poor farmer's family, Rong was sent to attend missionary schools at a very young age. Having studied at the Morri-

son Memorial Society School in Hong Kong for three years, he volunteered with two of his classmates to follow Rev. Samuel Brown, their teacher, to the United States for education in 1847. Unwilling to work as a missionary in China after graduation, Rong lost financial support from the missionary community and had to work to complete his education at the Yale College. As the first Chinese graduate from an American college, Rong returned to China in 1854 with a clear and ambitious plan to help more young Chinese have modern education so that they could help build a strong and powerful China.

Rong Hong devoted much of his life to having a large number of Chinese students educated in the United States. Receiving little attention from Chinese government in his early years, Rong had to work as a tea merchant to make a living. His knowledge and ability was finally appreciated by Zeng Guofan, one of the reform-minded top-ranking officials in the Qing Court in the early 1860s. Rong was sent by Zeng to the United States to purchase all the machineries needed for the Jiangnan Zhizaojiu (Jiangnan Arsenal), the first modern manufacturing enterprise in China, in 1863. He was successful in persuading Zeng to set up a technical training school within the arsenal to train technicians and engineers after his return to Shanghai. With the help from Zeng and other high-ranking officials, Rong finally received the approval from the Qing Court for his studying abroad scheme in 1871.

Following Rong's recommendation, the Chinese government sent 120 young students, its first educational mission in modern history, to the Untied States in four installments between 1872 and 1875. According to Rong's original plan, these students would stay in the United Sates for 15 years so that they could have complete education from elementary school to university. Leaving China around 13, they should be able to have a solid grasp of the English language and return to China as middle-aged men who could provide at least 20 years of service to their motherland. As the Deputy Commissioner of the Chinese Education Mission to the United States, Rong Hong took all the Chinese students to the New England and put them in local schools. However, Rong Hong was unable to complete his plan since the Qing Court recalled all Chinese students in 1881 in fear of the Americanization of Chinese students in the United States. Although only two students had graduated from college, many of the returned child students (*liuxue youtong*), as they were called in history, became leading figures in Chinese politics, military, science, engineering, finance, industry, and education.

Despite the setback, Rong Hong continued to support reform and reconstruction in China. He offered advice to Zhang Zhidong, the Commissioner of the Southern Ports, and other reformers during and after the Sino-Japanese War of 1894–1895. Rong drafted plans to establish a national bank and build a railroad to connect Tianjin and Zhenjiang. Neither plan worked because of internal fights and external intervention. Rong Hong had to leave China in 1902 when the Qing Court planned to arrest him for his close relations with Kang Youwei, Liang Qichao, and other reform leaders. He finally had the chance to return to China with a special invitation from Sun Zhongshan after the 1911 Revolution. However, the trip was never taken since Rong Hong died in the United States on April 22, 1912.

REFERENCES: Yung Wing, *My Life in China and America* (New York, 1909); Shi Ni, *Guannian Yu Beiju: Wanqing Liu Mei Youtong Mingyun Poxi [Ideals and Tragedy: An Analysis on the Fates of Chinese Child Students Sent to the United States in the Late Qing Dynasty]* (Shanghai, 1999); Guiyou Huang (ed.), *Asian American Autobiographers: A Bio-Bibliographical Critical Source Book* (Westport, CT, 2001).

Hongshan Li

Roosevelt, Franklin D. (1882–1945)

Franklin Delano Roosevelt served as President of the United States from 1933 to 1945 and presided over a critical time in U.S.-Chinese relations before and during World War II. Following Roosevelt's inauguration in January of 1933, the President embarked on a policy of appeasement toward Japanese aggression in China. Domestic concerns brought about by the Great Depression and isolationist feelings both in Congress and from the American public prompted Roosevelt to adopt this course of action, straining the U.S. relationship with the Chinese government and its leader, Jiang Jieshi.

Early in 1937, combat between Chinese and Japanese troops escalated on the Chinese mainland and developed into a major war. Roosevelt expressed sympathy for the Chinese people, but refused to alter American policy, despite a plea for assistance from Jiang. By 1940, Roosevelt had shifted the focus of his administration to the war in Europe, and aid to Great Britain was seen by the President as taking precedence over aid to China. The Japanese prompted Roosevelt to revise this policy in September of 1940, following Japan's signing of the Tripartite Pact with Germany and Italy. In the six months following the Tripartite Pact, the United States extended $95 million in purchasing credits to the Chinese, and in May 1941, China became eligible for the Lend-Lease program. After the Japanese attack on Pearl Har-

bor in December 1941, Roosevelt considered China an important ally in the war against Japan. However, he still considered the defeat of Germany to be of greater importance than the defeat of Japan and therefore, diverted the lion's share of economic and military aid to Great Britain. Roosevelt hoped China could help keep the Japanese at bay, while the U.S. and its Western allies focused on defeating Hitler. Following Pearl Harbor, Roosevelt and his administration had become extremely frustrated with Jiang's reluctance, at times, to fight the Japanese, and his oppressive internal policies aimed at consolidating power. Roosevelt's continued frustration with the Chinese war effort in October 1944 prompted him to demand a Chinese offensive and to insist that General Joseph Stilwell, Jiang's primary American military advisor, be placed in command of all Chinese forces. Jiang balked at the request and Roosevelt's hopes of China becoming a major theater in the war vanished. In the fall of 1944, as relations between Jiang's government and the Roosevelt administration deteriorated, relations between Roosevelt and the Chinese Communists seemed to improve. Roosevelt's advisors advised him that the Soviet Union was unlikely to support the Communist forces under Mao Zedong, and that there was a chance the Chinese forces could be unified peacefully at the conclusion of the war.

Despite the disagreements with Jiang, Roosevelt held fast to the belief that a post-war Communist China would not be in the best interests of the United States and hoped to direct a peaceful settlement of the internal Chinese struggle that would allow Jiang's government to retain power. While Roosevelt attempted to strengthen the position of Jiang and the Nationalists at the Yalta Conference in February 1945, he sent his personal envoy, Patrick Hurley, to attempt to persuade Jiang and Mao to form a coalition government headed by the Nationalists. Despite Roosevelt's belief that a coalition government was best for China, the President did not want to give the impression that his position had changed on who should rule China. Hurley made Roosevelt's intentions clear in a statement on April 2, 1945 that announced the United States would only support the Nationalist government of Jiang Jieshi.

Mao and the Communists were angered at the U.S. statement, coming on the heels of Hurley's meeting with Mao and Roosevelt's call for a coalition government. However, the Communists still expressed hope that Roosevelt would support a potential Communist regime, but that hope was soon dashed following Roosevelt's death on April 12, 1945.

See also World War II; Jiang Jieshi (1887–1975); Stilwell, Joseph W. (1883–1946); Mao Zedong (1893–1976).

REFERENCES: Warren I. Cohen, *America's Response to China: A History of Sino-American Relations* (New York, 2000); Robert Dallek, *Franklin D. Roosevelt and American Foreign Policy, 1933–1945* (New York, 1979); Wesley M. Bagby, *The Eagle-Dragon Alliance: America's Relations with China in World War II* (Newark, NY, 1992).

Mark Love

Roosevelt, Theodore (1858–1919)

As the 26th President of the United States, Theodore Roosevelt projected American economic and military power onto the international stage at the very beginning of the 20th century. Born into a wealthy New York family, Roosevelt compensated for his near-sightedness, asthma, and general physical frailty by dedicating himself to a regular regimen of athletic training. Despite the somewhat irregular schooling he had received from a succession of tutors, Roosevelt gained admission to Harvard, where he excelled in his studies and pursued his interests in naval history and natural science. After graduating from Columbia law school, Roosevelt began his political career, winning a seat in the New York state legislature, where he quickly established a reputation as a reformer. Then he suffered a bizarre conjunction of personal tragedies when his mother and his wife died within hours of each other. He went out West to recover his emotional equilibrium and formed an attachment to the Western wilderness that would define him personally and politically throughout the rest of his life.

After successful terms as a Commissioner of the National Civil Service and as the New York City Police Commissioner, Roosevelt was appointed Assistant Secretary of the Navy. Foreseeing the coming war with Spain, he was responsible for ordering the Pacific fleet to Hong Kong, from which it could easily interdict the Spanish fleet in the Philippines. After war was declared, he resigned his position, organized a volunteer company that soon became famous as the "Rough Riders," and charged with them up San Juan Hill into American history and into the American imagination. His subsequent fame led to his being elected governor of New York. But his hard-charging reforms led his enemies within his own party to devise to get him out of Albany by arranging his nomination as William McKinley's vice president. When McKinley was assassinated less than a year into his second term, Roosevelt became the youngest person ever to ascend to the presidency. As president, Roosevelt pursued an imperialistic foreign policy premised on American hegemony in the Western Hemisphere and especially in the Caribbean, on the dramatic enhancement and projection of American naval power, and on the aggressive expansion of American interests in the Pacific. The annexation of the Hawaiian Islands, the acquisition of the Philippines in the Spanish-American War, and the subsequent construction of the Panama Canal had made it possible for the United States to become a two-ocean power.

In 1905, Roosevelt interceded in the Russo-Japanese War, brokering the Treaty of Portsmouth, in which the Russians acknowledged Japanese influence in Korea and southern Manchuria and through which the Japanese were able to consolidate their gains before the war effort undermined their still developing industrial economy. In 1908, Roosevelt guided the Root-Takahira Agreement with Japan, defining the "Open Door Policy" toward China. Ostensibly meant to accelerate the modernization of the China by circumventing conflicts over competing spheres of interest in China, the agreement actually spared China from formal colonization while opening it to economic exploitation by any Western power that wished to establish a presence there.

REFERENCES: John Morton Blum, *The Republican Roosevelt* (Cambridge, MA, 1954); H. W. Brands, *T.R.: The Last Romantic* (New York, 1997); A. E. Campbell, *America Comes of Age: The Era of Theodore Roosevelt* (New York, 1971); Lewis L. Gould, *The Presidency of Theodore Roosevelt* (Lawrence, KS, 1991); George Grant, *Carry a Big Stick: The Uncommon Heroism of Theodore Roosevelt* (Elkton, MD, 1996); William Henry Harbaugh, *The Life and Times of Theodore Roosevelt* (New York, 1963); Stefan Lorant, *The Life and Times of Theodore Roosevelt* (New York, 1959); Delber L. McKee, *Chinese Exclusion versus the Open Door Policy, 1900–1906: Clashes over China Policy in the Roosevelt Era* (Detroit, MI, 1977); A. Gregory Moore, *The Dilemma of Stereotypes: Theodore Roosevelt and China, 1901–1909* (Kent, OH, 1978).

Martin Kich

Rusk, David Dean (1909–1994)

Dean Rusk served as U.S. Secretary of State from 1961 to 1969 under Democratic Party Presidents John F. Kennedy and Lyndon B. Johnson. During his State Department career, which began in 1945, Rusk focused upon Far Eastern affairs and was a strong critic of the People's Republic of China. Rusk's concerns regarding Chinese expansionism convinced the diplomat that United States military intervention in South Vietnam was justified.

Rusk was born February 9, 1909 in Cherokee County, Georgia. Following graduation from

Davidson College in 1931, Rusk was a Rhodes Scholar at Oxford for two years. From 1934 to 1940, he taught at Mills College in Oakland, California. During the Second World War, Rusk moved into the State Department, where in 1950 he was made Assistant Secretary for Far Eastern Affairs. Rusk advocated that the United States work with the United Nations to curtail North Korean aggression on the Korean peninsula. In 1952, he left the State Department to head the Rockefeller Foundation, but John Kennedy convinced him to resume his government service in 1961.

Rusk shared Kennedy's suspicions of Mao's China, and he sought to isolate the Chinese regime. At the same time, he encouraged American military escalation to halt the spread of Communism in Indochina. Risk failed to perceive the growing Sino-Soviet split as an opportunity for a rapprochement with China. Rusk concluded that Chinese support of world liberation struggles and an apparent disdain for the danger of nuclear war made Beijing a greater threat to world peace that Nikita Khrushchev's Kremlin. Rusk was convinced that Khrushchev's reckless behavior in the Cuban Missile Crisis was due to pressure from the Chinese to take a more aggressive stance against the West. In addition, the Chinese attack on India in October 1962 was perceived as further proof of Chinese aggression, even though Jiang Jieshi had also claimed the same disputed territory. Rusk was also concerned that continuing unrest in Laos was Chinese sponsored, and the Kennedy administration was prepared to meet what it viewed as growing Chinese influence in Indochina. Following Kennedy's assassination, there appeared to be some opportunity for reducing tensions with China when Roger Hilsman, Assistant Secretary of State for Far Eastern Affairs, suggested that the United States could coexist with Mao's China while retaining its commitment to Taiwan. Nevertheless, Rusk and President Lyndon B. Johnson never wavered from their belief that China was pursuing a war of national liberation in Vietnam; an exaggerated reading of events in Southeast Asia, which postponed any normalization of relations with China. Rusk believed that American security would be best served by a stable international order based upon accepted codes of behavior. The Secretary of State viewed the Chinese as a menace to this order, and he was prepared to make a stand against Chinese expansion in Southeast Asia, comparing Mao with Hitler as a danger to the civilized society. Mao, however, was more interested in internal matters, and in July 1966, the Chinese leader launched the Great Proletarian Cultural Revolu-

tion. Rusk was alarmed by Mao's policies, expressing concern that "a billion Chinese, armed with nuclear weapons" might emerge from the Cultural Revolution determined to carry out the nightmare visions of their leader. Accordingly, American foreign policy toward China changed little during the 1960s under Presidents Kennedy and Johnson. Their Secretary of State perceived China as a danger to international stability, and change in policy would come, instead, from the Republican administration of Richard Nixon.

Following the defeat of Hubert Humphrey in the 1968 presidential election, Rusk returned to private life. He taught international law at the University of Georgia in Athens (1976–1984). Rusk died on December 20, 1994.

See also Cold War.

REFERENCES: David Halberstram, *The Best and the Brightest* (New York, 1969); Dean Rusk, *As I Saw It* (New York, 1970); Thomas J. Schoenbaum, *Waging Peace and War: Dean Rusk in the Truman, Kennedy and Johnson Years* (New York, 1988); Thomas W. Zeiler, *Dean Rusk: Defending the American Mission Abroad* (Wilmington, DE, 2000).

Ron Briley

Russell and Company

Russell and Company was a 19th century American China trade firm, which specialized in tea and opium, and ultimately became the largest American firm on the Chinese coast.

In 1818 Connecticut commission merchant Samuel Russell (1789–1862) and several Rhode Island partners founded Samuel Russell & Co. in Guangzhou. In 1824 Russell broke with the Rhode Islanders and joined Philip Ammidon of Massachusetts to form a new firm, Russell & Co. In 1830, Ammidon left the partnership, Russell returned to Connecticut, and the firm merged with Perkins & Co. to create the largest American enterprise on the China coast. The alliance solidified Russell & Co.'s arrangements with members of the Howqua family, South Fujianese entrepreneurs who were based in Guangzhou and had long serviced Perkins & Co.'s accounts. Under the stewardship of Augustine Heard, Russell & Co. expanded from Sino-American trade into business ventures with India, the Philippines, and Great Britain. When Heard returned home for health reasons in 1834, Russell & Co. remained strong under partner John C. Green, who reorganized the company and regularly dispatched opium smuggling voyages up the China coast. Other long-serving Russell & Co. partners were Robert Bennet Forbes and Warren Delano, ancestor of President Franklin D. Roosevelt. The colorful Philadelphian William W. Wood, son of the actor of the same name, clerked briefly for the firm while writing *Sketches of China* (1830) and editing the *Canton Register* and *Chinese Courier*.

A major moral crisis facing the firm was the question of smuggling opium into China. Russell partners vigorously defended their business even though opium was an illegal addictive and severely debilitating drug. Opium smuggling was criticized by other American merchants who chose not to partake in it, notably New York's D. W. C. Olyphant. He characterized the trade as "an evil of the deepest dye." Russell partners in turn nicknamed Olyphant "holy Joe" and called his headquarters "Zion's corner." In a classic defense of a dishonorable profession, Russell partner John Murray Forbes wrote of Olyphant: "Protect me from all the hallowing influence of holy Joe — his ships are commanded by J-C — officered by Angels & manned by Saints ... Happy thrice happy is the ship even consigned to them." Russell & Co. weathered such criticism until Chinese Imperial Commissioner Lin Zexu halted the opium trade entirely. After the Opium War, Russell & Co. reentered the trade and expanded to Hong Kong and Shanghai. The firm finally went out of business in 1891, having outlasted all of their American competitors from the pre-Opium War days.

See also Opium Trade; First Opium War (1839–1842); Second Opium War (1856–1859).

REFERENCES: Jacques Downs, *The Golden Ghetto* (Bethlehem, PA, 1997); William C. Hunter, *The "Fan Kwae"* (London, 1882).

Jonathan Goldstein

San Francisco Conference (1945)

The San Francisco Conference of 1945 was a culmination of President Franklin D. Roosevelt's dream to establish a United Nations Organization, a successor to the League of Nations. Nearly 300 delegates representing 50 nations met in San Francisco from April to June 1945, and on June 25, 1945, the delegates approved the Charter of the United Nations.

Roosevelt had strong ideas about the organization of the United Nations, and the delegates eventually accepted his ideas. He wanted a more effective organization, and he believed the great powers needed a key role to enforce collective security and to prevent future wars. He also wanted to give these "policemen" the right to veto actions and policies they could not accept. To receive an invitation to the San Francisco Conference and thus to participate in the forthcoming United Nations Organization, nations had to accept the "Declaration by United Nations," issued in January 1942, no later than March 1945 and join the conflict against the Axis powers. There were several sets of issues that caused discussion among the participating delegates. Roosevelt called for a "Big Five" set of Great Powers, which, in addition to the Soviet Union and the United States included Great Britain, France, and China. France's record in the Second World War did not seem to support France as a Great Power, and there were similar concerns about China, but these five powers reflected Roosevelt's worldview and the American delegation would not yield on this point. Medium and smaller powers had concerns, chiefly relating to the veto powers and permanent standing on the Security Council of the five Great Powers. Perhaps surprisingly, the eventual UN organization reflected the draft that American, British, Soviet, and Chinese diplomats accepted during a meeting at Dumbarton Oaks in late summer 1944. Nonetheless, the small and middle powers proposed hundreds of amendments to the Dumbarton Oaks draft, and they questioned the wording of many clauses — in part, perhaps, if only to have influence in the deliberations establishing the United Nations rather than ascribing to a "done deal." In the end, the delegations voted overwhelmingly to approve of the new United Nations organization with six principal organs, including the Security Council. They also approved that the Charter would be effective on October 24, 1945, and that the first session of the UN General Assembly, also one of the six organs, would take place in January 1946 in London.

Sadly, Franklin Roosevelt died thirteen days before the conference opened and his successor, Harry S. Truman, had to direct America's diplomatic efforts. The U.S. delegation achieved its goals, and Jiang Jieshi's Nationalist regime still headquartered in Chongqing in southwest China received recognition as a Great Power, a recognition it retained more than 25 years after it lost the civil war and mainland China to Mao Zedong's Communist revolution in 1949.

See also United Nations.

REFERENCES: Robert Dallek (ed.), *The Roosevelt Diplomacy and World War II* (Huntington, NY, 1978); Townsend Hoopes, *FDR and the Creation of the UN* (New Haven, CT, 1997); Stephen C. Schlesinger, *Act of Creation: The Founding of the United Nations* (Boulder, CO, 2003).

Charles M. Dobbs

Schlesinger, James R. (1929-)

James Rodney Schlesinger was Director of the Central Intelligence Agency (CIA) from February 2, 1973 until July 2, 1973 when he became the U.S. Defense Secretary until November 2, 1975 under Presidents Richard Nixon and Gerald Ford.

Ford dismissed Schlesinger for his "arrogance." Nixon's dramatic trip to China in 1972 occurred just prior to Schlesinger's arrival at the CIA and Defense Secretary posts. Several events in the late 1960s and early 1970s, however, led China and the United States to reexamine their basic policies toward each other, which had been cordial at best.

After the signing of the Shanghai Communique, however, movement toward United States-China normalization during the 1970s saw only limited progress. However, Schlesinger wanted the Chinese to be treated more as a U.S. ally, rather than to remain as a neutral counterpart. Schlesinger was instrumental in setting up liaison offices in each other's capitals in 1973. Schlesinger set up the *People's Diplomacy* organization, which played an important role, as most exchanges of delegations were sponsored by friendship associations that helped the Chinese to look more favorably on the U.S. Chinese statements continued to express the view that both superpowers were theoretically adversaries of China, but they usually singled out the Soviet Union as the more dangerous of the two. In several visits to China during Schlesinger's tenure of office he continued to take a hard line against Russia and embraced a very friendly doctrine in favorable relations with China. It is at this point in time that Schlesinger clashed with most of President Ford's administration as they resisted to ally with China, and instead wanted to befriend the Soviets. Schlesinger pushed for strategic and economic cooperation with China, which would have given increased momentum to the normalization of Sino-American relations, which had been a major obstacle for most of the 1970s. In dealing with Sino-American relations Schlesinger believed that it was wise both as a deterrence to Soviet aggression and to build better relations with the Chinese if the U.S. developed good relations with China, and treated them as an ally. Credible strategic nuclear deterrence, the Secretary felt, depended on fulfilling several conditions, some of which included maintaining a highly survivable force that could be withheld or targeted against the Soviet Union's economic base in order to deter coercive or desperation attacks against U.S. population or economic targets. He believed the U.S. should establish a fast-response force that could act to deter additional enemy attacks. China was his ultimate plan to implement this philosophy. He thought that it would be very beneficial to set up such a quick response force in mainland China. To meet these needs, he built on existing ideas in developing a flexible response nuclear strategy, which, with the President's approval, Schlesinger made public by early 1974. Because Schlesinger regarded conventional forces as an equally essential element in the deterrence posture of the U.S., he was determined that the United States not fall seriously behind the Soviet Union and the American relationship to China was a huge part of the policy to heighten U.S. national security by gaining a closer relationship to the Chinese. Several visits to China during this period were unproductive for most of the administration because the Chinese were feeling as though the U.S. were only using China to gain a closer relationship to the Soviet Union. In late 1975 just after returning from a visit from China, Schlesinger was fired as Secretary of Defense.

REFERENCES: Neal Bernards and Lynn Hall, *American Foreign Policy: Opposing Viewpoints* (St. Paul, MN, 1987); Jean Edward Smith and Herbert M. Levine, *The Conduct Of American Foreign Policy Debated* (New York, 1990); James R. Schlesinger, *America at The Centuries End* (New York, 1989); Robert J. Art and Vincent Davis, *Reorganizing America's Defense: Leadership In War And Peace* (Washington, DC, 1985).

Steven Napier

Scowcroft-Eagleburger Mission (1989)

After Tiananmen Square Massacre in early June 1989, the administration of President George H. W. Bush imposed diplomatic, military, and economic sanctions on China including suspension of high-level official contacts with Beijing. Despite the tensions between the two nations, the White House wanted to defuse the emerging crisis in bilateral relations in order to preserve as much of the relationship as possible. One of the effective ways to achieve this goal was to reopen the lines of communication with China. In July 1989, Bush sent General Bret Scowcroft, the National Security Advisor and Lawrence Eagleburger, the Deputy Secretary of State on a mission to Beijing. The mission was a top secret because a visit to Beijing shortly after the bloody suppression at Tiananmen would be very unpopular if it were made public. Scowcroft and Eagleburger met with Chinese leader Deng Xiaoping and other senior officials. They conveyed two messages to the Chinese: Americans were concerned about the violations of human rights in China but the U.S. government wanted to prevent the setback of Sino-American relations.

Although the mission violated the ban on the top-level official exchanges between the two countries, the White House believed that it could be justified as an expedient way to break the deadlock. As Eagleburger explained, "Messages delivered below the level of the top leaders often get softened or altered on the way up the chain of command," whereas public statements "often engender public posturing, in which saving 'face' becomes more important than a sober consideration of the issues." He argued that though the trip was "neither easy nor pleasant," they delivered an "undiluted message from the President to the Chinese leadership about America's horror over Tiananmen."

The Chinese had believed the U.S. was responsible for the deadlock alone, but later in the fall of 1989, Beijing had begun to acknowledge that both sides, not just the United States, should take measures to move the relations forward. It was the change of the Chinese position that made the second mission possible. In December 1989, Scowcroft and Eagleburger went to China again. This time they intended to explore the possibilities of improving bilateral relations. Through their public toasts and private talks, they let the Chinese leaders know that President Bush considered Deng as his personal friend and China as more important to the United States than ever before. They also conveyed the message that the President would need some sign from the Chinese leadership that Beijing would reciprocate his gesture of good will.

The exchanges of conciliatory gestures from both sides produced great controversy in the United States over the wisdom of White House's policy. Among the published opinions, the defenders described the mission as an act of "courageous leadership," while the critics described the trip as "hailing the Butchers in Beijing." They also contended that the Bush administration acted deceitfully, compromised too much and got too little in return. The photos of Scowcroft toasting Chinese Premier Li Peng angered the nation. China's need to show the world that Beijing was not isolated after the Tiananmen tragedy seemed to lead it effectively "trap" Scowcroft in the photos. The backlash made it more difficult for Bush to improve the relationship between China and America.

See also Tiananmen Square Massacre.

REFERENCES: James Mann, *About Face: A History of America's Curious Relationship with China, from Nixon to Clinton* (New York, 1999); Harry Harding, *A Fragile Relationship: the United States and China Since 1972* (Washington, DC, 1992).

Yuwu Song

Second Indochina War

At the time the Geneva Accords of 1954 ended the First Indochina War, the Communist-led forces of the Viet Minh controlled most of Vietnam. Under these accords, Vietnam was split at the 17th parallel; all Viet Minh armed forces were to go to the North, while anti-Communist forces were go to the South. Elections were sup-

posed to be held in 1956, to choose a government under which Vietnam would be reunited. But these elections were blocked by Ngo Dinh Diem, who with U.S. support became President of the Republic of Vietnam (RVN) in the South. Diem's army and police hunted down the Communists in the South, who appealed to their leaders, now mostly in the North, for permission to launch a guerrilla war against Diem.

That permission came in 1959, and widespread activity by the guerrillas who soon came to be called the Viet Cong began in 1960. The Communist forces fighting in South Vietnam were made up almost entirely of native-born southerners in the early years of the war; they would be mostly northerners by the last years, in the 1970s. On the government's side, U.S. personnel began participating in combat on a small but significant scale in 1962, and on a large scale in 1965. China approved the Vietnamese Communists' initiation of the guerrilla war, and provided military aid. Many Americans greatly exaggerated the degree of Chinese influence on the Vietnamese Communists (actually weaker in the 1960s than it had been in the mid 1950s), even treating the Vietnamese as proxies in a Chinese effort to take over Southeast Asia. By 1964 the war was going very badly for the RVN, and the United States was thinking of attacking North Vietnam. The Chinese warned that they would defend North Vietnam if it were invaded, but they doubted the Americans would be deterred; the United States had ignored similar warnings given in 1950, over North Korea. Fearing that the crisis over Vietnam might trigger a Sino-American conflict even worse than the one that had occurred over Korea, the Chinese in 1964 began a very expensive program to shift industry away from the coast into the interior of China, to make it less vulnerable to U.S. bombing.

Systematic U.S. bombing of North Vietnam began in 1965, and intensified unevenly until 1968. The PRC put military personnel into North Vietnam, mostly the northernmost part of North Vietnam, beginning in 1965. The number is believed to have peaked in 1967, at about 170,000. They included antiaircraft gunners, and military engineers to improve roads and railways, and repair bomb damage. Probably their most important function was as a tripwire, a concrete warning to the United States that a U.S. invasion of North Vietnam could lead to a war with China. The United States did not invade North Vietnam, and seldom bombed the areas having the greatest concentrations of Chinese personnel. China criticized the DRV decision to begin peace talks with the United States in Paris, in 1968, and most of the Chinese military personnel pulled out of North Vietnam in 1969, but Chinese military aid in the form of munitions and supplies continued. Intertwined struggles in Vietnam, Laos, and Cambodia made up the Second Indochina War. Vietnamese Communist forces used base areas and supply lines in Laos and Cambodia. Vietnamese Communist forces aided local guerrillas, the Pathet Lao in Laos and the Khmer Rouge in Cambodia, in warfare against their governments. Indeed, the Vietnamese were the primary force fighting the Laotian government, and from 1970 to 1972 they were also the primary force fighting the Cambodian government. The United States bombed Communist forces in Laos massively from 1965 to 1973, and bombed Communist forces in Cambodia from 1969 to 1973, but made little use of ground troops in those countries. China aided the Pathet Lao and the Khmer Rouge, as well as the Vietnamese. A modest number of Chinese military personnel were in northern Laos, near the Chinese border, for most of the war. Nominally they were a road-building crew. The most important function seems to have been to create a buffer zone along the Chinese border, to keep active combat away from the border. When President Richard Nixon opened up U.S. relations with China in 1971 and 1972, one of his main motives was a hope of improving the U.S. position in the Indochina War. But he was unable to persuade the Chinese to press the Vietnamese Communists to be conciliatory in peace talks, the way they had at the Geneva Conference of 1954.

U.S. forces began to withdraw from Vietnam in 1969; they were mostly gone by the time the Paris Peace Agreement of January 27, 1973, ended U.S. combat action in Vietnam. U.S. bombing in Laos and Cambodia ended later in 1973. The fighting continued without the Americans until it was ended by Communist victories in 1975, first in Cambodia, then in South Vietnam, and finally in Laos.

See also First Indochina War; Geneva Conference (1954); Nixon's Visit to China; Cold War.

REFERENCES: William Turley, *The Second Indochina War* (Boulder, CO, 1986); Qiang Zhai, *China and the Vietnam Wars, 1950–1975* (Chapel Hill, NC, 2000).
Edwin Moise

Second Opium War (1856–1860)

The Second Opium War, known as the Arrow War (1856–1860), involved all the major powers of the world — China, Britain, France, the United States, and Russia. Rather than a result of a diplomatic dispute over the alleged insult to the British flag ascribed to the *Arrow*, a sailing vessel

registered in Hong Kong, the War manifested the irreconcilable conflicts between China and the West in the post-Opium War era: the British right to enter Guangzhou, the extension of foreign trade beyond the five treaty ports as agreed in the Treaty of Nanjing (1842), the legalization of opium, and the creation of diplomatic residence in Beijing.

In the mid 19th century, China was Britain's third and at times second most important trading partner in terms of imports. Under the pretext of free trade and respect for international law, Britain was determined to have opium legalized in China, to monopolize the free opium market, and to open China's interior to British trade. This could not be achieved until Chinese resistance against British interests was completely destroyed. Furthermore, there were significant political and economic interests in British India, notably Indian opium, which had to be defended at all costs in order to avoid a threat to the British colonial rule.

The Second Opium War originated from a minor diplomatic incident in Guangzhou involving a Chinese-owned, Hong Kong-registered sailing vessel, the *Arrow*. On October 8, 1856, Chinese officials boarded the *Arrow* to arrest 12 Chinese sailors suspected of piracy and smuggling. During the arrest, the British flag was torn. Harry Parkes, British Consul at Guangzhou, demanded from Chinese officials an apology to the flag and the release of the crew. The Chinese officials released the crew but refused to apologize. Consequently, Consul Parkes sent the British navy to bombard Guangzhou. By then, the *Arrow* incident escalated into an undeclared war. Hostilities led to the destruction of the foreign factories in Guangzhou, and the British community there withdrew to Hong Kong.

In response, Britain sent an expedition to China under the command of Lord Elgin. France sent another expedition under Baron Gros on the pretext of avenging the murder of a Catholic priest in Guangxi province. The Anglo-French forces overran Guangzhou, captured Governor-General Ye Mingchen (1807–1859), and set up a puppet government under Consul Parkes. They moved northwards to Tianjin and imposed on the Chinese the Treaties of Tianjin (1858), which permitted diplomatic residence in Beijing, opened 10 new ports to foreign trade, and required China to pay indemnities. By virtue of the most-favored-nation status, the United States and Russia gained similar treaties.

In 1859, Frederick Bruce, Lord Elgin's brother, came to exchange the ratifications. Insisting on exchanging them in Beijing instead of

Shanghai as the Chinese preferred, Bruce sailed north but the British forces were defeated by the Chinese troops at Dagu. After the incident, Britain and France sent another expedition to China, and they occupied Beijing, burnt the imperial gardens and drove the Emperor into exile.

Prince Gong, the Emperor's younger brother, signed the Convention of Beijing (1860), which increased the indemnities, confirmed diplomatic residence in Beijing, ceded Jiulong (Kowloon) peninsula to Britain, and permitted Christian missionaries to travel, purchase and rent properties, and build churches in all the provinces. The Convention of Beijing created a diplomatic framework for the expansion of Western political, economic and religious influences into China's interior throughout the late 19th century.

See also First Opium War (1839–1842).

REFERENCES: Mao Haijian, *Tianchao de bengkui [The Collapse of the Celestial Empire: A Reexamination of the Opium War]* (Beijing, 1995); John Y. Wong, *Deadly Dreams: Opium and the Arrow War (1856–1860) in China* (New York, 1998).

Joseph Tse-Hei Lee

Second Taiwan Strait Crisis (1958) *see* Taiwan Strait

Self-Strengthening Movement (1861–1895)

The self-strengthening movement refers to a series of administrative changes established by Qing Dynasty's leaders in response to the realization that Western powers had superior military and economic structures. The West gained the upper hand in China during a number of conflicts where they intervened especially in the two Opium Wars 1839–1842 and 1856–1860 and three rebellions including the devastating Taiping Rebellion 1851–1864. The treaty concessions made by defeated China were extensive and marked the opening of China by Western powers Britain, France, Russia and the United States. The protracted fourteen year Taiping Rebellion required British and French military intervention to restore order and cost China dearly both economically and in exposing the erosion of the effectiveness of the Qing. The presence of Westerners living in concession areas and the British occupation of Beijing confronted the Qing with the need for major reforms to meet the foreign challenge.

Following a coup in 1862, two dowagers (mother-empresses) and Prince Gong became co-regents to the reigning boy emperor and it was this context when the movement — Tongzhi

Restoration — gained approval by Empress Dowager Cixi. Diplomatically, the court ascertained that it needed time to rebuild. During the interval, a policy of cooperation with the West was established while the military was extensively upgraded. To accomplish these aims Prince Gong along with grand councilors and provincial leaders embarked on building an elaborate administrative structure to buttress its mission of diplomacy. For the first time, an office of foreign affairs was formed — the Zongli Yamen — or Office for General Management was to coordinate dealings with four foreign powers. To facilitate its functions, offices for developing foreign-language and science schools was one development and the second was the formation of Customs Inspector. Examples of additional practical steps included sending students on language and diplomatic missions, setting up factories in machine tools, matches, cotton and paper mills and establishing communication via telegraph lines. With treaty ports in operation, the office of Superintendents of Trade Affairs worked with the foreign legations (still considered barbarians) to resolve any issues/disputes, while Customs enforced the collection of import fees. In the educational sphere the court recognized they were wanting in knowledge of Western technology, science and language-fluency and in international legal codes. Beginning in the 1840s and continuing during the movement there were extensive translations of Western characteristics such as history, legal codes and geography. A window to the Western world was provided by an extensive fifty-volume work by Wei Yuan whose rationale was "to learn the superior techniques of the barbarians to control the barbarians," considered as the mantra of the Self-Strengthening Movement.

Other writers gradually emphasized that China was tradition-encrusted and needed to modernize in view of the advancements in the world. One glaring weakness was the dated technology used by the military. As a consequence a flurry of military-related developments was started in 1882 such as the formation of a navy, expansion of shipbuilding and gun manufacture at three dockyard and arsenals. Leading the way was Li Hongzhang, a provincial general who saw firsthand the obsolescence of Chinese military equipment and strategy. A pragmatist, it was Li who was responsible for putting many of the movement's goals in motion.

In spite of the innovations during the Self-Strengthening Movement, weak direction by the Empresses led to uneven and shallow, if not failed, developments. The focus on specific areas was not broad enough to trigger an industrial revolution as in France and England. In the end the shortage of currency was exacerbated by the further draining of resources in fending off further foreign intrusions. The defeat and concessions, following the Sino-Japanese War of 1894–1895, chipped away at the Movement's momentum and eventually led to the decline and end of the imperial system.

REFERENCES: Immanuel C.Y. Hsu, *The Rise of Modern China* (New York, 2000); Chien-chung Ma, *Strengthen the Country and Enrich the People: the Reform Writings of Ma Jianzhong, 1845–1900* (Richmond, UK, 1998); David Pong, *Shen Pao-chen and China's Modernization in the Nineteenth Century* (Cambridge, UK, 1994).

Jim Steinberg

Service, John Stewart (1909–1999)

Service was born in Chengdu, Sichuan Province, where his parents were YMCA missionaries. He attended high school in Shanghai, and, like many "mish kids" journeyed to the United States to attend college. After graduation from Oberlin College in 1932, Service returned to China where he married Caroline Schulz, a college classmate. He entered the Foreign Service, and in August 1943, he was assigned as a political officer to the staff of General Joseph Stilwell's headquarters in Chongqing.

Service was among the most outspoken of the "China Hands," a group of Foreign Service officers who grew increasingly disillusioned with the Nationalist government. In July 1944, he was the Foreign Service officer included in the initial nine-person "Dixie Mission" to Yanan, where he proved himself indispensable due to his language fluency. In the Communist base area, he wrote that he felt he had "come into a different country," one marked by diligence and cooperation in sharp contrast with Nationalist inefficiency, corruption, and general ineptitude. In an October "Double Tenth" Memo to Stilwell (which would later be used as evidence against him in the McCarthy era) Service openly castigated Jiang and his government. The imbroglio that developed after General Patrick Hurley, President Franklin D. Roosevelt's personal emissary to Chinese leader Jiang Jieshi, passed the memo to the Nationalists, served to push long-standing tensions to the breaking point and led to the recall of both Stilwell and Service. Service was able to return to his post, but soon found himself again at the center of controversy. He authored a February 28, 1945 telegram, which urged a realistic approach to China's internal problems by pressuring the Nationalists to make badly needed reforms and providing American aid to the Communists in the fight against Japan. Enraged by this seeming insubordination and with a view toward revenge, Hurley accused Service and his colleagues of harboring sympathy for the Communists and had them recalled.

Service's troubles deepened after he shared personal copies of secret documents with the editor of the left-leaning magazine *Amerasia*, in an attempt to air his side of the ongoing debate over China policy. *Amerasia* had been under FBI surveillance for the pilfering of sensitive government documents, and Service's admitted indiscretion led to his arrest in June 1945. Although a grand jury and an internal State Department hearing board exonerated the Foreign Service officer, the black marks on his record made him a convenient target for loyalty and security hearings, which began on an almost annual basis beginning in 1945 and which ultimately led to his dismissal in December 1951. Labeled as significantly responsible for the "loss" of China, Service refused to go quietly. He fought the State Department's ruling, and in a unanimous decision in 1957 the Supreme Court ruled that the Truman administration had exceeded its authority in its review of Service's case and his dismissal. To the surprise of many, he rejoined the State Department. Upon his retirement from an obscure post in the Liverpool consulate, Service enrolled in the University of California at Berkeley, where he received a master's degree in 1964 and became library curator of its Center for Chinese Studies. During this time, he authored and edited several books, including two that dealt with his career. After President Richard Nixon's visit to China in 1972, he revisited China several times before his death in 1999.

The eminent historian Warren Cohen considers the dismissal of Service and other China Hands "one of the most shameful and destructive episodes in the history of the United States." The absence of China experts like Service in the State Department had far-reaching effects. Former Defense Secretary Robert McNamara, in his memoir of decision-making in the Vietnam War, *In Retrospect*, attributed much of the failure of Washington policymakers to properly read Beijing's objectives or appreciate the particularities of Communist ideology in Asia to the irony that the careers of Service and his colleagues had been cut short when they were needed most.

See also China Hands; *Amerasia*; McCarthyism.

REFERENCES: Joseph Esherick, *Lost Chance in China: The World War II Dispatches of John S. Service* (New York, 1974); E. J. Kahn, *The China Hands: America's Foreign Service Officers and What Befell Them* (New York, 1975).

Matthew Young

Seventh Fleet

The U.S. Navy's Seventh Fleet was established on March 15, 1943 in support of the Southwest Pacific campaigns under General Douglas MacArthur in the war against Japan. In the postwar era, the fleet was stationed in Japan, Guam, and the Philippines. The latter is no longer a fleet base. At the start of the Korean War, President Harry S. Truman ordered the fleet into the Taiwan Strait for dual purposes: first, to prevent the invasion of Taiwan by the military of the Peoples Liberation Army (PLA), and second, to prevent action by the military forces on Taiwan against the mainland. This presidential order reversed American policy on identifying American interests as stretching from Japan to the Philippines.

The PLA was concentrating forces for a planned assault on Taiwan. The Taiwanese were bombing installations on the mainland. The presence of the Seventh Fleet interfered with the actions of both adversaries. Following the armistice in the Korean War, the fleet was engaged in support of U.S. diplomatic policy when the PLA began to shell the offshore islands of Jinmen and Mazu in 1954, in response to the U.S.-China Mutual Defense Treaty (1954). These islands served as symbols of the desire of the government of Taiwan to return to power on the mainland. The U.S. Congress authorized the President to use military force to secure Taiwan and the Penghu islands against armed attack. The United Nations Security Council adopted a cease-fire resolution to end this crisis. In 1955 the PLA also threatened the Dachen islands. These islands were evacuated by the Republic of China's (ROC) forces with American persuasion. The Seventh Fleet played a role in the evacuation. Jinmen and Mazu were attacked again in 1958. The UN did not play a role in this crisis as such a decision would have effectively recognized two Chinas. However, bilateral talks between the American and PRC officials in Warsaw defused this crisis. In 1996 the Peoples Republic of China (PRC) fired missiles at the Taiwan Strait during the elections for President of the Republic of China. The PRC had announced that any move towards independence of the ROC would result in the use of military force. Units of the Seventh Fleet were sent as support for the ROC in this test of wills. The American understanding is that the reunification of China should proceed by peaceful means. Should a reunification by force be attempted, the Seventh Fleet would be part of the American deterrent. In 1999 tensions heightened once again as air patrols by both the PRC and ROC flew in the Taiwan Strait. Both sides increased their military alert status. This crisis was triggered by (then) ROC President Li Denghui's statement on "state to state" relations with the PRC. The PRC has repeatedly stated that any policy, which jeopardizes reunification may be met with force. The American government sent two aircraft carrier groups to the South China Sea as an indicator of American concern for peaceful reunification.

Presently the Seventh Fleet has been tasked with three major assignments: Joint Task Force commander in the event of natural disaster or joint military operation; operational commander for all military forces in the region; and defense of the Korean peninsula. Units of the fleet may be found sailing in the Indian Ocean, the South China Sea, and the Pacific Ocean at any time.

See also Taiwan Strait; Taiwan Relations Act (1979); Neutralization of Taiwan; De-neutralization of the Taiwan Strait; Taiwan.

REFERENCES: John W. Chambers II (ed.), *The Oxford Companion to American Military History* (Oxford, 1999); Immanuel C. Y. Hsu, *The Rise of Modern China* (Oxford, 2000); Gordon H. Chang and He Di, "The Absence of War in the U.S.-China Confrontation over Jinmen and Mazu in 1954–1955: Contingency, Luck, Deterrence?" *The American Historical Review* (December 1993).

Katherine Reist

Shanghai Communique

A monumental diplomatic document signed by U.S. President Richard Nixon and China's Premier Zhou Enlai and announced in Shanghai on February 28, 1972 at the end of Nixon's week-long visit in China. It marked a turning point in Sino-American relations after more than twenty-two years of mutual isolation and hostility as well as a significant break-through in international relations during the Cold War. The document was the culmination of subtle changes in Nixon's foreign policy orientation and China's desire to break out of international isolation, particularly in light of its mounting tension with the Soviet Union.

Following the "ping pong diplomacy" in the spring of 1971, whereby American table-tennis players were invited to visit China and received extremely warm treatment, Nixon lost no time in responding to Beijing's olive branch. As both the U.S. and China were prepared to engage in serious discussions about their mutual relations, Henry Kissinger, Nixon's chief foreign affairs advisor, made a secrete trip to Beijing in July 1971, which laid the foundation for Nixon's visit the following February and outlined the general framework for the communique. Accompanied by an official entourage including Secretary of State William Rogers and Henry Kissinger, Nixon met with the paramount Chinese leader Mao Zedong and had a frank exchange of views on Sino-

American relations and other world affairs. Zhou Enlai, who commanded the respect of both Nixon and Kissinger with his political acumen and diplomatic skills, played a critical role in conducting earnest and fruitful discussions with the American delegation, particularly in dealing with the thorny issue of Taiwan.

The communique, first and foremost, stated the American acknowledgement that "there is but one China and that Taiwan is a part of China," though it also emphasized the U.S. interest in a "peaceful settlement of the Taiwan question by the Chinese themselves." It also announced Washington's intention of gradual reduction and eventual withdrawal of all American forces from Taiwan. In the meanwhile, the U.S. voiced its endorsement of the so-called "Five Principles of Peaceful Co-existence" that had long been advocated by the PRC government, which stressed the ideas of respecting other countries' national sovereignty and territorial integrity, and of non-interference of other states' internal affairs. Despite their profound ideological differences, both sides pledged in the communique that neither would "seek hegemony in the Asia-Pacific region" and, largely with the Soviet Union in mind, both parties made it clear that they would oppose any efforts at building "spheres of interests" in the world. Last but not least, the communique signaled the beginning of trade, cultural and education exchanges between China and the U.S.

The communique paved the way for the official establishment of Sino-American diplomatic relations in early 1979, thus ending a thirty-year mutual hostility during the peak of the Cold War. As tension in the Taiwan Strait has flared up time and again since the signing of this historic document, the issue of mainland relationship with Taiwan remains one of the major focal points of contention between China and the U.S. Consequently, the communique has often been invoked by Beijing to remind Washington of its commitment to the "one China" policy.

See also Nixon's Visit to China; One China Policy; Ping Pong Diplomacy; Cold War; Normalization.

REFERENCES: James H. Mann, *About Face: A History of America's Curious Relationship With China* (New York, 2000); Henry Kissinger, *Diplomacy* (New York, 1995); Michael Shaller, *The United States and China: Into the Twenty-First Century* (New York, 2002).

Yi Sun

Shen Chong Incident (1947)

The Shen Chong incident was a defining moment in the Sino-U.S. relations of the Chinese Civil War era. The event of two American soldiers raping a Chinese college girl on December 24, 1946 ignited widespread outrage and demonstrations in the ensuing weeks, as the seemingly personal crime was quickly transformed into one committed against the nation. To most of the Chinese people, the rape symbolized the violation of Chinese national integrity by the U.S. neocolonialism.

As the major ally to Chinese resistance against Japanese aggression, the United States began to send its military forces to China during World War II. The number reached about 113,000 by the end of 1945, and a year later there were still 12,000 American military personnel stationed in China to facilitate the repatriation of surrendered Japanese troops. In April 1946 a Sino-American draft agreement was reached, specifying that the U.S. military personnel were not subject to Chinese judicial proceedings, as their actions could only be held accountable before American military courts. With the outbreak of the Chinese Civil War in mid 1940s and the U.S. support to the Nationalists' government, an anti-American sentiment was brewing throughout China. As many incidents were reported in newspapers involving death, injury, and damage inflicted by some American soldiers stationed in China, their reckless behavior aroused bitterness among local citizens in Beijing, Shanghai, and other large Chinese cities. One editorial even commented that American offenses were comparable to that of the Japanese occupation forces.

The issue reached a climax on December 24, 1946 when Shen Chong, a first-year student of the Beijing University who came from a prominent family, was reportedly raped by two American Marines in Beijing. As the news of the crime began to spread, the event became a highly symbolic rallying point across the nation. Students from the Beijing University promptly organized protests, demanding that a tribunal with Chinese representation be set up; that U.S. Marine Corps authorities accept full responsibility for the criminal offences committed by their men, guarantee that such offences would not recur, and offer a sincere apology and compensation to Shen Chong; and that the United States immediately withdraw all of its forces from China. The university faculty also issued a joined telegram to American Ambassador John Leighton Stuart protesting the atrocious acts. Within a short period of time, a student strike was organized and a campaign to boycott American goods was launched. The anti-American protests rapidly spread throughout China, as people demonstrated their solidarity with students from Beijing and demanded an immediate U.S. withdrawal. While the Chinese Communist Party proclaimed that the incident represented the rape of the entire nation, the mainstream Chinese media also strongly condemned the barbarous acts, and questioned whether U.S. was China's friend, and whether President Harry S. Truman considered China to be a fully sovereign and equal nation.

As the United States continued to withdraw its military personnel from China, the country's anti-American sentiment was quickly replaced by a much deeper concern of deteriorating civil war in 1947. Nevertheless, the Shen Chong Incident not only stimulated harsh denunciation of American presence in China that led to a major re-evaluation of Sino-American relations, it also provided a focal point that thrusted the Chinese student movement to a new level of political activism.

See also Civil War (1945–1949).

REFERENCES: James A. Cook, "Penetration and Neocolonialism: the Shen Chong Rape Case and the Anti-American Student Movement of 1946–47," *Republic China* (1996); Jon W. Huebner, "Chinese Anti-Americanism," *Australian Journal of Chinese Affairs* (January 1987).

Wenxian Zhang

Shultz, George Pratt (1920-)

A U.S. veteran administrator, businessman, educator, and Republican politician, George Pratt Shultz was born in New York City on December 13, 1920. He earned his BA in Economics from Princeton University in 1942. After his graduation, he served in the Marine Corps Reserve during World War II until 1945. He received his Ph.D. in Industrial Economics from the Massachusetts Institute of Technology (MIT) in 1949. He then taught economics at MIT until 1957 when he joined the University of Chicago as a professor of industrial relations. He served as Dean of Graduate School of Business from 1962 to 1969. Besides being a faculty member, Shultz was appointed as a Senate Staff economist and an adviser to the President's Council on Economics during 1955–1956. Later, he served in a succession of federal posts, including Secretary of Labor from 1969 1970 in the Nixon administration. He was appointed director of the Office of Management and Budget in 1970–1972. From 1972 to 1974, he was Secretary of the Treasury. He left public office to become President of Bechtel Group, Inc. in 1975.

Shultz held the presidency of Bechtel until June 1982 when he was called back to Washington to replace Alexander M. Haig Jr. as Secretary of State in President Ronald Reagan's administra-tion. He continued to serve in that capacity during the second Reagan administration.

In order to win the People's Republic of China over to the U.S. side during the Cold War and also improve Sino-American relations, the Reagan administration addressed some issues (viewed by the Chinese as "obstacles") between the United States and China. Due to rising tensions resulting from the Taiwan Relations Act (1979), after eight months' negotiation with China, Shultz signed the Third Joint Communique on August 17, 1982. The U.S. declared it would limit arms sales to Taiwan to "the level of those supplied in recent years since the establishment of diplomatic relations between the United States and China," and would gradually reduce arms sales to Taiwan as well.

The Communique was sharply criticized both by members of Congress and by the Nationalist Government in Taiwan, which declared the statement to be "in contradiction of the letter and the spirit" of the Taiwan Relations Act. However, the Communique was welcomed by the People's Republic of China, which quoted this communique as one of the three corner stones for the "One China Policy" of Sino-U.S. relations. The 1982 Communique also marked a historic U.S. decision to increase the flow of technology, resources, investment, and trade to China and to assist China's economic development.

Shultz was also instrumental to the signing of the Intermediate Nuclear Forces Treaty eliminating medium and short-range nuclear weapons between the Soviet Union and the United States in 1987.

Less flamboyant than his predecessor Haig, he won respect for his steady professionalism and his preference for conciliation rather than conflict. Though also known for his ability to effect compromises, he was criticized for failing to oppose more strongly the operations that led to the Iran-contra affair during Reagan's presidency.

He is a member of the board of directors of Bechtel Group, Fremont Group, Gilead Sciences, and Charles Schwab & Co. He is Chairman of the International Council of J. P. Morgan Chase and chairman of the Accenture Energy Advisory Board. He was awarded the Medal of Freedom, the nation's highest civilian honor, on January 19, 1989, the Seoul Peace Prize in 1992, the Eisenhower Medal for Leadership and Service in 2001, the Reagan Distinguished American Award in 2002, and the American Foreign Service Association's Lifetime Achievement Award in 2003.

Shultz has written several books which include *Economic Policy Beyond the Headlines*, co-written with Kenneth Dam, and his best-selling memoir, *Turmoil and Triumph: My Years as Secretary of State*. His monograph, *Economics in Action: Ideas, Institutions, Policies*, was published in 1995 as a part of the Hoover Essays in Public Policy series.

See also Taiwan Relations Act (1979); One China Policy.

REFERENCES: Charles Moritz, *George Shultz in Current Biography Yearbook* (New York, 1988); Hoover Institution, "George Shultz: Thomas W. and Susan B. Ford Distinguished Fellow," *www-hoover.standford.edu/bios/shultz.html*; Marquis Who's Who LLC, *Who's Who in America* (Chicago, IL, 1988–1989).

Fu Zhuo

Sino-American Special Technical Cooperative Organization (SACO)

The Sino-American Special Technical Cooperative Organization, commonly known by its acronym SACO, was officially established in April 1943. However, the beginning of SACO should be traced to May 1942 when Commander Milton E. Miles of the United States Navy arrived in Chongqing to seek cooperation with Lieutenant General Dai Li, Director of the Bureau of Investigation and Statistics (BIS or *Juntong*) of the Military Commission of the Chinese Nationalist Government. Presenting himself as Naval Observer, Miles's official duty in China mandated him to help strengthen Navy's war effort in the Pacific through collaboration with the Chinese.

By the end of 1942, the "Friendship Project," the code name for Miles's mission in China, had grown into a full-scale cooperative operation that required an official agreement to formalize its existence and confer it legitimacy. After much deliberation and debate on both sides, the SACO Agreement came into being. The agreement defines the nature of the organization as an anti-Japanese war collaboration between Dai Li's *Juntong* and the U.S. Navy. While the Chinese would provide manpower and facilities, the U.S. would supply instructors and materiel. Secretary of the U.S. Navy, Frank Knox, and Chinese Foreign Minister, Song Ziwen, initialed the treaty. Both Dai Li and Miles also signed the agreement. This document significantly expanded the original plan of a small and relatively simple naval project and transformed it into a large and elaborate joint undertaking. Dai Li assumed the position of Director, with Miles serving as his deputy.

During the next three years until the end of the war, SACO continued to grow. Headquartered in Chongqing, the wartime capital of China, between 1942 and 1945, SACO established twelve training camps, along with numerous coast watch stations and intelligence centers. More than two thousand American officers and enlisted men from all military services came to serve in SACO, and most of them worked as training instructors for Dai's paramilitary and secret police forces. Fifty thousand Chinese troops underwent training, according to the official SACO record.

Not only was its size outstanding among American wartime organizations in China, its scope and nature of operations were also exceptional. Collaboratively, American and Chinese SACO members waged intelligence and clandestine warfare against the Japanese behind enemy lines inside China. They also penetrated into areas beyond China's border, engaging in secret wars against the Japanese and their collaborators in Indochina, Burma and Thailand. At the same time, Dai Li's U.S.-trained and equipped paramilitary troops also involved themselves in clashes against the Chinese Communists. This aspect of SACO wartime operations resulted in bitter memory against the Americans in postwar China, making SACO a symbol of American brutal intervention in China's national struggle against the reactionary forces represented by the Nationalist government.

While its legacy is still open to debate, institutionally speaking, SACO was strictly a wartime organization. As soon as the war ended, the majority of Americans left China immediately. Miles returned to the United States in September 1945, suffering from a severe case of battle fatigue. An official termination agreement went into effect on July 1, 1946, and the last American left China in October. By that time, Dai Li had died in a plane crash earlier that year, in March.

See also Office of Strategic Services (OSS); Intelligence Cooperation in World War II.

REFERENCES: Milton E. Miles, *A Different Kind of War: The Little-Known Story of the Combined Guerrilla Forces Created in China by the U.S. Navy and the Chinese During WW II* (Garden City, NY, 1967); Bureau of Intelligence, Defense Ministry, ROC, *Zhong-Mei hezuo-suo zhi [Official History of SACO]* (Taibei, 1970); Yu Shen, *SACO: An Ambivalent Experience of Sino-American Cooperation During World War II* (Ph.D. Dissertation, University of Illinois at Urbana-Champaign, 1995).

Yu Shen

Sino-Japanese War (1937–1945)

In 1931, the Japanese had occupied Manchuria and created Manchukuo, a puppet state nominally headed by Puyi, the last Manchu emperor. Although there were protests from the international community including the United States announcement of non-recognition of Manchukuo, the Japanese paid little attention to the international response. Japan had long had economic interests in Manchuria, and the Manchurian provinces had been a focal point for the competition between Japan and Russia (and then the Soviet Union) for influence in the region. So the Japanese seizure of the province was not truly surprising. Indeed, there was no military response from the Chinese themselves. The Chinese Guomindang government was preoccupied with subduing the autonomous warlords who, in the absence of a strong central government, had established power bases in most of the provinces of China. The Chinese Communists were re-gathering themselves after the Guomindang had turned against them and they had been forced to undertake the "Long March" to new strongholds in northwest China.

But when the Japanese invaded China "proper" in 1937, the menace of militaristic totalitarianism loomed over Europe and Asia, and the international response was much stronger than it had been to the seizure of Manchuria. The United States imposed a boycott on shipments of steel, rubber, and petroleum to Japan, and Japan found itself increasingly treated as a rogue state. The first phase of the war extended from 1937 to 1941, when the United States joined China and formally entered the war against Japan following the attack on the naval base at Pearl Harbor. During the first phase, the Japanese seized control of the provinces adjacent to Manchuria, those along the coast that included the major port cities, and those along the lower reaches of the major rivers flowing to the coast, including some of the richest agricultural lands in the country. As the Japanese advanced farther into China, there was a conspicuous escalation in the savagery of the fighting. The most notorious episodes were the indiscriminate bombing of Shanghai by the Japanese and their berserker through the Guomindang capital, which came to be known as the "Rape of Nanjing." The first phase of the war closed with the Japanese offensive having exhausted itself against the distances and unlimited manpower of China. The Guomindang forces under Jiang Jieshi could count only one major victory in the first four years of the war, but they had avoided the sort of catastrophic defeat that the Japanese army had hoped to inflict on them.

After the entry of the United States into the war, the Japanese first sought to consolidate their conquests in China, rather than to expand them dramatically. As the United States began to ship lend-lease supplies to the Guomindang through Burma, the Japanese forces in southeast China sought to broaden their control of the provinces at the Chinese end of the Burma Road, while those in Burma sought to force the Americans and British back into India. At the same time, the Japanese sought to clear the large number of pockets of Chinese resistance from their rear areas. Since many of the bases of the Chinese Communists were located behind Japanese lines, the Communists bore the brunt of this portion of the Japanese effort. The final phase of the Sino-Japanese War was defined by the last Japanese offensive campaign of the war. Initiated in April 1944, the Ichigo offensive lasted until the end of that year and set up localized offensives that continued through April 1945. Involving more than 800,000 of the two million Japanese troops in China, the Ichigo offensive had two main aims. First, the Japanese wished to overrun air bases at the eastern edge of the Guomindang territory, from which American B-29s could reach Japanese cities. Second, they wanted to seize control the corridors through which two railways ran, linking Indochina to Korea and providing an overland supply route through eastern China as the American campaign intensified against Japanese shipping in the western Pacific.

At great human cost, the Chinese did manage to tie up a large percentage of the Japanese army for the duration of the war, but at the conclusion of hostilities, the Japanese still controlled most of eastern China, including the largest population centers. The Japanese experience in China was broadly analogous to the Nazi experience in the Soviet Union, but even though the Japanese found the country too massive to subdue, the Chinese were never able to liberate their nation in the way that the Soviet armies eventually pushed the Nazis back to Berlin.

See also World War II.

REFERENCES: His-sheng Chi, *Nationalist China at War: Military Defeats and Political Collapse, 1937–1945* (Ann Arbor, MI, 1982); Lloyd Eastman, *Seeds of Destruction: Nationalist China in War and Revolution, 1937–1949* (Stanford, CA, 1984); Marius Jansen, *Japan and China: From War to Peace, 1894–1972* (New York, 1975); Lincoln Li, *The Japanese Army in North China, 1937–1941: Problems of Political and Economic Control* (New York, 1975); James W. Morley (ed.), *The China Quagmire: Japan's Expansion on the Asian Continent, 1933–1941* (New York, 1983); Michael Schaller, *The U.S. Crusade in China, 1938–1945* (New York, 1979); Kuikwong Shum, *The Chinese Communists' Road to Power: The Anti-Japanese United Front, 1935–1945* (New York, 1988).

Martin Kich

Sino-Soviet Pact (1950)

Sino-Soviet Pact or Sino-Soviet Treaty of Friendship and Alliance created a bilateral defense commitment, settled historic territorial issues between China and the Soviet Union, and initiated a modest program of Soviet aid to the People's Republic of China (PRC). The treaty was to remain in force for 30 years. The major goal of the pact was to establish a Sino-Soviet alliance to counterbalance the Japanese-American anti-Communist bloc in East Asia. In Article one, it stipulated that the treaty was to prevent the rebirth of aggression and imperialism on the part of Japan "or any other state which would unite with Japan directly or any other form in acts of aggression."

On December 16, 1949, Chinese Communist leader Mao Zedong made his first trip abroad to Moscow. He stayed in Russia for more than two months, during which he negotiated with Soviet leader Joseph Stalin on the terms of a Sino-Soviet treaty of friendship. In ideology, Mao had already joined the Soviet-led Communist bloc. But Stalin was suspicious of Mao, fearing that Mao would not submit to his dictation. Stalin's view was not changed until China sent troops to fight in the Korean War in October 1950. The major objective of the treaty was to establish a Sino-Soviet alliance to conterbalance the Japanese-American anti-Communist bloc in East Asia. Article 1 stipulated that the treaty was to prevent the rebirth of aggression and imperialism on the part of Japan "or any other state which would united with Japan directly or any other form in acts of aggression." Despite of Mao's weak negotiating position, some of the terms followed China's requests. Article 5 provided that Sino-Soviet economic and cultural cooperation should be developed in conformity with the "principles of equality, mutual interests, and also mutual respect for state sovereignty and territorial integrity and noninterference in the internal affairs of the other party." These were what Beijing later called the Five Principles of Peaceful Coexistence.

The Sino-Soviet treaty was short-lived. The first ideological conflict came in 1956 when the new Russian Communist leader Nikita Khruschev issued the "secret report" to the Communist Party of the Soviet Union Congress, denouncing Stalin as a dictator. Other conflicts between the two Communist giants emerged on issues of foreign policy. In the early 1960s, Moscwo withdrew its experts in China, unilaterally ended bilateral contracts, and cancelled projects of scientific and technological cooperation. The Chinese openly criticized the Russians of being anti-Marxist-Leninist revisionists. The denouement of the treaty came when armed conflicts between the two countries broke out in the boarder areas along the Ussuri River in 1969. On April 3, 1979, the PRC government declared that the treaty would expire without renewal.

See also Sino-Soviet Rift; Strategic Triangle of U.S.-Soviet-China Relations.

REFERENCES: Howard L. Boorman et al., *Moscow-Peking Axis: Strength and Strains* (New York, 1957); O. Edmund Clubb, *China and Russia: The "Great Game"* (New York, 1971).

Yuwu Song

Sino-Soviet Rift

After the founding of the People's Republic of China (PRC) in October 1949, Communist China embarked on the policy of forging a closer alliance with the Soviet Union in its quest for national security, economic development and an ambition to emerge as industrial and military power. In pursuit of this, Chairman Mao Zedong visited Moscow in November 1949, and signed the Sino-Soviet Treaty of Friendship and Alliance with the Soviet Union on February 14, 1950. During this visit, he not only advocated the imperative of leaning towards the Soviet Union but also induced his countrymen to follow the Soviet model of development.

Sino-Soviet relations started off on a positive note. Their common ideological outlook, shared geopolitical interests and mutual strategic necessity impelled them to build a strong partnership in order to counterbalance the U.S. power and influence infused through its network of military alliances like North Atlantic Treaty Organization (NATO, 1949), South East Asia Treaty Organization (SEATO, 1954) and Central Treaty Organization (CENTO, 1955). Initially, the Soviet Union played a constructive role in building China's military sinews and its economic development through massive military and economic assistance. However, Sino-Soviet bonhomie proved short-lived. After the death of the Soviet leader Joseph Stalin in 1953, the Sino-Soviet rift started surfacing due to a host of intermeshing factors such as the clash of personality between Mao and the new Russian leader Nikita Khrushchev, Moscow's reconciliatory overtures to the West, its de-Stalinization and their divergent perceptions and approaches to security, economic and developmental issues. For instance, China was growing disenchanted with inadequacy of Soviet cooperation on China's avowed goal of reunifying Taiwan, on Moscow's neutral stance during the 1962 Sino-Indian War and also backing out of its commitment to provide nuclear weapons technology to China. With regard to economic cooperation, Moscow withdrew its economic advisers from China in 1960 in reaction to China's launching of the Great Leap Forward (1958–1960).

The personality factor was also hanging heavily in the psyche of Mao who not only felt offended by disrespect shown to him by the Soviet leaders Khrushchev and Georgy Malenkov but also got disillusioned with their revisionist policy deviating from the core Marxist-Leninist ideology, eventually resulting in China's snapping of ties with the Communist Party of the Soviet Union in 1966. The Mao-led Great Proletarian Cultural Revolution (1966–1976) was highly critical of the Soviet style of "bureaucratic Communism" that contributed to further deterioration in the hitherto strained relations between China and the Soviet Union, fuelled by Chinese Red Guard's harassment of Soviet diplomats in Beijing. Not only this, Sino-Soviet ideological differences were sharpened on the territorial issues, which culminated in "bloody armed clashes" on their border in 1969 over the Damansky (Zhen Bao) Island in the Ussuri River. In brief, the factors that hindered the normalization of Sino-Soviet relations included the Soviet military build up in East Asia and Mongolia, its moral and material support to Vietnam's aggression against Cambodia, its invasion of Czechoslovakia — its ideological ally — in 1968 and of Afghanistan in 1979. These developments convinced China that the Soviet Union was transforming itself into a "socialist imperialist" power.

As a matter of fact, the Sino-Soviet rift created a fertile ground for Sino-U.S. rapprochement. President Richard Nixon went to China in February 1972. He and his National Security Advisor Henry Kissinger held intensive discussion on international and regional issues with Chairman Mao and Premier Zhou Enlai. They tried to convince the Beijing leadership that real threat to Beijing emanated from the Soviet Union rather than the United States. The net accomplishment of President Nixon's China visit was the signing of the joint Shanghai Communique on February 28, 1972, which committed the United States to "one China policy." Finally, China and the U.S. established full diplomatic relations in January 1979. This was a turning point in exacerbating the Sino-Soviet rift.

See also Nixon's Visit to China; One China Policy; Sino-Soviet Pact (1950); Strategic Triangle of U.S.-Soviet-China Relations.

REFERENCES: Henry Kissinger, *Observations: Selected Speeches and Essays, 1982–1984* (London, 1985); Richard Wich, *Sino-Soviet Crisis Politics: A Study of Political Change and Communication* (Cambridge, MA, 1980); Thomas W. Robinson, *The Sino-Soviet Border Dispute: Background, Development, and the March 1969 Clashes* (Santa Monica, CA, 1970).

Romi Jain

Smedley, Agnes (1892–1950)

Agnes Smedley was a journalist, writer and actitivist who emerged from a poverty-stricken and grim childhood in rural Missouri and the coal towns of Colorado to become a campaigner for workers' rights, birth control, women's rights and the Communist Revolution in China. She was imprisoned in the early 1920s for her work against British colonialism in India and for her work with Margaret Sanger establishing birth control clinics and disseminating birth control information.

Pulled from school to support her family by working as a maid at age 12, she followed her mother's advice and struggled for an education, also rejecting the fate of marriage and hopeless battles to provide for unwanted children. Motivated by her mother's early death, she helped to establish birth control information centers in the U.S. and Germany, and later tried unsuccessfully to get them set up in major cities in China. Her articles about Chinese women were interspersed with those about the Chinese Revolutionaries. Smedley also suffered from the sexism of men and women in revolutionary movements in India and China while she was raising money, calling the world's attention to the mistreatment of peasant and working populations, and struggling valiantly for social reform both inside the U.S. and in the rest of the world. She was simultaneously, like her contemporary and mentor, Emma Goldman, vilified for imagined promiscuity in the Western media and by colleagues and wives of her compatriots of India and China. Thus, while she worked closely in the 1920s in California with her "common law" husband Virendranath Chattopadhyaya to secure freedom from British rule for India in the 1920s, his colleagues saw her as "perverting" Chatto's vision. While she was one of a very few Western journalists to travel to Communist-controlled Yanan, China in mid 1930s, and was able to meet and interview both common soldiers and Communist leaders like Mao Zedong and Zhu De, revolutionary Chinese women arranged for her to be banished from Yanan.

Smedley wrote, in increasingly difficult circumstances, five books from 1941 to her death in 1950. With intimate knowledge gained on these travels, she documented the progress of the Chinese Communist endeavors in *The Red Army Marches, Chinese Destinies, China Fights Back*, and *The Battle Hymn of China*, and produced her most mature work, *The Great Road: The Life and Times of Chu Teh* (published posthumously). Possibly because of the hardships of her early life, exacerbated by the constant harassment by American and British officials, she often dealt with ill-health, including a stomach ulcer which eventually caused her death on May 6, 1950 after an operation in an Oxford hospital. During her life, she worked with some of the most famous writers in China such as Lu Xun, Ding Ling, Mao Dun as well as some of the most prominent China experts such as Edgar Snow and Anna Louise Strong, documenting China from the turn of the century through the beginning of the People's Republic of China.

Because of unproven accusations that she was a Soviet spy, rather than receiving the deserved recognition for her contributions to Western understanding of China in the 1940s and 1950s, she spent the last few years of her life seeing her works suppressed and her reputation impugned. These accusations were never proved, but, Ruth Price, in her 2005 biography, claims to have found evidence in both German and Chinese records, that support them. Efforts made possible by the second-wave women's movement, including the Feminist Press, and individuals like Zhou Enlai who praised her in a 1960s speech, have ensured the recovery of her reputation as a down-to-earth, clear eyed activist whose own working-class origin gave her a unique voice in articulating the struggles of Chinese women, but also the common workers, peasants, soldiers along with their political and military leaders found in the rest of the press. Her ashes are buried near Beijing and she has regained prominence in the history of 20th century Chinese American relations.

See also Snow, Edgar (1905–1972); Strong, Anna Louise (1885–1970).

REFERENCE: Janice MacKinnon and Stephen R. MacKinnon, *The Life and Times of An American Radical* (Berkeley, CA, 1988); Ruth Price, *The Lives of Agnes Smedley* (Oxford, UK, 2005); Agnes Smedley, *Daughter of Earth* (New York, 1973); Agnes Smedley, *Portraits of Chinese Women in Revolution* (New York, 1976); Agnes Smedley, *Battle Hymn of China* (New York, 1943); Agnes Smedley, *China Fights Back: An American Women with the Eighth Route Army* (New York, 1938); Agnes Smedley, *China's Red Army Marches* (New York, 1934); Agnes Smedley, *Chinese Destinies, Sketches of Present Day China* (New York, 1933); Agnes Smedley, *Daughter of Earth* (New York, 1973); Agnes Smedley, *The Great Road: The Life and Times of Chu Teh* (New York, 1956).

Janice M. Bogstad

Smith, Howard Alexander (1880–1966)

Howard Alexander Smith was born in New York City on January 30, 1880. He graduated from Princeton University in 1901 and from the Law Department of Columbia University in 1904. His political philosophy of internationalism was shaped by the influence of his professor Woodrow Wilson at Princeton.

From 1944 to 1959, Smith served as U.S. senator. As a Republican member on the Far Eastern Subcommittee of the Senate Committee on Foreign Relations, he helped formulate the contain-

ment policy against Communist expansion in East Asia. In 1949, Smith took a trip to East Asia. This trip convinced him that the United States was losing ground to Communists in that area because of Washington's erroneous foreign policies. In the late 1940s, as Chinese Communist forces swept through China during the civil war, Smith and other Guomindang (GMD) supporters raised a public outcry for the continuation of assistance to Nationalist leader Jiang Jieshi even as the Nationalist forces suffered incredible setbacks. This group included powerful people such as General Claire L. Chennault, publisher Henry Luce of Time-Life, Senators William Knowland (R-California), Kenneth Wherry (R-Nebraska), and Pat McCarran (D-Nevada), columnists Joseph and Stuart Alsop, and China expert George Taylor. They vehemently opposed the State Department's efforts to disengage the U.S. from Jiang's government. They urged the American government to provide more assistance to Jiang in the war against Mao's Communist forces. They even charged that the 1949 victory of the Chinese Communists over the Nationalists was aided by left-wing sympathizers and traitors in the State Department. Together they exerted great pressure on the White House to change its China policies. As a result of this pressure and other events such as the break-out of the Korean War, foreign policy makers in Washington abandoned their attempts of making accommodation with Communist China and turned to support Taiwan.

Throughout the 1950s, Smith called for strong measures to restore Jiang's Nationalist government to power on mainland China. He joined forces in opposing to seating Beijing in the United Nations. His unflinching support for GMD won him the nickname "Foremost Formosan."

See also Civil War (1945–1949).

REFERENCES: Ross Y. Koen, *The China Lobby in American Politics* (New York, 1974); Chen Jian, *China's Road to the Korean War: The Making of the Sino-American Confrontation* (New York, 1994).

Yuwu Song

Snow, Edgar (1905–1972)

Snow was born in Kansas City, Missouri, on July 19, 1905. He worked as a farm hand before his adventurer spirit caused him to travel to the West Coast taking odd jobs along the way. In the 1920s he studied briefly at a junior college in Kansas City and at the schools of journalism at the University of Missouri and Columbia University in New York where he took a job in advertising. He later became a correspondent for the Kansas City *Star*. Again the adventurer spirit took hold of him, and Snow decided to travel around the world.

In 1928 he arrived in Shanghai taking a "temporary" job as an assistant editor and reporter at *China Weekly Review*. He remained in China for the next thirteen years. In 1929 he traveled the entire Chinese rail network and visited Korea writing about his experiences in several guidebooks. In 1930 he became a correspondent for the Consolidated Press Association reporting from China, Southeast Asia, and India. In 1932, he married Helen Foster, an official at the American consulate in Shanghai. She also wrote about East Asia under the pseudonym Nym Wales; the couple divorced in 1949. He settled in Beijing where he continued to work as a journalist and teach occasional courses at Beijing University. In 1933 Snow published his first book, *Far Eastern Front*, about Japanese aggression in China. In 1936 Snow made it through the Nationalist blockade to the Chinese Communists in Shaanxi province. He became the first Western journalist to interview Mao Zedong, Zhou Enlai and other Communist leaders in their stronghold at Yanan. His finding resulted in his best known book *Red Star Over China* (1937) where he wrote about the Chinese Communist movement and its leaders noting that they were not crazed radicals, but dedicated revolutionary reformers who also wanted to stop Japanese aggression. Starting in 1937, Snow covered the Japanese invasion of China, and in the same year, he and his wife translated a collection of short stories by leading contemporary Chinese authors including Lu Xun in *Living China*. In 1941 he returned to the United States as an associate editor of the *Saturday Evening Post*, also becoming its foreign correspondent in the Soviet Union. After the war, he reported on Indian independence. During the McCarthy Era, Snow was charged as a Communist sympathizer particularly due to his earlier writings from China. Although never formally charged, the *Saturday Evening Post* wanted him to "tone down" his writing. He refused and left the journal in 1951. Being increasingly unable to find work in the United States, he moved to Switzerland where he continued to write. In all, he wrote over fourteen books and countless articles.

In 1960 *Look* magazine hired Snow to become the first American reporter to visit Communist China resulting in several articles and the book *The Other Side of the River: Red China Today* that was poorly received in the United States. He returned to China in 1964 and again in 1970, when he stood beside his friend Mao Zedong and other Chinese leaders on top of the gate of Tiananmen Square during the October 1 celebra-

tion of the founding of the People's Republic. Mao and Premier Zhou Enlai gave him a message to give to the United States government requesting talks between the two nations. Shortly before President Richard M. Nixon made his historic trip to China, Snow died in Eysins, Switzerland, on February 15, 1972, in the care of Chinese doctors sent from the People's Republic. Some of his ashes were later scattered on the campus of Beijing University.

See also Mao Zedong (1893–1976); McCarthyism; Smedley, Agnes (1892–1950); Strong, Anna Louise (1885–1970).

REFERENCES: John Maxwell Hamilton, *Edgar Snow: A Biography* (Bloomington, IN, 1988); Helen Foster Snow, *My China Years: A Memoir* (New York, 1984); Edgar Snow, *Journey to the Beginning* (New York, 1958).

Greg Ference

Song Meiling (1898–2003)

Song Meiling, known in the West as Madame Jiang Jieshi (Mme. Chiang Kai-shek), was born on December 2, 1898 in Guangdong, China. Song moved to the United States to attend boarding school at the age of eight. She started college at Wesleyan College in Macon, Georgia, but transferred to Wellesley College and graduated with honors in 1917 with a major in English literature and minor in philosophy. From her childhood in a rich Christian home and education at prestigious American colleges, Song acquired some of her fundamental social and political principles: the duty of the masses to follow the elite, the necessity and desirability of peaceful reforms as opposed to violent or sudden revolutionary changes, and the relevance of the American political and technological model to China's future development. An ambitious woman, she tried to bring Western influence to China after she returned home from the United States. From 1917 to 1927, she worked in Shanghai as a reformer in women's groups, and she relearned her native language and cultural background through a study of the Chinese classics. Although Song did not achieve spectacular successes in reform and politics, she was involved in these activities to a greater extent than most other upper-class Chinese women, partly as a result of her liberal Western education and family tradition. This period probably marks the beginning of Song's interest in politics and her desire to become actively involved, both of which figured strongly in her marriage to Jiang Jieshi, the Nationalist leader, in 1927. Her marriage to Jiang, who at the time had temporarily retired from politics, surely stands as the decisive event of her life. The Chinese militarist-turned-unifier, his beliefs, and his political associates would channel and occasionally obstruct her Western reformist instincts in the years to come.

To many, the marriage was a political match. Song, widely believed to be a power-hungry person, must have viewed the marriage as the first step on her own road to power. On his part, the marriage shows Jiang's dependence on and desire for support from the powerful Song family and their American connections. In 1934 Madame Jiang helped initiate China's New Life Movement, with the goal of the "physical, educational and moral rebirth of the Chinese nation," based on traditional Chinese values. In December 1936 Jiang Jieshi was detained in Xian by one of his subordinates, General Zhang Xueliang. Madame Jiang flew to Sian and successfully negotiated the Generalissimo's release on Christmas Day.

Before the Japanese attack on Pearl Harbor in 1941, Madame Jiang made her appeals and statements asking the international community to support China against the Japanese invasion through the American and British press. After 1941, she focused her publicity almost exclusively on America, the ally with the most interest in China's development as a power in the war and after the war. To some extent, she became the voice and eventually the symbol of Nationalist China to the West. Her efforts as unofficial ambassador expanded during the war culminating in the well-publicized 1943 trip to the United States and Canada. Madame Jiang stayed as a guest of the White House; addressed Congress; appeared on the cover of the *Time* magazine. Her U.S. trip was a great personal triumph and added immensely to her country's good image in America, but its effect on her power at home was negligible and possibly even detrimental. She could hardly have changed the Allies' Europe-first strategy and gained substantial increases in aid, yet her strength in China seemed based on scoring such successes. At the home front, Madame Jiang as the First Lady of China presided over an awesome number of projects. However, only in her efforts to increase women's war work and war relief activities, traditionally the sphere of women and politicians' wives, could she build a movement and use her power without incurring the wrath and jealousy of powerful conservatives in the government.

During the Chinese Civil War of the late 1940s, Madame Jiang tried to help her husband salvage the Nationalists' sinking ship. In 1948, on the eve of the collapse of the Nanjing regime, she flew to Washington against the best judgment of Jiang to meet President Harry S. Truman and ask for American aids. Her trip turned out to be a fiasco. After Jiang and his Nationalist government retreated to Taiwan, Madame Jiang continued her efforts to inform the American public about the dangers of world Communism by publishing books, delivering speeches, and appearing on TV interviews in the United States. She became the honorary chair of the American Bureau for Medical Aid to China, a Patron of the International Red Cross Committee, and First Honorary Member of the Bill of Rights Commemorative Society. Through the late 1960's she was included among America's 10 most admired women. After her husband's death in 1975, Madame Jiang moved to the U.S., residing in Lattington, New York. She died on October 23, 2003, at the age of 105 in New York City.

See also Jiang Jieshi (1887–1975).

REFERENCES: Emily Hahn, *The Soong Sisters* (New York, 1970); Sterling Seagrave, *The Soong Dynasty* (New York, 1985); Roby Eunson, *The Soong Sisters* (New York, 1975).

Yuwu Song

Song Qingling (1893–1981)

Song Qingling was born on January 27, 1893, in Shanghai. Her siblings included the financier and Nationalist official Song Ziwen; Song Ailing; wife of Kong Xiangxi, a financier and Nationalist official, and Song Meiling, Madame Jiang Jieshi. Her father, Charles Jones Song, a wealthy businessman and missionary, was educated by Methodist missionaries in China and spent eight years in the United States. Due to his American connections, his children grew up in a Westernized household and educated in the United States.

In 1908, Qingling and Meiling traveled to the United States. Qingling stayed for five years learning fluent English, and attended Wesleyan College in Macon, Georgia, graduating in 1913. Returning to China, she moved to Japan to become Sun Zhongshan's English language secretary after her sister Ailing left to marry Kong Xiangxi. Sun and the Song family had fled to Japan after a failed revolution attempt in China. In 1915, against the wishes of her family, she married Sun who was twenty-six years older than her, and who already had a wife and children. Qingling became Sun's confidant and assistant until he died in 1925. She supported his reorganization of his political party, the Guomindang (GMD) that cooperated with the Soviet Union and allowed Chinese Communists to join. On his deathbed in Beijing, she helped Sun write a letter in English to the Soviet Union that is considered one of his last testaments. After her husband's death, she supported the left wing of the GMD, and when it split into pro and anti-Communist factions in 1927, she denounced the party for forgetting her husband's ideals. When her brother Song Ziwen joined the anti-Communist faction of the GMD led by Generalissimo Jiang Jieshi whom her sister Meiling decided to marry, she left China in disgust for the Soviet Union. In 1929 she briefly returned to China for the state funeral of her late husband in a newly constructed mausoleum in Nanjing. Madame Sun returned again to China in 1931 and moved to Shanghai where she supported Chinese leftists. She spoke out against Japanese aggression in China urging a united front of Communists and Nationalists against it, while criticizing her brother-in-law Jiang Jieshi's Nationalist government for whom all her brothers and sisters worked. When the Sino-Japanese War began in 1937, she moved to Hong Kong where she established the China Defense League to collect aid for both the Nationalists and the Communists. In 1940 she joined the rest of her family in the Nationalist wartime capital of Chongqing to present a united front against the Japanese, and worked with her family in the war effort.

After the war she returned to Shanghai and during the Chinese Civil War 1945–1949, she again attacked the GMD and supported the Communists. Following the Communist victory in 1949, she became a vice-chair of the central government giving the regime the prestige of her late husband's legacy. She also held various other official and ceremonial positions. During the chaotic Cultural Revolution, she was denounced by the Red Guards but protected by Premier Zhou Enlai. Shortly before her death on May 29, 1981, the government made her honorary President of the People's Republic and a full member of the Chinese Communist Party.

See also Sun Zhongshan (1866–1925).

REFERENCES: Jung Chang with Jon Halliday, *Mme Sun Yat-sen* (New York, 1986); Sterling Seagrave, *The Soong Dynasty* (New York, 1985).

Greg Ference

Song Ziwen (1894–1971)

Song Ziwen, best known as T.V. Soong in the West, was born in Shanghai on December 4, 1894. His siblings included Song Ailing, wife of Kong Xiangxi, a financier and Nationalist official; Song Qingling, Madame Sun Zhongshan; and Song Meiling, Madame Jiang Jieshi. Methodist missionaries in China educated his father, Charles Jones Song, who then spent eight years in the United States and became a wealthy businessman and missionary upon his return to China. Due to their father's American connections, the Soong children grew up in Westernized surroundings and educated in the United States.

Song Ziwen became fluent in English and at-tended Vanderbilt University before transferring to Harvard University where he graduated with a degree in economics in 1915. He worked as a clerk in international banking in New York City and attended classes at Columbia. He returned to Shanghai in 1917 taking jobs in banking and business. By 1925, he had become important for financing the Guomindong (GMD), the political party of his brother-in-law Sun Zhongshan. He soon became a major political figure in GMD Nationalist government of Generalissimo Jiang Jieshi, another brother-in-law. He served as minister of finance and helped establish the Central Bank of China and the National Economic Council to modernize the country. He restructured the tax system, renegotiated China's debts, ended internal customs taxes, and reformed the currency. In 1928, he secured an agreement from the American ambassador to restore national tariff autonomy to China. His ties to the Shanghai banking and business communities helped finance Jiang's government in the 1930s.

In 1933, Jiang replaced Song as finance minister with their common brother-in-law Kong Xiangxi when the two disagreed over policy regarding Japanese aggression. Like his sister Madame Sun, he advocated fighting the Japanese, while Jiang preferred to attack and destroy the Chinese Communists before taking on the Japanese. Song continued to be active in business and finance, being appointed to head China's largest bank in 1935. When the warlord Zhang Xueliang seized Jiang Jieshi in Xian in December 1936, Song and his sister Meiling negotiated his release with the promises to end the fighting between the Nationalists and Communists and form a united front to fight the Japanese. After the start of the Sino-Japanese War in 1937, Song became more important to Jiang due to his command of English and knowledge of the United States. He was sent to America in 1940 to arrange a large loan before the presidential election of that year in case pro-China Franklin D. Roosevelt suffered defeat. He remained there for the next two years arranging for further American financial and military aid to China especially after the United States entered the war following Pearl Harbor. Before his return to China in late 1942, Jiang appointed him foreign minister. Later, when he returned to China, he became the equivalent of prime minister. In 1943, he negotiated with the United States and Britain the end of extraterritoriality (the rights of foreigners to govern themselves while in China) that had plagued China's sovereignty since the mid-1800s. In 1945, Song led the Chinese delegation at the founding of the United Nations in San Francisco being elected as chairman of the major committees. In August he traveled to Moscow to negotiate the Sino-Soviet Treaty of Friendship and Alliance. During the early stages of the Chinese Civil War of 1945–1949, he was involved with the Marshall Mission that attempted unsuccessfully to end the conflict between the GMD and the Communists in 1946. Due to this failure and other problems of the Nationalist regime, for which Song often became a scapegoat, he resigned from the central government taking the position of governor of Guangdong Province.

When China fell to the Communists in 1949, Song did not join the Nationalist regime on Taiwan, but rather moved to the New York City where he continued his banking and business career, living quietly. He died in San Francisco on April 24, 1971.

REFERENCES: Sterling Seagrave, *The Soong Dynasty* (New York, 1985); Parks M. Coble, *The Shanghai Capitalists and the Nationalist Government, 1927–1937* (Cambridge, MA, 1980).

Greg Ference

Soong, T.V. (1894–1971) *see* Song Ziwen (1894–1971)

Soong, Mayling (1898–2003) *see* Song Meiling (1898–2003)

Soong, Qingling (1893–1981) *see* Song Qingling (1893–1981)

South Korea *see* Republic of Korea (ROK)

South Manchurian Railway

Railways played pivotal roles in the formation and sustaining of imperialist enclaves in China, enabling diplomats to press for and monitor concessions and commercial entrepreneurs to access the resources, markets, and labor pools of hinterlands. As such, in addition to serving as arteries of transport and trade, railways facilitated encroachment upon Chinese sovereignty.

Perhaps the most developed rail network in China at liberation was that of the South Manchurian Railway (SMR). Not only was more than 40% of all of China's rail lines in 1949 located in Manchuria, but the SMR also left a legacy of economic and urban development that dwarfed the colonial projects of other powers. Indeed, Mantetsu, as the railway is popularly known in Japanese, was Japan's largest pre-war enterprise. Created in 1906, the SMR began with a wealth of

assets. The line itself had been recently built by Tsarist Russia, connecting the port of Dalian (Japanese: Dairen, Russian: Dal'ny) with the China Eastern Railway. Along with the line came coalmines and rights for the construction of railway towns as well for the stationing of troops that Russia had gained from the Qing court. The SMR, however, also faced substantial difficulties. The Japanese victory in the Russo-Japanese War (1904–1905) only gained control of the railway as far north as Japanese forces had established a presence, at Changchun. This left the Russians with a line running across northern Manchuria to Vladivostok, insuring continued Russian competition. Moreover, the Russian lines were of a different gauge than Japanese, and hostilities had left the SMR without much rolling stock and many of its bridges destroyed. Sensing an opportunity, Edward H. Harriman attempted to gain partial control of the SMR in 1905 (the "Harriman Affair"), but Japanese officials determined to make the line work by themselves. The Japanese government subsequently guaranteed investors' returns for five years in order to insure that the new company was fully capitalized.

The SMR proved successful. This was partly due to its administration, including many of Japan's promising young bureaucrats, who attempted to entice Chinese support through relatively enlightened policies. This meant not only running an efficient railway, but also promoting colonial development. The SMR eventually operated agricultural research facilities, hospitals, laboratories, factories, schools, universities, and a string of cities planned and maintained by their own personnel. The SMR also benefited from the global popularity of a local product — soybeans. Although first introduced to world markets via a river and portage network in the late 19th century, the soy trade mushroomed as the SMR aided production through providing scientific expertise and transportation infrastructure. Soybeans and their derivatives would account for the bulk of Manchuria's trade, and Manchurian soybeans accounted for a large percentage of the prewar global trade in the product. Soybeans enabled the SMR to expand its capabilities, including a substantial research effort that explored technical, economic, political, and social issues in Manchuria and the rest of northeast Asia. The SMR published extensive accounts of their projects in English, the most well known being their *Reports on Progress.*

As the SMR lay at the heart of the Japanese informal empire in Manchuria, Japanese paid close attention to efforts that might challenge the railway. Although some Chinese rail lines eventually succeeded in diverting some traffic from the SMR, these efforts proved abortive when, after September 18, 1931, elements of the Japanese army based in Manchuria, the Kantogun (also called the Kwantung Army) seized Manchuria, creating the "puppet state" of Manchukuo the following year.

See also Manchuria; Puyi (1906–1967); Manchukuo; Harriman Affair.

REFERENCES: Clarence B. Davis, "Railway Imperialism in China, 1895–1939," in Clarence B. Davis and Kenneth E. Wilburn, Jr. (eds.), *Railway Imperialism* (New York, 1991); Yoshihisa Tak Mazusaka, *The Making of Japanese Manchuria, 1904–1932* (Cambridge, MA, 2001); Ramon H. Myers, "Japanese Imperialism in Manchuria: The South Manchurian Railway Company, 1906–33," in Peter Duus, Ramon H. Myers, and Mark Peattie (eds.), *The Japanese Informal Empire in China, 1895–1937* (Princeton, NJ, 1989); Bill Sewell, "Reconsidering the Modern in Japanese History: Modernity in the Service of the Prewar Japanese Empire," *Japan Review Vol. 16* (2004); John Young, *The Research Activities of the South Manchurian Railway Company, 1907–1945: A History and Bibliography* (New York, 1966).

Bill Sewell

Spy Plane Incident (2001)

In April 2001, a routine reconnaissance flight quickly became an international incident. American Navy EP-3E spy planes had been flying eavesdropping missions in what the United States claims is international airspace off of China's coast. The People's Republic of China, however, claims the airspace extending 200 miles out from its shores—a claim that the U.S. does not recognize. During these flights, it was not uncommon for Chinese fighter aircraft to intercept and escort the American planes. Chinese pilots flying F-8 jets had on several occasions gotten very close to the American aircraft playing a deadly game of cat and mouse.

On April 1, two F-8s were scrambled from Lingshui air base on Hainan Island and intercepted an EP-3E piloted by Navy Lieutenant Shane Osborn. One of the Chinese pilots, Wang Wei, brought his plane too close and collided with the American aircraft. The tail of his jet struck the left outboard propeller of the EP-3E. Wang's plane broke in half and, in the process, sliced the nose off of the American plane and disabled its right inner engine. As Osborn fought to regain control of his aircraft, his crew prepared for a crash. Once he had the aircraft stabilized, the pilot chose to head to the closest landing field — the Chinese base on Hainan. His crew scrambled to destroy sensitive equipment and code information as the plane approached the runway. Twenty minutes after the collision, the plane rested on Chinese soil surrounded by Chinese troops. Fifteen minutes after landing, the American crew of 24 surrendered. Over a period of eleven days, the Americans remained captive on the island while the Chinese combed the aircraft for intelligence information. Tensions heightened as each nation insisted that the other was responsible for the incident. Hardliners on both sides created difficulties for diplomats who worked to resolve the stand off. U.S. officials insisted that the American plane was in international airspace and that Wang, who was killed in the collision, caused the crash. Chinese officials claimed that the aircraft was in Chinese territory at the time and blamed the collision on Osborn. The two nations negotiated a settlement that would allow the American crew to return to the United States. In a carefully worded statement, the U.S. government said that it was "very sorry" for the incident, but did not recognize China's claims that its airspace extended 200 miles beyond its coastline. The Chinese government released that crew, but retained control of the aircraft pending further negotiations. By early July, the plane was disassembled and shipped to the United States in a rented Russian AN-124 cargo.

It is difficult to assess the impact of this particular incident on overall Sino-American relations. Among the Chinese populace, it spurred an increase in nationalism and resentment of American operations along China's borders. For Americans, the incident was a foreign policy test for a new President and his administration. Hardliners on both sides did not get the concessions they sought from the settlement. While it is clearly in the best interests of both nations to be engaged in trade and other activities, incidents like this illustrate just how much tension still exists between the two governments.

REFERENCES: Xinhua News Agency, "China, U.S. Agree in Principle on EP-3's Return" (May 29, 2001); "Chinese Pilot Slammed His Plane into Navy Aircraft," *Congress Daily* (April 5, 2001); Jay Branegan, et. al., "Safe Landing: A Carefully Engineered Game Plan Helped Bush Bring the U.S. Flight Crew Home: An Inside Look," *Time* (April 23, 2001); Mark Thompson, "An 8,000-Ft. Plunge and a Tough Choice: Going Nose to Nose in the Sky," *Time* (April 23, 2001); Pamela Hess, "U.S., China Spy Plane Talks to Begin" from United Press International (April 17, 2001); Xinhua News Agency, "U.S. EP-3 Plane Dismantlement Finished" (July 3, 2001).

Anne M. Platoff

Stilwell, Joseph W. (1883–1946)

Raised in New York State by a highly educated father who became Vice President of a utility company, Joseph W. Stilwell entered West

Point in 1900 at the behest of his father who believed the military could discipline his unruly son. Upon graduation in 1904, Stilwell requested that the Army send him to the Philippines. After two years there, he returned to West Point as an instructor of modern languages where he taught English, French and Spanish. In 1911, the Army transferred Stilwell back to the Philippines where he had the opportunity to visit China during the revolution that overthrew the Qing Dynasty.

After U.S. entry into World War I, Stilwell deployed to France where he served as an intelligence officer. From 1920–1923, Stilwell served in Beijing as a member of the Military Intelligence Division. There, he studied Chinese and reported on conditions in China including observations of the warlord wars fought during that time. After attending the Command and General Staff School at Fort Leavenworth, Stilwell became battalion of the 15th Infantry regiment stationed in Tianjin. The assignment permitted Stilwell to witness the Nationalist revolution of 1928 in which China nominally unified under Jiang Jieshi. Stilwell also became reacquainted with George C. Marshall, the regiment's executive officer who would become the U.S. Chief of Staff. From 1929–1933, Stilwell worked as an instructor at the Infantry school at Ft. Benning where he earned the nickname "Vinegar Joe." Bored with a training assignment in San Diego, he requested transfer to Beijing in 1935 as military attache to the U.S. legation. He traveled extensively throughout China over the next couple years observing the Nationalist army's dispositions in the face of Japanese expansion and the presence of Chinese Communists. Stilwell grew contemptuous of Jiang Jieshi's military leadership, and increasingly admired the Communists for their fighting skill. During the first two years of the Sino-Japanese War, he formed a positive opinion of the Chinese soldier, but his opinion of Nationalist officers, especially Jiang Jieshi, remained negative.

After Pearl Harbor, Jiang became Supreme Commander of the China Theater, and requested that a top ranking U.S. officer become his Allied Chief of Staff. In 1942, Marshall selected Stilwell who was promoted to Lt. Gen. and named the Commanding General of U.S. Army Forces in the China-Burma-India Theater as well as Chief of Staff to Jiang Jieshi. Over the next two years, relations between Jiang and Stilwell became strained. Stilwell and his forces were chased out of Burma by the Japanese in what he described as a "hell of a beating." During the campaign and the months that followed, he and Jiang often differed in strategy. Stilwell wanted to reorganize the entire Chinese army, making it leaner and more

efficient, and intended to use that army to defeat Japan on the ground. Jiang opposed reorganization because it would weed out those commanders loyal to him and place the smaller army in the hands of men not so loyal. He also preferred to avoid major battle with Japan. At the advice of General Claire Chennault, longtime adviser who now commanded the 14th Air Force in China, Jiang wanted to rely on air power to defeat Japan and placed his best troops opposite those of the Communists. Stilwell and Chennault stood at such polar opposite positions on strategy that Franklin Roosevelt met with both commanders, took Chennault's side, and wanted to fire Stilwell. Marshall's opposition saved Stilwell. In 1944, Japan launched the Ichigo Offensive, which not only overran Chennault's airfields, but nearly entered Jiang's wartime capital in Chongqing. Fearing that Jiang would be knocked out the war, Roosevelt insisted that Stilwell become commander of all Chinese forces including those of the Communists upon whom Stilwell looked with favor. Jiang refused and demanded Stilwell's recall. Roosevelt complied, and Stilwell was replaced by General Albert Wedemeyer.

In June 1945, Stilwell took command of the 10th Army in the Pacific in preparation for the invasion of Japan, but Japan's surrender in August ended such planning. The next month, Stilwell stood by on the USS Missouri as Douglas MacArthur took the surrender of Japan. Days before the surrender, Stilwell urged his government to stay out of the conflict between the Nationalists and the Communists. In October 1946, Joseph W. Stilwell died from cancer.

See also World War II; Roosevelt, Franklin D. (1882–1945); Jiang Jieshi (1887–1975); Stilwell Road; China-Burma-India (CBI) Theater.

REFERENCES: Barbara W. Tuchman, *Stilwell and the American Experience in China, 1911–1945* (New York, 1970); Ronald H. Spector, *Eagle Against the Sun: The American War with Japan* (New York, 1985).

Stephen Craft

Stilwell Road

Stilwell Road was originally called Ledo Road. The 478-mile road links northeastern India with the Burma Road, an important strategic military route running from Burma to China. During World War II, U.S. Army engineers began to build Ledo Road in December 1942 to connect the railheads of Ledo (Assam, now in Arunachal Pradesh, India) and Mogaung (Burma). The Ledo road was constructed under direct supervision of American general Joseph W. Stilwell during the war. The Chinese troops also played a crucial role in the construction of the highway. The Ledo

Road crossed into Burma through the difficult Pangsau Pass of the Patkai Range. In January 1945, a connection via Myitkyina and Bhamo was finished to the Burma Road at Mu-se. Barely two years after Stilwell took responsibility for constructing the Ledo Road, it joined hands with the Burma Road and became a highway stretching from Assam to Kunming, 1,040 miles in length. Generalissimo Jiang Jieshi renamed the highway later in honor of Stilwell. After World War II, the American army abandoned the road in October 1945, but it is still used as a major internal route.

See also World War II; Roosevelt, Franklin D. (1882–1945); Jiang Jieshi (1887–1975); Stilwell, Joseph W. (1883–1946); Burma Road; China-Burma-India (CBI) Theater.

REFERENCES: Nathan N. Prefer, *Vinegar Joe's War: Stilwell's Campaigns for Burma* (Novato, CA, 2000); Barbara W. Tuchman, *Stilwell and the American Experience in China: 1911–1945* (New York, 1971).

Yuwu Song

Stimson Doctrine

The Stimson Doctrine is a policy of the American government, enunciated in a note to Japan and China in early 1932, of non-recognition of international territorial changes effected by force. Unsettled conditions in China had invited foreign intervention since the mid 19th century. With the collapse of the Manchu Dynasty in 1911, a series of governments followed that exercised only nominal authority against local warlords. This situation continued until the late 1920s when Jiang Jieshi and the Guomindang (Nationalists) established central authority in China. In consolidating power, Jiang tried to extend his rule into Manchuria, a northern province rich in raw materials that had been dominated by Russia and Japan since the late 1800s. This touched off an undeclared war between China and Russia in 1929, which the U.S. tried to mediate unsuccessfully by invoking the Kellogg-Briand Pact.

Nationalist aspirations to reassert Chinese authority in Manchuria convinced Japan that its rights in the area were endangered. For Japan, Manchuria offered a defensive buffer against Russia and raw materials for the import-hungry island nation. Japan, by the early 1930s, was experiencing nationalist movement of its own led by junior army officers. The economic hardship of the Great Depression, magnified by a Chinese boycott of Japanese goods, convinced a number of these military officers to seek control of Manchuria as a way to increase Japan's industrial base, alleviate food shortages, and absorb its surplus population. In mid-September 1931, a group of junior officers instigated the Mukden Incident,

an alleged act of Chinese sabotage against the Japanese-owned South Manchurian Railroad. This served as a pretext for Japan to occupy all of Manchuria by mid-1932 and establish a puppet regime of Manchukuo.

Japan's action violated earlier treaties to respect Chinese territorial integrity and political independence, but when China asked for assistance from the League of Nations and the United States, neither took effective action. The United States, in a stance consistent with its failure to join the League in 1920, wished to avoid any cooperation with the League on political issues that might cause it to assume leadership in world affairs. U.S. policy makers nonetheless faced a dilemma: previous American governments had supported the Open Door Policy but had also recognized Japan's primary interests in China (Root-Takahira and Lansing Ishii agreements). At first, Secretary of State Henry L. Stimson considered the matter a local incident. Upon realizing Japan's intention to seize Manchuria, Stimson tried to again invoke the Kellogg-Briand Pact, which Japan, like Russia earlier, ignored. He then hoped the League of Nations would resolve the matter, but it merely condemned the Japanese aggression. Stimson then pushed for economic sanctions to stop Japan's seizure of Manchuria. At the time, Japan sent approximately forty percent of its exports to the U.S. and purchased more than seventy-five percent of its oil from America. In the midst of the Great Depression, however, President Herbert Hoover feared that such a step would provoke a war. Instead, on January 7, 1932, the U.S. issued the Stimson Doctrine. Influenced largely by Secretary of State William Jennings Bryan's response to Japan's Twenty-One Demands in 1915, the United States refused to recognize any treaty, agreement, or situation that infringed upon American treaty rights, the Open Door Policy, China's territorial integrity, or violated the Kellogg-Briand Pact. In short, the U.S. would not recognize Japan's control over Manchuria. The announcement had no impact on Japan, which completed its seizure of Manchuria. Stimson tried to respond by threatening to discard the Nine-Power Treaty and build-up an American war fleet in the Pacific, but Hoover rejected such pressure, fearful that it would result in a complete breakdown of order in Asia. The League of Nations eventually embraced the Stimson Doctrine but Japan responded by withdrawing its membership from that organization. The failure of the Stimson Doctrine to stop Japan's seizure of Manchuria demonstrated the inadequacy of America's alternatives to relying on the League of Nations to maintain peace, namely, the Open Door Policy, disarmament, and the Kellogg-Briand Pact, because the Great Depression paralyzed its political will to defend those policies through the use of economic or military force.

See also World War II; Manchuria; Mukden Incident; Manchukuo; Open Door Policy.

REFERENCES: Robert H. Ferrell, *American Diplomacy in the Great Depression: Hoover Stimson Foreign Policy, 1929–1933* (New Haven, CT, 1957); Armin Rappaport, *Henry L. Stimson and Japan, 1931–33* (Chicago, IL, 1963); Henry L. Stimson, *The Far Eastern Crisis: Recollections and Observations* (New York, 1936); Christopher Thorne, *The Limits of Foreign Policy: The West, the League, and the Far Eastern Crisis of 1931–33* (New York, 1973).

Dean Fafoutis

Stimson, Henry Lewis (1867–1950)

From 1929 to 1933, Henry Lewis Stimson served as Secretary of State under President Herbert Hoover. The Stimson Doctrine formulated by the Secretary proposed non-recognition of territorial gains by Japan in China, but the policy failed to halt Japanese expansionism.

Stimson was born on September 21, 1867 in New York City. After attending Harvard Law School, Stimson was admitted to the bar in 1891. In 1906, he was appointed as the U.S. Attorney for the Southern District of New York by President Theodore Roosevelt, and five years later he was selected as Secretary of War in President William Howard Taft's cabinet. During World War I, Stimson served as an artillery officer in France, reaching the rank the colonel. Following the war, Stimson returned to private law practice. He was recalled to public service as President Calvin Coolidge's representative to Nicaragua, and from 1927 to 1929, he served as Governor General of the Philippines, whose independence he opposed. Assuming the office of Secretary of State under President Hoover, Stimson was confronted with the Japanese invasion of Manchuria in September 1931. The Japanese expansion was well timed, as the United States was more concerned with combating the Great Depression and collecting European war debts than supporting the territorial integrity of China. Recognizing that Japan had long exercised influence in Manchuria, the Hoover administration was not prepared to meet the Japanese attack with military or economic sanctions. Many in the United States, nevertheless, perceived Japanese aggression as a threat to the international peace system established following World War I by the League of Nations and Kellogg-Briand Pact outlawing war. Accordingly, Stimson embarked on a policy of moral diplomacy. In January 1932, Stimson informed the Chinese and Japanese governments that the United States would not recognize any infringement upon the territorial integrity or sovereignty of China. Non-recognition, however, failed to stop the Japanese army from attacking Shanghai with its large international community, including many Americans. In response to the assault upon Shanghai, Stimson sent a public letter to the Chairman of the Senate Foreign Relations Committee, William Borah, stating that Japanese aggression in China violated the Nine Power Treaty of 1922, and the United States would no longer be bound by the treaty's restraints on naval construction and the fortification of Pacific possessions. The League of Nations endorsed the non-recognition policy, but in March 1932, the Japanese puppet state of "Manchukuo" was proclaimed in Manchuria. Later that year, Japan withdrew from the League of Nations. Non-recognition failed to curtail the Japanese.

Stimson returned to private life with the electoral defeat of Hoover in 1932, but in 1940 he agreed to join the administration of Democrat Franklin D. Roosevelt as Secretary of War. Playing a crucial role in the U.S. military planning for the Second World War, Stimson strongly advised President Harry S. Truman to use the atomic bomb against the Japanese. He retired from public service in September 1945, and he died on October 20, 1950 in Huntington, New York.

See also Stimson Doctrine; Manchukuo; Nine Power Treaty (1922).

REFERENCES: Godfrey Hodgson, *The Colonel: The Life and Wars of Henry Stimson, 1867–1950* (New York, 1990); Elting Elmore Morison, *Turmoil and Tradition: A Study of the Life and Times of Henry L. Stimson* (Boston, 1960); Armin Rappaport, *Henry L. Stimson and Japan, 1931–33* (Chicago, 1963).

Ron Briley

Strategic Triangle of U.S.-Soviet-China Relations

The 1960s witnessed the beginnings of a U.S.-Soviet-China strategic triangle and over the years the motives affecting the three governments have changed greatly but the triangle continues although with evolving dynamics.

After the founding of the People's Republic of China (PRC) in 1949, Mao Zedong positioned China as a willing junior partner to the Soviet Union in its superpower competition with the United States. And soon thereafter, in late 1950, Chinese and American armed forces fought each other to a stalemate in Korea, further straining relations between the two countries. The decade of the 1960s brought about change. The Soviet Union engaged in a military buildup after the

Cuban missile crisis and its intervention in Czechoslovakia after the so-called Prague Spring seemed to indicate an activist foreign policy, the so-called Brezhnev Doctrine. The United States, while involved in an escalating conflict in Indochina, carefully kept that conflict from spilling over into China. And China, wracked by the Great Proletarian Cultural Revolution, worried about a possible Soviet preemptive strike amidst worsening Sino-Soviet relations. And so the government in Beijing became increasingly interested in a warmer relationship with Washington to counterbalance Moscow. President Richard Nixon traveled to China in 1972, and that helped open the Sino-American dialogue. Fear of the Soviet Union helped overcome Beijing's concern with America's policy on Taiwan and America's longstanding concerns with Communist China. During the Carter Presidency, for example, China permitted the United States to establish listening posts in Northwest China, and the two countries shared the intelligence these posts gathered. Soviet support for India in its war with Pakistan and for the Vietnamese invasion of Cambodia helped bring China and America closer, and they became closer yet with the Soviet invasion of Afghanistan in December 1979. The 1980s saw the emergence of a new power equation in international diplomacy that cast aside attempts by former U.S. Secretary of State Henry Kissinger to create a multipolar world of at least five power centers and that seemingly settled on a strategic triangle between the United States, the People's Republic of China, and the Soviet Union. While Sino-American relations continued to develop, there were issues about the status of Taiwan and of Sino-American trade. China held to its "one China" policy, and the United States continued to support the government in Taibei; similarly, China wanted the United States to drop its opposition to China's entrance into the World Trade Organization, while America had concerns about Chinese trading advantages and the use of convict labor to produce goods for sale in the United States.

As Sino-American relations cooled somewhat during the presidency of Ronald Reagan, the Chinese sought to lessen tensions with the Soviets to help balance the Americans. The Soviet Union was fading as a threat, and so China wanted to rebalance its relationships. The Reagan administration was friendly with Taiwan, and so it too wanted to rebalance its relationships. The resulting triangle at times seemed to match up with other triangles, including any two of the three great powers and the Korean peninsula, with America, China, and Japan, with America, China, and Taiwan, with America, China, and

Vietnam, with China, India, and the Soviet Union; with China, Pakistan, and the United States or, in other words, the emerging strategic triangle reflected the full range of issues, including trade, sale of military technology and weapons, and great power influence across the many countries and regions that border either on China or Russia. The strategic triangle became even more complex in the 1990s. The Soviet Union collapsed, and Russia was not the threat the old USSR had been. The Tiananmen Square bloodshed on June 4, 1989 in Beijing along with Chinese threats to Taiwan, the takeover of Hong Kong from Great Britain, Chinese intransigence over Tibet, and concerns for human rights all served to chill Sino-American relations. Meanwhile, the United States supported Russian President Boris Yeltsin and efforts to grow democracy in Russia. So, China and Russia began to speak again, to discuss differences, and to draw closer together.

Currently the strategic triangle continues and continues to evolve. In the aftermath of the terrorist attack on September 11, 2001, both China and Russia have potentially radical Turkic Islamic minorities that perhaps might draw together in a holy war. These mutual fears could help unite them, at least for this issue, with the United States, which is currently committed to combating such radical terrorism. The decision of the Bush administration to withdraw from the Anti-Ballistic Missile (ABM) Treaty has helped bring China and Russia closer together, fueled by PRC purchases of Soviet military equipment from Russia, especially modern fighter planes, submarines, and destroyers. This equipment helps China modernize its military, increase the pressure on Taiwan, and provides Russia with cash it needs. Meanwhile, the superpowers come and go together on nuclear proliferation in North Korea, the nuclear-fueled war of words between India and Pakistan, and the status of such Middle Eastern and Western Asian countries as Iran and Iraq.

See also Cold War.

REFERENCES: Gordon H. Chang, *Friends and Enemies: The United States, China, and the Soviet Union, 1948–1972* (Stanford, CA, 1990); William E. Griffith, *Cold War and Coexistence: Russia, China and the United States* (Englewood Cliffs, NJ, 1971); Ipyong J. Kim (ed.), *The Strategic Triangle: China, United States, and the Soviet Union* (New York, 1987); Robert S. Ross, *China, the United States, and the Soviet Union: Tripolarity and Policy Making in the Cold War* (Armonk, NY, 1993); Douglas T. Stuart and William T. Tow (eds.), *China, the Soviet Union, and the West: Strategic and Political Dimensions for the 1980s* (Boulder, CO, 1982).

Charles M. Dobbs

Strong, Anna Louise (1885–1970)

During the long course of her career, Anna Louise Strong was a free-lance journalist and social reformer who believed that socialism was the answer to many ills of the world's people. She was born in Friend, Nebraska to a father who was a Congregational minister. Her mother was college educated and active in church missionary organizations.poetry, *Storm Songs and Fables*, in the same year, she started work as a journalist for *Advance*, but went on to graduate school at University of Chicago, receiving a Ph.D. in Psychology at the age of 23 (1908). She also began a long career of social activism with work at Hull House, started by students in Chicago to help the inner-city poor and moved on to the work for children through the National Child Labor Committee and then the United States Children's Bureau (1912), then in Ireland (1914). While reporting for the *Seattle Union Call,* she was arrested along with the entire staff and this led to her first trip to Russia and a rich series of books, articles and lectures where she interpreted revolutions and civil wars around the world.

Over the rest of her life, she traveled to Spain, Mexico, Soviet Russia, Tibet, Vietnam, and China, where she spent most of her last twelve years. She was acquainted with a wide range of social reformers from Eleanor Roosevelt to Lenin, the Song sisters (Song Qingling and Song Meiling), and Mao Zedong. Like her younger contemporary, Edgar Snow, she took on the duty of explaining China to the outside world, and especially to the American public from 1925 to the early 1960s. She made her first visit to China in 1925, going to Guangzhou to meet with the Russian advisor Mikhail Borodin and observe the revolutionary activity of the Nationalist Party. She visited China again in 1927, producing from this visit the book *China's Millions* (1928, revised, 1936, into *China's Millions: The Revolutionary Struggle from 1927–1935* and condensed into a textbook.) This was the beginning of many visits to China, interspersed with visits to Russia and books on the progress of the Russian leadership, with which she became increasingly disillusioned. In 1946–1947, she met briefly with Mao in Yanan and continued to observe and write about the Communist-Nationalist conflicts, eventually published *Dawn Comes Up Like Thunder out of China* (1948) and *Tomorrow's China* (1948).and Strong transmitted this oft-quoted phrase to the world. Despite her obvious radical politics, and charges that her work was "mere propaganda," it was also very popular, if occasionally suppressed. She continued to travel to Russia, China, and even Vietnam and Laos in 1960, writing from there about "American Imperialism." From September 1962 until 1966, Strong wrote "Letters from China," which vividly describes daily life through the turbulent years as China broke with Russia. *I Change Worlds* was planned as the first book of three in her autobiography, the others being *Roving to Revolutions*, and *What I found in China*. She died before they were finished, but left behind more than 30 books and countless articles.

Strong's manuscripts and correspondence are in University of Washington Seattle's library and Beijing Library in China. Her passionate, vivid and personalized observations, her devotion to the story of everyday people, focus on women, children and the working class all contributed to the effectiveness of her writing as an alternative to mainstream accounts of revolutions and civil wars around the world.

See also Mao Zedong (1893–1976); McCarthyism; Snow, Edgar (1905–1972); Smedley, Agnes (1892–1950); Paper Tiger.

REFERENCES: Rewi Alley, *Six Americans in China* (Beijing, 1985); Amy Wai Sum Lee, "Anna Louise Strong," *Dictionary of Literary Biography: American Radical and Reform Writers* (Detroit, MI, 2005); Anna Louise Strong, *I Change Worlds: The Remaking of an American* (New York, 1935); Tracy B. Strong and Helen Keyssar, *Right in Her Soul: The Life of Anna Louise Strong* (New York, 1983).

Janice M. Bogstad

Stuart, John Leighton (1876–1962)

John Leighton Stuart, missionary, university president, and ambassador, was born in Hangzhou, China, to American Presbyterian missionary parents. He graduated from Hampden-Sydney College in 1896. He also attended Union Theological Seminary in Richmond, Virginia and graduated in 1902.

Stuart and his wife left America for China in 1904. He taught New Testament at Nanjing Theological Seminary from 1908 to 1919. He wrote *Essentials of New Testament Greek* in Chinese (1916) and a *Greek-Chinese-English Dictionary of the New Testament* (1918). From 1904 to 1946 he was a missionary under the Board of Foreign Missions of the Presbyterian Church in the United States in China. In 1919 Stuart became the first President of Yenching University, which was created by the merger of the most prestigious Beijing University and North China Union College.

Stuart was highly respected by the Chinese as a man of principle and humanitarianism. During the 1920s, Chinese nationalism was rising. Stuart was sympathetic to the movement, "My sympathies were early aroused against the humiliating terms of foreign treaties and the unfair privileges that the nationals of foreign countries enjoyed — including missionaries." Stuart called Chinese nationalism "in the main a thoroughly wholesome tendency." In early 1930s, Japan began to occupy northern China, which caused great concerns in Washington. As a China expert, Stuart was called to the White House by President Franklin D. Roosevelt in the spring of 1933. He gave advice to the President on what America could do short of war to prevent the Japanese from overrunning the whole of China. After Japan captured Beijing in 1937, Stuart turned down the request by the Japanese to fly the flag of the puppet government at Yenching. He also made great attempts to protect his students and professors in the university. Shortly after the United States declared war on Japan following the Japanese attack on Pearl Harbor, Stuart was interned in Beijing by the Japanese authorities. In early 1945 the Japanese offered him a release, but Stuart rejected it because it did not include two fellow prisoners. It took thirty-nine months before he was released in August 1945. Stuart resumed the presidency of Yenching University until 1946. To help end the Chinese Civil War (1945–1949) between the Communists and the Nationalists, General George C. Marshall was sent by President Harry S. Truman to China in November 1945. Marshall brought Stuart into the negotiations because he was a greatly respected personality in China. In 1946 Truman administration chose Stuart to be ambassador to China after the Communists had rejected the proposed appointment of General Albert Wedemeyer. As ambassador, he tried to maintain good relations with both the Communist leaders and the Nationalist leaders. Stuart also tried to carry out the sometimes contradictory State Department policies. The United States finally changed its policies to get the Communists and the Nationalists to form a coalition government and began to support Jiang Jieshi's Nationalist government in the civil war. Even with a great amount of American aid, Jiang's forces lost and the Communists prevailed in the war.

In August 1949 the State Department issued the *China White Paper* to let the American public know that the collapse of the Nationalist government in the Chinese Civil War was caused by its own shortcomings rather than a lack of sufficient U.S. support. Stuart was shocked and disappointed by its timing and contents, "I have felt acutely the irony of my having been my country's Ambassador to China at a time when all that I had previously accomplished in the country to which I was accredited was apparently being destroyed."

Stuart left his beloved China in August 1949. After 1949, he lived in Washington, DC. He published his memoirs, *Fifty Years in China* in 1954. The book earned critical acclaim, "No living American has over so long a period touched the Chinese so helpfully as has John Leighton Stuart." Stuart died in Washington in 1962.

See also Civil War (1945–1949); Marshall Mission; Yenching University; China White Paper.

REFERENCES: Yu-ming Shaw, *John Leighton Stuart: The Mind and Life of an American Missionary in China, 1876–1941* (Ph.D. Dissertation, University of Chicago, 1975); John Leighton Stuart, *Fifty Years in China: the Memoirs of John Leighton Stuart, Missionary and Ambassador* (New York, 1954); Kenneth W. Rea and John C. Brewer (eds.), *The Forgotten Ambassador: the Reports of John Leighton Stuart, 1946–1949* (Boulder, CO, 1981).

Yuwu Song

Sun Liren (1900–1990)

Sun Liren was an American-trained Chinese general who won fame in the Burma campaigns during World War II, and rose to become the commander in chief of the Chinese Army in 1950 in Taiwan. However, he was removed from his post in 1955 on charges of negligence in association with an alleged scheme against Nationalist leader Jiang Jieshi.

Born in Shucheng, Anhui Province, Sun learned Chinese classics and received a modern education during his childhood. He went to Qinghua College in Beijing, where he studied until 1923 when he left for the United States. Sun first studied civil engineering at Purdue University and earned a BS degree in 1924, and then enrolled at the Virginia Military Institute, where he graduated in 1927. After returning to China, he joined the National Revolutionary Army as a corporal.

Sun rose quickly in the Chinese military ranks, and by 1930 he was already a colonel and a regimental commander. In 1937 he was wounded in thirteen places while fighting with his regiment against the Japanese attack at Shanghai. By 1942 Sun was promoted the divisional commander of the New 38th Division, and participated in the first Burma campaign that spring. The steady advance of the forces under his command enabled the British Burma Division to escape enemy encirclement. While facing ferocious Japanese counter-attack, Sun masterminded a skillful evacuation into India under General Joseph Stilwell. In 1943 Sun was named the commander of the New First Army and took part in the second Burma campaign the following year. His victories were described by Stilwell as the first sustained offensive in Chinese history against a first-class enemy.

In 1945, Sun accepted an invitation from

General Dwight D. Eisenhower to inspect European battlefields. Shortly after, Sun and his army returned to China and accepted the surrender of the Japanese Twenty-third Army in Guangdong. In 1946 he was appointed deputy pacification commander for the Northeast region, and a year later deputy commander in chief of the Chinese Army. His appointment was welcomed in American military circles; many of them regarded Sun as one of China's outstanding young commanders. While facing disastrous defeat by the Communists in mainland China, Sun remained optimistic: "I am not the kind of man who gives up. Now we need American moral and material aid." Unlike other high-ranking nationalist officials, Sun had not been involved in the misuse of the American military supplies. In 1949 after Jiang and his forces fled to Taiwan, Sun became Taiwan defense commander, and played an important role in helping retrain the nationalist troops with American equipment. In 1950, Sun was promoted commander in chief of the Chinese Army. At that time, most United States diplomatic and military officials considered Sun an effective and modern-minded officer, a leader who combined military ability and personal honesty with moderate political views. It was speculated that some even view Sun a better alternative to Jiang Jieshi's autocracy and corruption.

However, Sun's authority was quickly challenged by Jiang's son Jiang Jingguo, whose political commissar system in the armed forces was strongly opposed by Sun. In 1954 Sun was removed from his post and named personal chief of staff to Jiang Jieshi. The following year he was placed under detention for an alleged plot against Jiang. The allegation included a troop petition to Jiang, calling for the abolition of the political officer system and the appointment of Sun as the Chief of Staff of the Nationalist armed forces. Nevertheless, many people believed that Sun's downfall was because he was perceived as a political rival and threat to the Jiang government in Taiwan. Sun's confinement finally came to an end in 1988, one year after Jiang Jingguo died, and the Control Yuan cleared Sun of any conspiracy against the Nationalist government. Sun passed away in Taiwan in 1990.

See also Jiang Jingguo (1910–1988); Jiang Jieshi (1887–1975); Stilwell, Joseph W. (1883–1946); China-Burma-India (CBI) Theater.

REFERENCES: Howard L. Boorman, *Biographical Dictionary of Republic China* (New York, 1970); "Sun Li-jen, War Hero in Burma Fighting, Dies," *New York Times* (November 21, 1990).

Wenxian Zhang

Sun Yat-sen (1866–1925) *see* Sun Zhongshan (1866–1925)

Sun Zhongshan (1866–1925)

Sun Zhongshan was a professional revolutionary and founding father of the Republic of China in 1911. Born into a family of peasants near Guangzhou in Xiangshan (now Zhongshan) county on November 12, 1866, Sun Zhongshan received a traditional primary education in village schools as a child. In 1879, at the age of thirteen, he went to Hawaii to join his older brother, and there he began Western education, graduating from Oahu College in 1883, when he was seventeen years old. This early Western influence significantly shaped his radical ideas and his future career as a revolutionary. After returning to China, Sun enrolled in the College of Medicine for Chinese in Hong Kong, graduating with a medical degree in 1892. During his student years in Hong Kong he furthered his study of English as well as of Chinese history and classics. At the time of his graduation he was one of the new breed of Western-trained Chinese professionals.

Also during those years in Hong Kong, Sun became increasingly disenchanted over the plight of China and the weakness and corruption of the Qing Dynasty. Deeply concerned about the fate of his country, he became even more radical in his thinking and actions. He repeatedly called upon local officials to reform and in 1894 he traveled to Tianjin to personally petition Li Hongzhang to stand strong in the face of foreign aggression. With his failure to change public policies, a thoroughly disappointed Sun returned to Hawaii and there began organizing the first revolutionary party, which became known as the Revive China Society (*Xingzhonghui*). Its aim was to overthrow the Qing Dynasty and establish a republic. With the help of secret society members, in 1895 Sun led a revolt against the Qing Dynasty in Guangzhou. With its failure and a price on his head, Sun fled to London where he narrowly escaped a plot to kidnap and ship him back to China to stand trial. He remained in London for another two years where he developed his ideas of nationalism, democracy, and people's livelihood, known as the Three Principles of the People (*Sanmin zhuyi*).

In 1905 Sun went to Japan where he helped to organize another revolutionary party, the United League (Tongmeng hui), the forerunner to Guomindang (Nationalist Party). Between 1907 and 1911, the United League and other revolutionary parties continually led uprisings against the dynasty. Finally, on October 10, 1911, one of those revolts in Wuchang succeeded and within a few months the Qing Dynasty collapsed. At the time of the Wuchang revolt Sun was in the United States fundraising for the revolution. He immediately rushed back to China, where his party chose him on January 1, 1912, as the provisional President of the newly formed Republic of China, with its capital in Nanjing. But within a month, for the sake of national unity, Sun stepped down in favor of Yuan Shikai, the strongman of north China. Over the following years Yuan persecuted Sun's followers in the Nationalist Party in his bid to reestablish a monarchy with himself as emperor. Sun once again went into exile abroad. After Yuan died in 1916, China disintegrated into a period of warlordism and Sun returned to China to build a new base in the south. Sun realized that he needed a strong base area to build up his own military force to defeat the warlords and reunite China. He turned to Europe and especially the United States for aid. But after the failure of the 1911 Revolution and death of Yuan Shikai, Washington doubted that Sun had the ability to build a new China based on his Three Principles of the People. President Woodrow Wilson looked down upon Sun and was unsympathetic to his cause. The United States failed to perceive Sun's great potential as a national leader.

With the failure to gain aid from the West, Sun turned to the newly formed Soviet Union for help in 1923. The Russians sent a number of advisors who helped Sun reorganize his party along Bolshevik lines and to establish the Huangpu (Whampoa) Military Academy, where Jiang Jieshi became commandant. The alliance with Russia also led to the first period of collaboration between the Nationalists and the Chinese Communists, which lasted until 1927. The newly reinvigorated Nationalist Party called for national unity and the abrogation of the unequal treaties. Once again the Americans underestimated Sun's growing strength and continued to refuse to make any concessions to him and his goals of treaty revision. Instead, the American government continued to insist on its treaty rights in China.

In the winter of 1924, already in poor health, Sun traveled to north China in an effort to make peace with the warlord government in Beijing. During that visit Sun died on March 12, 1925, at the age of fifty-nine. His goal of reuniting China had been left unfulfilled.

See also Chinese Revolution (1911); Guomindang; Jiang Jieshi (1887–1975).

REFERENCES: Lyon Sharman, *Sun Yat-sen, His Life and Its Meaning* (New York, 1934); Harold Schiffrin, *Sun Yat-sen and the Origins of the Chinese Revolution*

(Berkeley, CA, 1968); C. Martin Wilbur, *Sun Yat-sen: Frustrated Patriot* (New York, 1976).

Robert J. Antony

Taft, William Howard (1857–1930)

William Howard Taft is the only person to serve both as a U.S. President and a Justice of the Supreme Court. Born in Cincinnati, Ohio, and educated at Yale University, Taft served in a number of government positions during his career. Most relevant to relations with China, Taft gained an appreciation for Asia while acting as the chief civil administrator and Governor-General for the Philippines between 1900 and 1903. Subsequently, President Theodore Roosevelt appointed him as Secretary of War, a position in which he served until 1908. His tasks as Secretary of War included assisting with the peace mission during the Russo-Japanese War of 1904–1905. This conflict was fought over control of the Manchuria region and its resources in Northeast China. In 1908, Taft won the presidential election as a Republican, having been Roosevelt's handpicked successor.

As President, Taft took a keen interest in China, perhaps as a manifestation of his previous roles in Asia. But Taft would break away from the policies of the previous Roosevelt administration, despite his strong connection to Roosevelt. The issue regarding China was how the United States should cooperate with China, Japan, Russia, and other European powers in order to enhance America's economic interests in the region. The position of Theodore Roosevelt was that Japan had a vital interest in Manchuria, while the United States had only limited interest in the region and there was not enough at stake to threaten increased tensions with Japan or other powers in Manchuria.

However, the Taft administration viewed trade prospects with China to be vital and important for both countries. The term used to describe Taft's position regarding China is "Dollar Diplomacy." The Taft administration feared that Japan's power in China would grow too strong, and efforts needed to be taken to guarantee America's economic interests. Together with his Secretary of State Philander C. Knox, Taft led a push to encourage major American private investments into railroads in Manchuria. They believed this policy would help the United States to maintain an economic foothold and exercise more influence, while also providing the Chinese with important infrastructure. This plan was not a success. First, Japan and Russia cooperated with each other on the task of blocking Taft's railroad plans. Second, American businesses were not anxious at the time to invest in a region of the world with such risk and uncertainty.

Foreign policy toward Asia was one of many areas where Taft pushed for policies that dismayed Theodore Roosevelt. As such, Roosevelt ran in the 1912 election as a third party candidate, which pulled enough of the vote away from Taft to ensure that Woodrow Wilson could win the election for the Democrats.

See also Dollar Diplomacy; Knox, Philander C. (1853–1921); Knox Neutralization Scheme; Manchuria.

REFERENCES: Warren I. Cohen, *America's Response to China: A History of Sino-American Relations* (New York, 2000); Michael Schaller, *The United States and China in the Twentieth Century* (New York, 1990).

Wade D. Pfau

Taiping Rebellion (1850–1864)

The largest rebellion during the Qing Dynasty in China; it was even more destructive than the American Civil War, which it roughly paralleled. The Taiping Rebellion was the largest and most devastating of several rebellions against the Manchu Dynasty fought during the mid 19th century. The rebellion, which resulted from a series demographic, economic, ethnic, and religious tensions that had been brewing for over the preceding century in China, eventually engulfed over half of the Qing empire and destroyed the lives of at least 20 million people. The rebellion brought the Manchu regime to its knees and also came to embroil numerous Europeans and Americans in the conflict.

The leader of the Taiping movement was a peasant named Hong Xiuquan (Hung Hsiuch'uan), a mystic visionary who claimed to be the Son of God and younger brother of Jesus. After failing several times to pass the civil service examination, which would have enabled him to become an official, Hong began gathering followers in his home county near Guangzhou in the years following China's defeat in the Opium War (1839–1842). Later he moved to neighboring Guangxi province were he organized a God Worshippers' Society, which came to number in the tens of thousands, made up mostly of ethnically despised Hakkas like himself. As his movement grew he came into increasing conflicts with non-Hakka villagers and the government. Finally, in 1851 Hong declared his intention to rebel against the Manchu Dynasty by proclaiming the establishment of a rival Heavenly Kingdom of Great Peace (*Taiping tianguo*). In a short time his armies swept northward, taking Nanjing in March 1853, and making it his new capital. Although further expeditions were launched against the north the Taipings repeatedly failed to take Beijing, and a stalemate ensued over the following years.

The new Taiping society was revolutionary, actually presaging many of the later developments under the Communists. Puritanical in nature, Taiping leaders outlawed alcohol, opium, prostitution, and gambling, while they fostered the segregation of the sexes and the accumulation of wealth into public treasuries. They called for the leveling of society, the confiscation of land from the rich, and the equality of men and women, even allowing women to take civil service exams and obtain public office. They also banned footbinding and concubinage, although in practice many Taiping leaders (including Hong) kept large harems. This primitive Communism drew inspiration from both ancient Chinese classics and modern Western Christianity. The Taiping Rebellion was the greatest challenge not only to Qing rulership but also to the entire Confucian tradition before the 20th century.

During the turmoil many Westerners also became involved in the rebellion. Some foreigners, optimistic about Hong's declared Christian inspiration, joined with or otherwise supported the Taiping movement. At one time Hong had even studied with an American missionary named Issachar Jacox Roberts. Other foreigners remained less optimistic and opposed the rebels. In 1853, at the height of their power, Taiping rebels allied with Triads secret society members and seized the walled city of Shanghai, adjacent to the new foreign settlement, and held it for seventeen months. In response foreigners quickly organized an army of mercenaries (known as the Ever Victorious Army), first under the command of an American named Frederick. T. Ward and later under the famous British commander, C. G. "Chinese" Gordon. The army helped defeat the rebels around Shanghai. Even the Rev. Roberts, his former mentor, later rejected Hong and his pseudo-Christian beliefs. In the meantime, however, Britain and France took advantage of the situation to put pressure on the troubled Qing rulers to fully accept their treaty obligations. They declared war, the Second Opium War or the so-called Arrow War (1856), and in 1860 their joint expedition occupied Beijing. During those years, although the American government tried to remain aloof from the fighting, it nevertheless expressed its concerns and fears about the collapse of the Qing government and the break-up of China among the Western powers. In the end, however, Britain cooperated with the United States in supporting the Manchu regime against the Taiping rebels.

After 1853 the Taiping movement slowly declined. Although large numbers of workers and peasants joined the rebellion, few scholars and gentry joined the cause; this was a major reason for its ultimate failure. Furthermore, by 1856 the Taiping leadership nearly destroyed itself in a series of bloody internecine struggles. By 1864, under the leadership of regional commanders, like Zeng Guofan and Li Hongzhang, the Manchu armies were able to drive the rebels out of Nanjing and within a short time the entire movement collapsed.

See also Ward, Frederick T. (1831–1862); Second Opium War (1856–1860); Roberts, Issachar Jacox (1802–1871).

REFERENCES: Franz Michael, *The Taiping Rebellion* (Seattle, WA, 1966, 1972); S. Y. Teng, *The Taiping Rebellion and the Western Powers* (Oxford, 1971); Jonathan Spence, *God's Chinese Son* (New York, 1996).

Robert J. Antony

Taiwan

After China's defeat in the first Sino-Japanese War of 1894–1895, Taiwan became a Japanese colony, a concession in perpetuity by the Chinese empire. Following Japan's surrender at the end of World War II in 1945, Taiwan was returned to the Republic of China (ROC) under the Cairo Declaration (1943) by Allied leaders U.S. President Franklin D. Roosevelt, British Prime Minister Winston Churchill, and Chinese Nationalist leader Jiang Jieshi. In 1949, upon losing the Chinese Civil War to Mao Zedong's Chinese Communist Party, Jiang and his Guomindang (GMD) forces moved the Nationalist government in Nanjing to Taibei, while continuing to claim sovereignty over the mainland. On October 1, 1949, the Chinese Communists founded the People's Republic of China (PRC), claiming to be the successor state of both the mainland and Taiwan and portraying Jiang's government on Taiwan as an illegitimate entity. Initially, the Truman administration had abandoned the Nationalists and expected that the Chinese Communist forces would take Taiwan soon. However, with the outbreak of the Korean War in 1950, President Harry S. Truman ordered the Seventh fleet into the Taiwan Strait to protect Taiwan against Communist attacks. As the Taiwan Strait crises occurred in the 1950s, the United States made a commitment to defend Taiwan by signing the U.S.-China Mutual Defense Treaty in 1954.

In the 1960s and 1970s, Taiwan's economy began to take off. With massive American economic and military aid, the small island became one of the East Asian Tigers while maintaining an autocratic and totalitarian rule. In the context of the Cold War, the United States and most Western countries as well as the United Nations viewed Jiang's government on Taiwan as the sole legitimate government of China until the 1970s when most nations started switching recognition to the Communist government in Beijing. After the entry of the PRC into the United Nations in 1971, the United States modified its policy towards China. President Richard Nixon visited Beijing in 1972, and the United States recognized the PRC and ended diplomatic relations with Taiwan in 1979. Meanwhile, Congress passed the Taiwan Relations Act in 1979, which stated that the United States would provide any amount of arms necessary for Taiwan's self-defense. Since then the PRC and the United States have been contending over the issue of arms sales to Taiwan.

Political reforms started by Jiang Jieshi's successor Jiang Jingguo in the late 1970s liberalized Taiwan from a land of one-party rule into a multiparty democracy. The consolidation of political liberalization culminated in 2000 when the Nationalist's monopoly on power for more than seven decades was ended after Chen Shuibian, the independence-leaning candidate of the Democratic Progressive Party, won the ROC presidential election. Since Chen's victory, the Taiwan independence movement has grown more prominent, causing great tensions between the mainland and Taiwan. It also caused great concerns of the United States, which hopes the two sides will settle their differences peacefully. The political status of Taiwan remained and will continue to remain a thorny issue in the Sino-American relations for years to come.

See also Taiwan Strait; Neutralization of Taiwan; De-neutralization of the Taiwan Strait; Seventh Fleet; U.S.-China Mutual Defense Treaty (1954); Taiwan Relations Act (1979); Arms Sales to Taiwan.

REFERENCES: William Bueler, *U.S. China Policy and the Problem of Taiwan* (Boulder, CO, 1971); William Kintnerand and John Cooper, *A Matter of Two Chinas: The China-Taiwan Issue in U.S. Foreign Policy* (Philadelphia, PE, 1978); Thomas Stolper, *China, Taiwan, and the Offshore Islands* (Armonk, NY, 1985); Martin L. Lasater, *The Taiwan Conundrum in U.S. China Policy* (Boulder, CO, 2000).

Yuwu Song

Taiwan Anti-American Protest of 1957

On March 20, 1957, Sgt. Robert Reynolds, attached to the U.S. Military Assistance and Advisory Group-Taiwan (MAAG), murdered a Chinese man, Liu Tse-jan, in what he claimed was self-defense. Reynolds alleged he found Liu peeping through a window at his wife, and when Reynolds confronted the man, Liu threatened him with a stick. Chinese investigators, on the other hand, found nothing at the scene that could be construed as a weapon and were troubled by the fact that Reynolds chased the man and inflicted the gunshot that ultimately killed Liu. The dead man worked at the Institute of Revolutionary Practice, and left behind a wife and a baby daughter. The Chinese press and reliable Chinese sources in Taiwan described the murder as a revenge killing over either a black-market partnership gone sour or similar affections for a local Chinese woman. Chinese prosecutors investigating the case rejected Reynold's self-defense claims and insisted that Reynolds acted out of malice.

Naturally, Chinese authorities wanted to try Reynolds in their own courts. When MAAG forces went to Taiwan in 1951, U.S. military personnel in Taiwan were granted the equivalence of diplomatic immunity. In the months leading up to the murder, the United States stalled Status of Forces negotiations during which Chinese authorities demanded that U.S. military forces be tried in Chinese courts should they commit crimes. Making matters worse for the Americans was the Girard Case in Japan in which a U.S. shot a Japanese woman in the back. Nevertheless, U.S. authorities refused to hand Reynolds over to the Nationalist authorities, but instead convened a court-martial On May 23, after two days of trial, the court acquitted Reynolds of the charge of voluntary manslaughter.

On May 24, Liu's widow arrived outside the U.S. Embassy with a poster that said in both English and Chinese: "Killer Reynolds innocent? U.S. Court Martial decision unfair, unjust." Over the next couple of hours, a crowd of 150–200 people gathered outside the U.S. Embassy in Taibei. Around 1:00 PM, an angry mob that appeared to be organized and numbering in the hundreds arrived at the scene shouting slogans and carrying placards. At 1:30, the mob began to throw stones at the building. Minutes later, demonstrators attacked and wrecked the Embassy over a two-hour period. Around 4:00, a crowd of thousands gathered outside the United States Information Service Office in Taibei, and watched as 20–30 rioters ransacked the building. When police attempted to arrest three students, rioters attacked and set fire to the nearby Taibei Police Bureau Headquarters. Policemen opened fire on the mob, killing one and wounding 20. Later that evening, the Nationalist government on Taiwan declared a state of emergency and imposed martial law. By midnight, Nationalist military officials declared the situation to be under control, but actually did not have full control until later that morning.

The riot resulted in the injuring of nearly a dozen Embassy and MAAG personnel. Because the number of Chinese police sent to restrain the protestors were so few and that military units were slow to move, U.S. officials were convinced that the riot had been organized by the Nationalist government. Karl Rankin, the U.S. ambassador, immediately filed a protest to the Chinese authorities for failing to protect U.S. property and nationals, and demanded both compensation and an apology. The Nationalist government apologized, but denied that it staged the riot and claimed its police did not immediately use force in order to avoid bloodshed. The riot damaged U.S.-Nationalist relations to a certain extent, but not irreparably. Nevertheless, the riot inspired anti-Americanism throughout Asia and led many to question whether the United States was militaristic.

REFERENCES: *Foreign Relations of the United States, 1955–1957, Vol. 3* (Washington, DC, 1986).

Stephen G. Craft

Taiwan Relations Act (1979)

Passed on March 29, 1979, the Taiwan Relations Act of 1979 was seen as a way to assist Taiwan under the new One China Policy. The Act stated that the United States would make available any amount of arms necessary to maintain Taiwan's capability of self-defense. It also provided for Congress to have a role in determining the weapons and services provided.

Congress did not take control after the bill's passage into law. The authors of the bill immediately accused President Jimmy Carter of not implementing the legislation's military aspects. They saw this inaction as President Carter's placating "Red China." This lack of activity was a trend that continued into the Reagan, Bush, and Clinton administrations. Each sought to decrease the amount of military personnel and equipments sent to Taiwan. This was in reaction to threats from China hinting at invasions of Taiwan if the U.S. continued to offer military supports to what China considered to be a rogue province. The Taiwan Relations Act of 1979 remained mostly a means for securing trade and commerce between the two countries. While the Taiwanese government wanted the military supplies and equipments, they did not wish to be perceived as needy. Taiwan never sent a delegate to the United States to ask for help with national security and self-defense issues. Twenty years later, three Senators worked to make changes to the Act. On March 26, 1999, Concurrent Resolution 17 was reported to the Senate. It contained measures to reaffirm the United States' position on providing Taiwan with up to date military equipments. It also reaffirmed the pledge of the Taiwan Relations Act of 1979 that the United States was committed to protecting Taiwan's right of self-defense.

During the investigation of the Act's history it was found that Taiwan was the only country with which the United States provided military aid yet which it had no military relationship. There was no communication with Taiwanese intelligence. No military inspectors had been sent over to judge the condition of the equipments provided. There were no military personnel serving as a direct link between the United States and Taiwan. This situation was a direct result of pressure from China itself. In Resolution 17, the Senate added rules requiring a yearly report of the condition of Taiwan's military equipments and a report on what Taiwan would need and what the cost would be to keep them supplied with state of the art military equipments.

See also Taiwan Strait; One China Policy; Arms Sales to Taiwan; Taiwan.

REFERENCES: John F. Copper, *Taiwan* (Westminster, UK, 2003); Linda Chao and Ramon Myers, *The First Chinese Democracy: Political Life in the Republic of China on Taiwan* (Baltimore, MD, 1998); Willem Kemenade, *China, Hong Kong, Taiwan, Inc.: The Dynamics of the New Empire* (New York, 1998).

Arthur Holst

Taiwan Security Enhancement Act (1999)

Taiwan Security Enhancement Act (1999), a bill meant to reaffirm the U.S. security commitment to Taiwan, was introduced on March 24, 1999 in the 1st Session of the 106th Congress in both the Senate (693) and the House of Representatives (H.R. 1838) on March 24, 1999 and May 18, 1999 respectively. The original bill authorized the sale of "specific military items" such as theater missile defense equipment, surface-to-air missiles to Taiwan. It, however, came under the severe criticism from Congressmen. The House International Relations Committee Chairman Benjamin Gilman offered an amendment, as a compromise formula, eliminating all references to "specific weapons systems," although the bill required America to enhance training and exchange programs with the Taiwan military, and to establish direct, secure communications between the U.S. and Taiwan military commands. Representative Gilman's version was endorsed by the International Relations Committee in a 32–6 vote on October 26, 1999. While the full House passed the bill on February 1, 2000 by a vote of 341–70.

Taiwan Security Enhancement Act (TSEA) was the reaction of Republican Congressmen to China's refusal to give up the use of force to reunify the mainland and Taiwan and the continuance of U.S. ambiguity regarding the American defense of Taiwan. According to the bill, "it is in the national interest of the United States to eliminate ambiguity and convey with clarity the continued United States support for Taiwan, its people, and their ability to maintain their democracy free from outside coercion and force." It also finds that "the current defense relationship between the United States and Taiwan is deficient in terms of its capacity over the long term to counter and deter potential aggression against Taiwan by the People's Republic of China." The bill provides for "training of Taiwan military officers at professional military education schools including National Defense University and sale of defense articles and services to Taiwan; increase in technical staff of the American Institute in Taiwan; maintenance of sufficient self-defense capacity of Taiwan enhancement of programs and arrangements for operational training and exchanges of senior officers between the armed forces of the United States and the armed forces of Taiwan for work in threat analysis, doctrine, force planning, operational methods, and other areas; as well as communication between U.S. and Taiwan military commands."

The TSEA evoked strong reaction from China when the House of Representatives passed it. While reacting to the passage of the Act, Chinese government stated that it was a complete violation of the three Sino-U.S. joint communiques, a serious encroachment on China's sovereignty, and a gross interference in its internal affairs. China reaffirmed that an assurance of strong military support from the U.S. would only serve to encourage the secessionist forces in Taiwan to push for formal independence. China called upon the U.S. government to prevent the Act from becoming a law. Quite interestingly, the bill did not find favor with the Clinton administration itself. It rather threatened to veto the legislation if passed by the Senate as it would only serve to endanger Taiwan's security by provoking China into conflict and undermine the U.S. objectives for stability in Asia.

See also Taiwan; Taiwan Strait; U.S.-China Mutual Defense Treaty (1954); Taiwan Relations Act (1979).

REFERENCES: Law Librarians' Society of Washington, D.C. (LLSDC), "Hearing: Taiwan, the PRC, and the Taiwan Security Enhancement Act," *GPO Congressional Publications* (Washington, DC, September 15, 1999); *Taiwan Security Enhancement Act, www.taiwandc.org/nws-2000-04.htm.*

Romi Jain

Taiwan Strait

The Taiwan Strait separates the island of Taiwan from mainland China. Formerly called the

"Formosa Strait," after the old Portuguese name for Taiwan, the Strait has taken on military-political dimensions since the Communists gained control over mainland China in 1949. The defeated Nationalist government under Jiang Jieshi fled with remnants of the Nationalists Army to the island. Mao Zedong's People's Liberation Army (PLA) had been strictly a land-based military force, and was thus ill-prepared to launch an immediate invasion of the island. The United States moved its Seventh Fleet into the Taiwan Strait to counter any moves by the PLA to invade the island. Thus the Strait has come to be the dividing line between the two Chinese governments.

Taiwan is approximately 110 miles off the coast of China. However, several smaller islands in the Strait are also held by the Nationalist government and lie much closer to the mainland. These islands provide tempting targets for Beijing and are potential flashpoints for the resumption of open warfare. The Penghu (Pescadore) Islands lie roughly halfway between the mainland and the southern half of Taiwan. The islands of Jinmen and Little Jinmen are separated from the mainland by only about 2 miles of open water. About 150 miles north along the coast lay the Mazu island group.

There have been several crises in the Taiwan Strait in the second half of the 20th century. In 1954, the First Taiwan Strait Crisis took place when the Peoples Liberation Army launched heavy artillery attacks on the offshore island of Jinmen after the U.S. lifted its blockade of Taiwan, making possible Nationalist attacks on mainland China. In 1958 the PLA again used military pressure in an attempt to push the Nationalists off Jinmen and Mazu, which led to the second Taiwan Strait crisis. Each crisis was begun by an increase in rhetoric on radio broadcasts, followed by an increase in the strength of the PLA in the areas closest to the Strait, including MIG flights in the skies around the contested area. The 1954–1955 crisis inspired the passage of the Far East Resolution by the United States, which committed the United States to support the defense of all territory then controlled by the Nationalist Government. However, the U.S. was only to commit American forces for direct combat if the American President believed that an attack on Jinmen or the Penghu was the first stage in an invasion of Taiwan itself. The United States wanted to avoid allowing the Communists to take any offshore islands from the Nationalists, but at the same time it wanted to avoid being dragged into a war with Communist China to assist Jiang in his dream of re-conquering the mainland. Jiang Jieshi

added to tensions by placing about one-third of his army on Jinmen and Mazu — one hundred thousand men. Their placement did little to defend these islands, while their proximity to the mainland made their presence appear threatening to the Communist government. Eisenhower argued for much smaller garrisons, which would make the islands strong outposts, not massive garrisons, the lost of which would have been catastrophic. However Jiang believed the loss of the islands would lead to the loss of Taiwan itself and thus made the defense of every island an imperative. The vulnerability of Jinmen to blockade showed the folly of Jiang's placement of so much of his force on the island.

The Communist forces on August 23, 1958 began a campaign of bombardment of Jinmen and Little Jinmen, sending twenty thousand rounds onto the island the first day. Thereafter the daily toll averaged about eight thousand. Although Jiang claimed massive destruction and death resulted from the attacks, real damage was minimal. The Nationalist Army provided counter-battery artillery fire against their Communist adversaries on the mainland, but neither side seems to have inflicted much damage to the other. U.S. naval forces provided escort services to convoys from Taiwan to its beleaguered islands, although they remained beyond the three-mile limit of the beaches. During the autumn of 1958, the Communists began several weeks of ceasefire, during which the Nationalists moved enormous amounts of supplies to the islands. During October they began to shell Nationalist convoys only on odd days of the month, permitting re-supply only on even days. The U.S. remained aloof from convoy operations unless the Communists attempted to interfere on even numbered days. Gradually the Communists began to shell only on ceremonial occasions. Jiang decreased the number of his soldiers on the Jinmen by as much as twenty thousand, leaving what the U.S. considered to be still far too much of his force on the vulnerable outpost.

In 1996, PRC conducted military exercises in the Taiwan Strait in an apparent effort to intimidate the Taiwan electorate before the pending presidential elections, which triggered the third Taiwan Strait crisis. As a result, the United States dispatched two aircraft carrier battle groups to the region. Beijing's attempts at intimidation backfired. Arousing more anger than fear, it boosted the independence-prone candidate Li Denghui by 5% in the polls. The military exercises also strengthened the argument for further U.S. arms sales to Taiwan and resulted in the strengthening of military ties between the United

States and Japan, increasing the role Tokyo would play in defending Taiwan. The crisis, however, had a great impact in disrupting the economy in Taiwan. The stock market and real estate prices fell while capital fled the island. The government was forced to spend millions for economic recovery.

The Taiwan Strait remained a source of tension through the end of the 20th century and beyond. Rising political tensions between two Chinas are usually reflected by increased military tensions in the Strait.

See also Neutralization of Taiwan; De-neutralization of the Taiwan Strait; Taiwan; Seventh Fleet; U.S.-China Mutual Defense Treaty (1954); Taiwan Relations Act (1979); Arms Sales to Taiwan.

References: M.A. Rubinstein (ed.), *Taiwan: A New History* (Armonk, NY, 1990)

Barry Stentiford

Tang Shaoyi (1860–1938)

Born into a rich merchant family in Guangdong Province, Tang Shaoyi was sent by his father to join the China Educational Mission led by Chen Lanbin and Rong Hong. Arriving in the United States with the third group of students in 1874, Tang had elementary education in Springfield, Massachusetts and went to high school in Hartford, Connecticut. He was only able to study at Columbia University for a year before the Qing Court recalled the Educational Mission from the United States in 1881.

Soon after his return to China, Tang was sent to work as an apprentice in the new Korean customs house established by the Qing Court as part of China's effort to strengthen its claim over the client state. He was promoted to Consul in Seoul under the recommendation from Yuan Shikai, a prominent Qing official, in 1885 because of his outstanding performance in handling the 1884 pro-Japanese coupe. Tang stayed in Korea for over a decade to help Yuan in all foreign affair matters. After China lost control of Korea in the Sino-Japanese War in 1895, Tang returned to Seoul to serve as Consul General. His diplomatic service in Korea finally came to an end in 1898 when he was recalled by the Qing Court.

As an experienced diplomat and administrator, Tang moved up rapidly in the Chinese government. After serving as the Director to the Northern Railways, he was appointed Commissioner of Foreign Affairs in Shandong Province, helping Yuan to handle lawsuits brought by missionaries over their losses suffered during the Boxer Rebellion. Between 1901 and 1904, he was the Director of the Customs House in Tianjin, responsible for the running of the city. In 1904, Tang was appointed as the negotiator by the Qing Court to defend Chinese control over Tibet through the negotiation of a new treaty with Britain. Taking the advantage of the division among the English officials, Tang held a strong stand on China's sovereignty over Tibet and stalled the negotiation in Calcutta, India. When both sides met again in Beijing in 1906, situation became more favorable for China. The Anglo-Chinese Adhesion Agreement signed in April in Beijing restored the diplomatic recognition of China's sovereignty over Tibet.

Recognizing his success in defending China's sovereignty over Tibet, the Qing Court appointed Tang as Governor of Liaoning Province in 1907. As Governor, Tang tried to build a railroad from Xinmin to Fakumen and set up a development bank with American capital, including the Boxer Indemnity returned by the United States. His plan was defeated by William Rockhill, the American Minister to Beijing, and Liang Cheng, the Chinese Minister to Washington, who wanted to use the returned Boxer Indemnity to educate Chinese students in the United States. When he appealed to the State Department for financial support during his visit to Washington as the special envoy expressing China's gratitude for the return of the Boxer Indemnity in 1908, the response was negative. Tang left the post of Governor after his return to China and served as Minister of Postal Services.

During the Revolution of 1911, Tang represented Qing Court in the negotiation with the revolutionaries. When Yuan Shikai became the President of the Republic of China in 1912, Tang was appointed by Yuan as the first Prime Minister. However, Tang resigned within a few months because of Yuan's repeated violations of the new Constitution. When Yuan was working to make himself the new emperor, Tang was among the first to denounce such an attempt. In 1917, he served as Minister of Finance in the Nationalist government led by Sun Zhongshan. Although he played an active role in national politics, Tang's influence dwindled, especially, after the death of Sun Zhongshan in the mid-1920s. He was murdered in Shanghai in 1938.

References: Shi Ni, *Guannian Yu Beiju: Wanqing Liumei Youtong Mingyun Poxi [Ideals and Tragedy: An Analysis on the Fates of Chinese Child Students Sent to the United States in the Late Qing Dynasty]* (Shanghai, 1999); David Hinners, *Tong Shaoyi and His Family: A Saga of Two Countries and Three Generations* (Lanham, MD, 1999).

Hongshan Li

Tao Xingzhi (1891–1946)

As one of the best known educators in modern Chinese history, Tao received traditional as well as modern education in China and the United States. Growing up in a relatively poor family in Anhui Province, Tao was taught by his father at home until 15 years old. Having attended modern school for a few years, Tao entered Jinling University, a missionary school run by an American church in Nanjing in 1911, studying Chinese literature and philosophy. After his graduation, Tao borrowed money and went to the United States to further his education. Having earned a master degree in political science from the University of Illinois within a year, Tao entered the Teachers' College, Columbia University in 1915. Tao went back to China after finishing all the course work required by the Ph.D. program at Columbia in 1917.

Taking the professorship and dean's position at the Jinling Normal College right after his return, Tao rose quickly as one of the leading educators in China. Pressed by the dire needs for modern education in China's national reconstruction and survival, Tao joined other educators in starting the new education movement in China in 1919. As part of the effort to spread the new ideas for education, Tao initiated the publication of *The New Education* magazine and served as one of the chief editors since the very beginning. In order to provide stronger leadership for the movement, Tao worked with Guo Binwen, Huang Yanpei, and other leading educators in establishing the Chinese National Association for the Advancement of Education in 1921. As the Director General of the Association, Tao spent most of energy in promoting mass education. In 1923, he collaborated with Yan Yangchu, another famous educator, to found the National Association for the Advancement for the Common People's Education. In the same year, Tao and Zhu Jingneng edited and published the *Common People's Thousand Character Lessons* to help the average illiterate people to acquire basic language education within a few months.

Deeply concerned about the high illiteracy and poverty rate in rural areas, Tao put more focus on rural education. In order to get more peasants educated, Tao set up the Xiaozhuang Rural Experimental Normal School near Nanjing in March 1927. Within a few years, he managed to establish an educational network including kindergarten, elementary, and secondary schools in the area. Applying all his major educational and social ideas in these schools, Tao intended to turn the district into a model in education as well as in social, cultural, political, and economic reforms, which might be used as an example for the reconstruction for the whole nation. Although his experiments attracted numerous admirers throughout the nation and around the world, all the schools in the experimental district were closed by the Nationalist government in April 1930 and Tao was forced to seek shelter in the International Settlement in Shanghai as an arrest order was issued by the government for his alleged collaborations with rebels against the government.

Despite the setback in Xiaozhuang, Tao continued to devote his energy to the mass education during the difficult years of Japanese encroachment and invasion. With a new focus on science education, Tao edited and published many science books while staying in Shanghai in the early 1930s. Once the war with Japan officially started, he helped establish the Wartime Education Association and drew the wartime educational plan for the nation. As the war came to an end, Tao joined his friends in organizing the Chinese Democratic League in 1945 and served as the chairman for the Committee on Education and editor for the *National Education Monthly* and *Democratic Weekly*. He died on July 25, 1946.

REFERENCES: Don-chean Chu, *Patterns of Education for the Developing Nations: Tao's Work in China 1917–1946* (Tainan, Taiwan, 1966); Anhuisheng Tao Xingzhi Jiaoyu Sixiang Yanjiuhui [The Society of the Study on Tao Xingzhi's Educational Thoughts, Anhui Province], *Tao Xingzhi Yisheng [Life of Tao Xingzhi]* (Changsha, China, 1984); Tao Xingzhi, *Xingzhi Shuxinji [Correspondence of Xingzhi]* (Hefei, China, 1983).

Hongshan Li

Third Taiwan Strait Crisis (1996) *see* Taiwan Strait

Thomas, James Augustus (1862–1940)

James Augustus Thomas was a tobacco entrepreneur, philanthropist and Sinologist. A close friend and business associate of James and Benjamin Duke, the renowned industrialists and philanthropists, Thomas spent thirty years in China, managing operations for the British-American Tobacco Company in Asia. Between 1888 and 1922 he initiated the export of American cigarettes to China and other Asian countries. Initially, his interest in China was primarily commercial. However, he gradually became involved in a number of projects: he organized the Chinese-American Bank of Commerce; helped develop the partnership between Standard Oil and the Chinese government; established two schools for Chinese students; he also played an important role in the Chinese Red Cross. During the 1930s, he provided assistance in the management of China Child Welfare Inc. and China Famine Relief USA Inc. Thomas also served as Director of the China Society of America and an Executive Committee Member of the American Asiatic Society.

REFERENCES: The Papers of J. A. Thomas (William R Perkins Library, Duke University, 1905–1923).

Yuwu Song

Tiananmen Square Massacre

Tiananmen Square Massacre was the bloody culmination of six weeks of demonstrations for political liberalization and reforms by Chinese students, workers, professionals, and common citizens in Beijing against the Chinese Communist Party and the government on June 4, 1989.

The 1980s witnessed rapid market-oriented economic reforms and developments started by Chinese leader Deng Xiaoping, who masterminded and instituted the reform and opening policies in China. The reform led to the loss of the old value system, the feeling of dislocation, and confusion about the infiltration of the new Western liberal value system. In the meantime, inflation and official corruption ran rampant, triggering unprecedented social discontent. In April 1989, Hu Yaobang, the reform-minded party leader, who had been purged by the conservative party elders, died. Students took to the street in memory of Hu. This event quickly turned into a movement for political reforms. Protesters demanded freedom of speech, freedom of assembly, and democratic elections. They also urged the government to fight corruption and nepotism. The demonstrations were marked by million-strong street marches participated by people from all walks of life, a hunger strike, and the erection of the Goddess of Democracy modeled after the Statue of Liberty in the United States. The political temperature was getting higher and higher. Some people even demanded the step-down of Deng and Premier Li Peng. Alarmed and infuriated, the party leadership felt that they were cornered and had no choice but to crush the movement. In the night of June 3 and early morning of June 4, the People's Liberation Army marched into central Beijing. Hundreds of demonstrators were killed in the west of the capital and in the area around Tiananmen Square. The gory scenes covered by foreign news media shocked and horrified the whole world.

During the weeks of the protests, the Bush administration acted cautiously fearing that any American encouragement of the demonstrators would backfire and provide the Chinese government with excuses for cracking down on the demonstration. Now the bloodshed led to a huge public outcry in the United States. Heavy pressure was being put on the administration for action. The White House responded quickly by condemning the Chinese government's use of brute force. In the following weeks, the U.S. government announced the freeze on the military relationship with Beijing, suspended scheduled exchanges between the two countries, and banned high-level official visits. America also became a sanctuary for the leading protesters who fled the country and for the famed political dissidents Fang Lizhi and his wife who took refuge in the U.S. embassy in Beijing following the episode. China and the United States reached an unprecedented impasse over human rights and the Sino-American relations turned sour since President Richard Nixon's groundbreaking visit to Beijing in 1972.

See also Deng Xiaoping (1904–1997); Bush, George H. W. (1924-); Scowcroft-Eagleburger Mission (1989).

REFERENCES: Roger V. Des Forges, Luo Ning, and Wu Yen-bo (eds.), *Chinese Democracy and the Crisis of 1989: Chinese and American Reflections* (Albany, NY, 1993); Chu-yuan Cheng, *Behind the Tiananmen Massacre: Social, Political, and Economic Ferment in China* (Boulder, CO, 1990).

Yuwu Song

Tibet

Geographically, Tibet is a region in the Himalayas of Central Asia that is inhabited by the Tibetan people. Politically, the term is usually used to refer to the Tibet Autonomous Region of the People's Republic of China. Culturally, Tibet includes surrounding areas with large Tibetan populations where Tibetan influence has been historically strong. Portions of the current Chinese provinces of Sichuan, Yunnan and Qinghai could be considered part of cultural Tibet, as well as portions of India including Ladakh, Himachal Pradesh and Uttarunchal. The borders of the political entity called Tibet have varied throughout history. Tibetans are recognized as one of the minorities of the People's Republic of China (PRC) and have a distinctive language and culture. Their culture is closely integrated with a unique form of Buddhism. The temporal state was administered by lamas, with the reincarnation of the Dalai Lama considered to be head of state. Throughout much of its history, Tibet has been under the influence of outside powers such as the Mongols, the Chinese, the British, the Nepalese, and the Indians. However, there have also been significant periods of time when the government of Tibet controlled its own internal and external affairs. While the status of Tibet is still in dispute, in reality it is a territory controlled by the PRC government, which considers Tibet to be an integral part of China. Beijing traces its claim to Tibet to the historical relationship between Tibet and China dating back to the time when Mongol rulers were in control of much of this part of Asia.

There is also a Tibetan Government-in-exile led by the Dalai Lama, who fled to India in 1959. This government is headquartered in Dharamsala in northern India. As the traditional spiritual and temporal leader of Tibet, the Dalai Lama represents his people for much of the world while the government of China administers his homeland. The Tibetans counter Chinese claims to Tibet with the argument that, during the period from 1913 to 1951, Tibet governed its own affairs and was therefore an independent state. When the Chinese People's Liberation Army (PLA) entered the territory in 1949, Tibet met a number of the criteria that commonly are used to define a sovereign state. A distinctive Tibetan government that included a head of state, a cabinet of ministers, a national assembly, and a judicial system controlled the territory of Tibet during this time. The Tibetan government levied taxes, issued its own currency and postage stamps, and maintained a small army. In addition, the Government of Tibet maintained diplomatic relations with its neighbors including Nepal, Bhutan, Sikkim, Mongolia, China, and British India. It also had limited relations with Russia and Japan. Whether the action of the PLA was an invasion or a peaceful liberation is a matter of perspective. The result, though, was that from that point in time the People's Republic of China has had control over the territory of Tibet. During the transition period that followed, the Tibetan government attempted to retain some autonomy through negotiations with the Chinese government, most notably the 17 Point Agreement for the Peaceful Liberation of Tibet, signed in 1951. At the time the agreement was signed, Chinese troops were already occupying part of Tibet. After the Tibetan government in exile was formed, the Dalai Lama refuted the validity of this agreement citing that the Tibetan representatives who signed did not have the authority to enter into agreements, that the document was signed under duress, and that the Chinese government has not abided by the conditions of the agreement. Key points of the 17 Point Agreement stated that Tibet was a part of China, provided for the incorporation of the Tibetan armed forces into the PLA, and guaranteed religious freedom in Tibet. Since the departure of the Dalai Lama from Lhasa, the Chinese government has worked to modernize Tibet and integrate it into the People's Republic. The Chinese contend that great strides have been made in advancing Tibet from a feudal society to a society where education and medical services are provided to all. The Tibetan Government in Exile, on the other hand, has accused the Chinese of a number of human rights violations in the territory.

The Dalai Lama has enjoyed great popularity internationally for his struggle for Tibetan independence and was awarded the Nobel Peace Prize in 1989. Absent from most discussion of the Tibetan question, however, have been the influential powers of the West. The status of Tibet has been debated on a number of occasions by the General Assembly of the United Nations, but for the most part the nations of the world have only gone as far as to chastise China for violating Tibetan human rights. Over 50 years after the signing of the 17 Point of Agreement, the status of Tibet is still contested.

The policy of the United States does not recognize Tibet as an independent state. It reaffirms the status of Tibet as a part of China. However, during the time period between the flight of the Dalai Lama and President Richard Nixon's trip to Beijing in 1972, the U.S. Central Intelligence Agency provided support to Tibetan rebels who were resisting the Chinese control over Tibet. This strategy was part of Washington's Cold War policies in Asia and not an effort to help Tibetans to gain independence. As relations normalized between the United States and the People's Republic of China in the 1970s, U.S. policy regarding Tibet has placed an emphasis on the human rights situation in the region. The U.S. has frequently criticized China for human rights violations in Tibet and has encouraged the Chinese government to engage in a dialog with the Dalai Lama or his representatives.

See also Dalai Lama (1935-).

REFERENCES: Jane Ardley, *The Tibetan Independence Movement: Political, Religious and Gandhian Perspectives* (London, 2002); Stephen R. Bowers and Eva M. Neterowicz, *Tibet: Endurance of the National Idea* (Washington, DC, 1994); Melvyn C. Goldstein, *A History of Modern Tibet, 1913–1951: The Demise of a Lamaist State* (Berkeley, CA, 1989); John Kenneth Knaus, *Orphans of the Cold War: America and the Tibetan Struggle for Survival* (New York, 1999); Alex McKay (ed.), *Tibet and Her Neighbors: a History* (London, 2003); Tsepon W. D. Shakabpa, *Tibet: A Political History* (New Haven, CT, 1967); Nirmal Chandra Sinha, *Tibet: Considerations on Inner Asian History* (Calcutta, 1967); Michael C. van Walt van Praag, *The Status of Tibet: History, rights, and Prospects in International Law* (Boulder, CO, 1987); The Government of Tibet in Exile, *www.tibet.com.*

Anne M. Platoff

Tong Hollington K. (1887–1971) *see*
Dong Xianguang (1887–1971)

Trade Act of 1974

The Congress of the United States has been actively involved in legislating on trade issues since the beginning of the Republic. In 1930 it worsened the Great Depression with the passage of the protectionist Smoot-Hawley Act by imposing stiff tariffs on almost anything imported into the United States. However, in 1934 Congress began to move away from protection with passage of the Reciprocal Traded Agreements Act, which allowed the President to negotiate tariff reductions with other countries.

After World War II Congress steadily reduced tariffs and worked with the executive branch to reduce non-tariff barriers to trade. Beginning in 1945, agreements were made which created the General Agreement on Tariffs and Trade (GATT). The GATT was the predecessor to the World Trade Organization. In 1962 Congress passed the Trade Expansion Act. Congress allowed the Kennedy (Kennedy Round) administration to make major tariff reductions. When Congress adopted the Trade Act of 1974, it gave the President fast-track authority to quickly negotiate trade agreements. The authority enabled the United States to spearhead the development of an increasingly liberalized global trading system. An important addition to the Trade Act of 1974 was the Jackson-Vanik Amendment. It mandated a policy of requiring freedom of emigration as a condition for being granted Most Favored Nation (MFN) status if the country was a "non-market economy." While the amendment was focused on Jewish emigration from the Soviet Union it also applied to China. The President was required by law to grant Communist China trade benefits in exchange for free emigration. From the time that President Richard Nixon moved to restore relations with China it sought MFN. However, it was denied because of its human rights record even after it moved from a non-market economy to a market economy. There have been constant calls for repeal of the Jackson-Vanik Amendment on behalf of China and a restoration of normal trade relations.

Section 301 of the Trade Act of 1974 directs the President to identify countries that are engaging in unfair trade practices, and to take trade actions against those countries, including sanctions if necessary, to remedy the problem. Unfair trade practices included dumping, child labor violations, abuse of labor violations and other practices.

The Trade Act of 1974 is still the legal basis of trade between the United States and China. In 2004 the AFL-CIO filed a petition under Section 301 demanding that President George W. Bush pressure the Chinese government for engaging in unreasonable trade practices by their violations of workers' rights.

See also Most Favored Nation (MFN); General Agreement on Tariffs and Trade (GATT).

REFERENCES: Bill Clinton, *Permanent Normal Trade Relations for China: Message from the President of the United States Transmitting Legislation Authorizing the People's Republic of China to Terminate Application of Title IV of the Trade Act of 1974 to the People's Republic of China and Extending Permanent Normal Trade Relations Treatment to Products from China.* (Washington, DC, 2000); Bill Clinton, *Continuation of Waiver Under the Trade Act of 1974 With Respect to China: Communication from the President of the United States Transmitting Notification of His Determination That a Continuation of the Waiver Currently in Effect for the People's Republic of China Will Substantially Promote the Objectives of Section 402 of the Trade Act of 1974, Pursuant to 19 USC. 2432 (c) and (d).* (Washington, DC, 2000); Bill Clinton, *A Report to the Congress Concerning the Extension of Waiver Authority for the People's Republic of China: Communication from the President of the United States Transmitting Notification of His Determination That Continuation of the Waiver Currently in Effect for the People's Republic of China Will Substantially Promote the Objectives of Section 402 of the Trade Act of 1974, Pursuant to 19 USC. 2432 (c) and (d).* (Washington, DC, 1999); Bill Clinton, *Extension of Waiver Authority for the People's Republic of China: Communication from the President of the United States Transmitting Notification of His Determination That a Continuation of a Waiver Currently in Effect for the Peoples Republic of China Will Substantially Promote the Objectives of Section 402, of the Trade Act of 1974 — Received in the U.S. House of Representatives, May 31, 1996, Pursuant to 19 USC. 2432 (c), (d).* (Washington, DC, 1996).

Jack Waskey

Trade Act of 1988

In 1988 the Congress of the United States passed the Omnibus Trade and Competitiveness Act. The legislation passed Congress in mid-August and was signed into law by President Ronald Reagan on August 23, 1988. The purpose of the Trade Act of 1988 was to promote the competitiveness of American industry. The Act authorized the executive branch to negotiate reciprocal trade agreements, to aid the development of American trade strategy, to strengthen American trade laws, and to improve through trade the living standards of the world.

The Trade Act of 1988 enacted a number of changes in American trade law as it had been enacted in the Trade Act of 1978, which had modified earlier trade legislation. Major changes made by the Trade Act of 1988 to section 301 as it had been written in the Trade Act of 1978. The first major change to Section 301 was the adoption of a requirement that the U.S. Trade Representative (USTR) must identify unfair trade practices that would prevent fair competition for U.S. products in the markets of foreign countries. The U.S. Trade Representative was also required to investigate these practices. The second major change to Section 301 required the USTR to investigate countries that would not adequately protect intellectual property rights. This was a change to Section 182 of the Trade Act of 1974. It sought to approach the issues of marketing and protecting intellectual property. It authorized the USTR to negotiate improvements in foreign intellectual property regimes through bilateral and/or multilateral initiatives.

And the third major change required the USTR to review annually trade agreements that involve telecommunications products or services. The review was to determine if a country was failing to live up to the agreements that it had made or if it was engaging in unfair practices in the telecommunications market.

On November 9, 2001, President George W. Bush issued a memorandum of fact that the state trading companies of Communist China were engaged in unfair competition. The finding was based on the Trade Act of 1988. In the memorandum the President noted that China was seeking membership in the World Trade Organization (WTO). The condition of membership was an economic condition. The state trading companies of China must trade for purely economic motives and not for political advantages in a way that was harmful to trade. The president's memorandum however did not block China's entry into the WTO on December 11, 2001. However, this has not ended difficulties in U.S.-China trade relations.

China now accounts for seventeen percent of U.S. imports. This volume of imports is very significant to both countries. However, U.S. policy is resistant to simply allowing China to engage in trade with impunity. There are complaints that businesses that believe themselves to be aggrieved in some way can file that will impact U.S.-China trade. The future of the relationship is in part in the Trade Act of 1988 as amended and as enforced.

See also World Trade Organization (WTO); Trade Act of 1974.

REFERENCES: Gary Clyde Hufbauer and Yee Wong, *China Bashing, Policy Brief PB04–5* (Washington, DC, Institute for International Economics, 2004); *United States Code*, Title 19-Customs Duties, Chapter 12, Trade Act of 1974, Section 301, et al; *United States Code*, Title 19-Customs Duties, Chapter 19, Telecommunications Trade, Section 3101, et al.

Jack Waskey

Trade Embargo

Embargo refers to the use of the coercive economic measures or economic sanction against the People's Republic China (PRC) by the United States in pursuit of foreign-policy objectives during the Cold War. It lasted from the late 1940s to the early 1970s.

The embargo policy was initiated by the administration of President Harry S. Truman in 1949. Frustrated with Communist victory in China and loss of U.S. influence in mainland Asia, Washington imposed limited restrictions on investment in and trade with the newly founded PRC to prevent the possible Sino-Soviet alliance and pacify domestic criticism of the administration's loss of China. With the PRC military intervention in the Korean conflict, Washington implemented total embargo against China to punish China and undermine China's fighting capability. In 1952, through the newly established China Committee (CHINCOM) within the Coordinating Committee (COCOM) of the Consultative Group in Paris, Washington formulated the "China differential," a more extensive embargo list against the PRC than against the Soviet Union. After the Korean War ended, President Dwight D. Eisenhower continued Truman's embargo policy against China to foil the Beijing-Moscow cooperation and deter China's military operations in the Taiwan Strait and support to the North Vietnam. Nevertheless, lured by the China market, such major U.S. allies as Great Britain, France, Canada, and Japan called for relaxing China trade control. Pressured, the Eisenhower administration accepted the allies' decision to abolish the "China differential" in 1958 but insisted on its unilateral China embargo. After taking office, President John F. Kennedy considered a limited relaxation of China embargo to provide humanitarian relief for China's famine and ease Chinese hostility to the Americans. However, China's belligerent stand — particularly its military conflicts with India, its continued aid to the North Vietnamese, and its renewed threat to Taiwan — made the Kennedy administration hold the China embargo weapon. After the Kennedy administration, Washington's unilateral China embargo lasted till Nixon's visit to Beijing in 1972.

The U.S. embargo against the PRC represented an alternative to military operation or non-action. On the one hand, while inflicting bitter blow on China's economy, the U.S. multinational embargo was not very successful in directly stopping China's military aggressions and undermining the Chinese Communist regime but aroused China's greater hostility against America. On the other hand, however, the indirect influence of the embargo was far-reaching. To meet the challenge of the U.S. sanctions and overcome the difficulties caused by the embargo, Beijing was forced to centralize its political and economic systems and launch a series of radical political and economic campaigns, like the Great Leap Forward movement, which plunged China into disaster. More important, the embargo played an important role in the Sino-Soviet split in the early 1960s. Although the collapse of Beijing-Moscow alliance could be attributed to multiple reasons, the economic factor should be emphasized. It was the U.S. over-one-decade embargo that led to Beijing's over-dependence on Moscow's support and assistance. The continued over-dependence not only caused China's growing discontent with the Soviet dominance in the alliance relationship but also made the Soviets more and more unable to bear the China burden. Thus, the collapse of the Sino-Soviet alliance finally became inevitable. In this way, the embargo proved to be successful in the long run.

See also Cold War; China Committee (CHINCOM).

REFERENCES: Simei Qin, "The Eisenhower Administration and Changes in Western Embargo Policy against China, 1954–1958," in Warren Cohen and Akira Iriye (eds.), *The Great Powers in East Asia, 1953–1960* (New York, 1990); Sayuri Shimizu, *Creating People of Plenty: United States and Japan's Economic Alternatives, 1950–1960* (Kent, OH, 2001); Shu Guang Zhang, *Economic Cold War: America's Embargo against China and the Sino-Soviet Alliance, 1949–1963* (Stanford, CA, 2001).

Tao Peng

Transcontinental Railroad

In 1862, two U.S. companies, the Union Pacific and the Central Pacific undertook the most ambitious project that the nation had ever imagined: building a transcontinental railroad. The challenge was great: 1,800 miles across tough terrains and rugged granite walls of the Sierra Nevada and Rocky Mountains. The Union Pacific was in charge of laying track westward from Omaha, Nebraska while the Central Pacific took the section eastward from Sacramento, California. The construction was quite slow in the first two years because the job performance of the native workers was very poor and the two companies faced a severe labor shortage.

In February, 1865, Charles Crocker, chief of construction of the Central Pacific persuaded his company to Great Wall of China and invented gunpowder could no doubt build a railroad. In 1852, there were about 25,000 Chinese immigrants in California who escaped from poverty and famines in southeastern coast of China. In California, the immigrants helped each other through support networks, based on place of origin and kinship. They worked in agriculture, mines, and domestic services. And now they found that there came a new job opportunity. Employed by the railroad companies, the Chinese worked under grueling and treacherous conditions for less money than their white counterparts. The Chinese immigrant workers hired by Central Pacific got $26-$35 a month for a 12-hour day, 6-day work week without food and shelter, while the white workers received $35 a month and were provided with food and shelter. Despite the discriminatory treatment, the Chinese worked very hard. They were described as "quiet, peaceable, patient, industrious, and economical." By 1867, 12,000 of the 13,500 Chinese immigrants. The building of the railroad was difficult and dangerous. Accidents, avalanches, and explosions were numerous. Chinese immigrant workers among other construction jobs took the most dangerous task of hammering at the rocks on the cliffs and inserting dynamite. One out of ten Chinese workers died during the project. At the end of the arduous task, the Chinese were recognized with the honoring of laying the last rail. Reports from the National Park Service recorded the moment, "When the railroad was completed on May 10, 1869, an eight man Chinese crew was selected to place the last section of rail, a symbol to honor the dedication and hard work of these laborers. A few of the speakers mentioned the invaluable contributions of the Chinese...."

Despite their hard work and contributions, Chinese immigrants became victims of the discriminatory legal system and racial prejudice and violence in the United States. They were forbidden to appear as witnesses in court. They did not have the rights to vote or become naturalized citizens. Their children had to study in segregated schools. And as foreign nationals, they had to pay special taxes. After the completion of the Transcontinental Railroad, the situation for the Chinese became worse. The racial discrimination reached a crescendo in the form of the Chinese Exclusion Act of 1882, which suspended Chinese immigration for ten years.

See also Chinese Americans; Chinatowns; Chinese Exclusion Act of 1882.

REFERENCES: Stephen E. Ambrose, *Nothing Like It in the World: The Men Who Built the Transcontinental Railroad, 1863–1869* (New York, 2000); John Debo Galloway, *The First Transcontinental Railroad: Central Pacific, Union Pacific* (New York, 1950).

Yuwu Song

Treaty of Nanjing (1842)

The Treaty of Nanjing officially ended the First Opium War (1839–1842). The war between the British and the Chinese started in 1839 when the Chinese tried to stop the smuggling of opium into the country, while the British wanted free trade and diplomatic representation with China. After an earlier attempt at ending the war in 1841 failed, the Manchu official Qiying and the British plenipotentiary Sir Henry Pottinger negotiated the agreement. They signed the treaty for their respective countries on August 29, 1842, aboard a British warship anchored in the Yangzi River. The Chinese emperor approved it in September, followed by Queen Victoria in December 1842. This dictated treaty opened China to the outside world.

The treaty consisted of thirteen articles. Aside from ending the war, the British meant for the treaty to be punitive. Its terms included forcing China to pay an indemnity of 21 million Mexican silver dollars (for the cost of the war, confiscated British opium, and debts owed to British merchants), abolishing the Guangzhou System or Cohongs that had the monopoly on foreign trade, opening five ports to British trade (Guangzhou, Xiamen, Fuzhou, Ningbo, and Shanghai), allowing British officials to be stationed at these ports, granting these officials the right to communicate with Chinese officials on an equal footing, establishing low import and export tariffs, and ceding the island of Hong Kong to the British. Despite opium being the cause of the war, its status was not raised in the discussions. The Treaty of the Bogue, signed on October 8, 1843, also by Pottinger and Qiying, supplemented the Nanjing settlement. Among its provisions, it granted the British the right of extraterritoriality where British subjects in China were exempt from Chinese law and would be tried by British consuls under British law. It also gave Britain most-favored-nation status where China would automatically extend to it any privilege granted to other nations in the future. With the British success, other countries including the United States began pressuring China for similar treaties resulting in the American Treaty of Wangxia in 1844.

The Treaties of Nanjing and the Bogue would be followed by other forced agreements such as the Treaties of Tianjin in 1858 and the Conventions of 1860. It marks the beginning of the so-called "unequal treaties," due to their absence of reciprocity, where the Chinese lost much of their sovereignty to foreigners until the 1940s.

See also Treaty System; Treaty Ports; Treaty of Tianjin (1858).

REFERENCES: Harry G. Gelber, *Opium, Soldiers and Evangelicals: England's 1840–42 War with China and its Aftermath* (New York, 2004); Ssu-yu Teng, *Chang Hsi and the Treaty of Nanking, 1842* (Chicago, IL, 1944).

Greg Ference

Treaty of Nanking (1842) *see* Treaty of Nanjing (1842)

Treaty of Tianjin (1858)

Treaty of Tianjin (1858) is also called the Reed Treaty. In 1854 the American, British, and French wanted their earlier treaties revised to secure greater economic opportunities in China. The American 1844 Treaty of Wangxia granted the United States the right to renegotiate this agreement in twelve years. Due to the most-favored-nation clauses in the American, French and British treaties, it meant that the twelve years would apply to the British Treaty of Nanjing from 1842. The Chinese refused, and the three Western powers renewed their demands in 1856. The Chinese vacillated while focusing their energy into waging an intense struggle against the Taiping rebels in central China. Following two minor incidents later that year, Britain and France sent forces to China in 1857 in the Arrow War or Second Opium War, during which the United States remained neutral.

To try to stop the allies and put its resources against the Taipings, the Chinese signed four treaties, all of the same name, in 1858, with Russia (June 13), the United States (June 18), Great Britain (June 26), and France (June 27) in Tianjin. The four treaties were of different lengths, with the American having thirty articles. The American minister plenipotentiary William B. Reed, a politician and professor, received instructions to work with the French and the British, while assuring the Chinese that the United States continued to have no territorial demands and would not interfere in China's domestic affairs. He negotiated the American treaty with the Chinese officials Guilang, a Manchu, and Hua Shana, a Mongol. As compared to the British and French negotiations, the American discussions went well since the Chinese felt the American demands moderate. The American treaty was not a revision of the 1844 agreement, but guaranteed the concessions received in it. Among its provisions, it permitted official correspondence with the imperial government, a yearly visit by the American minister to Beijing, two more treaty ports open to American trade, the establishment of a fair tariff, and the toleration and protection of Protestantism, Christians and their converts.

Due to the most-favored-nation clause in all Western treaties, the American version meant little. As a result, the treaties opened eleven new treaty ports to trade, enabled foreigners to travel within China, standardized weights and measures, set the tariff at 2.5 percent, allowed diplomatic representation at Beijing, guaranteed Christian missionaries freedom of movement, toleration of the Christian religion, missionaries and converts, and legalized the sale and trade of opium.

For the British and the French, their treaties were supposed to end the Arrow War or Second Opium War, while the Russians wanted be perceived as the mediator between the belligerents and to ensure it would receive the same gains as Britain and France. Since the Chinese hesitated to put the treaties into effect, the war resumed and lasted until 1860.

The American Treaty of Tianjin was revised with eight articles in 1868 by the Burlingame Treaty. It reaffirmed Chinese sovereignty, pledged non-intervention by America in Chinese internal affairs, gave the Chinese the right to freely immigrate to the United States and guaranteed the Chinese in America civil rights. Bitter opposition to the latter two provisions resulted in an 1880 revision that could suspend but not prohibit Chinese immigration followed by the Chinese Exclusion Act of 1882.

See also Treaty System; Treaty Ports.

REFERENCES: Michael H. Hunt, *The Making of a Special Relationship: The United States and China to 1914* (New York, 1983); Te-kong Tong, *United States Diplomacy in China, 1844–60* (Seattle, WA, 1964).

Greg Ference

Treaty of Tientsin (1858) *see* Treaty of Tianjin (1858)

Treaty of Versailles (1919)

When the First World War broke out in August 1914, China proclaimed its neutrality. Japan, on the other hand, quickly joined the Allied powers of France, Great Britain and Russia, and seized the German concessions in Shandong province including the city of Qingdao that Germany acquired by the late 1890s. By the end of 1914, Japan had taken control of most of the province.

To retain permanent possession of the area, the Japanese presented the Twenty-One Demands to Yuan Shikai's government in Beijing in 1915,

made secret agreements with the warlord government in Beijing in 1918, and entered into a number of treaties with the Allied countries including the United States in 1917. To counter the Japanese, and to win Allied support for its claims to the former German lands and Japanese-controlled Shandong, the Chinese entered the war on August 14, 1917.

The Japanese with their treaties, and the Chinese, as an allied state, both came to the peace conference in Paris in 1919 prepared to get Shandong. Chinese diplomat Gu Weijun led China's Chinese delegation consisting of representatives of both the Guangzhou and Beijing governments to present unity during the negotiations. They believed their cause to be supported by the wartime idealistic rhetoric of American President Woodrow Wilson promoting democracy and self-determination. When the Japanese made their various agreements known, it caught the Chinese delegation off guard. The great power leaders at the Paris conference, minus President Wilson, backed Japan due to their earlier commitments. The president, though isolated, initially supported the Chinese position. However, the Japanese made it clear to him that they would champion the issue of racial equality and would leave the peace conference if their demands were not met. Wilson knew he could not allow both, and, following the advice of his own advisors and fellow Allied leaders, the President abandoned China. He believed it would be best to keep Japan in the negotiations and have it join the League of Nations and to back China's claims later. In late April 1919, the conference awarded Shandong to the Japanese. When this news reached Beijing, the Chinese felt deserted by the Americans, and lost any faith in Wilsonian beliefs. The news also caused mass student demonstrations against the treaty and the Japanese starting on May 4, in Beijing, which quickly spread to other areas of China, which became known as the May Fourth Movement or Incident.

The Chinese sent thousands of letters and telegrams to Paris urging their delegates to repudiate the treaty. Without any instructions from China, the delegates decided not to sign the treaty. In case some secret deal had been made, Chinese expatriates in France blockaded the delegation's hotel in Paris to keep it from attending the signing of the treaty on June 28, 1919, much to the disappointment of President Wilson. Orders from the Beijing government instructing the delegates not to sign the treaty arrived the next day.

See also Paris Peace Conference (1919); May Fourth Movement (1919).

REFERENCES: Bruce Elleman, *Wilson and China: A*

Revised History of the Shandong Question (Armonk, NY, 2002); Immanuel C.Y. Hsu, *The Rise of Modern China* (New York, 2000); Wunsz King, *Woodrow Wilson, Wellington Koo and the China Question at the Paris Peace Conference* (Leyden, 1959).

Greg Ference

Treaty of Wang-hsia (1844) *see* Treaty of Wangxia (1844)

Treaty of Wangxia (1844)

Treaty of Wangxia is also called Cushing's Treaty. It was the first treaty between the United States and China. Following British success in negotiating the opening of China with the Treaty of Nanjing that ended the First Opium War (1839–1842), and the Treaty of the Bogue that supplemented the earlier treaty, the United States also wanted an economic foothold in China. Until then, the United States had informal trade relations with China. Talks by United States naval officer Lawrence Kearney, commander of theEast Indian Squadron, played an instrumental role in the pre-negotiations especially since he emphasized that America did not support the smuggling or trading of opium nor desired territorial concessions. China became more favorably inclined to work with the United States and hoped to play the Americans and British off each other.

In 1843, the United States sent Caleb Cushing, a lawyer and politician, to China to negotiate an agreement on much the same terms as the 1842 Treaty of Nanjing and the supplementary Treaty of the Bogue. Cushing, with the help of the medical doctor and missionary Peter Parker and several other missionaries, began talks in Macao with the Manchu official Qiying who had also negotiated the Treaty of Nanjing. The resulting treaty of thirty-four articles was signed on July 3, 1844, in the small village of Wangxia (Wang-hsia) near Macao. It was approved by the Chinese emperor in September and ratified unanimously by the United States Senate in January 1845. Like its British counterparts, the treaty opened five port cities for American trade (Guangzhou, Xiamen, Fuzhou, Ningbo, and Shanghai), allowed American officials to be stationed at these ports, established low import and export tariffs, and granted right of extraterritoriality where Americans in China were exempt from Chinese law and would be tried by American consuls using American law. It also gave the United States most-favored-nation status where China would automatically extend to it any privilege granted to other nations in the future.

Unlike the British treaties, Treaty of Wangxia permitted the building and maintaining American hospitals, churches and cemeteries in the five port cities; Americans to hire Chinese language teachers and to purchase Chinese books; American warships to anchor for brief periods of time at non-treaty ports; and, forbade the trading of opium. The agreement included a provision that the treaty would be reviewed for possible renegotiation in twelve years. However, since the most-favored-nation clause was included in all treaties China signed, it granted these same rights to other countries. As a result, in 1854, the Americans, British and French wanted a revision of the Treaty of Nanjing, and subsequently their own treaties, to permit greater economic opportunities in China. The Chinese refused leading to the Second Opium War or Arrow War by Britain and France while the United States remained neutral.

Since the treaty was not forced, the Americans started to view themselves as the defender and friend of China. This "special relationship" would continue into the 20th century. The Treaty of Wangxia allowed increased economic and cultural ties with China, and would be replaced by the Treaty of Tianjin in 1858 during the Second Opium War.

See also Treaty System; Treaty Ports.

REFERENCES: William J. Donahue, "The Caleb Cushing Mission," *Modern Asian Studies* (April 1982); Te-kong Tong, *United States Diplomacy in China, 1844–60* (Seattle, WA, 1964); Ping Chia Kuo, "Caleb Cushing and the Treaty of Wang-hsia, 1844," *Journal of Modern History* (March 1933).

Greg Ference

Treaty Ports

The Treaty of Nanjing (1842) that ended the First Opium War (1839–1842) became the first in a series of "unequal treaties." Such treaties required China to open an increasing number of "treaty ports" and cede or lease territory, including inland towns, which became bases for foreign operations in China. These treaty ports eased the entry of foreign ideas, religions, material culture, and individuals. As the centers of foreign power, they became symbols of imperialism and, as such, the target of Chinese nationalists. But, ironically, the ports also became places to organize and imagine political and cultural alternatives to the imperial order (e.g., the Chinese Communist Party was founded in Shanghai in 1921).

The five ports stipulated in the Treaty of Nanjing — Shanghai, Ningbo, Fuzhou, Xiamen, and Guangzhou — immediately became the most important channels for introducing Western goods, customs, and ideas. The opening of the treaty ports and other annexed or leased territories also attracted increasing numbers of foreigners, not only traders but also missionaries, teachers, adventurers, and opportunists, their families, as well as troops to protect the newly acquired legal rights of foreign nationals. The number of treaty ports grew to nearly fifty by the time of the Revolution of 1911; and a few years later there were almost one hundred, spanning the entire coast of China and lining its major rivers. As expanding and interactive showcases for a new, Western-inspired, industrial culture, the treaty ports provided a vision of what was in store for the rest of China. These living showcases gave Chinese firsthand knowledge not only of foreign technology and ideas but also of the West's consumer and visual culture through department stores, advertisements, museums, zoos, parks, restaurants, dance halls, and many other businesses and forms of entertainment originally designed to serve foreigners. Many of these institutions had Chinese managers, who soon established equivalents for elite Chinese patrons. Chinese of any social class merely had to enter the city to experience aspects of this new culture. And enter they did, as urbanization accelerated in the late 19th and early 20th centuries. With or without new consumer goods and habits, a growing number of sojourners in these cities returned to their rural hometowns with stories of this urban-based culture. Likewise, new Chinese media, first established in the major treaty ports to avoid imperial censors, also extended awareness of this culture throughout China. In late 19th century Shanghai, for instance, an intellectual class emerged that made its living peddling words. These words and pictures reached Chinese through a quickly expanding mass media of newspapers and periodicals as well as through novels and books.

Britain and the United States finally abolished the last of the treaty ports in 1943, during the Second World War, partially in recognition of China as one of the "big four" Allied powers fighting Japan. The agreements were implemented at the war's end in 1945. But it took the chaos of the Chinese Civil War (1945–1949) and the early policies of the government of the People's Republic of China to finally expel Americans and other foreigners.

See also Treaty System.

References: Karl Gerth, *China Made: Consumer Culture and the Creation of the Nation* (Cambridge, MA, 2003); Albert Feuerwerker, *The Foreign Establishment in China in the Early Twentieth Century* (Ann Arbor, MI, 1976); Fei Chengkang, *Zhongguo zujie shi [A History of Chinese Concessions]* (Shanghai, 1991).

Karl Gerth

Treaty System

In the aftermath of the Napoleonic Wars, Western naval powers returned to China. With the demonstration of the Qing Dynasty's weakness with its defeat in the first Opium Wars in the early 1840s, these naval powers forced the so-called unequal treaty system on the hapless Manchu rulers of China. The treaty system featured the opening of Chinese ports to foreign trade, a 5% ad valorem tariff so that China could not protect infant industries against the competition of well-developed foreign manufacturers, extraterritoriality in criminal and civil matters, most favored nation so that any concession to one imperialist power soon accrued to every imperialist power, protection for western missionaries, the establishment of foreign "concessions"— really, independent enclaves controlled by foreign military, and very nearly the dividing of China into distinct territories, presaging, perhaps, the end of a unified Chinese empire.

The treaty system replaced the system of tributary relations that had lasted for centuries. To Chinese leaders, China was the center of the universe, symbolized by its name, Zhongguo or Middle Kingdom. Representatives of surrounding lands would come on an approved schedule to show their recognition of China's greatness. Where diplomacy assumes that all nations are equal, tributary relations necessarily assumes that in each relationship one country is superior and the other is inferior. In return for recognition of China's greatness, the visiting delegations received great gifts and an audience with the Emperor. The audience entailed a detailed protocol, but the gifts could make the visit financially profitable and merchants frequently sought to serve as representatives of their home countries.

When the modern West arrived after the end of the Napoleonic conflicts, foreign representatives sought diplomacy and met with a Qing Dynasty insistence on tributary relations. They would no longer accept the century-long Guangzhou System of Trade, which confined seafaring nations to the port of Guangzhou, Guangdong Province along the southeast China coast far from the capital in Beijing. The first Anglo-Chinese Opium War began a century of foreign dominance and imposition of the worst of diplomatic relations, the treaty system on China.

Great Britain imposed the treaty system on China, and was the first to benefit from its provisions. The Treaty of Nanjing, ending the brief war included opening of Chinese ports, extraterritoriality in criminal cases, most favored nation status, and an indemnity China had to pay for Great Britain. Other nations followed Britain's lead. The Second Opium War led to additional Chinese concessions, including ceding control over China's tariff to foreigners, especially the Chinese Maritime Customs Service and Sir Robert Hart. Britain achieved a kind of informal empire over China. In the 1850s, Russia began showing interest in Manchuria, as Britain moved along the Yangzi River, and later France began moving into southern China from Vietnam. By the 1890s, the nature of relations between the imperialist powers and China was changing, from informal to more formal empire. Previously, the foreign powers seemed content with rights to trade and to proselytize religion in distinct regions of China, and to accept indemnity payments from China for extracting these rights from China. That began to change as Russia forced the Chinese Eastern Railway Company on China to control Manchuria, as Germany seized concessions in Shandong, as Japan began to look at Fujian and Zhejiang provinces, as France moved into Yunnan, and as Britain moved from informal to more formal empire. By 1900, the process had moved so far from its beginnings, that the United States feared other powers would carve China into colonies and American merchants would be shut out of the China trade. The result was Secretary of State John Hay's call for an Open Door for trade, so that American merchants could compete with foreign merchants, a proclamation that most of the imperialist nations chose to ignore.

Thus, the treaty system in its largest sense would continue until the Second World War when the allies began returning their rights wrested a century before to keep Free China in the war against Japan.

See also Treaty Ports; Treaty of Nanjing (1842); Open Door Policy.

REFERENCES: Masataka Banno, *China and the West, 1858–1861: The Origins of the Tsungli Yamen* (Cambridge, MA, 1964); Jack Beeching, *The Chinese Opium Wars* (New York, 1977); John King Fairbank, *Trade and Diplomacy on the China Coast: The Opening of the Treaty Ports, 1842–1854* (Cambridge, MA, 1953, 1969); En-sai Tai, *Treaty Ports in China: A Study in Diplomacy* (Arlington, VA, 1976); J.Y. Wong, *Deadly Dreams: Opium, Imperialism, and the Arrow War in China* (New York, 1998).

Charles M. Dobbs

Treaty Tariff

In the aftermath of the First Opium War in the 1840s, China signed the Treaty of Nanjing and the supplemental Treaty of the Bogue with Great Britain. This was the first of a series of unequal treaties, first with Great Britain and later with the various imperial powers seeking to take advantage of the declining Qing Dynasty and a weakened China.

These treaties had a series of provisions that combined threatened China's sovereignty and paved the way for increasing foreign encroachments into all aspects of Chinese polity, economy, and society. Among the treaty conditions, China and Great Britain agreed to a "fair and reasonable" tariff on both exports and imports. In signing the treaty, Chinese government officials could neither guess nor predict the long-term, continuing negative impact of this ad valorem tariff whose rates varied from 4 to 13% and averaged about 5%. The two signatories agreed that they could not change the duties, the 5% tariff, except by mutual consent. Thus, for the ensuing 88 years, that is, until 1930, China was unable to fix its tariffs of its own free will. The key taxes, that is, the major sources of government income during the long Qing Dynasty era, were the salt *gabelle* or tax and the land tax, neither of which was particular onerous. This reflected both the low cost of government, including the famous *hsien* magistrate-based system and the reality that there were a great many irregular taxes, which provided much needed tax income. It seemed that taxes on imports and exports were not that important and did not appear that great a concession to the hated foreigners. In 1842, the Chinese did not realize the importance of their concession in the treaty. They did not foresee the industrial revolution, the need to protect infant industries, the huge influx of competing, and initially lower cost and better made foreign manufactures, the use of the tariff as a tool in trade negotiations or even a protective tariff as a means to finance industrialization or to protect infant industries.

There were two great outcomes. First, increasingly, the Qing Dynasty and the central government would lose control over the Chinese economy, especially in the coastal cities and along the great rivers, a situation that was further exacerbated by the foreign establishment of industries in China and by imperialist encroachments on Chinese territorial sovereignty. Second, to help collect the ad valorem tariff and to ensure its appropriate expenditure which mostly was paying of indemnity to the imperialist powers, the Chinese conceded the establishment of the Chinese Maritime Customs Agency by Great Britain, overseen by a succession of British administrators, most famously Sir Robert Hart with his famous "standing desk." The Shimonoseki Treaty with Japan in 1895 added the right for foreigners to develop manufactures in treaty port areas, thereby making it possible to use cheap Chinese labor and avoid even the modest tariffs that were imposed on outside products.

Finally, in 1930, as the Great Depression began its terrible havoc across the world, the imperialist powers returned tariff autonomy to China.

See also Treaty Ports; Treaty System; Treaty of Nanjing (1842).

REFERENCES: John K. Fairbank, *Trade and Diplomacy on the China Coast: The Opening of the Treaty Ports* (Cambridge, MA, 1953); Sheo-Ming Keh, *The Tariff System of China, 1843–1940* (Bloomington, IN, 1941); Rhoads Murphey, *The Treaty Ports and China's Modernization: What Went Wrong* (Ann Arbor, MI, 1970); En-Sai Tai, *Treaty Ports in China: A Study in Diplomacy* (Arlington, VA, 1976); Stanley Fowler Wright, *China's Struggle for Tariff Autonomy, 1843–1938* (Shanghai, 1938).

Charles M. Dobbs

Triangular Diplomacy *see* Strategic Triangle of U.S.-Soviet-China Relations

Truman Doctrine

As East-West tensions increased in the immediate post-World War II years American and Soviet spheres of influence emerged. The withdrawal of the United Kingdom from the Indian subcontinent, Near East, and the Balkans in 1947 prompted the United States to redraft its national security and foreign policies, which resulted in the Truman Doctrine first articulated publicly by President Harry S. Truman before a joint-session of the U.S. Congress that March. Although the impending British withdrawal from the "northern tier" of the Mediterranean and Soviet ambitions in the oil-rich Near East were the president's principle concern in early 1947 the policy of containing Communism central to his congressional address would influence American foreign policy world-wide until the early 1970s.

At the core of Truman's policy was American assistance to peoples resisting the encroachment of Communism. The National Security Council would make "containment" the United States' guiding principle towards all Communist nations with its policy document *NSC-68* in early 1950. In Asia this would translate into an effort to contain the People's Republic of China (PRC), as well as the Soviet Union. From the late 1940s onward, thus, the Truman Doctrine would put the United States and PRC on a collision course until the Nixon administration reversed American policy in 1972.

The first test of American resolve in Asia came with the 1949 Communist victory in the Chinese Civil War. Not until the following year,

however, with the outbreak of hostilities on the Korean peninsula would U.S. military forces be engaged in containing Communism. Yielding to domestic political pressure, Truman sought to isolate the PRC despite early indications of a fissure in the Sino-Soviet monolith as the 1950s dawned. In his threat to bring nuclear force to bear on the Democratic People's Republic of Korea, and her erstwhile ally, so as to conclude armistice talks in Korea, President Dwight D. Eisenhower continued his predecessor's policy towards the PRC. With the adoption of the National Security Council's *NSC-162/2* in 1953 the Eisenhower administration would move away from the conventional force implications of the Truman Doctrine. Instead, under Eisenhower's national security policy, the "New Look," American monies, military material and advisors, and the nation's nuclear arsenal would be at the forefront of the U.S. effort to contain Communism.

Nonetheless, the United States remained committed to isolating the PRC and diminishing Communist Chinese influence in Asia not only through its economic and military support of the Republic of China (Taiwan) but also through its regional alliance, the Southeast Asia Treaty Organization (SEATO). During the 1950s Taiwan received U.S. support during the Jinmen-Mazu crises of 1954–1955 and 1958. Further, the United States provided military aid to the Republic of Vietnam and other Southeast Asian nations, along with the Republic of the Philippines, in their efforts to defeat Communist insurgencies in a policy that continued the spirit of the Truman Doctrine.

See also Civil War (1945–1949); Taiwan Strait.

REFERENCES: Rosemary Foot, *The Practice of Power: U.S. Relations with China Since 1949* (Oxford, 1995); John Lewis Gaddis, *Strategies of Containment: A Critical Appraisal of Postwar American National Security Policy* (Oxford, 1982); June M. Grasso, *Truman's Two-China Policy* (Armonk, NY 1987); George C. Herring, Jr., *America's Longest War: The United States and Vietnam, 1950–1975* (Columbus, OH, 2001); Akira Iriye, *The Cold War in Asia: A Historical Introduction* (Englewood Cliffs, NJ, 1974); Ronald H. Spector, *Advice and Support: The Early Years of the U.S. Army in Vietnam, 1941–1960* (New York, 1985); Shu Guang Zhang, *Deterrence and Strategic Culture: Chinese American Confrontations, 1949–1958* (Ithaca, NY, 1992).

Paul D. Gelpi, Jr.

Truman, Harry S. (1884–1972)

Born in rural Missouri, elected to the U.S. Senate in 1934, and nominated Franklin D. Roosevelt's Vice President on the Democratic Party's winning ticket in 1944, Harry S. Truman became the nation's thirty-third President with Roosevelt's death in April 1945. Known more for his domestic concerns at the time, Truman inherited a presidency shaped by a series of foreign policy and military crises whose legacies were the use of the atomic bomb, the Marshall Plan, and the Truman Doctrine. Although his successful 1948 presidential campaign focused on his domestic agenda, twin crises in East Asia — the Communist victory in the Chinese Civil War and the Korean War — defined his last four years in office.

Early in his presidency, Truman relied upon many of Roosevelt's advisors and continued his predecessor's policies in Asia, especially U.S. support for Jiang Jieshi's Guomindang forces against Japan, as well as in their internecine fighting with the Chinese Communists. By early 1946, however, he had begun assembling his own cabinet and soon demonstrated a leadership style much removed from that of the patrician Roosevelt, especially with regards to the Jiang Jieshi government. As the Chinese Civil War drew to a close U.S. efforts to confront Communism were focused in Europe and the Truman administration mustered little support for the Guomindang. The withdrawal of the Guomindang to Taiwan and the establishment of the People's Republic of China, under the leadership of Mao Zedong, on the mainland, therefore, opened Truman to the domestic political charge that he had allowed China to "fall" to Communism. Always a staunch anti-Communist Truman had defined the conflict with the Soviet Union and global Communism, the Cold War, in stark ideological terms that resonated with his fellow Americans. Yet he maintained a cautious ambiguity with regards to events in China, a reflection of his administration's view that the principal threat to world security was the Soviet Union. After the establishment of the Republic of China on Taiwan, nevertheless, he initiated a two-China policy that would be a hallmark of Sino-American relations into the 21st century. His treatment of Sino-Soviet Communism as a monolithic threat and policy of isolation towards the People's Republic of China, moreover, set the parameters of U.S. national security policy until 1972.

Concerns similar to those that governed his approach to the Chinese Civil War dominated Truman's approach to events in Korea following World War II. The U.S. policy of containment, as articulated by the Truman Doctrine and NSC-68, did not consider Korea an area of national interest and U.S. military forces were withdrawn after the establishment of the non-Communist Republic of Korea under Syngman Rhee. Yet the invasion of the Republic of Korea by the North Korean Peoples' Army (NKPA) in June 1950 fundamentally altered U.S. foreign relations and military affairs in Asia into the 21st century. Throughout the Korean War, Truman sought to keep the conflict from expanding into a war with the PRC. When denied permission by Truman to risk war with China, General Douglas MacArthur, commander of UN/U.S. forces in Korea tried to bypass the President by writing the Speaker of the House of Representatives, thinking he could obtain Congressional support for his mission. Truman removed MacArthur from his command for unauthorized policy statements. The President also rejected all suggestions by his military commanders to bring Taiwan into the conflict. In doing so, he reaffirmed a two-China policy for the United States.

See also Cold War; Civil War (1945–1949); Marshall Mission; Korean War.

REFERENCES: Robert H. Ferrell, *Harry S. Truman: A Life* (Columbia, MO, 1994); Rosemary Foot, *The Practice of Power: U.S. Relations with China Since 1949* (Oxford, 1995); John Lewis Gaddis, *Strategies of Containment: A Critical Appraisal of Postwar American National Security Policy* (Oxford, 1982); June M. Grasso, *Truman's Two-China Policy* (Armonk, NY 1987); Alonzo L. Hamby, *Man of the People: A Life of Harry S. Truman* (New York, 1995); Akira Iriye, *The Cold War in Asia: A Historical Introduction* (Englewood Cliffs, NJ, 1974); David McCullough, *Truman* (New York, 1992); and Harry S. Truman, *Memoirs* (Garden City, NY, 1955–1956); Shu Guang Zhang, *Deterrence and Strategic Culture: Chinese American Confrontations, 1949–1958* (Ithaca, NY, 1992).

Paul D. Gelpi, Jr.

Tsungli Yamen *see* **Zongli Yamen**

Tuchman, Barbara (1912–1989)

An award-winning and popular American historian, Tuchman's formal education may have ended with a BA from Radcliffe College (1933), but her skills as a researcher who specialized in war writing won her a Pulitzer Prize in 1963 for the *Guns of August* and 1972 for *Stilwell and the American Experience in China, 1911–1945*. She first came to public attention for *The Zimmerman Telegram*, which places great responsibility for World War I on the heads of the European aristocracy. Tuchman went on to win other awards for such works as the controversial *A Distant Mirror: The Calamitous Fourteenth Century* and, in addition to historical works, wrote novels, essays and political texts.

Born in New York City in 1912, she married Lester R. Tuchman in 1940, raised three daughters and published 11 books, largely history, and many articles. Tuchman worked as a staff writer and foreign correspondent for *Nation* (1935–1938, including an assignment in Madrid), *The War* with Spain (1937), *New Statesman and Nation* (1939), and for the Office of War Information. She was a popular public speaker in the 1970s and 1980s, especially on topics of World War I and World War II. Her books were widely read even though they presented complicated political climates and convoluted governmental interactions. In general, she researched her subjects extensively but also was able to travel to some of the important sites of her later histories. Her narratives were praised for both their clarity and their basis in solid research, although they are sometimes criticized by more scholarly historians for this very accessibility associated with over-simplification.

She also became well-known for beginning to untangle the myriad accusations and counter-accusations about responsibility for America's failure to prevent Communism in China with her biographical work on Stilwell: *Stilwell and the American Experience in China, 1941–1945*. The book was based principally on material she gathered from reading Stilwell's extensive personal diaries at the invitation of his widow. Rather than concentrating on the war years of the 1930s and 1940s as the title suggests, she tells the story of this one man's progress from early youth to the position where he was the U.S. government's best choice to collaborate with the Chinese during World War II. She documents Stilwell's experiences in China from 1920–1923 where he learned the language and came to respect the common Chinese solider and through the intervening years before he was sent back in 1941. At this point, when it seemed that the success of the Western efforts to win the war in the Pacific hung on America's ability to negotiate military alliances with Chinese leader Generalissimo Jiang Jieshi's army, Stilwell was given the job. Then before he could finish, and in the face of Jiang's unwillingness to commit his forces to the war with Japan when he wanted them for the internal war with the Communists, Stilwell was recalled by President Franklin D. Roosevelt, almost three months after Jiang had requested it. His advice about Jiang and the corruption of the Guomindang was ignored, and he watched the progress of other generals from a post in the U.S.

From a perspective of 25 years in the future, Tuchman helps to recover Stilwell's reputation as a talented and knowledgeable military tactician from the recriminations of the 1950s over "American loss of China" to Communist rule. It is interesting to read personalized account in contrast with Chin-tung Liang, which rather articulates Stilwell's faults. Nevertheless, Tuchman's view of the situation has persisted in the Western imagination. As a result of the popularity of this work,

her thinking influenced the American public's view of foreign policy in Asia and she produced another popular but controversial work, *The March of Folly: From Troy to Vietnam (1985)*. She continued to lecture and write up until her death and her theses on the personal causalities for 20th century military mistakes are still taught, pondered and critiqued.

See also Stilwell, Joseph W. (1883–1946).

REFERENCES: Liang, Chin-tung, *General Stilwell in China, 1942–1944: The Full Story* (Jamaica, NY, 1972); "Barbara Tuchman," *Contemporary Authors Online* (2004); Barbara Tuchman, *Practicing History: Selected Essays* (New York, 1981); Barbara Tuchman, *Stilwell and the American Experience in China: 1911–1945* (New York, 1971).

Janice M. Bogstad

Twenty-One Demands

The so-called "Twenty-One Demands" were submitted secretly to the Chinese government by Japan on January 18, 1915, as part of the latter's expansion in East Asia during World War I. Divided into five groups of an increasingly imperial nature, the demands pressed China to relinquish control of the German leasehold in Shandong Province and to extend railway and port privileges to the Japanese there; to acknowledge Japan's "special position" in Manchuria and Mongolia and consult Japan on administration of internal matters; to grant special mining rights to the Japanese-financed Hanyehping Company; to prevent further territorial cessions along the Chinese coast; and to grant Japanese in China special rights, and Japan control of certain administrative and industrial functions.

The demands were grounded in both Japan's ongoing attempts to win entry in the China market equal to the Western powers, and in the unusual circumstances of World War I. With the outbreak of war in August 1914, Japan capitalized on its 1902 alliance with Great Britain and captured Germany's holdings at Jiaozhou. Paul Reinsch, American minister to Beijing, had warned that further expansion was probable, and gleaned enough information from private conversations with Chinese officials to conclude that the demands gravely violated both Chinese sovereignty and the Open Door policy. Though Tokyo passed the demands off as "requests," Washington prepared to defend the Open Door. But because the Wilson administration divided over what constituted tangible American interests in Asia, its response to the crisis was ambivalent. State Department policymakers, including William Jennings Bryan and Robert Lansing, discussed appeasing Japan, particularly with regard to its position in Manchuria, in order to avoid war. But President

Woodrow Wilson refused to barter Chinese rights to improve relations with Tokyo. Writing from Beijing at the same time, Reinsch agreed, shrilly denouncing Japan's secret and coercive diplomacy and calling for U.S. intervention. Nevertheless while the first note, sent on March 13, invoked American treaty rights in Manchuria, Mongolia, and Shandong, it weakened that position by acknowledging that, "territorial contiguity creates special relations between Japan and these districts."

Wilson eventually realized that the protest was inadequate, but already hampered by a dispute with Germany over neutral rights in World War I, he could not risk a breach with Japan. Wilson could only express the hope to protect China, and protest Japanese actions through diplomatic channels. By early April, following reports from Reinsch that Japan had been spreading the rumor in China that Washington approved the demands and the State Department's conclusion that Tokyo had been deceiving the United States, Wilson hardened his stance. On April 14, Wilson instructed Bryan to tell the Japanese ambassador informally that Washington considered the demands an attack on Chinese sovereignty and on the Open Door; by month's end, Wilson considered issuing a circular to stir up international opinion. By then, however, Tokyo had submitted a new list of demands, changed extensively in light of American protests. Wilson and Bryan, nevertheless, dispatched a new note on May 5 challenging nearly every one of the revised demands, reneging on some points in the protest of March 13, and threatening to denounce Japan's actions publicly. Another note, which outraged Japanese leaders hoping to satisfy American objections, followed on May 11 reiterating American commitment to the Open Door and Chinese sovereignty.

Seemingly an American victory, the Twenty-One Demands crisis cast a long shadow across Sino-American relations. Not only did it help to destabilize the government of Yuan Shikai, it soured the Chinese toward the United States, and led to the 1917 Lansing-Ishii negotiations, which formally recognized the "special relationship" between Japan and China. At the Versailles Conference in 1919, Chinese diplomats hoped for the return of Shandong, but agreements with Tokyo in 1915 and 1918 accepting the demands complicated negotiations. Shandong was not returned until 1922.

See also Treaty of Versailles (1919); Paris Peace Conference (1919); Open Door Policy; May Fourth Movement (1919).

REFERENCES: Burton Beers, *Vain Endeavor: Robert Lansing's Attempts to End the American-Japanese Rivalry* (Durham, NC, 1962); Frederick R. Dickinson, *War and National Reinvention: Japan in the Great War, 1914–1919* (Cambridge, MA, 1999); Noel H. Pugach, *Paul S. Reinsch: Open Door Diplomat in Action* (Millwood, NY, 1979).

Eric A. Cheezum

Two China Policy

The "Two China Policy" is an informal position employed by the United States for the purpose of maintaining separate trade and other relations with both the People's Republic of China (PRC) on the mainland and the Republic of China (ROC) on the island of Taiwan. While most associate the policy with President Richard Nixon, the policy goes back as far as the President Harry S. Truman's administration.

In 1949, at the culmination of the Chinese Civil War between Jiang Jieshi's Nationalists (GMD) and Mao Zedong's Chinese Communist Party (CCP), the GMD established a "provisional" capital on Taiwan. The U.S. National Security Council drafted a policy paper on October 25, 1949 proposing recognition of governments headed by the CCP and the GMD, thereby beginning the U.S. position toward two Chinas. Eventually, Truman opted for a hands-off policy toward Taiwan because he considered its fate part of the civil war and its capture by CCP forces inevitable. The Korean War changed the American position to one of staunch defense of Taiwan. The United States, the UN, and most other countries then recognized the GMD government in Taiwan as the sole legitimate government for all of China. Protection of Taiwan became an important American goal at the time of the Korean War and later Taiwan was an essential Asian ally during the Cold War.

It was not until the early 1970s that much changed about the world's view of the two Chinas. The new two China policy was developed by the United States as a means of maintaining representation for Taiwan when the UN changed its official recognition of China to the PRC. The U.S. proposal was rejected, and in October 1971, the UN expelled Taiwan and gave China's seat to the PRC. Taiwan's official global diplomatic status began a long period of erosion. Only months later, President Nixon made his historic visit to China, meeting with Chinese Premier Zhou Enlai and signing the Shanghai Communique on February 27, 1972. That document formalized the U.S. two China policy by stating, "the United States acknowledges that all Chinese on either side of the Taiwan Strait maintain there is but one China and that Taiwan is a part of China ... (The

U.S.) reaffirms its interest in a peaceful settlement of the Taiwan question by the Chinese themselves." During President Jimmy Carter's administration, the United States recognized the PRC government as the sole legal government of China and established formal diplomatic relations on January 1, 1979. The PRC, in exchange, acknowledged, "the people of the United States will maintain cultural, commercial, and other unofficial relations with the people of Taiwan." More recent American Presidents had different opinions with regard to the two China policy. In 1998, while visiting Chinese President Jiang Zemin, President Clinton outlined a policy that became known as the "three nos." It consisted of: "1) no U.S. support for an independent Taiwan, 2) no support for a two China or one China, one Taiwan policy, and 3) no support for Taiwan's admittance into any international organization that requires statehood for membership." In March of 2001, the Bush administration dropped the "three nos" policy, saying they would adhere to a one China policy, but not articulating American aims any further.

The United States is not alone in its unofficial dealings with two different Chinas. Taiwan still maintains trade offices with more than 60 countries where it lacks official relations. Even the World Trade Organization accepted Taiwan (Chinese Taibei) as a member starting in 2002. Both the PRC and Taiwan maintain a commitment to possible future reunification, however, Taiwan's Democratic Progressive Party has much support for a declaration of independence from China. The United States continues its official recognition of one China, but it is dealing with two.

See also Cold War; Shanghai Communique; One China Policy; United Nations; Taiwan.

REFERENCES: Wang Jisi, "The Origins of America's 'Two China' Policy," in Harry Harding and Yuan Ming (eds.), *Sino-American Relations 1945–1955: A Joint Reassessment of a Critical Decade* (Wilmington, DE, 1989); Wesley M. Bagby, *America's International Relations Since World War I* (New York, 1999); Franz Schurmann and Orville Schell (eds.), *Communist China: Revolutionary Reconstruction and International Confrontation 1949 to Present* (New York, 1967).

Catherine Forslund

Tz'u-hsi (1835–1908) *see* Cixi (1835–1908)

United China Relief

In late 1930s China was fighting the Japanese invasion. The heroic spirits of the Chinese people deeply touched Americans on the other side of the Pacific. Some prominent Americans began to get involved in informing the American public of what was going on in the Far East and in raising funds for Chinese troops and civilians. Major figures included Dr. Claude Forkner, Roger Greene, Dr. Edward H. Hume, Dr. John Earl Baker, Dr. B. A. Garside, Eugene E. Barnett, Thomas W. Lamont, James G. Blaine, Henry R. Luce, Pearl S. Buck, John D. Rockefeller III, Artemus G. Gates, and Raymont Rubicam. In order to coordinate efforts and work more effectively with various relief agencies, they founded the United China Relief on February 7, 1941 as a membership corporation in the state and county of New York. The officers were James G. Blaine (Chairman), Eugene E. Barnett (Vice Chairman), Artemus G. Gates (Treasurer), and B.A. Garside (Secretary).

The basic objectives of United China Relief were 1) to provide funds for relief and rehabilitation in China; 2) to demonstrate to the Chinese people the friendship of the people of America; 3) to educate the people of America about the importance of what was happening in Asia; and 4) to clarify the confusion which existed in raising funds for China. Eventually United China Relief consisted of representatives from the American Bureau for Medical Aid to China (ABMAC), the China Emergency Relief Committee, the China Aid Council, the American Committee for Chinese War Orphans, the Church Committee for China Relief, China Famine Relief, the American Committee for Chinese Industrial Cooperatives (Indusco, Inc.), and the Associated Boards for Christian Colleges in China (ABCCC). These agencies decided to establish a corporation that would carry on a joint fundraising campaign. Except for China Famine Relief, all of them elected to become cooperating agencies of the newly formed United China Relief, Inc. The goal was to raise $5 million. Many fund raising activities were held across America. United China Relief sent speakers out on the road, who delivered speeches at lunches, dinners, women's clubs, and college commencements. Henry R. Luce, editor-in-chief of *Time* magazine, made a personal contribution of $60,000 to meet the initial expenses and wrote a personal letter to all *Time* subscribers for financial contributions to the cause. The letter was a huge success and brought $200,000 in total. By the end of 1941, and after Japan attacked Peal Harbor, it had successfully reached its five-million-dollar goal. As soon as United China Relief was established, its China headquarters was set up in China's wartime capital Chongqing by Dwight W. Edwards. He organized and coordinated a committee composed of prominent Chinese and

Americans: Madame Song Qingling, the widow of Dr. Sun Zhongshan, Madame Jiang, the wife of President Jiang Jieshi, Hu Shi, and Lin Yutang. In 1942 United China Relief conducted a very successful campaign, raising approximately $7 million for relief in China. In 1943 it conducted most of its fundraising under the supervision of the National War Fund. This arrangement was a great financial success. Of the money raised, $12,611,000 went to relief and rehabilitation, $12,586,000 to medicine and health, $4,700,000 to child welfare, and $6,184,000 to aid education. A total of $36,081,000 was brought in to help China during the war. After the war in 1945, United China Relief turned its focus from war relief to projects with more long-term benefits, such as education. The directors felt that the best way to help China was to help the Chinese help themselves. Based upon this new mission, the board decided in 1946 to change the name of the corporation to United Service to China, Inc.

See also World War II.

REFERENCE: B. A. Garside, *Within The Four Seas* (New York: 1985); T. Christopher Jespersen, *American Images of China, 1931–1949*, (Stanford, CA, 1996); Patricia Neils, *China Images in the Life and Times of Henry Luce* (Savage, MD, 1990); Christopher Thorne, *Allies of a Kind: The United States, Britain and the War against Japan, 1941–1945* (Oxford, 1978); United Service to China Archives, *http://infoshare1.princeton.edu/libraries /firestone/rbsc/finding_aids/usc.html*, Princeton University.

Fu Zhuo

United Service to China *see* United China Relief

United Nations

When the United Nations was created at the end of World War II, the United States was trying to build up the Republic of China (ROC) as the major power of East Asia, so that government was given one of the five permanent seats, and the veto power that went with a permanent seat, on the UN Security Council.

The Chinese Communist Party, victorious in the Chinese Civil War, declared the establishment of the People's Republic of China (PRC) in 1949. The defeated Guomindang government withdrew to Taiwan, where it asserted that it was still the government of China, and that Taibei was now the capital of China. The United States, very much the dominant power in the United Nations in that period, was able to persuade the UN to accept this theory. The representative of the Soviet Union to the United Nations walked out in protest on January 13, 1950. On June 25, 1950,

North Korean armed forces invaded South Korea. The absence of a Soviet representative in the United Nations had left U.S. predominance even greater than usual, and the Security Council quickly voted to condemn the North Korean action. U.S. General Douglas MacArthur became officially head of a United Nations Command. Most of his troops were American, but some were contributed by other UN member states. After MacArthur had defeated the North Korean forces in South Korea, he led the United Nations forces in a retaliatory conquest of North Korea. The PRC warned it would not permit American troops to conquer North Korea. When these warnings were ignored, PRC forces intervened massively in November 1950, and drove MacArthur's forces back to the South. Although there was a pretense that the Chinese troops in Korea were not the official forces of the PRC, only "volunteers," the PRC was de facto at war against the United Nations Command from 1950 to 1953. After the Korean War, discussion of possible admission of the PRC to the United Nations resumed. It was repeatedly proposed in the General Assembly that the PRC replace the ROC, as the representative of China in the United Nations. The number of votes for this resolution gradually increased from year to year, until in 1965 it came close to passing. Then the Chinese Great Proletarian Cultural Revolution intervened, severely disrupting all of China's international relations.

In 1970, as China emerged from this period of self-isolation, the motion for the PRC to replace the ROC in the United Nations once again came close to passing, and it soon became apparent that the resolution would pass the next time it came up for a vote. The United States decided to offer an alternate resolution, under which both the PRC and the ROC would be represented in the United Nations, as separate governments. But the ROC considered itself the government of China, not just of the area it actually ruled (Taiwan), and rejected the "two China" policy as a "gross insult." The United States hesitated so long, before proposing a "two China" resolution against both ROC and PRC opposition that this resolution never came up for a vote. It was the resolution substituting the PRC for the ROC as the representative of China that was passed by the General Assembly, 76 to 35, in 1971.

See also One China Policy; Two China Policy; Taiwan.

REFERENCES: Max Hastings, *The Korean War* (New York, 1987); Henry Kissinger, *White House Years* (Boston, MA, 1979).

Edwin Moise

Universal Declaration of Human Rights

The Universal Declaration of Human Rights is a United Nations document adopted by the General Assembly on December 10, 1948. This document defines a common standard of human rights that apply to all human beings regardless of their citizenship. By joining the UN, all member nations agree to the principles of the UN Charter, including the organization's pledge "to reaffirm faith in fundamental human rights, in the dignity and worth of the human person, in the equal rights of men and women and of nations large and small." The Universal Declaration is an attempt to define "fundamental human rights."

According to the Universal Declaration of Human Rights, all people are entitled to a basic set of human rights regardless of race, color, sex, language, religion, political or other opinion, national or social origin, property, birth or other status. Among the rights guaranteed by the convention are life, liberty and security of person; freedom from slavery or servitude; freedom from torture or cruel punishment; freedom from discrimination; the right to trial; and freedom from arbitrary arrest, detention or exile. Other rights included in the Declaration are freedom of thought, conscience and religion; freedom of opinion and expression; and freedom of peaceful assembly and association. Many nations, including the People's Republic of China (PRC), contend that each member of the United Nations is entitled to deal with its own internal affairs without interference from other nations. Other nations contend that as member states, nations are obligated to abide by the UN Charter and the Universal Declaration of Human Rights when dealing with their own people. Each year the United States Department of State issues a human rights report for the People's Republic of China. The American government has criticized the Chinese for violations of many of the rights defined in the Universal Declaration of Human Rights, including the Chinese government's treatment of dissidents, religious groups, detainees, restrictions on the press, harassment of individuals working for governmental change, and the suppression of ethnic minorities. The reports are quite detailed and very critical of the People's Republic. On the other hand, the Chinese government asserts that economic rights and social mobility are among of the most basic human rights. The PRC has defended its record contending that economic reforms have improved conditions for millions of its citizens. China continues to counter its critics by demonstrating that citizens have greater freedom to travel, have increased opportunities for education and employment, and enjoy a higher standard of living.

While there is a lack of agreement among UN members on their obligations regarding the rights outlined in the Universal Declaration of Human Rights, the document has become the internationally recognized definition of "human rights." It forms the basis for the dialog that continues about China's treatment of its citizens.

See also Human Rights in China (HRIC); Human Rights.

REFERENCES: United Nations, *Charter of the United Nations*, www.un.org; Johannes Morsink, *The Universal Declaration of Human Rights: Origins, Drafting, and Intent* (Philadelphia, PA, 1999); "Universal Declaration of Human Rights," *General Assembly Resolution 217 A (III), December 10, 1948*, www.un.org; U.S. State Department, *Country Reports on Human Rights Practices*, www.state.gov/g/drl/hr/c1470.htm.

Anne M. Platoff

U.S.-China Business Council (USCBC)

On the one hand, the USCBC is a conventional interest group, promoting expanded opportunities for American companies to trade with and invest in China. On the other hand, because of the rocky nature of state-to-state relations between the two countries, USCBC has perforce taken on an additional role as one among dozens of private associations seeking to improve understanding between the United States and China. In both respects, it follows in the footsteps of its early 20th century predecessor, the American Asiatic Association.

Originally called the National Council for U.S.-China Trade, USCBC was founded in 1973, in a context where U.S.-China relations were steadily thawing and commercial relations were on the immediate agenda. Since that time, its activities have fallen under four headings— giving advice to American businesses, legislative lobbying, publishing a bimonthly magazine, and (as previously noted) promoting improved overall bilateral relations. The Council is a membership organization, individual corporations constituting its members and their dues providing its financial base. Members bring specific business-related questions to the Council's staff. Through this process and various member programs, USCBC accumulates experience-based information, which it can share with members, as needed. In addition to providing such consultation, USCBC promotes a legislative agenda that is favorable to increased business interaction between the United States and China. In particular, it has long championed Permanent Normal Trade Relations (PNTR) status for China, an effort that achieved a milestone (but not final success) with

China's 1999 accession to the World Trade Organization (WTO).

Since 1974, the USCBC has published *China Business Review*. The magazine's mission is "to help foreign companies understand China's business climate and identify market opportunities in the People's Republic of China." While the magazine is sponsored by the Council, it operates with relative commercial and editorial independence, financing itself with advertising revenue and recruiting outside writers. Each issue has a special focus, usually a region or market sector. A special issue in 2000 celebrated China's entry into the WTO. The Council's President (former academic Robert Kapp, for the past several years) contributes a "Letter from the President" to each issue. In part, these letters constitute one avenue through which the Council seeks to influence the overall tenor of U.S.-China relations. In the September-October 2000 issue, for example, Kapp addressed the two presidential candidates, "China must not be an American afterthought," he wrote, "Maintaining a productive relationship with China should rank high on the American agenda…. The greatest danger we face in our relations with China is the danger of unfamiliarity…. [The President must shun those who] present China as a morality play…. [He] should understand and draw upon the skills and insights of people of Chinese descent in the United States." Kapp has made similar statements in Congressional testimony and at various public forums.

See also **Permanent Normal Trade Relations; World Trade Organization (WTO).**

REFERENCES: Joyce K. Kallgren, "Public Interest and Private Interest in Sino-American Exchanges: DeTocqueville's 'Associations' in Action," in *Educational Exchanges: Essays on the Sino-American Experience* (Berkeley, CA, 1987); "China and the WTO," *China Business Review* (January-February 2000).

Norty Wheeler

U.S.-China Economic and Security Review Commission

The U.S.-China Economic and Security Review Commission was established in October 2000 by the Floyd D. Spence National Defense Authorization Act. The main purpose of the Commission is to assess the national security implications and impact of the bilateral trade and economic relationship between China and America to report its conclusions to the Congress. It also provides recommendations to Congress for the legislative and administrative action. The Commission is supposed to focus its work and study on nine major areas: proliferation practices,

economic reforms and U.S. economic transfers, energy, U.S. capital markets, corporate reporting, regional economic and security impacts, US-China bilateral programs, WTO compliance, and media control by the Chinese government. Each year, the Commission submits an assessment report to Congress, which covers the main themes of that year. For example, the 2002 report focused on conflicting national perspectives, managing U.S.-China economic relations (trade and investment), China's WTO membership, conflicting goals accessing U.S. capital markets, proliferation of weapons of mass destruction, cross-strait and regional relations, China's military economy, technology transfer and military acquisitions, etc.

REFERENCES: U.S.-China Economic and Security Review Commission, *www.uscc.gov*.

Yuwu Song

U.S.-China Mutual Defense Treaty (1954)

U.S.-China Mutual Defense Treaty of 1954 is the treaty concluded between the United States and the Republic of China (ROC) on December 2, 1954, effective on March 3, 1955, and terminated on December 16, 1978 following the U.S. recognition of the People's Republic of China (PRC). Its major objective was to "declare publicly and formally" the unity of the United States and the ROC against any potential aggressor in the West Pacific area. For this purpose, each party would keep and develop its individual and collective capacity and act against "an armed attack in the West Pacific area" on the territories of either of the parties. The United States made a definite commitment to the defense of Taiwan and the Penghu (Pescadores).

The Nationalist government started its defense treaty request to Washington in January 1953, in hope of a U.S. protection against the PRC attack. But Washington remained cautious in this regard, because such a treaty might not only involve the United States in Nationalist large-scale conflicts with the PRC but also restrain the Nationalist limited military operations against the mainland. The first Taiwan Strait crisis put these worries aside. In October 1954, Washington decided to negotiate a mutual defense treaty in exchange of the Nationalist acceptance of the UN cease-fire plan in the Taiwan Strait. Taibei accepted this tradeoff.

However, the negotiations became difficult. The difference arose first on the treaty scope. Taibei insisted that the U.S. support for the Nationalist efforts to counterattack the mainland should be at lease implicit in the treaty text, while Washington had no intention to expand its commitment to the mainland area. As a compromise, both agreed to add, "such other territories as may be determined by mutual agreement" to treaty areas, thus extending the possible application of the treaty to the mainland areas upon the U.S. agreement. More controversial was the issue on the degree of U.S. control over the deployment of Nationalist troops. The American side feared that once the United States was obligated by the treaty to come to Taiwan's assistance, the Nationalists might provoke a conflict with the PRC by initiating large-scale offensive operations against the mainland or by stationing large concentrations on the offshore islands. To prevent this, Washington insisted on notification prior to the Nationalist operations against the mainland, a veto power over these operations, and even the right to approve the Nationalist deployment of troops to the offshore islands. Taibei tried to reject these demands but failed. Finally, they accepted all of the U.S. demands because they needed the treaty protection. In return, the United States accepted the Nationalist proposal to include these issues in separate notes instead of the treaty text and keep them secret in Taiwan.

The U.S.-China Mutual Defense Treaty of 1954 carried out Washington's Asian Cold War containment strategy. Through the treaty, Taiwan was officially included in U.S. security alliance system in the West Pacific area. As the basis of U.S. support for the ROC government in Taiwan until the late 1970s, the treaty guaranteed the survival of the Nationalists but also damped their hope to recover the mainland.

See also Cold War; Neutralization of Taiwan; De-neutralization of the Taiwan Strait; Taiwan; Seventh Fleet; Taiwan Relations Act of 1979.

REFERENCES: Robert Accinelli, *Crisis and Commitment: United States Policy Toward Taiwan, 1950–1955* (Chapel Hill, NC, 1996); John W. Garver, *The Sino-American Alliance: Nationalist China and American Cold War Strategy in Asia* (New York, 1997).

Tao Peng

U.S.-Republic of China Economic Council

U.S.-Republic of China Economic Council (name changed to The U.S.-Taiwan Business Council in 2001) provides its members with access to a network of companies involved in business between Taiwan and the United States, and serves as an effective spokesman in dealing with business, trade, and investment matters. Mainly a private business council, it also makes suggestions to the American government on how to deal with the government of Republic of China (ROC) on Taiwan regarding business, foreign and economic affairs.

It was established in 1976 by David Kennedy, then U.S. Ambassador to NATO and once the Secretary of Treasure for two years in the Nixon administration, and by Y.S. Sun, then Minister of Economic Affairs and later the Premier. The council rapidly took on an important role in developing trade and business relationships between the United States and the ROC. Kennedy was the first elected chairman and William Morell was the first elected President of this council. In 1977, the First Annual Conference was held in Chicago. Many former American cabinet ministers and big company CEOs were elected chairmanship for this council. Caspar Weinberger; Dan Tellep; William Clark and Frank C. Carlucci all served as chairman in the past, a post currently held by William S. Cohen, former defense minister in the Clinton administration. The Council is located in Arlington, VA since 1999. The Council's counterpart in Taiwan is Republic of China (ROC)-USA Economic Council, which later changed its name to Taiwan-U.S. Business Council. Past Chairmen included T.K. Chang, C.F. Koo. Dr. Jeffrey L.S. Koo, a nephew of C.F. Koo. Chungyu Wang is the present chairman. The Council consists of the President's Office, Finance and Administration, Corporate Affairs (membership/research/services), Biotechnology Sector, Defense and Aerospace Sector, Semiconductors Sector, and a Sector in charge of other fields. One of a major services provided by the Council is the Chairman's Circle. Started by Caspar Weinberger, then Chairman of the Council, this Circle intends to gather a group of CEOs of American companies with major interests in U.S.-Taiwan business and trade. Its function is to do consulting work for member CEOs and maintain direct access to the highest levels of Taiwan's government and business community as well as to U.S. government both in the Executive Branch and in Congress.

When the United States was trying to normalize its relationship with the People's Republic of China in the late 1970's, in order to maintain and foster the U.S.-ROC relations, the Council was heavily involved in all aspects of and instrumental to the drafting and passing of the Taiwan Relations Act in April 1979. It is recognized by the U.S. and Taiwan governments and business leaders as the most important private organization in the entire range of unofficial relations between the U.S. and Taiwan.

Since the Council was established, it assisted U.S. companies to gain big contracts from the ROC government and business sectors, for instance, the sales of 150 U.S. F-16 jet fighters in 1992 to Taiwan, a nuclear power plant by General Electric in 1999, and a $200 million Intermodal Rail System project by Frederic R. Harris 1999. Apart from that, with the help of this Council, Boeing sold many of its passenger and cargo planes to Taiwan's airlines. It was also instrumental to the removal of Taiwan from the Section 301 Priority Watch List regarding violation of intellectual property rights.

REFERENCE: Financial Times Information, *2002 Taiwan-U.S. Economic Cooperation Confab Set For Sept. 9–12* (Taibei, 2002); U.S. Taiwan Business Council, *www.us-taiwan.org*; China External Trade Development Council, *Expanding U.S. Sales to Republic of China* (Taibei, 1979).

Fu Zhou

Vance, Cyrus (1917–2002)

Cyrus Vance was born on March 27, 1917 in Clarksburg, West Virginia. He graduated from Yale University with his Bachelor's degree in 1939 and then to Yale Law School where he graduated with his law degree in 1942. He enlisted in the Navy and served during World War II. He left the military in 1946 and went to New York City to work in a Wall Street law firm.

In 1960 he first stepped into a government role. He became the general counsel for the Department of Defense. He served in that role for two years before becoming the Secretary of the Army in 1962. He was then raised to Deputy Secretary of Defense under the administration of President Lyndon B. Johnson. In this role he was at first vehement supporter of the war in Vietnam. But a few years later in, 1968, his views changed and he urged President Johnson to pull out of that country. This change of stance earned him a spot as deputy chief delegate to the Vietnam peace talks in Paris. Vance returned to his private law practice as Johnson's term came to an end in 1969. Vance reentered politics at the request of President Jimmy Carter in 1976 when he was asked to serve as Secretary of State. It would prove to be his most famous role. Vance was key in pushing for talks with the Soviet Union. He argued for continued and increasing economic ties along with detente and worked on the SALT (Strategic Arms Limitation Talks) II Treaty. Often he clashed with the National Security Advisor, Zbigniew Brzezinski, with whom he shared opposing views. His influence was evident in President Carter's decision to return to the Canal Zone to Panama and the Camp David Accords agreement between Israel and Egypt. After the Camp David Accords, Vance's influence on the President began to wane as Brzezinski's rose. Vance believed that it was necessary to develop full diplomatic relations with China, however, he wished to establish relations for their own sake. He

feared that a sudden American recognition of Beijing would infuriate Moscow. But President Carter shared the opinions with Brzezinski, intending to play the "China card" as a counterweight against the Soviets. Eventually, Vance's role in talks with the People's Republic of China became insignificant and he was relegated to the outer circle.

Cyrus Vance died on January 12, 2002 after a long struggle with Alzheimer's disease.

See also Detente; Brzezinski, Zbigniew (1928-); Cold War.

REFERENCES: REFERENCES: David McLellan, *Cyrus Vance* (Lanham, MD, 1985); Cyrus Vance, *Hard Choices: Critical Years in America's Foreign Policy* (New York, 1983); David Hamburg, *Preventing Deadly Conflict.* (Washington, DC, 1997).

Arthur Holst

Vietnam

The relationship between China and Vietnam was historically an uneasy one. China had ruled the Vietnamese for more than a thousand years, and Vietnamese culture showed much Chinese influence, but many of the heroes and heroines of Vietnamese tradition had become famous by fighting Chinese invaders.

The United States was largely responsible for the decision to have the Republic of China occupy northern Vietnam at the end of World War II, and accept the surrender of the Japanese forces there. Jiang Jieshi picked units of South China warlords only loosely allied with him for this task. The Chinese occupation forces seemed primarily interested in stripping the Vietnamese of as much gold and other valuables as possible. The People's Republic of China, established in 1949, gained control of the areas bordering on Vietnam at the beginning of 1950. The Chinese soon began to provide arms, supplies, and military training to the Viet Minh, a Vietnamese nationalist movement under Communist leadership. This greatly strengthened the Viet Minh, who up to this time had faced a stalemate, at a fairly low level of guerrilla warfare, fighting against France in the First Indochina War. It also strengthened Chinese influence on the Vietnamese Communist movement; this remained strong until 1956. Many Americans greatly exaggerated the degree of Chinese control, even suggesting that the Viet Minh were serving as stooges in a Chinese effort to conquer Southeast Asia. Beginning in 1950 the U.S. provided substantial aid to the French forces fighting in Indochina, and speculated about the possibility of a direct Chinese invasion of Indochina. At the Geneva Conference of 1954, China pressured the Viet Minh to be conciliatory. The conference resulted in a division of Vietnam between the North, ruled by the Democratic Republic of Vietnam (DRV), Communist, and the South, ruled by the Republic of Vietnam (RVN), anti-Communist. Chinese advice played a major role in the disastrous land reform campaign of 1953–1956 in North Vietnam. Realization by the Vietnamese of how badly they had been led astray permanently reduced the influence of Chinese advisers in Vietnam. Communist-led guerrilla struggles against the governments of Laos and South Vietnam began in 1959 and 1960. These eventually spread to become the Second Indochina War.

From 1962 to 1965, China was much more supportive of these struggles than the Soviet Union was; this inclined the DRV to the Chinese side in the Sino-Soviet dispute. American leaders again spoke of the Vietnamese serving as cat's-paws in a Chinese effort to conquer Southeast Asia, which was even less true in the 1960s than it had been in the early 1950s. When the United States began large-scale bombing of North Vietnam in 1965, China put a substantial military force into the northern part of North Vietnam, as a concrete warning that if the United States invaded the North, it would find itself fighting China. These troops were withdrawn in 1969, when the U.S. threat to North Vietnam had subsided. The United States, remembering the lesson of the Korean War, limited its actions to avoid provoking a conflict with China. China criticized the DRV for entering peace negotiations with the United States in 1968. One of President Richard Nixon's motives in beginning detente with China was a hope of leverage against the DRV. For the most part he was disappointed; the Chinese did not apply the kind of pressure on the DRV to be conciliatory in Paris that they had applied at the Geneva Conference of 1954.

The Paris Peace Agreement of January 1973 ended U.S. participation in combat in Vietnam, but the war there went on, with the United States and China supplying arms and munitions to the RVN and DRV respectively, until the Communist victory of 1975. North and South Vietnam were re-united as the Socialist Republic of Vietnam (SRV), which aligned itself with the Soviet Union and was soon on very bad terms with China. From the late 1970s through the 1980s, China and the United States were united in extreme hostility to the SRV. China even invaded northern Vietnam briefly, in 1979. These tensions eased in the 1990s.

See also First Indochina War; Second Indochina War.

REFERENCES: Qiang Zhai, *China and the Vietnam Wars, 1950–1975* (Chapel Hill, NC, 2000).

Edwin Moise

Vincent, John Carter (1900–1972)

John Carter Vincent was a Foreign Service Officer who became known as one of the "China Hands," American diplomats who were dismissed in the 1950s based on accusations that their statements and actions had contributed to the Communist takeover in China in 1949.

John Carter Vincent was born in Seneca, Kansas, in 1900. He grew up in the South, attended Clemson University and graduated from Mercer University. He took the Foreign Service examination. After passing, he hoped to be assigned to a European Consulate, but he wound up in Changsha, China in 1924 instead. In 1931, he married Elizabeth Slagle, an American visiting China, and continued to work at posts in China until 1936. He returned to China in 1941. Vincent believed that the Nationalist Chinese were not fully committed to an all-out campaign against Japan. He also was open to the idea that Chinese Communist troops could play a role in the defeat of Japan. His contacts in China included leftwing Communists, and he drew the wrath of General Patrick Hurley and General Albert Wedemeyer. These emissaries frequently clashed with career diplomats in China and accused them of undermining American policies in China.

After the Communist takeover in China in 1949, Vincent and the other China Hands came under political attacks and were portrayed as Communists or Communist supporters. Reviews by State Department Loyalty Boards led to the dismissal of Vincent in January 1953. Most of the evidence came from a notorious informer, Louis Budeng, and the fact that as a student at Mercer in the 1920s, Vincent helped lead a campus strike as a member of a group that jokingly labeled itself "the Bolsheviks." The verdict of history regarding John Carter Vincent is still uncertain. Nationalist supporters continue to assert that his actions contributed to the Communist victory in China. Several scholars who have examined his career have absolved him of any guilt in that regard. It is certain that the shabby procedures used to fire him left America in the dark as it tried to formulate China policy in the 1950s. Diplomats like George F. Kennan claimed that all Foreign Service recruiting was crippled by the spectacle of the fate of Vincent and the China Hands. The Kennedy administration quietly took a few steps to redress the injustice perpetuated on Vincent and other diplomats, but no official apology has ever been issued. A discussion among members of the Retired Foreign Service Officer Association in the 1990s noted that, sadly, no one any longer shows interest in this dark chapter of American history.

Throughout his life, Vincent dealt with hardship with a quiet grace and determination. He defended his reputation, but never asked for pity. His fate contributed to U.S.-China isolation that would not relent for more than 20 years.

See also China Hands.

REFERENCES: Gary May, *China Scapegoat* (New York, 1987); E.J. Kahn, *The China Hands* (New York, 1975); Paul Gordon Lauren, *The China Hands' Legacy* (New York, 1987).

Michael J. Polley

Voice of America (VOA)

VOA is a multimedia broadcast service funded by the United States government. It broadcasts internationally through short and mid-range radio, satellite television, and streaming Internet. According to its website, VOA currently broadcasts 1,000 hours of international news, informational, educational, and cultural programs about the United States weekly to 96 million people worldwide. It was first broadcast from New York City on February 24, 1942, shortly after American entry into World War II. That day, the following was broadcast in German into Nazi Germany: "Here speaks a voice from America. Every day at this time we will bring you news of the war. The news may be good. The news may be bad. We shall tell you the truth." The service was first organized under the Office of Wartime Information. With the inception of the U.S. Information Agency (USIA) in 1953, however, VOA was placed under that agency. More recently, it came under the control of the International Broadcasting Board, a part of the Broadcasting Board of Governors created by the International Broadcasting Act of 1994.

Of the 44 languages in which VOA broadcasts, three are used for the people living in China: Mandarin, Cantonese, and Tibetan. All languages broadcast over the radio are now also offered through streaming Internet broadcasts. Mandarin is also included in VOA's television programming which offers a more limited selection of languages. Despite the Chinese government's efforts to jam the VOA broadcasts over the years, VOA has become very popular with the Chinese, especially with the young people in China, who listen to VOA for the purpose of getting to know the outside world or simply learning the English language. In general, VOA has played an important role in providing information to and enlightening the Chinese when news is heavily censored and manipulated by the Communist government.

Since the first broadcast of Radio Free Asia (RFA) in 1996, the two services have shared many resources and divided time on the airwaves. Together, they ensure that one or the other service is always broadcasting in Mandarin into China. At certain points each day they act as competitors, with different programming at the same time. The two services have also competed for funding. The combination of services, however, provides more broadcasting options for Asian listeners. The VOA has not always been popular. Critics argue that control by the USIA brings into question its degree of independence and its possible use as a U.S. propaganda tool. VOA was chartered to provide "accurate, objective, and comprehensive" news to areas of the world that lack it. The Board of Governors, however, was mandated by Congress to assure that international U.S. broadcasters serve clear foreign policy purposes. Critics believe the goals of serving a foreign policy purpose and being objective are inconsistent; the fact that all editorials require advance State Department approval could indicate that serving foreign policy purposes trumps objectivity. Beyond that, the Smith-Mundt Act of 1948, which prohibited VOA from broadcasting domestically, raises the question of whether VOA broadcasts information the government did not want the U.S. public to hear. Finally, critics believe that the appointment of the VOA director by the President of the United States politicizes the post.

VOA counters concerns about objectivity in various ways. First, all facts presented must be double sourced. Second, even though all editorials must be approved by the State Department, only two or three minutes out of an hour of news are dedicated to editorials which are clearly differentiated from the hard news. Third, VOA addresses the apparent contradiction in mandates by "telling the whole story," thereby, allowing listeners to think for themselves after hearing both positive and negative news.

VOA operates in a fluid manner, shifting the focus of its attention to different areas of the world as events change. During the Cold War for example, it focused on those countries under Communist control or under threat of Communist takeover. But more recently, it has expanded coverage in the Arabic speaking world in coordination with the U.S. war on terror. Over the years, other broadcast services such as Radio Free Europe/Radio Liberty (RFE/RL) and RFA were also developed to provide additional coverage to regions considered in need of free airwaves.

See also Cold War; Radio Free Asia.

REFERENCES: Alan L. Heil, *Voice of America: A History* (New York, 2003); Voice of America, *www.voa.gov*; Michael Nelson, *War of the Black Heavens: The Battles of Western Broadcasting in the Cold War* (Syracuse, NY,

1997); Holly Cowan Shulman, *The Voice of America: Propaganda and Democracy, 1941–1945* (Madison, WI, 1990); Laurien Alexandre, *The Voice of America: From Detente to the Reagan Doctrine* (Norwood, NJ, 1988).

Catherine Forslund

Voice of the Martyrs

Voice of the Martyrs is a nondenominational agency based in Bartlesville, Oklahoma, whose mission is to support persecuted Christian believers worldwide. Founded by Richard and Sabina Wurmbrand, who were imprisoned and tortured for fourteen years under the Communist government in Romania, the Voice of the Martyrs prints a newsletter on the persecution of Christians in China and elsewhere, urging believers in the U.S. to pray for those who suffer under restrictive political regimes (defined as places in which the government either actively suppresses Christian activity or is unable to shield believers from assault and property destruction), as well as for their persecutors and captors. In China, Voice of the Martyrs distributes Bibles via hot-air balloon and seeks amnesty for Christians imprisoned for their faith, while supporting persecuted families with financial and medical assistance where possible. In China at the turn of the 21st century, official figures recorded twelve million Chinese Catholics and up to twenty million Protestants; however, there were believed to be from sixty-three to 100 million Catholics and Protestants in China at that time. Through the Religious Affairs Bureau controlled by the Chinese Communist Party, the government in Beijing authorizes five religions: Protestantism, Catholicism, Buddhism, Islam, and Taoism. Other religions are unregistered or banned (e.g., Falun Gong). In 1999, China developed a set of laws that would permit the government to deem membership in a religious organization to be a threat to national security. If convicted, believers may be punished by incarceration for life or by execution.

Voice of the Martyrs supports families of those persecuted for membership in unregistered churches. The organization provides basic medical and survival supplies, such as cooking pots and blankets, as well as services, such as financial support to the families of imprisoned and martyred believers and medical treatment after assault. Voice of the Martyrs also organizes drives in the United States to raise public awareness, to inspire fervent prayer, and to notify Chinese diplomats of American interest in religious freedom in China.

REFERENCES: *Roundtable Before the Congressional-Executive Commission on China, 107th Congress* (Washington, DC, March 25, 2002); Voice of the Martyrs, *Statement of Faith* (Bartlesville, OK, 2004).

Tara Robbins

Wallace, Henry A. (1888–1905)

While serving as President Franklin D. Roosevelt's Vice President (1941–1945), Henry A. Wallace traveled to China in May 1944 for the purpose of negotiating a united front between Nationalist leader Jiang Jieshi and the Chinese Communists against the Japanese. Wallace's mission was no more successful than that of other American emissaries in convincing Jiang to abandon his extreme anti-Communist position and reform the Guomindang, Nationalist China's ruling party.

Wallace was born on October 7, 1888 on a farm near Orient, Adair County, Iowa. Following graduation from Iowa State College in 1910, he served on the editorial staff of *Wallace's Farmer* with his father Henry C. Wallace, who served as Secretary of Agriculture under President Warren G. Harding. Following in the footsteps of his father, Wallace, who was noted for his experimentation with breeding high-yielding strains of corn, was appointed Secretary of Agriculture by Franklin Roosevelt. Wallace served as Secretary of Agriculture from 1933 to 1940, when he resigned after being nominated as Roosevelt's Vice President. While many in the Democratic Party perceived Wallace as a dreamer and overly liberal, he earned the trust of Roosevelt. The President was growing increasingly frustrated with reports from China regarding Jiang's failure to aggressively pursue the war against Japan. According to General Joseph Stilwell, Jiang's U.S. military adviser, the Chinese leader was more concerned with using American military equipment to fight the Chinese Communists than resisting the Japanese.

Accordingly, Roosevelt dispatched Wallace to China in order to address five objectives with Jiang: bring hyperinflation under control, become more active in the war with Japan, unify military operations with the Chinese Communists in northern China, allow American military observers into Communist-controlled territories, and resolve outstanding differences with the Soviet Union in order to provide a sound foundation for post war stability in Asia. Wallace, who was most unimpressed with the poor status of Chinese peasant farmers under the domination of wealthy landlords, found it difficult to negotiate with the stubborn Jiang. The only concession, which the Vice President was able to wring from the Chinese leader, was a promise that military observers from the United States would be allowed into Communist-controlled regions. In exchange, Wallace agreed to request that Roosevelt send a person representative to Chunking as Jiang was frustrated in his dealings with Stilwell and U.S. Ambassador Clarence Gauss. After his talks with Jiang, Wallace spent three days as the houseguest of General Claire Chennault, a strong supporter of the Chinese leader. Chennault convinced the Vice President that Stilwell's constant criticism of Jiang was undermining the war effort in China. Wallace, who was hardly an expert on Chinese affairs, cabled Roosevelt urging that the President replace Stilwell. Wallace's mission to China was a failure, and he found Jiang reluctant to engage in the agrarian reform needed to raise the standard of living for the Chinese masses. Wallace enjoyed little more success with American politicians, as Roosevelt reluctantly agreed to Wallace's removal from the Democratic ticket in favor of Missouri Senator Harry Truman for the 1944 Presidential contest.

A bitter Wallace was appointed Secretary of Commerce, where he served from March 1945 to September 1946, until he was fired by President Truman for criticizing the administration's hard line stance on the Soviet Union. In 1948, Wallace challenged Truman for the Presidency, serving as the candidate of the Progressive Party. Wallace was accused of receiving the support of the American Communist Party, and his 1944 mission to China was offered as evidence of his Communist sympathies. Disgusted with what would become known as McCarthyism, Wallace retreated into private life and resumed his farming interests. He died on November 18, 1965 in Danbury, Connecticut.

See also Roosevelt, Franklin D. (1882–1945); Stilwell, Joseph W. (1883–1946); McCarthyism.

REFERENCES: John Morton Blum (ed.), *The Price of Vision: The Diary of Henry A. Wallace, 1942–1946* (Boston, MA, 1973); John C. Culver and John Hyde, *American Dreamer: The Life and Times of Henry A. Wallace* (New York, 2000); J. Samuel Walker, *Henry A. Wallace and American Foreign Policy* (Westport, CT, 1976).

Ron Briley

Waln, Robert, Jr. (1794–1825)

The Philadelphia merchant and author Robert Waln, Jr. may be considered America's first Sinologist because of research he did while residing in China and his subsequent stateside publications about that country.

Waln was born in Philadelphia in 1794, the son of export merchant Robert Waln, Sr. and Phebe Lewis Waln. The family's wealth and social position made it unnecessary for him to earn a living. He was self-educated, and at an early age turned to writing. Through his father's commercial connections, Robert Jr. made a voyage to China. Waln stayed in Guangzhou, the only port in China open to Westerners, from September 10, 1819, to January 3, 1820. Waln began to write extensively about China on his homeward voyage. In 1821 he published a series of articles in Philadelphia's *National Gazette*. His *magnum opus, China*, 475 pages long, was privately published in 1823. It bore the impressive if prolix title: China; comprehending a view of the origin, antiquity, history, religion, morals, government, laws, population, literature, drama, festivals, games, women, beggars, manners, customs, of that empire, with remarks on the European embassies to China; and the policy of sending a mission from the United States to the Court of Peking. To which is added, a commercial appendix, containing a synopsis of the trade of Portugal, Holland, England, France, Denmark, Ostend, Sweden, Prussia, Trieste, and Spain in China and India; and a full description of the American trade to Guangzhou, its rise, progress, and present state: with mercantile information, useful to the Chinese trader and general merchant.

Waln's scholarship is distinct because of his exposure of myth and advocacy of ways of improving Sino-American relations. He critiqued existing Western writings as a means of acquiring an "accurate" image of China. He also presented his readers with a "more authentic" account, having "refined out the 'chinomania' of the Romish writers or the immoderate incredulity of more modern travelers." Waln advocated that a low-key U.S. embassy, avoiding "all demands of favors," be dispatched to China to quietly negotiate improved trading conditions. Men of learning should accompany the embassy to "collect facts and information which the pride or policy of other travelers may have mutilated or concealed." Waln's proposals were perhaps twenty years ahead of their time and went unheeded. A United States Embassy was ultimately sent to China in 1844, nineteen years after his death.

Waln produced an amateurish kind of scholarship with a distinctly American thrust. His style was verbose, his footnotes were sometimes vague, and he never referred directly to a Chinese text. However, seen in the context of his day, his Sinology was innovative. David Rittenhouse's orrery cannot be compared to a modern astronomical observatory nor can Benjamin Franklin's kite to a 20th century electrical generator. Like Rittenhouse and Franklin, Waln offered his countrymen some highly specialized and relatively advanced "useful knowledge" with which to build the new nation.

REFERENCES: *Waln Family Papers*, Philadelphia's Library Company and Historical Society of Pennsylvania; Jonathan Goldstein, "A Philadelphia Author Turns to China: Robert Waln, Jr., as America's First Sinologist," *The American Asian Review No. 3* (2003).

Jonathan Goldstein

Wang Ching-wei (1883–1944) *see* Wang Jingwei (1883–1944)

Wang Jingwei (1883–1944)

A leader in the Guomindang (GMD) government of the early 20th century and a close associate of Dr. Sun Zhongshan, Wang Jingwei was better known as the head of a Japanese-sponsored puppet regime based in Nanjing, China during the Sino-Japanese War. Wang's ancestors were from Shaoxing, Zhejiang Province. Wang was born on May 4, 1883 in Guangzhou, Guangdong Province, the youngest of ten children of Wang Shu, a legal secretary in the imperial Qing government. During his early years Wang received a traditional education studying Chinese classics and history, and became resentful of the Manchu Dynasty that ruled China. In 1903 he passed the Guangdong provincial examination and won a government scholarship for study in Japan the following year. In 1906, he earned a degree from Tokyo Law College, where he studied constitutional laws and political theories. In Japan Wang joined the Tongmenghui, the new patriotic society founded in 1905 by anti-Manchu activists Dr. Sun Zhongshan and Huang Xing. From then on Wang became an ardent supporter of the republican movement, writing eloquent and fiery articles against the Qing government and the advocates of a Chinese constitutional monarchy. In 1910 he led a failed assassination against Prince Regent Zai Feng, and was arrested in Beijing. Wang's brave act and his brilliant quote, "It is a pleasure to face the killer's knife, knowing I have no regret in my young life" made him a hero of the Chinese nationalism. Wang was freed from the prison after the revolution in 1911, and married Chen Bijun the following year. In the late 1910s Wang became a member of the personal entourage of Dr. Sun, and in 1924 he was elected the second-ranking member of the Central Executive Committee of the GMD. In 1925 when Dr. Sun passed away, it was believed that Wang drafted Sun's final political testament. Though he was elected chairman of the national government based in Guangzhou shortly after, his power was rapidly eroded by Jiang Jieshi, the rising military

leader of GMD. Wang belonged to the left wing of the party and ruled briefly from Wuhan in 1927, where he cooperated with the Chinese Communists first but later expelled them following Jiang's steps. To Wang, the nationalist revolution was a quest for freedom and equality of China. Wang and his associates believed that imperialism was the root of China's affliction, and American capitalism was only an extension of European capitalism. Advocating a hard-line approach, Wang demanded abolition of the unequal treaties, and criticized GMD leaders for failing to secure an apology from the United States for the shelling of Nanjing in an incident, which took place on March 24, 1927. However, Wang dismissed the use of sheer force in dealing with imperialist nations. His view was a step-by-step process involving a concentration of political, diplomatic, and economic forces against the Western powers. Although Wang became the President of the Executive Yuan in the Nanjing government in early 1932, his rivalry with Jiang continued. In November 1935, Wang was wounded by an assailant, who resented Wang's appeasement policy toward Japan. He was forced to resign and sought medical treatment overseas. Wang returned to China after the Xian Incident in late 1936, however, his political influence was diminished.

After the Sino-Japanese War broke out in 1937, he became increasingly pessimistic about the eventual outcome of the conflict. Although Wang had previously denounced Japanese imperialism, he was not prepared to fight against Japan's aggression. On December 29, 1938 he issued a public declaration of his advocacy of peace, requesting the halt of armed resistance to Japan. In 1939 Wang went to Japan twice to work out an agreement for a Chinese administration in the Japanese-occupied China. On March 30, 1940, under Japan's notion of Pan-Asianism, which he formerly opposed, Wang established a pro-Japanese government in Nanjing. Although with only token authority, Wang believed he was Sun's rightful heir, and his government was the legitimate national government of China. On January 9, 1943, at the urge of Japan, his Nanjing government declared war on the United States and Great Britain. Suffering from ailing health caused by his would-be assassin, Wang went to Japan for medical treatment in 1944, and died at Nagoya on November 10. He was succeeded by Chen Gongbo, but the regime fell apart shortly after. His wife along with his associates was tried for treason following the Japanese surrender.

See also Sun Zhongshan (1866–1925); Jiang Jieshi (1887–1975); Guomindang (GMD).

REFERENCES: Howard L. Boorman, *Biographical*

Dictionary of Republic China (New York, 1970); Gerald Bunker, *The Peace Conspiracy: Wang Ching-wei and the China War, 1937–1941* (Cambridge, MA, 1972).

Wenxian Zhang

Ward, Frederick Townsend (1831–1862)

Descended from generations of seafaring men, Ward was born and raised in Salem, Massachusetts. He left high school after two years to become second mate on the clipper ship *Hamilton*, on which he traveled to China in 1847. After returning he resumed his studies but soon withdrew to become chief mate on the *Russell Glover*, which his father commanded. He arrived in San Francisco in May 1850 and spent a year on the west coast, apparently digging for gold. In late 1851 he set out for China, where the Taiping Rebellion offered opportunities for ambitious young men. After working on an opium ship he was hired in 1852 as first officer of a ship that transported "coolies" to Mexico, where he joined William Walker's private army. After Walker's failed attempts to establish governments in Mexico and Nicaragua the U.S. government declared Ward an outlaw. He joined the French army and fought in the Crimean War until he was forced to resign for insubordination. In 1857 he reappeared in China as first mate on a coastal steamer, but a year later he resigned to join his father's ship brokerage firm in New York. Dissatisfied with that sedentary existence, he returned to China in January 1860, accompanied by his brother Henry, who entered the commission trade at Shanghai. Frederick resumed his naval career as an officer on the steamer *Confucius*.

After the Taipings captured Suzhou in 1860, the Shanghai taotai, Wu Xu, and a wealthy comprador, Yang Fang, better known as Takee, hired Ward to recruit and train an army composed of Chinese and Filipino troops commanded by European and American officers. Provided with funds from a variety of sources, most notably customs revenue, Ward offered recruits higher pay than they could earn elsewhere, and the salaries were supplemented by bonuses and the opportunity to loot. Ward and Takee, whose daughter Ward married in 1862, formed a business partnership that allegedly made huge profits in acquiring supplies for the army, utilizing Henry Ward as "purchasing agent."

British and American officials, as well as foreign residents in the treaty ports, initially feared and loathed the army, and the *North China Herald*, the most influential of the treaty-port newspapers, declared it "a disgrace that such a gang should be allowed to set all laws at defiance because they are in the pay of the Taotai." One his-torian has aptly described the officers as "foreign rowdies and deserters" who were "sometimes drunk and always disorderly." Although Ward tried to maintain some degree of discipline, in some instances applying brutal punishment, he had only limited success, in no small part because of his reluctance to dismiss those who were loyal to him, even when they proved incompetent, as was true of his Chinese interpreter and a surgeon who was a hopeless alcoholic.

Ward himself was known as fearless, but reckless is a more accurate description, and he was wounded more than a dozen times. The army's first significant victory was the capture of Songjiang in July 1860 in a battle that impressed its sponsors but convinced many foreigners that its commander was "a dangerous filibuster [sic] and outlaw, perhaps even a lunatic." An imperial decree of 1862 awarded the force the flattering but inaccurate title of "Ever-Victorious Army." Despite winning some notable victories, the army also suffered ignominious defeats, as at Qingpu in August 1860. In victory or defeat, it invariably suffered high casualties, and Ward himself was mortally wounded in September 1862. The Chinese authorities gave him a state funeral and built a memorial temple in his honor at Songjiang.

See also Taiping Rebellion.

REFERENCES: Hallett Abend, *A God from the West: a Biography of Frederick Townsend Ward* (Garden City, NY, 1947); Holger Cahill, *A Yankee Adventurer: the Story of Ward and the Taiping Rebellion* (New York, 1930); Caleb Carr, *The Devil Soldier: the Story of Frederick Townsend Ward* (New York, 1992); Richard J. Smith, *Mercenaries and Mandarins: the Ever Victorious Army of Nineteenth Century China* (Millwood, NY, 1978).

Michael Sinclair

Ward Incident

As Mao Zedong's People's Liberation Army (PLA) swept through China during the Chinese Civil War against the Nationalists in 1948 and 1949, they began to harass Westerners in general and Americans in particular. As one of the major trade centers in China, Mukden was taken by the Communist troops in October 1948. In November, the Communists demanded that American Consul Angus Ward surrender the consulate's radio transmitter. Ward refused. In response, the Mao's troops surrounded the consulate, putting Ward and 21 staff members under house arrest. For months, without communication, water, and electricity, Ward and the other Americans were completely isolated under guard by the Chinese Communists.

The American government ordered the consulate closed and called for the withdrawal of Ward and his staff. But Ward was unable to do it because in June 1949 the Chinese charged the American consulate with serving as a headquarters for espionage. With the crisis worsening, the Truman administration called upon American allies to withhold recognition of Mao's newly established government. In response, the PLA troops arrested Ward, accusing him and his staff members of inciting a riot outside the consulate in October 1949. In November 1949, as Angus Ward was brought to trial, the American public anger verged on explosion. President Harry S. Truman, already under severe attacks for "losing" China to the Communists, could not afford to show weakness in the face of the Chinese Communist challenge. He met with his military advisors to discuss the feasibility of a rescue operation. However incensed with the Communists, Washington showed great restraints because it was still looking for opportunities for reaching an accommodation with the People's Republic of China (PRC). Secretary of State Dean Acheson conveyed the message to Beijing that the U.S. would not recognize the new Chinese government until all the Americans at Mukden were released. On November 24, 1949, Ward and his staff were charged with the inciting-to-riot and ordered to be deported. They finally left China in December 1949.

The crisis lasted for more than a year, by which time the already fragile U.S. relations with the Chinese Communists had been damaged virtually beyond repair. Any possibilities that might have existed for U.S. recognition of the PRC became remote. In retrospect, the Ward Case is the beginning of the confrontation between the United States and the People's Republic China.

See also Civil War (1945–1949).

REFERENCES: *New York Times* (March 14, 1949); Gordon H. Chang, *Friends and Enemies: The United States, China, and the Soviet Union, 1948–1972* (Stanford, CA, 1990); Jian Chen, *China's Road to the Korean War: The Making of the Sino-American Confrontation* (New York, 1994).

Yuwu Song

Warlordism

"Warlordism" defines a particularly chaotic era in China's tumultuous 20th century history. Despite its vague, even misleading intimations, its cachet insures popular retention. "Warlord" arises from the pejorative Chinese *junfa*, a military man who selfishly looks after his own interests at society's expense. Chinese, however, prefer *dujun*, a military governor or regional militarist. "Warlord," however, fits the times. China between the revolution of 1911 and the Northern Expedition (1926–1928) was an era of violence and disarray, and the term represents well the image of military men focused on building alliances, plotting expansion, and insuring mutual destruction.

The warlords were a varied lot, and no simple moniker suits all. Some, like Zhang Zongchang, the "dog meat general" were thugs who plundered their domains. Others were reactionary, like Zhang Xun, the "pig-tailed general"—so called because of his retention of the queue as a symbol of imperial loyalty—whose troops pillaged republican Nanjing in 1913. Yet not all were irredeemably violent. Some, though conservative, demonstrated reformist aspirations, like Wu Peifu. Although Wu massacred striking railway workers in 1923, he denounced foreign ties and promoted the reunification of China through convening national assemblies. Similar was Zhang Zuolin, a Manchurian bandit who gained regional supremacy with Japanese aid but recoiled from those connections. Another was Yan Xishan, who embarked upon a series of paternalistic reforms to make his province self-sufficient and modern. Rounding out the most famous was Feng Yuxiang, the "Christian general" widely thought to be interested in social reforms.

These were only the top of the heap—below lay an array of lower-echelon officers and common soldiers who maintained their own hopes for themselves and society. Some, like Zhu De, gave up being mercenaries and dedicated their lives to revolutionizing China—in Zhu's case by helping to create the People's Liberation Army. The most obvious commonality evident here is a willing recourse to violence. All resorted to arms to establish local peace, under their leadership, and to expand the area they controlled. Beyond that, however, many shared certain inclinations. Even if they could not be expected to meet alliance obligations, many were committed to some concept of China as a nation deserving of international respect. Although they fought for individual hegemony, they also fought to reunify China in order to better deal with the host of problems besetting China. They were even in general agreement about what the problems confronting society were: technical and industrial weakness, foreign meddling, regionalism, and the lack of a moral compass. This helps explain why despite their differences, most were committed to re-energizing China, not only economically, but socially as well. Warlordism proved unable to reunite China—its very nature prevented the effective organization and application of power. That said, it continued into the Nationalist era, as many of Jiang Jieshi's allies after 1926 were former warlords. It was not until the People's Republic that the challenge of vestigial warlordism was surmounted and a more integrated state created. During the warlord era, the nationalist anti-foreign sentiment was fierce in China, threatening American and other powers' interests under the unequal treaty system. The chaos and disturbances caused by the movements of anti-imperialism and the warfare between the warlords prompted the United States, Japan, and other Western nations to cooperate in the defense of their interests, lives, and property. In 1921 the United States established a Yangzi River patrol to protect American privileges. In 1923 Washington acted with other nations by sending warships to Guangzhou in the name of protecting the foreign administration of Chinese customs. In 1927 the Chinese civil war became more intense, the U.S. government sent 35 warships, along with the navies of other powers, to Shanghai to protect foreign economic interests.

Warlordism is historically significant because it structured, in part, the Nationalist government — an American ally — as well as the milieu that Mao Zedong would describe as one where "political power grows out of the barrel of a gun." As a result, warlordism impacted indirectly not only American relations with but also perceptions of China.

It is worth noting that this was not the only era in Chinese history that China devolved into a fractured network of local strongmen, as the dissolution of central power was followed several times by eras of incessant strife. That said, each era proved shorter than the previous, the "warlord" era lasting only a scant eighteen years.

REFERENCES: Edward L. Dreyer, China at War, 1901–1949 (New York, 1995); Edward Allen McCord, The Power of the Gun: The Emergence of Modern Chinese Warlordism (Berkeley, CA, 1993); Edward A. McCord, "Warlords Against Warlordism: the Politics of Anti-Militarism in Early Twentieth-century China," *Modern Asian Studies* (October 1996); James E. Sheridan, "The Warlord Era: Politics and Militarism under the Peking Government," in John K. Fairbank (ed.), The Cambridge History of China: Volume 12: Republican China 1912–1949, Part I (Cambridge, MA, 1983); Ronald Suleski, *Civil Government in Warlord China: Tradition, Modernization and Manchuria* (New York, 2002).

Bill Sewell

Warsaw Talks

Fifteen years of ambassadorial discussions, starting in Geneva in 1954 between the Peoples Republic of China (PRC) and the United States, consisted of 136 meetings, are commonly known as the Warsaw Talks. More than half of the talks took place in Geneva before moving to Warsaw in August 1955 and the talks ended in February 1970. The process of raising the Geneva talks to an ambassadorial level was initiated by PRC Premier Zhou Enlai at the African-Asian conference in Bandung, Indonesia in April 1955. Lower level talks were already occurring in Geneva in 1954 over the repatriation of approximately forty to fifty Americans imprisoned in China and an estimated 200 Chinese nationals restricted from leaving the U.S., offering the setting and precedent to raise the level of contact to the ambassadorial level. The talks were conducted by the U.S. ambassador to Czechoslovakia U. Alexis Smith and the PRC's ambassador to Poland Wang Bingnan.

The Geneva/Warsaw talks were representative of the PRC's foreign policy practice of establishing special institutions to manage diplomatic relationships. Though the initiative was publicly led by Zhou, Mao Zedong, the Chinese Communist Party chairman, was the ultimate decision-maker in mainland foreign policy. John Foster Dulles, President Dwight D. Eisenhower 's Secretary of State was the major, but far from the only player in shaping the U.S. China policy. Though traditionally viewed as ideologically driven, Dulles was sensitive to outside pressure on American policies in Asia leading to a more pragmatic interpretation of his actions. Protection of the Republic of China (ROC) on Taiwan was central to Eisenhower's Asia policy, driven by anti-Communist elements in Congress and the ROC's lobbying efforts. However, European allies and Japan were increasingly unwilling to risk conflict, and continued economic loss due to the American-led trade embargo with the mainland in order to live up to its commitments to Taiwan.

Therefore, Dulles was open to discussions with the PRC, but only on a very limited agenda. Extending the original Geneva discussions on repatriations resulted in the only agreement of these meetings, signed September 10, 1955. This concordant recognized that citizens on each side were entitled to return to their home, and called for developing appropriate measures allowing them to exercise the right of repatriation. The second agenda item, though characterized as other substantive issues involved Taiwan. Efforts to negotiate a renunciation of force agreement in Taiwan Strait failed after six drafts agreements were proposed during thirty-five meetings from October 1955 to July 1956. The Americans proposed three drafts in an effort to convince the PRC to abandon force in its effort to gain control of Taiwan. The U.S. view was in line with the United Nations Charter and international law that force could not be used in China's efforts to regain control the island. Further, the draft language affirmed that all disputes be settled by peaceful means without resorting to the threat or use of force. Despite the PRC's view that Taiwan was an internal dispute, Zhou proposed a foreign ministers' meeting to settle disputes in the Taiwan area to raise the level of official contact with the U.S.

Through the John F. Kennedy and Lyndon B. Johnson administrations of the 1960s, the talks continued on an erratic schedule of monthly, bimonthly meetings, some years having only one or no meetings at all. This is reflective of no unifying agenda or exchange of proposals. The lack of face-to-face encounters during the dramatic events—China's war with India, Sino-Soviet conflict, the Chinese Great Proletarian Cultural Revolution, the Vietnam War—in these years suggests other developments were shaping Sino-American relations.

Despite a quiet ending and lack of dramatic breakthroughs, the Sino-American Ambassadorial Talks provided an important mechanism to conduct diplomacy, resolve conflicts, and coordinate policies. The Warsaw Talks modernized, stabilized and most importantly moderated the relationship.

See also Cold War.

REFERENCES: Zhang Baijia and Jia Qingguo, "Steering Wheel, Shock Absorber, and Diplomatic Probe in Confrontation: Sino-American Ambassadorial Talks Seen from the Chinese Perspective," in Robert S. Ross and Jiang Changbin (eds.), *Re-Examining the Cold War: U.S.-China Diplomacy 1954–1973* (Cambridge, MA, 2001); Steven M. Goldstein and Steering Wheel, "Dialogue of the Deaf?: The Sino-American Ambassadorial-Level Talks, 1955–1970," in Robert S. Ross and Jiang Changbin (eds.), *Re-Examining the Cold War: U.S.-China Diplomacy 1954–1973* (Cambridge, MA, 2001).

Lynn Brown

Washington Naval Conference (1921–1922)

The American Secretary of State, Charles Evans Hughes, organized a conference of postwar naval powers, officially the Conference on the Limitation of Armaments, to meet in Washington, DC, beginning in late 1921. Hughes wanted to end a naval building boom and, as a consequence, reduce U.S. government expenditures, of which spending on the U.S. Navy comprised 40+% of the immediate postwar government budget. The conference began in November 1921 and concluded with the signing of the last of several agreements in February 1922. There were three major treaties.

The Four Power Treaty (1921) sought to lower tensions between the major Pacific Ocean naval powers. The Four Power Treaty, which the United States, Great Britain, Japan, and France

signed on December 13, 1921, helped prevent an extension of the Anglo-Japanese Alliance of 1902 which would run its course in 1922; this treaty potentially could put Great Britain and the United States at war because of Britain's alliance with Japan. The Treaty stipulated that all the signatories would be consulted in the event of a controversy between two of them over "any Pacific question." An accompanying agreement stated the signatories would respect one another's rights regarding the various Pacific islands and mandates that they held which benefited Japan since it had the most possessions in the Pacific. Finally, these agreements ensured that a consultative process to keep possible stress points from boiling over to war.

The Five Power Treaty (1921), signed on February 6, 1922, the day the conference ended, sought to halt a naval building boom, and yet preserve the relative strengths of major navies. It likely was the best known of the three treaties. The United States, Great Britain, Japan, France and Italy agreed to a ten-year moratorium on battleship and aircraft carrier production (since one way to make aircraft carriers was to alter existing battleships)—that is capital ships of more than 10,000 tons and with guns of 8 inch calibers or greater—and reduce their capital ship gross tonnage on a ratio of 5:5:3:1.75:1.75. The agreement would last for ten years. Thus, the United States would reduce its battleship tonnage to 525,000 gross tons, scrapping twenty six capital ships, Great Britain would scrap twenty four, and Japan sixteen, and so on and so forth according to the ratios. While France and Italy had some qualms, Japan wanted a higher ratio fearing potential collusion between the two English-speaking naval superpowers, United States and Great Britain, in a future conflict, and so both governments agreed, as a concession, not to fortify any of their respective Pacific holdings west of the Hawaiian Islands and north of Singapore.

Finally, the Nine Power Treaty, also signed the day the Conference adjourned, encompassed all the countries that had interests of one sort or another in China. The signatories guaranteed China's independence, sovereignty, and territorial integrity in the aftermath of the rush for spheres of influence prior to the First World War. The signatories also accepted the American idea of an "Open Door" for trade, and lastly they agreed to review Chinese tariff policies, since the long established 5% ad valorem tariff continued to inhibit Chinese industrialization.

One must note, however, that, while these treaties dealt with major issues in the Pacific and in China, the government of China did not participate meaningfully in these discussions and none of the treaties sought to reduce or return the rights and advantages the foreign imperialists enjoyed in China. Rather, these treaties sought to create a framework for a more peaceful and hence more profitable exploitation of China and the Chinese people.

See also Four Power Treaty (1921); Five Power Treaty (1921); Nine Power Treaty (1922).

REFERENCES: Thomas H. Buckley, *The United States and The Washington Conference, 1921–1922* (Knoxville, TN, 1970); Wen-ssu Chin, *China at the Washington Conference, 1921–1922* (New York, 1963); Akira Iriye, *After Imperialism: The Search for a New Order in the Far East, 1921–1931* (Cambridge, MA, 1965); Westel W. Willoughby, *China at the Conference, A Report* (Baltimore, MD, 1922).

Charles M. Dobbs

Wedemeyer, Albert Coady (1897–1989)

Albert Wedemeyer's personality and career invites sharp contrasts. While General Joseph W. Stilwell denounced him as the "world's most pompous prick," military historian John Keegan praised him as "one of the most intellectual and farsighted military minds America has ever produced." The grandson of German immigrants, Wedemeyer left his native Nebraska for West Point where he graduated in 1919 near the bottom of his class. He went on to serve in the 15th Infantry Regiment in Tianjin, where he learned some Mandarin and completed two tours of duty in the Philippines.

After service in East Asia, Wedemeyer distinguished himself at the Command and General Staff School at Fort Leavenworth. As Europe blundered toward war, he attended the *Kriegsakadamie*, the German Army General Staff School, from 1936–1938. His reputation as a talented strategist led to his assignment in the War Plans Division of the General Staff, where he became one of the two principal authors of the Victory Program, the United States' comprehensive blueprint to defeat the Axis powers in the event of war. The leak of the plan of which only five copies existed, and subsequent publication of its most sensitive aspects in the *Chicago Tribune* three days before Pearl Harbor brought Wedemeyer under suspicion of treason. He was ultimately exonerated after an extensive FBI investigation.

A protege of General George C. Marshall, Wedemeyer accompanied the Chief of Staff to most of the Allied conferences. Almost immediately after his promotion to general in October 1943, he was, he later wrote, "eased out to Asia" to become Lord Louis Mountbatten's Chief of Staff for planning for the Southeast Asia Command. Following the recall of General Joseph W. Stilwell

precisely a year later, he became Chinese leader Jiang Jieshi's Allied Chief of Staff, commander of U.S. Army forces in China and administrator of American aid to China. Wedemeyer employed "honey instead of vinegar" with Jiang; this led to a better relationship than Stilwell had enjoyed, but did not produce any more tangible results. Wedemeyer admired Jiang as a "Christian gentleman" and shared his uncompromising antipathy to Communism, but at the same time was not blinded to the Nationalist regime's inept leadership, corruption, and insensitivity to the needs of the people.

After leaving Jiang's staff in 1946, Wedemeyer dealt primarily with the repatriation of Japanese troops and civilians. Following Marshall's failed mission in 1947, President Harry S. Truman dispatched Wedemeyer to make an appraisal of the state of the rapidly deteriorating Nationalist government. Upon the end of his brief visit, Wedemeyer publicly criticized the regime, stating that victory over the Communists would not be decided on the battlefield, but through effective economic and political reform. His report of the situation in China and Korea warned of an imminent Communist triumph in China unless greater U.S. support was given to the Nationalists, and envisioned UN guardianship for Manchuria, which would include the Soviet Union. The recommendations were deemed so sensitive that their publication was suppressed for two years, and were released only after the Truman administration came under attack for the "loss" of China. Despite these criticisms, Wedemeyer ultimately attributed the Communist victory to Marshall and Truman's failure to support Jiang adequately.

After Wedemeyer's retirement from the military in 1951, he continued as an active member of the China Lobby, and was associated briefly with the John Birch Society. He testified against his wartime political advisor, John Service, before Senator Pat McCarran's Senate Subcommittee for Internal Security. In 1952, he served as national chairman for Senator Robert Taft's bid for the Republican nomination against rival Dwight D. Eisenhower. Four years before his death in 1989, Wedemeyer received the Medal of Freedom from President Ronald Reagan.

See also Civil War (1945–1949); Wedemeyer Mission; Jiang Jieshi (1887–1975); Stilwell, Joseph W. (1883–1946); Service, John Stewart (1909-).

REFERENCES: Albert C. Wedemeyer, *Wedemeyer Reports* (New York, 1958); William Stueck, *The Wedemeyer Mission: American Politics and Foreign Policy During the Cold War* (Athens, GA, 1984); E. J. Kahn, Jr., *The China*

Hands: America's Foreign Service Officers and What Befell Them (New York, 1975).

Matthew Young

Wedemeyer Mission

Albert C. Wedemeyer was a lieutenant general in the U.S. Army who succeeded General Joseph W. Stilwell as Chinese leader Jiang Jieshi's chief of staff in China during the Second World War. He reported honestly the problems of Jiang's Nationalist regime, including the corruption and inefficiency, and he tried to bring about change, but he also treated Jiang with sympathy that Stilwell clearly lacked.

On July 9, 1947, President Harry S. Truman instructed General Wedemeyer to go to China on a fact-finding mission, and to return with recommendations for U.S. policy. Republican Congressman Walter Judd, who had been a missionary in China and who remained a strong friend and supporter of Jiang, suggested such a mission to Truman. The civil war was intensifying, and Manchuria was emerging as a key battleground. Despite U.S. support, it seemed that the Nationalists were losing the battle for the hearts and minds of the Chinese people, and perhaps losing the military conflict as well. And, as the fortunes of Jiang's Guomindang worsened, Republicans and China Lobby members at home increased their attacks on the Truman administration. Moreover, in March 1947, President Truman called for aid for Greece and Turkey to resist Communist aggression, the Truman Doctrine, and in June 1947, Secretary of State George C. Marshall called upon the countries of Europe to rebuild themselves with American assistance, the so-called Marshall Plan. There were no similar announcements of new and expansive military and/or economic aid for China and southern Korea. Truman faced pressure from the China Lobby, and sending Wedemeyer to China might divert that pressure.

Wedemeyer was dismayed when he returned to China after an absence of only two years. He found that Jiang remained resistant to reforming his government and his military, that corruption remained rampant, and that the tide of war was turning ever more rapidly against the Guomindang. He remained for a month in China. He would recommend rather dramatic action.

When Wedemeyer arrived in the United States, he reported honestly, and recommended continuation of economic and military aid to Jiang and the Nationalist regime. Indeed, he also called for either a five-power guardianship of Manchuria or else making it into a United Nations "trusteeship." Manchuria, by that point, had become the main battleground between Jiang's U.S.-trained and -equipped divisions and Mao's guerrillas; he wanted a vast military and economic aid effort. Wedemeyer recommended some 10,000 American military advisors, which might well presage the introduction of U.S. armed forces into this civil war. He recognized the risks, but thought there were few alternatives.

However, Secretary of State George C. Marshall rejected this advice. A former U.S. Army Chief of Staff, Marshall had visited China earlier and he recognized the futility of aiding Jiang. More importantly, in this era of small U.S. government budgets and a small military, Marshall wanted to keep America focused on containing the Soviet Union in Europe, and he did not want to provide the Soviets with a model for neutralizing Greece, where a civil war also was threatening the U.S.-backed government. There were only one and a third U.S. Army divisions in the United States, given demobilization after 1945; committing two-thirds of a division to China would have left the U.S. without troops. Of course, the U.S. State Department China Hands were already seeking to distance the U.S. Government from the fate of Jiang's Guomindang regime and to create conditions for dealing with Mao's Communist government headquartered in Yanan. And so, Marshall recommended and Truman accepted largely rejecting Wedemeyer's recommendations. The U.S. Government approved some additional military and economic aid, but not of the scope that Wedemeyer recommended and without the introduction of a vast number of American military advisors. Soon thereafter, the Nationalists suffered a dramatic series of losses in Manchuria, and subsequently at the Battle of the Huaihai, and the Communists surged to victory throughout China in 1949.

See also Civil War (1945–1949); Jiang Jieshi (1887–1975); Wedemeyer, Albert Coady (1897–1989).

REFERENCES: Peng Deng, *China's Crisis and Revolution Through American Lenses, 1944–1949* (Lanham, MD, 1994); Suzanne Pepper, *Civil War in China: The Political Struggle, 1945–1949* (Lanham, MD, 1999); Chonghai Petey Shaw, *The Role of the United States in Chinese Civil Conflicts, 1944–1949* (Salt Lake City, UT, 1991); William Stueck, *The Wedemeyer Mission: American Politics and Foreign Policy during the Cold War* (Athens, GA, 1984).

Charles M. Dobbs

Wei Jingsheng (1950-)

Born in 1950, shortly after the Communist victory in China, Wei Jingsheng had a privileged upbringing. The son of two party members, Wei's father was a high-ranking official in the Ministry of Foreign Affairs. Not surprisingly, Wei was politically involved from a very young age. In 1966, at the beginning of the Chinese Great Proletarian Cultural Revolution, Wei joined the Red Guards and began traveling across China. During these travels, he witnessed first-hand the poverty of the countryside, and began questioning the direction of the Communist party leadership. Nevertheless, he remained committed to the ideals of the Cultural Revolution, eventually joining one of the most radical and violent Red Guard units. His activities, extreme even by Red Guard standards, resulted in his being arrested and detained for four months in 1967. In 1969, as Red Guard units were being disbanded and "sent down" to the countryside, Wei joined the military. Four years later he left the military, moved to Beijing, and found a job as an electrician for the Beijing Zoo. While working at the zoo, Wei met and fell in love with a young Tibetan woman, whose father had been imprisoned on charges of being a spy. Consequently, Wei became further disillusioned with the government, questioning its policies in Tibet.

During the late 1970s, Chinese leader Deng Xiaoping began advocating his "Four Modernizations," which included agriculture, industry, defense, and science and technology. He hoped his pragmatic approach would help him become the preeminent leader of the post-Mao era. Taking advantage of this changing of the guard, Beijing intellectuals spoke out for the first time in years. Many called for greater democracy, writing their thoughts on posters and displaying them in public. In late 1978, they covered a particular wall in downtown Beijing with such posters, earning it the moniker "Democracy Wall." Wei Jingsheng frequented the wall to read the attached essays and poems, eventually authoring an essay of his own. Cleverly titled "The Fifth Modernization," Wei called on Deng to add democracy to his list of modernization projects.

Wei's poster brought him immediate recognition, allowing him to publish follow-up articles in the small magazine, *Exploration* (*Tansuo*). In these articles, Wei pointed out that China and other socialist nations were the poorest in the world and that until the party tolerated democracy and individualism, the Chinese would remain enslaved and deprived of meaningful lives. Most dangerously, Wei publicly attacked Deng Xiaoping by name. In March 1979, four months after he called for the "fifth modernization," authorities arrested Wei and sentenced him to 15 years in prison. For most of the next 15 years, Wei endured bitter treatment at the hands of his prison guards. When student protesters in Tiananmen Square demanded his release in 1989, they too found themselves in prison or, in many cases, killed. In 1994, with less than one year of his term remaining, Wei was released from prison. His release, not coincidentally, occurred as Beijing was bidding to host the 2000 Olympic Games. Far from repentant, however, Wei used his newfound freedom to speak out against the government and the lack of liberties in China. Consequently, the government arrested Wei once again and sentenced him to an additional fourteen years in prison. With the death of Deng Xiaoping in 1997, Wei was re-released, placed on an airplane, and sent to the United States to live in exile.

Since 1997, Wei has remained an active critic of the Chinese government. He is a familiar voice on Radio Free Asia, Voice of America, and the BBC. Because of his status and connections, Wei will remain a powerful voice for human rights for the foreseeable future.

See also Cultural Revolution; Tiananmen Square Massacre; Deng Xiaoping (1904–1997); Democracy Wall Movement (1978–1979); Four Modernizations.

REFERENCES: Ian Buruma, *Bad Elements: Chinese Rebels from Los Angeles to Beijing* (New York, 2003); Philip Caputo, "The Wei that Wasn't," *New York Times Magazine* (June 1998); Leslie Chang, "A Chinese Dissident Turns Freedom in U.S. Into a Prison of Sorts," *Wall Street Journal* (November 2000); "The Wall: Over and Out," *Asiaweek* (April 2000); Wei Jingsheng, *Courage to Stand Alone: Letters from Prison and Other Writings* (New York, 1998); Charles Wilbanks, "No More Heroes," *Asiaweek* (July 1998).

David Kenley

Wen Ho Lee "Spy" Case

On March 8, 1999, 59-year-old computer scientist Wen Ho Lee was dismissed from his post in the department handling nuclear weapons design at the Los Alamos National Laboratory in New Mexico. A Taiwanese-born, naturalized American citizen, Lee was dismissed because he had refused to cooperate with an FBI investigation. Suspected of being a spy for the People's Republic of China, he was eventually indicted on 59 felony charges. Concerns over rising Chinese economic and military power, about nuclear proliferation, and about security at American research institutes and production facilities had dovetailed with a pre-election intensification of Republican criticism of President Bill Clinton's handling of issues related to national security and foreign affairs. Separate Congressional and Department of Energy investigations revealed evidence that security was lax at the Los Alamos facility and at other facilities devoted to nuclear-weapons research and development. The subsequent FBI investigation reportedly revealed that Lee had violated security protocols by downloading information about the W88 warhead used on the Trident II submarines and had carried the information off site.

The evidence of Lee's guilt seemed to grow by the week as the government prepared its case against him. It was reported that he had had unauthorized contacts with Chinese scientists, that these contacts had occurred over an extended period, perhaps over several decades, that he had solicited invitations to visit Chinese scientific institutes, and that he had failed a polygraph test. But, from the beginning of the case, there were those who felt that Lee, if not completely innocent, had become a convenient scapegoat serving all sorts of political and bureaucratic agendas. Evidence emerged that Lee had initially come under suspicion simply because of his ethnicity. In response to this ethnic profiling, Asian-American groups would ultimately contribute more than $400,000 to a fund established to finance Lee's defense. Moreover, as the auditing of data at the Los Alamos facility continued, all sorts of materials were found to be missing. Some disks and hard drives containing classified materials were eventually found in non-secure locations within the facility, where they had been casually stored or simply left. These revelations served to undermine the sense that Lee's violations of security protocols were egregious. There was a further erosion of the sense of the singularity of the Lee case when the media began to report on a number of corporations that had apparently been selling the Chinese cutting-edge technical devices, despite the devices' sophisticated military applications. Then, experts emerged who argued that the information that Lee had removed from the laboratory was neither sensitive nor secret. In fact, much of it was readily available in specialized reference books and journal articles, and some of it was even available on the Internet. In any case, the information that the Chinese had acquired was simply not directly traceable to Lee's department, for the laboratory had distributed it to almost 550 people serving in all sorts of capacities throughout the Departments of Defense and Energy.

As Lee was about to be tried, the government unexpectedly but judiciously offered him a plea bargain. All charges but one, for downloading classified material onto a non-secure computer, were dropped, and Lee was sentenced to the time he had already spent in federal custody, 278 days served in solitary confinement. As part of the plea bargain, Lee was required to provide investigators with information on the contents of seven computer tapes that he had erased after he had come under investigation.

REFERENCES: Peter Grier, "The Lessons of the Fizzled Wen Ho Lee Spy Case," *Christian Science Monitor* (September 12, 2000); Wen Ho Lee, with Helen Zia, *My Country versus Me: The First-Hand Account by the Los Alamos Scientist Who Was Falsely Accused of Being a Spy* (New York, 2001); "Statement of Attorney General Janet Reno and FBI Director Louis J. Freeh on Investigation and Prosecution of Dr. Wen Ho Lee," *Essential Speeches* (2003); Dan Stober and Ian Hoffman, *A Convenient Spy: Wen Ho Lee and the Politics of Nuclear Espionage* (New York, 2001); Bruce Juyan Zhang and Glen T. Cameron, "Study Finds Sourcing Patterns in Wen Ho Lee Spy Case," *Newspaper Research Journal* (Fall 2003).

Martin Kich

Wen Jiabao (1942-)

Wen Jiaobao became the Premier of the State Council, of the People's Republic of China in March 2003, thus taking over from Zhu Rongji the primary running of the economy and the state bureaucracy. Since taking office, Wen has been a key person in the Fourth Generation leadership.

Regarded as quiet and unassuming, Wen Jiabao is a good communicator and is known as a "man of the people." Wen has worked to reach out to those who seem left out of decades of economic growth in rural and western China. He oversaw a diverse set of critical issues such as agriculture, poverty relief, forestry, and water resources. He was unusually visible in the media when he led flood relief efforts in the summer of 1998 and recommended a ban on logging on major rivers. In February 1999, he urged a crackdown on forest destruction. Wen Jiabao gained in Chinese public approval as a result of what was seen as his open management of the SARS crisis in early 2003. In November 2003, he became the first major Chinese official to publicly address the problem of AIDS, which has devastated the rural provinces. By doing so, Wen appeared to be attempting to reverse years of policies of denial. Sometimes labeled a "latter-day Zhou Enlai," Wen has an extraordinary ability to convert complicated issues into straightforward policy recommendations.

Wen Jiabao, a native of Tianjin, was born in September 1942. He joined the Chinese Communist Party in April 1965. That same year, Wen graduated from the Beijing Institute of Geology, where he also obtained his Master's degree in 1968. His career took off when he was recruited into the Gansu provincial hierarchy, where he was sent during the Cultural Revolution. He then went to Beijing in 1982, first serving as head of the Policy and Regulations Research Section, then as vice minister until 1985 in the Ministry of Geology and Mineral Resources, and ultimately appointed deputy chief of staff for then Party chief Hu Yaobang. Wen survived the purges of two of his superiors, Hu Yaobang and Zhao Ziyang during the 1980s, by virtue of his managerial competence, team spirit, political savvy, and technical expertise. He went on to serve Jiang Zemin for three years. In 1995, he headed the team for drafting the nation's Ninth Five-Year Plan (1996–2000), the "blueprint for the twenty-first century."

Premier Wen Jiabao is presiding over a major government reorganization — the third major consolidation of government bureaucracy in the past two decades — that will have significant implications for government personnel and policies. As head of the new Central Work Commission on Finance, Wen supervised the reformation and recapitalization of China's banks, the stabilization of China's securities markets, and the reorganization of the Ministry of Finance. He recommended that China's monetary policy play a greater role in promoting the reform and development of state-owned enterprises, and has urged the financial sector to support development of China's western regions, focusing on infrastructure projects, ecological improvement, rational utilization of natural resources and education. In 2004, Wen Jiabao pledged to further consolidate the achievements of macro-economic control policy in the Chinese economy. This is part of his plan to ease the country's too rapid growth rate without reducing China's demand for imports.

Wen Jiabao has met with many state leaders throughout the world, including British Prime Minister. Visiting the U.S. for the first time in December 2003, Wen said U.S.-China relations are "the most important state-to-state relations in our world" and persuaded U.S. President George W. Bush to issue a mild rebuke to Taiwan regarding possible moves toward independence.

REFERENCES: Barry Naughton, "The Emergence of Wen Jiabao," *China Leadership Monitor Vol. 6* (Spring 2003); Cheng Li, *China's Leaders* (Boulder, CO, 2001); Andrew J. Nathan and Bruce Gilley, *China's New Rulers: The Secret Files* (New York, 2003).

Elizabeth Van Wie Davis

White, Theodore H. (1915–1986)

The journalist Theodore "Teddy" White played a central role in reporting events in wartime China and in shaping the postwar controversy over the "loss" of China to Communism. White received the greater part of his fame for accomplishments later in his career, including a Pulitzer Prize for *Making of the President: 1960* and his role as Jackie Kennedy's willing accomplice in building the myth of Camelot, but his rise to journalistic prominence began in China in the late 1930's. This hard-working and ambitious son of working-class immigrants received a Harvard education funded in part with a scholarship for newsboys. As the only undergraduate majoring in Chinese history, White was tutored by John King Fairbank, who was at the time one of newest additions to the Harvard faculty and who would become the most famous American Sinologist in the 20th century. After graduating with top honors in 1938, White made his way to China with the aid of a postgraduate fellowship, where he was hired by John Hersey to cover the ongoing war with Japan for *Time* magazine.

White was one of a small coterie of journalists who countered the wartime American view of Nationalist China as a promising, albeit beleaguered, democratic regime sympathetic to American values. In a May 1944 *Life* magazine article White described the Nationalists as a "corrupt political clique that combines some of the worst features of Tammany Hall and the Spanish Inquisition." White's experiences in China during World War II became the basis for his first book, *Thunder Out of China*, co-authored with Annalee Jacoby and published in 1946. The best-selling book's unflattering portrait of Generalissimo Jiang Jieshi and its biting, but nonetheless insightful and prescient critique of the Nationalist government revealed the fault lines that would soon emerge over the "loss" of China and which naturally led to direct conflict and an eventual parting of ways with his boss and friend, the press lord Henry R. Luce.

Even more difficult times came when White found himself the target of loyalty board hearings brought on by his willingness to testify on behalf of a friend, the State Department official John Paton Davies. While ultimately exonerated, White confessed that the venomous atmosphere of the McCarthy era damaged his typically indomitable self-assurance; he did not turn his attention to China again until he accompanied the American press corps on Nixon's 1972 visit. By his own admission White willingly suspended judgment on those he admired. Aside from John F. Kennedy, the journalist reserved his greatest admiration and affection for two very different personalities he encountered in China, General Joseph W. Stilwell and Chinese Communist leader Zhou Enlai. White spent a great deal of time with Zhou while the latter served as the head Chinese Communist Party representative in Chongqing. As a *Time* correspondent, White recognized that Zhou most likely saw him as an opportunity to influence his magazine. Even so, White considered Zhou his mentor on Chinese politics, and considered Zhou's eventual acknowledgement that White was "on the threshold of beginning to understand [China]" a great accolade. Along with fellow correspondent Brooks Atkinson, White developed a privileged relationship with General Stilwell, whom he favored in his reporting on the political infighting that characterized the China-Burma-India Theater. After Stilwell's death in 1946, White was invited by the general's wife to edit his personal papers.

White characterized himself as being fascinated with power, and sought a career, which would make it possible for him to watch history as it unfolded. With regard to China from its war with Japan and on through the ensuing civil war, White nimbly placed himself near the various loci of political and military power; the books he authored based on personal experience remain important sources on the events and personalities of this period.

See also Jiang Jieshi (1887–1975); Stilwell, Joseph W. (1883–1946); Zhou Enlai (1898–1976).

REFERENCES: Thomas Griffith, *Harry and Teddy: The Turbulent Friendship of Press Lord Henry R. Luce and His Favorite Reporter, Theodore H. White* (New York, 1995); Theodore H. White, *In Search of History: A Personal Adventure* (New York, 1978); Theodore H. White and Annalee Jacoby, *Thunder Out of China* (New York, 1946).

Matthew Young

Wilkie, Wendell (1892–1944)

Wendell Wilkie was born in Elwood, Indiana, on February 18, 1892. In 1940, the Republican Party tapped Wilkie, a lawyer and utilities executive, to run against President Franklin D. Roosevelt, even though Wilkie was a former Democrat. On the election day, Roosevelt got 27 million votes to Wilkie's 22 million, and in the Electoral College, Roosevelt beat Wilkie 449 to 82. Although having many different political views from the President, Wilkie shared with Roosevelt an unwavering opposition to America's neutrality in the global crisis. He was a strong supporter of some of Roosevelt's controversial initiatives such as the Lend-Lease Act. In 1941, he visited Britain and the Middle East as FDR's personal representative, and in 1942 traveled to the USSR and China in the same capacity.

During his China trip, he was warmly received. Knowing that Wilkie was favoring a Pacific First strategy, a policy stance countering FDR's Europe First strategy by stressing the need to defeat Japan before Hitler, the Chinese tried hard to gain his support in changing American policies. Wilkie was impressed by Chinese leader Jiang Jieshi and his wife Song Meiling. The good impression left on Willkie by Madame Jiang prompted him to tell the Chinese, "Someone from this section with brains and persuasiveness and moral force must help educate us about China ... Madame would be the perfect ambassador. Her great ability—and I know she will excuse me for speaking so personally—her great devotion to China, are well known in the United States. She would find herself not only beloved, but immensely effective. We would listen to her as to no one else. With wit and charm, a generous and understanding heart, a gracious and beautiful manner and appearance, and a burning conviction, she is just what we need as a visitor." Wilkie's trip to China as the Presidential emissary did help pave the way for Madame Jiang's visit to America in 1942 and 1943, which turned out to be quite a success for publicizing China's cause against Japan. In 1943, Wilkie wrote *One World*, a plea for international peacekeeping after the war. He expressed his belief that it was vital for Americans to understand the problems of Asia and the viewpoint of its people, and that the future peace of the world would lay in a just solution of the problems of the Orient after the war. *One World* became a best-seller, the book sold millions of copies and helped to bring the U.S. out of its isolationist slumber. In 1943, together with Eleanor Roosevelt and other prominent Americans worried about the increasing threats to peace and democracy, Wilkie helped to establish Freedom House.

On October 8, 1944, Wilkie died at age fifty-two. Eleanor Roosevelt in her October 12, 1944 "My Day" newspaper column eulogized Wilkie as a "man of courage [whose] outspoken opinions on race relations were among his great contributions to the thinking of the world." She concluded, "Americans tend to forget the names of the men who lost their bid for the presidency. Wilkie proved the exception to this rule." Shortly before Willkie died, he told a friend, that if he could write his own epitaph and had to choose between "here lies a president" or "here lies one who contributed to saving freedom," he would prefer the latter.

See also Jiang Jieshi (1887–1975); Song Meiling (1898–2003).

REFERENCES: Dennis Kavanagh (ed.), *A Dictionary of Political Biography: Who's Who in Twentieth Century World Politics* (New York; 1998); Sterling Seagrave, *The Soong Dynasty* (New York, 1985); Barbara W. Tuchman, *Stilwell and the American Experience in China: 1911–1945* (New York, 1971).

Yuwu Song

William, Maurice (1881–1973)

Born in Kharkov, Russia in 1881, Maurice William immigrated with his family to New York at the age of eight, where he attended school. He later worked in a dairy shop, in a printing plant, and then as a messenger and clerk, and still later as a guard. As William's biographer writes, it was during this time that William had close encounters with the working class. Hoping to remake society, William got deeply involved in the socialist movement. He began to study law part time believing he would reform the society by practicing law. But when he heard Meyer London, a socialist lawyer-congressman denouncing lawyers as "parasites," he quit the study of law. While he was pondering his future career, William was advised by an acquaintance, "Become a dentist, comrade. Under the most perfect system of society, there will still be rotten teeth."

In 1907, William got his degree of doctor of dental surgery. Later he set up his own independent practice. It was William's first hand experience with the exploitation of working class New Yorkers, and his disillusionment with World War I, that led him to rethink the critical issues in Marxism and to write and publish The Social Interpretation of History in 1920. It turned out that this book had a tremendous influence on Dr. Sun Zhongshan, the Father of modern China.

William's main critique of Marxism is that Marx's theory was out of date. To him, it was the consumer that was the motive force of history rather than the industrial proletariat whom Marx believed would play the leading role in revolutionizing the modern society. The attraction of William's simple but prescient concept for Sun is easy to see. Sun could easily realize that the Chinese industrial working class early in the 20th century was so miniscule that it would not be able to lead the socialist movement. Before reading William's book, Sun's ideology was indebted to Socialism and Marxism. The Nationalist Party founded and led by Sun often took advice from the Comintern (Communist International) for guidance. William's book completely changed Sun's worldview. Since he read William's book, he tuned down his enthusiasm for Marxism and wrote and spoke more in terms of "Livelihood" that were obviously influenced by William's ideas. Harley Farnsworth MacNair, a renowned China scholar in the 1930s wrote, "In paragraph after paragraph, Dr. Sun either quoted, almost word for word, or paraphrased, the arguments, which he had found in the Social Interpretation of History. He now repudiated several of his own earlier theories, substituting therefore the system of thought which he had recently discovered in Dr. William's work."

In the late 1930s and early 1940s, William, the social critic, became William, the social activist. In response to Japanese full-scale aggression against China in 1937, many Americans took actions organizing to aid China. Maurice William became a great China sympathizer and played an active role in organizing and fundraising for the Chinese. He served as an officer in the American Bureau of Medical Aid to China set up in 1937. He also became chairman of the fundraising committee of the United Council for Civilian Relief in China, which was the largest and most influential organization of its kind at that time. The United Council included prominent members such as Albert Einstein, Herbert Hoover, and Henry Luce.

See also Sun Zhongshan (1866–1925).

REFERENCES: Maurice Zolotow, *Maurice William and Sun Yat-sen* (London, 1948); John R. Watt, *A Friend in Deed: ABMAC and the Republic of China, 1937–1942* (New York, 1987); "Anniversary of an Idea," *New York Times* (August 3, 1949); Paul W. Mortiz, "American Book that Remade China," *Christian Science Monitor* (November 17, 1945); James T. Shotwell, "Sun Yat-sen and Maurice William," *Political Science Quarterly* (March 1932).

Yuwu Song

Williams, Edward Thomas (1854–1944)

Edward Thomas Williams was a missionary worker, diplomat, and expert of American Sinology. He attended Bethany College and later became a minister in the Disciples of Christ Church. In 1887 he went to China as a missionary worker under the Foreign Christian Missionary Society in China. While working in China, he became fascinated with Chinese history, philosophy, and culture. From 1896 to 1898, he worked for the American consul general in Shanghai as a translator and then vice-consul-general. In 1901, he served as Chinese secretary of the U.S. legation in Beijing. He rose to become consul general in Tianjin in 1908. Williams also worked in the Far Eastern Affairs Division in Washington, D.C. for a short period of time. In 1913 Williams was named the chief of Far Eastern Division of the State Department. In that capacity, he vigorously showed support for U.S. minister to China Paul S. Reinsch to launch a consistent effort to expand American business influence in China. He also tried hard to protect China's integrity and independence against the encroachments of the Western powers in general and Japan in particular. In 1915, he warned the American government against Tokyo's Twenty-One Demands on China pointing out that it would hurt American interests in the long run if Japan would get what it wanted. In 1918 Williams quit his government job and accepted an offer from the University of California at Berkeley to be a professor of Oriental Languages and Literature. He held this professorship until his retirement in 1927. As the leading American China scholar and expert, he was called back to service by the U.S. government to work as a technical advisor to the American delegation at the Versailles Conference after the First World War in 1919. He also worked for the U.S. government at the Washington Naval Conference in 1921 and 1922.

Williams was considered to be an excellent teacher and an accomplished speaker. He authored a few well-received books on modern Chinese politics and history. His publications include such works as *China Yesterday and Today* (1923), *A Short History of China* (1928), *Recent Chinese Legislations* (1904), *The State Religion under the Manchus* (1913), and many monographs and articles. He was a member of several learned societies and was decorated twice for his achievements by the Chinese government in1918 and in 1936. As an expert of Chinese affairs, Williams showed spectacular foresight. He predicted a possible second world war as far back as 1919 when he denounced the decision on Shandong at the peace conference before a U.S. Senate Committee "as constituting a standing menace to the whole world which might lead to another world conflict." He also visualized the development of the imperial expansion by Japan in East Asia as the outcome of a strategic policy agenda shaped in 1854 when Commodore Perry of the United States Navy, obtained the opening of Japan to international trade and the establishment of foreign concessions.

See also **Twenty-One Demands.**

REFERENCES: Edward Thomas Williams, *A Short History of China* (New York, 1928); Edward Thomas Williams, *China: Yesterday and Today* (New York, 1923).

Yuwu Song

Wilson, Woodrow (1856–1924)

Born on December 29, 1856, in Staunton, Virginia, Woodrow Wilson served as President of the United States from 1913 to 1921. Like many contemporaries, Wilson believed China a prime recipient of Christianity and self-government, and promoted those values as the basis for his China policy. Believing the Open Door Policy an effective bulwark against Western and Japanese imperialism, Wilson gradually learned that tangible American interests in Asia were few, and that measures beyond mere goodwill were necessary to protect Chinese sovereignty.

In March 1913, as Wilson settled into the White House, the extension of an international loan consortium developed by the outgoing Taft administration came before the cabinet. Wilson quickly rejected renewal of the loan, which he condemned as "dollar diplomacy" infringing upon Chinese administrative integrity. In rejecting the consortium, Wilson portrayed his administration as anti-imperialistic and reversed America's traditional relationship with China, which had long rested on international cooperation. Wilson's unilateralist approach to China initially bore good relations with Beijing, especially after he authorized the recognition of the Yuan Shikai's government in May 1913. Wilson's minister to Beijing—Paul S. Reinsch, a political scientist from Madison, Wisconsin, and expert on Far Eastern affairs—embodied this policy of benevolence. Wilson admired Reinsch's anti-imperialism, support for the Open Door, and commitment to China's uplift. American goodwill to China reached its zenith in 1914 when the two countries renegotiated the Boxer Indemnity so that payments to the United States would support Chinese students studying there.

With the outbreak of World War I in 1914, Wilson's China policy shifted focus away from Beijing, toward Tokyo. At Beijing's request, the State Department considered advocating neutralization of the Asian theater. But Japan, hoping to consolidate its foothold on the Asian mainland, invoked its 1902 alliance with Britain, invading Germany's territorial holdings in the Pacific, including their base at Jiaozhou, in Shandong. China appealed to Washington for protection, but even though Wilson recognized that America was the only bulwark against Japanese imperialism, he felt unable to intervene. The Twenty-One Demands crisis of spring 1915, during which Japan attempted secretly to expand its hegemony over China, further demonstrated American paralysis in Asia. With America's neutral status already at issue with the European belligerents, Secretary of State William Jennings Bryan protested the demands, but conceded that Japan possessed special rights in China.

Having lost the initiative against Japan, Wilson took more interest in relations with Asia in May 1915, proclaiming that the United States would not recognize any agreement between China and Japan that infringed either on American rights in China, or on Chinese sovereignty. Wilson's stance hardened more toward Japan in 1916, with a return to the international approach favored by earlier policymakers. That year he consented to American participation in another international loan consortium, although due to its war obligations the United States did not join until

June 1918. That consortium, while America's first line of defense in China, proved generally ineffective. Another indication of Wilson's growing multilateralism was the Lansing-Ishii Agreement of November 1917. In an effort to force Japanese recognition of the Open Door Policy, Wilson authorized Secretary of State Robert Lansing to negotiate an adjustment of American and Japanese claims, although the agreement's meaning remained ambiguous. Wilson believed that it had staunched Japanese imperialism, while Japanese leaders believed they had finally satisfied American objections and used it to justify further expansion.

China was encouraged to join the Allies in 1917, and the resolution of the Shandong question became a focal point of the postwar settlement at Versailles. Although Wilson planned to reject Japanese demands and restore Shandong to China at the peace talks, Japan's threat to decline membership in the League of Nations led him to sacrifice Chinese interests. Conceding to Japanese imperialism cost Wilson during the ratification debates for the Versailles Treaty. The Shandong settlement proved a major argument against approval of the treaty in the Senate, and explaining his actions formed the centerpiece of Wilson's speaking tour defending the document in the western states in late 1919. Wilson died in Washington, DC, on February 3, 1924.

See also Open Door Policy; Twenty-One Demands; World War I; Treaty of Versailles (1919).

REFERENCES: Roy Watson Curry, *Woodrow Wilson and Far Eastern Policy, 1913–1921* (New York, 1957); Russell H. Fifield, *Woodrow Wilson and the Far East: The Diplomacy of the Shantung Question* (New York, 1952); Tien-yi Li, *Woodrow Wilson's China Policy, 1913–1917* (Kansas City, MO, 1952)

Eric A. Cheezum

Woodcock, Leonard (1911–2001)

Leonard Woodcock was a U.S. labor leader who became the first United States Ambassador to the People's Republic of China (PRC) in 1979. Woodcock was born on February 15, 1911, in Providence, Rhode Island, but moved to Germany as a child. When World War I began, Woodcock and his mother went to England where he attended school. Woodcock returned to the U.S. in 1926 and in the early 1930s obtained work as a machine assembler.

Early in his career Woodcock showed a taste for, and skill at, union politics. He became active in the United Auto Workers (UAW) Union. He helped lead the organizing drive at the General Motors Fisher Body plant in 1941. He became the international Vice President in 1955, serving until 1970, when he became President of the UAW. UAW members elected Woodcock to a full term at the union's 23rd Constitutional Convention in April 1972 and reelected him in 1974. Woodcock's tenure as UAW President came at the height of union power in the United States, and right before the American auto industry suffered some of its most serious challenges from higher gasoline prices and Japanese competition. Under Woodcock's leadership, the UAW acquired benefits for workers unprecedented in American labor history. Woodcock was involved with other organizations geared towards benefiting the working classes in the United States, including the Committee for National Health Insurance, National Commissions on Productivity and on Supplies and Shortages, the Labor Management Advisory Council, and the National Urban Coalition.

Woodcock retired from the presidency of the UAW in 1977. Following his retirement, President Jimmy Carter selected Woodcock to lead a diplomatic team to Vietnam in an attempt to resolve the issue of American soldiers listed as missing in action from the Vietnam War. In July 1977, President Carter sent Woodcock to Beijing to become the Chief of Mission, with a mandate to negotiate a full normalization of relations between the U.S. and the PRC. Carter chose Woodcock in part because of his long background of fighting for workers' rights and benefits within the American labor and capitalist systems. In the fall of 1978, Woodcock negotiated directly with Deng Xiaoping. Normal diplomatic relations began in January 1979 and Woodcock became the first U.S. ambassador to the PRC. Woodcock did not remain ambassador for long. In 1981 he left Beijing, but remained committed to improving relations between the U.S. and China. Upon his return from China, Woodcock accepted a position in the Center for Chinese Studies at the University of Michigan. In the fall of 1989, he traveled to Beijing in part to attempt the release of Chinese astrophysicist Fang Lizhi, who was living in the U.S. embassy after seeking sanctuary following the Tiananmen Square Massacre. On the 1989 trip, Woodcock again met with Deng.

From his first appointment as Chief of Station in Beijing, Woodcock became a zealous champion of U.S.-China trade and cultural exchange. Woodcock consistently supported the renewal of China's Most Favored Nation trading status. In his zeal for bilateral trade, he opposed the UAW's emphasis on blocking access to American markets to lower-priced Chinese goods. Woodcock urged Congress in 2000 to grant permanent normal trade relations with China and supported

China's entrance into the World Trade Organization. Organized labor, as represented by the AFL-CIO, vehemently opposed such a move, but Woodcock argued that increased trade with China would benefit workers in both countries in the long run. Woodcock died January 16, 2001, at his home in Ann Arbor, Michigan at the age of 89.

REFERENCES: Leonard Woodcock, *China-United States Relations in Transition* (Washington, DC, 1982); John Barnard, *The American Vanguard: The United Auto Workers During the Reuther Years* (Detroit, MI, 2004).

Barry Stentiford

World Trade Organization (WTO)

The World Trade Organization (WTO), established on January 1, 1995, is the global international organization that creates and enforces the rules of trade between countries. The WTO was set up by the General Agreement on Tariffs and Trade (GATT), during the Uruguay Round of 1986–1994. At its core are the WTO agreements—known as the multilateral trading system — negotiated and signed by most of the world's trading countries and ratified by their governments. These agreements are the legal ground-rules for international commerce, which guarantee member countries principal trade rights and require national trade policies to remain within agreed limits.

China became a member of the WTO on December 11, 2001, after 14 years of bilateral negotiations with the requesting original 37 WTO members and some 900 pages of legal text. Major progress was made towards China's WTO accession when the United States and China reached a bilateral agreement on November 15, 1999, that required China to substantially lower barriers on agricultural products, industrial goods, and services by the end of 2004. The United States also secured a number of significant concessions from China that protect U.S. interests during China's WTO implementation stage that ends on December 11, 2007. By contrast, the United States did not make any specific new concessions to China.

China has undertaken a series of important commitments in accordance with WTO rules. Some of the commitments undertaken by China included providing non-discriminatory treatment to all WTO members. WTO members are required to grant one another most favored nation status, called normal trade relations in the United States. All foreign individuals and enterprises must be accorded treatment no less favorable than that accorded to Chinese domestic enterprises with respect to trade. The WTO Agreement also required China to continue to revise its existing domestic laws and enact new legislation to assure full compliance with the WTO Agreement.

Trade relations are likely to remain an important bilateral issue for the United States and China as the trade between the two countries increases. The WTO will serve as an important instrument to insure that the inevitable trade disputes that arise are dealt with in a fair and equitable manner. Trade friction is channeled through the WTO's dispute settlement process where the focus is on interpreting agreements and commitments, and on ensuring that countries' trade policies conform to them. Therefore, the risk of trade disputes spilling over into political or military conflict is diminished.

See also General Agreement on Tariffs and Trade (GATT).

REFERENCES: *Mitsuo Mazushita, The World Trade Organization* (New York, 2003); World Trade Organization, *www.wto.org*; *Bernard Hoekman, The Political Economy of the World Trading System* ((New York, 2001).

Elizabeth Van Wie Davis

World War I

Soon after the fighting began in Europe in summer 1914, the conflict drew in the infant Republic of China and the Japanese Empire. Japan quickly declared war on Germany. But, China demurred, for there was little that China could contribute to the war, and some in China favored the Central Powers once it was clear that Japan was fighting with the Allies. However, many young Chinese men volunteered to help the Allied effort, and many of them engaged in various support activities in France.

Within days of the outbreak of war in Europe, Japan took action in the Pacific. Meeting its obligations under the Anglo-Japanese Alliance of 1902, the island nation demanded Germany surrender its Pacific fleet, and hand over its concession in China's Shandong peninsula and its Pacific island holdings to Japan. When Germany resisted, Japan entered the First World War. Initially China tried to remain neutral, and was unable to prevent Japan from seizing the German concession and taking it over. As the attention of Europe and of those countries that Europeans helped colonize focused on the fighting, especially the trench warfare in the west, Japan tried to gain informal empire over China. On January 18, 1915, the Japanese minister to China, Hioki, presented the so-called "Twenty-One Demands" to Chinese leader, Yuan Shikai, all to ensure Japan's position in China. These demands fell into five groupings, including Japan taking over Germany's concession in the Shandong peninsula, Manchuria and

Mongolia being set aside for Japanese economic exploitation and colonization, that China grant no more concessions to other imperialist powers, that energy poor Japan control China's main coal reserves, and that Japan gain quasi-control over China's future military and economic dealings. And the Japanese demanded secrecy. The negotiations did not go well either for Japan or China. Yuan's government leaked the demands, and both Great Britain and the United States made known their concerns. Still, Japan became tired of Chinese stall tactics and on May 7 demanded acceptance, which came on May 25. In the end China accepted three overall demands, recognizing Japan's sphere of influence in Shandong, Japan's economic position in South Manchuria, and Japan's emerging influence in Fujian province across the straits from Japanese-controlled Formosa (present-day Taiwan). When Yuan died suddenly on June 6, 1916, China lost its single voice to the outside world and it began to devolve into a period of warlordism. There really was no other leader capable of bringing the various military leaders together and creating an effective central government. This weakness helped Japan push its agenda while the other imperial powers were caught up in the war in Europe. On August 14, 1917, China finally declared war on Germany. Already, by 1916, thousands of Chinese peasants had labored in the British and French military zones in Western Europe. The Chinese declaration brought little advantage to the Allies and to China, but China would at the very least be present at the postwar peace negotiations to press its case for the return of the German concession. After the guns fell silent in Europe, the victorious and losing powers met in Paris to negotiate the peace. It was a victors' peace, and it undid the Germany victory over Russia. The Japanese delegation wanted a statement on racial equality as a basis for the League of Nations, which the British delegation had to decline owing to strong opposition from the Dominions, especially Australia. To assuage the Japanese, the negotiators offered Japan all of Germany's holdings in the Pacific and China

The offer of Germany's paramount interests in Shandong to Japan inflamed Chinese opinion. Thousands of Chinese students from thirteen higher education institutions in and around Beijing broke out in protest on May 4, 1919, and soon thereafter urban Chinese joined the demonstrations. Students in Paris surrounded the home of the chief Chinese delegate, Gu Weijun, preventing him from attending the treaty signing ceremony. Thus the May 4th Movement, as it was known, marked the beginnings of modern Chinese nationalism and the flowering of the New Culture Movement. Boycotts of Japanese-made goods indicated the depth of feeling, as two opposing views of nationalism would soon clash in Eastern Asia.

See also May Fourth Movement.

REFERENCES: Barbara J. Brooks, *Japan's Imperial Diplomacy: Consuls, Treaty Ports, and War in China, 1895–1938* (Honolulu, HW, 2000); Jerome Chen, *Yuan Shih-k'ai*, (Stanford, CA, 1972); Peter Duus, Ramon H. Myers, and Mark R. Peattie (eds.), *The Japanese Informal Empire in China, 1895–1937* (Princeton, NJ, 1989); Bruce A. Elleman, *Wilson and China: A Revised History of the Shandong Question* (Armonk, NY, 2002); Thomas E. LaFargue, *China and the World War* (New York, 1973); Ernest Young, *The Presidency of Yuan Shih-k'ai* (Ann Arbor, MI, 1977).

Charles M. Dobbs

World War II

Hostilities between Japan and China began a decade before the United States entered the Second World War. On September 18, 1931, the Japanese army in southern Manchuria, the Kwantung Army, claimed that Chinese bandits blew up tracks of the South Manchurian Railway (SMR) near Mukden. During the next year, Japanese forces seized all of Manchuria on the pretext of chasing Chinese bandits and securing the SMR.

Over the next four years, Japan expanded its area of control in Inner Mongolia and northeast China. Japanese forces took a few Chinese northern provinces, Chahar, Suiyan, and Jehol, and began moving into Shansi and the remainder of Shandong. In part, Japan seized additional territory hoping to return that land for Chinese recognition of its seizure of Manchuria. And, for Chinese Nationalist leader Jiang Jieshi, one of the few weapons he possessed was non-recognition of Japan's gains. On July 7, 1937, at the Marco Polo Bridge south of Beijing, a Japanese force clashed with a local Chinese garrison and as this minor incident escalated, Japanese army leaders in China soon took all of Beijing, the port of Tianjin, and cut China's overland communications with the Soviet Union. Between the summer of 1937 and December 7, 1941, Japan gained control over virtually all of North China and the lower Yangzi River valley, including most of the major cities, ports, and communications in China. Jiang's Nationalist armies mostly gave ground to the advancing Japanese. The Soviet-Japanese Treaty of April 1941 helped the Soviet Union and Japan concentrate again potential conflicts with Nazi Germany and the United States respectively. The U.S. entry into the war greatly affected the situation in China. China had absorbed a great deal of Japanese resources, and Japan sought to take advantage of the German victories in Western Europe in 1940 and gain the resources needed to compel China's surrender. However, Japan found itself compelled to divert resources to meet the twin axes of the U.S. advance in the Southwest and the Central Pacific.

In China, there was a strange three-way conflict. Jiang's government relocated eventually in Chongqing in Sichuan Province, and the economy of so-called Free China nearly collapsed, brought on by a ruinous monetary inflation. Peasants were restless, which weakened Jiang's claim on power as it created potential new converts to Mao's agrarian Communist movement. Mao seized the mantle of nationalism by his movement's clear stand against Japanese aggression. But, for the most part, Jiang and Mao watched each other warily and sought to gain from one another and left the important task of defeating Japan to America. Japanese forces did launch several offensives. Right after Pearl Harbor, they attacked to secure a north-south corridor from Beijing to Guangdong. In 1943, they attacked toward Chongqing, but Nationalist armies stopped them, and they also tried to seize Hunan, and failed. In 1944, Japan tried once again with the Ichigo Offensive. The Japanese captured airfields used by U.S. flyers, and finally secured the Beijing-Guangdong rail line. Late in 1944, Chinese divisions in Southwest China cooperated with other forces on the long-awaited offensive against Japanese positions in Burma, and thereafter they were able to press back Japanese units throughout China until the war's end. The United States underwent a change of opinion with respect to China. President Franklin D. Roosevelt viewed China as a major power, and the American military at first thought it would need to invade Taiwan or the East China coast to have a staging area to invade Japan. But America's hopes were not realized. Jiang was very willing to accept American aid but not American advice and certainly not risk his American-equipped and-trained divisions against the Japanese army. And, as America's offensive across the Pacific moved ahead, the need for a base in China for the invasion of Japan lessened. Meanwhile, a U.S. Army observer group, the so-called Dixie Mission, spent time with Mao's resistance movement headquartered in Yanan. They reported a relatively honest, efficient, and effective anti-Japanese force that merited additional American aid, and presaged America's challenge when the civil war reerupted after the Japanese surrender.

When Japan surrendered on September 2, 1945, the situation in China was unclear. The Soviet Red Army had seized Manchuria on its way to Korea. Japanese troops remained in China, and 50,000 American marines went into North China to facilitate their surrender and repatriation. China suffered some 11 million dead, mostly civilian casualties. Jiang demanded American logistical support to move his best divisions over North China to fight for Manchuria, and thus the seeds of his defeat in the postwar civil war were already sown in the final act of World War II in China.

REFERENCES: Wesley M. Bagby, *The Eagle-Dragon Alliance: America's Relations with China in World War II* (Newark, DE, 1992); John Hunter Boyle, *China and Japan at War, 1937–1945: The Politics of Collaboration* (Stanford, CA, 1972); His-sheng Chi, *Nationalist China at War: Military Defeats and Political Collapse, 1937–1945* (Ann Arbor, MI, 1982); James C. Hsiung and Steven I. Levine, editors. *China's Bitter Victory: The War with Japan, 1937–1945* (Armonk, NY, 1992); Dick Wilson, *When Tigers Fight: The Story of the Sino-Japanese War, 1937–1945* (New York, 1982).

Charles M. Dobbs

Wu, Harry (1937-) *see* Wu Hongda (1937-)

Wu Hongda (1937-)

Wu Hongda (Hongda Harry Wu) was born in Shanghai, China in 1937. After emigrating to America, he reached a wide public audience in 1991 when he provided information for a CBS "60 Minutes" program on September 15, 1991 on China's forced labor camps. He subsequently testified before U.S. Congress Subcommittee on International Operations on September 8, 1995 on his nineteen years in these camps and his later research.

Wu was born into a privileged Shanghai family and, until the early 1950s, enjoyed a peaceful, ordered childhood, completing grammar school at a prestigious Jesuit institution, St. Francis School in Shanghai. There he became interested in science and also in becoming a Roman Catholic.

It was in the 1952 that this idyllic life began to disintegrate as, in the wake of the 1949 transformation of China to a Communist state, his father, a banker, was first arrested and then demoted at his bank. Family finances quickly became strained and family members suffered the social stigma, which the Communist cadres attached to people from the former "upper classes," or class enemies. Wu and his siblings were allowed to attend school, but his older brother was assigned work in a remote area of China and Wu, accepted at the Beijing College of Geology, was constantly observed and criticized for his questionable class background.

Encouraged to speak his mind, he, like many other young people during the Hundred Flowers Movement (1957), finally spoke out against the oppression of his family and, upon the eve of his graduation, found himself imprisoned on the pretext of theft. There followed nineteen years of transfers from one labor camp to another and many tests of his ability both to survive and to hold onto his humanity. He was finally released in 1979 and given a job as a teacher at China Geo-science University in Wuhan (1980–1985) but found that he could neither forget the individuals left behind in the camps nor keep silent about the abuses they and he suffered. He was finally given a visa to take a temporary position at Berkeley, CA in 1985–1987 and then the Hoover Institution at Stanford in 1987. He also found the Laogai (Convicted Labor Reform) Research Foundation in 1987 and this is the platform from which he goes on lecture tours, does research and writes about the extensive system of labor camps that he asserts are essential to China's booming economy.

Wu has published three books on the *laogai* phenomenon. His works give both personal and statistical accounts of a the tiered systems known as Convicted Labor Reform (CLR or *laogai* in Chinese), Re-education by Labor (RTL or *laojiao*) and Forced Job Placement (FJP or *jiuye*) that serve as China's prison system for everything from petty to serious criminals and from low-level (like Wu) and important (like Jiang Qing or Madame Mao Zedong) political prisoners. His most troubling assertions are that this system is largely secret, very extensive as it affects millions of prisoners, and also essential to the current Chinese economy. In his first published book, *Laogai: the Chinese Gulag*, he reports on his clandestine visit back to China in 1991 to gather evidence about the camps. He estimates for the number of prisoners who suffered in the camps since 1949 (over 50 million) and how many are still there (2–5 million), as well as documenting over 900 camps on maps. He also provides the political and legal history of this institutionalized production method.

His second, *Bitter Winds*, is largely autobiographical and chronological, starting with his childhood, chronicling and explaining his arrest in 1960 and his 19 years in different camps, his release in 1980 and ending with his 1991 CBS appearance and the *Newsweek* article that followed. It is both graphic and effective in giving a personal face to the institutionalized abuse, mismanagement, and corruption under which he and his fellows suffered. His third, *Troublemaker*, describes his attempt to enter China in 1995 to do further research. This book details his arrest in 1995 and the two months of incarceration that followed. This incident again brought him to the attention of the American public and raised awareness of his social agenda to halt the purchase of prisoner-made goods in the U.S. as it coincided (not by his intention, he asserts) with Hilary Clinton's planned visit to the Fourth UN Conference on the Status of Women. His release was secured by the U.S. State Department's threat to cancel her visit. Wu continues to write, lecture, give interviews, and do research in his effort to expose, and perhaps close down, the forced labor camps, especially by emphasizing that they will exist as long as they are economically advantageous to China within the world economy.

See also Human Rights; Human Rights in China.

REFERENCES: Kate Saunders, *Eighteen Layers of Hell* (London, 1997); Hongda Harry Wu and Carolyn Wakeman, *Bitter Winds: A Memoir of My Years in China's Gulag* (New York, 1994); Hongda Harry Wu and Ted Slingerland, *Laogai: the Chinese Gulag* (Boulder, CO, 1992); Hongda Harry Wu and George Vecsey, *Troublemaker: One Man's Crusade Against China's Cruelty* (New York, 1996).

Janice M. Bogstad

Wu Tingfang (1842–1922)

Born as an immigrant son in Singapore in 1842, Wu Tingfang returned to Guangdong Province with his farther at age of four. Unable to find the suitable education in a safe environment in his hometown, Wu had to go to Hong Kong for school. Having graduated from St. Paul's College and worked as interpreter for the colonial government in Hong Kong for over a decade, Wu entered the Lincoln's Inn, one of the best law schools in England, in 1874. Wu became the first Chinese lawyer after receiving L.L.D. from the Lincoln's Inn and passing the necessary examination in England in 1876.

Between 1877 and 1882, Wu practiced law in Hong Kong and became a leading figure in the Chinese community. With strong support from local Chinese leaders as well as Sir John Hennessy, the British Governor of Hong Kong, Wu became the first Chinese Justice of the Peace in 1878 and member of the Legislative Council in 1880. Although his stay in Hong Kong was relatively brief, he made great contribution to the Chinese political participation in the British colony. Accepting the appointment from Li Hongzhang, Governor General of Hebei, Wu moved to Tianjin in 1882 to help Li handle foreign affairs and manage modern enterprises. Deeply impressed by his diplomatic skills displayed in the negotiation with Japan in Shimonoseki in 1895, the Qing court appointed Wu as Chinese Minister to the United

States, Spain, and Peru the next year. Arriving in Washington in 1897, Wu worked hard to protect rights and interests of Chinese immigrants in the Untied States. Taking advantage of his legal, diplomatic, and language skills, Wu sent numerous memorandums to American officials, made speeches in various occasions, and published articles in American journals to expose the mistreatment of the Chinese and denounce the American violation of the treaties between the two nations. Having completed an extended term in the Untied States, Wu returned to China in 1902 and became the chief negotiator for new commercial treaties between China and the United States and Japan. In the following years, he served as deputy minister of Ministries of Commerce, Justice, and Foreign Affairs, and as justice at International Court at The Hague. In 1907, Wu was appointed again as the Minister to the United States, Mexico, Peru, and Cuba. It was during his second term that the negotiation for the return of the Boxer Indemnity was completed and remission was started in January 1909.

Wu supported the Chinese Revolution of 1911 and served as Minister of Justice and Foreign Affairs in several revolutionary governments. Sharply disagreeing with the leaders in the Beijing government, Wu joined Sun Zhongshan in the Nationalist revolutionary effort in Guangdong, serving as Minister of Foreign Affairs and Finance. Wu died as Governor of Guangdong Province on June 23, 1922, while fighting the rebellion launched by General Chen Jiongming.

REFERENCES: Linda Pomerantz Shin, *China in Transition: The Role of Wu Ting-fang* (Los Angeles, CA, 1970); Zhang Yunqiao, *Wu Tingfang Yu Qingmuo Zhengzhi Gaige [Wu Tingfang and Political Reforms in the Late Qing]* (Taibei, 1987); Linda Pomerantz-Zhang, *Wu Tingfang (1842–1922): Reform and Modernization in Modern Chinese History* (Hong Kong, 1992); Zhang Liheng, *Cong Xifang Dao Dongfang: Wu Tingfang Yu Zhongguo Jindai Shehui De Yanjin [From the East to the West: Wu Tingfang and the Modernization of the Chinese Society]* (Beijing, 2002).

Hongshan Li

Wu Xueqian (1921-)

Vice Premier Wu Xueqian's distinguished 44 years of service on behalf of the People's Republic of China took him across five continents. His travels made him a well-known diplomatic figure during an era when the Communist Chinese government was isolated diplomatically from much of the world, excluded as a voting member of the United Nations, and not recognized as a legitimate regime by a number of Western governments.

A member of the Central Committee of the Communist Party of China as well as the powerful Political Bureau of the Central Committee, Wu Xueqian was born in Shanghai on December 12, 1921. He joined the Communist Party at age 17 in June 1939 — a full decade before Mao Zedong won control of the mainland and declared the People's Republic. As a young underground revolutionary, Wu was involved in the organizing of Shanghai students. In June 1949 at age 27, he made his first international trip as the official Chinese National Federation of Democratic Youth's representative to the World Federation of Democratic Youth in Prague, Czechoslovakia, a nation that newly Communist itself. Upon the founding of the People's Republic, he served as Deputy Director General, then Director General from 1949 until 1958 of the International Liaison Department of the Central Committee of the Youth League, later renamed the Communist Youth League. From 1958 until 1982, he was the Director General, then Vice Minister of the International Liaison Department of the Communist Party's Central Committee. Then for seven months in 1982, he served as the First Vice-Foreign Minister. During those 24 years, he traveled extensively at a time when China was excluded from many diplomatic circles. He was a frequent visitor to African and West Asian countries, persuading them to consider establishing relations with China — often to the alarm of the Western powers. In November 1982, he was elevated to the post of Foreign Minister, then in June 1982 was appointed to serve simultaneously as State Councilor — making him roughly the Chinese equivalent of the United States' Secretary of State and National Security Advisor. In that dual position, he served as the head of the PRC's delegation to the United Nations and visited over 50 countries throughout Asia, Africa, Europe and the Americas, including Argentina, Brazil, Canada, Finland, France, Hungary, Japan, Egypt, Kenya, Malaysia, North Korea, Romania, Sweden, the United States, West Germany and Zambia. Among his diplomatic accomplishments were the 1986 signing of the Sino-Finland and Sino-Sweden Agreements on Avoidance of Double Taxation and Prevention of Tax Evasion, and the Sino-Hungarian Consular Treaty. He is also credited with historic negotiations to resolve boundary disputes with both the Soviet Union and India. He is cited as one of the key diplomats involved in the decades-long negotiations with Great Britain to secure the return of Hong Kong to Chinese sovereignty.

In March 1988, he was named Vice Premier of China's State Council and as one of his first official acts led the Chinese delegation to the funeral of Pakistan's President Haq. In 1990, he attended the independence celebration of Namibia, formerly the Republic of South Africa's administrative territory of Southwest Africa, and signed the Sino-Namibia Joint Communique establishing diplomatic relations. In the same year, he visited Gabon and Nigeria, and attended the enthroning ceremonies of Japan's new Emperor Akihito. Wu retired in March 1993 at the age of 72 and resides in Beijing.

REFERENCES: Rick Chu, "Diplomacy is China's Weak Suit," *Taibei Times* (Taibei, March 12, 2000); Jonathan Dimbleby, "A Sense of Betrayal," *The Times of London,* (London, July 6, 1997); Michael E. Marti, *China and the Legacy of Deng Xiaoping: From Communist Revolution to Capitalist Evolution* (Dulles, VA, 2002); David Shambaugh, "Europe's Relations With China: Forging Closer Ties," a paper presented at the symposium "Blue Horizon: United States-Japan-PRC Tripartite Relations, Part I: Security" (Maxwell Air Force Base, Alabama: Institute for National Strategic Studies, National Defense University, 1996); Robert Shuey and Shirley A. Kan, "Chinese Missile and Nuclear Proliferation: Issues for Congress," Congressional Research Service: Issue Brief, IB92056 (Washington, DC, November 16, 1995).

Rob Kerby

Yalta Conference (1945)

The Yalta Conference was a meeting of the leaders of the big three wartime Allies from February 4 to 11, 1945 at Yalta, the key Black Sea port on the Crimean peninsula in the Soviet Union. U.S. President Franklin D. Roosevelt, British Prime Minister Winston Churchill, and Soviet Premier Joseph Stalin reached agreement on a series of issues related to the conduct of the war in Europe and Asia, and the postwar world. At this point, the Soviets were triumphant in the land war against Germany, while Japan remained a formidable foe whose defeat, especially the invasion of the home islands, could well cost more than a million American casualties.

The agreements were very important. The Big Three wartime allies came to agreement on the fate of postwar Germany, German reparations, the future United Nations, the status of the postwar Polish government, which reflected the Red Army's control of Eastern Europe and the relative powerlessness of the Western Allies east of the Elbe and Danube Rivers, and the status of Yugoslavia. They also reaffirmed their demand for unconditional surrender of the remaining Axis partners. And Stalin committed the Soviet Union to the fight against Japan once the Allies had successfully concluded the war against Germany. However, since the agreements on Japan presaged military action, the Big Three decided to keep those agreements secret.

In return for this commitment, Stalin gained major concessions. Roosevelt and Churchill accepted that, in return for Soviet entry, Stalin could regain Russia's position lost after the Russia-Japanese War of 1904–1905, including Sakhalin Island, significant interests in Lushun (Port Arthur) and Dalian (Dairen) in Manchuria, giving the Soviet Navy all-year, warm water ports in Northeast Asia, and Russia's former railway holdings, the Chinese Eastern Railway, that spur of the Trans-Siberian Railway that reduced the long trip from Moscow in the west to Vladivostock in the far east by more than 800 miles by cutting across Manchuria. In addition, they agreed that the Soviet Union could keep its control over Outer Mongolia and seize the Kurile Islands north of the main Japanese islands, which had always been Japanese. Of course, the gains came at the expense of Japan, the wartime enemy, and China, the wartime ally, and likely presaged the future of Korea, divided between the emerging Cold War adversaries and postwar superpowers. In a larger sense, to reward Stalin for Russia's sacrifices against Germany and for his commitment to enter the war against Japan, the Western Allies agreed to the re-establishment of Soviet rights in China when, at nearly the very same moment, they were retroceding their own imperialist rights back to the Nationalist government, headquartered in Chongqing.

China was not a participant at the Yalta Conference, and Jiang's government complained about the resulting accords. While President Roosevelt promised Stalin that he would consult with Jiang and obtain his approval, there truly was little discussion. Roosevelt told Churchill and Stalin that the Chinese could not keep secrets. The government in Chongqing noted that it had no input into the decision, and that its Allies sacrificed the sovereignty China just regained to reward Stalin. Stalin, for his part, promised to respect Chinese sovereignty in Manchuria and, for example, to agree to join Chinese-Soviet management of the Chinese Eastern Railway. Later as the wartime allies became Cold War adversaries, critics would charge that Roosevelt gave away too much at Yalta, and they would accuse a young man seen in many photographs over Roosevelt's shoulder, Alger Hiss, of being a spy who aided the Soviets.

See also **Chinese Eastern Railway; Manchuria; World War II; Cold War.**

REFERENCES: Russell D. Buhite, *Decisions at Yalta: An Appraisal of Summit Diplomacy* (Wilmington, DE, 1986); Diane Shaver Clemens, *Yalta* (New York, 1970); Richard F. Fenno, *The Yalta Conference* (Boston, MA, 1955); Hugh Thomas, *Armed Truce: The Beginning of the Cold War, 1945–1946* (London, 1986).

Charles M. Dobbs

Yao Ming (1980-)

Yao Ming was born on September 12, 1980 in Shanghai, to parents who were both professional basketball players. By age 9 the quiet, bookish boy — a devotee of Chinese military history — had grown to 5'7" (1.7 m) tall, and was recruited for a sports school to be drilled in basketball skills. His professional career began in 1997, when he joined the Shanghai Sharks, a mediocre team in his hometown. In the 2000–2001 season, he scored an outstanding average of 27 points and 19 rebounds per game, for which he won the title of Most Valuable Player of the Chinese Basketball Association. He played to some acclaim on the Chinese national team in the 2000 Sydney Summer Olympics, and in the 2001–2002 season led the Sharks to a CBA championship. During a playoff game that followed this victory, Yao thrilled his fans and set a record by making every one of the 21 shots he attempted.

In 2002, he became eligible for the U.S. National Basketball Association (NBA) draft, and impressed scouts by his performance at a draft camp. Selected as a center by the team with the number one overall draft pick — the Houston Rockets — this gigantic Chinese player, at 7' 6" and 310 lbs, the fourth tallest man in the NBA, instantly focused worldwide attention. In the United States where basketball originated, great players had always been homegrown; although Yao was not the first Chinese player to be recruited by the NBA (Wang Zhizhi was hired in 2001 by the Dallas Mavericks), his height and record fueled wide-ranging speculation. In China news about Yao's U.S. hiring was subdued, for fear that he would eventually prove an embarrassment to himself and his compatriots. Yao's performance during his rookie season was one of the best in NBA history. He earned a place on the NBA All-Rookie First Team with a more than respectable average of 13.5 points and 8.2 rebounds per game. Some of the highlights of the season were his head-to-head battles with the star center Shaquille O'Neal of the reigning Los Angeles Lakers. Since then, Yao has consistently improved his overall statistics. At the beginning of his second season, the Rockets hired a new coach, Jeff Van Gundy, who tailored the team's offense to spotlight Yao. In the off-season, Yao plays for the Chinese national team in the International Basketball Association World Championships.

Yao's meteoric rise to mega-stardom in China is explained in part by the widespread popularity of basketball icons such as Michael Jordan; the sudden appearance of a native son on a hallowed stage caused Chinese public attention to basketball to skyrocket. Within the U.S., a number of factors contributed to Yao's steep and sudden rise to household recognition status. The Chinese press attributes Yao's popularity in part to a savvy campaign headed by a Yao relative, who holds an MBA from Harvard University. No doubt the NBA itself recognizes the value of its product overseas, and salivating at the size of the Chinese market, it promotes Yao as a prize commodity. Yao himself is easily promoted: clean-cut, good-natured, polite, and endowed with an endearing sense of humor, he is a counterfoil to the rampant images of the "bad-boys of sports" — egotistic, self-aggrandizing, foul-mouthed, and often in trouble with the law. He also benefits from the cerebral, high-achieving stereotype of Asian Americans in the U.S.: whereas sports heroes commonly market athletic gear, Yao has effectively marketed Apple Computers, Visa, and McDonald's.

Yao's third major international role besides in sports and commerce is diplomatic. At a time in which U.S. xenophobia and paranoia is at a post-Cold War high, and China's own explosive economic growth thrusts it onto U.S. radars as a potential competitor if not enemy, Yao's friendly face helps to familiarize an otherwise faceless "other." His behavior is carefully and bilaterally stellar: he exhibits behavior considered exemplary in the U.S. as well as in China. He lives with his mother in Houston (filial affection pleases the Chinese); she runs the "Mama Yao Restaurant" (entrepreneurship pleases both the Chinese and the Americans). Half of his multi-million dollar NBA salary is dutifully turned over to China each year (his U.S. success produces a base-level, tangible benefit to his homeland). During the off-season in 2003, he hosted a multinational telethon in China to battle SARS. He held the flag for the Chinese delegates at the Athens Olympics in August 2004 and played on the Chinese national team, demonstrating his undying love of his homeland. He co-starred with Magic Johnson, the Lakers legend diagnosed HIV-positive, in a public service spot televised in Hong Kong, urging by example, sharing take-out Chinese food with Johnson, that one should not fear casual contact with people with AIDS and demonstrating U.S.-Chinese compassion and friendship.

Beginning in 2005, Yao will be a key representative of "Basketball without Borders," the NBA's primary international outreach program featuring players as coaches in basketball camps for youth, now expanded to four continents including inaugural events in China. These camps also provide opportunities for young people from different countries to discuss important social issues as identified by the organizers. Yao Ming has clearly been co-opted by both the United States and China to promote the values dear to each.

REFERENCES: David J. Blythe, "Foreign Stars & Foreign Relations," (Unpublished Paper, 2004); U.S. National Basketball Association, *www.nba.com/player file/yao_ming*; *Time*, *www.time.com/time/asia/2003/heroes/yao_ming.html*.

Cynthia Ning

Ye Gongchao (1904–1981)

Ye Gongchao is known in the West by the anglicized name of George Kung-chao Yeh or George K.C. Yeh. He was a Chinese diplomat, scholar, and statesman. Ye was born on September 12, 1904, (or possibly October 20) in Guangzhou, China. Ye's father, Ye Taosen was a bureaucrat in the Manchu Dynasty government. His family had been previously involved in scholarly activity. His mother was Zhao Huating. Ye attended preparatory school in China before going in 1919 to Amherst College in Massachusetts to study English literature. His poetic ability was noticed by Robert Frost. He graduated in 1924 with a BA in English. Attended Cambridge University in England for graduate study, Ye graduated in 1926 with a MA in Indo-European Linguistics. After returning to China, he began a fourteen year teaching career as a professor of English at Beijing University (1926–1927); the National Jinan University (1927–1929); and at Qinghua University (1929–1935). He returned to Beijing University in 1935 as head of the English Department.

With the outbreak of war with Japan, Beijing University retreated to Chongqing where it merged with the National Southwestern Associated University. Ye taught there until 1939. During this time he translated into English a short story by the Chinese poet Bian Zhilin. The translation was published in a British literary periodical, *Life and Letters Today* (October 1939). In 1940 Ye went to Shanghi on personal business. He was arrested by the Japanese and jailed for a while before being rescued. In 1941 he was recruited by the Guomindang to work for the party. He was posted to Malaya as Director of the Malaya Office of the Chinese Ministry of Information. In 1942 he went to London as Director of the United Kingdom Office of the Chinese Ministry of Information. He also served as councilor to the Chinese Embassy. While in London he gave several talks that were subsequently published in pamphlet form on Chinese religions and their implications for the war effort. Among these was "The Confucian Conception of Jen" (1943).

Ye returned to China in 1946 as director of the European affairs department of the Ministry of Foreign Affairs. He was sent to Rangoon as Ambassador Extraordinary to resolve territorial claims of China on its border with Burma. Ye was appointed Minister for Foreign Affairs in September 1949 shortly before the Nationalists' retreat to Taiwan. As foreign minister, he negotiated a peace treaty with Japan (1952) and a mutual defense pact with the United States (1954). Ye was also chairman of the Nationalist government's delegation to the United Nations. In 1950 when Outer Mongolia was allowed to join the United Nations, he abstained. Jiang Jieshi dismissed him after the vote, but soon restored him to office. In 1958 he was appointed Ambassador to the United States from the Republic of China. He served until 1962 when he was made Minister without Portfolio. This title he held until 1978. Ye was the author of several books including *Cultural Life in Ancient China*, and *Introducing China* (1948) with C. P. Fitzgerald. Shorter works in English include *Social Forces in English Literature*, *Communism in China* (1954), and *Communism Versus the Humanistic Tradition* (1961).

Ye was decorated with the Grand Cordon of the Order of the Brilliant Star and was a member of the Royal Asiatic Society of the United Kingdom. Ye died of a heart attack on November 20, 1981, in Taibei, Taiwan.

Sse also U.S.-China Mutual Defense Treaty (1954).

REFERENCES: George K.C. Yeh and C. P. Fitzgerald, *Introducing China* (London, 1948); George K.C. Yeh, *Satellization Is War* (Taibei, 1953); George K.C. Yeh, *Collection of Speeches Made in the United States of America from September 1954 to February 1955* (Taibei, 1955); George K.C. Yeh, *Foreign Policy Speeches, 1955* (Taibei, 1956); Zhou Gu (ed.), *Diplomatic Documents from Hu Shih and George K.C. Yeh's Visit to the United States* (Taibei, 2001).

Jack Waskey

Yenching University

Yenching University represented a model of Christian higher education in China. It not only was an agency of Sino-Western cultural exchange but also portrayed the ideal of integration between Christianity and Chinese culture. Yenching University originated with the merger of four Christian schools—Beijing University, North China Union College, North China Union College for Women, and School of Theology—from 1915 to 1920. John Leighton Stuart, then a faculty member in the Nanjing Theological Seminary, was selected as president.

Yenching University, in many ways, reflected the educational efforts and ideals of President Stuart. Stuart's realization of a bicultural Christian campus was vividly demonstrated at the anti-Christian movements of the 1920s. Mission schools were criticized for being under the protection of the unequal treaties, and for failing to conform to the requirements of the Chinese educational system. Stuart allowed Wu Lei-chuan become the chancellor of Yenching while he continued to use the name of President to manage the university. The university took various other steps to comply with the new educational regulations. First, it decided to offer a wide range of courses on religion as electives. Second, Stuart created the Yenta Christian Fellowship (Yenching University Christian Fellowship) as "the center of the direct expression of Christian life and service." Stuart believed that the witness of Christian faculty and students in their life was the best way to reach the Christianization of the campus. Third, many departments, especially those of the social sciences, used research and investigation in China for their case studies. In Stuart's mind, this was another way of contextualization of a Christian university in China. One of Yenching's most noticeable achievements was its China Studies. The Chinese Department's strong faculty and the creation of the Harvard-Yenching Institute of Chinese Studies in 1928 were another important step in reaching the goal of cultural synthesis. Later the Harvard-Yenching Institute produced many impressive results, such as the *Harvard-Yenching Sinological Index Series*, *Yenching Journal of Chinese Studies*, and the *Harvard-Yenching Monograph Series*. The successful advancement of Stuart's educational goals came from his leadership, his noble personality, his persistence in his ideals, and his charisma. He built friendships and received financial support from important figures both abroad and local. Stuart's personal connection assisted him in making Yenching University a unique place that survived many turbulent times.

When Beijing fell into Japanese hands in 1937, Yenching University, using the American flag as protection, continued to operate. Its relative autonomy came to an end after Pearl Harbor in December 1941. Stuart was put into confinement for three years and eight months. During this period, some of Yenching's professors and students moved to southwest China and resumed education in Chengdu, Sichuan. After Stuart was released at the end of the war, he managed to reinstate the university to its original place in Beijing. Stuart later left China when the Chinese Communists took control of China in 1949. In 1952, Yenching University merged with Beijing University and the latter moved into Yenching's campus.

See also Stuart, John Leighton (1876–1962).

REFERENCES: Dwight Woodbridge Edwards, *Yenching University* (New York, 1959); Shaw Yu-ming, *American Missionary in China: John Leighton Stuart and Chinese-American Relations* (Cambridge, 1992); John Leighton Stuart, *Fifty Years in China; the Memoirs of John Leighton Stuart, Missionary and Ambassador* (New York, 1954); Philip West, *Yenching University and Sino-Western Relations, 1916–1952* (Cambridge, 1976).

Chen-mian Wang

Yin He Incident see *Galaxy (Yin He)* Incident

Yoke Force

In February 1942, General Joseph W. Stilwell was appointed Commander of the Headquarters, American Armed Forces, China-Burma-India Theater. He also served as Chief of Staff to the Supreme Commander, China Theatre, Generalissimo Jiang Jieshi, and Deputy Commander in Burma to General Sir Archibald Wavell, British Commander in Chief for India and Burma. Later he served in the same capacity to Admiral Lord Mountbatten, the head of South East Asia Command, which was a reconfiguration of the China-Burma-India Theater in 1943. Stilwell had had previous military experience in China in the 1920s as a language officer and in serving with the Fifteenth Infantry in Tianjin; he had returned to China as military attache in the 1930s. Stilwell and Jiang often disagreed on goals and methods in the war against the Japanese in China and Burma. These divergent views reflected the differing goals of the United States and China as to the prosecution of the war, as well as personality differences between the two men. Stilwell believed that with proper training and equipment, and proper leadership, Chinese troops would prove to be very effective in military action. The British, among others, were skeptical.

Three Chinese Divisions were sent to India for training and equipping by Americans. These troops were the Yoke Force, a group for whom Stilwell's goal was to be a professional, apolitical military organization. Jiang obviously disagreed with this goal, as political loyalty was highly valued in the Chinese command structure. Stilwell pushed the Chinese to intervene in Burma, and to secure the area where the Ledo Road was to be constructed since the Burma Road had been closed by the Japanese. This supply road and pipeline to southern China was begun in 1943 and completed in early 1945. Jiang preferred to concentrate on problems within China, especially the flow of Lend-Lease supplies, and the air units under General Clare Chennault, who had boasted that air power alone would defeat the Japanese. This view was much more acceptable to Jiang than those expressed by Stilwell, which emphasized the need for ground forces to be used directly against the Japanese. Major problems in China in Stilwell's view were those of the need for reorganization, the elimination of political influence and corruption, and the concentration of authority within a small group. Jiang did not admit the need for major changes.

The first Sino-American-British operations in Burma in early 1942 were failures. Therefore, the training base at Ramgarth (India) was established in December 1943. The Yoke Force participated in the Burma campaign with British forces and Merrill's Marauders (the 5307 Composite Group), beginning in May 1944. Although Jiang frequently countermanded Stilwell's orders, leaving Chinese commanders and Stilwell frustrated, these forces countered the Japanese drive towards India and cleared North Burma of Japanese control. The Yoke force assisted in the capture of the Japanese air base at Myitkyina. The collapse of Jiang's forces in the summer of 1944 in response to the Japanese Ichigo campaign, which attacked Chinese positions in central and southern China in a push towards the American air bases in southern China and the Chinese wartime capital of Chongqing in central China, led most American planners to discount further operations in China. The Yoke forces were reabsorbed into the Chinese army. At Jiang's insistence, Stilwell was recalled to the U.S. in late 1944.

See also China-Burma-India (CBI) Theater; Stilwell, Joseph W. (1883–1946).

REFERENCES: John Costello, *The Pacific War* (New York, 1982); G.L. Weinberg (ed.), *A World At Arms* (New York, 1994); Barbara W. Tuchman, *Stilwell and the American Experience in China, 1911–1945* (New York, 1971); Theodore H. White (ed.), *The Stilwell Papers* (New York, 1991).

Katherine Reist

Yoshida Letter

The "Yoshida Letter" refers to the December 24, 1951 letter that Japan's Prime Minister Yoshida Shigeru sent to John Foster Dulles, who at the time was consultant to Secretary of State Dean Acheson. In the letter Yoshida expressed his willingness to negotiate a peace treaty with Jiang Jieshi's Nationalist Government in Taiwan. Yoshida's aim was to facilitate U.S. Senate ratification of the San Francisco Peace Treaty. Dulles had just returned from a trip to Tokyo with John Sparkman and Alexander H. Smith, respectively the chair and ranking Republican member of the Senate Subcommittee on Far Eastern Relations, who had expressed to Yoshida privately and to the press publicly their desire that Japan sign a treaty with Jiang's government. Dulles let the two key senators read the draft of the Yoshida Letter; furthermore, he conveyed to Yoshida that the letter's commitment to sign a peace treaty with Jiang's government was the minimum statement without which Senate ratification of the San Francisco Peace Treaty was probably impossible. The letter gained Yoshida's objective of Senate ratification of the San Francisco Peace Treaty that restored sovereignty to Japan. In this context, Yoshida's letter, along with Japan's ensuing 1952 peace treaty with the Republic of China, was widely regarded as recognizing Jiang's regime as the legitimate government of China. In reality, despite intense efforts by Taiwan's government, Yoshida skillfully limited the scope of the letter and the treaty to "territories which are now, or which may hereafter be, under the control" of Jiang's government. In restricting the scope to the de facto situation of the time, Yoshida sought to maintain Japan's option to negotiate separate treaties with the People's Republic of China in Beijing.

Declassified documents reveal that the negotiations leading up to the letter were also more complex than conventionally realized. Dulles engaged in extensive discussions with Acheson, British officials (particularly British Foreign Secretary Herbert Morrison), the American Charge d'Affaires in Taibei (Karl Lott Rankin), the American ambassador in Tokyo (William J. Sebald), as well as with Japan's Vice Minister of Foreign Affairs Iguchi Sadao. However, when he decided that Yoshida had not moved close enough to his own position, he drafted the "Yoshida Letter" himself with some help from Sebald. Even though he made some modifications in response to Yoshida's reservations, the letter was essentially Dulles'; nonetheless, Yoshida agreed to sign it.

In securing the letter and the commitment therein, Dulles went beyond instructions from Secretary of State Acheson, who sought to lessen conflicts with Britain over East Asian policy; therefore, Acheson wanted treaty negotiations dealing only with practical matters, like trade, rather than a peace treaty. Having acted contrary to Acheson's policy and instructions, Dulles made misleading statements in his reports to his superior about the letter and his role. Moreover, his reports presented a case for satisfying conservative senators to ensure treaty ratification and for resisting British pressure to return to the spirit of Dulles' agreement with Morrison. It is clear that he misled Acheson: Dulles reported that he did not have the letter and did know its specifics—even though he brought back a copy in his briefcase and had received a telegram from Sebald with news that Yoshida had agreed to Dulles' modifications to the letter. Thus, although some historians emphasize continuity in U.S. foreign policy from Acheson to Dulles, the case of the Yoshida Letter demonstrates Dulles' departure from the style and substance of Acheson's policies.

See also Dulles, John Foster (1888–1959).

REFERENCES: U.S. Department of State, *Foreign Relations of the United States, 1951: Asia and the Pacific Vol. 6* (Washington, DC, 1977); Zhonghua Minguo waijiao wenti yanjiuhui [Research Society for Problems of the Republic of China's Foreign Affairs] (ed.), *Jinshan hoyue yu Zhong-Ri hoyue di guanxi [Relationship between the San Francisco Peace Treaty and the Sino-Japanese Peace Treaty]*, Vol. 8 of *Zhong-Ri waijiao shiliao congbian [Historical documents of Sino-Japanese foreign relations]* (Taibei, 1966); Tian Hao (Hoyt Tillman), "Wushi niandai chuqi Meiguo de dui Hua zhengce," ["U.S. Policy toward China in the Early 1950s,"] *Lishi yanjiu [Historical Research]*, journal of the Chinese Academy of Social Sciences in Beijing (October 1983).

Hoyt Tillman

Young, John Russell (1840–1899)

Journalist, diplomat, and ultimately Librarian of Congress, Young was born in Ireland but moved with his family to America before his first birthday. At the age of fifteen he began working as a proofreader in his uncle's publishing company in Philadelphia, and six years later he became a copy boy at the *Philadelphia Press*. Promoted to reporter, he gained fame for his reports on the Battle of Bull Run, and at the age of twenty-six he was appointed managing editor of Horace Greeley's *New York Tribune*. In 1872 he joined the *New York Herald* and became a correspondent in London and Paris, which enabled him to become acquainted with many European statesmen and celebrities.

Former President Ulysses Grant, beginning his world tour, visited London in 1877 and invited Young to accompany him. Young was fascinated by his experience in China, where he met the legendary Viceroy Li Hongzhang, and in 1882 Grant secured his appointment as U.S. minister to Beijing. Many prominent newspapers declared him unqualified and characterized the appointment as flagrant patronage, but he performed as well as most and better than many who held the position. While generally cooperating with his fellow Western diplomats, Young sought to persuade the Chinese that the United States differed from the European powers in that it did not pursue an imperialist policy and was committed to China's independence. He took great pride in asserting the intimacy of his relationship with Li Hongzhang, but Li — justifiably, as events proved — doubted that the United States would provide significant assistance to China and was deeply offended by Congress' passage in 1882 of legislation suspending Chinese immigration. As Secretary of State Frederick T. Frelinghuysen provided little or no direction, Young had considerable freedom to set policy.

During his tenure at Beijing the most important issue with which he dealt was the Sino-French dispute of 1883–1885. For Young this was a difficult time; in July 1883 his second wife, to whom he had been married for seventeen months, died shortly after giving birth to a son in Paris. He nevertheless decided to remain in Beijing. While maintaining an "official" policy of restraint, he did not conceal his disapproval of French policy, for which he was severely criticized by the Western residents in the treaty ports. Although he rebuffed Li Hongzhang's requests for military assistance, he did repeatedly urge Frelinghuysen to authorize U.S. mediation of the dispute, and in July 1884 he arranged the "sale" of the China Merchants' Steam Navigation Company's ships to the American firm of Russell and Company, a ruse that prevented the French from seizing those vessels, which were returned to the Chinese after the dispute was settled. Young's action, combined with his known sympathy for the Chinese side, provoked the French to declare that he had disqualified himself to mediate the dispute, and they never seriously considered agreeing to mediation. Despite his personal sympathies he consistently warned the Chinese authorities that a prolonged war would prove disastrous and urged them to accept French peace terms, but the Chinese stood firm until Sir Robert Hart, the Inspector-General of Chinese Customs, negotiated peace in the summer of 1885. Later that year, when Grover Cleveland became the first Democrat elected President since the Civil War, Young, aware that the new administration preferred to assign a Democrat to Beijing, resigned and rejoined the *New York Herald*. In June 1897 President William McKinley appointed him Librarian of Congress, and he oversaw the transfer of the collection from the Capitol Building to its present quarters, a process that had not been completed when he died in January 1899.

Young was short and plump, with a thick moustache. Quiet and reserved by nature, he was said to be a man of exceptional charm.

REFERENCES: David L. Anderson, *Imperialism and Idealism: American Diplomats in China, 1861–1898* (Bloomington, IN, 1985); Michael H. Hunt, *The Making of a Special Relationship: The United States and China to 1914* (New York, 1983); John Russell Young, *Around the World with General Grant* (New York, 1879); John Russell Young, *Men and Memories: Personal Reminiscences* (New York, 1901).

Michael Sinclair

Young Men's Christian Association (YMCA)

The YMCA was rooted in the social gospel movement, a style of Protestantism that combined social service with soul saving and that attracted millions Americans in the late 19th century. These evangelical Christians saw their mission as global, and dozens of them went to China from the 1880s through the 1920s. In 1885 and 1886, the first two YMCA chapters were established in China. The YMCA diverged from the strategy of earlier Protestant missionaries, who concentrated almost exclusively on conversion, making little attempt to learn about Chinese culture or to provide helpful social services. In this divergence, the YMCA's social gospel-inspired leaders harked back to the 16th century experience of Catholic Jesuit missionaries such as Matteo Ricci. By 1895, there was sufficient financial support in the U.S. and sufficient interest among the Chinese to send missionary David Willard Lyon to Shanghai as the YMCA's first official secretary in China. Eventually, Lyon made Tianjin the organization's Chinese base of operations, largely because of the large number of English-speaking students there.

The YMCA operated in China under a broad strategy called "indigenization," which implied both obtaining as much Chinese financial support as possible and setting policy based on local conditions rather than on mandates from the United States. One significant result of indigenization was that the YMCA in China took on an even greater social service orientation (at the expense of religious evangelism) than it did in the U.S. According to historian Shirley Garrett, "The spirit of the Chinese Association, no matter what letters were sent home to prospective backers, was one of service, not conversion." Unlike missionary churches, the YMCA did not require conversion as a condition of participation in any of its programs.

By 1907, the YMCA had branches in eight Chinese cities, and it involved members in an array of service programs for the next two decades. It helped students who wanted to study overseas. It provided a hospitable environment for Chinese students, businessmen, and reformers who wanted to congregate and discuss social reforms. Though officially apolitical, the YMCA allowed Sun Zhongshan's revolutionary literature in its reading rooms during the first decade of the 20th century. It introduced physical education into China, which helped fill the void left by the 1905 abolition of the examination system. In 1912, 30 students inspired by a YMCA conference undertook an investigation of the condition of coolies. Local reformers joined American YMCA staffers in organizing a variety of creative, multi-media public health campaigns — using cartoons, calendars, sandwich board signs, and even giving outdoor prizes to generate interest. The Association's most sustained, and probably most influential, service project was promoting mass literacy. It was the YMCA that, in 1920, appointed James Yen to lead a mass literacy campaign, which he eventually publicized in his 1925 book, *The Mass Education Movement in China*. Despite its largely constructive role in China, the YMCA came under attack by radicals from 1925 onward as a representative of Western domination. By the end of the 1920s, its role in China was greatly diminished.

REFERENCES: Shirley Garrett, *Social Reformers in Urban China: The Chinese YMCA, 1895–1926* (Cambridge, MA, 1970); Jun Xing, *Baptized in the Fire of Revolution: The American Social Gospel and the YMCA in China, 1919–1937* (Bethlehem, PA, 1996).

Norty Wheeler

Yuan Shih-k'ai *see* Yuan Shikai (1859–1916)

Yuan Shikai (1859–1916)

Yuan Shikai was born on September 16, 1859 in Xiangchen County, Henan Province, China and died on June 6, 1916. Yuan joined the Chinese military when he was still a teenager and worked his way up with the help from his family members first, and then, through his own hard work and smart maneuvering among different military leaders in China. Yuan was first known as the Chinese military leader who commanded the suppression of 1882 Korean Soldiers' Riot and the Progressive reformers' coup in Korea (1884). He was also one of the Chinese commanders fighting the Seoul campaign and Pyongyang campaign in Korea during the Sino-Japanese War (1894–1895). After China's humiliating defeat at the Japanese hand and the signing of the Treaty of Shimonoseki, Yuan returned and was authorized by the Qing Court to be in charge of developing and training China's modern "New Army" outside of Beijing.

In 1898, he was recruited by the reform-minded emperor, Guangxu to help put through their "Hundred-Day Reform." But he soon betrayed the emperor and helped the conservatives headed by Empress Dowager Cixi to crack down on the reformers. After a few years of staying out of limelight, Yuan became the Prime Minister of the Qing court in 1911, controlling the imperial government, including the Imperial Guards. At the same time, he also secretly dealt with the revolutionaries led by Dr. Sun Zhongshan who had started their revolution and established their revolutionary government in southern China. The next year, Yuan "persuaded" the imperial family to let the young Xuantong (Puyi) emperor to step down, thus ended China's imperial rule for good. Then Yuan himself became the first President of the new Republic of China. However, Yuan was never a believer in republicanism. His conservative views and personal ambition led him to force the Congress to make himself "President-for-Life," and then, in December 1915, declared that he would become the emperor of a new dynasty. But faced with the strong opposition and numerous rebellions across the country, Yuan had to end his imperial rule in March 1916. He died soon after.

After his death, the power struggle among his Beiyang Army generals actually cast China into the long "Warlord Era" (1816–1928). Yuan is remembered in Chinese history as the founder of China's first modern army, a traitor of China's reform effort, and the biggest warlord who was ambitious enough to try turning the history backward and died miserably.

See also Sun Zhongshan (1866–1925); Chinese Revolution (1911).

REFERENCES: Jerome Chen, *Yuan Shih-k'ai* (Stanford, CA, 1972); Jerome Chen, *Yuan Shih-k'ai, 1859–1916: Brutus Assumes the Purple* (London, 1961); Husheng He (ed.), *Ten Great Warlords of Republican China* (Beijing, 1995); Stephen R. MacKinnon, *Power and Politics in Late Imperial China: Yuan Shih-k'ai in Beijing and Tianjin, 1901–1908* (Berkeley, CA, 1980); Ernest P. Young, *The Presidency of Yuan Shih-k'ai: Liberalism and Dictatorship in Early Republican China* (Ann Arbor, MI, 1977).

Xiansheng Tian

Yung Wing (1828–1912) *see* Rong Hong (1828–1912)

Zhao Ziyang (1919–2005)

Zhao Ziyang was a prominent Chinese Communist Party (CCP) leader and the Premier of the People's Republic China in the 1980s. He was born under the name of Zhao Xiusheng in Hua County, Henan Province in November 1919 (Some sources indicate he was born in 1918). His father was a prosperous landlord and grain merchant. Zhao began his elementary education in his hometown; he then attended secondary schools in Kaifeng and Wuhan, where he became attracted to the underground Communist Youth League. In 1932 Zhao officially joined the league, and in 1938 he became a member of the Chinese Communist Party, and subsequently fought with Communist guerrillas against the Japanese invasion. During the civil war between the Communists and the Nationalists, Zhao served as a local party official in the Communist-held areas in central China, engaging in rural land reforms.

After the establishment of the People's Republic of China in 1949, Zhao was assigned to Guangdong Province to oversee the redistribution of land to poor farmers. Serving as the rural work director of the local government in the early 1950s, he gained valuable experience in managing agricultural issues. Over the next decade, Zhao rose steadily in the party hierarchy, and by 1965 he was named First Secretary of the CCP in Guangdong Province. However, during the turbulent years of the Chinese Great Proletarian Cultural Revolution (1966–1976), Zhao was purged in 1967 because he supported the progressive policies of more pragmatic party leaders such as Liu Shaoqi and Deng Xiaoping, and opposed the radical measures of Chairman Mao Zedong. In 1972 he was "rehabilitated," and in 1975 named First Secretary of CCP in Sichuan Province. Based on his experience, Zhao quickly restored the local economy by drastically reducing central control and using various incentives to promote productivity. Within a few years a miracle in Sichuan was created as severe famine diminished, and the industrial production rose eighty percent between 1976 and 1979. *Zhao's achievements in Sichuan caught the attention of Vice Premier Deng Xiaoping, who had emerged as the dominant figure in the Chinese leadership after Mao's death in 1976. *Zhao was promoted a full member of* the Politburo of CCP in 1979, and the Premier of the Chinese State Council a year later, succeeding Mao's designated heir Hua Guofeng. Deng and Zhao, along with CCP General Secretary Hu Yaobang, adopted a new economic policy for modernizing the country. Under Zhao, the free market and tax systems were introduced in China, foreign investment was welcomed, and the central government was streamlined.

During this period China also experienced dramatic expansion of trade and scientific and cultural exchanges with Western countries, particularly the United States. Unlike the confrontation-style diplomacy of the 1960s, Zhao's foreign policy was peaceful and productive. In 1982 the Chinese government signed a joint communique with the Reagan administration, which reaffirmed Beijing as the sole legitimate government of China, and the U.S. government pledged to gradually reduce arms sales to Taiwan. In January 1984, Zhao made a sixteen-day, diplomatic visit to the United States. Being the first Chinese Communist Premier to visit America, Zhao commented: "As a friendly envoy of the Chinese people, I have come to visit your country for the purpose of seeking increased mutual understanding, stabilizing the relations between our two countries, enhancing Chinese-American friendship, and helping to preserve world peace.... The Taiwan issue is the major difference between China and the United States, or in other words, the principal obstacle to the growth of Sino-U.S. relations.... United States and China, both being big countries, should be aware of their heavy responsibility for the maintenance of world peace." During his visit, Zhao talked with President Ronald Reagan on the issues of nuclear energy cooperation and non-proliferation, arms sales, trade restrictions. The two leaders voiced their joint opposition to the Soviet aggression in Central Asia. In Washington, Zhao signed the Industrial and Technological Cooperation Agreement with the Reagan administration. Three months later, while hosting Reagan's reciprocal visit to China, Zhao also signed a comprehensive tax and investment treaty with Reagan in Beijing.

In 1987 Zhao succeeded the popular Communist leader Hu Yaobang as General Secretary of CCP, following an initial student demonstration in the previous year. In 1989 a new round of pro-democracy demonstrations broke out after the sudden death of Hu, which escalated into a massive movement for political and social reform in China. Zhao visited fasting students and insisted on moderate measures in dealing with the demonstrators. However, when the conservative hardliners took control, he was stripped of all his positions and placed under house arrest. Zhao remained under detention until he passed away in 2005.

During this period China also experienced dramatic expansion of trade and scientific and cultural exchanges with Western nations, particularly the United States. Unlike the confrontation-style diplomacy of the 1960s, Zhao's foreign policy was peaceful and productive. In 1982 the Chinese government signed a joint communique with the Reagan administration, reaffirming Beijing as the "sole legal government of China." In 1983, Zhao made a month-long, ten-nation tour of Africa, promoting China's support for Third World countries. In January 1984, Zhao made a sixteen-day visit to the United States, and hosted Reagan's reciprocal visit to China three months later. During the same year he also visited nine European countries to stimulate trade relations and foreign investments in China. In December 1984 Zhao and British Prime Minister Margaret Thatcher signed the historical agreement on Hong Kong, which specified that the Chinese sovereignty would be restored by July 1997. Under Zhao, China also stabilized its relationship with the former Soviet Union, with whom China shares a long and vulnerable border.

In 1987 Zhao succeeded the popular Communist leader Hu Yaobang as General Secretary of CCP, following an initial student demonstration in the previous year. In 1989 a new round of pro-democracy demonstrations broke out after the sudden death of Hu, which escalated into a massive movement for political and social reforms in China. Zhao visited fasting students and insisted on only moderate measures in dealing with the demonstrators. However, when the hardliners took control, he was stripped of all his powers and placed under house arrest. Zhao remained under detention until he passed away in 2005.

See also Tiananmen Square Massacre.

REFERENCES: Charles Moritz, *Current Biography Yearbook* (New York, 1984); David Shambaugh, *The Making of a Premier: Zhao Ziyang's Provincial Career* (Boulder, CO, 1984); *Encyclopedia of China: the Essential Reference to China, Its History and Culture* (New York, 1999); Pak-wah Leung, *Political Leaders of Modern China: A Biographical Dictionary* (Westport, CT, 2002).

Wenxian Zhang

Zhou Enlai (1898–1976)

As one of the top Chinese Communist Party (CCP) leaders and founder of new China's diplomacy, Zhou Enlai formed CCP branches in France in 1920–1924. On his return to China in 1924, he became director of the political department at Huangpu Military Academy during the first CCP-Guomindang (GMD) alliance. After the two parties split, Zhou joined General Zhu De and led an armed revolt within the GMD army in Nanchang to establish a Communist military force on August 1, 1928, now celebrated as the founding day of the People's Liberation Army (PLA). He was elected to the CCP Politburo in 1928 and as secretary of the Central Bureau in 1931. When Mao Zedong emerged as the CCP's leader, Zhou became his chief supporter and closest working colleague throughout his political career. Together, they led the Communist forces in the historic Long March from central China to northwest China in 1934 and 1935.

During World War II, as the chief CCP representative with the GMD government, Zhou successfully negotiated a second CCP-GMD united front to fight against Japan's invasion. He became vice chairman of the CCP Central Military Commission (CMC) in 1937 and head of the political department of the Military Committee in the GMD government in Chongqing in 1938. After the Pearl Harbor Attack in 1941, he initiated official contact with the U.S. government, resulting in the dispatch of the Dixie Mission to the CCP headquarters at Yanan. When World War II was over, Zhou, representing CCP, got involved in talks with GMD with General George C. Mashall as mediator for a settlement between the two parties. After the negotiations failed in 1946, Zhou returned to Yanan and served as the acting chief of the PLA's general staff.

When the PRC was founded in 1949, Zhou became its first Premier, foreign minister, and vice chairman of the Central Government Military Commission. He was third in the hierarchy after Mao and Liu Shaoqi, and the second most important figure in foreign affairs after Mao. Optimistic and modest, he instinctively kept a middle position in the central leadership and tried to hold the party together by persuasion and without challenging Mao's major foreign policy decisions, such as sending Chinese troops to the Korean War in 1950. Despite differing worldviews, he usually kept silent in the shadow of Mao's strong influence in foreign policy-making and merely tried to implement Mao's policies through skillful diplomacy. In 1951, he established a friendship with India, persuading it to accept China's policy toward Tibet and to serve as mediator for the PRC and the United States during the Korean truce talks. Zhou developed the well-known "Five Principles of Peaceful Co-existence," which marked the beginning of a new period of Chinese diplomacy and has become the foundation of China's foreign policy since 1954. As a diplomat recognized worldwide, his flexible approach and pleasant personality broke through cold war hostilities and improved China's international relations as he led the Chinese delegations to the 1954 Indochina conference at Geneva and 1955 Asian-African conference at Bandung. Zhou survived the Chinese Cultural Revolution from 1966 to 1976 as he tried to make compromises between radical idealists and conservative pragmatists.

In 1971, Zhou bent his new efforts toward improving relations with the U.S. since the Soviet Union posed a direct threat to China. In July, he secretly met Henry A. Kissinger to arrange for President Richard Nixon to visit the PRC. In February 1972, Zhou met Nixon at the Beijing airport and, a week later, signed the Shanghai Communique, which normalized PRC-U.S. relations after twenty-three years of hostility. In September, he met the Japanese Prime Minister Tanaka Kakuei in Beijing to establish diplomatic relations. Though diagnosed with cancer in 1973, he continued to meet American officials. He received George H.W. Bush as the chief representative of Washington in 1974. He talked with President Gerald Ford during his state visit to Beijing in 1975. At the Fourth National People's Congress in 1975, Zhou made important domestic policy changes by emphasizing the economic development and the nation's modernization. Zhou died in Beijing on January 8, 1976.

See also Nixon's Visit to China; Kissinger, Henry (1923-); Shanghai Communique.

REFERENCES: Kuo-kang Shao, *Zhou Enlai and the Foundations of Chinese Foreign Policy* (New York, 1996); Ronald C. Keith, *The Diplomacy of Zhou Enlai* (New York, 1989); A. Doak Barnett, *The Making of Foreign Policy in China* (Boulder, CO, 1985).

Li Xiaobing

Zhou-Stuart Conversations

In December 1945, General George C. Marshall, the retired Army Chief of Staff, traveled to China to mediate and bring an end to the civil war between the Chinese Nationalists and the Chinese Communists. Though Marshall achieved peace for a short time in early 1946, the negotiation came to a deadlock at the end of June as heavy fighting broke out in northern China and Manchuria.

The critical difference between the Guomindang (GMD) and the Chinese Communist Party (CCP) was in the administration of the local governments in regions from which the Communists agreed to evacuate their forces. Marshall noticed that the negotiations gradually switched to the political affairs of China, which was not a familiar subject to him. He thus recommended that John Leighton Stuart, then the President of Yenching University, be appointed as U.S. ambassador to China. Stuart, having lived in China for many years, enjoyed a good reputation there, and spoke fluent Chinese. He seemed to be an appropriate candidate to assist Marshall in dealing with political matters. On July 11, 1946, Stuart became the ambassador, and he soon held a series of meetings with Zhou Enlai, the CCP representative, from late July to mid-November. In order to break the impasse in negotiations, Stuart proposed a five-man committee composed of two representatives from each side with Stuart as mediator. This committee, according to its original design, would work toward establishing an effective State council concurrently with a cessation of hostilities. Although pleased with this proposal, Zhou refused to move forward with it once he learned that Jiang Jieshi, the Nationalist leader, stipulated a five-point prerequisite on it. Jiang insisted that the Communist troops withdraw from certain strategically important areas and move into regions in Manchuria proposed by Jiang. Zhou rejected this demand because Jiang said nothing about the local governments that the Communists had already set up in their territory. Two more issues also obstructed the possibility of the five-man committee. One regarded the number of seats that Communists and their friendly allies could have in the State Council. Of the total forty seats, the Nationalists only agreed to allow, at most, thirteen seats while the Communists wanted fourteen, more than one third and enough to constitute a veto in all decisions. Another issue was that Zhou thought that Jiang unjustifiably announced the convocation of the National Assembly at the same time that Nationalist troops attacked Zhangjiakou (Kalgan), a strategic Communist stronghold.

Stuart, basically playing a role of messenger, shuttled between the two sides. All his talks with Zhou revolved around the above issues. He found great distrust and suspicions on both sides, especially among the Communists. Zhou found an evil purpose in all Nationalist moves. For example, Marshall and Stuart worked very hard to obtain a ten-day truce before the Nationalist takeover of Zhangjiakou. Zhou on the other hand raised a series of conditions for future negotiations. Zhou, in a way to show his displeasure of Jiang's demands, withdrew to Shanghai for several weeks. In order to pressure both sides, Stuart and Marshall twice released a joint statement about the current development of their negotiations. The second statement, which came out on October 8, sought to push the Communists back to reason. Stuart and Marshall also asked people of the third parties to bring Zhou back to the conference table. Yet with the opening of the National Assembly, Zhou saw no hope for further negotiations, and bid his farewell to Stuart and Marshall on November 16, 1946 right before his departure to Yanan.

Though their conversations failed to bring out any positive results, Stuart and Zhou left a good impression on each other. Zhou considered Stuart to be honest and Stuart thought Zhou possessed a brilliant mind and rare personal charm.

See also Civil War (1945–1949); Stuart, John Leighton (1876–1962); Zhou Enlai (1898–1976).

REFERENCES: George C. Marshall, *Marshall's Mission to China, December 1945-January 1947: The Report and Appended Documents* (Arlington, VA, 1976); Shaw Yu-ming, *American Missionary in China: John Leighton Stuart and Chinese-American Relations* (Cambridge, MA, 1992); John Leighton Stuart, *Fifty Years in China; the Memoirs of John Leighton Stuart, Missionary and Ambassador* (New York, 1954); Zhou Enlai, *Zhou Enlai yi jiu si liu nian tan pan wen xuan [Selcted Works of Zhou Enlai on Negotiations of 1946]* (Beijing, 1996).

Chen-main Wang

Zhu Rongji (1928 -)

Zhu Rongji was born at Changsha, Hunan Province on October 1, 1928. He graduated from the prestigious Qinghua University with a degree in electrical engineering. Afterwards, he worked for the Northeast China Department of Industries as deputy head of its production planning office. From 1952 to 1958, he worked in the State Planning Commission as group head and deputy division chief.

In 1958, Zhu was labeled as a rightist by the State Council Personnel Department and was kicked out of the Chinese Communist Party because he expressed his own ideas on economic policies and criticized the policies held during the Great Leap Forward. Zhu was sent to rural area to feed pigs and clean toilets for five years. In 1962, Zhu went back to Beijing as a teacher at Beijing's State Cadre Training School after the Anti-Rightist Campaign was over. In 1965, during the Chinese Great Proletarian Cultural Revolution (1966–1976), Zhu was labeled as a capitalist and was sent to work in the rural area again. In 1975, Zhu was assigned to the Ministry of Oil Industry. In 1978, party leader Deng Xiaoping, who had stepped down during the Cultural Revolution, regained power. Deng began a re-evaluation of the government's policies in the past. Zhu was taken out of the rightist category. In 1979, Zhu became division chief of the State Economic Commission, and later became deputy director of this Commission. This allowed him to accumulate more experience related to economy and economic policies.

In 1983, Zhu was transferred to Shanghai as Deputy Party Secretary and worked under Jiang Zemin. Between 1988 and 1991, Zhu became Shanghai municipal secretary and mayor. In 1990, Zhu, as Shanghai's mayor, visited the United States. This was seen as an important diplomatic move after the Tiananmen Square Massacre of 1989. Zhu allowed the American International Group (AIG), an international insurance and financial services company, to establish a branch in Shanghai. He believed that Chinese insurance companies would learn more about insurance management from AIG. In 1991, Zhu became Vice Premier of the State Council and mainly dealt with issues of economy and finance, which Deng believed that only Zhu could do it right for a market economy. In 1998, Zhu was elected Premier by the National People's Congress. He retired from this post after the end of his five-year term. During this period, Zhu guided China from a planned economy to a market economy. He reformed the banking system in China, and allowed the growth of private enterprises. Zhu also paved the road for China to enter the World Trade Organization by reforming China's economic system and changing economic policies. In April 1999, Zhu visited the United States, although he faced opposition from the senior leaders in the Communist party. Zhu's trip was to talk with the United States about the accession of China to the World Trade Organization, and he hoped to gain the support from the United States. Zhu proposed terms about expanding access for U.S. businesses in China, cutting tariffs, and opening the Chinese domestic telecommunication industry for U.S. participation. Although Zhu's terms were seen as a breakthrough from the Chinese viewpoint, no agreement was made at that time. It was not until November 15, 1999 when an economic agreement with which Zhu had helped negotiate was reached. In 2003, Zhu's term as Premier was due, and he retired from his post.

REFERENCES: Laurence J. Brahm, *Zhu Rongji and The Transformation of Modern China* (Singapore, 2002); David M. Lampton (ed.), *The Making of Chinese Foreign and Security Policy in the Era of Reform, 1978–2000* (Stanford, CA, 2001); Robert L. Suettinger, *Beyond Tiananmen: The Politics of U.S.-China Relations, 1989–2000* (Washington, DC, 2003).

Edy Parsons

Zongli Yamen

The Zongli Geguo Shiwu Yamen (Office for the Administration of the Affairs of Different Nations), abbreviated as Zongli Yamen, was established as a foreign office in 1861. After her military defeat in the Second Opium War (1856–1860), China signed the Convention of Beijing (1860), which gave foreign powers the right to diplomatic residence in Beijing. Foreign legations were established in Beijing in 1861, and foreign representatives required a highly centralized bureaucratic body in the Qing government in handling foreign affairs in China.

The Zongli Yamen operated as a special committee on foreign affairs under the Grand Council. A Manchu prince was appointed by the Emperor as its head, and several ministers as its members. The number of the ministers increased from three in 1861 to thirteen in 1884, all of whom were high-level officials. Under the ministers were 16 secretaries, half of them being Manchu and the other half Han Chinese. Under the Zongli Yamen were five bureaus: Russian, British, French, American, and Coastal Defense. A foreign language school called Tongwenguan and the Inspectorate-General of Customs were affiliated with it. Initially perceived as a temporary office without authority to make policy (only the Emperor and the Grand Council had such authority), the influence of the Zongli Yamen depended on the power and status of its head and ministers. Because Prince Gong, the long-serving head of the Zongli Yamen, and Wenxiang, the chief minister, were senior ministers of the Grand Council, the Emperor usually approved their proposals during the 1860s and 1870s. Throughout the late 19th century, the Zongli Yamen successfully imposed a nationwide standard in dealing with a wide range of issues in relation to foreign affairs, the most prominent being cases of anti-missionary and anti-Christian violence, and cases of commercial disputes involving foreign merchants in China.

However, after Wenxiang's death in 1876 and Prince Gong's dismal in 1884, the Zongli Yamnen's influence began to decline, whereas Li Hongzhang, the statesman and leading modernizer, was appointed by the Empress Dowager Cixi to take charge of foreign affairs. After the Boxer Rebellion, a new Ministry of Foreign Affairs (Waiwubu) was created to replace the Zongli Yamen.

See also Li Hongzhang (1823–1901).

REFERENCES: Banno Masataka, *China and the West, 1858–1861: The Origins of the Tsungli Yamen* (Cambridge, MA, 1964); Jennifer M. Rudolph, *Negotiating Power and Navigating Change in the Qing: Zongli Yamen, 1861–1901* (Ph.D. Dissertation, University of Washington, 1999).

Joseph Tse-Hei Lee

Appendix I. American Chiefs of Mission to China

(Source: U.S. State Department)

Edward Everett. Title: Commissioner. Appointment: March 3, 1843.
Commissioned to China. Declined appointment.

Caleb Cushing (Massachusetts). Title: Envoy Extraordinary and Minister Plenipotentiary; Commissioner. Appointment: May 8, 1843. Presentation of Credentials: about June 12, 1844. Termination of Mission: Left Macao, August 27, 1844.
Commissioned to China. Was issued two separate commissions during a recess of the Senate, one as Commissioner and one as Envoy Extraordinary and Minister Plenipotentiary; after confirmation on June 17, 1844, re-commissioned as Commissioner only. Presentation of credentials to the Chief of State upon arrival did not become the normal procedure for U.S. diplomatic representatives in China until 1898. The date in brackets represents establishment of an official relationship with appropriate Chinese authorities, not necessarily including communication to them of a letter of credence.

Alexander H. Everett (Massachusetts). Title: Commissioner. Appointment: March 13, 1845. Presentation of Credentials: October 26, 1846. Termination of Mission: Died at post, June 28, 1847.
Commissioned to China. Presentation of credentials to the Chief of State upon arrival did not become the normal procedure for U.S. diplomatic representatives in China until 1898. The date in brackets represents establishment of an official relationship with appropriate Chinese authorities, not necessarily including communication to them of a letter of credence. Nominated February 26, 1845, to be Envoy Extraordinary and Minister Plenipotentiary; the Senate did not confirm this nomination.

John W. Davis (Indiana). Title: Commissioner. Appointment: January 3, 1848. Presentation of Credentials: October 6, 1848. Termination of Mission: Left post, May 25, 1850.
Commissioned to China. Presentation of credentials to the Chief of State upon arrival did not become the normal procedure for U.S. diplomatic representatives in China until 1898. The date in brackets represents establishment of an official relationship with appropriate Chinese authorities, not necessarily including communication to them of a letter or credence.
Peter Parker served as Chargé d'Affaires ad interim, May 1850–July 1853.

Joseph Blunt (New York). Title: Commissioner. Appointment: October 15, 1851.
Commissioned during a recess of the Senate. Commissioned to China. Declined appointment.

Humphrey Marshall (Kentucky). Title: Commissioner. Appointment: August 4, 1852. Presentation of Credentials: July 4, 1853. Termination of Mission: Left post, January 27, 1854.
Commissioned to China. Presentation of credentials to the Chief of State upon arrival did not become the normal procedure for U.S. diplomatic representatives in China until 1898. The date in brackets represents establishment of an official relationship with appropriate Chinese authorities, not necessarily including communication to them of a letter or credence.

Robert J. Walker (Mississippi). Title: Commissioner. Appointment: June 21, 1853.
Commissioned during recess of the Senate. Commissioned to China. Declined appointment.

Robert M. McLane (Maryland). Title: Commissioner. Appointment: October 18, 1853. Presentation of Credentials: November 3, 1854. Termination of Mission: Left post, December 12, 1854.

Commissioned during recess of the Senate; re-commissioned after confirmation on December 6, 1853. Commissioned to China. Presentation of credentials to the Chief of State upon arrival did not become the normal procedure for U.S. diplomatic representatives in China until 1898. The date in brackets represents establishment of an official relationship with appropriate Chinese authorities, not necessarily including communication to them of a letter or credence.

Peter Parker (Massachusetts). Title: Commissioner. Appointment: August 16, 1855. Presentation of Credentials: July 15, 1856. Termination of Mission: Left China August 25, 1857.

Commissioned during a recess of Senate; re-commissioned after confirmation on May 26, 1856. Commissioned to China. Presentation of credentials to the Chief of State upon arrival did not become the normal procedure for U.S. diplomatic representatives in China until 1898. The date in brackets represents establishment of an official relationship with appropriate Chinese authorities, not necessarily including communication to them of a letter or credence.

William B. Reed (Pennsylvania). Title: Envoy Extraordinary and Minister Plenipotentiary. Appointment: April 18, 1857. Presentation of Credentials: May 3, 1858. Termination of Mission: Left China, November 11, 1858.

Commissioned during a recess of the Senate; re-commissioned after confirmation on January 14, 1858. Commissioned to China. Presentation of credentials to the Chief of State upon arrival did not become the normal procedure for U.S. diplomatic representatives in China until 1898. The date in brackets represents establishment of an official relationship with appropriate Chinese authorities, not necessarily including communication to them of a letter or credence.

John E. Ward (Georgia). Title: Envoy Extraordinary and Minister Plenipotentiary. Appointment: December 15, 1858. Presentation of Credentials: August 10, 1859. Termination of Mission: Left Hong Kong, December 15, 1860.

Commissioned to China. Presentation of credentials to the Chief of State upon arrival did not become the normal procedure for U.S. diplomatic representatives in China until 1898. The date in brackets represents establishment of an official relationship with appropriate Chinese authorities, not necessarily including communication to them of a letter or credence.

Anson Burlingame (Massachusetts). Title: Envoy Extraordinary and Minister Plenipotentiary. Appointment: June 14, 1861. Presentation of Credentials: August 20, 1862. Termination of Mission: Appointment terminated, November 21, 1867.

Commissioned during a recess of the Senate; re-commissioned after confirmation on July 15, 1861. Commissioned to China. Presentation of credentials to the Chief of State upon arrival did not become the normal procedure for U.S. diplomatic representatives in China until 1898. The date in brackets represents establishment of an official relationship with appropriate Chinese authorities, not necessarily including communication to them of a letter or credence.

J. Ross Browne (California). Title: Envoy Extraordinary and Minister Plenipotentiary. Appointment: March 11, 1868. Presentation of Credentials: September 29-October 28, 1868. Termination of Mission: Left post, July 5, 1869.

Commissioned to China. Presentation of credentials to the Chief of State upon arrival did not become the normal procedure for U.S. diplomatic representatives in China until 1898. The date in brackets represents establishment of an official relationship with appropriate Chinese authorities, not necessarily including communication to them of a letter or credence.

William A. Howard (Michigan). Title: Envoy Extraordinary and Minister Plenipotentiary.
Commissioned to China. Took oath of office, but did not proceed to post.

Frederick F. Low (California). Title: Envoy Extraordinary and Minister Plenipotentiary. Appointment: September 28, 1869. Presentation of Credentials: April 27, 1870. Termination of Mission: Left post, July 24, 1873.
Commissioned during recess of the Senate; re-commissioned after confirmation December 21, 1869. Commissioned to China. Presentation of credentials to the Chief of State upon arrival did not become the normal procedure for U.S. diplomatic representatives in China until 1898. The date in brackets represents establishment of an official relationship with appropriate Chinese authorities, not necessarily including communication to them of a letter or credence.

Benjamin P. Avery (California). Title: Envoy Extraordinary and Minister Plenipotentiary. Appointment: April 10, 1874. Presentation of Credentials: November 29, 1874. Termination of Mission: Died at post, November 8, 1875.
Commissioned to China. Presentation of credentials to the Chief of State upon arrival did not become the normal procedure for U.S. diplomatic representatives in China until 1898. The date in brackets represents establishment of an official relationship with appropriate Chinese authorities, not necessarily including communication to them of a letter or credence.

George F. Seward (California). Title: Envoy Extraordinary and Minister Plenipotentiary. Appointment: January 7, 1876. Presentation of Credentials: April 24, 1876. Termination of Mission: Superseded, August 16, 1880.
Commissioned to China. Presentation of credentials to the Chief of State upon arrival did not become the normal procedure for U.S. diplomatic representatives in China until 1898. The date in brackets represents establishment of an official relationship with appropriate Chinese authorities, not necessarily including communication to them of a letter or credence.

James B. Angell (Michigan). Title: Envoy Extraordinary and Minister Plenipotentiary. Appointment: April 9, 1880. Presentation of Credentials: August 16, 1880. Termination of Mission: Left post, October 4, 1881.
Commissioned to China. Presentation of credentials to the Chief of State upon arrival did not become the normal procedure for U.S. diplomatic representatives in China until 1898. The date in brackets represents establishment of an official relationship with appropriate Chinese authorities, not necessarily including communication to them of a letter or credence.

John Russell Young (New York). Title: Envoy Extraordinary and Minister Plenipotentiary. Appointment: March 15, 1882. Presentation of Credentials: August 17, 1882. Termination of Mission: Relinquished charge, April 7, 1885.
Commissioned to China. Presentation of credentials to the Chief of State upon arrival did not become the normal procedure for U.S. diplomatic representatives in China until 1898. The date in brackets represents establishment of an official relationship with appropriate Chinese authorities, not necessarily including communication to them of a letter or credence.

Charles Denby (Indiana). Title: Envoy Extraordinary and Minister Plenipotentiary. Appointment: May 29, 1885. Presentation of Credentials: October 1, 1885. Termination of Mission: Presented recall, July 8, 1898.
Commissioned during a recess of the Senate; re-commissioned after confirmation on January 13, 1886. Commissioned to China. Presentation of credentials to the Chief of State upon arrival did not become the normal procedure for U.S. diplomatic representatives in China until 1898. The date in brackets represents establishment of an official relationship with appropriate Chinese authorities, not necessarily including communication to them of a letter or credence.

Henry W. Blair (New Hampshire). Title: Envoy Extraordinary and Minister Plenipotentiary. Appointment: February 27, 1891.

Commissioned to China. Took oath of office under recess appointment, but did not proceed to post; the Government of China having objected to his appointment.

Charles Page Bryan (Illinois). Title: Envoy Extraordinary and Minister Plenipotentiary. Appointment: November 10, 1897.

Took oath of office under recess appointment, but did not proceed to post; nomination of January 5, 1898 was withdrawn before the Senate acted upon it.

Edwin H. Conger (Iowa). Title: Envoy Extraordinary and Minister Plenipotentiary. Appointment: January 19, 1898. Presentation of Credentials: July 8, 1898. Termination of Mission: Left post, April 4, 1905.

Commissioned to China.

William Woodville Rockhill (District of Colombia). Title: Envoy Extraordinary and Minister Plenipotentiary. Appointment: March 8, 1905. Presentation of Credentials: June 17, 1905. Termination of Mission: Relinquished charge, June 1, 1909.

Commissioned to China.

Charles R. Crane (Illinois). Title: Envoy Extraordinary and Minister Plenipotentiary. Appointment: July 23, 1909.

Took oath of office, but did not proceed to post.

William James Calhoun (Illinois). Title: Envoy Extraordinary and Minister Plenipotentiary. Appointment: December 21, 1909. Presentation of Credentials: April 21, 1910. Termination of Mission: Normal relations interrupted, February 12, 1912; new Government of China still unrecognized by the United States when Calhoun left post, February 16, 1913.

Commissioned to China.

Paul S. Reinsch (Wisconsin). Non-career appointee. Title: Envoy Extraordinary and Minister Plenipotentiary. Appointment: August 15, 1913. Presentation of Credentials: November 15, 1913. Termination of Mission: Left post, September 15, 1919.

Commissioned to China.

Charles R. Crane (Illinois). Non-career appointee. Title: Envoy Extraordinary and Minister Plenipotentiary. Appointment: March 22, 1920. Presentation of Credentials: June 12, 1920. Termination of Mission: Left China, July 2, 1921.

Commissioned to China.

Jacob Gould Schurman (New York). Non-career appointee. Title: Envoy Extraordinary and Minister Plenipotentiary. Appointment: June 2, 1921. Presentation of Credentials: September 12, 1921. Termination of Mission: Left post, April 15, 1925.

Commissioned to China.

John Van A. MacMurray (New Jersey). Foreign Service officer. Title: Envoy Extraordinary and Minister Plenipotentiary. Appointment: April 9, 1925. Presentation of Credentials: July 15, 1925. Termination of Mission: Left post, November 22, 1929.

Commissioned during a recess of the Senate; re-commissioned after confirmation on December 17, 1925. Commissioned to China.

Nelson T. Johnson (Oklahoma). Foreign Service officer. Title: Envoy Extraordinary and Minister Plenipotentiary. Appointment: December 16, 1929. Presentation of Credentials: February 1, 1930. Termination of Mission: Promoted to Ambassador Extraordinary and Plenipotentiary.

Commissioned to China.

Nelson T. Johnson (Oklahoma). Foreign Service officer. Title: Ambassador Extraordinary and Plenipotentiary. Appointment: June 18, 1935. Presentation of Credentials: September 17, 1935. Termination of Mission: Left post, May 14, 1941.
Commissioned to China.

Clarence E. Gauss (Connecticut). Foreign Service officer. Title: Ambassador Extraordinary and Plenipotentiary. Appointment: February 11, 1941. Presentation of Credentials: May 26, 1941. Termination of Mission: Left post, November 14, 1944.
Commissioned to China.

Patrick J. Hurley (New Mexico). Non-career appointee. Title: Ambassador Extraordinary and Plenipotentiary. Appointment: November 30, 1944. Presentation of Credentials: January 8, 1945. Termination of Mission: Left post, September 22, 1945.
Commissioned to China.

J. Leighton Stuart (New York). Non-career appointee. Title: Ambassador Extraordinary and Plenipotentiary. Appointment: July 12, 1946. Presentation of Credentials: July 19, 1946. Termination of Mission: Left post, August 2, 1949
Commissioned to China.
Karl L. Rankin served as Charge d'Affaires ad interim, August. 1950-April. 1953.

Karl L. Rankin (Maine). Foreign Service office. Title: Ambassador Extraordinary and Plenipotentiary. Appointment: February 27, 1953. Presentation of Credentials: April 2, 1953. Termination of Mission: Appointment terminated, December 30, 1957.
Commissioned to China; resident at Taipei.

Everett F. Drumright (Oklahoma). Foreign Service officer. Title: Ambassador Extraordinary and Plenipotentiary. Appointment: February 17, 1958. Presentation of Credentials: March 8, 1958. Termination of Mission: Left post, March 8, 1962.
Commissioned to China; resident at Taipei.

Alan G. Kirk (New York). Non-career appointee. Title: Ambassador Extraordinary and Plenipotentiary. Appointment: June 7, 1962. Presentation of Credentials: July 5, 1962. Termination of Mission: Left post, January 18, 1963.
Commissioned to China; resident at Taipei.

Jerauld Wright (District of Colombia). Non-career appointee. Title: Ambassador Extraordinary and Plenipotentiary. Appointment: May 3, 1963. Presentation of Credentials: June 29, 1963. Termination of Mission: Left post, July 25, 1965.
Commissioned to China; resident at Taipei.

Walter P. McConaugthy (Alabama). Foreign Service officer. Title: Ambassador Extraordinary and Plenipotentiary. Appointment: June 16, 1966. Presentation of Credentials: June 28, 1966. Termination of Mission: Left post, April 4, 1974.
Commissioned to China; resident at Taipei.

U.S. Liaison Office in Peking (now Beijing)

The following persons headed the U.S. Liaison Office in Peking (now Beijing) between May 1973 and March 1979.

David K.E. Bruce (Virginia). A non-career appointee. Appointment: March 15, 1973. Entered on Duty: May 14, 1973. Termination of Mission: Left post, September 25, 1974.

George H. W. Bush (Texas). A Non-career appointee. Appointment: September 26, 1974. Entered on Duty: October 21, 1974. Termination of Mission: Left post, December 7, 1975.

Thomas S. Gates, Jr. (Pennsylvania). A non-career appointee. Appointment: April 14, 1976. Entered on Duty: May 6, 1976. Termination of Mission: Promoted to Ambassador Extraordinary and Plenipotentiary.
   The U.S. Liaison Office officially became an Embassy on March 1, 1979.

Leonard Unger (Maryland). Foreign Service officer. Title: Ambassador Extraordinary and Plenipotentiary. Appointment: March 14, 1974. Presentation of Credentials: May 25, 1974. Termination of Mission: Left post, January 19, 1979
   Commissioned to the Republic of China; resident at Taipei. The United States established diplomatic relations with the People's Republic of China, and terminated them with the Republic of China, on January 1, 1979. Embassy Taipei closed February 28, 1979.

Leonard F. Woodcock (Michigan). Non-career appointee. Title: Ambassador Extraordinary and Plenipotentiary. Appointment: February 27, 1979. Presentation of Credentials: March 7, 1979. Termination of Mission: Left post, February 13, 1981.
   Commissioned to the People's Republic of China.

Arthur W. Hummel, Jr. (Maryland). Foreign Service officer. Title: Ambassador Extraordinary and Plenipotentiary. Appointment: July 30, 1981. Presentation of Credentials: September 24, 1981. Termination of Mission: Left post, September 24, 1985.
   Commissioned to the People's Republic of China.

Winston Lord (New York). Non-career appointee. Title: Ambassador Extraordinary and Plenipotentiary. Appointment: November 6, 1985. Presentation of Credentials: November 19, 1985. Termination of Mission: Left post, April 23, 1989.
   Commissioned to the People's Republic of China.

James Roderick Lilley (Maryland). Non-career appointee. Title: Ambassador Extraordinary and Plenipotentiary. Appointment: April 20, 1989. Presentation of Credentials: May 8, 1989. Termination of Mission: Left post, May 10, 1991.
   Commissioned to the People's Republic of China.

J. Stapleton Roy (Pennsylvania). Foreign Service officer. Title: Ambassador Extraordinary and Plenipotentiary. Appointment: July 2, 1991. Presentation of Credentials: August 20, 1991. Termination of Mission: Left post, June 17, 1995.
   Commissioned to the People's Republic of China.

Jim Sasser (Tennessee). Non-career appointee. Title: Ambassador Extraordinary and Plenipotentiary. Appointment: December 19, 1995. Presentation of Credentials: February 14, 1996. Termination of Mission: Left post July 1, 1999.
   Commissioned to the People's Republic of China.

Joseph W. Prueher (Tennessee). Non-career appointee. Title: Ambassador Extraordinary and Plenipotentiary. Appointment: November 16, 1999. Presentation of Credentials: December 15, 1999. Termination of Mission: Left post May 1, 2001.
   Commissioned to the People's Republic of China.

Clark T. Randt, Jr. (Connecticut). Non-career appointee. Title: Ambassador Extraordinary and Plenipotentiary. Appointment: July 12, 2001. Presentation of Credentials: July 28, 2001.

Appendix II. Chinese Chiefs of Mission to the United States Since Normalization

Chai Zemin (1979–1982)
Zhang Wenjin (1983–1985)
Han Xu (1985–1989)
Zhu Qizhen (1989–1993)

Li Daoyu (1993–1998)
Li Zhaoxing (1998–2001)
Yang Jiechi (2001–2005)
Zhou Wenzhong (2005-)

Appendix III. Correspondence of Wade-Giles to Pinyin

The table below is based on the "Correspondence of Wade-Giles to Pinyin" list created by the Library of Congress. It shows the relationship between Wade-Giles and pinyin romanizations.

Wade-Giles	Pinyin	Wade-Giles	Pinyin	Wade-Giles	Pinyin
a	a	k'ai	kai	pu	bu
ai	ai	kan	gan	p'u	pu
an	an	k'an	kan	sa	sa
ang	ang	kang	gang	sai	sai
ao	ao	k'ang	kang	san	san
cha	zha	kao	gao	sang	sang
ch'a	cha	k'ao	kao	sao	sao
chai	zhai	ken	gen	se	se
ch'ai	chai	k'en	ken	sen	sen
chan	zhan	keng	geng	seng	seng
ch'an	chan	k'eng	keng	sha	sha
chang	zhang	ko	ge	shai	shai
ch'ang	chang	k'o	ke	shan	shan
chao	zhao	kou	gou	shang	shang
ch'ao	chao	k'ou	kou	shao	shao
che	zhe	ku	gu	she	she
ch'e	che	k'u	ku	shen	shen
chen	zhen	kua	gua	sheng	sheng
ch'en	chen	k'ua	kua	shih	shi
cheng	zheng	kuai	guai	shou	shou
ch'eng	cheng	k'uai	kuai	shu	shu
chi	ji	kuan	guan	shua	shua
ch'i	qi	k'uan	kuan	shuai	shuai
chia	jia	kuang	guang	shuan	shuan
ch'ia	qia	k'uang	kuang	shuang	shuang
chiang	jiang	kuei	gui	shui	shui
ch'iang	qiang	k'uei	kui	shun	shun
chiao	jiao	kun	gun	shuo	shuo
ch'iao	qiao	k'un	kun	so	suo
chieh	jie	kung	gong	sou	sou
ch'ieh	qie	k'ung	kong	ssu	si
chien	jian	kuo	guo	su	su
ch'ien	qian	k'uo	kuo	suan	suan
chih	zhi	la	la	sui	sui
ch'ih	chi	lai	lai	sun	sun
chin	jin	lan	lan	sung	song
ch'in	qin	lang	lang	ta	da
ching	jing	lao	lao	t'a	ta
ch'ing	qing	le	le	tai	dai
chiu	jiu	lei	lei	t'ai	tai
ch'iu	qiu	leng	leng	tan	dan
chiung	jiong	li	li	t'an	tan

Wade-Giles	Pinyin	Wade-Giles	Pinyin	Wade-Giles	Pinyin
ch'iung	qiong	liang	liang	tang	dang
cho	zhuo	liao	liao	t'ang	tang
ch'o	chuo	lieh	lie	tao	dao
chou	zhou	lien	lian	t'ao	tao
ch'ou	chou	lin	lin	te	de
chu	zhu	ling	ling	t'e	te
ch'u	chu	liu	liu	teng	deng
chü	ju	lo	luo	t'eng	teng
ch'ü	qu	lou	lou	ti	di
chua	zhua	lu	lu	t'i	ti
chuai	zhuai	lü	lü	tiao	diao
ch'uai	chuai	luan	luan	t'iao	tiao
chuan	zhuan	lüan	luan	tieh	die
ch'uan	chuan	lüeh	lue	t'ieh	tie
chüan	juan	lun	lun	tien	dian
ch'üan	quan	lung	long	t'ien	tian
chuang	zhuangma	ma	ting	ding	
ch'uang	chuangmai	mai	t'ing	ting	
chüeh	jue	man	man	tiu	diu
ch'üeh	que	mang	mang	to	duo
chui	zhui	mao	mao	t'o	tuo
ch'ui	chui	mei	mei	tou	dou
chun	zhun	men	men	t'ou	tou
ch'un	chun	meng	meng	tu	du
chün	jun	mi	mi	t'u	tu
ch'ün	qun	miao	miao	tuan	duan
chung	zhong	mieh	mie	t'uan	tuan
ch'ung	chong	mien	mian	tui	dui
en	en	min	min	t'ui	tui
erh	er	ming	ming	tun	dun
fa	fa	miu	miu	t'un	tun
fan	fan	mo	mo	tung	dong
fang	fang	mou	mou	t'ung	tong
fei	fei	mu	mu	tsa	za
fen	fen	na	na	ts'a	ca
feng	feng	nai	nai	tsai	zai
fo	fo	nan	nan	ts'ai	cai
fou	fou	nang	nang	tsan	zan
fu	fu	nao	nao	ts'an	can
ha	ha	nei	nei	tsang	zang
hai	hai	nen	nen	ts'ang	cang
han	han	neng	neng	tsao	zao
hang	hang	ni	ni	ts'ao	cao
hao	hao	niang	niang	tse	ze
hei	hei	niao	niao	ts'e	ce
hen	hen	nieh	nie	tsei	zei
heng	heng	nien	nian	tsen	zen
ho	he	nin	nin	ts'en	cen
hou	hou	ning	ning	tseng	zeng
hsi	xi	niu	niu	ts'eng	ceng
hsia	xia	no	nuo	tso	zuo
hsiang	xiang	nou	nou	ts'o	cuo
hsiao	xiao	nu	nu	tsou	zou
hsieh	xie	nü	nü	ts'ou	cou
hsien	xian	nuan	nuan	tsu	zu
hsin	xin	nüeh	nue	ts'u	cu

Wade-Giles	Pinyin	Wade-Giles	Pinyin	Wade-Giles	Pinyin
hsing	xing	nung	nong	tsuan	zuan
hsiu	xiu	o	e	ts'uan	cuan
hsiung	xiong	ou	ou	tsui	zui
hsü	xu	pa	ba	ts'ui	cui
hsüan	xuan	p'a	pa	tsun	zun
hsüeh	xue	pai	bai	ts'un	cun
hsün	xun	p'ai	pai	tsung	zong
hu	hu	pan	ban	ts'ung	cong
hua	hua	p'an	pan	tzu	zi
huai	huai	pang	bang	tz'u	ci
huan	huan	p'ang	pang	wa	wa
huang	huang	pao	bao	wai	wai
hui	hui	p'ao	pao	wan	wan
hun	hun	pei	bei	wang	wang
hung	hong	p'ei	pei	wei	wei
huo	huo	pen	ben	wen	wen
i	yi	p'en	pen	weng	weng
jan	ran	peng	beng	wo	wo
jang	rang	p'eng	peng	wu	wu
jao	rao	pi	bi	ya	ya
je	re	p'I	pi	yai	yai
jen	ren	piao	biao	yang	yang
jeng	reng	p'iao	piao	yao	yao
jih	ri	pieh	bie	yeh	ye
jo	ruo	p'ieh	pie	yen	yan
jou	rou	pien	bian	yin	yin
ju	ru	p'ien	pian	ying	ying
juan	ruan	pin	bin	yo	yo
jui	rui	p'in	pin	yu	you
jun	run	ping	bing	yü	yu
jung	rong	p'ing	ping	yüan	yuan
ka	ga	po	bo	yüeh	yue
k'a	ka	p'o	po	yün	yun
kai	gai	p'ou	pou	yung	yong

The Contributors

Robert J. Antony is professor of history at Western Kentucky University. He is the author of *Like Froth Floating on the Sea: The World of Pirates and Seafarers in Late Imperial South China* and co-editor with Jane Kate Leonard of *Dragons, Tigers, and Dogs: Qing Crisis Management and the Boundaries of State Power in Late Imperial China.*

Patrick Belton is an academic at Oxford University. He serves as president of the Nathan Hale Foreign Policy Society and has been featured on ABC, CNN, NPR, and in *Washington Post* and *New York Times* as a frequent media commentator on foreign policy.

Janice M. Bogstad is professor and head of Collection Development at University of Wisconsin-Eau Claire McIntyre Library.

Ron Briley received his education at West Texas State University and University of New Mexico. He is a history teacher and assistant headmaster at Sandia Preparatory School in Albuquerque, New Mexico, where he has taught since 1978. Briley is also adjunct professor of history at the University of New Mexico Valencia Campus. His scholarly work has appeared in numerous academic journals, reference works, and anthologies. Briley is the author of *Class at Bat, Gender on Deck, and Race in the Hole: A Line Up of Essays on Twentieth-Century Culture and America's Game.*

Ray Lynn Brown is a current MA candidate in history at the University of Central Oklahoma (UCO) in Edmond, OK and a graduate of Northeastern State University in Tahlequah, OK with a BA in Political Science. Currently serving the final of two years as a graduate assistant in the history Department at UCO while pursuing research interests in U.S. diplomatic history, propaganda and public diplomacy. He will begin the Ph.D. history program at Northern Arizona University in fall 2005.

Laura M. Calkins holds a Ph.D. in Modern International History of Asia from the School of Oriental and African Studies, University of London, UK. She has held a National Science Foundation Post-Doctoral Fellowship at the University of Michigan, and is now an Oral Historian at the Vietnam Archive, Texas Tech University.

Eric A. Cheezum is a doctoral candidate in U.S. history at the University of South Carolina, Columbia; his dissertation explores the conservatism of Woodrow Wilson. Cheezum is the coauthor of *Woodrow Wilson* with Kendrick A. Clements; he is also conducting research on the relationship between the environment and local identity in Maryland.

Jinxing Chen received his Ph.D. in history from the University of Toledo in 1997. He now is assistant professor of history at Edgewood College in Madison, Wisconsin, where he teaches East Asian history.

Errol MacGregor Clauss is professor of history at Salem College, Winston-Salem, NC.

Stephen G. Craft is assistant professor of social sciences at Embry-Riddle Aeronautical University, Daytona Beach, and is the author of *V.K. Wellington Koo and the Emergence of Modern China.*

Elizabeth Van Wie Davis is professor of Politics at Asia-Pacific Center for Security Studies. She focuses on Chinese politics and security. Dr. Davis' books include *Islam, Oil & Geopolitics in Central Asia* (pending), *Chinese Perspectives on Sino-American Relations* and *China and the Law of the Sea Convention.* Her articles appear in journals around the world.

Charles M. Dobbs is a professor of history at Iowa State University. He is the author of *The Unwanted Symbol* and *The United States and East Asia Since 1945* and more than twenty articles on U.S. diplomatic and military history.

Eric H. Doss attended The Citadel, The Military College of South Carolina, graduating in 2002 with a BA in History. He is currently pursuing a MA in History at Clemson University, with particular interest in military, Southern, and educational history.

Cord Eberspaecher is currently teaching at the University of Oldenburg, Germany. He earned his MA in history, sinology and political science and Ph. D. at the University of Hamburg. His research focuses on Military History, China and the West and Modern German History. He is author of *Die deutsche Yangtse-Patrouille [The German Yangzi Patrol].*

David G. Egler is currently professor of East Asian history at Western Illinois University. He was educated at the University of Chicago, Vanderbilt University, University of Michigan and University of Arizona. He received Fulbright and Yoshida International Education fellowships for study at Waseda University in Japan and was research scholar at the Social Sciences Institute, Tokyo University.

Nilly Kamal El-Amir is a researcher at Center for Asian Studies of Cairo University, Egypt. She earned her University degree in political science in 2000. She is preparing her master degree on "Trans-regionalism: A Case Study of the Asia — Europe Relations." She has participated at research projects and conferences on the Asian affairs.

Robert Elder recently received his MA from

Clemson University and is now a Ph.D. student at Emory University in the field of American history.

Dean Fafoutis is a specialist in U.S. diplomatic history. He teaches at Salibury University (MD), and also serves as the editor of *International Social Science Review*.

Gregory C. Ference is professor of history at Salisbury University in Maryland. He received his Ph.D. and MA in History, as well as an MLS from Indiana University. He earned his BA in History from the University of Pittsburgh with a Certificate in Russian and East European Studies.

Catherine Forslund is associate professor of history at Rockford College. Her book, *Anna Chennault: Informal Diplomacy and Asian Relations* has been followed by articles exploring editorial cartoon coverage of the Korean War. She was assisted in this project by Joshua Parker.

Paul D. Gelpi, Jr. has degrees from the University of New Orleans and The University of Alabama. He is now associate professor of history at Grambling State University.

Karl Gerth received his Ph.D. from Harvard, teaches modern Chinese history at the University of South Carolina. He is author of *China Made: Consumer Culture and the Creation of the Nation* and is currently researching the dismantling of market culture in urban China during the first decade of the People's Republic.

Jonathan Goldstein is a Research Associate of Harvard University's Fairbank Center for East Asian Research and a Professor of East Asian History at the University of West Georgia. His books include *Philadelphia and the China Trade, 1682–1846*, *America Views China*, *China and Israel*, and *The Jews of China*.

Arthur M. Holst received his Ph.D. in Political Science from Temple University. He is Government Affairs Manager for the City of Philadelphia and teaches in the MPA Program at Widener University. He has written extensively on Politics, Public Administration, History and the Environment.

B.M. Jain is professor and research scientist in Political Science, South Asia Studies Center at the University of Rajasthan in Jaipur, India. He has widely traveled abroad in North America, Europe and Asia for lectures and conferences, and has also been Visiting Fellow at the University of Pennsylvania (Philadelphia), University of Hong Kong, Henry L. Stimson Center (Washington, D.C.). He has written over one dozen books and has published over six dozen articles in various journals including *Pacific Affairs*, *The Round Table*. He has been featured in an entry in the *Marquis WHO's WHO in the World*, 16th edition, and 1999.

Romi Jain is formerly associated with South Asia Studies Center, University of Rajasthan in India, has specialized in international relations, the U.S. and major powers. She has published articles in several journals, including U.S.-China Relations in *Asian Profile*. Currently, she is working on a book tentatively entitled as *Strategic Triangular Partnership: U.S.A, China, and Pak-*

istan, and has contributed a book chapter entitled *India and SAARC* for the International Research Forum-SAARC Project sponsored by Japan Peace Foundation and Sountry Cultural Foundation (Japan).

Linus Kafka is a doctoral candidate at the University of California, Los Angeles studying American intellectual history, especially as it relates to a global context. His dissertation is entitled *The World and Henry Adams: Cosmopolitan Intellectuals and the Making of Modern America*. He is a former attorney with a BA in History and American Studies from Rutgers, an MA in history from NYU, and a JD from the University of Arizona.

David Kenley received his Ph.D. from University of Hawaii. He is associate professor of history at Elizabethtown College. He is the author of *New Culture in a New World: The May Fourth Movement and the Chinese Diaspora, 1919–1932* and other works dealing with Chinese intellectual history and diasporas in world history.

Rob Kerby is an alumnus of the University of Tulsa and did post-graduate work at TU and the University of Arkansas at Little Rock. He has published or been the lead editor on more than 50 books including *Blood In, Blood Out* with Art Blajos and *Give Me Back My Dignity* with Nicky Cruz, documenting the Los Angeles riots. He has been a recent contributor to *First, Second and Third Industrial Revolutions; The Encyclopedia of World Geography*.

Martin Kich is professor of English at Wright State University — Lake Campus. He has received the university's Trustees' Award for sustained excellence in teaching, scholarship, and service. He is the author of *Western American Novelists* and *A Companion to Emerging American Novelists* (Facts on File, forthcoming). He is editing two forthcoming volumes of the *Dictionary of Literary Biography* on American and British horror novelists, and his other publications include contributions to several dozen reference works on literary, cultural, and historical topics.

Leigh Kimmel has degrees in Russian language and literature, library science, and history. She has written on a wide variety of topics, ranging from ancient Mesopotamian law codes to modern Soviet playwrights.

Tong Lam received his Ph.D. degree in History at the University of Chicago in 2003. He is currently assistant professor of history at the University of Richmond. His research and teaching interests include nation and empire, war and memory, and the history of social science.

Joseph Tse-Hei Lee received his Ph.D., School of Oriental and African Studies, University of London. He is associate professor of history at Pace University in New York, and author of *The Bible and the Gun: Christianity in South China, 1860–1900*.

Keith A. Leitich is an independent researcher and consultant on Central Asian geopolitics and South Korean politics based in Seattle, WA. Mr. Leitich has contributed articles to: *Encyclopedia of Religion and War*,

Supplement to the Modern Encyclopedia of Russian, Soviet Eurasian History, Encyclopedia of Modern Asia, McGill's Guide to Military History and has been published widely, including in *Contemporary Education, Education, International Education Forum, International Journal of Central Asian Studies,* and *the Journal of Central Asian Studies.*

Hongshan Li teaches at the History Department of Kent State University.

Xiaobing Li is professor of history and associate director of Western Pacific Institute at the University of Central Oklahoma. He is the editor of *American Review of China Studies,* author and co-author of numerous books, including *Voices from the Korean War* and *Mao's Generals Remember Korea.*

Hsiang-Wang Liu earned his Ph.D. from Pennsylvania State University. He is teaching at Kutztown University of Pennsylvania.

Mark Love is assistant professor of Library Services at Central Missouri State University. He holds degrees in History from Texas A&M University and Sam Houston State University and a degree in Library Science from the University of North Texas. His essay on the Farmers' Holiday Association was published in the *Encyclopedia of the Great Depression.*

James I. Matray is professor and chair of the History Department at California State University, Chico. He has published more than forty articles and book chapters on U.S.-Korean relations during and after World War II. Author of *The Reluctant Crusade: American Foreign Policy in Korea, 1941–1950* and *Japan's Emergence as a Global Power,* his most recent books are *Korea Divided: The 38th Parallel and the Demilitarized Zone* and *East Asia and the United States: An Encyclopedia of Relations Since 1784.*

D. E. "Gene" Mills, Jr. is currently serving as adjunct faculty in Religion at Tallahassee Community College, a Ph.D. student in American religious History at Florida State University and as the Senior Assistant to the Editors of the academic journal *Church History: Studies in Christianity and Culture.*

Edwin E. Moise has degrees from Harvard and the University of Michigan. He is now professor of history at Clemson University. He is the author of *Tonkin Gulf and the Escalation of the Vietnam War* and other books on Vietnam and China.

Steven Napier is a political scientist, historian, and writer of philosophy. He holds a BA and MA from Marshall University. In addition, he is the author of *FDR's Monetary Policy* (pending), and *Property And Commercial Law In British India: A Comparative History* (pending).

Cynthia Ning is associate director of the University of Hawaii's Center for Chinese Studies, and executive director of the Chinese Language Teachers Association. She is the author of *Communicating in Chinese,* a series of textbooks for beginning level instruction in Mandarin Chinese; and *Exploring in Chinese* (forthcoming), a video-based series for Mandarin Chinese

instruction at the intermediate level. She also teaches and writes about Chinese comic literature and film, and has a growing interest in sports as a social phenomenon.

Meredith Oyen is Meredith Oyen is currently completing her Ph.D. in U.S. Diplomatic History at Georgetown University. Her research centers on the role of immigration and the overseas Chinese in U.S.-Chinese relations.

Edy Parsons is a Ph.D candidate at Department of History, Iowa State University.

Tao Peng is currently assistant professor of history in Minnesota State University at Mankato, receiving Ph.D, from the University of Georgia in 2002. Research areas include postwar Sino-American relations and U.S.-Japan security alliance.

Wade D. Pfau completed his Ph.D. in Economics at Princeton University in 2003. He has bachelor's degrees in Economics, Political Science, and History from the University of Iowa. He is now associate professor at the National Graduate Institute for Policy Studies in Tokyo, Japan. His primary research interests are in pension reform and the implications of aging populations.

Anne M. Platoff has a BA in history and political science from Kansas State University. She earned an MA in historical studies from the University of Houston — Clear Lake and an MS in library science from the University of North Texas. She is currently employed as a librarian at the University of California, Santa Barbara. She has authored a historical monograph for NASA, as well as articles in history and information science.

Vincent Kelly Pollard teaches political science and Asian studies courses at the University of Hawaii at Manoa. Pollard earned graduate degrees at the Universities of Chicago and Hawaii-Manoa. A student of social movements and Fulbright Scholar, Pollard specializes in comparative politics and world politics.

Michael Polley is associate professor of history at Columbia College of Missouri. He has published numerous encyclopedia articles in the areas of East Asian history and military history.

Edgar A. Porter serves as Interim Dean of the School of Hawaiian, Asian and Pacific Studies at the University of Hawaii. He is the author of *The People's Doctor: George Hatem and China's Revolution, Foreign Teachers in China: Old Problems for a New Generation, 1979–1989* and editor of *Journalism From Tiananmen.*

Rogerio Miguel Puga is a lecturer at Instituto de Educacao e Ciencias and a researcher at Universidade Nova (Lisbon, Portugal). He has published several articles and book chapters on the History of Macau and the Portuguese, English and American presences in Macau.

Katherine K. Reist is associate professor of history, and head of the Department of History at the University of Pittsburgh at Johnstown. A graduate of The Ohio State University, she specializes in modern Chinese history. Although her teaching encompasses a broad range of courses, her research focuses on the American military presence in China in the first half of the twentieth century.

Tara Robbins is a Ph.D. candidate at the University of Chapel Hill and a graduate of Swarthmore College.

Bill Sewell is associate professor of history at Saint Mary's University, Halifax, Nova Scotia, Canada where he teaches East Asian and urban history. His research focuses on northeast China in the late nineteenth and the first half of the twentieth centuries. He is a founding list editor for H-NEAsia.

Yu Shen teaches at the Department of History at Indiana University Southeast.

Michael Sinclair received his Ph.D. from Stanford University in 1973. He is professor of history at Wake Forest University. His research interests include Sino-Western relations and the history of Shanghai. He is currently completing a book on the Sino-French War of 1883–1885.

Yuwu Song received his Ph.D. in History from the University of Alabama at Tuscaloosa and an MA in Library and Information Science from the University of Texas at Austin. He works at Arizona State University Libraries. He authored the book: *Building Better Web Sites: A How-To-Do-It-Manual For Librarians*. He is now working on two book projects: *Chinese Feature Films, 1913–1949: A Filmography* and *Chinese Stamps*.

James Steinberg is associate professor of Sociology at Wright State University-Lake Campus, where he teaches a range of sociology courses and regional studies courses on modern China, ancient China, and modern Japan.

Barry M. Stentiford has graduate degrees from the University of Montana and the University of Alabama. He is professor of history at Grambling State University. He is the author of *The American Home Guard: The State Militia in the Twentieth Century* as well as several articles on Military History and the Far East.

Yi Sun received her undergraduate education at Nankai University in China, and her Master's and doctoral degrees in American history from Washington State University. She is currently tenured associate professor at the University of San Diego, teaching U.S.-Asian relations and Asian history. She has published over twenty articles in both English and Chinese, on subjects ranging from Sino-American relations to globalization to Chinese women and economic modernization. Presently she is working on a book manuscript on contemporary Chinese women.

Antonio Thompson is ABD at the Department of History, University of Kentucky, specializing in American Foreign Policy, U.S. Since 1865, Modern Germany, and International Relations.

Xiansheng Tian teaches at the History Department of Metropolitan State College of Denver.

Hoyt Cleveland Tillman received his Ph.D. from Harvard. He is professor of Chinese cultural history at Arizona State University. Most of his publications focus on the history of Confucian thought, especially during the Song period; his interests in the Yoshida Letter were developed during a seminar with Edwin Reischauer and James Thomson.

Chen-mian Wang, the Fifth European Chair of Chinese Studies at the IIAS, is professor of history at the Graduate Institute of History, National Central University in Taiwan. His main research interests include the Ming-Qing transition in 17th century China; U.S.-China diplomatic history; and Protestant churches in Republican China.

Andrew J. Waskey has degrees from Georgia Institute of Technology, the University of Southern Mississippi, and Austin Presbyterian Theological Seminary. He is now associate professor of social sciences at Dalton State College. He is the author of several hundred encyclopedia entries and articles; has contributed book reviewer for the *Chinese Journal of Political Science*; and is co-author of *Political Perspectives: A Reader*.

Norton Wheeler is a business executive currently working in China and also a Ph.D. candidate at the University of Kansas. He is author of "Improving Mainland Society and U.S.-China Relations: A Case Study of Four Chinese American-led Transnational Associations," in *The Expanding Roles of Chinese Americans in U.S.-China Relations*.

Michael D. Wilson is associate professor of history, Vanguard University of Southern California. Ph.D. History, UCLA (1996). BA Vanguard University of Southern California (1983). Plan to publish: "United States Policy and the Nationalist Revolution, 1925–1928" (Ph.D. dissertation). Michael has traveled and taught fairly extensively in China since his first stint as an English teacher in Nanchang, Jiangxi from 1984–1986.

Yusheng Yao received his Ph.D. in history from University of Minnesota and now teaches in the History Department of Rollins College. His articles on Chinese history and literature are published in *Modern China* and *Twentieth Century China*.

Matthew Young has degrees from Kenyon College and Bowling Green State University. He is currently associate professor of history at Marietta College, where he teaches courses in American and East Asian history.

Maochun Yu holds degrees from the University of California at Berkeley, Swarthmore College and Nankai University. He is now associate professor of East Asia and military history at the United States Naval Academy in Annapolis, Maryland. He is the author of *OSS in China-Prelude to Cold War*, and numerous articles on military and intelligence history of World War II and the Cold War.

M. Cristina Zaccarini is professor of United States history and Modern Chinese history at Adelphi University and co-director of the Asian Studies Program at Adelphi University. In addition to her book, *The Sino-American Friendship as Tradition and Challenge: Ailie Gale in China, 1908–1950*, Zaccarini has published articles on the relationship between United States and China in the 20th century. She is currently researching the impact of missionaries on Western medicine during the Nationalist decade in China, as well as the impact of Chinese medicine on American doctors and the public.

Wenxian Zhang received a BA from the Peking University in Beijing, China, and his MLS and MS from the Southern Connecticut State University in New Haven, Connecticut. He is currently serving as associate professor and the head of Archives and Special Collections at the Olin Library, Rollins College in Winter Park, Florida. His research interests include international librarianship, and Chinese history and cultures.

Fu Zhuo is assistant professor and Librarian at James C. Kirkpatrick Library of Central Missouri State University, received his MLIS from the University of Alberta and MEd from the University of Western Ontario in Canada. He enjoys doing library public service and research.

Bibliography

Acheson, Dean. *Present at the Creation; My Years in the State Department.* New York: Norton, 1969.

Anderson, Irvine, Jr. *The Standard-Vacuum Oil Company and United States East Asian Policy, 1933–1941.* Princeton, NJ: Princeton University Press, 1975.

Bachrack, Stanley. *The Committee of One Million: The "China Lobby" and U.S. Policy, 1953–1971.* New York: Columbia University Press, 1971.

Bagby, Welsey. *The Eagle-Dragon Alliance: America's Relationship with China in World War II.* Newark: University of Delaware Press, 1992.

Barnett, A. Doak. *China and the Major Powers in East Asia.* Washington, D.C.: Brookings Institution, 1977.

_____. *Communist China and Asia: A Challenge to American Foreign Policy.* New York: Harper, 1960.

_____, and Edwin O. Reischauer. *The United States and China: The Next Decade.* New York: Praeger, 1970.

Barrett, David D. *Dixie Mission: The United States Army Observer Group in Yenan, 1944.* Berkeley: Center for Chinese Studies, University of California, 1970.

Beldon, Jack. *China Shakes the World.* New York: Monthly Review Press, 1949.

Blair, Clay. *The Forgotten War: America in Korea, 1950–1953.* New York: Times Books, 1987.

Blum, Robert. *Drawing the Line: The Origin of the American Containment Policy in East Asia.* New York: Norton, 1982.

_____. *The United States and China in World Affairs.* New York: McGraw-Hill, 1966.

Boorman, Howard, ed. *Biographical Dictionary of Republican China.* New York: Columbia University Press, 1968.

Borg, Dorothy. *The United States and the Far Eastern Crisis of 1933–1938: From the Manchurian Incident Through the Initial Stage of the Undeclared Sino-Japanese War.* Cambridge, MA: Harvard University Press, 1964.

_____, and Waldo Heinrichs, eds. *Uncertain Years: Chinese-American Relations, 1947–1950.* New York: Columbia University Press, 1980.

Brzezinski, Zbigniew. *Power and Principle: Memoirs of the National Security Advisor, 1977–1981.* New York: Farrar, Straus, Giroux, 1983.

Bueler, William. *U.S. China Policy and the Problem of Taiwan.* Boulder: Colorado Associated University Press, 1971.

Burns, Richard, and Edward Bennett, eds. *Diplomats in Crisis: United States-Chinese-Japanese Relations, 1919–1941.* Santa Barbara, CA: ABC-Clio, 1974.

Caldwell, Oliver. *A Secret War: Americans in China, 1944–45.* Carbondale: Southern Illinois University Press, 1972.

Chang, Gordon H. *Friends and Enemies: The United States, China, and the Soviet Union, 1948–1972.* Stanford, CA: Stanford University Press, 1990.

Chang, Hsin-hai. *America and China: A New Approach to Asia.* New York: Simon and Schuster, 1965.

Chen, Jian. *China's Road to the Korean War: The Making of the Sino-American Confrontation.* New York: Columbia University Press, 1994.

_____. *Mao's China and the Cold War.* Chapel Hill: University of North Carolina Press, 2001.

Chennault, Claire Lee. *Way of a Fighter.* New York: G.P. Putnam's Sons, 1949.

Chong, Key Ray. *Americans and Chinese Reform and Revolution, 1898–1922: The Role of Private Citizens in Diplomacy.* Lanham, MD: University Press of America, 1984.

Christensen, Thomas J. *Useful Adversaries: Grand Strategy, Domestic Mobilization, and Sino-American Conflict, 1947–1958.* Princeton, NJ: Princeton University Press, 1996.

Clark, Elmer T. *The Chiangs of China.* New York: Abingdon-Cokesbury Press, 1943.

Cohen, Warren I. *America's Response to China: A History of Sino-American Relations.* New York: Columbia University Press, 2000.

_____. *East Asian Art and American Culture: A Study in International Relations.* New York: Columbia University Press, 1992.

_____. ed. *New Frontiers in American-East Asian Relations: Essays Presented to Dorothy Borg.* New York: Columbia University Press, 1983.

Cohen, Warren, and Akira Iriye, eds. *The Great Powers in East Asia, 1953–1960.* New York: Columbia University Press, 1990.

Conklin, Jeffrey Scott. *Forging an East Asian Foreign Policy.* Lanham, MD: University Press of America, 1995.

Cray, Ed. *General of the Army, G. C. Marshall: Soldier and Statesman.* New York: Norton, 1990.

Crow, Carl. *China Takes Her Place.* New York: Harper, 1944.

Davies, John Paton. *Dragon by the Tail.* New York: Norton, 1972.

Dudden, Arthur. *The American Pacific: From the Old China Trade to the Present.* New York: Oxford University Press, 1992.

Dulles, Foster Rhea. *American Policy Toward Communist China, 1949–1969.* New York: Crowell, 1972.

Eastman, Lloyd. *The Abortive Revolution.* Cambridge, MA: Harvard University Press, 1974.

_____. *Seeds of Destruction: North China in War and Revolution, 1937–1949.* Stanford, CA: Stanford University Press, 1984.

Edwards, Lee. *Missionary for Freedom: the Life and Time of Walter Judd.* New York: Paragon House, 1990.

Epstein, Israel. *The Unfinished Revolution in China.* Boston: Little, Brown and Company, 1947.

Esherick, Joseph. *Lost Chance in China: The World War Two Dispatches of John S. Service.* New York: Random House, 1974.

Eunson, Roby. *The Soong Sisters.* New York: Franklin Watts, 1975.

Evans, Paul. *John Fairbank and the American Understanding of Modern China.* New York: Blackwell, 1988.

Fairbank, John King. *China Perceived.* New York: Knopf, 1976.

_____. *Chinabound: a Fifty-year Memoir.* New York: Harper, 1982.

_____. *The United States and China.* Cambridge, MA: Harvard University Press, 1979.

Feis, Herbert. *The China Tangle: The American Effort in China from Pearl Harbor to the Marshall Mission.* Princeton, NJ: Princeton University Press, 1953.

Foot, Rosemary. *The Practice of Power: U.S. Relations with China since 1949.* New York: Oxford University Press, 1995.

Furuya, Keija. *Chiang Kai-shek: His Life and Times.* New York: St. John's University, 1981.

Gallicchio, Marc. *The Cold War Begins in Asia: American East Asian Policy and the Fall of the Japanese Empire.* New York: Columbia University Press, 1988.

Garver, John W. *China's Decision for Rapprochement with the United States, 1968–1971.* Boulder, CO: Westview Press, 1982.

_____. *Face Off: China, the United States, and Taiwan's Democratization.* Seattle: University of Washington Press, 1997.

Gibert, Stephen P., and William M. Carpenter. *America and Island China: A Documentary History.* Lanham, MD: University Press of America, 1989.

Grasso, June. *Truman's Two-China Policy.* Armonk, NY: M.E. Sharpe, 1987.

Grayson, Benson Lee. *The American Image of China.* New York: Ungar, 1979.

Gregor, A. James. *Arming the Dragon: U.S. Security Ties with the People's Republic of China.* Washington, D.C.: Ethics and Public Policy Center, 1987.

_____. *The China Connection: U.S. Policy and the People's Republic of China.* Stanford, CA: Stanford University Press, 1986.

Gu, Weijun. *Gu wei jun hui yi lu [Memoir of V. K. Wellington Koo].* Beijing: Zhonghua shu ju, 1983–1985.

Gurtov, Melvin. *The First Vietnam Crisis: Chinese Communist Strategy and United States Involvement.* New York: Columbia University Press, 1967.

Halperin, Morton. *China and the Bomb.* New York: Praeger, 1965.

Harding, Harry. *A Fragile Relationship: The United States and China Since 1972.* Washington, D.C.: Brookings Institution, 1992.

Harding, Harry, and Ming Yuan, eds. *Sino-American Relations, 1945–1955: A Joint Reassessment of a Critical Decade.* Wilmington, DE: SR Books, 1989.

Harland, Bryce. *Collision Course: America and East Asia in the Past and the Future.* New York: St. Martin's Press, 1996.

Harris, Theodore. *Pearl S. Buck: A Biography.* New York: John Day, 1971.

Hawes, Grace. *The Marshall Plan for China: Economic Cooperation Administration 1948–1949.* Cambridge, MA: Schenkman, 1977.

Head, William. *America's China Sojourn: America's Foreign Policy and Its Effects on Sino-American Relations, 1942–1948.* Lanham, MD: University Press of America, 1983.

Hinton, Harold C. *Peking-Washington: Chinese Foreign Policy and the United States.* Beverly Hills: Sage Publications, 1976.

Hseuh, Chun-tu, ed. *Revolutionary Leaders of Modern China.* New York: Oxford University Press, 1971.

Hsiao, Gene T., ed. *Sino-American Detente and Its Policy Implications*. New York: Praeger, 1974.

Hunt, Michael H. *The Making of a Special Relationship: The United States and China to 1914*. New York: Columbia University Press, 1983.

Iriye, Akira. *Across the Pacific: An Inner History of American-East Asian Relations*. New York: Harcourt, 1967.

_____, and Warren Cohen, eds. *American, Chinese, and Japanese Perspectives on Wartime Asia, 1931–1949*. Wilmington, DE: SR Books, 1990.

Jespersen, T. Christopher. *American Images of China, 1931–1949*. Stanford, CA: Stanford University Press, 1996.

Jiang, Xiangze. *The United States and China*. Chicago: University of Chicago Press, 1988.

Jones, Howard. *Quest for Security: A History of U.S. Foreign Relations*. New York: McGraw-Hill, 1996.

Kahn, E.J., Jr. *The China Hands: America's Foreign Service Officers and What Befell Them*. New York: Viking, 1972.

Kalicki, J. H. *The Pattern of Sino-American Crises: Political-Military Interactions in the 1950s*. London: Cambridge University Press, 1975.

Keeley, Joseph Charles. *The China Lobby Man: the Story of Alfred Kohlberg*. New Rochelle, NY: Arlington House, 1969.

Kennedy, Scott, ed. *China Cross Talk: The American Debate Over China Policy Since Normalization: A Reader*. Lanham, MD: University Press of America, 2003.

Kerr, George H. *Formosa Betrayed*. Boston: Houghton Mifflin, 1965.

Kintner, William, and John Cooper. *A Matter of Two Chinas: The China-Taiwan Issue in U.S. Foreign Policy*. Philadelphia: Foreign Policy Research Institute, 1978.

Kissinger, Henry. *White House Years*. Boston: Little, Brown and Company, 1979.

Koen, Ross Y. *The China Lobby in American Politics*. New York: Harper, 1974.

Kosnitiz, Leonard. *Public Opinion and Foreign Policy: America's China Policy, 1949–1979*. Westport, CT: Greenwood Press, 1984.

Kubek, Anthony. *How the Far East Was Lost: American Policy and the Creation of Communist China, 1941–1949*. Chicago: H. Regnery Co., 1963.

Lasater, Martin L. *The Taiwan Issue in Sino-American Strategic Relations*. Boulder, CO: Westview Press, 1984.

Lauren, Paul Gordon, ed. *The China Hands' Legacy: Ethics and Diplomacy*. Boulder, CO: Westview Press, 1987.

Leary, William. *Perilous Missions: Civil Air Transport, The Chinese War, and CIA Covert Operations in East Asia, 1946–1955*. Tuscaloosa: University of Alabama Press, 1983.

Liang, Chin-tung. *General Stilwell in China, 1942–1944: The Full Story*. Jamaica, NY: St. John's University Press, 1972.

Liu, Ta-Jen. *U.S.-China Relations, 1784–1992*. Lanham, MD: University Press of America, 1997.

Liu, Xiaoyuan. *A Partnership for Disorder: China, the United States, and Their Policies for the Postwar Disposition of the Japanese Empire, 1941–1945*. New York: Cambridge University Press, 1996.

Lu, Ning. *The Dynamics of Foreign-policy Decision-making in China*. Boulder, CO: Westview Press, 1997.

MacFarquhar, Roderick, ed. *Sino-American Relations, 1949–1971*. New York: Praeger, 1972.

MacKinnon, S. R., and Oris Friesen. *China Reporting: An Oral History of American Journalism in the 1930s & 1940s*. Berkeley: University of California Press, 1987.

Madsen, Richard. *China and the American Dream: A Moral Inquiry*. Berkeley: University of California Press, 1995.

Mann, James. *About Face: A History of America's Curious Relationship with China, from Nixon to Clinton*. New York: Knopf, 1999.

Martin, Edwin W. *Divided Counsel: The Anglo-American Response to Communist Victory in China*. Lexington: University Press of Kentucky, 1986.

_____. *Southeast Asia and China: The End of Containment*. Boulder, CO: Westview Press, 1977.

May, Ernest. *The Truman Administration and China, 1945–1949*. Philadelphia: Lippincott, 1975.

May, Gary. *China Scapegoat: The Diplomatic Ordeal of John Carter Vincent*. Washington, D.C.: New Republic Books, 1979.

Mayers, David Allan. *Cracking the Monolith: U.S. Policy Against the Sino-Soviet Alliance, 1949–1955*. Baton Rouge: Louisiana State University Press, 1986.

Mosher, Steven. *China Misperceived: American Illusions and Chinese Reality*. New York: Basic Books, 1990.

Mosley, Leonard. *Marshall: Hero for Our Times*. New York: Hearst Books, 1982.

Nathan, Andrew J., and Robert S. Ross. *The Great Wall and the Empty Fortress: China's Search for Security*. New York: Norton, 1997.

Newman, Robert. *Owen Lattimore and the "Loss" of China*. Berkeley: University of California Press, 1992.

Nixon, Richard M. *RN, the Memoirs of Richard Nixon*. New York: Grosset & Dunlap, 1978.

Purifoy, Lewis. *Harry Truman's China Policy: McCarthyism and the Diplomacy of Hysteria*. New York: New Viewpoints, 1976.

Rankin, Karl Lott. *China Assignment*. Seattle: University of Washington Press, 1964.

Reardon-Anderson, James. *Yenan and the Great Powers: The Origins of Chinese Communist Foreign Policy, 1944–46*. New York: Columbia University Press, 1980.

Rodman, Peter W. *Broken Triangle: China, Russia, and America after 25 Years*. Washington, D.C.: Nixon Center for Peace and Freedom, 1997.

Romanus, Charles F., and Sunderland Riley. *Stilwell's Mission to China and Stilwell's Command Problems*. Washington, D.C.: Office of the Chief of Military History, Department of the Army, 1953–1956.

Ross, Robert. *Negotiating Cooperation: The United States and China, 1969–1989*. Stanford, CA: Stanford University Press, 1995.

Rusk, Dean. *As I Saw It*. New York: Norton, 1990.

Ryan, Mark. *Chinese Attitudes toward Nuclear Weapons: China and the United States during the Korean War*. Armonk, NY: M.E. Sharpe, 1989.

Sanders, Sol W., ed. *The U.S. Role in the Asian Century: A Panel of Experts Looks at the National Interest in the New Environment*. Lanham, MD: University Press of America, 1997.

Schaller, Michael. *Douglas MacArthur: The Far Eastern General*. New York: Columbia University Press, 1989.

_____. *The U.S. Crusade in China, 1938–1945*. New York: Columbia University Press, 1979.

_____. *The United States and China in the Twentieth Century*. New York: Oxford University Press, 1979.

_____. *The United States and China: Into the 21st Century*. New York: Oxford University Press, 2002.

Seagrave, Sterling. *The Soong Dynasty*. New York: Harper, 1985.

Service, John S. *The Amerasia Papers: Some Problems in the History of U.S.-China Relations*. Berkeley: Center for Chinese Studies, University of California, 1971.

Shambaugh, David. *Beautiful Imperialist: China Perceives America, 1972–1990*. Princeton, NJ: Princeton University Press, 1991.

Shaw, Yu-ming. *An American Missionary in China: John Leighton Stuart and Chinese-American Relations*. Cambridge, MA: Council on East Asian Studies, Harvard University, 1992.

Sheean, Vincent. *Between the Thunder and the Sun*. New York: Random House, 1943.

_____. *Personal History*. New York: Doubleday, 1934.

Shewmaker, Kenneth E. *Americans and Chinese Communists, 1927–1945, A Persuading Encounter*. Ithaca, NY: Cornell University Press, 1971.

Smith, Bradley. *The War's Long Shadow: The Second World War and Its Aftermath: China, Russia, Britain, America*. New York: Simon and Schuster, 1986.

Snow, Edgar. *Red Star Over China*. New York: Random House, 1944.

Snow, Lois Wheeler. *Edgar Snow's China*. New York: Random House, 1981.

Soloman, Richard, ed. *The China Factor: Sino-American Relations and the Global Scene*. Englewood Cliffs, NJ: Prentice-Hall, 1981.

Spencer, Jonathan D. *The Search for Modern China*. New York: Norton, 1990.

Starr, John B., ed. *The Future of U.S.-China Relations*. New York: New York University Press, 1981.

Steele, A. T. *The American People and China*. New York: McGraw-Hill, 1966.

Stolper, Thomas. *China, Taiwan, and the Offshore Islands*. Armonk, NY: M.E. Sharpe, 1985.

Stuart, Douglas, and William Tow, eds. *China, the Soviet Union and the West: Strategic and Political Dimensions of the 1980s*. Boulder, CO: Westview Press, 1982.

Stuart, John Leighton. *Fifty Years in China; the Memoirs of John Leighton Stuart*. New York: Random House, 1954.

_____. *The Forgotten Ambassador: the Reports of John Leighton Stuart, 1946–1949*. Boulder, CO: Westview Press, 1981.

Stueck, William. *The Road to Confrontation: American Policy toward China and Korea, 1947–1950*. Chapel Hill: University of North Carolina Press, 1981.

_____. *The Wedemeyer Mission: American Politics and Foreign Policy during the Cold War*. Athens: University of Georgia Press, 1984.

Sutter, Robert. *The China Quandary: Domestic Determinants of U.S. China Policy, 1972–1982*. Boulder, CO: Westview Press, 1983.

_____. *China-Watch: Toward Sino-American Reconciliation*. Baltimore: Johns Hopkins University Press, 1978.

Swaine, Michael D., and Ashley J. Tellis. *Interpreting China's Grand Strategy: Past, Present, and Future*. Santa Monica, CA: Rand, 2000.

Swanberg, W. A. *Luce and His Empire*. New York: Scribner, 1972.

Szulc, Tad. *The Illusion of Peace: Foreign Policy in the Nixon Years*. New York: Viking Press, 1978.

Tang, Tsou. *America's Failure in China: 1941–1950*. Chicago: University of Chicago Press, 1963.

Thompson, James C., Peter Stanley, and John Perry. *Sentimental Imperialists: The American Experience in East Asia*. New York: Harper, 1981.

Thomson, James C. *While China Faced West: American Reformers in Nationalist China, 1928–1937*. Cambridge, MA: Harvard University Press, 1969.

Tuchman, Barbara W. *Notes from China*. New York: Collier Books, 1972.

_____. *Stilwell and the American Experience in China: 1911–1945*. New York: Macmillan, 1970.

Tucker, Nancy Bernkopf. *Patterns in the Dust: Chinese-American Relations and the Recognition Controversy*. New York: Columbia University Press, 1983.

_____. *Taiwan, Hong Kong, and the United States, 1945–1992: Uncertain Friendships*. New York: Twayne Publishers, 1994.

Tyler, Patrick. *A Great Wall: Six Presidents and China: An Investigative History*. New York: Public Affairs, 1999.

Valone, Stephen. *"A Policy Calculated to Benefit China": The United States and the China Arms Embargo, 1919–1929*. Westport, CT: Greenwood Press, 1991.

Varg, Paul. *The Closing of the Door; Sino-American Relations, 1936–1946*. East Lansing: Michigan State University Press, 1973.

_____. *Missionaries, Chinese and Diplomats; the American Protestant Missionary Movement in China, 1890–1952*. Princeton, NJ: Princeton University Press, 1958.

Vogel, Ezra F., ed. *Living with China: U.S.-China Relations in the Twenty-first Century*. New York: Norton, 1997.

Westad, Odd. *Cold War and Revolution: Soviet-American Rivalry and the Origins of the Chinese Civil War*. New York: Columbia University Press, 1993.

White, Theodore. *In Search of History: A Personal Adventure*. New York: Harper, 1978.

_____, and Annalee Jacoby. *The Thunder Out of China*. New York: William Sloane Associates, Inc, 1946.

_____, ed. *The Stilwell Papers*. New York: William Sloane Associates, 1948.

White, Vaughan. *Our Neighbors, the Chinese*. New York: Rhinehart, 1946.

Whiting, Allen. *China Crosses the Yalu*. Stanford, CA: Stanford University Press, 1960.

Willkie, Wendell L. *One World*. New York: Simon and Schuster, 1943.

Xiang, Lanxin. *Recasting the Imperial Far East: Britain and America in China, 1945–1950*. Armonk, NY: M.E. Sharpe, 1995.

Young, Arthur. *China and the Helping Hand*. Cambridge, MA: Harvard University Press, 1963.

Young, Kenneth. *Negotiating with the Chinese Communists: The United States Experience, 1953–1967*. New York: McGraw-Hill, 1968.

Yu, Maochun. *OSS in China: Prelude to Cold War*. New Haven, CT: Yale University Press, 1997.

Zhai, Qiang. *China and the Vietnam Wars, 1950–1975*. Chapel Hill: University of North Carolina Press, 2000.

_____. *The Dragon, the Lion, and the Eagle: Chinese, British, American Relations, 1949–1958*. Kent, OH: Kent State University Press, 1994.

Zhang, Shu. *Deterrence and Strategic Culture: Chinese-American Confrontations, 1949–1958*. Ithaca, NY: Cornell University Press, 1993.

Zhang, Shuguang. *Deterrence and Strategic Culture: Chinese-American Confrontations, 1949–1958*. Ithaca, NY: Cornell University Press, 1993.

_____. *Economic Cold War: America's Embargo Against China and the Sino-Soviet Alliance, 1949–1963*. Stanford, CA: Stanford University Press, 2000.

Index

*Cited in **boldface** are pages on which the primary entry on a topic may be found*